THE OXFORD HANDBOOK OF

STRATEGY

Volume II

CORPORATE STRATEGY

The Oxford Handbook of Strategy, Volume I:
A Strategy Overview and Competitive Strategy
is also available (ISBN 0-19-878255-1).

Both volumes are also available as a set (ISBN 0-19-925017-0).

THE OXFORD HANDBOOK OF

STRATEGY

VOLUME II

CORPORATE STRATEGY

Edited by

DAVID O. FAULKNER

AND

ANDREW CAMPBELL

OXFORD

UNIVERSITY PRESS

OXFORD

UNIVERSITY PRESS

Great Clarendon Street, Oxford OX2 6DP

Oxford University Press is a department of the University of Oxford.
It furthers the University's objective of excellence in research, scholarship,
and education by publishing worldwide in

Oxford New York

Auckland Bangkok Buenos Aires Cape Town Chennai
Dar es Salaam Delhi Hong Kong Istanbul Karachi Kolkata
Kuala Lumpur Madrid Melbourne Mexico City Mumbai Nairobi
São Paulo Shanghai Taipei Tokyo Toronto

Oxford is a registered trade mark of Oxford University Press
in the UK and in certain other countries

Published in the United States
by Oxford University Press Inc., New York

© Oxford University Press, 2003

British Library Cataloguing in Publication Data

Data available

Library of Congress Cataloging in Publication Data

Data available

ISBN 0-19-924864-8

1 3 5 7 9 10 8 6 4 2

Typeset by Kolam Information Services Pvt. Ltd, Pondicherry, India
Printed in Great Britain
on acid-free paper by
T. J. International, Padstow, Cornwall

Contents

List of Figures   vii

List of Tables   x

List of Boxes   xi

List of Contributors   xii

Abbreviations   xvii

17. Introduction to Volume II: Corporate and International Strategy, Change, and Flexibility   1
ANDREW CAMPBELL AND DAVID FAULKNER

PART III CORPORATE STRATEGY

18. Why Diversify? Four Decades of Management Thinking   17
MICHAEL GOOLD AND KATHLEEN LUCHS

19. The Rationale for Multi-SBU Companies   43
C. K. PRAHALAD AND YVES L. DOZ

20. The Role of the Parent Company   72
ANDREW CAMPBELL

21. Mergers and Acquisitions: Motives, Value Creation, and Implementation   95
RICHARD SCHOENBERG

22. Cooperative Strategy: Strategic Alliances and Networks   118
DAVID FAULKNER

PART IV INTERNATIONAL STRATEGY

23. International Strategy   159
DAVID FAULKNER

24. Strategies for Multinational Enterprises   183
ALAN RUGMAN AND ALAIN VERBEKE

25. Globalization and the Multinational Enterprise   206
PETER BUCKLEY

PART V CHANGE

26. Managing Strategic Change   237
RICHARD WHIPP

27. Turnarounds   267
PETER MCKIERNAN

28. Organizational Structure   319
RICHARD WHITTINGTON

29. Strategy Innovation   349
PETER J. WILLIAMSON

PART VI FLEXIBILITY

30. Game Theory in Strategy   383
J. H. POWELL

31. Strategy, Heuristics, and Real Options   416
BRUCE KOGUT AND NALIN KULATILAKA

32. Strategic Flexibility: Creating Dynamic Competitive Advantages   447
HENK W. VOLBERDA

Index   507

FIGURES

18.1 Growth-share matrix   24
18.2 Evolution of thinking on corporate strategy and diversification   37
19.1 A framework for wealth creation   45
20.1 Four ways in which parents attempt to create value   74
20.2 Corporate strategy framework   88
21.1 Global merger and acquisition activity   97
21.2 Achieving earnings per share enhancement via acquisition
      using highly rated shares   99
21.3 Primary determinants of acquisition performance   103
21.4 Value creation within acquisitions   107
21.5 Types of acquisition integration approaches   110
22.1 The prisoners' dilemma   120
22.2 Federated enterprises are developing from both directions   122
22.3 The make/buy/ally matrix   123
22.4 Coop strategies fall into two distinct types   125
22.5 Different forms of cooperation   127
22.6 Strategic alliance forms   133
22.7 The best alliances should aim for both strategic and cultural fit   136
22.8 Almost all alliances involve both cooperation and competition   138
22.9 Communications in an equal partner network   149
22.10 The communication pattern in the dominated network   151
23.1 Configuration/coordination matrix   160
23.2 The Stopford and Wells (1972) matrix   163
23.3 An 'integration-responsiveness' grid   164
23.4 The international corporate structure matrix   173
23.5 Common organizational forms   179
24.1 Porter's three generic strategies   184
24.2 Porter's global strategies   185
24.3 Porter's extended generic strategies framework for global industries   186
24.4 Principal categories of efficiency-based strategies   190
24.5 Business networks in international strategic management   196
25.1 Internationalization of firms: conflict of markets   207
26.1 Change director   238

26.2	Processes of change within orthodox organization theory	244
26.3	Making change happen	246
26.4	Organizational change	248
26.5	Strategic change processes	250
26.6	Types of crisis management	255
26.7	Resistance to change	259
26.8	Strategic change matrix	264
27.1	Six stages of turnaround	269
27.2	A full marketing communications model	275
27.3	Decline chain factors	277
27.4	Triggering action	285
27.5	Reactions to declining performance	286
27.6	The dangers from delay	287
27.7	Actual performance affects acceptability	287
27.8	The extended Cyert and March model (see Grinyer and McKiernan 1990 for a fuller version)	293
27.9	Relationship between operating state and recovery state	304
27.10	Simple learning loop	310
28.1	Structural change and performance at Unilever	324
28.2	The five stages of growth	325
28.3a	The changing structures of DuPont: DuPont's functional structure, 1919–1921	328
28.3b	The changing structures of DuPont: DuPont's new divisional structure, August 1921	329
28.3c	The changing structures of DuPont: DuPont's divisional structure, 1999	329
28.4	The Financière Agache holding company structure	330
28.5	Types of organizational structure	331
28.6	Organizational structures in large Western European industrial firms, 1950–1993	332
28.7	International structures	334
28.8	Traditional structures for international business	335
28.9	The transnational structure	335
28.10	Softbank: a cyber-keiretsu?	337
28.11a	ABB group organizational chart, 1997	340
28.11b	ABB group organizational chart, 1998	341
29.1	ROCE, P/E, and strategy decay	355
29.2	Strategy convergence	357
29.3	The hidden constraints: narrow capabilities and market knowledge	361
29.4	The trader—'aware but incapable'	362
29.5	The prisoner—'capable but unaware'	364
29.6	Creating strategic options at Acer	367

29.7	The strategy innovation pipeline	373
29.8	The life cycle of an option on the future	377
30.1	Extended game tree for product/market investment game, pay-offs to (Row, Column), respectively	393
30.2	Starting from the BATNA point, P, the parties move up and right towards a final negotiated position which is better for both of them than their BATNAs	403
30.3	A can increase her portion either by increasing her BATNA or by decreasing B's BATNA	404
30.4	Powergraph network structure	408
30.5	Powergraph model of battle for Trafalgar	410
31.1	Correspondence of technology and organization	426
31.2	The implications of hysteresis on the choice of new techniques	427
31.3	Choice of capability set 'static case'	434
31.4	Static and dynamic hysteresis	437
31.5	Expanded capability sets	438
31.6	Effects of learning	439
32.1	Different modes of strategy depicted as a constellation of the degree of environmental turbulence, the comprehensiveness of planning activities, and the extent of organizational activities	456
32.2	The paradox of flexibility	464
32.3	A strategic framework of flexibility	468
32.4	Types of flexibility	469
32.5	The rigid organization form	476
32.6	The planned organization form	477
32.7	The flexible organization form	478
32.8	The chaotic organization form	480
32.9	A typology of alternative flexible forms for coping with hypercompetition	481
32.10	Single trajectories of revitalization	484
32.11	A dual-trajectory revitalization for multi-unit firms facing extreme competition	486
32.12	KLM Cargo: a trajectory of radical transformation	490
32.13	Permanent flexible multi-unit firms	492
32.13a	The network corporation	493
32.13b	The dual corporation	494
32.13c	The oscillating corporation	497
32.13d	The balanced corporation	498
32.14	The flexibility trajectory of successful firms of the twenty-first century	501

TABLES

20.1 Company backgrounds   82

22.1 Differences between different organizational forms   142

23.1 Global strategy: an organizing framework   167

27.1 Symptoms of corporate decline   274

27.2 Main secondary causes of decline   278

27.3 'Generic' turnaround strategies   306

28.1 The world's largest firms by revenues, 1999   321

28.2 Evolving types of multi-divisional   339

29.1 Designing a portfolio of options for the mobile telephone business   371

30.1 Normal form game of product/market investment, pay-offs to (Row, Column), respectively   392

30.2 *Prisoners' dilemma* game, pay-offs to (TrustCo, CheatCo), respectively   394

30.3 Market entry *Chicken* game, pay-offs to (ImproverCo, AspirantCo), respectively   396

30.4 *Hawk-Dove* game, pay-offs to (A, B), respectively   400

30.5 *Rendezvous* game, pay-offs to (Emma, Dai), respectively   405

31.1 Strategizing as cognitive frames   420

31.2 T_{ij} and Ω_{lm} switching cost pairs   433

32.1 Developments within strategic management and their contributions to organizational flexibility   460

32.2 Examples of internal and external types of flexibility   471

BOXES

20.1	Value creation insights	84
20.2	Typical reasons for parenting opportunities	89
20.3	ABB: parenting advantage statement (mid-1990s)	90
23.1	McKinsey: a mini-case	177
24.1	Shelter-based strategies	189
24.2	The global shipbuilding industry	189
26.1	The BBC	239
28.1	Wal-Mart's structure	321
28.2	Complementary structural change at Unilever	323
28.3	Structuring Netscape	326
28.4	Ove Arup's structural reformation	327
28.5	DuPont discovers the M-form	328
28.6	Polycentricity at Procter & Gamble	336
28.7	ABB—Beyond the M-form?	340
28.8	Microsoft 'Reorgs'	342
30.1	The battle for Trafalgar	409
32.1	The Red Queen effect	449
32.2	GM's competence trap: extreme exploitation	462
32.3	Apple's renewal trap: extreme exploration	465
32.4	The tensions between exploitation and exploration within KLM	466
32.5	Dual migration paths within the Dutch PTT Post	488
32.6	Mini-case: radical transformation of KLM Cargo	489
32.7	Balancing acts in 3M, HP, and Motorola	498

Notes on Contributors

Peter Buckley is Professor of International Business and Director of the Centre of International Business at the University of Leeds. He is a visiting professor at the Universities of Paris I (Pantheon-Sorbonne), Rennes I, Groningen, and Reading. He has published nineteen books, many of which have been translated into other languages, and was elected a Fellow of the Academy of International Business in 1985 for 'outstanding achievements in international business'. He is also a fellow of the British Academy of Management and the Royal Society of Arts, and was awarded an Honorary Professorship to the University of International Business and Economics in Beijing, China. e-mail: pjb@lub.leeds.ac.uk

Andrew Campbell is a Director of Ashridge Strategic Management Centre and active as a consultant on strategic issues for major corporate clients. He is also a visiting professor at City University. Previously he was a Fellow in the Centre for Business Strategy at the London Business School. Before that he was a consultant for six years with McKinsey & Co., working on strategy and organization problems in London and Los Angeles. He also spent three years as a loan officer with Investors in Industry. Andrew Campbell holds an MBA from the Harvard Business School where he was a Harkness Fellow and a Baker Scholar. His books include: *Synergy* (1998), *Core Competency-Based Strategy* (1997), *Breakup!* (1997), *Corporate-Level Strategy* (1994), *Strategic Synergy* (1992), *A Sense of Mission* (1990), *Strategies and Styles* (1987). e-mail: andrew.campbell@ashridge.org.uk

Yves Doz is Associate Dean for Executive Education and Timken Chaired Professor of Global Technology and Innovation at INSEAD. He has been on the faculty at HBS, and held visiting appointments at Stanford and Aoyama Gakuin University in Japan. He has a doctorate from Harvard University and is a graduate of the École des Hautes Études Commerciales. His research on strategy and organization of MNCs, examining high tech industries, has been published widely in such journals as the *Strategic Management Journal* and *Harvard Business Review*, in book chapters, and in books. e-mail: yves.doz@ insead.fr

David Faulkner is a Tutorial Fellow and Member of the Governing Body of Christ Church, Oxford, and Oxford University Lecturer in Strategic Management at the Saïd Business School where he is a former Director of the MBA. His specialist research area is international Cooperative Strategy and Acquisitions, on which

subject he has written, edited, or co-authored a number of books including: *Strategies of Cooperation: Managing Alliances, Networks, and Joint Ventures* (1998); *Co-operative Strategy: Economic, Business and Organizational Issues* (2000); *The Dynamics of International Strategy* (1999); *Strategic Alliances: Cooperating to Compete* (1995); *The Management of International Acquisitions* (2001). He is an Oxford educated economist by background, who has spent much of his early career as a strategic management consultant with McKinsey & Co. and Arthur D. Little.
e-mail: david.faulkner@christ-church.ox.ac.uk

Michael Goold is a director of the Ashridge Strategic Management Centre. His research interests are concerned with corporate strategy and the management of multi-business companies, and he runs the Centre's programme on Strategic Decisions. His publications include: *Synergy: Why Links between Business Units Often Fail and How to Make Them Work* (1998), *Corporate-Level Strategy: Creating Value in the Multibusiness Company* (1994), and *Strategic Control: Milestones for Long-Term Performance* (1990).

Bruce Kogut is the Felix Zandman Professor of Management at the Wharton School, University of Pennsylvania, and co-Director of the Reginald H. Jones Center. He works in the areas of international competition, strategy and real options, and globalization. Recent articles and projects include: *Redesigning the Firm* (1996), co-authored with E. Bowman, studies of small worlds in Germany (*American Sociological Review*, 2001), open source (*Oxford Review of Economic Policy*), and a forthcoming book on the Global Internet Economy.
e-mail: kogut@wharton.upenn.edu

Nalin Kulatilaka is a Professor of Finance at Boston University, School of Management. He is the Research Director of the Global Mobility Innovations and Insights (GMII), a multi-university research programme to study the impact of the mobile Internet. His current research examines the strategic use of real options by integrating operating and financial aspects of a firm. He is the co-author of *Real Options: Managing Strategic Investments in an Uncertain World* (1999). For more details visit http://people.bu.edu/nalink

Kathleen Sommers Luchs is a business researcher and writer. She has been a research associate at Ashridge Strategic Management Centre in London and at Harvard Business School. Her publications include *Strategic Synergy* (1992), co-authored with Andrew Campbell, and *Managing the Multi-business Company* (1996), co-authored with Michael Goold. She has an MBA from London Business School and a Ph.D. from Yale University.

Peter McKiernan is the Professor of Management at the University of St Andrews and Visiting Professor in Strategic Management at the Universities of Strathclyde and Warwick in the United Kingdom. His specialist research interests are corporate

turnaround, scenario thinking, and SMEs. He edited the double volume on the *Historical Evolution of Strategic Management* (1996) and his other books include: *Sharpbenders: The Secrets of Unleashing Corporate Potential* (1998), *Inside Fortress Europe* (1984), and *Strategies of Growth* (1992). He is a past winner of prizes from the British Academy of Management, IBM, the UK Pharmaceutical Industry, and Fife Enterprise for his research in strategic management. He acts as a strategy coach to several governments and major MNCs. He is currently the Vice-Chairman of the British Academy of Management and a Vice-President of the European Academy of Management.

John Powell is Senior Lecturer in Strategy at the School of Management, Bath University. Before taking a Ph.D. at Cranfield University and subsequently starting his academic career, he held a number of board-level positions in the defence industry, and bases his research (in the modelling and management of major inter-company conflicts) on those experiences and his active consultancy. He holds HM the Queen's Gold Medal for academic excellence and the President's Medal for the OR Society of UK. e-mail: j.h.powell@bath.ac.uk

C. K. Prahalad is the Harvey C. Fruehauf Professor of Corporate Strategy and International Business Administration at the University of Michigan's Graduate School of Business Administration in Ann Arbor; and Senior Faculty Associate of the William Davidson Institute at the University of Michigan Business School. He studies the role and value added of top management in large, diversified, multi-national corporations. He has been a visiting research fellow at Harvard, a professor at the Indian Institute of Management, and a visiting professor at the European Institute of Business Administration (INSEAD). Professor Prahalad, with Yves Doz, wrote *The Multinational Mission: Balancing Local Demands and Global Vision* (1987), and he is also the co-author of many articles that have appeared in the *Harvard Business Review*, including 'Do You Really Have a Global Strategy?' (1985), 'Collaborate with Your Competitors and Win' (1989), 'Strategic Intent' (1989), 'Core Competence of the Corporation' (1990), 'Corporate Imagination and Expeditionary Marketing' (1991), and 'Strategy as Stretch and Leverage' (1993). 'Strategic Intent' and 'Core Competence of the Corporation' won McKinsey Prizes in 1989 and 1990, respectively. His paper 'Dominant Logic', co-authored with Richard Bettis, was chosen as the best article published in the *Strategic Management Journal* during the period 1980–1988. His book *Competing for the Future* (1994) was co-authored with Gary Hamel.

Alan M. Rugman is L. Leslie Waters Chair of International Business and a professor at the Kelley School of Business, Indiana University, Bloomington. He is also a fellow of Templeton College, University of Oxford. He has published numerous books and articles dealing with the strategic management of multinational enterprises and trade and investment policy. He is co-editor of the *Oxford Handbook of*

International Business (2001), *Multinationals as Flagship Firms* (2000), and *Environmental Regulations and Corporate Strategy* (1999), all published by Oxford University Press. Previously he was a professor at the University of Toronto in Canada.

Richard Schoenberg is Senior Lecturer in International Business Strategy at Imperial College Management School, University of London, and was previously a University Lecturer at The Judge Institute of Management, University of Cambridge. Prior to joining academia, Dr Schoenberg held industrial positions with ICI plc and Ford of Europe Inc. He is an active researcher in the area of European Mergers and Acquisitions, on which he holds a prize winning Ph.D. from the University of London. His work has been published in a number of leading management journals and he is a regular presenter on M&A at conferences organized by the Strategic Management Society, the Academy of International Business and the British Academy of Management. e-mail: r.schoenberg@ic.ac.uk

Alain Verbeke is Professor of International Business Strategy and holds the McCaig Chair in Management at the Faculty of Management, University of Calgary, Canada. He is also an Associate Fellow of Templeton College, University of Oxford. Formerly he was a Professor of International Strategic Management and Public Policy at the Solvay Business School, University of Brussels (VUB), where he was director of the MBA programme. He is the author of numerous articles in major refereed journals, and fourteen books. He consults for the European Commission and leading multinational corporations in the area of strategic management and transportation policy.

Henk W. Volberda is Professor of Strategic Management and Business Policy of the Rotterdam School of Management, Erasmus University, where he teaches strategic management, strategy implementation, corporate entrepreneurship, and strategic flexibility. He has been a visiting scholar at the Wharton School at the University of Pennsylvania and City University Business School, London. Professor Volberda obtained his doctorate *cum laude* in Business Administration of the University of Groningen. His research on organizational flexibility and strategic change received the NCD Award 1987, the ERASM Research Award 1994, the Erasmus University Research Award 1997, and the Igor Ansoff Strategic Management Award 1993. For his work on alliance capabilities (together with Ard-Pieter de Man and Johan Draulans) he received the Dutch ROA Award 1999 (best consultancy article). Moreover, his research on absorptive capacity and internal networks (together with Raymond van Wijk and Frans van den Bosch) received an honorable mention of the McKinsey/SMS Best Conference Paper Prize. Professor Volberda has worked as a consultant for many large European corporations and published in many refereed books and journals. He is director of the Erasmus Strategic Renewal Program, programme director of the Erasmus Institute of Management (ERIM), board member of the VSB (Dutch Strategic Management Society), board member of the Rotterdam School of Management, secretary of the Dutch-Flemish Academy

of Management, and external adviser of Stroeve securities bank. He is also editor-in-chief of *M&O* and *Management Select*, senior editor of *Long Range Planning*, and member of the Editorial Board of *Organization Science* and *Tijdschrift voor Bedrijfsadministratie* (TBA). His book, *Building the Flexible Firm: How to Remain Competitive* (1998), published by Oxford University Press, received wide acclaim. His new book, together with Tom Elfring, *Rethinking Strategy* (2001) has been published recently.

Peter Williamson is Professor of International Management and Asian Business at the INSEAD in Fontainebleau, France, and Singapore. His research and publications span globalization, strategy innovation, and alliances. His latest book, with Yves Doz and José Santos, *From Global to Metanational: How Companies Win in the Global Knowledge Economy* (2001), sets out a blueprint for how multinationals can prosper in the global knowledge economy by developing their capability for 'learning from the world'. His other books include: *Managing the Global Frontier* (1994), co-authored with Qionghua Hu; *The Economics of Financial Markets* (1996), co-authored with Hendrik Houthakker; and *The Strategy Handbook* (1991), co-authored with Michael Hay. Formerly at the Boston Consulting Group, he acts as consultant to companies in Europe, Asia, and the Americas and serves on the boards of several listed companies. He holds a Ph.D. in Business Economics from Harvard University. e-mail: peter.williamson@attglobal.net

Richard Whipp is a professor and deputy director at Cardiff Business School. He is the current chair of the British Academy of Management. His MA is from Cambridge and his Ph.D. from Warwick University. He has taught and researched at Aston Management Centre and Warwick Business School. His book publications include: *Innovation and the Auto Industry* (1985), co-authored with Peter Clark; *Patterns of Labour* (1990); *Managing Change for Competitive Success* (1991), with Andrew Pettigrew; and *A Managed Service* (2002), co-authored with Ian Kirkpatrick and Martin Kitchener. His current research centres on the temporal aspects of strategic management as seen in the volume *Making Time* (2002), edited with Adams and Sabelis. e-mail: Whippr@cardiff.ac.uk

Richard Whittington is Millman Fellow in Management at New College and University Reader in Strategy at the Saïd Business School, University of Oxford. He is the author of *Corporate Strategies in Recession and Recovery* (1989), *What is Strategy—and Does it Matter?* (1993/2000), and *The European Corporation: Strategy, Structure and Social Science* (2000), co-authored with Michael Mayer. He has also published two co-edited volumes, *Rethinking Marketing* (1999) and *The Handbook of Strategy and Management* (2001). He is Associate Editor of the *British Journal of Management* and serves on the editorial boards of *Long Range Planning* and *Organization Studies*. His current research is on the practice of strategy, and how strategists learn to strategize. e-mail: richard.whittington@new.ox.ac.uk

ABBREVIATIONS

BATNA   best alternative to a negotiated agreement
BCG   Boston Consulting Group
CSA   country-specific advantage
EVA   economic value analysis
FDI   foreign direct investment
FSA   firm-specific advantage
IJV   international joint venture
LB   location bound
MNE   multinational enterprise
NLB   non-location bound
OBR   operating patterns, beliefs, and rules
OLI   ownership, location, internalization
P/E   price/earnings
PUV   perceived use value
RDP   resource dependency perspective
ROCE   return on capital employed
ROE   return on equity
ROI   return on investment
SBU   strategic business unit
SDR   strategy decay rate
TCA   transaction cost analysis
TSR   total shareholder returns

CHAPTER 17

INTRODUCTION TO VOLUME II

CORPORATE AND INTERNATIONAL STRATEGY, CHANGE, AND FLEXIBILITY

ANDREW CAMPBELL

DAVID FAULKNER

17.1 INTRODUCTION

THE *Oxford Handbook of Strategy* is a compendium of chapters by prominent academics addressing some of the most important issues in the field of strategic management at the beginning of the twenty-first century. It is produced in two volumes, the first describing a number of different approaches to strategy, and the essence of competitive or business strategy; the second dealing with corporate strategy, change, and flexibility. All the contributors are practising academics, mostly currently researching in the area in which they have written their chapters for the Handbook. The volumes are part of an important new series of Handbooks that Oxford University Press is developing across the social sciences and human-

ities, including several in business and management. The first of these is *The Oxford Handbook of International Business* edited by Professor Alan Rugman and Professor Tom Brewer. These Handbooks aim to address key topics in their field and to identify the evolution of debates and research on these topics.

The Oxford Handbook of Strategy is targeted at an advanced group of academics, researchers, and graduate students for whom it aims to be a useful resource, sitting between the specialist journal article or monograph and the extensive range of established textbooks in the field. It is intended to provide the graduate student, researcher, or strategy lecturer with a well-informed and authoritative guide to the subject and to the current debates taking place in the field of strategy. It aims to be a blend of mature thinking and cutting-edge speculation. For example it revisits the traditional issue of the boundaries of the firm in the light of the New Economy, focuses on dynamic capabilities and organizational learning as issues vital to the maintenance of competitive advantage, and considers the impact on the mainly static tools of strategic analysis of the turbulent economic conditions inherent in the globalized world of today. The Handbook also deals with the more traditional subjects of competitive analysis, the role of the corporate centre, and international strategy amongst others. Teachers and students of strategy will find both much of the traditional material for their presentations contained in the Handbook, as well as illustrations of how to introduce the newer issues of debate into their teaching and research.

This second volume is divided into four sections—Corporate Strategy, International Strategy, Change, and Flexibility. Whereas many of the issues in Volume I relate to the marketplace and strategy at the business level, the issues in this volume are all corporate-level concerns: ones that affect the whole organization.

17.2 CORPORATE STRATEGY

So far as corporate strategy has existed as a topic separate from business-level strategy, it has had a chequered existence. Only in the last ten years has a rigorous consensus emerged.

The opening chapter by Goold and Luchs provides a valuable scan of thinking in the corporate strategy area over the last forty years. The topic rises to prominence with the arrival of the conglomerates. Before the creation of highly diverse companies such as Harold Geneen's ITT, the issue of multi-business companies was only addressed in passing. In the 1960s the topic of strategy itself was only just taking form and there was little understanding of the distinction between strategy at the marketplace level and strategy at the firm level.

The concept of general management skills that could be applied across a range of businesses did exist as did the concept of synergy. In fact for the next thirty years these two concepts were two paths along which thinking developed, with very little attempt at integration. In trying to understand conglomerates, the Boston Consulting Group developed the BCG Matrix, Boston Box, or growth/share matrix. Its elegance, managerial language (cash cows, dogs, etc.), and simplicity caused the Boston Box to dominate the teaching of corporate-level strategy. This tool was followed by other major consultancies with their own variants, notably McKinsey and Arthur D. Little, who were determined not to be left behind in the race to acquire prestigious multinational clients.

With hindsight the ideas spawned by the matrix—portfolio balance and diversification—proved to be disastrous. Many companies in the 1970s and 1980s set off on the path of diversification eager to create a portfolio that could finance itself while delivering a stream of 'quality earnings growth'. The strategy was attractive to managers, because it suggested that they could create a portfolio that would not be subject to the vagaries of the capital markets. But they also believed that this was the right thing to do based on the best academic thinking.

The story of failure is best illustrated by the major oil companies, who energetically entered new businesses starting with the first oil crisis in 1974/5. Having tried almost every industry, these companies spent the last years of the 1980s and the early part of the 1990s licking their wounds and returning to the only business they had proved competitive in—the oil industry.

While the world was experimenting with diversification, the synergy logic was still alive. The frustration was that it continuously failed to submit to the rigours of academic thinking. Rumelt (1982) showed that 'related' diversification outperformed 'unrelated' diversification, demonstrating a critical flaw in the Boston Box. But the results were hard to replicate. The case for relatedness had the same tautological attractiveness as the case for portfolio balance, but, since neither could be demonstrated to be superior to the satisfaction of the academic world, they existed alongside each other, allowing managers to find a theory to support whatever they wanted to do and academics to teach whatever they wanted to.

Enlightenment was slow in coming. It was given a huge indirect boost by the re-emergence of the resource-based view of strategy after a gap of twenty-five years from its first introduction by Penrose in 1959. Picked up by Wernerfelt (1984) and later by Prahalad and Hamel in the form of 'core competencies' (1990), the synergy school now had some managerial language and better theory with which to fight the portfolio school. Prahalad and Hamel were pushing on an open door. Managers found that their diversification efforts were underperforming and desperately needed a new logic for guiding their decisions.

The merging of the synergy and portfolio schools came in the early 1990s. The three leading teams working on the topic (Prahalad and Doz, Goold and Campbell,

and Collis and Montgomery) came to the same conclusion: that corporate-level strategy was about achieving a fit between three elements:

(1) the value creation logic for having multiple businesses under one management team;
(2) the choice of businesses to have in the portfolio; and
(3) the skills, processes, and structures used to manage the portfolio.

The portfolio school did not make sense if the logic was balance or risk spreading. These rationales were demonstrated not to be a value-creating logic. The shareholder is in a better position than managers to balance and spread risk. The portfolio school did make sense if the logic was based on added value.

The synergy school was also challenged. Instead of looking for relatedness in the nature of the businesses, synergy could depend on skills, processes, and structures of the parent company. Success occurred when the businesses were 'related' to the skills of the parent, which were themselves built on an understanding of how to create value. Each team inevitably developed its own language and framework, but a robust intellectual framework had finally been agreed.

In Chapter 19, Prahalad and Doz explore the different kinds of economic logic that can sustain a diversified company and link these to different governance mechanisms. One of the messages from this work is the importance of the CEO, a theme that also runs through the work of Goold and Campbell. Since the economic logic for the company must come from the top, there is a tough strategy demand put on the CEO. Moreover, since the economic logic must fit with the skills of the corporate centre, the skills of the CEO being a dominant element, the economic logic is often constrained by the CEO's personal skills. Corporate strategy starts to look almost like career strategy for the CEO.

This tight link between the concept of corporate strategy and the skills of the individuals in the corporate parent is taken up in Chapter 20 by Andrew Campbell—'The Role of the Parent Company'. This chapter summarizes the contributions made by Goold and Campbell to the theory of corporate strategy. This version—parenting theory—places equal emphasis on value destruction and value creation. The task, Campbell argues, is not only to develop a value creation logic but also a logic for avoiding 'value destruction'. There must not only be a fit between the businesses in the portfolio and the skills of the parent, there must also be an absence of major misfit.

This might seem like playing with words. But the theory is based on many years of observation, which pointed out that parent companies have a big impact on the decisions made in the businesses they own. This creates the potential for value creation and destruction. In fact value neutrality is the one state that is most rare. Value destruction is avoided by ensuring that parent managers have 'sufficient feel' for the businesses they own. The most engaging analogy is that of the specialist doctor. He or she develops some medicine or way of interacting with patients that

have a particular health issue. Value is created when this medicine is applied to a patient with the health issue. Value is destroyed if the medicine has side effects and is applied to patients without the health problem or if the side effects are more severe than the beneficial effects in certain patients. The best doctors only give the medicine to patients who will experience a net gain, and the ideal situation is to give the medicine only to patients for whom the net gain is greater than that available from other solutions to their health problem. Parenting theory is, therefore, built on the concept of 'parenting advantage' just like competitive strategy theory is built on the concept of competitive advantage.

With agreement about the integrated view of corporate-level strategy, much of the interesting work currently underway takes these evolving theories and applies them to particular issues such as acquisitions, alliances, organization design, and organization renewal.

Schoenberg's 'Mergers and Acquisitions', Chapter 21, provides further evidence for the integrated view. Acquisitions frequently fail. In fact the numerous studies on success rates come to a remarkably consistent view that less than half of acquisitions succeed. Much of the blame can be laid at the feet of ambition, hubris, and incompetence. But for many it is a lack of a sufficient understanding of the rules of the game—of the integrated view of corporate-level strategy.

To add a business to the portfolio through acquisition, the buyer must believe that he or she can outbid other interested buyers without overpaying for the business. Assuming the other bidders are rational, they will be prepared to pay a price close to the value of the business to them. To outbid others, the buyer must believe that the target business is worth more to the buyer than to any other bidder. In the language of parenting theory, the buyer must believe that he or she has parenting advantage. The 1999 fight between Royal Bank of Scotland and Bank of Scotland for National Westminster Bank was a classic. The Royal Bank won because it was able to convince the institutions that it could do more with the National Westminster assets.

Schoenberg also describes the importance of integration management. Integration is the mechanism by which the buyer creates additional value from the acquisition. But too much integration can destroy value and too little can leave value on the table. Knowing the appropriate level of integration is an essential part of a parent company's skill set—a skill that the parent must be better at than others at least for certain kinds of acquisitions. As Schoenberg points out, the handling of employee resistance following an acquisition is one part of integration management that requires particular attention.

A similar logic can be used to address cooperative strategies, such as alliances and networks: only network or ally with businesses where the combined value is greater than that available to any other combination of partners. However, as Faulkner points out, in Chapter 22, there are other forces at work. In acquisitions, the buyer typically pays full value plus a premium for the target company. In alliances and networks there

is often no payment as such, just an agreement to commit to work together. Advantage can, therefore, be gained by choosing partners with as much attention on how to deprive competitors as on how to maximize value from the partnering. In fact a game theory perspective as illustrated by Powell in Chapter 30, is a useful one not only in understanding the rationale for cooperation but also in thinking about partners.

Faulkner notes the rapid growth in popularity of alliances in response to the increase in globalization of markets in recent years. The growth of international strategic alliances has in fact been one of the phenomena of the last decade. Apart from finding a partner with complementary assets able to realize synergies, he emphasizes the importance of trust and commitment by the partners to the enterprise, if the alliance is to be successful in the longer term. The chapter also considers the allied but distinct area of strategic networks, and their importance in assisting the globalization of enterprises. This view leads us to the next section of the book—international strategy.

17.3 INTERNATIONAL STRATEGY

International strategy can be viewed as being a subset of corporate-level strategy, on the one hand, and competitive strategy, on the other. As a part of competitive strategy, international strategy is about situations where the international sources of advantage make it impossible for locally focused businesses to survive. In most cases this is because the economies of scale from serving multiple markets are critical to competitive success. For companies in small countries, most businesses need to be international to survive. For companies in the United States or Germany the number is much smaller.

Viewed as part of corporate strategy, international strategy is about diversifying into other countries in order to create additional value. The operations in the other countries are additional units in a portfolio and can be analysed with the same framework as corporate-level strategies. Is there a value-creating logic for having multiple units in one portfolio? Does the parent organization have skills, resources, structures, and processes that are well designed to exploit the value opportunity? Do the businesses in the portfolio benefit significantly from the medicine the parent organization is offering? Finally, does the benefit exceed that available from any other parent company?

Unfortunately, the field of international strategy has developed largely independent of corporate strategy. Hence few writers in international strategy are attempting a synthesis. When this comes, it will give a big boost to the topic of corporate

strategy, because there are many more academics studying international issues than corporate issues.

In Chapter 23, Faulkner attempts to provide some answers to the question of how multinational corporations configure and coordinate their international strategies, by examining various approaches to internationalization as a strategy process. This analysis includes considering the stages models of internationalization, studies of the link between strategy and structure in MNCs, and more recent organizational models of multinational organizational forms, including that of the most modern, the transnational. Finally Faulkner introduces a model to summarize and discuss the four basic multinational forms described.

Since the terrorist attacks on the World Trade Center in September 2001 and the protests at Summits of world leaders, much has been written about the pros and cons of globalization. What Faulkner's chapter shows is that the forces of globalization are simple economic ones connected with scale and skill benefits. The result is greater value creation, which should make it possible to benefit all stakeholders. The tragedy of the anti-capitalist and anti-internationalist forces is that they may slow the process of value creation.

We should recall that challenges to economic forces have been made many times before. The market economy was viewed with great suspicion as recently as the 1940s. In 1942, Joseph Schumpeter, along with other economists, commentators, and even industrialists, forecast the demise of capitalism. In *Capitalism, Socialism and Democracy* Schumpeter wrote in the preface: 'a socialist form of society will inevitably emerge from an equally inevitable decomposition of capitalist society'. Later in the book he reinforces the thought: 'Can capitalism survive? No, I do not think it can. One may hate socialism or at least look upon it with cool criticism, and yet foresee its advent.' At the time, there was a strong view that capitalism = competition = waste.

Yet we have learned since that competition is the engine of progress: the fuel of value creation. We should hold faith with globalization for the same reasons.

Rugman and Verbeke, in Chapter 24, criticize Porter by showing that his generic global strategies are 'neither global nor generic'. In their place Rugman and Verbeke offer a new framework of four generic strategies based on distinguishing between location bound and non-location bound sources of value on one dimension and the number of home bases on the other. There have been many attempts to develop generic strategies and Rugman's certainly has value. However, like the others, there is a danger of oversimplifying. In practice each company needs to understand the sources of internationalization value, and develop strategies that are stronger the more they are uniquely tailored to the company's specific resource endowment.

Rugman and Verbeke also develop a framework for understanding the role that transnational networks can fulfil in a context of global competitiveness. This framework distinguishes between intra-organizational and inter-organizational networks. It also looks at the number of home bases. The weakness in the Porter frameworks is the assumption of only one home base, whereas 'most of the

interesting research issues in international business stem from the complexities of organizing a multinational enterprise across multiple home bases'.

Buckley, in Chapter 25, uses standard economic theory to examine the impact of multinational companies on the global economy and vice versa. He notes that the global economy has more shocks than it used to have, and these shocks are more rapidly distributed around the world system. Multinationals play a role not only in responding to these shocks, but also in generating them and transmitting them. The implication for the multinational is a need for increased flexibility in strategies, organization, and firm boundaries. The issue of flexibility is picked up again in the last section of this book.

First, however, there are four chapters on the subject of change.

17.4 CHANGE

Change is a topic of such importance to strategy that it is almost synonymous with management itself. If management is anything other than the creation of bureau-cracies, it is about the management of change. Change is not, therefore, a topic limited to corporate-level issues. It is central to almost all strategy. If all changes were possible, there would be very few constraints on the strategy development process. At the business level, it would be possible to analyse the needs of each marketplace, identify what competencies are needed to succeed, and put the competencies in place. At the corporate level, it would be possible to analyse the needs of each business, determine what parenting skills are needed, and put them in place. Unfortunately, resources and competencies are hard to change and the marketplace is competitive. Hence the management of change is about the imple-mentation of strategy; how to build the resources and skills needed to outperform competitors in the marketplace or other parent companies seeking to own similar businesses? If the changes needed are too difficult, the strategy will fail. If the strategy is not ambitious enough, competitors will get ahead. The problem is never ending and, as such, never completely solvable. This is why, despite huge improvements in the management of change, the task does not appear to get any easier. Managers still find it difficult to achieve the changes they need. In fact they always will. However good our change technology, the challenge is fundamentally a competitive one. Unless a company has major advantages over its competitors, it will find the management of change to be a tough challenge.

Whipp, in Chapter 26, underlines this point with the words, 'It is apparent that managers continue to regard strategic change as an area fraught with problems,

notwithstanding the rhetoric on some book covers which would seem to indicate otherwise.' Whipp argues that those trying to understand change need three perspectives. First, the discipline has a long and intertwined history. It is important to locate authors in their contexts, if the reader is to understand and use their insights. Second, the reader needs to be aware that many writers fail to distinguish sufficiently between different points on the continuum of change—from the status quo at one end to transformational change at the other. Prescriptions and observations of one type of change are often of little use if applied to another type of change. Third, the reader needs to be sensitive to the process view of change.

This view has become the bedrock of many of the most notable examinations of strategic change. The main benefit has been to show that a step by step approach to change is not relevant. It is a much more serendipitous and chaotic activity. Managers can be ambitious to nudge the change process and even provide conditions favourable to the direction of change desired. But managers cannot be ambitious to be in control of change.

McKiernan, in Chapter 27, addresses the question of change in the specific conditions of a turnaround situation. He is interested in change when the survival of the company is at stake. He develops a six-stage model for the turnaround process—causes, triggers, diagnosis, retrenchment, recovery, and renewal. Stage process models are now a generally accepted approach to the subject. McKiernan adds causes, triggers, and renewal to the more normal diagnosis, retrenchment, recovery model.

McKiernan gives particular attention to the behaviour of the dominant coalition, explaining what actions to expect and when, but, more importantly, why they occur. He uses the lenses of learning systems and complexity theory. He points out that each situation needs a unique solution. Corporate cultures and learning systems differ for each firm calling for a different approach to turnaround, a theme at the root of most good thinking about strategy as well.

Whittington, in Chapter 28, tackles the issue of organization structure. Whittington's chapter illustrates the limited state of theory on the subject of structure. Contingency theory is the bedrock of structural analysis, but contingency theory says very little in theory terms. It denies the idea that there is one right structure for all organizations. But it fails to define the variables that managers should use to design their organizations. Whittington identifies some of the variables that are commonly cited as relevant—size, technology, environment, strategy, degree of internationalization—but all of these variables are too imprecise and unquantified to give specific guidance to a manager faced with a tough design decision.

Certainly there are plenty of models of types of organization, but there is as yet no generally agreed theory. It is generally agreed that organizations should be less hierarchical, more networked, and more customer focused, but not why. We do not have a theory that explains why these variables are the right ones to focus on.

Whittington's discussion of future organization structures underlines the problem. Unable to predict the direction of organizational development from an

understanding of the theory, he focuses on current trends: 'If present trends provide at least a hint about the future . . .'. One might speculate that some of the problems encountered in the field of change generally may lie in our poor understanding of what is often referred to as one of the 'hard Ss'. If we do not know how to design the hard Ss, how are we going to manage the soft ones?

Williamson, in Chapter 29, tackles the topic of strategic renewal. He demonstrates that strategies decay, and provides four measures of strategic decay:

(1) divergence between revenue growth and earnings growth;
(2) rising ROCE but falling P/E multiple;
(3) a high ratio of rents to new value creation; and
(4) convergence of strategies in the industry.

Avoiding strategic decay is about having a portfolio of options to expand both capabilities and markets. While the work on corporate strategy and international strategy emphasizes value creation logic for expanding markets or capabilities, Williamson's logic is that of strategic renewal. Unless the company grows in some direction it will die. The synthesis between the two ways of thinking is missing, but some of the ideas from the strategic renewal school are compelling.

One such idea is the innovation pipeline. Companies it is argued need a pipeline of options at different stages of development. The concept fits well with the financial tool of 'real options pricing'. The options are valued either with financial tools or using management judgement. As their value increases, more can be invested in them, the objective being to avoid investing too much in creating the options that will provide the solution to the renewal problem. The pipeline consists of:

(1) a portfolio of ideas;
(2) a portfolio of experiments;
(3) a portfolio of ventures;
(4) a portfolio of businesses.

These four portfolios match the four stages that take an idea from 'imagination', through 'testing', 'launching', and 'investing'. The skill is to move the options through the pipeline at the right speed, so matching the investment with the rate of customer acceptance and technical development.

17.5 FLEXIBILITY

The last section of the volume contains three chapters associated with the concept of flexibility. Like the management of change, flexibility is a topic that seems always to be receding rather than arriving. As companies learn to be

more flexible, the demands for flexibility seem to increase another notch, so that the prize is always out of reach. Flexibility also has a cost. Undoubtedly the best way of exploiting today's environment is to choose a strategy and build an organization that best fits with it. Unfortunately, the strategy and organization quickly become less than perfect as the environment, competitors, or strategic priorities change.

Powell, in Chapter 30, demonstrates how a successful strategy depends not just on what makes marketplace sense, but also on the response of competitors. Game Theory recognizes that a game takes place between the main players. In economist terms this is a theory that applies only to oligopolistic situations. In perfect or commodity markets there is no game. A game only exists where a few players can influence the decisions that the others take. Since success in oligopolistic situations is determined as much by the behaviour of competitors (remember that one of Porter's five forces is 'rivalry'), strategies need to be developed for the game as much as for the marketplace. Developing an advantage over competitors is only part of the battle. The other part is persuading the competitors to act sensibly.

Kogut and Kulatilaka, in Chapter 31, deal with real option theory. This is about decision-making in the face of options. It has been developed from finance theory and it involves analysing when to make a decision, rather than keep options open. Since new information is arriving all the time, there is a strong logic for avoiding choices until the last possible moment. Flexibility is gained by waiting. Investment decisions should not be made according to a planning cycle, but only when necessary. The trick is to calculate when a decision needs to be made.

Chapter 32 is by Volberda. He points out that 'there are several equally good ways to match high variety and speed of managerial capabilities with an adequate organization design to resolve the constructive tension between developing capabilities and preserving stability within the organizational conditions'. He develops a strategic framework of flexibility that identifies three drivers of the choice of flexibility solution. The drivers are the 'managerial task' (variety and speed), the competitive forces (dynamism, complexity, and unpredictability) and the organization design task (controllability). This leads to four types of organizational form— rigid, planned, flexible, and chaotic. The ideal is to have a mix of planned and flexible solutions. He claims that there are four ways of achieving this mix—the network corporation, the dual corporation, the oscillating corporation, and the balanced corporation. All of these are acceptable solutions to the flexibility challenge.

It is appropriate that we end with a discussion of flexibility. Few issues can be more perplexing. Probably the biggest source of flexibility is the market economy. It provides for birth and death in a way that ensures value destroying firms do not hold us back for too long, and new ideas and forms can quickly gain support. Are we even asking the right question as we pursue flexibility within the firm?

An alternative view is to rely much more heavily on the market. An analogy is that of the theatre business on Broadway. Each play is written, cast, and presented. Adjustments may be made to the script or the casting, but the basic play does not change: there is only incremental not transformational change. The play may have a run of a few weeks or several years, but at some time the audiences start to decline and the play is withdrawn. At that point the cast disperse, the director looks for a new script, and the theatre for a new play. The resources are put back into the marketplace and a new combination is created. In this way New York presents a stream of excellent theatre.

We could aim for a similar solution in business in general. Each organization would be built around a strategy and designed to fit that strategy as closely as possible. Once the strategy starts to fail, the organization should be dissolved and the resources recombined into other organizations. Flexibility within the firm would not even be a management preoccupation.

The purpose of this last example is not to try to undermine the work of all those mastering flexibility, but rather to point out that we are in the very early days of this particular topic. We should expect some radical twists in the road ahead, before we can claim to understand how to design an economic system that is nimble and responsive to the needs of all the stakeholders involved.

17.6 VOLUME I OF *THE OXFORD HANDBOOK OF STRATEGY*

The Oxford Handbook of Strategy has two volumes. Volume I, the companion to this volume, focuses on competitive or business unit strategy rather than corporate strategy. The two volumes are presented as a set. Volume I starts with a discussion of a number of different approaches to strategy, and then examines a number of issues relating to analysis and formulation at the business unit level. Volume I contains the following chapters:

1. Introduction to Volume I   D. O. FAULKNER AND A. CAMPBELL

Part I Approaches to Strategy

2. The History of Strategy and Some Thoughts about the Future   J. KAY, P. MCKIERNAN, AND D. FAULKNER
3. The Boundary of the Firm   M. SLATER
4. Evolutionary Theory   D. BARRON

5. Institutional Theory   R. LOVERIDGE
6. The Strategic Management of Technology   D. TEECE
7. Strategy and Valuation   P. JOHNSON
8. The Knowledge-Based View of the Firm   R. GRANT

Part II Competitive Strategy

9. Analysing the Environment   R. PITKETHLY
10. Strategic Groups: Theory and Practice   J. MCGEE
11. Scenario Thinking and Strategic Modelling   R. G. COYLE
12. Analyzing Internal and Competitor Competences: Resources, Capabilities, and Management Processes   R. SANCHEZ
13. Dynamic Capabilities   S. TALLMAN
14. Formulating Strategy   C. BOWMAN
15. Organizational Learning   J. CHILD
16. Strategy in Service Organizations   S. SEGAL-HORN

REFERENCES

PRAHALAD, C. K., and HAMEL, G. (1990). 'The Core Competence of the Corporation'. *Harvard Business Review*, May–June: 79–91.

RUMELT, R. P. (1982). 'Diversification Strategy and Profitability'. *Strategic Management Journal*, 3: 359–69.

WERNERFELT, B. (1984). 'A Resource-Based View of the Firm'. *Strategic Management Journal*, 5: 171–80.

PART III

CORPORATE STRATEGY

CHAPTER 18

WHY DIVERSIFY?

FOUR DECADES OF
MANAGEMENT THINKING

MICHAEL GOOLD

KATHLEEN LUCHS

18.1 Introduction

Large, diversified corporations have been under critical scrutiny for many years. In 1951 the prevailing view in America was summarized in an article in the *Harvard Business Review*: 'The basic presumption is that a company turning from one type of activity to another is up to no good, especially if in the process it has become "big business"' (Andrews 1951: 94). Such companies were accused of being too powerful, and, in particular, of cross-subsidizing their different businesses in order to force competitors from the field. They were therefore seen as anti-competitive.

Today, diversified companies are also regarded by many commentators as being 'up to no good', but for just the opposite reason; they are now charged with being uncompetitive. The problem is not that they are over-mighty competitors, but that

This chapter is a revised version of Michael Goold and Kathleen Luchs, 'Why Diversify? Four Decades of Management Thinking', *Academy of Management Executive*, 7/3 (1993), 7 et seq. Reprinted with permission.

they add no value to their businesses. In 1987 Michael Porter wrote of the failure of many corporate strategies:

I studied the diversification records of 33 large, prestigious US companies over the 1950–1986 period and found that most of them had divested many more acquisitions than they had kept. The corporate strategies of most companies have dissipated instead of created shareholder value. By taking over companies and breaking them up, corporate raiders thrive on failed corporate strategies. (Porter 1987: 43)

How has thinking about the rationale for diversified companies evolved during this period of time? Why has fear of the power of diversified companies been replaced with scepticism about their results? What have we learned, both about diversification strategies that work and those that do not work? There have been relatively few influential ideas about what constitutes a successful strategy for a diversified company. This paper explores the development of these ideas, and examines current thinking about corporate-level strategy.

18.2 DIVERSIFICATION AND CORPORATE STRATEGY IN THE 1950S AND 1960S

An important and enduring justification for the diversified company is the argument that the managers of these companies possess general management skills that contribute to the overall performance of a company. Kenneth Andrews argued that there had been a steady growth of executive talent in America, equal to the task of managing diversity. The establishment of business schools in the early twentieth century created the basis for the education of professional managers, and the divisionalized structure of large corporations provided the opportunities for younger managers to gain the requisite experience (Andrews 1951, 1969).

18.2.1 General Management Skills

The idea that professional managers possessed skills that could be put to good use across different businesses rested on the assumption that different businesses nevertheless required similar managerial skills. This assumption received support from management theory. During the 1950s and 1960s much scholarly attention focused on identifying basic principles of management, useful to all managers and applicable to all kinds of enterprises. Peter Drucker, in *The Practice of Management*, argued that 'intuitive' management was no longer sufficient. He encouraged man-

agers to study the principles of management and to acquire knowledge and analyse their performance systematically (Drucker 1968: 21).

The interest in investigating and analysing underlying management principles continued into the 1960s. Harold Koontz wrote of the 'deluge of research and writing from the academic halls'. According to Koontz (1961: 175), it was the management process school, which aimed to identify universal principles of management, that held the greatest promise for advancing the practice of management.

Theorists such as Koontz and Drucker naturally emphasized the issues and problems which were common across different types of businesses, since their aim was to help all managers improve their skills and the performance of their businesses. Although they did not explicitly claim that professional managers could manage any business, it was not a great leap to conclude that, if all managers face similar problems, professional managers might be able to use their skills in different businesses. Simple observation, as well as theory, supported this idea. A writer in the *Harvard Business Review* noted that 'We are all familiar with those "professional managers" who are becoming the prototypes of our modern executive world. These men shift with great ease and with no apparent loss in effectiveness, from one industry to another. Their human and conceptual skills seem to make up for their unfamiliarity with the new job's technical aspects' (Katz 1955: 37). There was widespread respect for management skills, and businessmen were encouraged to apply their general management skills to improve the effectiveness of charities, universities, and government (Langlie 1960; Jones 1960; Andrews 1969; and Shetty and Perry 1976).

In Europe, too, there was interest in general management skills. The founding of business schools in the United Kingdom and in France during the 1960s, and the growing interest in management training, was in part motivated by the perceived need to provide European managers with the same kind of general management skills as their US competitors. Indeed, there was concern in Europe that the management skills of US companies were so powerful that Americans would take over large chunks of European industry (Whitley, Thomas, and Marceau 1981; Servan-Schreiber 1968).

18.2.2 Rise of Conglomerates

During the 1960s, the growth of conglomerates, with their numerous acquisitions of unrelated businesses across different industries, provided almost laboratory conditions in which to test out the idea that professional managers could apply their skills to many different businesses. Conglomerates such as Textron, ITT, and Litton not only grew rapidly, but also profitably, and top managers of these companies

perceived themselves as breaking new ground. For example, David Judelson of Gulf & Western claimed, 'Without the high degree of sophistication, skill, and effectiveness that management has developed only in the last two decades, the conglomerate could not exist. These management techniques provide the necessary unity and compatibility among a diversity of operations and acquisitions' (Judelson 1972: 458). Harold Geneen (1984) used a system of detailed budgets, tight financial control, and face-to-face meetings among his general managers to build ITT into a highly diversified conglomerate. In 1967 Royal Little, who masterminded Textron's broad diversification, explained that the company succeeded because 'we are adding that intangible called business judgement' (Berg 1973: 16). Textron had common financial controls, budgetary systems, and capital allocation procedures across its many businesses, but it provided few central services and had only a very small corporate office. The group vice-presidents, who were responsible for a number of divisions, were appointed from outside the company. They acted as overseers and consultants to the divisions.

These new American conglomerates were admired abroad. In the United Kingdom, one writer wrote glowingly of Litton Industries and its spectacular growth across high-tech industries, claiming that the company was 'a technological achievement of its own, an operation in the technology of management as much as the management of technology' (Heller 1969: 378). Several British companies, such as Slater Walker, embarked upon a strategy of conglomerate diversification during the 1960s and 1970s. The emphasis in Britain, however, was more on identifying and buying companies whose assets were worth more than their stock market price and less on the application of sound, underlying general management principles by the top management group (Slater 1977: 91).

Did the conglomerates add value to their numerous businesses across different industries? The practices of at least some conglomerates such as Textron held up well under academic scrutiny. Norman Berg argued that corporate executives in such companies were fulfilling new roles as 'managers of managers'. While he admitted that it was too early to draw firm conclusions about the long-term success of conglomerates, Berg (1969) suggested that corporate strategies based on improving the performance of a diverse collection of businesses would have important implications for the practice of management and also for public policy.

For over twenty years, faith in general management skills seemed to justify a kind of virtuous circle of corporate growth and diversification. Andrews summarized the basic premiss, arguing that 'successful diversification—because it always means successful surmounting of formidable administrative problems—develops know-how which further diversification will capitalise and extend' (Andrews 1951: 98). The conglomerate movement of the 1960s, involving extensive diversification across a wide variety of industries, seemed to demonstrate that the specialized skills and practices of corporate general managers enabled them to manage ever greater complexity and diversity.

18.2.3 Conglomerates and Performance Problems

There was little reason to question the belief that general management skills provided a sufficient rationale for diversified companies while such corporations were performing well and growing profitably. But by the late 1960s, conglomerates were encountering performance problems. In early 1969, the stock prices of conglomerates such as Litton, Gulf & Western, and Textron fell as much as 50 per cent from their highs a year earlier, compared to a 9 per cent decline in the Dow Jones Industrial Average over the period, and one observer foresaw a round of conglomerate divestitures if such companies were to survive. Even ITT's consistent record of increased quarterly earnings over 58 quarters during the 1960s and 1970s was broken in 1974 (Attiyeh 1972; Geneen 1984: 43).

What became apparent was that sound principles of organization and financial control, coupled to a corporate objective of growth, were not, alone, sufficient to ensure satisfactory performance in highly diversified companies. Indeed, General Electric, a leader in the development of sophisticated techniques and principles for the management of a diverse portfolio of businesses, found by the early 1970s that its management approach had resulted in an extended period of what GE called 'profitless growth'. For example, the company's sales increased 40 per cent from 1965 to 1970, while its profits actually fell (Goold and Quinn 1990; Hamermesh 1986: 3; Hall 1978: 17).

By the late 1960s, there was therefore an increasing awareness that a new approach to the management of diversity was needed.

18.3 DIVERSIFICATION AND CORPORATE STRATEGY IN THE 1970S

As a response to the increasing recognition that large and diversified companies present particular management problems, increasing attention was devoted to the question of the issues on which general managers should focus their efforts.

18.3.1 The Concept of Strategy

One theme that emerged with increasing force during the 1960s and 1970s was the need for senior managers to focus their attention on the 'strategies' of their

companies. Strategy was more than long-range planning or objective setting; it was a way of deciding the basic direction of the company and preparing it to meet future challenges (Drucker 1959; Ansoff 1965; Sloan 1986; Chandler 1982; Mace 1965).

C. Roland Christensen, one of the creators of the Business Policy course at Harvard Business School during the 1960s, argued that the concept of strategy made it possible to simplify the complex tasks of top managers (Learned et al. 1965). A focus on strategy prevented senior executives from meddling in operating details and day-to-day issues, which should be left to more junior managers with direct responsibility for them. It allowed them to concentrate on the most important issues facing their companies. And it simplified management by providing a framework for decisions.

CEOs readily accepted that strategy should be their main and unique responsibility. During the late 1960s and 1970s many companies established formal planning systems, and the appropriate structure and uses of such systems received much attention from academics (Vancil and Lorange 1975; Lorange and Vancil 1977; Ringbakk 1969; Berg 1965). In the early 1970s, Louis Gerstner remarked on how quickly strategic planning had been adopted by companies, noting that 'Writer after writer has hailed this new discipline as the fountainhead of all corporate progress' (Gerstner 1972: 5).

The strategic frameworks, models, and tools being developed by academics and consultants focused mainly on strategic issues at the level of the business unit, and they were, therefore, less relevant in helping to define an overall strategy for companies with many different businesses. Andrews (1980: 35), however, defined the main task of corporate-level strategy as identifying the businesses in which the firm would compete, and this became the accepted understanding of corporate strategy. This general concept of corporate strategy, though, did not provide much practical guidance to some of the problems managers of diversified companies confronted. In particular, it did not help them decide how resources should be allocated among businesses, especially when investment proposals were being put forward by a large number of disparate businesses, each with its own strategy. This problem was exacerbated when the aggregate demand for resources exceeded what was available.

18.3.2 Problems with Resource Allocation

Resource allocation decisions in diversified companies are a key part of corporate strategy. But they present particular difficulties. The corporate centre must take a view on the relative merits of investment proposals coming from a range of businesses in different sectors, with different time horizons, different competitive

positions, and different risk profiles, not to mention management teams with differing credibilities. This can be complex. In the early 1970s, for example, a company such as ITT had to attempt to allocate resources between businesses that included telecommunications, insurance, rental cars, bakeries, and construction. With many divisions competing for funds, how could a company be sure it was investing in the best projects for future growth (Berg 1965)?

Joseph Bower explored in detail how a large, diversified firm allocated resources. His research highlighted the gulf between financial theory, which saw the manager's task as choosing projects with the highest returns, and corporate reality, where all proposed projects showed at least the return required by the corporate hurdle rate for investment. In practice, divisional managers only proposed projects with acceptable forecast returns, and corporate-level managers had little basis on which to choose between projects.

Bower (1986) argued that investment decisions should not be made on a project-by-project basis, but had to be integrally related to a business's strategic product/market decisions. During the 1970s, the new techniques of portfolio planning that were introduced by the Boston Consulting Group and others gained wide acceptance because they helped corporate executives resolve practical problems of capital allocation in the context of an overall corporate strategy (Bower 1986; Hamermesh 1986).

18.3.3 Portfolio Planning

Portfolio planning provided corporate managers with a common framework to compare many different businesses. The industry attractiveness-business position matrix developed at GE, the Boston Consulting Group's growth-share matrix (Figure 18.1), and variations developed at other consultancies were used to classify businesses in terms of their strategic position and opportunities. These classifications helped managers both to set appropriate objectives and resource allocation strategies for different businesses, and to determine the overall cash requirements and cash generation of the corporate portfolio (Hall 1978; Day 1977).

The helicopter view provided by portfolio planning techniques was widely perceived as useful. For example, one CEO explained:

Portfolio planning became relevant to me as soon as I became CEO. I was finding it very difficult to manage and understand so many different products and markets. I just grabbed at portfolio planning, because it provided me with a way to organise my thinking about our businesses and the resource allocation issues facing the total company. I became and still am very enthusiastic. I guess you could say that I went for it hook, line, and sinker. (Hamermesh 1986: 30)

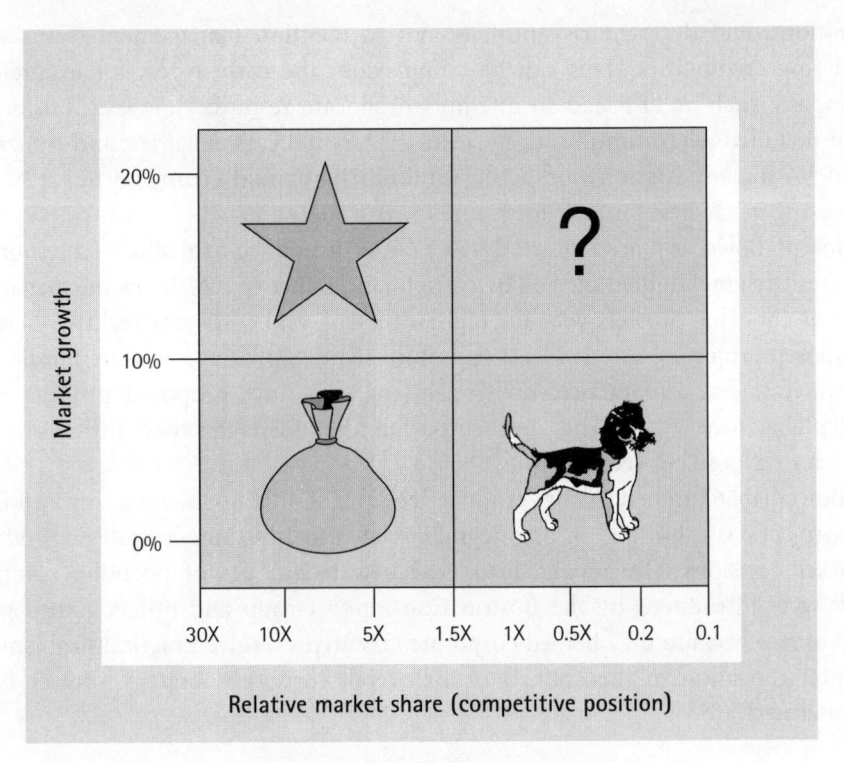

Fig. 18.1 Growth–share matrix

During the 1970s, more and more corporations adopted portfolio planning, with the largest diversified companies among the earliest adherents. A survey sponsored by the *Harvard Business Review* showed that by 1979, 45 per cent of the Fortune 500 companies were using some form of portfolio planning (Haspeslagh 1982).

In many companies, portfolio planning techniques became more than analytical tools to help chief executives direct corporate resources towards the most profitable opportunities: they became the basis of corporate strategy itself. The key concept here was the idea of a 'balanced' portfolio: that is to say, a portfolio made up of businesses whose profitability, growth, and cash flow characteristics would complement each other, and add up to a satisfactory overall corporate performance. 'Imbalance' could be caused, for example, either by excessive cash generation with too few growth opportunities or by insufficient cash generation to fund the growth requirements elsewhere in the portfolio (Hedley 1977; Hofer and Schendel 1978). Often, the first step towards balancing the corporate portfolio was to identify businesses that were a drain on corporate resources. Monsanto, for example, used portfolio planning to restructure its portfolio, divesting low-growth commodity chemicals businesses and acquiring businesses in higher growth industries such as biotechnology (Hamermesh 1986: 71).

Portfolio planning reinforced the virtuous circle of corporate growth and diversification that had been originally founded on general management skills. It helped corporate-level managers correct past diversification mistakes, leading to the divestiture of weak businesses, and it encouraged them to invest in a mix of businesses, with different strategic (and cash) characteristics to balance their corporate portfolios and ensure future growth.

18.3.4 Problems with Portfolio Management

But even as an increasing number of corporations turned to portfolio planning, problems emerged in managing 'balanced' portfolios (Bettis and Hall 1983). Companies discovered that while certain businesses appeared to meet all the economic requirements of the corporate portfolio, they did not fit easily into the corporate family. It turned out to be extremely difficult, for example, for corporate managers with long experience of managing mature businesses in a particular industry sector to manage effectively their acquired growth businesses in new, dynamic, and unfamiliar sectors.

Research on how companies actually used portfolio planning confirmed the difficulties of managing businesses with different strategic characteristics, missions, or mandates. Philippe Haspeslagh investigated whether companies adjusted their systems of financial planning, capital investment appraisal, incentive compensation, or strategic planning to fit the requirements of their different businesses. The focus of his study was on the role played by general management, rather than on specific business-level strategies. He found that companies made few changes in their formal corporate-level systems, but corporate-level managers in successful companies did make informal attempts to adapt these systems to their businesses (Haspeslagh 1982). In another study on the effectiveness of portfolio planning techniques, the authors discovered that cash cows performed better in an organizational context of autonomy while fast growing businesses benefited from more control. They concluded that the administrative context was an important variable in explaining business performance, and that many companies were taking the wrong approach to some of their businesses (Hamermesh and White 1984).

The recognition that different types of businesses had to be managed differently undermined the argument that general management skills, buttressed by the common frameworks of strategy and portfolio planning, provided the rationale for diversified companies. Many companies discovered that common systems and approaches, when applied to different kinds of businesses, could detract value from those businesses. Portfolio planning helped corporate executives sort out the contribution of each of their businesses to the corporate portfolio, but it did not answer the other critical question confronting a diversified company: what contribution should the corporation make to each of its businesses?

18.4 DIVERSIFICATION AND CORPORATE STRATEGY IN THE 1980S

During the 1980s, there was widespread scepticism about the ability of companies to manage and add value to diverse, conglomerate portfolios. Raiders such as Carl Icahn and T. Boone Pickens demonstrated that they could acquire even the largest companies, break them up, and realize huge profits. The takeover activity of the 1980s prompted a rethinking of both the role of the corporate centre in large companies, and of the kinds of strategies which were appropriate for diversified companies.

18.4.1 Cost-cutting at Headquarters

What seemed most obvious about the corporate level in many companies was not its contribution, but its cost. Thus, attention shifted onto cutting headquarters costs. Some companies turned central services into profit centres, charged with selling their services to the business units, while other companies disbanded some central functions altogether. The pruning of corporate staffs often meant devolving more authority to line managers in decentralized units (Kanter 1989: 94; More 1987).

Cost-cutting and the downsizing of corporate staffs, however, were not alone sufficient to demonstrate that corporate centres could add value to their businesses, and the overall performance of large, diversified corporations also came under increasing scrutiny. Michael Porter (1987) published a study showing the high rate of divestiture of acquisitions among American corporations, arguing that the diversification strategies of many companies had failed to create value. And, the wave of takeovers caused executives to pay increasing attention to their company's stock price as analysts and raiders identified 'value gaps', or the difference between the current stock market price of a company and its break-up value (Young and Sutcliffe 1990).

18.4.2 Value-based Planning

Faced with the threat from raiders and the criticism of academics such as Porter, chief executives devoted themselves increasingly to the task of creating shareholder value. Managers were encouraged to evaluate corporate performance in the same terms as the stock market (and raiders), using economic rather than accounting

measures, and to take whatever actions were necessary to improve their company's stock price. Value-based planning, using the financial tools of discounted cash flow, ROE spreads, and hurdle rates, provided corporate managers with a fresh perspective on the linkages between stock prices and competitive strategy (Rappaport 1986; Reimann 1987).

A company's stock price, according to proponents of value-based planning, is determined by the value of the strategies of its businesses. However, it can be very difficult for managers to assess the strategies of dissimilar businesses: 'corporate level planners facing a portfolio of four, ten, dozens, or dozens and dozens of units do not know—probably cannot know—enough about each unit's competitive position, industry, rivals, and customers to make this determination' (Alberts and McTaggart 1984; Arzac 1986). One of the appeals of value-based planning is that, like portfolio planning, it offers corporate-level executives a means of evaluating many different businesses using a common framework. The corporate level can require business units to make strategic choices on the basis of economic returns, and doing this systematically across all units, it is argued, provides the corporate centre with the basis for making decisions on capital allocation.

Value-based planning techniques gained many adherents, especially among American corporations. In 1987 an article in *Fortune* described how 'managements have caught the religion. At first reluctant, they pound at the door of consultants who can teach them the way to a higher stock price—a price so high it would thwart even the most determined raider' (Curran 1987: 24).

But value-based planning also has limitations as a guide to corporate strategy. It can help corporate managers to focus on the goal of increasing shareholder wealth and to understand the criteria that must be met to do so. But it does not provide much insight into the kind of corporate strategies that should be pursued to meet these criteria. A higher stock price is a reward for creating value. But the key question remains: how can corporations add value to diverse business portfolios? Perhaps the most influential view on this vital topic to have emerged during the 1980s is that they should 'stick-to-the-knitting'.

18.4.3 Stick-to-the-Knitting

The concept of corporate success based on core businesses, or 'stick-to-the-knitting', gained popularity with the publication in 1982 of Peters and Waterman's *In Search of Excellence*. Successful corporations, they observed, did not diversify widely. They tended to specialize in particular industries and focused intently on improving their knowledge and skills in the areas they knew best (Peters and Waterman 1982).

'Stick-to-the-knitting' advice was also a reaction against the analytical techniques and impersonal approach of much of strategic and portfolio planning. Bob Hayes and Bill Abernathy voiced these concerns in their article 'Managing Our Way to Economic Decline'. In their view, too many American corporations were being run by 'pseudo-professional' managers, skilled in finance and law, but lacking in technological expertise or in-depth experience in any particular industry. They warned that portfolios diversified across different industries and businesses were appropriate for stocks and bonds, but not for corporations (Hayes and Abernathy 1980). The need for experience and deep knowledge of a business was also emphasized by Henry Mintzberg, who criticized the 'thin and lifeless' strategies that result from treating businesses as mere positions on a portfolio matrix. He argued that instead of broad diversity, we need 'focused organisations that understand their missions, *know* the people they serve, and excite the ones they employ; we should be encouraging "thick" management, deep knowledge, healthy competition and authentic social responsibility' (Mintzberg 1989: 373).

The widespread conviction that companies should 'stick-to-the-knitting' increased scepticism about the ability of corporations to manage and add value to diverse portfolios. It reinforced the practical pressures created by the corporate raiders and contributed to a wave of retrenching. From the mid-1980s onwards, a goal for many corporations has been to rationalize their portfolios to overcome the perceived disadvantages of broad diversification.

18.4.4 Corporate Restructuring

Restructuring (whether voluntary or not) has frequently led to the disposal of corporate assets. In 1985, for example, General Mills announced its intention to focus on its core businesses of consumer foods and restaurants, and the company sold off its toy and fashion businesses (Porter 1988). More recently, General Signal embarked on a strategy of 'back to the basics', retreating from its earlier major investments in high-tech businesses to focus on its traditional 'boring' products such as industrial mixers (Lubove 1992: 106).

Restructuring has been widely regarded as a salutary correction to the excesses of broad diversification. Michael Jensen has argued that corporate break-ups, divisional sell-offs, and LBOs are critical developments that can prevent the wasteful use of capital by managers of large public corporations, and other recent academic studies support the view that restructuring does help improve the performance of corporations (Jensen 1989; Chatterjee 1992; Bhagat, Shleifer, and Vishny 1990). But restructuring implies a sense of which businesses a company should retain and which it should divest. How should the 'core' businesses be selected?

One answer is that companies should restructure to limit their businesses to one, or a few, closely related industries. In this way, managers stick to what they know well, and are best able to exploit corporate expertise. This approach is consistent with 'stick-to-the-knitting' advice, but it is not a complete answer. Successful companies such as GE, Hanson, and Cooper Industries nevertheless have businesses in many different industries. Furthermore, sticking to a single industry does not necessarily limit complexity or ensure that companies expand into areas they 'know'. During the 1980s, companies such as Prudential and Merrill Lynch sought to combine different types of financial services businesses. They discovered that businesses such as insurance, stockbroking, and banking, though all in the financial services industry, nonetheless required very different approaches, resources, and skills (Grant 1988, 1991*a*).

Another reservation about a 'stick-to-the-knitting' strategy based on limiting diversification to closely related businesses is that, despite extensive research, empirical evidence on the performance of companies pursuing more and less related diversification strategies is ambiguous and contradictory. Many studies have compared the performance of single-product firms, companies that diversify into related products, markets, or technologies, and unrelated conglomerates, but no firm relationship between different diversification strategies and performance has been discovered.[1]

Some concept of what constitutes a 'core portfolio'—or the corporate 'knitting' —is required, though, if restructuring is to result in long-term improvement in corporate performance.

18.5 DIVERSIFICATION AND CORPORATE STRATEGY IN THE 1990s

The main issues for corporate strategy in the 1990s have therefore emerged as how to identify the businesses that should form a core portfolio for a corporation, and how to find ways of adding value to those businesses.

Three main alternative answers to these questions have received support in current management thinking:

(1) diversification should be limited to those businesses with 'synergy';
(2) the corporate focus should be on exploiting 'core competencies' across different businesses;

---

[1] There is an extensive literature on this topic. See Rumelt 1974, 1982; Bettis 1981; Christensen and Montgomery 1981; Johnson and Thomas 1987; Seth 1990.

(3) successful diversification depends on building a portfolio of businesses that fit with the managerial 'dominant logic' of top executives and their 'management style'.

18.5.1 Synergy

Synergy occurs when the performance of a portfolio of businesses adds up to more than the sum of its parts. The concept of synergy is based in part on economies of scale; two or more businesses can lower their costs if they can combine manufacturing facilities, use a common sales force, or advertise jointly, and in this way the combined businesses are worth more than they would be on a stand-alone basis (Ansoff 1965).

In much of the current management literature, synergy has become virtually synonymous with corporate-level strategy. Michael Porter views the management of interrelationships between businesses as the essence of corporate-level strategy, arguing that without synergy a diversified company is little more than a mutual fund (Porter 1985). Rosabeth Moss Kanter (1989: 90), too, argues that the achievement of synergy is the only justification for a multi-business company. In a review of the literature on mergers, Friedrich Trautwein (1990), a German academic, found that managers almost always justified diversification moves in terms of the synergies available, and that most of the advice in the management literature on diversification was based on the concept of realizing synergies.

In practice, however, many companies have found it very difficult to gain benefits from a corporate strategy based on synergy (Ramanujam and Varadarajan 1989; Campbell and Luchs 1992). Acquisitions aimed at realizing synergies can be especially risky; for example, two academic commentators have noted that anticipated synergy benefits 'show an almost unshakeable resolve not to appear when it becomes time for their release' (Reed and Luffman 1986: 34). Quantitative evidence appears to support the observation that synergies are hard to achieve; a recent study on takeovers concluded that most gains arise from asset disposals and restructuring rather than from synergy (Chatterjee 1992).

Those who view synergy as the essence of corporate-level strategy, including Porter and Kanter, acknowledge that companies find it difficult to gain synergy benefits and that the failure rate is high. Much of the current literature, therefore, focuses on implementation—what companies have to do in order to gain benefits from sharing skills or activities across businesses. Porter, for instance, discusses the need for the evolution of a new organizational form, which he calls the 'horizontal organization'. Horizontal organizations facilitate interrelationships across different businesses by overlaying horizontal structures, systems, and managerial approaches onto the vertical relationships which currently characterize the ties between business units and the corporate centre (Porter 1985). Kanter (1989) describes the

emergence of the 'post-entrepreneurial corporation', which aims to create the relationships and management processes required for cross-business cooperation. Christopher Bartlett and Sumantra Ghoshal argue a similar case for the complex problems facing multinationals attempting to make the most of their businesses in different countries. In their view, multinationals need to develop new organizational capabilities so that components, products, resources, people, and information can flow freely between interdependent units. Bartlett and Ghoshal (1989) describe such an integrated network as a 'transnational' organization.

Transnational or horizontal or post-entrepreneurial organizations, by definition, capture many synergy benefits because they have the organizational capabilities to manage complex interrelationships across businesses. There are, however, very few examples of companies that represent these new kinds of organizations, at least in fully-fledged form. Consequently, much of the advice on synergy remains theoretical and prescriptive.

There is evidence, furthermore, that managing complex interrelationships to create synergies across businesses is not the only means of creating value. Michael Goold and Andrew Campbell (1987), in their study of strategic management styles, found in the 1980s that companies such as Hanson and Courtaulds, which placed very little emphasis on synergy as a source of corporate value added, performed at least as well as companies which placed more emphasis on linkages across businesses. These findings are reinforced by successful multi-business companies such as KKR, the leveraged buy-out specialist, and Berkshire Hathaway, managed by the renowned investor Warren Buffet, which are collections of independent businesses, and whose strategies are not based on exploiting synergies across their businesses. The assumption that synergy is the only rationale for a group of companies does not fit the available evidence, and this suggests that not all corporations need focus their efforts on constructing and managing portfolios of interrelated businesses.

Synergy remains a powerful concept in our understanding of corporate strategy, but it is difficult to accept that it is the 'one best way' to create value in a multi-business company. For some companies, the advantages of managing stand-alone businesses may outweigh the long-term investment required to create linkages among those businesses, and the potential for synergy may simply not exist in some corporate portfolios. We need to discover more about when synergy is an appropriate corporate strategy, and we need to learn more about how companies successful at managing interrelationships across businesses go about it.

18.5.2 Core Competencies

Another approach to corporate strategy stresses building on the core competencies of the corporation. This can be seen as a particular case of synergy, with corporate

value creation dependent on exploiting unique skills and capabilities across a portfolio of businesses. Gary Hamel and C. K. Prahalad focus on technological competencies. They argue that the corporate portfolio should not be perceived simply as a group of businesses, but also as a collection of such competencies. In managing the corporate portfolio, managers must ensure that each part draws on and contributes to the core competencies the corporation is seeking to build and exploit. Even a poorly performing business may be contributing to an important core competence, and if managers divest such businesses they may also be discarding some of their competencies. If corporations are unable to transfer a core competence from one business to another, then they are wasting their resources. According to Prahalad and Hamel (1990; Hamel and Prahalad 1989), many of the current management approaches of Western corporations, including SBUs, decentralization, and resource allocation practices, undermine the ability of corporations to build core competencies, since autonomous businesses seldom have the resources or vision to build world-class competencies.

Hiroyuki Itami (1987), a Japanese academic, focuses on building the corporation's 'invisible assets', such as expertise in a particular technology, brand names, reputation, or customer information. Such assets, he argues, can be employed throughout the firm without being used up, and they are the only sustainable source of competitive advantage. Philippe Haspeslagh and David Jemison, authors of a recent study on acquisitions, support a capabilities-based view of corporate value creation, defining core capabilities as managerial and technological skills gained mainly through experience. Such capabilities can be applied across the corporation's businesses and make an important contribution to customer benefits (Haspeslagh and Jemison 1991: 23). It can be difficult to define a corporation's capabilities objectively, but understanding what they are can provide important insights into its sources of competitive advantage and the strategic options of the firm (Grant 1991b; Campbell 1991; Stalk, Evans, and Shulman 1992).

The work on core skills, capabilities or resources, has generated much interest. Walter Kiechel, in *Fortune* magazine, described how some executives are perceiving their role, and that of the corporate centre, as guardians and promoters of the company's core skills, and sums up the current understanding of these concepts: 'To the extent that such skills can be exploited by each of the company's businesses, they represent a reason for having all those businesses under one corporate umbrella—a much better reason, the experts add, than the fabled synergies that multibusiness companies of yore were supposed to realise but seldom did' (Kiechel 1988: 20).

But corporations, which do base their strategy on core competencies, have to be careful that the overall competence-based strategy does not become an excuse for poor performance or poor judgement. IBM, for example, acquired Rolm in order to gain access to the smaller company's expertise in PBX systems. Five years later, however, following heavy losses, IBM sold a majority stake in Rolm to Siemens. Some commentators feel that IBM was too optimistic about Rolm's competencies

and potential and not sufficiently knowledgeable about changes underway in the PBX market or within Rolm (Hof and Keller 1989: 82–4). It can be difficult to judge when an investment in a business is justified in terms of building a core competence, particularly if it means suspending normal profitability criteria and if the investment is in an unfamiliar business area.

Another danger with the competence approach to corporate strategy is that businesses may require similar core competencies, but demand different overall strategies and managerial approaches. Texas Instruments, for example, attempted to exploit the core competence it had developed in its semi-conductors business in areas such as calculators, watches, and home computers. It failed in these new areas not because it lacked the core semi-conductor competence, but because its top management had no experience in managing such consumer-oriented businesses (Prahalad and Bettis 1986: 495).

Similarly, Procter & Gamble applied its skills in product innovation and consumer promotion to a soft drinks business, Crush, but eventually divested the business because it ran into unfamiliar problems managing the local bottlers who largely control distribution of soft drinks (Winters 1989). Core competencies may add value in specific areas in a variety of different businesses, but this is no guarantee that, overall, a company will be able to manage those different businesses successfully.

The work on core competencies and capabilities broadens our understanding of a corporation's resources, and points out the important role of the corporate centre in building such resources and ensuring that they are used to best advantage. As with synergy, however, it is difficult to accept that this is the only way to add value to a corporate portfolio. Corporate centres are concerned not only with building skills and competencies in their businesses, but also with allocating resources to them, approving their plans and strategies, and monitoring and controlling their results. These important 'planning and control' functions can also be a source of added value, if done well. Some companies, such as Berkshire Hathaway and Hanson, lay far more stress on these planning and control functions than on competence building; and, in all companies, the planning and control functions occupy a vital place, even where the management of core competencies is also a focus of attention.

18.5.3 Dominant Logic and Management Style

A third approach to corporate success focuses on how the corporate centre adds value to a portfolio of businesses, in particular in its planning and control role. C. K. Prahalad and Richard Bettis argue that the more diverse a firm, the more complex the problems in managing it. Diversity, however, cannot be defined simply in terms

of the number of product/markets in which a firm competes; the strategic variety of the firm's businesses is a more significant measure of its diversity.

With firms in strategically similar businesses, the centre can use common methods and approaches, using a single managerial dominant logic: 'A dominant general management logic is defined as the way in which managers conceptualise the business and make critical resource allocation decisions—be it in technologies, product development, distribution, advertising, or in human resource management' (Prahalad and Bettis 1986: 490).

When managerial dominant logic does not match the needs of the business, tensions and problems arise. The corporate centre is liable to appoint the wrong managers to the business, to sanction inappropriate plans and investments, to control against the wrong targets, and to interfere unproductively in the managing of the business.

Goold and Campbell's work on strategic management styles shows how dominant logic works in specific companies. In their research on large, diversified companies they identified different types of strategic management styles, with the main styles being Financial Control, Strategic Control, and Strategic Planning. The different styles each added value, but in different ways and to businesses with different characteristics and requirements. Financial Control companies, for example, have distinctive administrative and control systems, emphasizing the setting and meeting of annual budget targets. Although they may invest in a wide variety of industries, the portfolios of businesses of successful Financial Control companies share common characteristics (Goold and Campbell 1987). Hanson was a good example: 'The company's strategy is to focus on mature, stable businesses: "We avoid areas of very high technology. We do not want to be in businesses which are highly capital intensive, where decision-making has to be centralised or which rely on huge and sometimes expensive research with a prospect of a return sometime or never"' (Campbell, Devine, and Young 1990: 242).

In this view, the dominant logic or management style of the corporate management group is central to the performance of a diversified firm, and a group of businesses is best managed when the dominant logic of top managers matches the strategic characteristics and requirements of the businesses. The importance of the 'fit' between top managers and the businesses in the corporate portfolio has also been emphasized by executives. Orion Hoch of Litton, for example, explained the reasons for Litton's extensive divestments and restructuring: 'Our aim was to go back to businesses that we could be comfortable with. . . . We wanted to get back to doing what we were good at doing' (*Barron's,* 20 May 1991). Gary Roubos, CEO of Dover Corporation, argued that the company was a successful conglomerate because it invested only in businesses in which it had considerable management 'feel', even though these businesses were highly diverse: 'Automatic lifts and toggle clamps are different—but they have much more in common than, say, investment banking and selling soap' (Aguilar 1988).

18.5.4 Dominant Logic, Management Style, and Success

Dominant logic may help explain why conglomerate diversification can succeed, and also why diversification based on synergy or core competencies can fail. If conglomerate diversification, such as that of Hanson, is based on businesses with a similar strategic logic, then it is possible for the corporate centre to take a common approach and to add value to those businesses. On the other hand, businesses with opportunities for sharing activities or skills, or ones requiring the same core competence, may nonetheless have different strategic logics. This makes it difficult for a corporate centre to realize synergy or exploit a core competence across the businesses. Oil companies that diversified into other extractive, energy or natural resource businesses in pursuit of synergies or core competencies tended to find that the benefits they sought were overwhelmed by the problems caused by dissimilarities in strategic logic between the new businesses and the core oil businesses.

The concepts of dominant logic and management style offer some promising insights into both successful and unsuccessful diversification efforts, but there are unanswered questions (Goold and Campbell 1991: 115–17). Should diversified corporations aim to build portfolios of strategically related businesses, to ensure that top management and corporate systems and approaches do add value? Or should corporations seek to differentiate their approaches—develop 'multiple dominant logics'—in order to manage businesses with different strategic characteristics successfully?

Goold and Campbell discovered that companies tend to adopt a particular strategic management style, even though the style was usually implicit. They observed that it was difficult for managers to cope with a variety of approaches or styles. They argued that CEOs should aim to focus their portfolios on the kinds of businesses which would gain benefits from their strategic management style (Goold and Campbell 1987). On the other hand, authorities on multinationals argue that the increasing complexities of globally spread businesses and international competition require corporations to develop new capabilities to manage businesses facing different strategic issues. C. K. Prahalad and Yves Doz (1987: 261) maintain that the winners in the struggle for global competitive advantage will be those companies that can develop differentiated structures, management processes, and systems appropriate to the wide variety of their businesses. Bartlett and Ghoshal describe how the 'administrative heritage' of companies emphasizes a particular approach to issues such as coordination across businesses, but they argue that the idealized transnational company should be able to combine different approaches and develop 'a full arsenal of coordinating processes, practices, and tools, and to use those mechanisms in the most effective and efficient manner' (Bartlett and Ghoshal 1989: 166).

The question of whether it is possible to add value to many different kinds of businesses is critical. Bartlett and Ghoshal found evidence that some companies are seeking ways to encompass much more variety, but none had yet become a true transnational. Goold, Campbell, and Alexander (1994) found that the most

successful diversified companies were those not attempting to add value to different fields of business. The most successful companies, like Rio Tinto the mining company or Unilever the consumer products company, were applying a consistent managerial formula to a portfolio of similar kinds of businesses. The authors concluded that these firms had 'parenting advantage': their corporate centres were better at adding value to certain kinds of business than rivals. These firms were also worse than rivals at adding value to businesses that did not fit their 'medicine'. As a result they had divested these businesses to rival parent companies. Sadtler, Campbell, and Koch (1997) reinforced this conclusion by studying spinoffs, demergers, and break-ups. They noted that the success of spinoffs and demergers was due to the management improvements that came about when a division or business was released from the inappropriate influence of its previous parent. They even developed a break-up index, showing which companies most needed to break up. These were companies with portfolios containing different kinds of businesses.

As the trend for focus has gathered momentum, it appears that companies are abandoning their attempts to manage highly complex, differentiated portfolios. It appears to be easier to add value to a portfolio of like businesses. The companies with portfolios of different kinds of businesses need very large synergies to justify the complexity costs and the risks of inappropriate planning and control.

18.6 THE CHALLENGE OF DIVERSIFICATION

During the last four decades, managers and academics have sought both to understand the basis of successful diversification and to address the problems created by such diversification. Figure 18.2 summarizes the evolution of thinking and practice during this time.

From the 1950s onwards, the development of management principles and the professional education of managers led to the belief that general management skills provided the justification for diversification. Diversified companies and conglomerates were seen to add value through the skills of their professional top managers, who applied modern management techniques and generalized approaches to a wide variety of businesses across different industries. During the late 1960s, however, the performance of many conglomerates weakened, and a new approach to corporate management of diversity was sought. The concepts of strategy and strategic management provided a new focus for senior management's attention during the 1970s, but soon proved unable to resolve many of the choices and trade-offs involved in resource allocation in the multi-business firm. Portfolio planning techniques helped many companies improve capital allocation across businesses with different

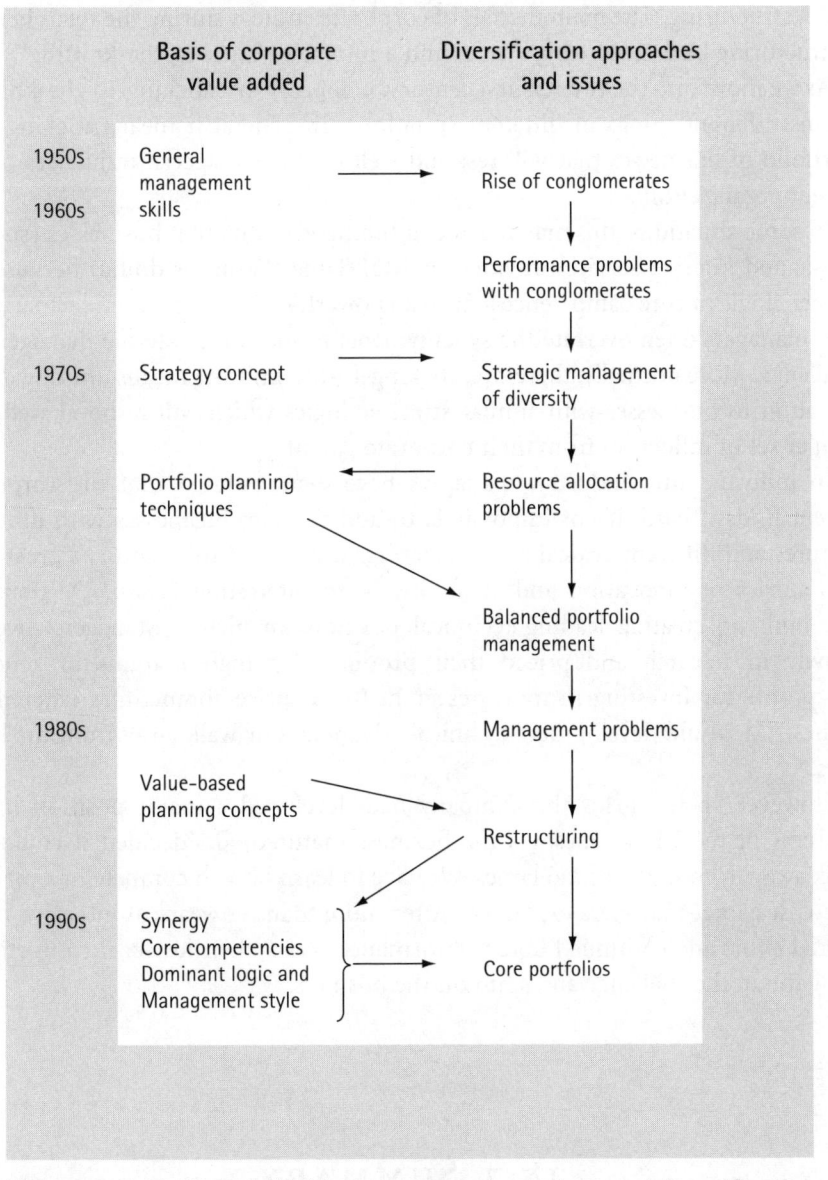

Basis of corporate value added

Diversification approaches and issues

1950s 1960s	General management skills	→ Rise of conglomerates
		Performance problems with conglomerates
1970s	Strategy concept	→ Strategic management of diversity
	Portfolio planning techniques	← Resource allocation problems
		Balanced portfolio management
1980s		Management problems
	Value-based planning concepts	Restructuring
1990s	Synergy Core competencies Dominant logic and Management style	→ Core portfolios

Fig. 18.2 Evolution of thinking on corporate strategy and diversification

strategic positions, and led on to the idea of balanced portfolio management. But such analytical approaches overlooked the problem of manageability. Many companies found it difficult to manage businesses facing different strategic issues, and during the 1980s poor corporate performance again became a critical issue. Raiders, executives, and academics realized that many diversified corporations were not creating shareholder value, and there was a wave of takeovers, corporate break-ups,

and restructuring. The main themes of corporate strategy during the 1980s became restructuring back to core businesses and a resolve to 'stick-to-the-knitting'.

As we move into the twenty-first century, it appears that sticking-to-the-knitting means different things in different situations. In general it means sticking to a portfolio of businesses that will respond well to the managerial influences of the parent organization.

In some situations, this may mean combining very different businesses (such as music and internet service providers as AOL Time Warner is doing) because the synergy logic or core competence logic is so powerful. However, experience suggests that managers often overrate the synergy benefits and underrate the management challenge. More normally, therefore, sticking-to-the-knitting means limiting diversification to businesses with similar strategic logics which will respond well to a similar set of influences from their corporate parent.

In industry after industry, managers have demonstrated that the corporate parent finds it hard, if not impossible, to add value to businesses with different cultures and different critical success factors. 3M, one of this century's great success stories of innovation and creativity, is an interesting lesson. 3M's success was built on creating leading technical positions in niches. Managers invested heavily in research and priced their products for high margins to generate the profits for investing in more research. If low price competitors entered the niches, 3M would develop new technical advantages or walk away from the business.

However, in the 1980s the company had developed a major position in the business of recording tapes. As the business matured, 3M decided it could not walk away from it. It was too large. 'We have to learn how to compete in a mature, low-cost game,' managers explained. After more than ten years of intensive managerial effort and continued underperformance versus their low-cost competitors, 3M gave up the challenge and spun off the business.

18.7 SUMMARY

After four decades of management thinking, we are beginning to arrive at a consensus about diversification. Businesses should not be retained in the portfolio or added to the portfolio unless the parent company can create more value from the businesses than they could create on their own or with any other parent.

We are also beginning to understand the limitations of parent company skills. The dominant logics observed by Prahalad and Bettis prove to be entrenched and more limited than most management thinkers had hoped. Or to take a more

positive view, the intensity of competition between parent companies is becoming so great that it is only possible to 'create more value' when the portfolio is tightly focused on similar kinds of businesses.

References

AGUILAR, F. J. (1988). 'Groen: A Dover Industries Company'. HBS Case 9–388–055.

ALBERTS, WILLIAM W., and McTAGGART, JAMES M. (1984). 'Value Based Strategic Investment Planning'. *Interfaces,* Jan.–Feb.: 138–51.

ANDREWS, KENNETH R. (1951). 'Product Diversification and the Public Interest'. *Harvard Business Review,* July: 91–107.

——— (1969). 'Toward Professionalism in Business Management'. *Harvard Business Review,* Mar.–Apr.: 49–60.

——— (1980). *The Concept of Corporate Strategy* (1971, revised edn.). Homewood, Ill.: Richard D. Irwin, Inc.

ANSOFF, H. IGOR (1965). *Corporate Strategy.* New York: McGraw-Hill.

ARZAC, ENRIQUE R. (1986). 'Do Your Business Units Create Shareholder Value?' *Harvard Business Review,* Jan.–Feb.: 121–6.

ATTIYEH, ROBERT S. (1972). 'Where Next for Conglomerates?' *Business Horizons,* Dec. 1969: 39–44. Reprinted in John W. Bonge and Bruce P. Coleman (eds.), *Concepts for Corporate Strategy.* New York: Macmillan.

BARTLETT, CHRISTOPHER A., and GHOSHAL, SUMANTRA (1989). *Managing Across Borders: The Transnational Solution.* Boston: Harvard Business School Press.

BERG, NORMAN A. (1965). 'Strategic Planning in Conglomerate Companies'. *Harvard Business Review,* May–June: 79–92.

——— (1969). 'What's Different about Conglomerate Management?', *Harvard Business Review,* Nov.–Dec.: 112–20.

——— (1973). 'Textron, Inc.'. HBS Case Study 373–337.

BETTIS, RICHARD A. (1981). 'Performance Differences in Related and Unrelated Diversified Firms'. *Strategic Management Journal,* 2: 379–93.

——— and HALL, WILLIAM K. (1983). 'The Business Portfolio Approach—Where it Falls Down in Practice'. *Long Range Planning,* 16/2 (Apr.): 95–104.

BHAGAT, S., SHLEIFER, A., and VISHNY, R. (1990). 'Hostile Takeovers in the 1980s: The Return to Corporate Specialization'. Brookings Papers on Economic Activity: Microeconomics.

BOWER, JOSEPH L. (1986). *Managing the Resource Allocation Process.* Boston: Harvard Business School Press, 1970. Harvard Business School Classics Edition, 1986.

CAMPBELL, ANDREW (1991). 'Building Core Skills'. Research Report, Ashridge Strategic Management Centre.

——— and LUCHS, KATHLEEN (1992). *Strategic Synergy.* Oxford: Butterworth-Heinemann.

——— DEVINE, MARION, and YOUNG, DAVID (1990). *A Sense of Mission.* London: Hutchinson.

CHANDLER, ALFRED D., Jr. (1982). *Strategy and Structure* (1962; reissued 1982). Cambridge, Mass.: MIT.

CHATTERJEE, S. (1992). 'Sources of Value in Takeovers: Synergy or Restructuring—Implications for Target and Bidder Firms'. *Strategic Management Journal*, 13/4 (May): 267–86.

CHRISTENSEN, KURT H., and MONTGOMERY, CYNTHIA A. (1981). 'Corporate Economic Performance: Diversification Strategy Versus Market Structure'. *Strategic Management Journal*, 2: 327–43.

CURRAN, JOHN J. (1987). 'Are Stocks Too High?' *Fortune*, 28 Sept.

DAY, GEORGE S. (1977). 'Diagnosing the Product Portfolio'. *Journal of Marketing*, Apr.: 29–38.

DRUCKER, PETER (1959). 'Long-Range Planning: Challenge to Management Science'. *Management Science*, 5/3: 238–49.

—— (1968). *The Practice of Management* (1955; reissued 1968). New York: Pan Books.

GENEEN, HAROLD, with MOSCOW, ALVIN (1984). *Managing.* New York: Doubleday & Co. Inc.

GERSTNER, LOUIS V. (1972). 'Can Strategic Management Pay Off?' *Business Horizons*, 15/6 (Dec.).

GOOLD, MICHAEL, and CAMPBELL, ANDREW (1987). *Strategies and Styles.* Oxford: Basil Blackwell Ltd.

———— (1991). 'Brief Case: From Corporate Strategy to Parenting Advantage'. *Long Range Planning*, 24/1 (Feb.): 115–17.

—— and QUINN, JOHN (1990). *Strategic Control.* London: Hutchinson and Economist Publications.

—— CAMPBELL, ANDREW, and ALEXANDER, MARCUS (1994). *Corporate Level Strategy.* New York: John Wiley and Sons, Inc.

GRANT, ROBERT M. (1988). 'On "Dominant Logic," Relatedness and the Link between Diversity and Performance'. *Strategic Management Journal*, 9/6 (Nov.–Dec.): 639–42.

—— (1991a). 'Diversification in the Financial Services Industry: Why are the Benefits of Synergy so Elusive?' Research Paper.

—— (1991b). 'The Resource-Based Theory of Competitive Advantage: Implications for Strategy Formulation'. *California Management Review*, Spring: 114–35.

HALL, WILLIAM K. (1978). 'SBUs: Hot, New Topic in the Management of Diversification'. *Business Horizons*, Feb.: 17–25.

HAMEL, GARY, and PRAHALAD, C. K. (1989). 'Strategic Intent'. *Harvard Business Review*, May–June: 63–76.

HAMERMESH, RICHARD G. (1986). *Making Strategy Work.* New York: John Wiley & Sons.

—— and WHITE, RODERICK E. (1984). 'Manage Beyond Portfolio Analysis'. *Harvard Business Review*, Jan.–Feb.: 103–9.

HASPESLAGH, PHILIPPE (1982). 'Portfolio Planning: Uses and Limits'. *Harvard Business Review*, Jan.–Feb.: 58–73.

—— and JEMISON, DAVID B. (1991). *Managing Acquisitions.* New York: Free Press.

HAYES, BOB, and ABERNATHY, BILL (1980). 'Managing Our Way to Economic Decline'. *Harvard Business Review*, July–Aug.: 67–77.

HEDLEY, BARRY (1977). 'Strategy and the "Business Portfolio"'. *Long Range Planning*, Feb.: 9–15.

HELLER, R. (1969). 'The Legend of Litton'. *Management Today*, Oct. 1967. Reprinted in H. Igor Ansoff (ed.), *Business Strategy.* Harmondsworth: Penguin Books, 1969.

HOF, ROBERT D., and KELLER, JOHN J. (1989). 'Behind the Scenes at the Fall of Rolm'. *Business Week*, 10 July: 82–4.

HOFER, CHARLES W., and SCHENDEL, DAN (1978). *Strategy Formulation: Analytical Concepts.* New York: West Publishing Company.

ITAMI, HIROYUKI (1987). *Mobilizing Invisible Assets.* Cambridge, Mass.: Harvard University Press.

JENSEN, MICHAEL (1989). 'The Eclipse of the Public Corporation'. *Harvard Business Review,* Sept.–Oct.: 61–74.

JOHNSON, GERRY, and THOMAS, HOWARD (1987). 'The Industry Context of Strategy, Structure and Performance: The U.K. Brewing Industry'. *Strategic Management Journal,* 8: 343–61.

JONES, THOMAS ROY (1960). 'Top Management's Responsibility to the Community', in H. B. Maynard (ed.), *Top Management Handbook.* New York: McGraw-Hill.

JUDELSON, DAVID N. (1972). 'The Conglomerate—Corporate Form of the Future'. *Michigan Business Review,* July 1969: 8–12. Reprinted in John W. Bonge and Bruce P. Coleman (eds.), *Concepts for Corporate Strategy.* New York: Macmillan, 1972.

KANTER, ROSABETH MOSS (1989). *When Giants Learn to Dance.* London: Simon & Schuster.

KATZ, ROBERT L. (1955). 'Skills of an Effective Administrator'. *Harvard Business Review,* Jan.–Feb.

KIECHEL, WALTER (1988). 'Corporate Strategy for the 1990s'. *Fortune,* 29 Feb.

KOONTZ, HAROLD (1961). 'The Management Theory Jungle'. *Academy of Management Journal,* 4/3 (Dec.): 174–88.

LANGLIE, ARTHUR B. (1960). 'Top Management's Responsibility for Good Government', in H. B. Maynard (ed.), *Top Management Handbook.* New York: McGraw-Hill.

LEARNED, E. P., CHRISTENSEN, C. R., ANDREWS, K. R., and GUTH, W. D. (1965). *Business Policy: Text and Cases.* Homewood, Ill.: Richard D. Irwin.

LORANGE, P., and VANCIL, R. F. (1977). *Strategic Planning Systems.* Englewood Cliffs, NJ: Prentice-Hall.

LUBOVE, SETH (1992). 'Dog with Bone'. *Fortune,* 13 Apr.

MACE, MYLES L. (1965). 'The President and Corporate Planning'. *Harvard Business Review,* Jan.–Feb.: 49–62.

MINTZBERG, HENRY (1989). *Mintzberg on Management.* New York: Free Press.

MORE, THOMAS (1987). 'Goodbye, Corporate Staff'. *Fortune,* 21 Dec.

PETERS, THOMAS J., and WATERMAN, ROBERT H. (1982). *In Search of Excellence.* New York: Free Press.

PORTER, M. E. (1985). *Competitive Advantage.* New York: Free Press.

—— (1987). 'From Competitive Advantage to Corporate Strategy'. *Harvard Business Review,* May–June: 43–59.

—— (1988). 'General Mills, Inc: Corporate Strategy'. HBS Case Study 9–388–123.

PRAHALAD, C. K., and BETTIS, R. A. (1986). 'The Dominant Logic: A New Linkage between Diversity and Performance'. *Strategic Management Journal,* 7: 485–501.

—— and DOZ, YVES L. (1987). *The Multinational Mission.* London: Free Press.

—— and HAMEL, GARY (1990). 'The Core Competence of the Corporation'. *Harvard Business Review,* May–June: 79–91.

RAMANUJAM, VASUDEVAN, and VARADARAJAN, P. (1989). 'Research on Corporate Diversification: A Synthesis'. *Strategic Management Journal,* 10: 523–51.

RAPPAPORT, ALFRED (1986). *Creating Shareholder Value: The New Standard for Business Performance.* New York: Free Press.

REED, RICHARD, and LUFFMAN, GEORGE A. (1986). 'Diversification: The Growing Confusion'. *Strategic Management Journal*, 7: 29–35.

REIMANN, BERNARD C. (1987). *Managing for Value*. Oxford: Basil Blackwell.

RINGBAKK, K. A. (1969). 'Organized Planning in Major U.S. Companies'. *Long Range Planning*, 2/2 (Dec.): 46–57.

RUMELT, RICHARD P. (1974). *Strategy, Structure and Economic Performance*. Boston: Harvard Business School Press.

——(1982). 'Diversification Strategy and Profitability'. *Strategic Management Journal*, 3: 359–69.

SADTLER, DAVID, CAMPBELL, ANDREW, and KOCH, RICHARD (1997). *Breakup! Why Large Companies Are Worth More Dead Than Alive*. Oxford: Capstone Publishing.

SERVAN-SCHREIBER, J.-J. (1968). *The American Challenge*, trans. Ronald Steel. London: Hamish Hamilton.

SETH, ANJU (1990). 'Value Creation in Acquisitions: A Re-Examination of Performance Issues'. *Strategic Management Journal*, 11: 99–115.

SHETTY, Y. K., and PERRY, NEWMAN S., Jr. (1976). 'Are Top Executives Transferable across Companies?' *Business Horizons*, June: 23–8.

SLATER, JIM (1977). *Return to Go: My Autobiography*. London: Weidenfeld and Nicolson.

SLOAN, ALFRED P. (1986). *My Years with General Motors*. New York: Doubleday, 1963; reissued Harmondsworth: Penguin Books, 1986.

STALK, GEORGE, EVANS, PHILIP, and SHULMAN, LAURENCE E. (1992). 'Competing on Capabilities'. *Harvard Business Review*, Mar.–Apr.: 57–69.

TRAUTWEIN, FRIEDRICH (1990). 'Merger Motives and Merger Prescriptions'. *Strategic Management Journal*, 11: 283–95.

VANCIL, R. F., and LORANGE, P. (1975). 'Strategic Planning in Diversified Companies'. *Harvard Business Review*, Jan.–Feb.: 81–90.

WHITLEY, RICHARD, THOMAS, ALAN, and MARCEAU, JANE (1981). *Masters of Business? Business Schools and Business Graduates in Britain and France*. London: Tavistock Publications.

WINTERS, PATRICIA (1989). 'Crush Fails to Fit on P&G Shelf'. *Advertising Age*, 10 July.

YOUNG, DAVID, and SUTCLIFFE, BRIGID (1990). 'Value Gaps—The Raiders, the Market or the Managers?' Research Paper, Ashridge Strategic Management Centre, Jan.

CHAPTER 19

THE RATIONALE FOR MULTI-SBU COMPANIES

C. K. PRAHALAD
YVES L. DOZ

19.1 INTRODUCTION

IN the last fifteen years greater recognition has been given to the importance of the CEO and top management in large, diversified companies. The sharp rise in their pay and their increasing public prominence are examples.

The role of top management is now seen as being essentially entrepreneurial, in other words about wealth creation. An administrative view, involving control, monitoring, and coordination is now seen as insufficient. Top management needs to develop an economic logic for its role, one that explains why the company has chosen this portfolio of businesses, and why management has chosen this particular set of governance and internal management processes.

An earlier draft of this paper was presented at the Twentieth Anniversary Conference of Euroforum, El Escorial, Spain, in September 1995. Support from Euroforum in preparing this paper is gratefully acknowledged.

At the same time as the top jobs have been getting greater recognition, so has the need for companies, particularly diversified companies, to articulate an economic logic that explains why they exist, and to continually reinvent the logic as circumstances change.

The need for an economic explanation has arisen not just because companies operate in an economic system, but also because many diversified companies and many diversification strategies have failed. Previous logics that drove companies to build diversified portfolios—the need to spread risk, the benefit of providing smooth earnings growth, the value of balance, and the need for long-term survival—have all been questioned if not abandoned. Top managers are, therefore, now expected to create their own logics—to explain how their particular configuration of business and governance process will create value. They are also expected to adjust their logics in the face of change.

In this chapter we will explore this task of the top management of a diversified firm. First, we will outline a framework for thinking about wealth creation in a diversified firm. Second, we will identify some of the key dilemmas that the CEO and the top management group face.

19.2 The Wealth Creation Process

Our understanding of the process of sustained wealth creation can be conceptualized as the interaction of three interlinked elements, as shown in Figure 19.1.

Sustained wealth creation requires the mobilization of a bundle of resources and assets that is appropriate to the environment. In a changing environment managers need to periodically re-evaluate the configuration of assets and resources that they want to own or access. Invariably, therefore, portfolio reconfiguration is high on the list of CEOs seeking to improve performance. A portfolio configuration choice carries with it, explicitly or not, value creation logic: How does this particular bundle of assets create value, over and beyond each business or/and each category of assets? The portfolio configuration sets the specifications of the value creation logic; while, in turn, the value creation logic sets rules for inclusion and exclusion in the asset portfolio. A thoughtful CEO works on both portfolio configuration and value creation logic at the same time.

The portfolio composition and value creation logics also drive the internal governance processes within the firm: the organizational, administrative, and political reflection of the value creation logic. Governance is about deciding the basic organizational building blocks that constitute the diversified firm, as well as the processes and values that govern the performance demanded from the units,

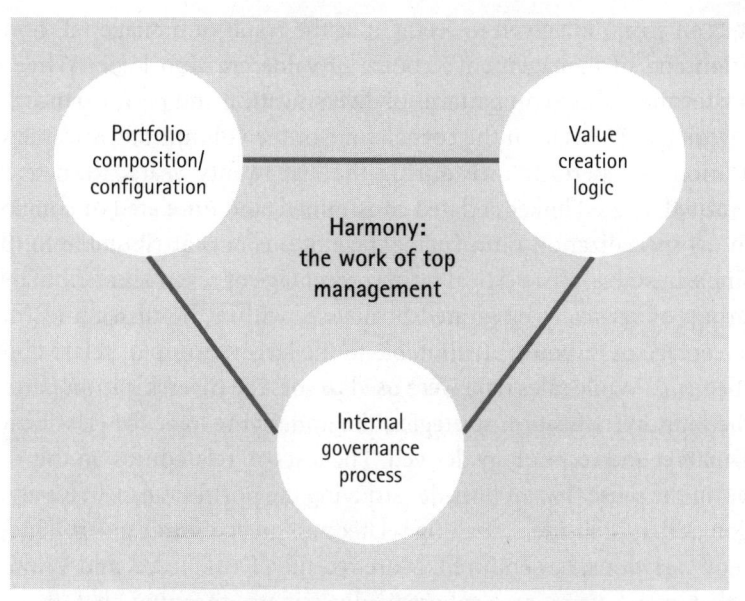

Fig. 19.1 A framework for wealth creation

strategic and operational priorities, inter-unit relationships, and the appropriate internal dialogues and behaviours. Internal governance defines how the asset portfolio is managed and conditions the capacity of the firm to create wealth.

Wealth creation demands constructive and harmonious interactions between portfolio configuration, value creation logic, and internal governance process. Building, maintaining, and evolving such interactions in the face of changing circumstances is the essence of the work of top management. To better understand this work we will first examine the three elements of wealth creation in some detail, stressing that they need to be considered as separate, but that any top management choices can only be made from a consideration of their interdependencies.

19.2.1 Assets and Resources: The Portfolio Configuration

Portfolio reconfiguration is perhaps the most visible manifestation of CEO action in almost all major firms. Many firms have divested businesses that they had acquired only a few years earlier. Companies that diversified during the 1970s and early 1980s frequently refocused their portfolios in the late 1980s and early 1990s (Markides 1995). What is the rationale?

In almost all cases, portfolio reconfiguration is based on a fresh assessment of the meaning, basis, and value of relatedness among businesses in the portfolio, often resulting from a new value creation logic. Relatedness is hardly a new concept in strategic management, but the emphasis in considering relatedness is shifting from

seeing it as an economic given to seeing it as the result of managerial thought and imagination and of management's choice of value creation logic. While Wrigley (1970) started the research on patterns of diversification and performance, Rumelt's seminal work (1974) has been the cornerstone of the voluminous research work on diversification and performance during the last twenty years. Rumelt classified firms as related, related linked, related constrained, and unrelated or conglomerate, based on (a) specialization ratio (percentage of business attributable to the firm's largest single business), (b) vertical ratio (percentage of revenues attributable to the largest group of vertically integrated businesses within the firm), and (c) related ratio (percentage of revenues attributable to the largest group of related businesses within the firm). While sales data were used to sort the diversification patterns into one of the four diversification strategies, the underlying logic for classification was product-market and technology derived. The tests of 'relatedness' in this schema is 'objective' in the sense that an outsider studying the portfolio can arrive at the same conclusion as that of insiders, making relatedness an economic given. This scheme, with minor variations, has endured. More recently, Dosi, Teece, and Winter (1994) showed that many firms are 'coherent' diversifiers, meaning that their pattern of diversification is consistent with their learning and skill base. This pattern of diversification is path-dependent and idiosyncratic with respect to the firm. What might appear to be unrelated diversification in the earlier Rumelt schema may appear to be 'coherent' here. This view of diversification is derived from the history of the firm. It raises the possibility that 'relatedness' as seen by managers may be different from an 'objective outsider's' perspective.

19.2.2 Types of Relatedness

Relatedness, though, once no longer seen as a given, may be defined along various dimensions, not just the learning and skill development path of the firm.

1. Business selection. Perhaps the simplest form of corporate relatedness is merely to select 'good' businesses. Although there is a lot more to General Electric's success, selecting businesses in leading positions, or with the potential to achieve leading positions, with activities sheltered from the most ruthless forms of competition, is one of the cornerstones of the company's strategy. This value creation logic was clearly articulated by CEO Jack Welch. It is based on dominating an industry— being number 1 or 2, or out. Less clearly stated, but well understood, are the other assumptions behind the logic: relentless cost reduction, picking businesses not subject to intense Japanese (and Korean) competition, and where the playing field favours Americans. All these criteria for value creation can be applied to the entire portfolio of GE. Every one of the businesses, as stand-alone entities, can apply these tests and so can corporate. When Jack Welch became CEO, many

of its businesses were already dominant players with world scale (if not worldwide) operations such as lighting, appliances, and medical systems. Welch had a varied enough portfolio to buy and sell businesses. Relentless cost-cutting prepared many of them for effective global competition. These underlying strengths allowed the creation of much shareholder value from selective divestments and acquisitions.

Conversely, the plight of Philips stems largely from inescapable exposure of its core businesses to ruthless Asian competition and to starting positions that had eroded over time with little portfolio redeployment and insufficient selectivity.

2. Industry consolidation. Business selection logic can also start with industry consolidation. Fragmentation can lead to weak general management skills, under investment in technologies, and an inability to capture economies of scale that may be invisible to the incumbents. Industry consolidation can also build barriers to entry unavailable to a fragmented one. Hence, a portfolio of assets can be assembled (often through acquisitions), with the goal to rationalize an industry and extract value from the process of industry consolidation. This approach was common in many industries during the 1960s and 1970s (e.g. elevators, cement, and retailing in the USA and in the UK) and is becoming common again (e.g. financial services, entertainment, telecom, airlines). ABB's strategy of consolidating the electrical power business is a good example of this perspective on portfolio consolidation. Corning's very successful entry into medical diagnostics labs was predicated on a similar logic.

3. Parenting similarities. Creating value from an unrelated corporate portfolio is easier when the businesses share common strategic and managerial characteristics. For example, Hanson Trust has always been described as an unrelated diversifier with businesses as diverse as brick making, coal, jacuzzis, and chemicals. Hanson managers, though, believed that their businesses had common characteristics and required similar management skills. Hanson's criteria for fit into their portfolio were: basic businesses providing good, essential products, not high tech, not people-intensive business, good management at the operating level, reasonable asset backing, stable rate of change, good cash flow, and discrete businesses (Haspeslagh and Taubmann 1992). This view is based on what Goold and Campbell (1994) have called the parenting advantage: the capacity of corporate management to add value to the business units based on a common set of corporate capabilities. Interestingly, though, Lord Hanson was not sufficiently convinced that Hanson's advantage was corporate rather than individual and would survive the death of his partner and his own imminent retirement. In early 1996 he announced the split of Hanson Trust into four separate companies in different sectors.

4. Core competencies. Considering relatedness from the standpoint of core competencies (Prahalad and Hamel 1990) yields a totally different view from that of parenting advantage. A very diversified portfolio such as Cargill's (commodity

trading, meat, chicken and pork processing, salt, fertilizer, petroleum trading, mini steel mills, financial services, citric acid, orange juice, animal feeds, and seeds) would be classified as unrelated. But top managers inside the firm may think and act otherwise, as reported by Cargill's CEO Whitney MacMillan:

Experience in the handling of bulk commodities, knowledge of trading, processing expertise, international understanding, risk management; these are the attributes of Cargill that underpin all our businesses. These core competencies represent the collective learning and judgement of all our 125 years of experience in all our businesses. They have been built over the years as the result of an unending process of refinement and improvement. They help hold us together and give us a sense of unity of purpose that would otherwise be difficult to define. They drive our development of new business opportunities and shape our ability to respond to future challenges.

What is the largest risk facing a multi-product line, multi-geography, multi-cultural, multi-lingual, multi-national corporation in maintaining core competencies and developing new ones? In my opinion, the largest threat is in our own organisational insularity. We must guard against the trap of becoming so locked into being diverse lines of business and different geographies that we lose the ability to leverage our resources and expertise to their full potential.

Relatedness, in Cargill, for example, is not based on product-market configuration, nor technology similarities, but on shared competencies and knowledge assets. Different businesses within Cargill demand different parenting skills from the parent, in contrast to Hanson's logic, but all share a common set of core competencies. Cargill is not alone in taking this approach. Many other seemingly diversified firms see competence logic for their portfolios. 3M, Canon, NEC, Sony, P&G, and ABB are some examples.

5. Interbusiness linkages. In some portfolios, managing the interlinkages provides value. For example, the distribution efficiencies and the clout that P&G has with retailers is different from what any one of its businesses can command. But this value would not be realized if its businesses independently negotiated terms with retailers such as Wal-Mart. Similarly, ABB has major contracts in emerging economies such as China or India that require the involvement of many of its different businesses, and GE adds the strength of its financial service operations to support deals by its other businesses. P&G, ABB, and GE have to manage their businesses differently from Hanson. Hanson would consciously ignore benefits from such coordination and prefer the accountability to performance that their system provides. Hanson made no pretence of constructing synergies between his acquisitions, as illustrated by the operation of two of his subsidiaries, Imperial Tobacco Limited and Elizabeth Shaw (a chocolate firm). Both were based in Bristol, England, and delivered goods to newsagents and corner shops throughout the United Kingdom. Yet Hanson was opposed to any sharing of distribution resources on the ground that any economies of scale would likely be outweighed by 'the general sloppiness that would result if each company

thought that distribution was the other's problem' (Haspeslagh and Taubmann 1992).

6. Complex strategic integration. Core competencies not only create the basis for value creation, but also aid the identification of new business opportunities which draw on competencies from multiple units (Burgelman and Doz 1997). The goal here is to create a portfolio that is capable of internally generating new businesses; yielding a capacity for self-revitalization. Hewlett-Packard with a clear focus on creating businesses at the intersection of Measurement, Computing, and Communications (its so-called MC2 strategy) represents one such portfolio. In 1994, more than 60 per cent of the sales of Hewlett-Packard came from businesses that did not exist in 1990. Nearly all the growth came from internal development of new products and new businesses. Value creation in such a portfolio is as much about growth and proactively reinventing the business portfolio based on core competencies as about rationalizing existing assets or defending existing businesses.

Our quick review of various types of portfolio configuration logics suggests that relatedness, contrary to the view in the literature, may not be an economic given but remain very dependent on the cognitive framework of top managers (Prahalad and Bettis 1986; Stimpert and Duhaime 1997).

Identifying the appropriate configuration of the portfolio, in contrast to deciding whether a portfolio is related or unrelated based on simple, universal tests, is a top management task. But how to assess a portfolio logic? Once one escapes the simplifying assumption of objective relatedness to accept the view that relatedness is in the eyes of the beholders, the burden of creating a robust logic is put squarely back on the shoulders of management.

19.2.3 Portfolio Logic

Creating the portfolio configuration logic is, therefore, a vital top management task. It involves asking the following questions:

1. What is the value of a bundle of assets and businesses as compared to the value of these businesses as independent units? The portfolio must benefit business units, and the business units must add value to the portfolio. The relatedness among the businesses in the portfolio may not be obvious at a first cut analysis. Often, the most valuable dimensions of relatedness need to be discovered. Top managers must be able to articulate the value of relatedness or the reason for a business to belong to the portfolio.

2. Which underlying value creation logics are at play (from the selection of well-positioned businesses to the discovery of new opportunities through complex strategic integration)? While some CEOs, such as Lord Hanson, focus on one logic, others, such as Percy Barnevik at ABB, attempt to develop a composite

value creation logic. How good is the match between the portfolio of assets and the value creation logic being applied?

The portfolio logic will force two kinds of questions: (a) what kinds of assets do I want and (b) what connections between these do I need? It is obvious that these questions are interrelated. The logic of the portfolio is a result of the history of the company (the cards that one is dealt) and the creative interpretation of opportunities by the top management of the firm (how well one can play the hand).

19.3 THE VALUE CREATION LOGIC: TOP MANAGEMENT'S THEORY OF RELATEDNESS

Implicit in the choice of portfolio configuration, if not explicitly articulated by the CEO, are assumptions about how the firm will compete and create value over and beyond what separate businesses could achieve. Value creation logic is about understanding the business model, resource intensity, risks, and the critical competencies needed for success as a diversified corporation. To clarify the point, let us consider some explicit statements of the value creation logic.

19.3.1 Hanson's Value Creation Logic

Each one of Hanson Trust's businesses was strategically defensible and differentiated. Each commanded significant market share. These businesses were unlikely to attract new competitors or be subject to radical technological change. Under these circumstances, good general management disciplines, budgeting, controls, incentives, autonomy, and low overheads can provide opportunities for extraordinary value creation. From the perspective of a business, the advantage of belonging to the Hanson portfolio is derived from the general management disciplines provided (imposed) by the parent. From the perspective of the group, it is having strategically defensible businesses that enjoy monopoly types of advantage. Further, high quality managerial skills might not be available to the businesses as stand-alone entities in some mature industries. In sum, Hanson is able to attract and retain better managers than 'member' companies could on their own and to give them better management tools.

19.3.2 GE's Value Creation Logic

To an extent General Electric follows a similar logic, but on a global scale. GE is in a wide variety of businesses—from lighting to financial services. The original portfolio logic was business selection, the simplest in our categories of portfolio relatedness. GE sold businesses where the number 1 or 2 criteria could not be met, such as consumer electronics, and built up its activities where it could, such as in medical imaging. The portfolio restructuring at GE, during Jack Welch's regime, was accomplished by divestment of more than $7 billion worth of businesses and acquisition of more than $17 billion. More than 52 per cent of GE today is in financial services. Second, the GE management process imposed discipline on the various businesses and improved their performance. Third, and this is where it increasingly departs from the value creation logic of Hanson and other conglomerates, GE is able to selectively move to managing inter-business linkages, for instance using its finance arm to lease large systems such as jet engines, power plants, or medical systems.

GE, though, was unable to move to create new opportunities. In emerging businesses such as 'factory automation', being number 1 or 2 had no meaning. When GE invested in it, the factory automation industry was just emerging, boundaries of businesses were unclear and GE faced non-traditional competitors. In this business, GE went for scale, as in other businesses. A series of acquisitions were made, and after some experimentation, GE quit the business. GE's logic of number 1 and 2 applies only to maturer businesses with reasonably clear boundaries. Being number 1 in the multimedia industry, at today's stage of evolution, for example, means very little, so did it in factory automation ten years ago.

While the value creation logic at GE is clear (and is now blindly adopted by many CEOs as a model for their own company), it is important to recognize that Welch started with unique endowments. Not all firms, nor CEOs, do. For instance, the value creation logic at Motorola is quite different. Since it never enjoyed such a rich endowment of businesses as did Welch at GE, nor businesses which could be sheltered from Japanese and European competition, its value creation logic is based on quality ('6 sigma'); continuous and radical improvements ('10 X'); positioning oneself at the beginning of the wave of growth in emerging businesses such as (successively) semiconductors, mobile and cellular communication, and in emerging markets such as China, the ASEAN countries, and India; and integrating technologies and markets into mutually supportive patterns. Implicit in Motorola's value creation logic is the capacity to bet on new products, scale up, grow rapidly, price aggressively, be global, and obsolete oneself. This is a very different logic from GE's.

The value creation logic a top management team can feasibly follow is thus the result not just of the theory of relatedness adopted, but also of other factors, such as the starting portfolio of the firm, the compatibility of different parts of the portfolio with the value creation logic, and the administrative and leadership skills in the company. Mature businesses are compatible with GE's value creation logic,

emerging ones perhaps not; limited endowments forced Motorola to design a value creation logic to build strength in emerging businesses and markets. Motorola's logic, though, is strategically and organizationally very demanding, in the sense that it attempts to maximize value creation from limited assets in a competitively exposed situation.

19.4 VALUE CREATION LOGIC: DYNAMIC EVOLUTION

In order to co-select their portfolio configuration and their value creation logic, particularly the most demanding ones, managers must develop a point of view about likely patterns of industry evolution. Intellectual leadership of an industry is a critical ingredient in developing new businesses (Hamel and Prahalad 1994). Examples of inventing new value creation models, even in old established industries, for single businesses are numerous. Consider the following:

- Swatch took leadership in the wristwatch business by bringing high fashion, European design, excellence, and low cost in manufacturing and technology, and continuous product development to an industry where the Swiss had lost leadership. It is the marriage of high fashion with high technology; fashion and efficiency that represents a new model of value creation. Seiko and Citizen did understand and optimize on efficiencies—their model of value creation—but did not see the industry ready for fashion à la Swatch.
- Nike has brought advertisement intensity, design, advanced technology, market segmentation, global logistics, to an old, traditional industry—sports shoes.
- Levi is experimenting with mass customization, with uniquely 'fitted' jeans, 'just for you', based on new information technology and new manufacturing and logistics capability.
- Benetton, Charles Schwab, Wal-Mart, CNN, Southwest Airlines, and British Airways are all examples of firms who invented a new value creation logic for a business, and the Internet has created a host of others.

19.4.1 Industry Foresight

How does one know that the new logic is appropriate? In order to discover a new value creation model, one needs to develop industry foresight (a unique point of

view regarding the patterns of industry evolution) through a thoughtful and imaginative assessment of underlying market drivers, trends, and critical discontinuities. Given a perspective, managers need to validate it through a process of market-based experiments at low cost (Hamel and Prahalad 1994). Ultimately, it is the market that validates a new model. Top managers must ensure that the industry foresight is based on deep understanding of the forces of change, rather than their stylistic preferences. This calls for a process of discovery inside the firm—one that involves a large number of people at all levels in the organization such that a wide variety of inputs are gathered and synthesized (Hamel 1996). The goal of this process is not one of analysis but of creating a new synthesis; identifying new opportunities that are often 'invisible' to industry incumbents. Developing such a new value creation logic can be compared to disciplined imagination (Szulanski and Doz 1995).

Moving from individual businesses to related, but diverse, competencies and markets, adds a further level of complexity, and, as we suggested, few firms seem to have a clear interbusiness value creation logic: HP, Motorola, and Kodak may be exceptions. Part of the difficulty stems from how tightly the portfolio logic and the value creation logic are intertwined. Discovering new opportunities and innovative business model(s) impacts the portfolio logic. On the other hand, a decision on the portfolio suggests implicit value creation logic. Hanson and Hewlett-Packard are distinct both in their portfolio, their opportunity horizon, and therefore, their value creation logic. Most top managers do not deal with this interrelationship explicitly. While the portfolio is frequently reconfigured, the underlying value creation logic is not explicitly re-examined. Identifying a set of business opportunities based on an existing portfolio of core competencies and identifying a set of core competencies that will be needed to manage a desired portfolio of businesses in the future is a creative task. Different managers can discover new patterns of relationships, based on competency assessment, across existing businesses in their portfolio as well as new businesses that could be added to it (Burgelman and Doz 1997).

19.4.2 Linking Portfolio and Governance

Once made explicit, the value creation logic becomes the intellectual link between the actual business portfolio and the governance of the firm. For example, in a portfolio where value is created by continuous development of new products and businesses drawing on competencies and expertise dispersed between existing business units, as in Motorola, Kodak, or HP, it is important to manage interbusiness unit relationships, as well as to continuously reconfigure resources to address emerging opportunities (Galunic and Rodan 1997). Stability in the remits of each business unit is not a virtue here. In fact, it may become a limiting factor (Galunic

and Eisenhardt 1996). In contrast, the business units in Hanson Trust could have highly stable remits. Hanson's value creation logic was based on each business operating as a stand-alone entity focusing on achieving the lowest cost position. The extent and form of encouragement and incentives to interunit cooperation are also a function of the value creation logic, and so is the balance between strategies that are guided by the centre and ones that are autonomously developed by the businesses.

19.5 VALUE CREATION LOGIC: ARTICULATING THE REASON FOR THE PORTFOLIO

Articulating the link between portfolio configuration and value creation logic is not easy for CEOs. First of all, the two are often treated separately in their minds. While CEOs are willing to discuss the logic for the portfolio very explicitly, they do not often articulate a model of value creation. The value creation logic is either ignored or remains implicit. GE, Hanson, and Motorola are exceptions. By considering the value creation logic managers can develop a framework for assessing all the decisions they make. They can also discover new and more complex ways of creating value. Ways that become harder and harder for others to copy.

Second, generic logics of value creation are widely accepted by managers, causing them to avoid taking a strategic look at their portfolios. Restructuring and re-engineering are the most popular generic value creation logics. They provide a denominator driven, cost reduction model. Cycle time reduction is another. While attention to cost, productivity, and cycle time are crucial, these focus on efficiencies. Wealth creation is also about growth and new business development the numerator. Internationalization (acquisition of similar businesses in other countries) is a generic logic that focuses on the numerator. Backward or forward integration is another. Diversification used to be a third until its failings were exposed in the 1980s. These generic logics are not wrong, but they often discourage managers from thinking more deeply and hence discovering logics that create more value.

Third, the portfolios of firms are not always amenable to a coherent value creation logic. Consider Kodak. Kay Whitmore, Kodak's CEO in the early 1990s, had struggled to identify and validate a portfolio logic, but some of his assumptions, such as the advantage of being active both in chemicals and pharmaceuticals, were questioned from the start. Kodak's portfolio, in 1993, consisted of chemical

imaging (film and paper), copiers, printers, medical reagents, over-the-counter and proprietary drugs, bulk chemicals, and cleaners. Under the new CEO, George Fisher, the portfolio has been pruned to an Imaging Business (chemical and electronic) which can capitalize on linkages and new opportunities. Other businesses have been divested—Eastman Chemicals, Sterling Drugs, and Lysol Cleaners. The value creation logic in fast-moving imaging businesses is certainly different from that in bulk chemicals!

Fourth, the process of creating a value creation logic is such an individual and time dependent process, mistakes can and often do happen. For example, Daimler Benz diversified all through the 1980s due to the conviction of Edzard Reuter and his team that they would become a 'one stop shop' for all communication needs of society—be it motor, air, or rail transportation or telecommunications. Similar visions of one stop shopping for financial services or multimedia products abound. However, consumers may want to have a choice and not be constrained by choices made for them by one vendor. Daimler Benz may have assembled, via a series of acquisitions, all the skills needed to be a 'one stop shop for transportation' but the customers may not wish to give it so much power. A reality check, therefore, is in order. Reuter's successor, Jürgen Shrempp, quickly started shedding businesses (Fokker and Dornier in commuter planes, most of AEG's businesses in electronics) and putting others into joint ventures with partners for whom they are more strategic (rail transportation with ABB, missiles and satellites with Matra), perhaps as a prelude to divestment. In contrast to Daimler Benz under Reuter, other companies may suffer from CEOs whose value creation logic is too tame, putting too much emphasis on sub-unit autonomy, but in so doing leaving too many opportunities where interunit linkages are unexploited. AT&T's travails in international development and its ultimate demerger into three companies may be an example of underachievement by design: the portfolio—telecoms and computers—called for a logic of integration, but the governance choice emphasized business unit autonomy.

Fifth, value creation logics become obsolete, and CEOs do not always notice it. Intel had become much more successful at microprocessors than at memories before its CEO noticed (Burgelman 1994; Burgelman and Grove 1996). In the airline industry, British Airways, among all European airlines, noted the importance of information technology and adopted yield management innovations much earlier than its competitors who remained wedded to a technical (e.g. Lufthansa) or political (e.g. Air France) logic of value creation (Lehrer 1997). Swissair became an outstandingly successful caterer before its top management became aware of how the way it created value had changed. Conversely, in the early 1990s, Gould's CEO decided to redeploy his company from traditional automotive components to fast-growing electronic ones, a laudable undertaking but one that ignored the deep differences between the two businesses and led Gould into deep trouble, bankruptcy and an emergency takeover by a Japanese company. Product types may evolve

incrementally in ways that are hard to notice at first (Intel), the business may not ostensibly change but the foundational knowledge key to value creation may (airlines), the centre of gravity of a firm's activities may move incrementally (Swissair), or management teams may wrongly emphasize continuity and miss out on discontinuities (Gould).

Last but not least, value creation logics and portfolio choices are almost never independent exercises performed by the CEO alone. They emerge at least partly from the strategy process and the interplay of sub-unit and corporate perspectives. In that sense tomorrow's value creation logic results from yesterday's internal governance process, seldom an ideal situation! In many companies vested interests and concerns about centralization and corporate vs. sub-unit roles cloud the debate and prevent incumbent CEOs from discovering or implementing new value creation logics. The CEO is hostage of the existing governance logic.

19.6 INTERNAL GOVERNANCE LOGIC: VALUE CREATION IN ACTION

Internal governance structures define the parts and their relationships to the whole. How are the parts defined? How do they relate to corporate management as well as to each other? How is the governance logic conditioned by the portfolio and value creation logic? These are some of the critical questions that CEOs face. An internal governance process that is inappropriate to the value creation logic will result in the firm not realizing the inherent potential of the portfolio.

We believe that a systematic approach to understanding the internal governance logic is a necessity. Such a logic is based on four building blocks:

(1) structural clarity based on a determination of basic administrative units into which the firm is divided;

(2) administrative processes that allow for dialogue across units, enforcement of accountability, measurement, and consolidation of performance;

(3) basic premises or key assumptions about the nature and quality of interactions between the building blocks of the company;

(4) values, beliefs, and behaviours that all employees are expected to understand and conform to.

We will examine each one of these below.

19.6.1 Structural Clarity

Irrespective of the portfolio configuration of the firm, a large company has to disaggregate itself into smaller administrative units for management. It is also important to note that one needs to manage product and business areas, functional expertise, and geographies. In many situations, programme or project management can also be a unit of disaggregation. But at least in all large firms, there is a need for product, geography, and functional building blocks. (We have deliberately excluded from this analysis the need for managing conceptual overlays such as core competencies. We focus only on the three basic dimensions of structure—product, geography, and function).

In most firms, the debate is not about the need for three dimensions, but about the relative roles of the three dimensions, and which to pick to structure subunits, and along which to manage interactions between units. The issue of matrix organizations (the tensions over relative influence of the three dimensions and the pathologies accompanying unresolved conflicts) are sufficiently well documented not to deserve special attention here (Davis and Lawrence 1977; Prahalad and Doz 1987; Ghoshal and Bartlett 1990).

Choices about what units to have revolved around three issues: How small or big should a unit be? Should each administrative unit have the complete set of resources it needs? And finally, how self-contained should its mission be?

Some companies have rather deliberately broken themselves up into many small units to set up an internal selection environment, either among existing activities (part of Barnevik's motive in choosing ABB's decentralized organization) or among new growth initiatives proposed by individual managers (e.g. Johnson & Johnson, 3M, Matsushita). While a firm is going through a process of rationalization and selection, disaggregating the firm into small, self-contained units can make sense. It provides a focus and clear accountability for cost reduction. In other words the value creation logic of portfolio selection is consistent with decentralization into small units. It is less consistent with a logic built on linkages and core competencies. ABB, for instance, is now backing out of its extreme decentralization. And obviously, where critical decisions are few but big as in chemicals or aerospace, an internal selection process is hardly appropriate. Aerospace groups, which may be relatively diversified, but often have only a dozen key product programmes, cannot be decentralized in the same way as 3M with its sixty thousand products.

Yet, it is important to recognize that no resource allocation process can enable top managers to cope with choices in any substantive depth if the number of subunits exceeds 30 to 45, a cognitive limit which CEOs of many large firms are intuitively coming to terms with. This does not mean that senior managers responsible for sectors or large units cannot allocate resources to smaller business units within their sectors—a multi-stage, multilevel resource allocation process. Further, intermediate level managers can encourage business units to collaborate with others

for growth by identifying opportunities that transcend their individual business scope but may be beneficial to each. Very small business units can also lead to under investment in critical technologies and in emerging markets. So while firms such as ABB can describe their approach to decentralization as managing a very large number of entrepreneurial units, the demands of internal growth and the increasing pressure for resource shifts across major businesses and geographies in most firms will require top managers to deal with fewer and larger aggregations. This calls for the maintenance, or resetting of intermediate levels of organizational aggregation. In other words, the portfolio and value creation logic will determine and limit the choices one can make in organization.

In a decentralized diversified company, managers responsible for an administrative unit (be it an SBU or a territory) will argue for a self-contained mission and a complete complement of resources. This makes them operate as if they were independent units and selectively draw on corporate services only as they deem fit. This approach to governance may be fine for Hanson (given its portfolio and value creation logic) but is it also acceptable for HP or Kodak? Are there too many opportunities that cut across any given configuration of administrative unit lines (say, a large project that cuts across several SBUs, or global account management that crosses several countries) such that any one-time determination of the boundaries and missions of SBUs (and national or regional organizations) will result in too many missed opportunities? The organization may need semi-permeable membranes separating the administrative units rather than brick walls. But then what is the meaning of a unit? a temporary project? a focal point for concentrating efforts and allocating resources? While R&D organizations have for long operated in that way, can the approach be generalized to a whole corporation?

19.6.2 Administrative Processes

Significant research attention has been bestowed on the administrative processes, such as budgeting, planning, performance appraisal, measurements, incentives and rewards, and the supporting technical infrastructure of communication, information, and control systems. Without trying to review the abundant management control literature nor relate it to our argument in this paper, let us just argue that the nature of dialogue between administrative units and corporate management needs to be contingent on the value creation logic adopted by the CEO. The administrative and the technical infrastructure provides a formal basis and framework for dialogue within the firm such as plans for the year, budgets for the quarter, performance expectations, or common design disciplines (based on common CAD tools). The design of the infrastructures supporting these processes and the way they are used can have significant influence on the nature of the dialogue as well as

the ability to build a corporate architecture that adds value. The dialogue can be arm's length as in the case of Hanson. White, one of the Vice Chairmen of Hanson, had this to say: 'I don't even know all the presidents of our companies. I know their names, but I have never been to any of our plants. I've never visited our headquarters in Iselin, New Jersey, either. There is no need for me' (Haspeslagh and Taubmann 1992). In this approach to governance, the dialogue is primarily through the administrative systems and hence the need for strong budgeting controls and a strong management team at the business units. There is an assumption of 'few surprises'—possible in slow-moving, mature businesses. Conversely, to take an opposite example, the approach at Canon is best described as 'heart-to-heart, mind-to-mind' communication. Consensus decision-making, deep personal knowledge of the businesses and markets by all levels is a prerequisite at Canon. The administrative control process can act as the backbone but not a substitute for intense and frequent personal communications across levels of management. In either case, Hanson Plc or Canon, Inc., the need for a strong and appropriate administrative and technical infrastructure for facilitating the dialogue is critical. However, the nature and the complexity of the administrative infrastructure, and how much of the sub-unit–corporate dialogue it encompasses, will be different depending on the nature of the portfolio and value creation logics.

While structural clarity and administrative processes provide the anatomy and the physiology of the company, the psychology of the company—how it acts within the broad framework of structure—is determined by the basic premisses and the values, beliefs, and behaviours.

19.6.3 Basic Premisses

What we call basic premisses within the company are key expectations imposed by the CEO and top managers. For example, in GE, after the initial decentralization, Jack Welch has built a basic premiss about 'boundaryless' behaviour to share information and best practices across boundaries, hierarchical levels, countries, and businesses within the company. In this case the premiss that a large firm represents a laboratory of good practices and that there is value in sharing these across boundaries transcends expectations of full autonomy created by the structural and administrative processes. In Hanson, another decentralized firm, conversely, the premiss of autonomy of the business units implies that they need not talk to each other. The boundaries are sacrosanct. In HP and 3M, for example, there is an expectation of continuous business renewal measured as a percentage of sales from new businesses. This premiss imposes an expectation of growth, but more importantly, an expectation of internal growth. Line managers, in these firms, have an obligation to leverage their resources in terms of both efficiency and innovation.

At Motorola, 6 sigma, as a premiss, suggests that they will strive for perfection in all they do and in all their relationships—including with their suppliers. Ford 2000 is an expectation that the European and North American operations will collaborate. This is a dramatic change in expectations for Ford from its ninety-year history of working separately across the Atlantic. Ford 2000 represents structural and administrative changes, but the big change is in the expectation of a qualitatively different dialogue across building blocks, imposed on the organization by the new CEO, Alex Trottman. For a company that historically was very US-oriented, AT&T's premiss of 'anytime, anywhere' suggests a globalization intent. The new premiss at Philips is 'Let's make things better'. It is about 'taking the next step and making whatever it is you are making, better.... So, when people say 'let's make things better', they speak from the head, and from the heart. And while we've long been known for making better things, perhaps from now on we'll be known for making things better'.

The goal for a CEO of setting and communicating basic premisses in an organization is to indicate the nature and quality of interactions between structural building blocks as well as the limits to the use of administrative processes. It provides a way to interpret and temper the behavioural signals given by the structure and the administrative process. The structure may provide clarity to boundaries, but it should not restrict the capacity of an organization to create wealth. The premisses provide an expectation of quality of interactions (that cannot be described in structural terms nor fully encompassed in measurement and control systems) among the building blocks.

Each basic premiss has to be accepted by the whole company to be useful. It is often a CEO-sponsored initiative to implant them in the whole organization. It is a statement of how the CEO expects to create value and differentiate his or her firm from others who may be similarly organized. Basic premisses force the organization to go beyond a sterile interpretation of relationships in the firm based exclusively on the formal structure and administrative processes. The roles and responsibilities of managers must be creative and evolving to incorporate adaptive behaviour. This expectation leads to a focus on values and behaviours.

19.6.4 Values and Behaviours

While structure and administrative processes provide the basic framework for organizing and monitoring the resources of the company, behaviours are critical to create an adaptive learning environment that allows for creative combination of resources to address new opportunities.

Two preconditions force the need for clearly understood values and behaviours. First, in a volatile industry environment, no structure can predetermine the nature

of adjustments that need to be made. Managers must go beyond predefined roles using matrices as mindset not a structure (Ghoshal and Bartlett 1990). Second, as CEOs adopt more demanding portfolio logics, there is a growing need to constantly discover new opportunities which allow managers to leverage competencies creatively. Constant reconfiguration of competencies to address new opportunities will force frequent changes in structure. Business unit boundaries may have to be redrawn. Given such a precondition for leverage and value creation, values and norms of behaviour become the anchor of stability and clarity, more than the formal structure. In an era of constant change in competitors, products, prices, customers, and resources, organizations need anchors to provide stability and comfort. Deeply held values and behaviours are the pillars of such stability.

There is a shifting emphasis in most firms from formal structures and administrative processes, critical as they are, to basic premises; and values and behaviours. Flexibility in resource reconfiguration, ability to learn and adapt continuously, to innovate and address new market opportunities—all at the heart of value creation—requires emphasis on the 'values and processes'. However, internal governance is about seeking the right harmony between the four aspects described in this section.

19.7 THE SEARCH FOR HARMONY

The CEO and top management are at the heart of managing this harmony. The CEO is always plagued with issues such as: 'How much do I rely on structure? on values and behaviours? How do I convince the organization that these values are critical and that I expect them to be followed in their daily work? What personal example should I set? Do I penalize managers for not supporting and living these values, even if their performance exceeds budgets? How do I communicate standards of behaviour as a prerequisite for standards of performance?' These questions are at the heart of managing apparent contradictions such as the need for short-term performance and longer-term creativity and growth. Contradictions are about predictability of performance and, at the same time, promoting change, about providing clarity to the existing configuration of business opportunities (existing SBU structure) and, at the same time, creating new 'white space' opportunities, about managing within a structure and creating opportunities that lie outside the existing structure.

The key to internal governance is understanding the implications of the portfolio configuration and value creation logics and using the four elements of governance to continually harmonize the complex and conflicting demands. The search is not for a static but a dynamic and evolving harmony. The CEO must search for both a harmony between the three logics as well as a harmony between the four elements of the internal governance process.

In searching for harmony, the CEO may reach different stable configurations of interactions between the three logics, or strive for a dynamic evolutionary capability. Hanson Trust constituted a harmonious but static relationship between the portfolio composition logic, the value-creating theory and the internal governance process selected by Lord Hanson. Hewlett-Packard, or Canon, on the other hand, constitutes evolving configurations, where the harmonious relationship is around change processes. Where Hanson put emphasis on formal structures and processes, Canon and HP emphasize values and norms and basic premises and principles. HP's or Canon's value creation logics are of distributed entrepreneurship and evolving business portfolios, built around core competencies. While they maximize adaptation, they may not optimize the relationships between the three logics at any point in time.

19.7.1 Maintaining Harmony

Maintaining strategic harmony is a demanding action agenda for the CEOs, whose traditional approaches to internal governance were too often based on one of two approaches: in one, the stylistic preferences of the CEO drive the process. The CEO's preferred style, control driven, details oriented (e.g. Harold Geneen at ITT) or hands off, decentralized ('if you meet the budget, you are out of trouble') prevails irrespective of the portfolio and value creation logics. In the other, tools are sometimes mistaken for personal leadership, as an increasingly formal approach to internal governance is fuelled by the ground swell of enthusiasm for decentralization. Consulting firms promote it. The desire to measure the contribution of a business unit by economic value analysis (EVA) makes decentralization a prerequisite. CEOs seem to like it as well. Is disaggregating a firm into stand-alone business units (the result of decentralization in most firms as well as the necessity to apply EVA methodology) necessarily appropriate in all cases? We believe not. We believe that it is dysfunctional to endow governance principles such as SBUs, matrix organization, teams, EVA, decentralization or any other, with quasi-religious sanctity. They all must be discussed, evaluated, and adopted, or not, in the context of a portfolio and value creation logic.

19.8 The Ceos' Intervention Capabilities: The Dilemmas

In the process of searching for harmony between the three logics, the CEO must concern himself/herself with the bandwidth of intervention modes available to him/her. A CEO has at his/her disposal all the internal governance tools but must recognize that there are no universal solutions. No single package is useful in all cases, as it is likely to impose a dominant logic as a straitjacket on all businesses (Prahalad and Bettis 1986). Neither can governance, in a diversified firm, be totally geared to the unique requirements of single businesses. That would be impossible to manage. Neither can the process be idiosyncratic and bound by the stylistic preferences or personality of the CEO. It must be geared to the needs of the portfolio and the value creation logic, and encompass a range of differentiated intervention models.

Increasing the repertoire of intervention modes suggests that a CEO must start with a framework to define internal governance. It is useful to start with the following questions to develop such a framework:

1. What in the internal governance process is non-negotiable and mandatory? There may be three kinds of issues that are mandatory. First, applying the formal 'rules of the game'. In all the firms we know, accounting procedures are non-negotiable. But, only in some, the technical architecture, often a critical precondition for sharing competencies and components across business units, is a non-negotiable. Secondly, a few achievements or performance standards are non-negotiable. In most firms, meeting budgets is one such non-negotiable. Performing better than one's cost of capital is another. Thirdly, where you put your efforts is becoming non-negotiable. For example, in some firms where CEOs have thought deeply about values, they are non-negotiable. A deep breach of value, even when achieving outstanding performance, is not acceptable. In some, commitments to customers and total quality are non-negotiable.

2. What aspects of the internal governance can be unique and tailor-made for a specific business unit, function, or a geography? For example, compensation for attracting the right talent for a specific business can be a local decision.

3. What is the role of perceived fairness in the system? It is very important that all employees see the system as being inherently fair. Building employee commitment, loyalty, and excitement requires a deep commitment to fairness. But fairness is as much perception as reality. In allowing for uniqueness, a CEO must worry about it being interpreted as unfair practice. But fairness is not the same as uniformity of systems and procedures (Kim and Mauborgne 1993). Uniformity can easily be seen as lack of fairness and courage, for instance when all units, no matter how successful, are required to cut investment.

4. How can mixed signals in the organization be avoided? In the desire to fine-tune the system, one can easily create multiple interpretations of the expectations imposed on the organization by top managers. The more a CEO uses precedents for establishing shared premises the greater the risk of mixed signals. For example, a demand for growth and at the same time pressure for profit improvement can be seen as a mixed (up!) signal if it is not properly explained to the organization. Mixed signals can paralyse an organization. However, creating the right level of tension and anticipation cannot be achieved without complex signals. The right balance is the key to high performance.

5. What aspects of the mix of governance mechanisms have the most impact? Which have the most associated costs? How do we understand the 'invisible and hidden costs'? For example, what are the consequences of re-engineering, downsizing, and multiple restructuring on the motivation of employees?

6. What is the level of due process built into the governance mix? Do people have a voice? How personally expensive is it for people to have their voice heard? Does the system provide for fair treatment of employees at all levels?

7. What is the balance between the investment in continuity and stability of the enterprise and the investment in change and flexibility? Continuity and stability to the team and processes within the firm dramatically reduce the costs of transactions as individuals start to work with each other, establish patterns of interactions, develop trust, and accumulate intellectual assets. Continuity is a critical factor for knowledge accumulation and exploitation. On the other hand, overemphasis on stability in the context of dramatic changes in the external environment will create paralysis. Change and flexibility, which alter the pattern of interactions, work flow, and skill mix in the organization are critical for survival.

8. Management is not about providing a static efficiency but continuous capability development. Efficiency at a point in time is critical to a high performance system. However, the building of the next round of advantages, the next practice, the next layer of efficiency and advantage, is equally critical. Quality of harmony between the various logics is measured not just by how well they knit together at a given point in time but by the ability of the system to push the next round of capability development.

19.8.1 Harmony and Substantive Issues

In thinking about his/her role in harmonizing portfolio configuration, value creation logic, and governance process, the CEO must recognize the inherent difficulties. The issues outlined above are the critical dilemmas. In addition, CEOs have to deal with substantive issues. For example, a significant part of the wealth creation opportunity is centred around stretching the imagination of the organiza-

tion and focusing it on aspirations that are outside the range of the current resources of the company (Hamel and Prahalad 1994). But stretch can become fear and anxiety if not properly managed. Stretch is very motivational if employees voluntarily commit to it because of their understanding of the rationale for it and turn imposed stretch into personal reach. Reach works if there is a compelling view of the future that is associated with it; if it provides personal meaning to every employee. On the other hand, if stretch is imposed administratively (as in budgets), it can lead to fear, anxiety, and dishonesty in the organization where managers stop being candid and start hiding slippage and sandbagging numbers. In some cases, an expectation of stretch targets by top management can create a sense of euphoria in the organization. Too much enthusiasm for growth, and change can also have the same effect as fear. Managers start feeding targets that are not grounded in reality. Hope is not a stretch target. Enthusiasm, like fear, can also create dishonesty in the organization. Reach is about commitment and not compliance, about voluntarism—giving the discretionary time, effort, and imagination on the part of the employee.

Similarly, a CEO in a large organization must strive to provide clarity to the tasks, values, performance expectations, and standards. The roles of various units must be clear and understood. This is the function of 'keeping the machine well oiled and reducing the frictional losses' in the system. However, clarity must coexist with a capacity for experimentation. Overemphasis on clarity can kill enthusiasm for experimentation. Experiments that are likely to change the way the system is currently managed and challenge the dominant logic are a very critical element of longer-term vitality in a large firm. CEOs must balance a commitment to the current system and at the same time provide support to the seeds that will challenge it.

Unless they are very careful, CEOs are likely to become too distant from the reality of the businesses that they are managing. A check on the calendar of a CEO can provide very useful hints on the distance that exists. Outside commitments, routine corporate reviews and corporate calendar, personal style and preferences, can leave very little time for in-depth understanding of the emerging opportunities—be it in the laboratories, in manufacturing, or in the changing mix of customers. Distance is a natural outcome of the job but staying informed of the key issues is a result of active management of one's time and of installing ad hoc processes that bypass and transcend the formal ones. The expectation is not that CEOs must be gluttons for detail but must have enough understanding of the emerging detail to extract a sense of the essence. For example, a CEO today must know what is happening in the information technology business to recognize the impacts it will have on distribution and retailing, customer interface, focused marketing, logistics, distance collaboration, the nature of dialogue between individuals, teams, and administrative units, and the cost structure of businesses. The goal is not to become an expert on the details of 'virtual reality' or large database construction techniques, but to recognize the implications of these to the businesses

(value creation logic) and to the internal governance processes. The goal is for the CEO to listen to the arguments, suspend judgement, and recognize that he/she cannot and need not have a solution to all the problems that the organization faces. Many of the solutions evolve and the CEO must unburden himself/herself from the self-imposed (and sometimes culturally imposed) burden of 'knowing the answer' to all questions.

19.9 CEO EFFECTIVENESS AND PUBLIC IMAGE

It is obvious that the CEOs must creatively manage the harmony of the interactions between the three logics. But harmony depends not just on analytical skills but also on the capacity to motivate and provide an emotional dimension to the company. Analytics and passion, clarity and experimentation, efficiency and innovation must all coexist. Ideally, CEOs must be able to constantly and creatively balance these factors.

19.9.1 CEOs' Limitations

The reality is that CEOs, like others, have limitations. We can identify two major sources of limitations. One widely recognized source of limitation is the background and the stylistic preferences (limitations) of the CEO. While many a CEO intellectually recognizes the impact his/her stylistic preferences have on the internal governance processes, few have the persistence to modify them (Kets de Vries and Miller 1984). The difficulty is in modifying behaviour patterns and managerial frames that one has grown up with. The search for an outside CEO is often triggered by an intuitive feel, on the part of directors, for the demands of a rapidly changing portfolio and value creation logics. These changes require a different internal governance logic. Boards come to the conclusion, often painfully, that nobody from the inside can break away from the ingrained managerial frames and styles fast enough. Employing an outsider becomes a way of dealing with the limitations of the incumbent CEO and his team. The changes in Alcatel, IBM, Kodak, Sears, K Mart, and American Express are just some examples of this process.

There is another, somewhat subtle, limitation to the effectiveness of a CEO in balancing the three logics. The public image of the CEO can both facilitate or limit

his/her capacity for managing the quality of interactions between the three logics. The public image is built by either a conscious decision on the part of the CEO to use it to influence the organization (to cut through layers of bureaucracy and reach the rank and file with his/her message directly) or a public persona is created by the press, with or without the cooperation of the CEO. The public image of the CEO has the same characteristics as the public image of a politician. CEOs cannot ignore their public image that evolves over time—it can be an advantage as it sets expectations, but can also act as a limiting factor (Sutton and Galunic 1996).

19.9.2 CEOs' Public Image

The public image of the CEO is reflected in the organization. All employees have access to that image and interpret it. For example, employees at GE, based on the public image of their CEO Jack Welch ('Neutron Jack' as he was called in the press) can come to the conclusion that profits at any cost are a must; being a dominant player is a must (number 1 or 2), that outsourcing is acceptable, that lack of internal growth may be tolerated, divestment of businesses is part of corporate strategy, and that the corporation is not committed to any single business, that there is no loyalty between employees and the firm, and the 'new social contract' is about assuring employability, not employment, and so on. Let us for the time being assume that this list is a by-product of the public image of the CEO—his statements to the press, the Harvard cases, the video tapes, and the book by Tichy and Sherman (1993), all publicly available material. Employees can learn a lot about what is valued in the company and what is the meaning of success. For example, whether there is value attached to protecting core competencies or keeping a technology edge, managing a small business with good profits but not a dominant market share, managers can learn to justify continuous profit increases in the face of no growth and/or cyclical businesses including in industries with excess capacity. There can be an increased awareness of what skills are lost as people are let go. Employees learn much about what aspects of management can be sacrificed to accomplish financial goals.

The public image of Bill Gates is growth, market dominance, establishing products as the industry standard, 'take no prisoners, winner take all', a wide scope of businesses, enormous technical and market foresight and imagination, brashness and irreverence—somewhat different from GE. Microsoft employees recognize that individual contributions are greatly valued; that their firm is constantly increasing the scope of what it does and challenging incumbents in major industries such as banking, education, by changing the dynamics of that industry. (For example, Microsoft's failed attempt to acquire Intuit—of Quicken fame—was an attempt to enter the financial services business and pose a challenge not only to traditional banks but brokerage services as well.)

The other side of the public image is one of weak management, indecision, unwillingness to change, protecting the past, not in touch with the realities of new competition—an image that the press had created for Gérard Worms at Suez. For example, it was felt that he could not find the appropriate balance between the portfolio of businesses he put together with new demands of governance. Given such a public image, are employees willing to commit to change in the absence of confidence in their CEO? Do they believe that radical changes will be supported and experiments allowed under his leadership? Do they feel that the CEO and top management know where they are going? (That was never in doubt in GE or Microsoft.) On top of these nagging doubts about the capacity of the CEO to lead and allow the organization to be innovative, questions of personal integrity can paralyse the system, as at Alcatel.

19.9.3 Attributes of Public Image

The public image of the CEO has many important attributes. For example:

1. It can build stockholder confidence. Welch (GE) and Goizueta (Coca Cola) have built impressive reputations as allies of stockholders and builders of market value. They may get there using different approaches but both have this reputation. On the other hand, Jordan (Westinghouse) does not. Does the public image (matched, over time by performance) increase market value of firms?

2. It can scare competitors. Being number 1 or 2, or as in the case of Bill Gates's approach to launching 'Windows 95' can give second thoughts to competitors. 'Do I want to take these guys on?'

3. It can inspire confidence in the company. The public image of the CEO can inspire confidence as in the case of Bob Galvin during the 1980s at Motorola and George Fisher at Motorola and at Kodak now, or of Percy Barnevik at ABB.

Public image for the CEO is a mixed blessing. Once a strong public persona is created, it is not easy for the CEO to provide a credible, conflicting message to the organization. The CEO becomes hostage of the image. How long do public images linger? Should we be thinking about public image as a 'brand franchise' with all its attendant benefits and limitations?

There are also very visible companies with very clear public images such as Hewlett-Packard, 3M, Marriott, Rubbermaid, and Motorola (now), but the public image of the CEO is not very clear or pronounced. Why is this so? We suggest that public image is sought and often given to CEOs who are involved in dramatic restructuring and re-engineering efforts (or those who run businesses with very dominant market shares). Such efforts provide for drama. On the other hand, neither HP nor Motorola nor 3M have been involved in major restructuring. They have not made big and dramatic takeover bids. Their growth has been

internal. Their strategic change is based on a longer-term view of the industry, its evolution, and the role their organization will play in it. The reinventing of the company is an ongoing, intense, but 'low decibel', effort. Their change efforts are 'middle-out' efforts (efforts of middle-level managers). This process is akin to treating the firm as 'distributed intelligence' working within a shared, common strategic architecture, a much less visible process than the traditional strategizing at the top followed by restructuring of portfolio and organization.

19.9.4 Visibility: Low or High

While the low visibility CEO can have more degrees of freedom to communicate and manage the balance between the three logics within the firm, the high visibility CEO can use the public image as an amplifier to his message. The contemporary CEO has to ask the following questions:

1. What is the evolving public image (and the corresponding image among employees)? What is the consistency between my values, concerns, goals and the emerging public persona? What are the implications of a 'misfit' between the two? Can I afford to ignore the public image that may be emerging, its impact on the firm or on my abilities to manage?

2. Where do employees, customers, suppliers, investors take their cues from? What is the impact of a 'barrage' of publicity on the CEO as a person?

3. What degrees of flexibility do I want to preserve in challenging the organization to focus on different issues; for example, from a focus on restructuring to growth. This can become a problem, especially when the CEO has ten or more years in the job and must change the key message more than once (e.g. message at GE focusing more on soft issues since 1991).

4. When does the external (public) message gain more credibility than internal messages? Why does this happen?

19.10 CONCLUSION

The CEO has become critical in the wealth creation process. Simultaneously, employees at all levels have become significant contributors to the competitiveness of the firm. High quality leadership, it appears, is a prerequisite to enable empowered employees to function. The CEO has to take responsibility for creating the right environment. We believe that this process of creating the right environment

consists of first developing harmony between the portfolio, value creation, and governance logics. It is an evolving, dynamic process. Secondly, we believe that there are inherent dilemmas in managing this delicate process. It demands a good sense of timing, sequencing, social and interpersonal and intercultural sensitivity. Stylistic preferences (limitations) must be understood. Finally, CEOs must ask themselves if they can avoid a public image or whether they can use it purposefully. They must also consider the implications of this image-creating process (voluntary and involuntary), and the image on sustained vitality and capacity for growth and wealth creation.

References

BURGELMAN, R. A. (1994). 'Fading Memories: A Process Theory of Strategic Business Exit in Dynamic Environments'. *Administrative Science Quarterly*, 39/1 (Mar.): 24–56.

——and DOZ, Y. L. (1997). 'Complex Strategic Integration in the Lean Multibusiness Corporation'. INSEAD Working Paper, 97/03/SM.

——and GROVE, A. (1996). 'Strategic Dissonance'. *California Management Review*, 38/2 (Winter): 8–28.

DAVIS, S. M., and LAWRENCE, P. R. (1977). *Matrix*. Boston: Addison-Wesley.

DOSI, G., TEECE, D., and WINTER, S. (1994). 'Understanding Corporate Coherence'. *Journal of Economic Behavior & Organization*, 23: 1–30.

DOZ, Y. L., and CHAKRAVARTHY, B. (1995). 'Managing Core Competence Dynamically'. Draft paper presented to the Strategic Management Society International Conference, Mexico City.

GALUNIC, C., and EISENHARDT, K. M. (1996). 'The Evolution of Intracorporate Domains: Divisional Chanter Losses in High-Technology, Multi-divisional Corporations'. *Organization Science*, 7/3: 255–82.

——and RODAN, S. (1997). 'Resource Combinations in the Firm: Knowledge Structures and the Potential for Schumpeterian Innovation'. INSEAD Working Paper, 97/75/OB.

GHOSHAL, S., and BARTLETT, C. A. (1990). 'Matrix Management, Not a Structure, a Frame of Mind'. *Harvard Business Review*, July–Aug.: 138–45.

GOOLD, M., and CAMPBELL, A. (1994). 'How Corporate Parents Add Value to the Stand-Alone Performance of their Business'. *Business Strategy Review*, 5/4 (Winter): 33–56.

HAMEL, G. (1996). 'Strategy as Revolution'. *Harvard Business Review*, 74/4 (July–Aug.): 69–83.

——and PRAHALAD, C. K. (1989). 'Strategic Intent'. *Harvard Business Review*, 67/3: 63–76.

————(1994). 'Competing for the Future'. *Harvard Business Review*, 72/4 (July–Aug.): 122–30.

HASPESLAGH, P., and TAUBMANN, C. (1992). *Hanson Plc*. INSEAD case study.

KETS DE VRIES, M., and MILLER, D. (1984). *The Neurotic Organization*. San Francisco: Jossey-Bass.

KIM, W. C., and MAUBORGNE, R. (1993). 'Making Global Strategies Work'. *Sloan Management Review*, 34/3 (Spring): 11–27.

LEHRER, M. (1997). 'Comparative Institutional Advantage in Corporate Governance and Managerial Hierarchies: The Case of European Airlines'. Ph.D. dissertation, INSEAD.

MACMILLAN, W. (1990). 'Cargill's Vision: A View to the Future'. An Address to Cargill's Senior Managers by Whitney MacMillan, Chairman and CEO (12 July).

MARKIDES, C. C. (1995). 'Diversification, Restructuring and Economic Performance'. *Strategic Management Journal*, 16/2 (Feb.): 101–18.

PRAHALAD, C. K., and BETTIS, R. A. (1986). 'The Dominant Logic: A New Linkage between Diversity and Performance'. *Strategic Management Journal*, 7: 485–501.

—— and DOZ, Y. L. (1987). *The Multinational Mission: Balancing Local Demands and Global Vision*. New York: Free Press.

—— and HAMEL, G. (1990). 'The Core Competence of the Corporation'. *Harvard Business Review*, May–June: 79–91.

RUMELT, R. P. (1974). *Strategy, Structure and Economic Performance*. Boston: Harvard University Press.

SONG, J. H. (1992). 'Diversification Strategies and the Experience of Top Executives of Large Firms'. *Strategic Management Journal*, 3/4 (Oct.–Nov.): 377–80.

STIMPERT, J. L., and DUHAIME, I. M. (1997). 'In the Eyes of the Beholder: Conceptualization of Relatedness Held by the Managers of Large Diversified Firms'. *Strategic Management Journal*, 18/2 (Feb.): 111–26.

SUTTON, R. I., and GALUNIC, D. C. (1996). 'Consequences of Public Scrutiny for Leaders and Their Organization'. *Research in Organizational Behavior*. Greenwich, Conn.: JAI Press, 18: 201–250.

SZULANSKI, G., and DOZ, Y. L. (1995). 'Strategy Formulation as Disciplined Imagination'. INSEAD Working Paper, 95/56/SM.

TICHY, N. M., and SHERMAN, S. (1993). *Control Your Destiny, or Someone Else Will: How Jack Welch is Making General Electric the World's Most Competitive Corporation*. New York: Doubleday.

WRIGLEY, L. (1970). 'Divisional Autonomy and Diversification'. Ph.D. dissertation, Harvard Business School.

CHAPTER 20

THE ROLE OF THE PARENT COMPANY

ANDREW CAMPBELL

20.1 INTRODUCTION

MANY corporate parent companies destroy value. The businesses in the corporate portfolio would be better off as independent companies or as part of other corporate portfolios. This is the disturbing conclusion after ten years of research and consulting on the subject of corporate-level strategy and the role of the corporate centre.

The main evidence lies in the hundreds of stories and situations where the corporate parent's influence over a business unit has caused the managers in the unit to make the wrong decisions, or at least to make poorer decisions than they would have made without the parent's influence.[1] It is these value-destroying interventions that so often give rise to the groundswell of complaint and resentment that business-unit managers express when talking about their corporate centres. This body of anecdotal evidence is supported by analysts' reports, and the activities

This chapter contains excerpts from Andrew Campbell, Michael Goold, and Marcus Alexander, 'The Value of the Parent Company', *California Management Review*, 38/1 (Fall 1995). Reprinted with permission.

[1] Much of our research was aimed at finding situations where value is being created by the influence of the parent. We would ask business-unit managers: 'What value are you getting from being part of the group and more specifically from your relationship with the corporate centre?' More often than not, they would start by saying: 'That's a hard question to answer. I can tell you about the disadvantages, costs, and constraints. But value received, well. . . .'

of raiders, which show that many large companies have a market value lower than their break-up value. The continuing success of management buy-outs, where business units blossom when freed from the grasp of some large corporation, also demonstrates how widespread value destruction by corporate parents is (see e.g. Green and Berry 1991; Jensen 1991; and Young and Sutcliffe 1990).

On the other hand, there are some companies where the parent is clearly creating value, where the business-unit managers have high respect for the corporate centre and the influence it has over their businesses, and where the company's market value is greater than the sum of its parts. The stories, the atmosphere, and the results in these successful corporate parents are completely different, underlining both the shortcomings in many large companies and the opportunities for those who get their corporate-level strategies right.

This chapter will focus on the role and influence of corporate parents in multi-business companies. The corporate parent consists of all managers and staff not assigned to a business unit, including not only the corporate headquarters but also division, group, region, and other intermediate levels of management. Do these parent managers and staff create or destroy value? This issue lies at the heart of the justification for multi-business companies.

Unless the parent company is creating value greater than its cost, the business units would be better off as independent companies. The observation that many parent companies today are actually destroying value adds urgency to the need to identify the conditions under which value is likely to be created.[2]

20.2 Four Ways to Destroy Value

Parent companies affect value in four ways—through stand-alone influence, through linkage influence, through central functions and services, and through corporate development activities.[3] In each of these areas, it is possible for parent companies to create value. Often, however, these areas of influence do result in value destruction (see Figure 20.1).

---

[2] See Goold, Campbell, and Alexander 1994, for a fuller description of our conclusions and the research on which they are based.

[3] This categorization of the ways in which parents affect value is collectively exhaustive but not mutually exclusive: particular actions can fall into one or more categories. The categorization has, however, proved practically useful. It is similar to categorizations developed by David Collis, 'Managing the Multi-Business Company', teaching note, Harvard Business School; McKinsey & Co. 'Corporate Centre Design', *McKinsey Quarterly*, 1991, No. 3; Bain & Co., internal corporate strategy practice document, on 'The Role of the Centre'.

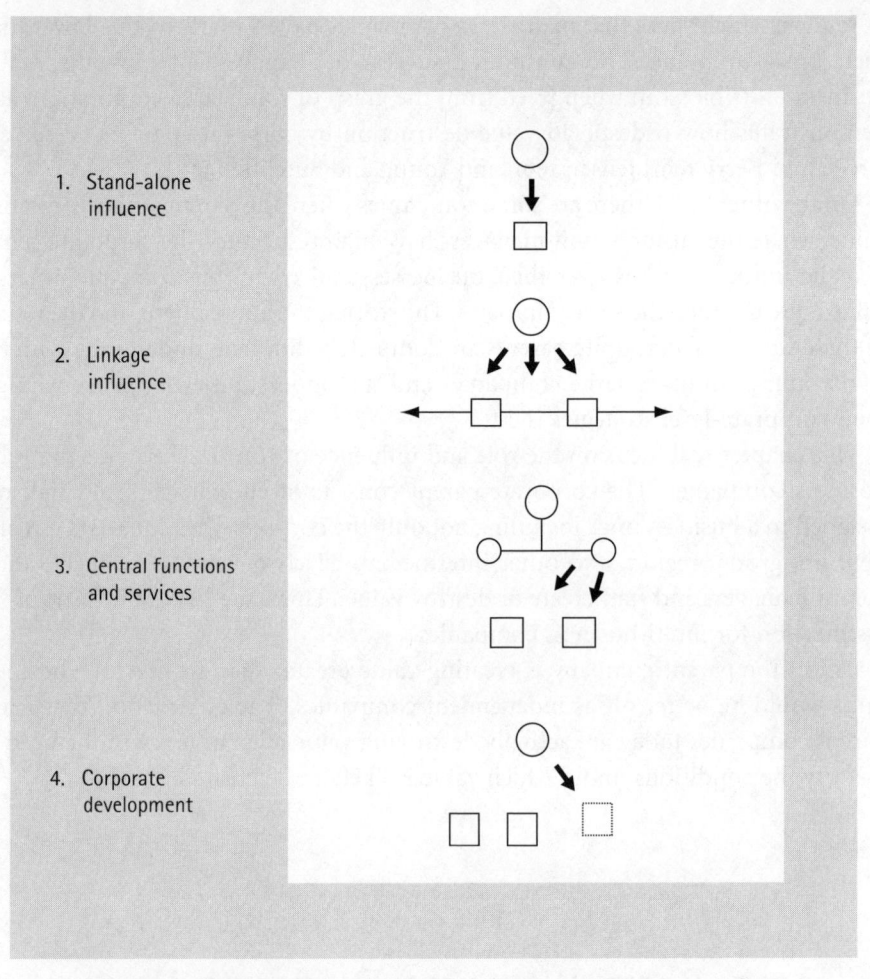

1. Stand-alone influence

2. Linkage influence

3. Central functions and services

4. Corporate development

Fig. 20.1 Four ways in which parents attempt to create value

20.2.1 Stand-Alone Influence

After the 1970s oil crisis, many of the oil majors decided to diversify into new businesses, which would provide more growth and opportunity than their core oil businesses. A popular new area was minerals, which was seen as drawing on skills in natural resource exploration and extraction that were related to their base businesses. In the event, almost all the oil companies have found that they destroyed shareholder value through their minerals diversifications. The root cause of the problem was that parent company managers from the oil industry did not understand the subtle differences between the oil businesses and the minerals businesses, and ended up by influencing the strategies of their minerals businesses in ways that caused them to perform worse, not better.

For example, we were told by a manager who had been part of British Petroleum's (BP's) minerals business: 'The problem was that the BP managing directors couldn't really get to grips with the minerals business or feel that they understood it. There was always that vestige of suspicion about the business, that in turn led to a temptation to say "no" to proposals from the business, or, alternatively, if they said yes, to say yes for the wrong reasons.' The impact on performance was dramatic. During the mid-1980s, the minerals businesses of Atlantic Richfield, BP, Exxon, Shell, and Standard Oil had an average pre-tax return on sales of −17 per cent, while the average independent minerals companies (i.e. companies not parented by the oil majors) achieved a positive return on sales of 10 per cent.

This is an example of what we call stand-alone influence. Stand-alone influence is about the parent's impact on the strategies and performance of each business in the parent's ownership, viewed as a stand-alone profit centre. All parents exert considerable stand-alone influence on their businesses. At a minimum, they are involved in agreeing and monitoring performance targets, in approving major capital expenditures, and in selecting and replacing the business-unit chief executives. These activities, in themselves, are powerful influences on the businesses. Many parents, however, go further, exercising influence on a wider range of issues, such as product-market strategies, pricing decisions, and human resource development. While corporate parents can create value through stand-alone influence, they often destroy value instead. By pressing for inappropriate targets, by starving businesses of resources for worthwhile projects, by encouraging wasteful investment, and by appointing the wrong managers, the parent can have a serious adverse effect on its businesses. The potential for value creation must therefore always be balanced against the risk of value destruction.

20.2.2 Linkage Influence

Linkage influence can be just as destructive. Through linkage influence, the corporate parent seeks to create value by fostering cooperation and synergy between its businesses. But the search for linkages and synergies so often leads to problems that Guy Jillings, Head of Strategic Planning of Shell International Petroleum, has coined the term 'anergy'. He believes that avoiding anergy is often a more essential goal than pursuing synergy.[4]

The problem of anergy is illustrated by a global consulting company which had made acquisitions in two new areas of consulting services to add to its traditional core. Senior managers believed that synergy could be created in a number of ways. First, economies of scale could be achieved by sharing back-office systems such as

---

[4] Most authors on the topic of synergy have commented that it frequently fails to occur in practice. For example, Porter 1985; Kanter 1989; Wells 1984.

client billing and data processing. Second, a more powerful identity could be established by sharing a brand name. Third, more business could be generated by appointing client managers for the company as a whole who could deepen client relationships, coordinate approaches, and cross-sell a broad range of consulting services.

In reality, the pressure for linkages nearly destroyed one of the acquisitions and hampered the efforts of all the other businesses. The shared billing system was complicated by the different needs of each business; after several million dollars of development cost, a compromise solution was reached which most units felt was inferior to their original systems, and which was no cheaper to run. Attempts at joint branding were abandoned because the individual brands were each strong and associated with particular services, whereas the amalgam brand was hard for clients to relate to, and was rejected by staff who felt loyal to the brand values of the specific organization they had joined. Cross-selling was not increased by the new layer of client managers, who were insufficiently familiar with the full range of services available. Worse still, clients resented the imposition of a gatekeeper between them and the specialist service providers they were used to dealing with, and few valued the supposed advantages of one-stop shopping. Eventually, poor performance forced the company to drop many of its linkage initiatives and to reaffirm clearly distinct lines of business.

In many companies, the problems associated with linkage initiatives have made business managers so cynical about the efforts of their parent that they deliberately conceal linkage opportunities. To avoid the risk of parental intervention, managers in these companies prefer to do business with outsiders rather than with insiders.

20.2.3 Central Functions and Services

Parents can also destroy value through establishing central functions and services that undermine, rather than support, business effectiveness. This is not simply a matter of excessive overhead costs. It is also about delayed decisions and substandard or unresponsive support. ABB's chief executive, Percy Barnevik, has acquired many companies where these problems had been rife. His dramatic response in cutting headquarters staff has led to an ABB rule of thumb: by taking out 90 per cent of the centre, you can usually improve business performance as well as save cost. This rule has been applied to Brown Boveri's headquarters, and to acquisitions such as Combustion Engineering in the United States and Strömberg in Finland. Typically, Barnevik removes 30 per cent of the central functions and staff on the grounds that they are adding little except cost. A further 30 per cent are set up as service units that must compete directly with outside suppliers. If they are cost-

effective, their services are purchased. Otherwise, they rapidly shrink or are disbanded. Thirty per cent of the central staff are put under the direct control of the individual businesses. If they fulfil a valid role in the business, they stay. If not, they are replaced or fired.

This approach addresses one of the main problems of central functions and services: that their privileged status protects them from the rigours of the market. By treating the divisions as clients whose business must be won, service levels are sharpened and improved. Unless this sort of relationship exists, the hoped-for economies of scale in central functions often prove illusory, and their influence can hamper rather than help the businesses.

20.2.4 Corporate Development

The final way in which parents destroy value is through corporate development activities—acquisitions, divestments, alliances, business redefinitions, and new ventures. Many corporate parents believe that they create substantial value in their corporate development activities, for example by spotting opportunities to buy businesses cheaply, by creating new ventures that provide profitable future growth opportunities, or by redefining businesses in ways that lead them to be more competitive in their marketplaces. We have found, however, that such initiatives frequently misfire. Parents overpay for acquisitions, support losing ventures, and redefine businesses in the wrong way. The weight of research evidence indicates that the majority of corporately sponsored acquisitions, alliances, new ventures, and business redefinitions fail to create value.[5] In particular, corporate histories are littered with stories of acquired businesses which turned out to be worth much less than expected, and so were sold subsequently for a fraction of the purchase price.

An extreme case concerns Ferranti, a medium-sized electronics company. During the 1980s, Ferranti performed well, developing a variety of sound businesses in defence electronics and other areas. However, in 1987, Ferranti paid $670 million to acquire the US International Signal and Communication (ISC) Group, with a view to becoming a major player in international defence markets. In 1989 it was discovered that ISC had entered into various fraudulent contracts, which led to losses of around $500 million for Ferranti. As a result, Ferranti was severely weakened and eventually forced into receivership after GEC had offered to buy the company for only one penny a share. A single acquisition brought Ferranti to its knees and wiped out all of the value created during the previous decades.

[5] There is a large literature on the poor record of acquisitions, alliances, and new ventures: see e.g. Porter 1987; or Franks and Harris 1989.

20.3 WHY VALUE DESTRUCTION IS SO COMMON

While corporate managers recognize that mistakes can be made at the headquarters in the same way as they can be made at other levels of management, few would accept our proposition that many corporate centres are systematically destroying value. They point to economies of scale in financial reporting, fund raising, liaising with the shareholders, tax, and other areas. They identify the lower cost of debt that large companies can provide. They talk about the value of providing an informed challenge and second opinion to the narrow perspective of business-unit managers. They refer to the task of allocating resources across the portfolio. Clearly, they argue, the corporate centre has a valid role and can contribute to performance.

We agree. There are economies of scale. The cost of debt can be lowered. An informed second opinion and a wise allocation of capital can add value. However, for reasons we will explain, the net influence of the parent in many companies is still negative. Inappropriate interference on linkage issues can outweigh the economies of scale in financial reporting. Wise resource allocation decisions can be fewer than foolish ones. Damage from over-ambitious or under-ambitious performance targets can be more significant than the benefits of lower interest on debt. Value-destroying influences can be greater than value-creating ones. Why is this so?

The reason why value destruction occurs is that it is hard for parent organizations to influence their businesses in ways that improve on the decisions of the managers running the businesses. As we shall see from examining each of the four ways parent organizations affect value, it is not as surprising as it might seem that the parent's influence will make decisions worse, not better. In fact it is only under particular conditions that we can expect the parent's influence to be positive.

20.3.1 The 10% versus 100% Paradox

With stand-alone influence, the assumption is that parent managers know better what is right for a business than the unit's own managers. Is this a realistic assumption? In a multi-business organization, managers in the parent can devote only a small percentage of their attention to the affairs of each business, while the managers in the businesses are fully engaged in their own units. Why should the parent managers, in 10% of their time, be able to improve on the decisions being made by competent managers who are giving 100% of their efforts to the business? The idea that part-time managers at one remove (or more) will be able to enhance the performance of the business's own dedicated management is, in some sense, paradoxical. We refer to this as the '10% versus 100%' paradox.

The 10% vs 100% paradox is compounded by principal/agent problems arising from placing a parent organization between the business managers and the providers of capital (see Jensen and Meckling 1976; Baiman 1982). In a hierarchy, the business-level managers are not motivated primarily by the objective of maximizing the performance of their businesses. They are motivated primarily by the objective of gaining favour, rewards, and career opportunities from their parent bosses. Unless the parent can mimic the influence of the providers of capital, the ownership relationship will result in different motivations and different objectives. Altering the motivations and objectives of business-level managers is one of the ways the parent can add value, but it can also result in value destruction as the business managers play a game of cat and mouse, hiding information and disguising outcomes, to persuade parent managers that they are high-quality individuals.

20.3.2 The Enlightened Self-Interest Paradox

With linkage influence, the assumption is that the parent managers can identify benefits of linkages between businesses that would not be perceived or implemented by the businesses' own managers. But, given the business managers' much greater understanding of their businesses, it is likely that they will have more knowledge about linkage opportunities and how to realize them than parent managers do. The difficulty of value creation from linkage influence therefore stems from another paradox. Why should the parent managers be able to perceive linkage opportunities, if they have not already been perceived as a result of mutual self-interest on the part of energetic business-unit managers? We call this the 'enlightened self-interest' paradox. The existence of this paradox explains why corporately inspired synergy initiatives often prove unsatisfactory.

20.3.3 The Beating the Specialists Paradox

With central functions and services influence, the assumption is that central staffs can provide better functional guidance, or better value-for-money services, than are available from businesses' own staff or from outside suppliers. But the trend in many large companies is now to decentralize or outsource central functions and services. This trend brings out another paradox. A specialist, external supplier stands or falls by its ability to provide the most responsive and cost-effective expertise in its chosen field, whether it be market research, manufacturing advice, or strategic planning. Why should an in-house staff department be able to create more value than specialist competitors who undertake similar tasks and services on

a third-party basis? It is this 'beating the specialists' paradox that has led many companies to disband large parts of their corporate functions and services.

20.3.4 The Beating the Odds Paradox

Finally, with corporate development activities, the assumption is that the parent can buy businesses for less than they are worth, sell businesses for more than they are worth, and launch new ventures or redefined businesses in ways that increase value. Yet the odds are against this happening. Given that the market for buying and selling businesses is sophisticated, and the competition to develop businesses in new areas is usually fierce, why should the parent expect to be able to create value through corporate development? We refer to this as the 'beating the odds' paradox.

These four paradoxes—10% vs 100%, enlightened self-interest, beating the specialists, and beating the odds—explain why it is hard to create value from the corporate centre; nevertheless, the best corporate parents do create substantial value. What conditions must exist to overcome the paradoxes? What conditions lead to value creation?

20.3.5 The Conditions for Value Creation

The first condition is that the businesses in the company's portfolio must have some opportunity to improve performance with which the parent company can help. If the businesses are performing at their optimum, there is no opportunity to add value. The parent can only add something if the business offers a 'parenting opportunity'.

Second, the parent must possess some special capabilities or resources that will enable it to improve performance and exploit the parenting opportunity. These parenting characteristics are the engine of value creation.

Third, the parent must have a sufficient understanding of the critical success factors in the business to make sure that it does not influence the business in inappropriate ways. Managers often refer to this understanding as having a 'feel for the business'. We have observed that it can take a parent manager a number of years, typically including experience of a business over a complete economic cycle, before a sufficient feel develops.

With these three conditions, we can see some analogy between the roles of the corporate parent and of medical experts. Medical specialists can only make a contribution if there are people whose health could be improved. Without this 'opportunity', their expertise is not valuable. To make a contribution, the medical expert must have skills and resources that match the patient's needs. An ear, nose, and

throat specialist is unlikely to contribute much to a patient with depression. Moreover, a specialist on depression must understand sufficiently about the overall health of this patient to be sure that the drugs he prescribes will not have side effects that will make the patient worse off on balance. For the medical expert to succeed, the same three conditions must exist: there must be an opportunity, the expert must have skills and resources that fit the opportunity, and the expert must understand the patient well enough to avoid negative side effects that outweigh the beneficial influences.

20.4 SUCCESSFUL PARENT COMPANIES

Successful parent companies not only meet these basic conditions for value to be created, they are particularly good at creating value. The best parents have unusual insights about certain kinds of parenting opportunities and focus their influence and activities on creating value from these insights. They have what we call 'value creation insights'. The best parents also have special skills and resources that fit particularly well with their value creation insights. These skills and resources are normally superior to those of other similar parents. They have what we call 'distinctive parenting characteristics'. Finally, the best parents limit their portfolios to businesses where their parenting will create a substantial amount of value. They are more effective at doing this because they have clear criteria defining which businesses fit well with the parent and which do not. They have what we call 'heartland' criteria.

20.4.1 Value-Creating Insights

At the time of our research, ABB, Canon, and Emerson were good illustrations of these concepts. They represented a cross-section of the successful diversified companies in our research sample. All three were recognized as world leaders and exemplars of their particular management styles. All three also had excellent performance records (Table 20.1). We will, therefore, illustrate our concepts by explaining the value creation insights these companies had, the distinctive parenting characteristics that supported their insights, and the heartland criteria these companies used to limit their portfolios. Readers should recognize, however, that things change. Insights that are valuable in one decade may not be valuable in the next. Hence these three companies, despite having exemplar parent organizations in the late 1980s and early 1990s, may become problem companies ten years later.

Table 20.1 Company backgrounds

	ABB	Canon	Emerson
Corporate headquarters	Switzerland	Japan	USA
Origins	Merger of ASEA (Sweden) and Brown Boveri (Switzerland) (1988)	Research laboratory focusing on precision optics (1933)	Electrical manufacturing (1890)
Industries	Power plants, power transmission, power distribution, transportation, general industrial	Business machines, cameras, other optical equipment	Electrical-electronic products and systems such as motors, process control instruments, appliance components, etc.
Size (1994)			
sales ($bn)	30	15	8
employees (000)	210	67	69
Performance (10 years)			
sales growth	NA*	250%	200%
earnings growth	200%**	150%	200%
share price growth	300%**	150%	300%

* ASEA and Brown Boveri merged in 1988.
** Based on ASEA (ASEA owns 50% of ABB).

One value creation insight at ABB involved linking nationally focused businesses into a global network: rationalizing production across countries, cross-selling products, sharing technical developments, and transferring best practice. ABB focused much of its parental influence on getting previously isolated national managers to work together across borders.

A second value creation insight at ABB concerned raising the commercial skills and orientation of managers. In large, engineering-dominated companies, managers can become more interested in their engineering prowess and in being involved in prestigious projects than they are in profit. Such companies often do not calculate profit except at high levels of aggregation. Most units are cost centres. The ABB parent discovered that commercial performance could be transformed if the profit ethic could be driven into the hearts of the managers and engineers in the local businesses. Many of ABB's parenting activities are, therefore, focused on achieving this value-creating objective.

A third value creation insight at ABB concerned overheads. Proud, previously rich, and nationally prominent companies have a tendency to build large central overheads that can cost as much as 20 per cent or more of profit. Much of ABB's parent activity, in the first year or two following an acquisition, was designed to reduce these overheads and release the value they had trapped. In later years ABB maintained the pressure on overheads ensuring that excessive costs did not build up again.

In Canon, one value creation insight was about developing new products. Technologists and product developers normally see themselves within the confines of a particular technology or product type. This puts bounds on their thinking defined by the accepted wisdom of the areas they are working in. Canon managers, however, discovered that it is possible to develop more creative products by blending and mixing technologies in, for example, fine optics and precision mechanics, and by challenging product development teams to produce customer solutions well beyond the scope of existing products.

Canon's second value creation insight was based on another parenting opportunity resulting from the bounded thinking of managers. In companies with traditional business-unit structures, managers are influenced by the competitors and critical success factors of the industry they see themselves competing in. They are influenced by the accepted industry logic and, therefore, play into the hands of the industry leaders. Canon managers discovered that it is possible to break out of the accepted logic and develop winning strategies by avoiding traditional business-unit structures and challenging managers to find new ways of competing.

Emerson's value creation insights were based on sharpening the strategic thinking of sound and profitable businesses. Emerson found that, in certain electrical and electronic businesses, it could push profit margins up from 5 to 10 per cent to in excess of 15 per cent at the same time as gaining market share. These improvements stemmed from re-examining of competitive positions and growth opportunities, detailed analysis of the components of cost and revenue in the businesses, and Emerson's special focus on manufacturing cost reductions. Emerson drove these improvements through business strategy reviews, which had been developed to focus on the issues of greatest potential. Emerson is by no means unusual in conducting strategy reviews with its businesses: what is unusual is the way in which the process zeroes in on opportunities to improve performance, rather than simply being a routine re-examination of the businesses' plans.

ABB, Canon, and Emerson had value creation insights that provided a focus for the parent's activities. All three companies had clarity about how the parent can create value. This clarity was built on insights they gained about opportunities to build or improve businesses and about how the parent can contribute. The insights affected the focus of parenting activities, the design of the parent organization, and the type of businesses in the company's portfolio. At the time of writing the parent organizations of all three companies are still partly driven by these insights. But they

are also influenced by new insights developed in the last ten years. ABB has developed new insights about growing businesses in Asia; Emerson has developed insights about developing new businesses; and Canon has developed insights about globalization. What distinguishes successful companies is that they have insights (see Box 20.1).

Box 20.1 Value creation insights

Value creation insights are at the root of all successful corporate-level strategies. They typically involve understandings by parent managers about how to improve the performance of businesses. Insights are based on unique knowledge or experience of:

(1) reasons why certain kinds of businesses have performance problems or fail to maximize their potential;
(2) ways in which a parent organization can influence the businesses so as to raise performance.

Value creation insights are extraordinarily diverse. Each of the successful companies we researched had its own, different value creation insights.

Value creation insights are about major areas of improvement: raising performance by 50% or 100%, not just 10%; doubling the value of a business, not just making marginal differences. Value creation insights are not, therefore, about providing a wise second opinion, gaining economies of scale in managing shareholder relationships or raising debt 10% cheaper. Value creation insights are about taking return on sales from below 10% to above 15% (Emerson), doubling sales volumes through linkages into an international network (Unilever and ABB), creating new businesses out of leveraging technologies (Canon and 3M), doubling shareholder value by buying mixed portfolios and unbundling them (KKR).

Value creation insights are linked to specific sorts of businesses that have underperformance opportunities and critical success factors which the parent managers understand. They are, therefore, expressed in terms such as: 'In businesses that make higher added value, safety critical engineering components and systems, a parent can create value by putting together international businesses out of previously separate national entities'; or 'In long-term, technically complex natural resource businesses, a parent can create value by transferring technical and functional expertise around the world'. Thus, the general form of a value creation insight is: 'In certain sorts of businesses, a parent can create value by...'. The value creation insight identifies both the businesses in which the parent can create value, and the means by which it does so.

Value creation insights are not always explicit. Sometimes they are embedded in the parent organization's culture and way of working. What is important is that they describe how the parent's corporate strategy leads to major value creation.

The final point about value creation insights is that they often take years of experience to develop and refine. Sometimes they appear to have sprung newly formed from the mind of a visionary chief executive or from a strategic planning process. However, more normally, they emerge from a long process of learning and experience.

20.4.2 Distinctive Parenting Characteristics

The second feature of successful diversified companies is their distinctive parenting. Emerson's distinctive parenting characteristics start with its planning process. At the heart of the process is the 'planning conference', an annual meeting between parent managers and businesses that is unusually combative and challenging. The degree of preparation done by both sides is unusual; the forty required charts and analyses are unusual; and the expertise of Chuck Knight, Emerson's CEO, based on twenty years' experience with running these meetings and monitoring Emerson's kind of businesses, is unusual. It is through the planning conference that Knight tests the thinking and the goals of the businesses, pressing for improvements and helping to identify ways of achieving them. By design, the atmosphere is confrontational. 'Emerson is a contact sport,' commented one manager. 'Knight invites people to punch back. He takes positions to provoke a response and expects one.' The debates are often heated, but the parent managers have the skills to make them open and constructive. In the second half of the 1990s, Emerson's planning process focused more on growth and less on profit margin and Chuck Knight developed a new process, 'the growth conference'. This reflected the new insights about growing businesses.

Canon has many distinctive parenting characteristics. Probably most important is Canon's uncompromising corporate commitment to developing its core technologies that goes back to its roots as a research laboratory. Professor Yamanouchi, previously a Canon employee, explained, 'R&D drives Canon's strategic thinking and is central to Canon's behaviour. As an example, the medium range plan of each product group is drawn up by the development centre of the product group. Canon's R&D staff, therefore, believe that their work is essential for the growth of Canon' (see Yamanouchi 1989). This commitment is linked to Canon's very large corporate staff which includes over 1,000 central research staff. Commitment to technology is also revealed in Canon frequently being among the top three companies registering new US patents.

Another distinctive parenting characteristic is Canon's ability to reduce rigidity in organizational boundaries by encouraging networking and cross-company linkages. The organization operates as a 'hub and spoke' system, with matrix lines that bind the spokes together. At the centre there is a 22-man corporate executive committee which meets weekly, bringing together the central managers, the heads of product divisions, the heads of sales organizations, and the heads of functions. This level of contact is unusual and greatly helps the effective management of the matrix. Canon also has many other mechanisms, such as heavyweight task forces, product development teams, and career management processes, designed to bring people together and move them across functional and organizational boundaries.

ABB, our third example, also has distinctive parenting characteristics. Percy Barnevik, ABB's chief executive, developed his parenting approach by turning

round ASEA in the late 1970s and early 1980s. ABB's 'lean matrix' of business areas and country managers topped by a corporate centre with around 100 staff has been written about frequently (see Taylor 1991; see also Kennedy 1992). It is designed to break previously monolithic, national companies into small, focused business units linked to similar units in other countries, but still benefiting from a strong national presence. Business area managers are part of the parent organization. They make decisions about rationalizing production across countries and spend their lives visiting business units to persuade unit managers to share technical developments, cross-sell products, and pick up on best practice.

Supporting this highly decentralized structure is a central monitoring and control system, Abacus, that provides profit statements and balance sheet information for every business unit and profit centre (5,000 in total). Units can compare themselves, and senior managers can rapidly identify anomalies or problem areas. This profit-focused information system combined with the small size of most business units, often less than 200 people and sometimes as few as 50, helps drive a commercial, profit-focused attitude into the culture of the lowest level engineer or manager. ABB's parenting systems and structures are distinctive and are linked to the value creation insights that provide a focus for all of ABB's parenting activities.

Successful parent companies, therefore, have a clear focus for their parenting activities, based on value creation insights. They also have distinctive parenting characteristics that enable them to create the value they focus on. In addition, successful companies have a portfolio of businesses that fit with their parenting. They are clear about the criteria that define what we call their 'heartland businesses', the businesses that will benefit most from the centre's parenting influence, and they focus their portfolios on such businesses. In these businesses, they are able to create high value and to avoid value destruction.

20.4.3 Heartland Businesses

Emerson's heartland is businesses that manufacture electrical, electromechanical, or electronic products of medium technology and capital intensity where there is potential to raise performance. Emerson avoids consumer markets: 'Our ability to strategize in consumer products is less good. We like a slower rhythm. We don't like advertising and short product cycles.' Canon's heartland includes businesses where precision mechanics, fine optics, and microelectronics are important technologies, where technical innovation and creative market positioning are important sources of advantage, and where there is a sufficiently large market to justify intensive technical development. ABB's heartland includes engineering-intensive, electro-technical businesses where there is potential to create linkages across national borders and which involve selling complex systems to large industrial companies or to governments.

20.5 Developing Successful Corporate Strategies

ABB, Canon, and Emerson were, and at the time of writing still are, successful parent companies with value-creating corporate strategies. They have value creation insights and distinctive parenting characteristics, and by focusing on a clearly defined heartland they avoid the value-destroying pitfalls that afflict many companies. But how can other companies that are currently less successful develop similarly powerful corporate strategies? We will end this article by proposing a criterion, parenting advantage, that should guide companies, and a framework that can be used to structure their search for successful corporate strategies.

We have argued that success is dependent on the value created or destroyed by the parent organization. By doing so we are identifying the parent as an organization that is separate from the business units, and that stands between the business units and the investors. This separate organization needs to justify its existence as an intermediary. Moreover, the parent organization is in competition with other parent organizations and other intermediaries for the ownership of businesses. To succeed, a parent organization needs to create value and it needs to be better at creating value than rivals—it needs to have what we call 'parenting advantage'.

20.5.1 Parenting Advantage

Parenting advantage is a criterion for guiding corporate strategy development, in the same way that competitive advantage is a criterion for guiding business strategy development. In business strategy, the key objective is to outperform competitors, and the concept of competitive advantage has proved immensely useful in assessing and developing business strategies. In corporate strategy, the key objective is to outperform rivals and other intermediaries, and the concept of parenting advantage has similar power to help assess and develop corporate strategies.

In the increasingly active market for corporate control that exists in Anglo-Saxon economies, parenting advantage is the only robust logic for a parent company to own a business. Without parenting advantage, a company is potentially exposed to the hostile attentions of other, superior rivals, and can often enhance shareholder value simply by selling businesses to other owners. Parenting advantage is the goal and criterion that should guide both the selection of businesses to include in the portfolio and the design of the parent organization.

As companies search for parenting advantage, they need to analyse and assess a number of inputs. They need to understand the strengths and weaknesses of the existing parent organization: what are the current characteristics of the parent?

They need to understand the nature of the businesses currently owned by the parent: what are the parenting opportunities in these businesses? They need to know enough about rival parents to be able to assess which parents might be better owners of any of the current businesses. Finally, they need to understand the trends and possible scenarios for the future that might affect the other three inputs. Developing corporate strategy, therefore, involves four inputs (Figure 20.2).

These inputs do not provide answers. Rather they provide understandings that are useful in the search for value creation insights. This search is an essentially creative process guided by the objective of parenting advantage: the strategist is searching for a strategy that will give the company parenting advantage. The outputs of this strategy development process are decisions about which businesses to include in the portfolio and decisions about how the parent organization should be designed.

20.5.2 Five Steps towards a Better Strategy

A useful first step in developing a new corporate strategy is to identify areas where the parent is currently destroying value. By divesting businesses or changing the parent's behaviour, these situations can be avoided. For many companies this first step greatly enhances shareholder value.

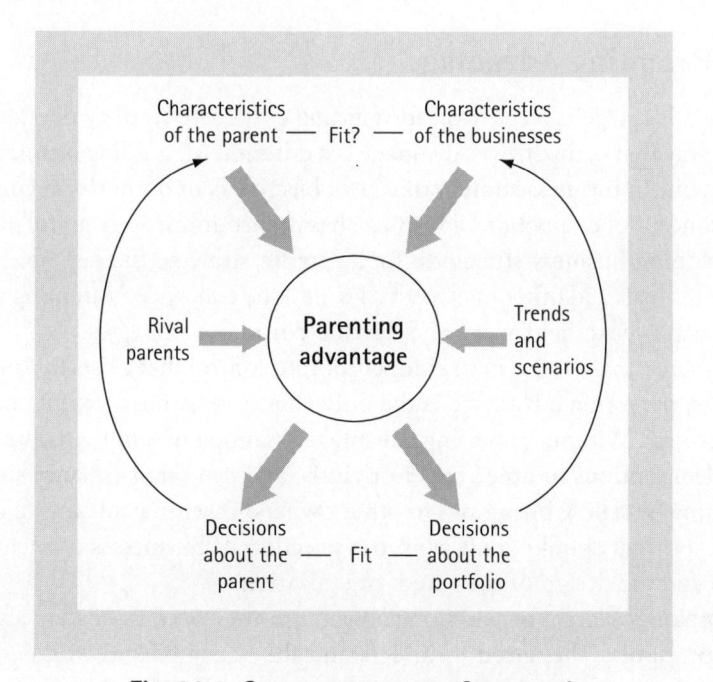

Fig. 20.2 Corporate strategy framework

The second step is to start searching for 'parenting opportunities'. These are opportunities to improve performance through the involvement of a parent company. For example, a business may have low levels of manufacturing skills because it is dominated by marketing managers. A parent company with a manufacturing capability can, therefore, help redress the balance. Or a business may be too small, causing its costs to be too high. By combining it with another business, a parent company can cure the scale problem. Box 20.2 describes some of the common reasons why businesses underperform in ways that provide parenting opportunities.

The third step is to assess whether and how the company can grasp the parenting opportunities. This involves creating groupings of businesses with similar parenting opportunities. Each grouping is then assessed for its fit with the parent organization. Could the capabilities and resources in the parent fit with the parenting opportunities in the group of businesses? If fit does not currently exist, the

---

Box 20.2 Typical reasons for parenting opportunities

1. **Wrongly defined business.** The managers in the business have a wrong conception of what the business should be and, therefore, have too narrow or too broad a product market scope, and too much or too little vertical integration. The trend to outsourcing and alliances is changing the definitions of many businesses, creating new parenting opportunities.
2. **Size and age.** Old, large, successful businesses often build up bureaucracies and overheads that are hard to eliminate from the inside. Small, young businesses may have insufficient functional skills, managerial succession problems, and lack of financial resources to ride a recession. In both cases parenting opportunities exist.
3. **Temptations.** Some businesses tempt their managers to make mistakes. Mature businesses often lead managers into over-diversifying. Businesses with long product cycles cause managers to rely too much on old products. Cyclical businesses cause managers to over-invest in the upswing. In all cases there are opportunities for a parent to provide corrective influence.
4. **Linkages.** Where businesses can create value through linking with other businesses, blockages often exist preventing this from happening between independent companies. Parent organizations can remove these blockages.
5. **Major changes.** Industries undergoing change, for example from local to international or from single-product to system, require managers with real expertise at making these changes. A parent organization that develops this expertise can provide important assistance to businesses it owns.
6. **Special expertise.** Special expertise can be created by exposing managers to a number of businesses either facing similar strategic issues, such as declining sales or the need to professionalize management, or involved in similar products and markets, but in different countries. A parent organization owning these similar businesses can build the expertise.

question is what changes would be necessary in the parent organization to create a fit. Achieving a good fit may take a number of years of searching for parenting opportunities and developing capabilities and resources to match.

Once a concept of parenting advantage has been developed and the basis for a corporate strategy agreed, the fourth step is to capture this in a parenting advantage statement (see statement for ABB in Box 20.3). This statement identifies the value creation insights and distinctive parenting characteristics on which the strategy will be built, and the heartland businesses within which parenting advantage will be sought. The parenting advantage statement captures the essence of a value-creating corporate strategy, and provides a succinct view of how and why parenting advantage will be achieved.

The fifth step is to convert the chosen strategy into an action plan, involving decisions about the parent organization and decisions about the portfolio of businesses. The implementation of these decisions will, in turn, feed back into changes in the parenting characteristics and the business characteristics. The ongoing corporate strategy development process thus requires continuous adjustment of the parent company and the portfolio of businesses to bring about a closer fit, and to adjust to unplanned changes in any of the important factors.

Box 20.3 ABB: parenting advantage statement (mid–1990s)

Value creation insights	• Most companies make direct trade-offs between centralization and decentralization, or scale and focus. There are opportunities for a parent that can combine the various benefits in new ways.
	• Many European engineering businesses have been relatively fragmented in global terms. Consolidation can reduce costs while increasing coverage and global muscle.
	• Many engineering businesses do not have a strong commercial focus, and are prone to increase sales volume and product range at the expense of margin. A parent can help redress the balance.
Distinctive parenting characteristics	• Ability to combine decentralized small business units into a global network through the ABB matrix structure.
	• Systems and corporate initiatives that focus on profitability, customer needs, and simplification of operations.
	• Ability to integrate acquisitions and improve their performance rapidly.
	• Ruthless approach to cutting of overhead costs.
Heartland businesses	• Engineering-intensive, electro-technical businesses, usually involving complex integration into systems. Customers are large industrial or governmental institutions.

For companies whose corporate-level plan has traditionally been little more than an aggregation of the plans of the businesses, together with a page or two describing the company's overall ambitions and objectives, the corporate strategy development process we are suggesting is radically different. It puts the role of the parent in creating, and destroying, value at centre stage; it insists that decisions that impact the capabilities and resources of the parent are just as essential components of corporate strategy as portfolio choices; and it derives choices about the corporate strategy from assessment of their likely impact on net value creation and parenting advantage. As such, it forces companies to face up to the fact that they are likely to be destroying value in many of their businesses, and to search for ways in which they can become better parents for all of their businesses.

The parenting advantage framework can also lead to very different conclusions from other, more conventional theories of corporate strategy. For example, object-ives such as portfolio balance, spread of risk, and growth take second place to parenting advantage. Decisions that improve balance, or increase spread of risk, or raise the rate of corporate growth cannot, in our view, be justified if they at the same time damage parenting advantage. Many of the large chemical companies that diversified away from bulk chemicals into specialty chemicals, in search of faster growth, more spread, and greater balance, have subsequently regretted their deci-sions. They have found that they were not able to parent the specialty businesses well, and that their results have therefore been disappointing. A focus on parenting advantage in corporate strategy development would have prevented many of these decisions.

20.5.3 Parenting Advantage versus Core Competences

Parenting advantage thinking has more in common with core competencies thinking (Prahalad and Hamel 1990). But there are important differences. The parenting advantage framework puts the emphasis on the capabilities and resources of the *parent* (parenting competencies), and the impact of these on the businesses. The core competencies logic does not distinguish so clearly between parent competencies and business competencies, and simply encourages companies to base their corporate strategies on competencies that are or could become common across the portfolio. As a result, the development of core competencies can sometimes conflict with the pursuit of parenting advantage. Texas Instruments, for example, attempted to exploit technical competencies it had developed in its semi-conductor businesses in areas such as calculators, watches, and home computers. It failed in these new areas not because it did not possess the requisite technical skills, but because senior managers in the parent company lacked experience and skills in parenting such consumer-oriented businesses. Similarly, Minebea, the Japanese leader in miniature

ball bearings, attempted to move into semiconductors, on the basis of its skills in precision manufacturing of miniature components. It has found, however, that this undoubted competence has not proved sufficient to allow it to become successful in the semiconductor business, and in 1991 it reported a loss of ¥5 billion from its semi-conductor subsidiary. In both cases, although the diversifications drew on common technical competencies, they were not successful because the corporate centre lacked the appropriate parenting competencies to avoid the mistakes that were made.[6]

Conversely, corporate strategies that build on the capabilities and resources in the parent company, but do not involve the sharing of operating competencies between the businesses, can be less easy to understand from a core competencies perspective. BTR, the British-based industrial manufacturing company, voted best managed company in Britain in 1993, had a corporate strategy based on clear sources of parenting advantage, but it did not go in for sharing marketing, technical, or engineering skills across its businesses. BTR's success with a portfolio of more than 1,000 business units in more than fifty countries was not based on core competencies. Like Emerson, it was based on the influence the parent organization exerted to raise performance in its businesses. Interestingly in the second half of the 1990s after more than twenty years of success, BTR's strategy ran out of steam, its performance declined and it was taken over. Its market had become much more global. Its strategy of focusing on technical niches wilted as these niches disappeared at the hands of more broadly focused competitors. BTR's rags to riches to takeover candidate is a warning to all companies that the role of the parent needs to evolve as the environment changes.

20.5.4 The Role of the Parent and E-commerce

The explosion of e-commerce and e-ventures in 1999 and 2000 poses a particularly interesting challenge for the role of the parent and corporate-level strategy.

E-commerce ventures have characteristics that are very unlikely to fit easily with the characteristics of the parent company. A simple analysis might suggest that most companies, therefore, should ignore e-commerce ventures in order to avoid doing harm with inappropriate parenting. However, the logic of parenting is about relative advantage—parenting advantage.

---

[6] Similar arguments help to show why 'relatedness' is not a sufficient basis for corporate strategy. Different businesses may be related in terms of technologies, markets, or customers, but the real issue is whether the corporate parent has the ability to add any value to the businesses. Relatedness does not necessarily mean that there are any parenting opportunities, or that the corporate parent has the skills or resources to realize any parenting opportunities there may be. We believe that it is for this reason that research to demonstrate that related corporate strategies lead to better performance than unrelated corporate strategies has proved somewhat inconclusive. See Rumelt 1974 for a basic statement of the 'relatedness' thesis, and Rumelt 1989 for a summary of the large body of subsequent research.

A company such as General Motors might rightly consider itself to be a poor parent for a new e-commerce venture, yet it may still be better than rivals. As a result, most companies have launched major efforts to develop new e-commerce businesses.

As soon as these businesses are successfully launched and able to develop on their own, it usually makes sense to spin them off into a separate company. While the parent company may have had parenting advantage in launching e-commerce ventures, such as General Motors' component purchasing alliance, it is likely to have a net negative impact on the venture once it is launched: the characteristics misfit becomes more of an issue once the initial resource support has been added. Not surprisingly it is common for companies with successful e-ventures to demerge them and float them as independent companies.

20.6 SUMMARY

The parenting advantage framework represents an approach to the issues of corporate strategy that not only explains the past but also helps with today's challenges. It helps corporate parents avoid common corporate strategy mistakes, and discover ways of moving forward that increase the probability of success. This chapter has pointed out why it is so hard for corporate parents to add value to a portfolio of different businesses. It has also shown how some companies like ABB, Canon, and Emerson succeed despite the difficulties.

The central message is that corporate-level strategy should be built on insights that corporate-level managers have about how to create value from owning a portfolio of businesses. Without such insights, the corporate level is likely to destroy more value than it creates; the company is better broken up into separate businesses.

References

BAIMAN, S. (1982). 'Agency Research in Managerial Accounting: A Survey'. *Journal of Accounting Literature*, 1: 154–213.

FRANKS, JULIAN, and HARRIS, ROBERT (1989). 'Shareholder Wealth Effects of Corporate Takeovers: The UK Experience'. *Journal of Financial Economics*, 23: 225–50.

GOOLD, MICHAEL, CAMPBELL, ANDREW, and ALEXANDER, MARCUS (1994). *Corporate-Level Strategy: Creating Value in the Multi-Business Company*. New York: John Wiley.

GREEN, SEBASTIAN, and BERRY, DEAN F. (1991). *Cultural, Structural and Strategic Change in Management Buyouts.* Basingstoke: Macmillan.

JENSEN, MICHAEL (1991). 'Corporate Control and the Politics of Finance'. *Journal of Applied Corporate Finance,* 4/2 (Summer): 13–33.

—— and MECKLING, W. H. (1976). 'Theory of the Firm: Managerial Behavior, Agency Costs and Ownership Structure'. *Journal of Financial Economics,* 3: 305–60.

KANTER, ROSABETH MOSS (1989). *When Giants Learn to Dance.* London: Simon and Schuster.

KENNEDY, CAROL (1992). 'ABB: Model Manager for the New Europe'. *Long Range Planning,* 24/15: 10–17.

PORTER, MICHAEL (1985). *Competitive Advantage: Creating and Sustaining Superior Performance.* New York: Free Press.

—— (1987). 'From Competitive Advantage to Corporate Strategy'. *Harvard Business Review,* May–June: 43–59.

PRAHALAD, C. K., and HAMEL, GARY (1990). 'The Core Competence of the Corporation'. *Harvard Business Review,* 3 (May–June): 79–93.

RUMELT, RICHARD P. (1974). *Strategy, Structure and Economic Performance.* Boston: Division of Research, Harvard Business School.

—— (1989). 'Research and Corporate Diversification: A Synthesis'. *Strategic Management Journal,* 7 (Nov./Dec.): 523–51.

TAYLOR, WILLIAM (1991). 'The Logic of Global Business: An Interview with ABB's Percy Barnevik'. *Harvard Business Review,* Mar.–Apr.: 90–105.

WELLS, JOHN (1984). 'In Search of Synergy'. Ph.D. diss., Harvard University, No. 8502578.

YAMANOUCHI, TERUO (1989). 'Breakthrough: The Development of the Canon Personal Copier'. *Long Range Planning,* 22/5: 11–21.

YOUNG, DAVID, and SUTCLIFFE, BRIGID (1990). 'Value Gaps—Who is Right?—The Raiders, the Market or the Managers?'. *Long Range Planning,* 23/4: 20–34.

MERGERS AND ACQUISITIONS

MOTIVES, VALUE CREATION, AND IMPLEMENTATION

RICHARD SCHOENBERG

21.1 INTRODUCTION

MERGERS and acquisitions (M&A) provide a popular means of achieving rapid growth and market entry. As we entered the new Millennium, companies were spending in excess of three trillion US dollars annually on over 30,000 M&A transactions, equivalent to the completion of one deal every 17 minutes. The objectives of this chapter are to explore the motives underlying this form of activity, to review the empirical evidence on M&A performance, and to discuss the factors determining acquisition outcome from a practical, yet research-based, perspective. The material is presented in six main sections: Acquisition Activity and its Drivers, Firms' Motives for Acquisition, Acquisition Performance, Value Creation within Acquisitions, Post-Acquisition Integration, and Employee Resistance to Acquisition.

21.2 ACQUISITION ACTIVITY
AND ITS DRIVERS

An acquisition may be defined as the purchase by one company, the 'bidder', of a controlling interest in another company, the 'target'. Typically, the bidding firm offers either cash or its own shares in exchange for the shares of the target company. Once the acquisition is completed, the bidding company controls all of the assets, both tangible and intangible, of the target entity and for this reason acquisitions are often referred to as takeovers.

In contrast to acquisition, a merger should be viewed as a combination of two previously separate organizations rather than a takeover of one by the other. A merger involves two companies, often of approximately similar size, coming together to combine all of their assets. The result of a merger is the formation of a new legal entity that encompasses the combined assets of the two previously independent companies. Shareholders in the two merging companies become the joint owners of the new entity. The merger of Glaxo Wellcome and SmithKline Beecham, for example, resulted in shareholders of both companies receiving new share certificates in the combined entity, Glaxo SmithKline.

However, while the terms 'acquisition' and 'merger' do have precise meanings in certain contexts, e.g. legal structures, they generally share common motives and criteria for success and therefore the terms are often used interchangeably in practice. In the interests of simplicity, the terms will also be used synonymously within this chapter.

Mergers and acquisitions should be viewed as an alternative to strategic alliances and organic growth as a means of achieving corporate growth. While each of these three routes for growth have their relative merits depending on the precise competitive environment and resource base of the company concerned, acquisitions can hold the advantage of overcoming the relatively long time scales and potential resource constraints of organic growth and do not involve the dilution of control inherent within strategic alliances.

The importance that companies attach to acquisitions is evidenced by the high volume of transactions completed each year. Global M&A activity in the year 2000 represented a total investment by companies of $3,500 billion. Figure 21.1 illustrates the strongly rising trend in acquisition activity seen throughout the 1990s. Transactions within Europe account for around one-third of the global total. One notable feature within European M&A is that cross-border company purchases now account for approximately half of all transactions as firms seek to build pan-European market positions to exploit the opportunities provided by the Single European Market.

Inspection of historical data on M&A activity reveals a number of periods of particularly high activity, which have become known as merger waves. Four merger

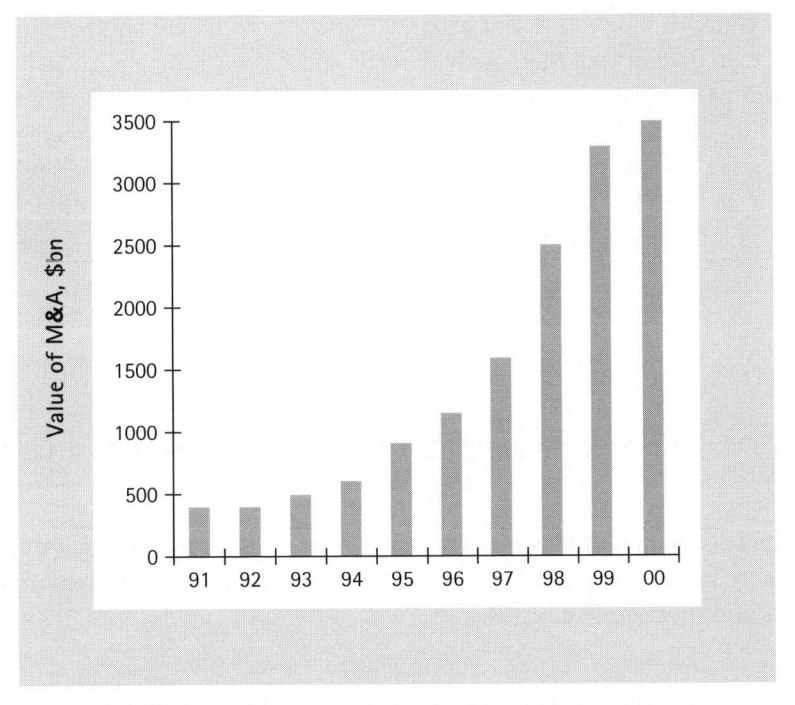

Fig. 21.1 Global merger and acquisition activity

Source: Thomson Financial.

waves have been identified with their peaks of activity, in terms of both number and value of transactions, occurring in 1899, 1929, 1968, and 1988. It is likely that the high levels of M&A experienced in the late 1990s represent a fifth wave. The principal drivers of these merger waves appear to be buoyant stock market conditions and low interest rates, with overall economic prosperity also exerting an influence. High share prices may make companies more inclined to undertake acquisitions in order to exploit their own increased p/e ratios (see Section 21.3.2 below) while the existence of low interest rates will reduce the cost of capital for debt-financed acquisitions. Certainly, both of these macro environmental factors were in place in the late 1990s with stock markets reaching record highs on both sides of the Atlantic and interest rates at historically low levels (Yagil 1996; Golbe and White 1993).

A further feature of these merger waves is that within each wave the acquisition activity tends to be concentrated within certain industry sectors. The high volumes of M&A in the late 1990s were particularly seen in the pharmaceutical, banking, and electricity sectors within the United Kingdom, while other sectors such as medical equipment, education, and ordnance experienced little or no activity. Studies into the industry-level determinants of acquisition activity have found that high rates of acquisitions tend to occur in industries that are characterized by good growth rates

and low concentration ratios. The external regulatory climate is another important influence on both overall M&A activity levels and those within a particular industry. More permissive and laissez-faire national merger regulation policies in the United Kingdom and United States were a major catalyst to the 1980s merger wave. Similarly, the deregulation of certain UK industry sectors following their privatization, or as the result of EU legislative changes, has been a major cause of high M&A levels within the affected industries during the 1990s (Schoenberg and Reeves 1999).

21.3 FIRMS' MOTIVES FOR ACQUISITION

Individual companies can have a wide range of motives for making an acquisition. These may broadly be classified into three groups: strategic motives, financial motives, and managerial motives.

21.3.1 Strategic Motives

A firm may undertake an acquisition in order to increase its penetration of an existing product market, to enter a new product market, to enter a new geographical territory, or to diversify away from its core business.

Acquisitions may be a particularly attractive means of achieving such strategic developments under certain conditions. In mature industries containing a number of established players, expansion or entry via acquisition can avoid the competitive reaction that can accompany attempts to grow by organic growth; rather than intensifying the rivalry by adding further productive capacity, the potential competition is purchased. In some industries economies of scale are central to a competitive cost structure and the purchase of an enterprise that is already of the requisite scale can provide entry without the risk of starting at a cost disadvantage. In consumer goods industries this argument can be extended to securing distribution channels. A frequent barrier to a product range expansion or a move into a new product area is the premium attached to retailers' shelf space. Acquisition of a company that is already operating in the desired product area gives immediate access to an established distribution channel and its valuable shelf space in addition to its other assets such as manufacturing capacity and brand name. Similarly, the speed with which acquisitions can provide an established market position can be very useful if a firm believes it is a late entrant relative to its competitors into a particular product or geographic market.

Companies may also undertake an acquisition because they wish to strengthen their existing resource base in a specific area or because they lack a particular competence that would be needed to develop their strategy by internal means. For example, when AOL merged with Time Warner it gained access to their back-catalogues of books and films, an asset that would have been virtually impossible to develop internally. Similarly, an acquisition might be used to gain a leading-edge product or process technology, an established brand name, access to a distribution channel, or managerial know-how. The latter factor can be especially relevant to cross-border acquisitions where the bidding company often lacks any operating experience in the overseas market and is keen to exploit the local market knowledge of the target firm's management team.

21.3.2 Financial Motives

Financially, acquisitive growth may be particularly attractive to a publicly quoted company if its price:earnings ratio is relatively high compared to that of potential target companies. Under such circumstances an acquisition funded by shares can provide an immediate earnings per share enhancement to the acquiring firm, as the simplified data in Figure 21.2 illustrate.

This type of financial logic also extends to the acquisition of companies in order to exploit their accumulated tax credits or high balance sheet liquidity. A company making healthy profits may be attracted to acquire a target firm that has built up losses over a period of time. Once the acquisition is completed, and if the appropriate

	GoAhead plc p/e ratio = 30 share price = 300p	Steady plc p/e ratio = 10 share price = 100p		GoAhead +Steady
Profit after tax	£10m	£10m		£20m
Shares in issue	100m	100m	GoAhead acquires Steady by way of 1 for 2 share offer (50% bid premium)	150m
Earnings per share	10p	10p		13.3p

Fig. 21.2 Achieving earnings per share enhancement via acquisition using highly rated shares

Source: David Norburn, Imperial College Management School.

accounting conditions are met, the accumulated losses of the target can be set against the future profits of the acquirer so reducing the latter's corporation tax liability. Similarly, a firm that possesses a cash-rich balance sheet or is in a highly cash generative business may make an attractive takeover target for a company that has promising investment opportunities of its own. The acquirer is able to raise the rate of return on the target company's cash by investing it in its own business or to extend its own borrowing capacity by virtue of its enhanced cash flow position. This logic can even be reversed whereby acquirers with very strong balance sheets and an associated high credit rating take over a highly geared business and subsequently enhance profits by refinancing the debt within the acquired company at a lower interest rate.

Finally, some acquirers are motivated to make acquisitions in the hope that they can purchase a company at a bargain price and later sell it on, either whole or in its constituent parts, at a profit. While few, if any, pure 'asset-stripping' opportunities remain today, a modern variant is the practice of 'unbundling'. This involves acquiring an existing conglomerate, the stock market value of which is less than the sum of the individual constituent businesses. The businesses are then sold off piecemeal, creating a surplus over the acquisition cost.

21.3.3 Managerial Motives

Companies seeking shareholder approval for an acquisition invariably outline the strategic and financial logic of the transaction and link this with shareholder value maximization. However it has been suggested that some takeovers are undertaken in the interests of the firm's managers rather than its shareholders. An acquisition can help to advance a manager's own position through a rapid increase in the size of the company that the manager is responsible for, or through an increased dependence on the manager's particular skills via the purchase of a target business which is reliant on those skills (Berkovitch and Narayanan 1993).

Acquisitions that are motivated primarily by the self-interest of the managers of the acquiring firm are unlikely to be value maximizing for its shareholders. This is for two reasons. First, managers driven to make acquisitions for personal reasons may be less concerned to make a careful economic analysis of whether the acquisition has the potential to create shareholder value. Second, they may be prepared to pay a higher price for the acquisition than would be justified on purely economic grounds. Direct research into this 'empire building' theory of acquisitions is, of course, very difficult given the natural reluctance of executives to admit that personal motives may have played a role in a corporate decision. However, there is tangential support available from research which shows that firms with strong CEOs but weak corporate governance structures tend to pay higher premiums for

their acquisitions. Where a strong CEO was also chairman of the board, or where the board of directors contained a low proportion of non-executive (external) directors, the acquisitions made by the firm exhibited higher bid premiums and inferior shareholder returns. Put more positively, the findings do also suggest that the presence of a strong board of directors can limit the ability of executives to pursue acquisitions for their own motives (Hayward and Hambrick 1997).

21.4 ACQUISITION PERFORMANCE

The performance record of acquisitions is mixed at best. Research undertaken from a strategic management perspective has sought to establish how well acquisitions have performed from the viewpoint of the acquiring firm. A study by McKinsey & Company reveals that 43 per cent of international acquisitions fail to produce a financial return that meets or exceeds the acquirer's cost of capital; put another way 43 per cent destroy shareholder value for the acquiring firm (Bleeke and Ernst 1993).

Other studies have adopted broader definitions of performance, typically assessing the outcome of an acquisition against the original objectives set for it, both financial and non-financial. These assessments are usually carried out three to five years following the completion of the acquisition and are conducted using input from the acquiring company. Recent research along these lines indicate that 45 to 55 per cent of acquirers are 'neutral to highly dissatisfied' with the overall performance of their acquisitions. Interestingly, the failure rates are similar for domestic and cross-border acquisitions and show no improvement over figures reported in 1974 from the first such study.

The subsequent fate of an acquisition may also provide an indication of its performance. Data show that approximately 45 per cent of all acquired firms are divested after an average of seven years under the ownership of the acquirer. Divestment has sometimes been taken to signify acquisition failure, but it could also indicate that an acquirer wishes to realize its profits following a successful restructuring of the acquired company. Indeed, research data further show that 40 per cent of divestitures are sold on at a price in excess of their acquisition cost, so this is perhaps not a particularly reliable performance measure (Kaplan and Weisbach 1992).

Separately, financial economists have investigated the impact of M&A on overall wealth generation. These researchers have typically relied on stock market measures of performance. Wealth generation is calculated from the change in the share prices of the bidder and target around the time of the acquisition announcement,

appropriately adjusted for the expected change taking account of movements in the overall stock market. If one accepts market efficiency arguments, these 'abnormal returns' represent the market's accurate predictions of the changes in wealth that will result from the acquisition. The results of such studies reveal that, overall, acquisitions create negligible or only very small wealth gains. However, the distribution of any gain between the shareholders of the bidding and target companies is not even.

For example, one in-depth study of 429 British acquisitions completed between 1980 and 1990 found that target companies gained approximately 30 per cent in value, while shareholders in bidding companies lost approximately 5 per cent. In order to calculate the total wealth gain, these share price movements must be weighted by the companies' starting point market capitalizations. This revealed that the acquisitions had produced overall wealth gains of only 2 per cent, (reflecting the fact that the majority of bidders have significantly greater market capitalizations than their targets). A further interpretation of this result is that at the level of the overall economy acquisition activity represents little more than a transfer of wealth from bidder to target shareholders (Sudarsanam, Holl, and Salami 1996).

Stock market based measures of acquisition performance do have some limitations from a purely managerial perspective. These measures are only applicable to cases involving publicly quoted companies, and, more importantly, only give information about investors' *expectations* as to the performance of the acquisition. Investors may have difficulty in making accurate judgements at the time of the acquisition announcement regarding the organizational issues that can influence an acquisition's outcome. Often issues such as the level of employee resistance or the choice of integration strategy only become apparent some months after the acquisition has been completed, and even then may not be immediately apparent to those external to the firm.

However, it is interesting to note that while the stock market based studies have tended to show that on average bidders' returns are negative, within this most do report that around 50 per cent of individual bidders show positive abnormal returns. This again confirms the summary finding that only approximately one in two acquisitions can be classified as successes for the acquiring company.

This mixed performance record has generated significant academic interest in M&A. A host of empirical studies have been conducted to investigate the role of a wide range of potential strategic, financial, and organizational factors that may have an influence on acquisition outcome. Taken together, these studies reveal that acquisition performance depends on three broad factors: the acquisition's potential for value creation, the post-acquisition integration of the acquired company, and the level of employee resistance to the acquisition. These primary determinants of acquisition performance are illustrated in Figure 21.3 and are discussed in turn in the three sections that follow (Larsson and Finkelstein 1999).

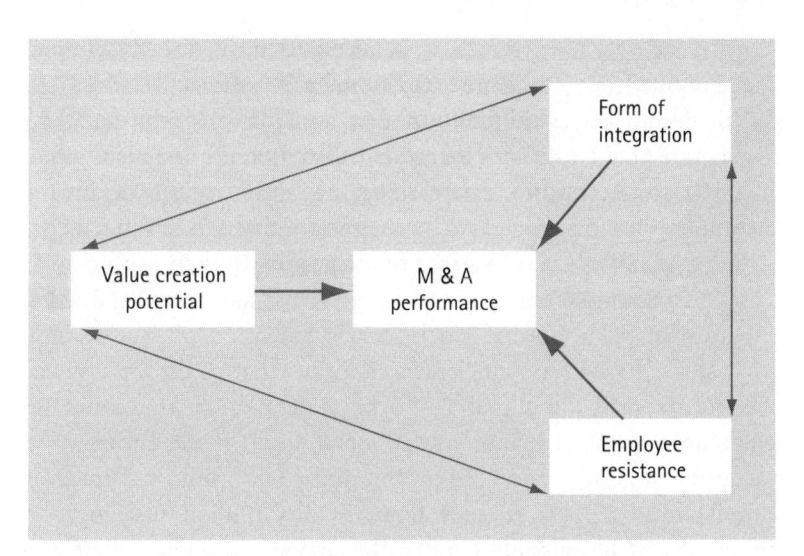

Fig. 21.3 Primary determinants of acquisition performance

Source: Adapted from the research of Larsson and Finkelstein (1999).

21.5 VALUE CREATION WITHIN
ACQUISITIONS

We have seen above that the share price of a target company tends to rise on the announcement of an acquisition. This is because the shareholders of a target company almost always demand a premium over and above the current share price before they will agree to accept a takeover offer. This premium is known as the 'bid premium'.

This is one area where there are important distinctions between the different types of M&A. The average bid premium for British takeovers involving publicly quoted companies has been around 35 per cent for friendly (agreed) acquisitions in recent years, whereas hostile acquisitions have attracted premiums of around 45 per cent. The higher premiums paid in hostile takeovers reflect both the greater resistance to the bid approach and that there may be competition amongst more than one bidder. This is one reason why hostile acquisitions have been found to perform less well than friendly transactions from the perspective of the acquiring company (Healy, Palepu and Ruback 1997). In a pure merger it may be that no bid premium is required, as managers and shareholders of both parties wish the transaction to proceed and will continue to have a stake in the control and ownership of the

merged entity. As yet, no research is believed to have directly compared the performance of pure mergers against traditional acquisitions.

Clearly, the need to pay a bid premium puts a major constraint on an acquirer's ability to generate positive returns for its own shareholders as a result of an acquisition. In order to successfully create value the future cash flow stream of the acquired company has to be increased by an amount that exceeds the bid premium, plus the often overlooked costs incurred in integrating the acquisition and making the bid itself. To illustrate this point further let us take the simplified example of a company that has a pre-bid stock market valuation of £100 million. If we assume that stock markets are efficient, this means that investors have accurately valued the future cash flows that could be generated by the company under its present management as being worth £100 million. If the company is subsequently acquired at a 35 per cent bid premium for £135 million, it means that the acquirer must raise the future cash flows by £35 million just to recover the bid premium that it has already paid to the previous owners. In effect, the bid premium is a portion of future value that is paid in advance to the previous owners. The acquisition will only generate value for the acquirer if future cash flows are raised by *more* than £35 million. Many acquisitions fail simply because insufficient value is created to recoup the bid premium. This has led to considerable research efforts to understand the antecedents of value creation within acquisitions.

21.5.1 Strategic Fit and Value Creation

Early studies into value creation focused on the link between financial performance and the strategic attributes of the combining firms, in particular the extent to which a target company's business should be related to that of the acquirer. The foundation of these studies lay in the argument that the more closely related two merging businesses are in terms of their products, markets, and technologies, the greater the potential to create value by exploiting synergies based on economies of scale and scope and increased market power. However, the results of these studies were less than conclusive. While some researchers confirmed that related acquisitions were associated with greater total wealth creation, others reported higher returns in unrelated acquisitions, and others still concluded that there were no significant differences in the performance of the two types. This lack of consensus has been attributed in part to methodological difficulties in the measurement of 'relatedness'. An external assessment of the overlap in product markets and technologies at best can provide only a crude measure of the ability to actually transfer value-creating capabilities between the companies post-acquisition. (For reviews of the relatedness studies, see Seth 1990; Flanagan 1996.)

These 'strategic fit' studies also investigated the influence of a number of other strategic factors, including the relative size of the acquisition and the target company's previous performance. The findings highlight that the acquisition of a company that is either very small or very large in relation to the size of the purchaser is associated with inferior financial performance. Small acquisitions can absorb as much management time as larger ones but for a much smaller incremental impact on the acquirer's overall performance, while a very large acquisition runs the risk of overstretching the purchaser both managerially and financially. In terms of the prior performance of the target company, higher returns are generally derived from the purchase of strongly performing businesses. This applies especially to cross-border acquisitions where any attempt to turn around a weak business can be hindered by unfamiliar cultural and legal contexts (Bleeke and Ernst 1993).

21.5.2 Generic Value Creation Mechanisms

One criticism that is sometimes levelled at the 'strategic fit' studies is that they tend to assume that *similarities* between the acquiring and acquired firms are the primary driver of potential value creation. Of course, *differences* between the two companies may also be a sound basis for value creation as the strengths of one company complement a different set of strengths in the other. The ultimate driver of value creation within acquisitions is the ability to leverage the individual resources and capabilities of the combining companies, whether this be based on organizational similarities or differences.

These arguments have led to a more generalized model of acquisition value creation (Haspeslagh and Jemison 1991; Porter 1987). This states that there are four generic mechanisms through which value can be created from an acquisition, as outlined below. There is an obvious overlap between these mechanisms and the strategic and financial motives for acquisition outlined in Sections 21.3.1 and 21.3.2 above. Where an acquisition is undertaken for true economic reasons, then one or more of the mechanisms discussed below must be present to a degree that allows the acquirer to more than recoup any bid premium paid. The four mechanisms are:

1. *Resource Sharing*, in which certain operating assets of the two companies are combined and rationalized, leading to cost reductions through economies of scale or scope. Resource sharing is generally based on the existence of similarities between the two organizations and is frequently employed within intra-industry acquisitions. For example, the merger of the pharmaceutical companies Glaxo Wellcome and SmithKline Beecham sought to achieve annual cost-savings of £1 billion through the combination of the two R&D organizations and from reducing the overlap in administration, selling, marketing, and manufacturing facilities.

2. *Knowledge (or skills) Transfer*, where value-adding knowledge such as production technology, marketing know-how, or financial control skills is transferred from the acquiring firm to the acquired, or vice versa. Additional value is created through the resulting reduction in costs or improvement in market position leading to enhanced revenues and/or margins. The effective transfer of functional knowledge involves both a process of teaching and learning across the two organizations, and therefore tends to be a longer term process than resource sharing. Nevertheless knowledge transfer is often a key source of value creation within cross-border acquisitions, in which the opportunities to share operational resources may be limited by geographic distance.

3. *Combination Benefits*, where an increase in market power or a reduction in competitive intensity is achieved, or where financial resources are beneficially combined. A company making a large acquisition within its existing industry, or a series of smaller ones, may succeed in raising profit margins by effecting a transformation of the industry structure. The emergence of a dominant player within the industry should reduce the extent of competitive rivalry, as well as provide increased bargaining power over both suppliers and customers for the acquiring company. For example, a further stated benefit of the GlaxoSmithKline merger was that the combined company would gain global leadership of the pharmaceutical industry and through its greater marketing and sales resources it would achieve an increased share of voice with healthcare professionals and so maximize its market opportunities.

In other instances financially based combination benefits may be available. As has been discussed above in Section 21.3.2, these may include the use of an acquirer's superior credit rating to reduce the interest charge of an indebted target, the consolidation of a target's losses to reduce tax liability, or the exploitation of various balance sheet positions.

4. *Restructuring* is applicable when the acquired company contains undervalued or underutilized assets. Here acquirers seek to exceed their acquisition costs by divesting certain assets at their true market value and by raising the productivity of the remaining assets. The latter may be accompanied by closing down surplus capacity, reducing head office staff, or rationalizing unprofitable product lines. Very often the two elements are combined; for example, the closure of surplus capacity may lead to a vacant factory site which can be sold off at a premium for redevelopment. A further form of restructuring is the concept of 'unbundling' as described in Section 21.3.2. Restructuring is essentially financially based, in that it requires little strategic capability transfer between the two firms. Rather, the skill of the acquirer is in recognizing and being able to realize the true value of the target's assets.

Research is continuing into the efficacy of these value creation mechanisms, especially the frequency and impact of resource sharing and knowledge transfer,

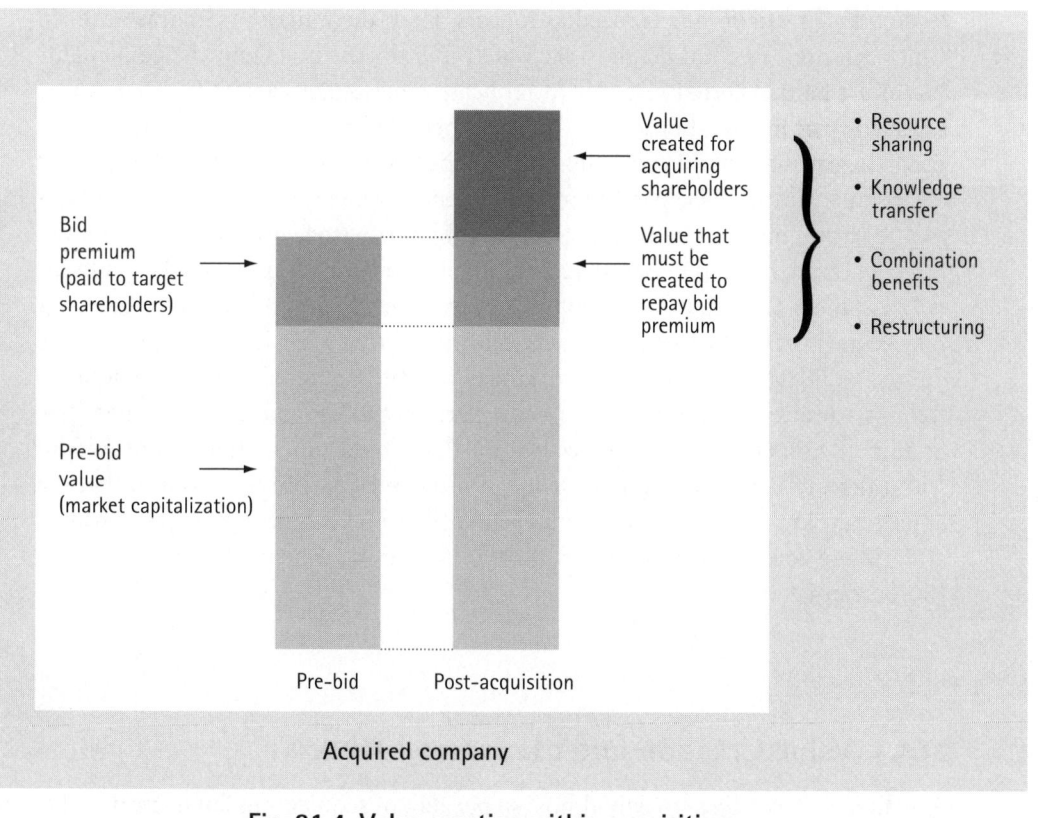

Fig. 21.4 Value creation within acquisitions

the two primary sources of operational synergy. Emerging results suggest that acquirers generally find it more beneficial in terms of value creation to rationalize their own assets upon combination rather than those of the target, and to transfer elements of their own knowledge base to the target company rather than vice versa. This is perhaps not surprising as an acquirer will almost always have a more in-depth understanding of their own assets and knowledge base than the target company's, and therefore can identify more accurately where cost-savings and knowledge transfers can most readily be implemented. However, the data reveal that in practice assets of the target company are three to five times more likely to be divested than those of the acquirer (Capron 1999).

Other research suggests that acquirers also consistently overestimate their ability to transfer knowledge. A survey of British cross-border acquisitions showed that while almost 80 per cent of acquirers actively sought 'some or more' knowledge transfer within the marketing function, only 60 per cent had attained this level three to five years later. Similar shortfalls were evident across the other main functional areas. A large body of literature is available separately on the subject of knowledge management, but two explanations to account for these difficulties in know-

ledge transfer can be summarized as follows. First, there may be circumstances in which acquirers find it difficult to accurately identify the exact knowledge elements that must be transferred in order to replicate a particular capability. This can be especially true in cross-border acquisitions where differences in cultural and market contexts may make it difficult to understand the knowledge elements that lie behind a particular functional capability in an unfamiliar geographic market; what works in one nation may not be readily translated by those from others. Second, knowledge, particularly tacit knowledge, is frequently embedded in specific key individuals within an organization and its transfer between bidder and target or vice versa may require a personal exchange between the current knowledge holder and the desired recipient. These personal exchanges may be hampered if there are negative feelings towards the acquisition on the part of the individuals concerned (see Section 21.7 on employee resistance below). The implication is that acquirers who wish to create value through knowledge transfer must ensure at the outset that the appropriate knowledge can be accurately identified and captured and that a positive atmosphere conducive to its successful transfer can be generated post-acquisition (Schoenberg 2001).

21.5.3 Value Creation and Managerial Hubris

A further explanation as to why almost 50 per cent of acquisitions fail to create value is that managers may suffer from 'hubris' when estimating their ability to exploit value creation opportunities. It has been argued that when highly confident managers evaluate an acquisition opportunity an exaggerated self-belief in their own management ability causes them to overestimate the value-creating benefits that will flow from the transaction and so pay an excessive bid premium. Research evidence from 100 large US acquisitions supports the occurrence of managerial hubris. It was found that the size of bid premium was positively related to the recent performance of the acquiring firm, recent media praise for the CEO, and the CEO's self-importance as reflected in their pay level compared to other board members. Collectively, the greater these three measures of hubris, the higher the bid premium that was paid for any acquisition, but the lower the subsequent returns that accrued to acquiring firm shareholders (Hayward and Hambrick 1997).

In a similar vein, others have suggested that external advisers, particularly investment banks, can produce considerable external pressure for the acquirer to complete their acquisition evaluation prematurely so that the transaction can be finalized as soon as possible. Investment banks often receive the same fee for their M&A advice regardless of the time it takes to finalize the deal, or in many cases they may be on a success-based fee. External advisers, perhaps acting unconsciously in their own self-interest, can therefore become a driving force for a successful completion. This may be

compounded if the acquisition is in the public eye and is attracting wide press coverage. Interestingly, corporate clients of the same investment bank have been shown to pay similar bid premiums for their acquisitions (Haunschild 1994; Haspeslagh and Jemison 1991).

21.6 POST-ACQUISITION INTEGRATION

The process adopted towards post-acquisition integration of the newly acquired firm is the second major determinant of acquisition performance. The presence of value creation opportunities does not in itself guarantee acquisition success. Plans have to be effectively implemented before the benefits can be realized in practice. The discussion in Section 21.5.2 above highlighted how the realization of operational synergy frequently involves substantial organization change. Manufacturing or service facilities may have to be rationalized, and redundancies made, without reducing the motivation of retained employees. Financial reporting and control systems may need to be integrated without imposing inappropriate information demands on the newly acquired firm. Technical experts may have to be relocated to facilitate knowledge transfer, yet must remain willing to share their expertise with those who were previously perhaps intellectual as well as commercial rivals. Such changes need to be implemented in a manner which creates additional value but without a level of organizational disruption that threatens to destroy the inherent value within the individual businesses.

Clearly, acquirers face a difficult challenge in deciding the degree to which the two organizations should be integrated following an acquisition. Under-integration may hinder the transfer of strategic capabilities necessary for value creation, while over-integration may cause unnecessary organizational conflict so adding to implementation costs. Contingency frameworks have been developed to help acquirers assess the most appropriate form of integration for a given acquisition. The underlying assumption of these frameworks is that generic forms of integration can be identified, and that the optimum form and degree of integration must be chosen to maximize acquisition performance.

The popular framework derived by Haspeslagh and Jemison (1991) from extensive case-study research argues that the appropriate form of integration will depend on the balance and trade-off between two key requirements. First, the value creation mechanism driving the acquisition will determine the degree of *strategic interdependence* that needs to be established between the two companies. In general, resource sharing and knowledge transfer imply high to moderate strategic interdependence is required, while the less operational forms of value creation,

combination benefits and restructuring, imply a lower requirement for interdependence. Second, the extent to which it is necessary to maintain the autonomy of the acquired firm in order to preserve its distinctive capabilities will determine the need for *organizational autonomy*. For example, where the innovative capability of a high technology business is embedded in a free-thinking and team orientated culture it may be important to preserve that culture if the rate of innovation is to continue post-acquisition. Consideration of these two requirements can guide the choice of the most appropriate form of integration from four basic approaches.

Absorption integration, where the aim is to achieve full consolidation of the operations, structure, and culture of both organizations, ultimately dissolving all boundaries between the two firms. Absorption integration is indicated where the value creation task requires high strategic interdependence, but there is a low requirement for the organizational autonomy of the acquired firm to be preserved. In absorption integration the intent is to closely integrate every aspect of the acquired business into the parent organization, so the managerial decisions are more to do with timing and communication than with which aspects of the business to integrate. An analysis of UK acquisitions completed in the first half of the 1990s found that 15 per cent had been subject to absorption integration. These acquisitions saw widespread changes, including substantial executive departure, with an emphasis on cost reduction through resource sharing (Angwin 2000).

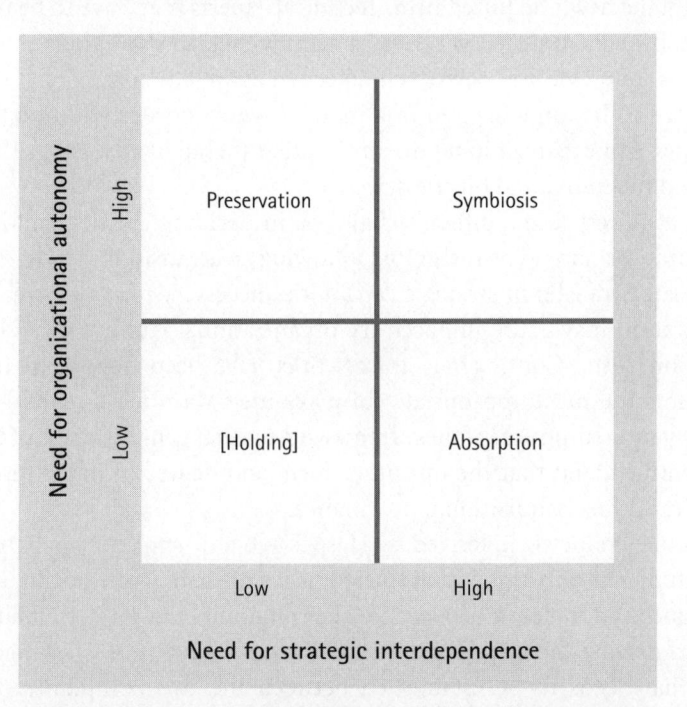

Fig. 21.5 Types of acquisition integration approaches

Source: Haspeslagh and Jemison 1991: 145, fig. 8.1.

Preservation integration, where the acquired organization is granted a high degree of autonomy and there is a low need for strategic interdependence between the combining businesses. This form of integration typically involves positioning the newly acquired firm as a stand-alone subsidiary with care taken to maintain the organizational environment within which the acquired firm's capabilities are embedded. The managerial challenge is to ensure that a sufficient level of value creation takes place whilst resisting any unnecessary interference in the new subsidiary. Preservation integration performs best where both firms have a capacity for organizational learning and valuable knowledge transfer can take place even at low levels of operational interaction. Alternatively, this form of integration may be appropriate where financially based combination benefits are an important source of value creation. Preservation is the most common form of integration in the United Kingdom, adopted for 49 per cent of all acquisitions.

Symbiosis integration is where the acquiring firm attempts to achieve a balance between preserving the organizational autonomy of the acquired firm while transferring strategic capabilities between the two businesses. Symbiotic integration is called for when the value creation mechanism dictates a high degree of strategic interdependence between the two businesses, but the acquired firm also needs to retain its autonomy because its existing capabilities are embedded in an organizational environment that is different from that of the acquiring firm. These conflicting needs make symbiotic integration a complex management task. Often such acquisitions will initially be managed in a manner similar to preservation integration and over time a mutual interdependence will gradually be built up. The skill of the acquiring management is to judge where and when the planned operational synergies can be implemented without jeopardizing or threatening the core cultural and organizational values of the acquired firm. Symbiosis integration was found to be used in only 9 per cent of UK acquisitions, perhaps reflecting the inherent management difficulties. It is notable that the chief executive of the acquired firm tends to be retained in preservation and symbiotic acquisitions as they are often the most appropriate gatekeepers to protect the original organizational environment and capabilities of the acquired firm.

Holding integration, where low levels of strategic interdependence are required but simultaneously the acquired firm is granted low levels of autonomy. Surprisingly, data show that holding integration is adopted in 27 per cent of UK acquisitions, although this form of integration is probably best utilized where the acquired firm needs to undergo a business turnaround and the dominant value creation mechanism is restructuring. In such cases there is often little need for strategic interdependence beyond general management knowledge transfer and the implementation of tight financial control. Further, the underperformance of the acquired company means there is little requirement to preserve the existing organizational environment; rather, a wholesale culture change may be required to effect the turnaround (Angwin 2000).

The originators of the above integration typology point out that the four forms of integration should be seen as broad 'metaphors' that can help to guide the post-acquisition strategy. Large or complex acquisitions may contain business units or sets of capabilities that vary in the trade-offs required between strategic interdependence and organizational autonomy and therefore will benefit from the use of more than one integration approach. Similarly, the most appropriate form of integration may change over the course of an acquisition and a progression from preservation to symbiotic integration is frequently observed in practice.

While the trade-off between strategic and organizational needs will be the key determinant of the form of integration, other factors may also exert an influence on the chosen balance. For example, acquirers of different nationalities have been shown to favour particular value creation strategies and integration approaches. Anglo-Saxon acquirers tend to derive performance improvements in their acquisitions through the introduction of differentiated products, a stronger marketing image, and a relatively high level of operational autonomy. In contrast, Japanese acquirers appear to favour the implementation of price-based competitive strategies coupled with low levels of operational and strategic autonomy, with changes of this type associated with performance improvement in the acquired firm. French acquirers, meanwhile, have a tendency to successfully introduce tighter cost control and an open and autonomous environment (Child, Pitkethly, and Faulkner 1999).

21.7 Employee Resistance to Acquisition

Employee resistance is the third major determinant of acquisition performance. In many instances employee resistance hinders the ability of the acquirer to create the planned value and achieve the necessary degree of post-acquisition integration. Employees frequently feel high levels of anxiety and uncertainty when a merger or acquisition is announced as concerns are voiced over issues ranging from changes in management style to possible redundancies. These concerns are often compounded once the acquisition is completed and new reporting hierarchies, management structures, and control systems are actually introduced. Staff and managers within the acquired firm can feel alienated and marginalized by the changes themselves and also by the implications for planned career paths and previously familiar and comfortable working patterns. These negative feelings can manifest themselves as increased employee stress, reduced work performance and commitment, acts of non-compliance, and in some cases even deliberately disruptive behaviours.

The impact of employee resistance is confirmed by research conducted within newly acquired US firms. Human resource problems, including absenteeism, staff turnover, conflict levels, and reduced work quality, rose in line with the degree of change that followed an acquisition. The occurrence of these human resource problems, in turn, had a clear negative impact on the subsequent performance of the affected acquisitions (Shanley 1994).

One obvious sign of employee resistance is a high rate of staff turnover within the acquired firm. Indeed, the turnover of managers within newly acquired companies has been found to be over twelve times higher than in non-acquired companies during the first year, with, on average, 25 per cent of the previous top management team departing post-acquisition. Of course, not all of these departures will have been voluntary. The acquirer may have weeded out underperforming managers or imposed its own management team as part of the acquisition integration process. This is particularly true where the acquired firm has been performing poorly prior to the acquisition and where absorption or holding integration are adopted. Overall, however, high rates of management turnover are associated with inferior acquisition performance. The loss of substantive experience from the acquired firm is not easily recovered (Cannella and Hambrick 1993).

Culture clashes can be a major cause of employee resistance. M&A involve the coming together of two separate organizational cultures which had previously defined the rituals and routines of working life within their respective companies. The marriage of different and incompatible cultures can foster feelings of uncertainty and insecurity amongst employees as differences in the philosophies, values, and practices of the two companies become exposed in the post-acquisition period. Large sample research studies show that, after controlling for other factors, the greater the difference in organizational cultures between the two combining companies the worse the subsequent performance of an acquisition.

Issues of culture clashes can be especially complex within cross-border acquisitions. Not only do these acquisitions bring together two separate organizational cultures, they also bring together the two national cultures of the firms concerned. The importance of this issue is illustrated by practitioner surveys which report that up to 90 per cent of unsuccessful cross-border acquisitions experience major unforeseen difficulties due to cultural differences. National culture exerts an influence on many aspects of a firm's organization and behaviour, for example its openness to strategic change, its decision-making style, and even its choice of acquisition integration strategy as we have seen above. Several empirical studies have found that differences in the national cultures of the bidder and target are associated with inferior acquisition outcome, although the separation of the influences of organizational and national culture is a methodological difficulty faced by such studies (Schoenberg 2000).

Emerging research suggests that out of this range of possible cultural differences, the two companies' attitudes towards risk may exert a particularly key influence in

terms of cultural compatibility and the ultimate performance of an acquisition. Interestingly, where cultural differences are present it has been found that isolating the acquired company is not a viable strategy for avoiding the negative consequences of those differences. Data reveal that cultural differences can reduce acquisition performance even where preservation integration is adopted and the acquired firm is managed as a stand-alone subsidiary (Schoenberg 2000).

However, differences in culture should not automatically be associated with negative consequences. Other recent research indicates that where the bidder's culture is perceived to exhibit relative attractiveness to target company employees, the combination of dissimilar cultures can in fact provide a positive influence on performance. There is also some evidence that the level of delegated autonomy and participation endorsed by the acquirer's culture may be an important determinant of its perceived attractiveness. Acquired firm employees have been shown to display greater commitment to achieving successful post-acquisition integration where they believe that the acquisition will increase their level of participation and autonomy (Very, Lubatkin, Calori, and Veiga 1997; Cartwright and Cooper 1996).

In addition to an evaluation of cultural compatibility, research from the human resource field suggests a number of other approaches that can be adopted to reduce employee resistance. Where redundancies are to occur as a result of the acquisition, careful communication of how the terminated employees were selected and treated is crucial. The perception of retained employees as to how well terminated colleagues have been treated has been shown to be a key factor in determining their attitudes towards changes in their own work situation. Similarly, systematic communication of the positive future of the combined company and the associated career opportunities can be helpful. Frequently, a major source of resistance amongst managerial and professional staff is a perception that their career may be thwarted as a result of acquisition, either because of rationalization or because their skills will be less valued henceforth. As well as deliberate communication efforts, the promotion of at least one acquired firm executive to a top management position in the post-acquisition firm has been found to exert a beneficial effect. The symbolic importance that is attached to personnel moves should not be underestimated (Fried et al. 1996; Cannella and Hambrick 1993).

Finally, the climate created during the negotiation stage of an acquisition can have a notable influence on the subsequent level of employee resistance. Ambiguity is often present during the purchase negotiations between the bidder and target on matters such as performance expectations, plant and staff rationalization, and future reporting relationships. This ambiguity may ease the negotiation process and precipitate early agreement, but it can lead to conflict and resentment when expectations and assumptions about the other side fail to be upheld post-acquisition. The resulting lack of trust and heightened organizational concern can fuel employee resistance and may seriously slow down the implementation of the acquisition. More positively, a higher incidence of acquisition success has been found to occur in

situations where bidders communicate a clear vision of the future, especially regarding the interfaces between the parent and new subsidiary, and rigidly adhere to assurances given during negotiation. This is supported by the finding that friendly acquisitions generally outperform hostile acquisitions where by definition the negotiation process has been fraught and highly charged (Haspeslagh and Jemison 1991).

21.8 CONCLUSION

This chapter has examined the subject of mergers and acquisitions from a strategic management perspective. We have seen that M&A are an increasingly popular means of corporate expansion, motivated by a variety of strategic, financial, and managerial objectives. Yet despite their popularity, M&A have a mixed performance record and a range of methodologies has confirmed that approximately one in two are classified as failures for the acquiring firm. An integration of the research highlights three major determinants of M&A performance. First, sufficient additional value must be created within the combined entity to more than offset any bid premium paid and the associated costs of combination. Second, an appropriate degree of integration must be achieved between the two businesses following the merger. The challenge here is to implement the changes necessary for value creation but without causing a level of organizational disruption that could damage the inherent capabilities of the two individual businesses. Finally, employee resistance to the combination must be minimized in order to avoid long-term human resource problems and the loss of key personnel.

It is noteworthy that the average failure rate of acquisitions has stood constant at around 50 per cent for the past twenty-five years. One implication that follows from this static failure rate is that either the research evidence and associated prescriptions are not reaching corporate executives, or that widespread managerial hubris is causing many executives to mistakenly believe that their acquisition will be one of the 50 per cent that succeeds. Certainly, the current high activity levels will act as a catalyst for further research on the topic. There is significant ongoing effort to increase our understanding of resource sharing and knowledge transfer as value creation mechanisms and the best practice in their implementation. A further promising research direction concerns the area of employee resistance and the exact role and processes by which cultural differences impact acquisition performance.

Although it is probable that activity levels will decline somewhat over the coming years as we pass the peak of the economic cycle, the flow of M&A transactions is

nevertheless set to remain reasonably buoyant. The deals of today that ultimately fail to deliver their promise will become the divestments and acquisitions of tomorrow. Similarly, the advancing globalization in many industries will see M&A continue as competitors are forced to consolidate. This may be a particularly significant driving force within continental Europe where many industries are currently notably more fragmented than in the United States or United Kingdom. Finally, the high rate of entrepreneurial start-ups seen in recent years can be expected to lead to a steady flow of available M&A targets as the entrepreneurs or their successors seek an exit route. M&A appear set to remain a central component of the corporate strategy agenda.

References

ANGWIN, D. (2000). *Implementing Successful Post-Acquisition Management.* London: Financial Times–Prentice-Hall.

BERKOVITCH, E., and NARAYANAN, M. (1993). 'Motives for Takeovers: An Empirical Investigation'. *Journal of Financial and Quantitative Analysis*, 28/3: 347–61.

BLEEKE, J., and ERNST, D. (1993). *Collaborating to Compete: Using Strategic Alliances and Acquisitions in the Global Marketplace.* New York: J. Wiley & Sons.

CANNELLA, A., and HAMBRICK, D. (1993). 'Effects of Executive Departures on the Performance of Acquired Firms'. *Strategic Management Journal*, 14: 137–52.

CAPRON, L. (1999). 'The Long Term Performance of Horizontal Acquisitions'. *Strategic Management Journal*, 20/11: 987–1018.

CARTWRIGHT, S., and COOPER, C. (1996). *Managing Mergers, Acquisitions and Strategic Alliances: Integrating People and Cultures.* Oxford: Butterworth-Heinemann.

CHILD, J., PITKETHLY, R., and FAULKNER, D. (1999). 'Changes in Management Practice and the Post-Acquisition Performance Achieved by Direct Investors in the UK'. *British Journal of Management*, 10/3: 185–98.

FLANAGAN, D. (1996). 'Announcements of Purely Related and Purely Unrelated Mergers and Shareholder Returns: Reconciling the Relatedness Paradox'. *Journal of Management*, 22: 823–35.

FRIED, Y., TIEGS, R., NAUGHTON, T., and ASHFORTH, B. (1996). 'Managers' Reactions to a Corporate Acquisition: A Test of an Integrative Model'. *Journal of Organisational Behaviour*, 17: 401–27.

GOLBE, D., and WHITE, L. (1993). 'Catch a Wave: The Time Series Behaviour of Mergers'. *Review of Economics and Statistics*, 75: 493–9.

HASPESLAGH, P., and JEMISON, D. (1991). *Managing Acquisitions: Creating Value through Corporate Renewal.* New York: Free Press.

HAUNSCHILD, P. (1994). 'How Much is that Company Worth? Inter-organizational Relationships, Uncertainty, and Acquisition Premiums'. *Administrative Science Quarterly*, 39: 391–411.

HAYWARD, M., and HAMBRICK, D. (1997). 'Explaining the Premiums Paid for Large Acquisitions: Evidence of CEO Hubris'. *Administrative Science Quarterly*, 42: 103–27.

HEALY, P., PALEPU, K., and RUBACK, R. (1997). 'Which Takeovers Are Profitable? Strategic or Financial?'. *Sloan Management Review*, 38/4: 45–57.

KAPLAN, S., and WEISBACH, M. (1992). 'The Success of Acquisitions: Evidence from Divestitures'. *Journal of Finance*, 57/1: 107–38.

LARSSON, R., and FINKELSTEIN, S. (1999). 'Integrating Strategic, Organisational, and Human Resource Perspectives on Mergers and Acquisitions: A Case Survey of Synergy Realization'. *Organization Science*, 10/1: 1–26.

PORTER, M. (1987). 'From Competitive Advantage to Corporate Strategy'. *Harvard Business Review*, 65/3: 43–59.

SCHOENBERG, R. (2000). 'The Influence of Cultural Compatibility within Cross-Border Acquisitions: A Review'. *Advances in Mergers and Acquisitions*, 1: 43–59.

——(2001). 'Knowledge Transfer and Resource Sharing as Value Creation Mechanisms in Inbound Continental European Acquisitions'. *Journal of Euromarketing*, 10/1: 99–114.

——and REEVES, R. (1999). 'What Determines Acquisition Activity within an Industry?'. *European Management Journal*, 17/1: 93–8.

SETH, A. (1990). 'Value Creation in Acquisitions: A Re-examination of Performance Issues'. *Strategic Management Journal*, 11/2: 99–116.

SHANLEY, M. (1994). 'Determinants and Consequences of Post-Acquisition Change', in G. von Krogh, A. Sinatra, and H. Singh (eds.), *The Management of Corporate Acquisitions*. London: Macmillan, 391–413.

SUDARSANAM, S., HOLL, P., and SALAMI, A. (1996). 'Shareholder Wealth Gains in Mergers: Effect of Synergy and Ownership Structure'. *Journal of Business Finance and Accounting*, 23: 673–98.

VERY, P., LUBATKIN, M., CALORI, R., and VEIGA, J. (1997). 'Relative Standing and the Performance of Recently Acquired European Firms'. *Strategic Management Journal*, 18: 593–614.

YAGIL, J., (1996). 'Mergers and Macro-Economic Factors'. *Review of Financial Economics*, 5/2: 181–90.

COOPERATIVE STRATEGY

STRATEGIC ALLIANCES AND NETWORKS

DAVID FAULKNER

22.1 INTRODUCTION

THE objectives of this chapter are to establish the rationale for cooperation between companies, to investigate the motives for developing cooperative relationships, to identify the nature and functioning of strategic alliances, and to identify the nature and functioning of strategic networks.

In recent times cooperative forms of doing business have grown rapidly, and continue to do so as firms of all sizes and nationalities in an increasing number of industries and countries perceive value in such arrangements. At this moment in history the companies of the East are showing themselves to be able to compete successfully against those of the West in an increasing number of industries. Despite the West's claims to be the birthplace of the industrial capitalist system, its economic dominance for the nineteenth century and the first half of the twentieth, and its emergence from World War II in a position of supreme power, world leadership in automobiles, electronics, steel, textiles, shipbuilding, and pharmaceuticals either

has passed or arguably is in the process of passing to the East, despite somewhat of a hiccup in recent years.

If there is one key difference between the West and the East in business philosophies, it is that the West is individualistic and competitive right down to a person to person level, whilst the East is collective and cooperative within dense networks of relationships. Perhaps, many commentators argue, this is the basis of its strength. If so, it is important that the West understand this philosophy, and if it is to be competitive perhaps adopt those aspects of it that are culturally congruent with its own way of doing things.

22.2 THE RATIONALE FOR COOPERATION

Cooperative activity between firms has become increasingly necessary due to the limitations and inadequacies of individual firms in coping successfully with a world where markets are becoming increasingly global in scope, technologies are changing rapidly, vast investment funds are regularly demanded to supply new products with ever-shortening life cycles, and the economic scene is becoming characterized by high uncertainty and turbulence. Strategic alliances, joint ventures, dynamic networks, constellations, cooperative agreements, collective strategies, and strategic networks all make an appearance and develop significance. In tune with the growth of cooperative managerial forms, the reputation of cooperation has over the last decade enjoyed a notable revival, to set against the hitherto dominant strength of the competitive model as a model of resource allocation efficiency.

Why is this revival of the popularity of cooperation coming about, since the obvious problem with cooperating with your competitor is that he may steal your secrets? If this is the case, then how can cooperation be justified? A look at the situation found in the Prisoners' Dilemma situation described below shows how cooperation can be the best policy for both partners.

In 1951 Merrill Flood of the Rand Corporation developed a model later termed the Prisoners' Dilemma by Albert Tucker. It addresses the issue of how we individually balance our innate inclination to act selfishly against the collective rationality of individual sacrifice for the sake of the common good including ourselves. John Casti in his book *Paradigms Lost* (1991) illustrates the difficulty effectively:

In Puccini's opera Tosca, Tosca's lover has been condemned to death, and the police chief Scarpia offers Tosca a deal. If Tosca will bestow her sexual favours on him, Scarpia will spare her lover's life by instructing the firing squad to load their rifles with blanks. Here both Tosca and Scarpia face the choice of either keeping their part of the bargain or double-crossing the other. Acting on the basis of what is best for them as individuals both Tosca and Scarpia try a

double-cross. Tosca stabs Scarpia as he is about to embrace her, while it turns out that Scarpia has not given the order to the firing squad to use blanks. The dilemma is that this outcome, undesirable for both parties, could have been avoided it they had trusted each other and acted not as selfish individuals, but rather in their mutual interest.

Analytically as shown in Figure 22.1 below, there are two parties and both have the options of cooperating (C) or defecting (D).

If the maximum value to each of them is 3 (a positive benefit with no comprom-ise involved) and the minimum value 0, then the possible outcomes and values for A are as shown below:

- *A defects and B cooperates.* A scores 3 (and B scores 0: Total 3). Tosca gets all she wants without making any sacrifices. This would have happened if Tosca had killed Scarpia, and Scarpia had loaded the rifles with blanks thus enabling Tosca's lover to escape.
- *A cooperates and B cooperates.* A scores 2 (and B scores 2: Total 4). Tosca, although saving her lover's life, has to submit sexually to Scarpia in order to do so, which it is presumed represents a sacrifice for her. Similarly Scarpia's com-promise involves not killing Tosca's lover.
- *A defects and B defects.* A scores 1 (and B scores 1: Total 2). This is what happened. At least Tosca has killed the evil Scarpia, but he in turn has killed her lover. Not a

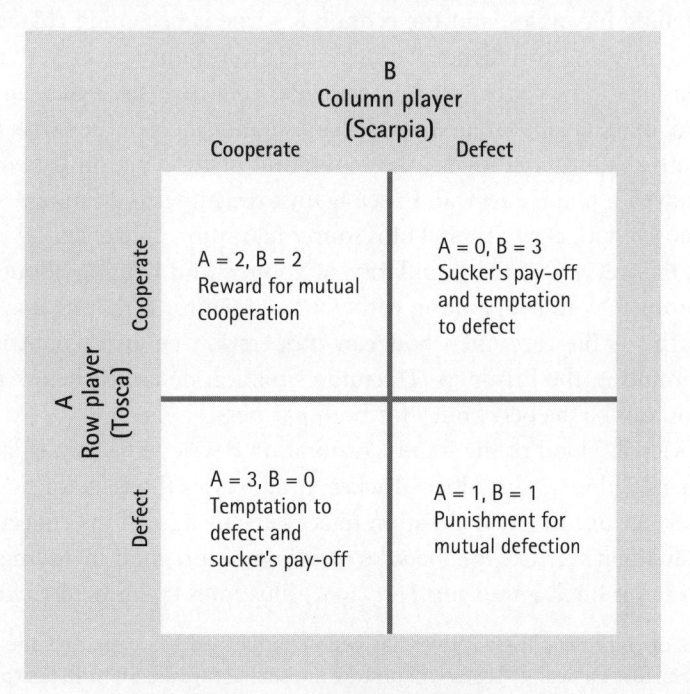

Fig. 22.1 The prisoners' dilemma

Note: The pay-offs to the row are listed first.

successful outcome for Tosca or Scarpia, however, but marginally better for her than the fourth possibility.

- *A cooperates and B defects.* A scores 0 (and B scores 3: Total 3). This is the worst outcome from Tosca's viewpoint. She has surrendered herself to Scarpia, but he has still executed her lover. This is the 'sucker's pay-off', and to be avoided if possible at all costs.

The dilemma is that, since Tosca (A) does not know what Scarpia (B) will do, she is likely rationally to defect in order to avoid the sucker's pay-off. Thus, she may score 3 if Scarpia is as good as his word and she can make him the sucker. She will at least score 1. However, if both cooperate they will each score 2 which is the best joint score available. Yet in the absence of trust it is unlikely to be achieved.

In the situation of a cooperative agreement then, the optimal joint score can only be achieved through genuine trusting cooperation; yet this may be difficult to achieve if both parties in the alliance are overly concerned not to be the sucker, and are thus reluctant to release their commercial secrets, for fear that their partner will defect with them. One prisoner defects because he fears that the other one will, and he will end up as the 'sucker'.

However, the pay-off listed above only applies to a single shot game. In a situation where the partners intend to work with each other over an indeterminate period, the situation changes. In this case, trust can be built and the potential synergies from cooperation can be realized. Furthermore, reputation comes into the equation. If one partner is seen to defect, he may find it difficult to attract further partners in the future. And if both partners are still reluctant to cooperate in a genuine fashion, the risk–reward ratio can be changed deliberately. If, in the Tosca defection situation, the defector immediately forfeits his or her life the incentive to defect is radically reduced. In the more prosaic world of business, this might mean that a potential defector automatically forfeits a large sum of money or shares in the event of defection. Thus, the situation can be constructed in such a way that the dominant strategy is one of cooperation. A cooperative strategy can then become a stable way of combining the competences of multiple partners to achieve a competitive strategy with competitive advantage. In sum:

1. The rational strategy of defection (competition) applies on the assumption of a zero-sum game, and a non-repeatable experience, i.e. if you are only in business for a single trade (e.g. buying a souvenir in a bazaar in Morocco), defection is a rational strategy for you.

2. As soon as the game becomes non zero-sum, e.g. through scale economies, and/or it is known that the game will be played over an extended time period or defection is costly, the strategy of defection is likely to become sub-optimal, i.e. to cooperate and keep your bargain is a better strategy for both players. At the very least if you defect, it will harm your reputation. You will become known as a player not to be trusted.

3. In these circumstances then, forgiving cooperative strategies are likely to prove the most effective.

Corporate organizational form has also been dramatically influenced by the globalization of markets and technologies, through a decline in the automatic choice of the integrated multinational corporation as the only instrument appropriate for international business development. The movement away from the traditional concept of the firm is accentuated by the growth of what Handy (1992) describes as 'The Federated Enterprise' seen both in the form of newly created joint ventures between existing companies and in the development of so-called virtual corporations where a number of companies cooperate in producing a single-product offering generally under a distinct brand name.

The recent growth of alliances and networks approaches the flexible transnational structure from the other end, i.e. the amalgamation of previously independent resources and competencies in contrast to the unbundling into a federal structure of previously hierarchically controlled resources and competencies (of Figure 22.2). Where the traditional concepts of firm, industry, and national economy start to become concepts of declining clarity, and thus to lose their exclusive usefulness as tools for strategic analysis, the need for an adequate theory of strategic alliances and other cooperative network strategies assumes increased importance.

The search for sustainable competitive advantage is of course what the whole game is about. Yet this is a factor that can often not be measured directly. Its extent can only be inferred from the measurement of other factors like profit, market share, and sales turnover. It is nonetheless the Holy Grail which all firms seek to find and to maintain. Coyne (1986) identifies it as stemming from:

(1) customers' perception of a consistent superiority of the attributes of one firm's products to its competitors;
(2) this being due to a capability gap;
(3) the capability gap being durable over time;

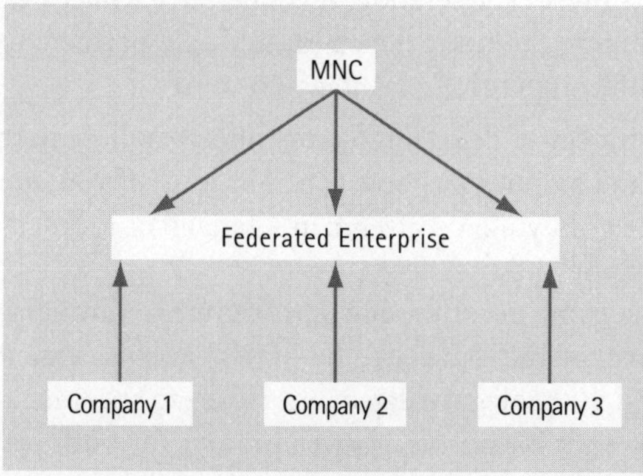

Fig. 22.2 Federated enterprises are developing from both directions

(4) the superiority being difficult to imitate.

It is this configuration of knowledge, skills, core competencies, and superior products that strategic alliances and networks seek to achieve, where the partners believe that they cannot achieve it alone.

Cooperative activity is frequently implicitly founded on the resource-based theory of competitive advantage. This theory (Grant 1991) holds that competitive advantage is most productively sought by an examination of a firm's existing resources and core competencies, an assessment of their profit potential, and the selection of strategies based upon the possibilities this reveals.

The task is then to assess the current core competencies the firm has, and fill whatever resource or competency gap is revealed by the inventory-taking of existing resources and competencies, in relation to the perceived potential profit opportunities. This is where strategic alliances and networks come in. The matrix below suggests how the make/buy/ally decision should be influenced both by the strategic importance of the activity in question and by the firm's competence at carrying it out. Under this schema, alliances should be formed if the activity is at least moderately strategically important, and the firm is only fairly good at carrying it out (cf. Figure 22.3).

The resource-based theory of competitive advantage suggests that a firm should not invest in an enterprise not strongly related to its own core competencies. Only strategies based upon existing core competencies could, it would hold, lead to the acquisition and maintenance of sustainable competitive advantage. The

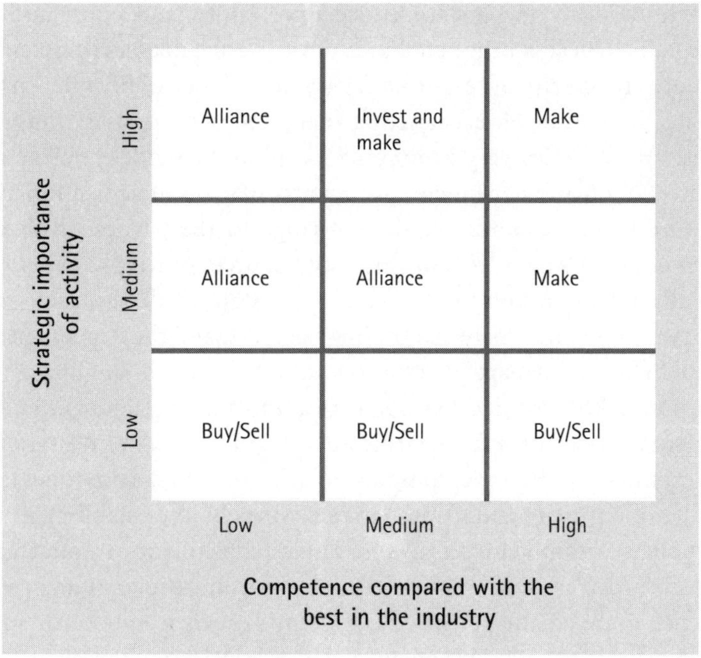

Strategic importance of activity		Low	Medium	High
	High	Alliance	Invest and make	Make
	Medium	Alliance	Alliance	Make
	Low	Buy/Sell	Buy/Sell	Buy/Sell

Competence compared with the best in the industry

Fig. 22.3 The make/buy/ally matrix

resource-based approach emphasizes that firms do not always tend towards similarity, and markets towards commodity status, in a situation of stable equilibrium. If the opportunity requires certain competencies in addition to those already present within the firm, a strategic alliance with a partner with complementary skills and resources or a network of complementary companies may represent a low risk way of overcoming that deficiency.

The resource dependency perspective (RDP) theory (similar to but different from the resource-based theory of the firm) (Pfeffer and Salancik 1978) proposes that the key to organizational survival is the ability to acquire and maintain resources, rather than to make profit. Thus, in the last resort it is organizational power, and the capacity of the organization to preserve itself, that determines competitive survival, not merely organizational efficiency. The unit of analysis for the RDP is the organization: environment relationship not the individual transaction. To deal with this uncertainty, firms attempt to manage their environment by cooperating with key parts of it, e.g. by cooperating with other companies owning key resources for them. An RDP approach treats the environment as a source of scarce resources, and therefore views the firm as dependent on other firms also in the environment. Resource dependency theory stems from the much earlier theory of social exchange which holds that where organizations have similar objectives, but different kinds or different combinations of resources at their disposal, it will often be mutually beneficial to the organizations in the pursuit of their goals to exchange resources. Classical international trade theory is based on similar foundations. Organizations have as their rationale to seek to reduce uncertainty, and enter into exchange relationships to achieve a negotiated and more predictable environment. Sources of uncertainty are scarcity of resources, lack of knowledge of how the environment will fluctuate, of the available exchange partners, and of the costs of transacting with them. These are all factors very commonly found in the modern business world.

The degree of a firm's dependence on a particular resource is a function of the critical nature of the resources in the exchange to the parties involved, and of the number of and ease of access to alternative sources of supply. Where few alternatives exist, and the resources are essential, a state of dependency exists. This creates a power differential between trading partners, and the dependant firm faces the problem of how to manage its resources with the concomitant loss of independence, since unchecked resource dependence leads to a state of strategic vulnerability. Such strategic vulnerability can be tackled in a number of ways. Western firms may do it for example by multiple sourcing of materials and components, internal restructuring, merger or acquisition; Japanese ones by the establishment of semi-captive suppliers within keiretsu groups. The establishment of a strategic alliance can thus be regarded as an attempt by a firm or firms to reduce strategic vulnerability, and hence to overcome perceived constraints on their autonomy in choosing their strategic direction. Strategic alliances and networks can be seen as attempts by firms to establish a negotiated environment, and thus to reduce uncertainty. On the

basis of this argument, alliances and networks will occur most when the level of competitive uncertainty is greatest.

In RDP motivated alliances and networks, all parties typically strive to form relationships with partners with whom balance can be achieved at minimum cost, and with a desirable level of satisfaction and determinacy. Thus, wherever possible they will link up with firms of a similar size and power in order to avoid being dominated and hence have their vulnerability increased.

Strategic alliances are frequently formed from resource dependency motives, and the ability of the partners to achieve and sustain competitive advantage in their chosen market is strongly influenced by the degree to which they place corporate learning as a high priority on their alliance agenda, and seek to cause the alliance to evolve in a direction based on that learning. In a sense, corporate learning can be seen as the dynamic counterpart to the resource dependency theory of the firm. Thus, a firm will diagnose its resource and skill deficiencies in relation to a particular external challenge, and through the process of deliberate and planned corporate learning set about remedying its weaknesses. Truly strategic alliances are generally competence driven, i.e. explicitly adding to either the task or the knowledge system or to the organizational memory of each partner. The idea of the organization as a residuary for learning is a popular one. Decision theory emphasizes the importance of the search for information to enable organizations to make informed choices. Prahalad and Hamel (1990) stress the role of learning as a source of competitive advantage, through the development of unique competencies.

Strategic networks, on the other hand, are more likely to be formed for skill substitution reasons, e.g. company A forms a network with companies B and C who carry out specific functions, e.g. R&D or sales and marketing, whilst A does the production. Figure 22.4 illustrates the differing situations of networks and alliances.

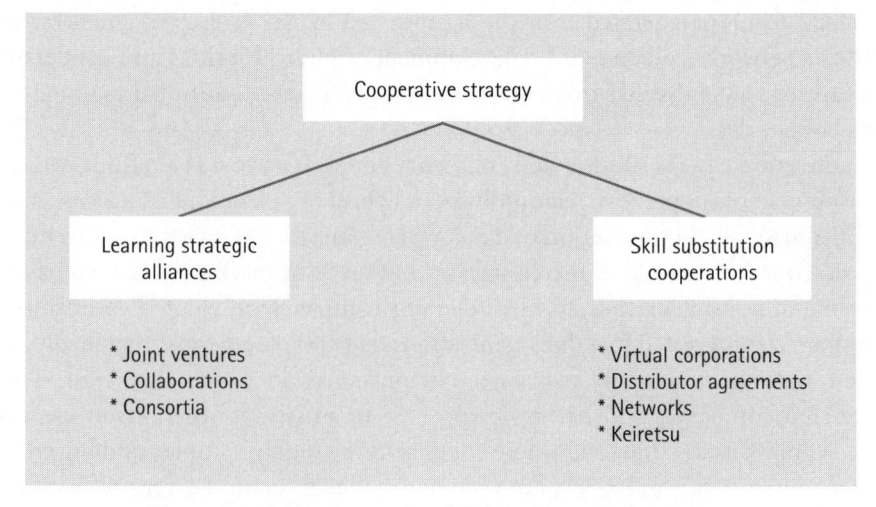

Fig. 22.4 Coop strategies fall into two distinct types

Even faced with success stories of the evolution of an alliance through mutual learning leading to competitive advantage, nagging doubts may well remain about the role of value appropriation in the form of learning by the partners, and of the consequent stability of the alliance. It is often suggested in fact that the alliance is an inherently unstable and transitory arrangement, and undoubtedly, given opportunistic attitudes by the partners, it can be, particularly in alliances between erstwhile competitors.

The often cited comparison of an alliance with a marriage is pertinent here. Marriages could be regarded as unstable as they currently have a high failure rate. In fact they have many of the qualities of strategic alliances. The partners retain separate identities but collaborate over a whole range of activities. Stability is threatened if one partner becomes excessively dependent on the other, or if the benefits are perceived to be all one way. But none-the-less, successful marriages are stable, and for the same reason as successful alliances. They depend upon trust, commitment, mutual learning, flexibility, and a feeling by both partners that they are stronger together than apart. Many businesses point to the need to negotiate decisions in alliances as a weakness, in contrast to companies, where hierarchies make decisions. This is to confuse stability with clarity of decision-making, and would lead to the suggestion that dictatorships are more stable than democracies.

In this analogy, it is commitment to the belief that the alliance represents the best available arrangement that is the foundation of its stability. The need for resolution of the inevitable tensions in such an arrangement can as easily be presented as a strength, rather than as an inherent problem. It leads to the need to debate, see, and evaluate contrasting viewpoints. Similar points arise in relation to strategic networks although to a lesser degree, since the closeness and interdependence of a network is typically lower than that of an alliance.

The movement of enterprises away from a simple wholly-owned corporate structure to more federated forms is accentuated by the growth of alliances, and strategic networks, which aid the development of global loyalties and cooperative endeavours, quite distinct from those encouraged by the traditional national and firm boundaries.

Transaction costs is another body of theory applied to provide a rationale for the development of cooperative relationships, or hybrid organizations as they are called by TCA theorists. In transaction cost analysis organizational forms are conventionally described on a scale of increasing integration with markets at one end as the absolute of non-integration, to hierarchies or completely integrated companies at the other. It is suggested that the organizations that survive are those that involve the lowest costs to run in the particular circumstances in which they exist. Thus, integrated companies will be the lowest cost in situations when assets are very specific, markets are thin, and where conditions are highly complex and uncertain, opportunism is rife and assets are very specific, as it would be very difficult and therefore costly to handle transactions in a fragmented, marketplace way. At the

other extreme, transactions are best carried out in markets where no one deal implies commitment to another, and relationships are completely at arm's length. This is most commonly the case when the product is a frequently traded commodity, assets are not specific, market pricing is needed for efficiency, there are many alternative sources of supply, and the costs of running a company would be very high.

Between the extremes of markets and integrated companies, there are a range of interorganizational forms of increasing levels of integration, which have evolved to deal with varying circumstances, and where they survive, may be assumed to do so as a result of their varying appropriateness to the situation. All forms between the extremes of markets and hierarchies exhibit some degree of cooperation in their activities. It is even likely that most hierarchies include internal markets within them in order to create situations where market pricing will improve efficiency, e.g. a Strategic Business Unit (SBU) may be empowered to use third party marketing advice if it is not satisfied with that available internally. Figure 22.5 illustrates forms of ascending interdependency all of which are cooperative except that of markets.

Hence, arm's length market relationships may develop into those with established suppliers and distributors, and then may integrate further into cooperative networks. Further up the ladder of integration come the hub-subcontractor networks like Marks & Spencer's close interrelationships with its suppliers. Licensing agreements come next, in which the relationship between the licensor and the licensee is integrated from the viewpoint of activities in a defined area, but both retain their separate ownership and identities.

Between licensing agreements and completely integrated companies, where rule by price (markets) is replaced by rule by fiat (companies), comes the most integrated form of rule by cooperation, namely that found in strategic alliances.

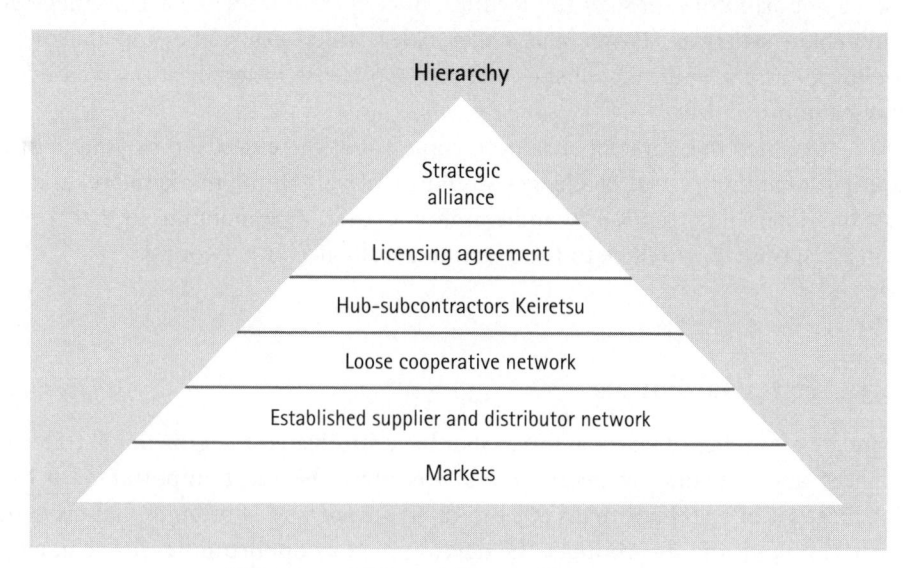

Fig. 22.5   Different forms of cooperation

Alliances may be preferred organizational forms where sensitive market awareness is required, the price mechanism remains important, risks of information leakage are not considered unacceptably high, scale economies and finance risks are high, but where there is resource limitation, and flexibility is important.

22.3 THE MOTIVATION FOR COOPERATION

The most common motivations behind the development of cooperation between companies as suggested by Porter and Fuller (1986) are:

(1) to achieve with one's partner, economies of scale and of learning;
(2) to get access to the benefits of the other firm's assets, be they technology, market access, capital, production capacity, products, or manpower;
(3) to reduce risk by sharing it, notably in terms of capital requirements, but also often R&D;
(4) to help shape the market, e.g. to withdraw capacity in a mature market.

Another motive behind the conclusion of cooperative strategies is the need for speed in reaching the market. In the current economic world, first mover advantages are becoming increasingly important, and often the conclusion of an alliance between a technologically strong company with new products and a company with strong market access is the only way to take advantage of opportunities. There may also be opportunities through the medium of cooperation for the achievement of value chain synergies (Porter and Fuller 1986) which extend beyond the mere pooling of assets, and include such matters as process rationalization, and even systems improvement.

It is suggested that for cooperation to come about there needs to be at least one external force in play that challenges would-be players in the marketplace, and at least one internal perception of vulnerability or need in responding to that force. Such a response may well be to form a strategic alliance or network.

22.3.1 External Forces

There are a number of external forces that have stimulated the growth of strategic alliances and networks in recent years. Amongst the most important are the globalization of tastes and markets, the rapid spread and shortening life cycle of new technology and its products, the development of opportunities for achieving major economies of scale, scope, and learning, increasing turbulence in inter-

national economies, a heightened level of uncertainty in all aspects of life and declining international trade barriers.

Theodore Levitt (1960) was credited over forty years ago with first having drawn attention to the increasing homogenization of tastes, leading to the development of the 'global village'. Since that time the globalization movement has spread to an increasing number of industries, and as Kenichi Ohmae (1989) points out, it is now possible to travel from New York to Paris and on to Tokyo, and to see very similar articles on display in all three cities at least in some industries like electronics, computers, or automobiles.

After World War II, trade barriers between nations placed a limit to the development of a world economy. With the dramatic economic recovery of the major combatant nations, the move towards increasing international trade was stimulated by international agreements to reduce trade barriers, and thus increase overall economic welfare by allowing greater specialization on the basis of comparative costs and the development of global brand names as easily recognizable in Tokyo as in New York or London.

GATT (now the WTO), the EU, EFTA, and other trading agreements and common markets enabled national firms to develop opportunities internationally, and to grow into multinational corporations. More recently the 1992 EU legislation, the reunification of Germany, the establishment of NAFTA, and the break-up of the communist bloc have accelerated this movement, and in so doing stimulated the growth of strategic alliances between firms in different nations.

However, not only are markets rapidly becoming global, the most modern technologies, namely microelectronics, genetic engineering, and advanced material sciences are, by now, all subject to truly global competition. The global technologies involved in the communications revolution have also succeeded in effect in shrinking the world, and led to the design and manufacture of products with global appeal, due to their pricing, reliability, and technical qualities. But, not only is technology becoming global in nature, it is also changing faster than previously, which means a single firm needs correspondingly greater resources to be capable of replacing the old technology with the new on a regular basis.

The globalization of markets and technologies leads to the need to be able to produce at a sufficiently large volume to realize the maximum economies of scale and scope, and thus compete globally on a unit cost basis. Although one effect of the new technologies is, through flexible manufacturing systems, to be able to produce small lots economically, the importance of scale and scope economies is still critical to global economic competitiveness in a wide range of industries. Alliances are often the only way to achieve such a large scale of operation to generate these economies. The advantages of alliances and networks over integrated firms are in the areas of specialization, entrepreneurship, and flexibility of arrangements, and these characteristics are particularly appropriate to meet the needs of today's turbulent and changing environment.

The oil crises of 1973 and 1978, the Middle East wars, and the subsequent aggravated economic cycles of boom and recession, coupled with ever-shortening product life cycles, have made economic forecasting as hazardous as long-term weather forecasting. Strategic vulnerability due to environmental uncertainty has become a fact of life in most industries. Cooperative strategy helps to reduce that vulnerability, by enabling 'cooperative enterprises' to grow or decline flexibly, to match the increasing variability of the market situation.

22.3.2 Internal Conditions

A range of external conditions and challenging situations may stimulate the creation of strategic alliances and networks. However, firms will only enter into such arrangements when their internal circumstances make this seem to be the right move. These internal circumstances have most commonly included a feeling of resource and competence inadequacy, in that cooperative activity would give a firm access to valuable markets, technologies, special skills, or raw materials in which it feels itself to be deficient, and which it could not easily get in any other way.

In conditions of economic turbulence and high uncertainty, access to the necessary resources for many firms become a risk, which raises the spectre of potential strategic vulnerability for even the most efficient firm. This leads to the need to reduce that uncertainty, and secure a more reliable access to the necessary resources, whether they be supplies, skills, or markets. Strategic alliances or a developed network with firms able to supply the resources may then develop where previously market relationships may have dominated.

For cooperation to be appropriate, both partners must be able to provide some resource or competence the other needs, or reach a critical mass together that they each do not reach alone. If the needs are not reciprocal, then the best course of action is for the partner in need to buy the competence or resource, or, if appropriate, buy the company possessing it. Cooperative arrangements require the satisfaction of complementary needs on the part of both partners, and thereby lead to competitive advantage.

There are many forms of resource dependency that provide the internal motivation for cooperation:

1. *Access to markets* is a common form. One firm has a successful product in its home market, but lacks the sales force, and perhaps the local knowledge to gain access to other markets. The alliance between Cincinnati Bell Information Systems of the United States and Kingston Communications of Hull in England was set up from CBIS's viewpoint in order to gain market access into the European Community, with the purpose of selling its automated telecommunications equipment. The

market motivator is also a strong one in the current spate of Eastern Europe and former USSR alliances with Western firms.

2. *New technology* is another form of resource need. Thus, in forming Cereal Partners to fight Kellogg's domination of the breakfast cereals market, Nestlé has joined forces with General Mills principally to gain access to its breakfast cereals technology.

3. *Access to special skills* is a form of resource need similar to access to technology. The special skills or competences may be of many types, and include the know-how associated with experience in a particular product area.

4. *Access to raw materials* is a further form. Thus, for example, Monarch Resources has allied with Cyprus Minerals to gain access to Venezuelan gold mines. Although this motivation was a very common one in past decades when the developed nations sought allies in less developed areas, it is currently less common.

Other internal circumstances that have stimulated the search for alliances have included the belief that running an alliance would be less costly than running and financing an integrated company, or the belief that an alliance, or a series of alliances, would provide strong protection against takeover predators. Others may be that firms believe it is the best way to limit risk, or to achieve a desired market position faster than by any other way. Transaction cost theory encompasses these motivations within its orbit. However, accurate calculation of the costs involved in various organizational forms is very difficult to compute, since it involves assigning costs to some unquantifiable factors, e.g. opportunism or information asymmetry. The lowest cost concept is still valuable in determining whether a particular activity is best carried out by internal means, by purchasing it in the market, or by collaboration with a partner. Where the transaction cost perspective is taken as the justification for the development of the alliance, this suggests the priority is to improve the firm's cost and efficiency rather than quality position.

Alliances are also frequently formed as a result of the need to limit risk. The nature of the risk may be its sheer size in terms of financial resources. Thus, a £100 million project shared between three alliance partners is a much lower risk for each partner than the same project shouldered alone. The risk may also be portfolio risk. Thus, £100 million invested in alliances in four countries probably represents a lower risk than the same figure invested alone in one project. The trade-off is between higher control and lower risk. An acquisition represents a high level of control but is expensive, and however well the acquirer may have researched the target company before purchase, it may still receive some unexpected surprises after the conclusion of the deal. A strategic alliance involves shared risk, is probably easier to unravel if it proves disappointing, and enables the partners to get to know each other slowly as their relationship develops.

The need to achieve speed is a further internal reason for alliance formation. Many objectives in the business world of the 1990s can only be achieved if the firm

acts quickly. In many industries there is a need for almost instantaneous product launches in the retail markets of London, Tokyo, and New York if opportunities which may not last forever are not to be missed. This suggests the need for alliances, which can be activated rapidly to take advantage of such opportunities.

Alliances and networks are not all formed with expansionary aims in mind, however. Many are the result of fear of being taken over. Thus, in the European insurance world, AXA and Groupe Midi of France formed an alliance and eventually merged to avoid being taken over by Generali of Italy. General Electric of the United Kingdom has formed an alliance with the its namesake in the United States for similar defensive reasons.

22.4 STRATEGIC ALLIANCES

A strategic alliance has been defined as: 'a particular mode of inter-organisational relationship in which the partners make substantial investments in developing a long-term collaborative effort, and common orientation' (Mattsson 1988). This definition excludes projects between companies that have a beginning and preordained end, and loose cooperative arrangements without long-term commitment. In establishing the 'collaborative effort and common orientation', the alliance partners forsake a competitive strategy in relation to each other in agreed areas of activity and embark on a cooperative one.

22.4.1 Types of Alliance

Alliances can be classified along three dimensions that define their nature, form, and membership:

1	Nature	Focused	Complex
2	Form	Joint venture	Collaboration
3	Membership	Two partners only	Consortium

Figure 22.6 illustrates the options available from which a choice may be made.

22.4.1.1 *Focused Alliances*

The focused alliance is an arrangement between two or more companies, set up to meet a clearly defined set of circumstances in a particular way. It normally involves only one major activity or function for each partner, or at least is clearly defined and

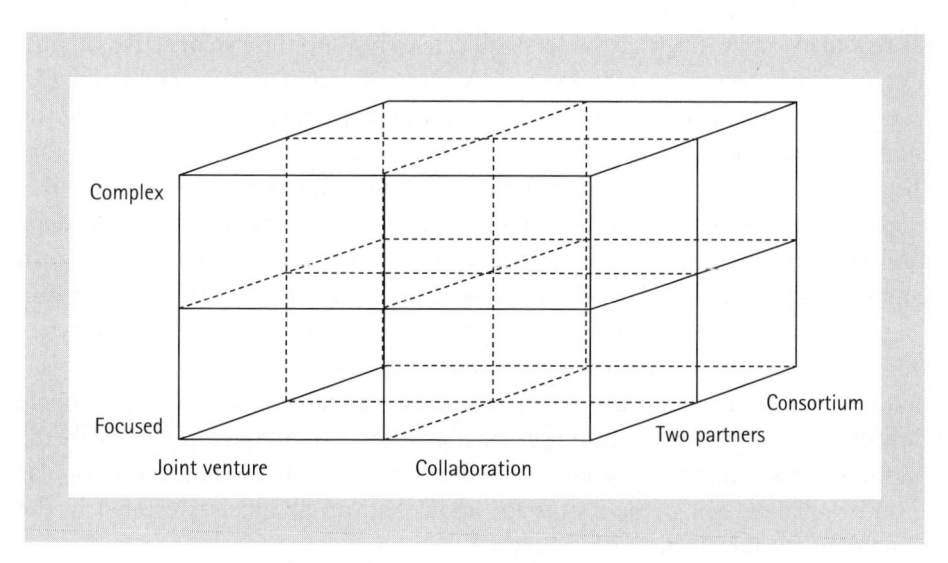

Fig. 22.6 Strategic alliance forms

limited in its objectives. Thus, for example, a US company seeking to enter the EU market with a given set of products may form an alliance with a European distribution company as its means of market entry. The US company provides the product, and probably some market and sales literature, and the European company provides the sales force and local know-how. The precise form of arrangement may vary widely, but the nature of the alliance is a focused one with clear remits, and understandings of respective contributions and rewards.

22.4.1.2 *Complex Alliances*

Complex alliances may involve the complete activity cost chains of the partners. The companies recognize that together they are capable of forming a far more powerful competitive enterprise than they do apart. Yet they wish to retain their separate identities and overall aspirations, whilst being willing to cooperate with each other over a wide range of activities. The alliance between the Royal Bank of Scotland and Banco Santander of Spain is a good example of a complex alliance. It includes exchange of banking facilities in the respective host countries, partnership in an electronic European foreign funds transfer conglomerate, and joint participation in a number of third country joint ventures. It remains separate, however, in the critical marketing and sales areas in the partners' respective home countries, and both companies retain clearly distinct images.

22.4.1.3 *Joint Ventures*

Joint ventures involve the creation of a legally separate company from that of the partners. The new company normally starts life with the partners as its

shareholders, and with an agreed set of objectives in a specific area of activity. Thus, a US company may set up a joint venture with a UK company to market in the EU. The partners provide finance and other support competences and resources for the joint venture in agreed amounts. The aim of the joint venture is normally that the new company should ultimately become a self-standing entity with its own employees and strategic aims, quite distinct from those of its parent shareholders. Unilever is a good example of a joint venture set up by a Dutch and an English company in the 1920s, and which has grown into a major multinational enterprise. Joint ventures usually involve non-core activities of the partners, and are characterized by having clear boundaries, specific assets, personnel, and managerial responsibilities. They are not generally set up in such a way that their products compete directly with those of the founding partners. Ultimately, they are divestable by the partners in a way that the non-joint venture form is not. They are the most popular form of alliance, being responsible for about half of all alliances created in the samples of several alliance researchers.

22.4.1.4 *Collaborations*

The collaborative alliance form is employed when partners do not wish to set up a separate joint venture company to provide boundaries to their relationship. This might be because they do not know at the outset where such boundaries should lie. Hence, the more flexible collaborative form meets their needs better. Collaborative alliances are also preferred when the partners' core business is the area of the alliances, and therefore assets cannot be separated from the core business and allocated to a dedicated joint venture. The collaborative form can be expanded or contracted to meet the partners' needs far more easily than can a joint venture. Royal Bank/Banco Santander is a classical example of the collaboration form of alliance.

22.4.1.5 *The Consortium*

The consortium is a distinct form of strategic alliance, in that it has a number of partners, and is normally a very large-scale activity set up for a very specific purpose, and usually managed in a hands-off fashion from the contributing shareholders. Consortia are particularly common for large-scale projects in the defence or aerospace industries where massive funds and a wide range of specialist competences are required for success. Airbus Industrie is a consortium where a number of European shareholders have set up an aircraft manufacturing company to compete in world markets with Boeing/McDonnell Douglas. The European shareholders, although large themselves, felt the need to create a large enough pool of funds to ensure they reached critical mass in terms of resources for aircraft development, and chose to form an international consortium to do this. A consortium may or may not have a legally distinct corporate form. Airbus Industrie originally did not have one, but is now restructuring itself to have one.

There are then eight possible basic configurations of alliance covering the alliance's nature, its form, and the number of partners it has, e.g. focused/two partner/ joint venture, complex/consortium/collaboration, and so forth. The alliance type that involves setting up a joint venture company is currently by far the most popular method. There are also well trodden paths by which alliances evolve. For example, focused alliances that are successful frequently develop into complex alliances, as the partners find other areas for mutual cooperation. Two partner alliances often recruit further partners, and develop into consortia, as the scale and complexity of opportunities become apparent. Alliances, initially without joint venture companies, frequently form them subsequently, as they experience difficulty in operating in a partially merged fashion, but without clear boundaries between the cooperative and the independent parts. It is also quite common for one partner in a joint venture to buy out the other. This need not mean the alliance was a failure. It may have been a considerable success, but the strategic objectives of the two companies may have moved onto different paths.

Other paths of evolution, however, are probably less likely to be followed. Consortia are unlikely to reduce to two partner alliances. Alliances with joint venture companies are unlikely to revert to a non-joint venture situation, but to keep the alliance in being. Thirdly, complex alliances are unlikely to revert to a simple focused relationship between the partners.

It is not possible to predict definitively which form of alliance will be adopted in which specific set of circumstances, since certain companies show policy preferences for certain forms rather than others, irrespective of their appropriateness. However, most alliances fall into three types:

(1) two partner joint ventures;
(2) two partner collaborations;
(3) consortium joint ventures.

Firms seeking strategic alliances generally choose between these three forms, before moving on to define their relationships in a more specific way.

22.4.2 Selecting a Partner

The creation of a strategic alliance does not of course guarantee its long-term survival. Research by the consultancy firms McKinsey and Coopers & Lybrand (now PricewaterhouseCoopers) has shown that there is no better than a 50 per cent survival probability for alliances over a five-year term. This conclusion is, however, put in perspective when considered against Porter's (1987) research into the success of acquisitions, which concluded that the success rate of acquisitions is even lower. Undoubtedly the 50 per cent failure rate of alliances could be considerably reduced, if firms learned the managerial skills necessary to develop and

maintain successful cooperative relationships, an aspect of management theory given only limited emphasis at business schools.

One of the keys to a successful alliance must be to choose the right partner. This requires the consideration of three basic factors:

(1) the synergy or strategic fit between the partners;
(2) the cultural fit between them; and
(3) the existence of only limited competition between the partners.

The importance of strategic fit and cultural fit can be illustrated in Figure 22.7 below.

22.4.2.1 *Strategic Fit*

A high degree of strategic fit is essential to justify the alliance in the first place. Strategic fit implies that the core competences of the two companies are highly complementary. Whatever partner is sought, it must be one with complementary assets, i.e. to supply some of the resources or competences needed to achieve the alliance objectives. These complementary needs may come about in a number of circumstances:

1. *Reciprocity.* Where the assets of the two partners have a reciprocal strength, i.e. there are synergies such that a newly configured joint value chain leads to greater power than the two companies could hope to exercise separately.

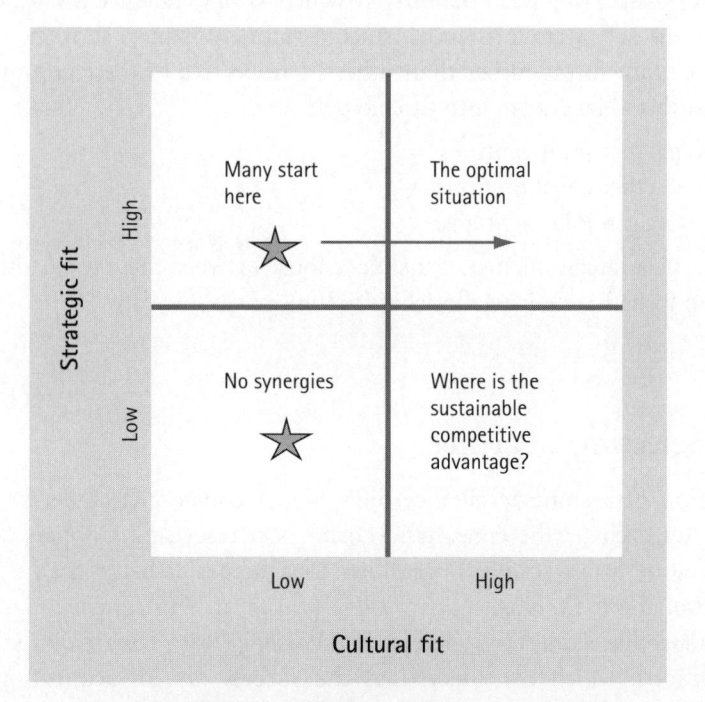

Fig. 22.7 The best alliances should aim for both strategic and cultural fit

2. *Efficiency.* Where an alliance leads to lower joint costs over an important range of areas: scale, scope, transaction, procurement, and so forth, then, this provides a powerful stimulus to alliance formation.

3. *Reputation.* Alliances are set up to create a more prestigious enterprise with a higher profile in the marketplace, enhanced image, prestige, and reputation.

4. *Legal requirements.* In many developing countries it is legally required that international companies take a local partner before being granted permission to trade.

Strategic fit, of some form or another, is normally the fundamental reason that the alliance has been set up in the first place. It is important both that it is clearly there at the outset, and that it continues to exist for the lifetime of the alliance. Strategic fit implies that the alliance has or is capable of developing a clearly identifiable source of sustainable competitive advantage. Garrette and Dussauge (1995) classify strategic fit into two forms of alliance, scale (where two competitors come together to achieve scale economies) and link (where two companies at different points in the value chain link up to reduce transaction costs). Clearly the tensions and risks of cooperation alliances will generally be greater in scale than in link alliances. Whatever partner is sought, it must be one with comple-mentary assets, i.e. to supply some of the resources or competences needed to achieve the alliance objectives. Cooperative arrangements require the satisfaction of complementary needs on the part of both partners, leading to competitive advantage.

22.4.2.2 *Cultural Fit*

However, for the alliance to endure, cultural adaptation must take place, leading the most successful alliances to graduate to the top right-hand box of Figure 22.7. Cultural fit is an expression more difficult to define than strategic fit. In the sense used here, it covers the following factors: the partners have cultural sensitivities sufficiently acute and flexible to be able to work effectively together, and to learn from each other's cultural differences. The partners are balanced in the sense of being of roughly equivalent size, strength, and consciousness of need. One is not therefore likely to attempt to dominate the other. Also, their attitudes to risk and to ethical considerations are compatible.

Cultural difficulties are very frequently cited as the reason for the failure of an alliance, but the question of compatible cultures is rarely explicitly addressed when an alliance is being set up. Additionally clearly different cultures (e.g. UK/Japan) often make for better alliances than superficially similar ones (e.g. UK/US). Indeed in support of this point, research has shown that an ethnically Chinese American national has a far more difficult task running a US/Chinese joint venture in China than an explicitly Caucasian American. Less tolerance is accorded to the ethnically Chinese American for cultural lapses in China.

22.4.2.3 *Limited Competition*

It is also important that the partners are not too competitive, cf. Figure 22.8.

Alliances in the top left-hand box should be relatively stable, since their areas of cooperation are far stronger than those of competition. Alliances in the bottom left do not have strategic fit and are likely to dissolve over time. The top right-hand box alliances may be very dynamic, and significant mutual learning may take place. However, the high level of potential competition between the partners renders them ultimately unstable, and they are likely to have a future of either complete merger or break-up to reduce this competitive tension. Partners in the bottom right-hand box have strong competitive characteristics and only weak cooperative ones. Such a situation is likely to lead to the appropriation of key skills by one partner or the other. It is generally fairly simple to analyse the situation at the outset of an alliance, and avoid the dangerous bottom right-hand box. However, situations change with time and alliances can slip unnoticed into this box after starting out in the more healthy top-level boxes. Such changes need to be guarded against by constant monitoring of the situation.

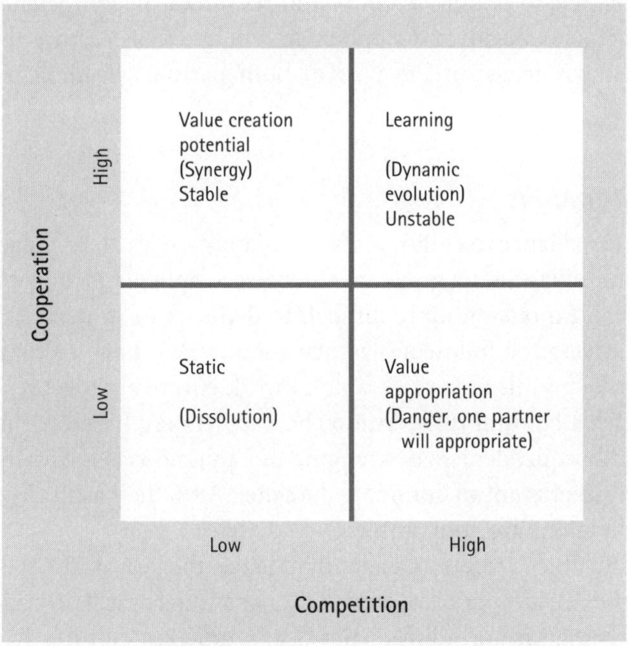

Fig. 22.8 Almost all alliances involve both cooperation and competition

22.4.3 The Management of Alliances

The management of an alliance consists of two primary factors:

(1) the systems, mechanisms, and organization structure chosen to operate the alliance;

(2) the attitudes of the partners towards each other.

Much the same concerns apply to a network, but in a rather looser way. Although the mechanisms chosen will obviously vary widely according to the cooperative form chosen, the attitudes necessary for success are similar in all forms. The relationship of the partners, as in a marriage, is a key to the success of the arrangement. It may not be a sufficient factor by itself, since the successful alliance needs positive quantifiable results, but it is certainly a necessary condition. An appropriate attitude has two major components: commitment and trust.

Lack of commitment can kill an alliance in a very short time. Alliances have failed because the partners have not allocated their best people to the project, have placed it low on the priority agenda, or have set up too many relationships, in the hope that at least some would succeed. These attitudes have the seeds of failure within them.

Trust is the second key factor for survival. Unless this develops early on in the partnership, the alliance soon ceases to be the best organizational arrangement for the partners, as they spend increasing amounts of time and resources monitoring each other's activities as a result of their mutual lack of trust. Trust may be classified in three forms.

1. Calculative trust, which exists at the outset of a relationship because the partners perceive that it is in their self-interest to set up the relationship, and to do so they must accord their partner some measure of trust.

2. Predictive trust develops as the partners discover by working together that each is as good as their word, and their actions may therefore be accurately predicted to be as they commit to them.

3. Bonding trust or a warm human relationship may then develop over time, but does not necessarily do so in all business relationships. If it does, however, it is the best guarantor of a successful relationship.

Trust does not imply naive revelation of company secrets not covered by the alliance agreement. It implies the belief that the partner will act with integrity, and will carry out its commitments. The appropriate attitude must be set from the start. During the negotiation stage, friendliness should be exhibited, and a deal struck that is clearly 'win–win'; qualities quite different from those that often characterize takeover negotiations.

Cultural sensitivity can also be the key to alliance success as mentioned earlier in the section on selecting a partner. Many alliances have failed purely as a result of cultural incompatibility. Cultural compatibility does not necessarily imply the existence of similar cultures. Indeed, partners have more to learn from differences

than from similarities. It does however require a willingness to display cultural sensitivity, and to accept that there is often more than one acceptable way of doing things. A comparison of the partners' cultural profiles will often highlight possible areas of future cultural discord.

Goal compatibility is vital to the long-term success of a partnership. Of course, the specific goals of the alliance will evolve over time. However, if the goals of the partners at a basic level fundamentally clash, the alliance cannot but be a short-term opportunistic affair. Compatibility does not necessarily mean the partners' goals must be identical. There is no fundamental incompatibility in having different sets of goals so long as they do not conflict, as did those of Courtaulds Coatings and Nippon Paint when both conceived of the ambition to be the world number one in marine paints.

The mechanisms for running a joint venture are quite distinct from those of a collaboration. A joint venture, whether two partner or consortium, involves the creation of a separate company to those of the partners. There are therefore two types of relationship to cope with, i.e. the relationship between the partners, and the relationship between each partner and the joint venture company. The most appropriate systems for running a joint venture are also the simplest. The venture should be set up with sufficient resources, guaranteed assistance by the partners whilst it is young, and allowed to get on with the job of realizing its objectives and targets. Involvement by the partners should be limited to board level, except at the request of the venture company. A chief executive should be appointed and given sufficient autonomy to build the joint venture company. Although this seems common sense, it is surprising how many joint ventures falter or fail through the unwillingness of the partners to give them sufficient autonomy and assets, and to realize that the venture will inevitably not have fully congruent objectives with those of the partners. Joint venture companies inevitably develop cultures, lives, and objectives of their own, and owner partners frequently find this fact difficult to adjust to. The now retired managing director of the EVC joint venture between ICI and Enichem is on record as claiming that both partners expected him to pursue their interests rather than those of the joint venture company he was employed to run, and both accused him of being biased in favour of the interests of their partner.

The relationship between the partners is different in nature between partners in collaborations. Here the 'boundary spanning' mechanism is the area crucial for success. The interface between the companies is the area where culture clashes, or conflict of objectives, will probably show themselves first. The establishment of a 'gateway' executive or office, as a channel for all contacts between the partners at least during the settling down period of the alliance, is a good way to avoid unnecessary misunderstandings.

In all circumstances, a good dispute resolution mechanism should be established before the alliance begins to operate. If this is left to be worked out as necessary, there is a high risk that its absence will lead to a souring of the relationship between the partners at the ultra-sensitive early stage of the partnership.

An effective system for disseminating alliance information widely within the partner companies is a further important factor for ensuring that both or all partners gain in learning to the greatest degree possible from the cooperative arrangement.

Finally procedure for divorce should be considered at the outset of an alliance in the event of a wish by either party to end the alliance, since this will increase the feeling of security by both parties that an end to the alliance does not represent a potential catastrophe.

22.4.4 Alliance Evolution

Bleeke and Ernst in a 1995 article in the *Harvard Business Review* claim that there are six possible outcomes to alliances including the dissolution of the alliances and the swallowing of one partner by the other. Only one solution of these was that the alliance continue successfully largely unchanged over an indefinite time period, and it is certainly true to say that two firms running an enterprise may well lead to an ultimate outcome of the simpler 'one firm running it' type. However this is not necessarily the case.

One key factor in the life of an alliance seems to be that, if it ceases to evolve, it starts to decay. The reality of a successful alliance is that it not only trades competences but also demonstrates synergies. Whereas the resource dependency perspective identifies a key part of a company's motivation for forming an alliance, the successful evolution of that alliance depends upon the realization of synergies between the companies, and the establishment of a level competitive advantage for the partners, that each could not as easily realize alone. Important conditions for evolution include:

(1) perception of balanced benefits from the alliance by both partners;
(2) the development of strong bonding factors;
(3) the regular development of new projects between the partners; and
(4) the adoption of a philosophy of constant learning by the partners.

22.5 Strategic Networks

Strategic networks differ from alliances in that they generally involve a lower level of interdependence between the members, and the learning factor is rarely so important. Members provide their own skills, and leave other members to provide theirs. Table 22.1 illustrates the differences between different organizational forms on a number of dimensions.

22.5.1 The Nature of Strategic Networks

There is then a clear distinction between the idea of a network with its implication of close but non-exclusive relationships, and that of an alliance which, however loosely, implies the creation of a joint enterprise at least over a limited domain. The term 'network' is in fact often very loosely used to describe any relationship from an executive's 'black book' of useful contacts to an integrated company organized on internal market lines (cf. Snow, Miles, and Coleman 1992). Johanson and Mattsson (1991) make a useful additional distinction between network theory and the form of strategic alliance theory that is based upon transaction cost analysis. Alliances may be concluded for transaction cost reasons, but networks never are, they believe.

Networks, like alliances, generally exist for reasons stemming from resource dependency theory, i.e. one network member provides one function which is complementary to and synergistic with the differing contribution of other members of the network, and provides other members with privileged access. Although costs enter into the calculus of who to admit and persevere with as network members, the existence of the network and the loose bonding implied by it, emphasizes autonomy and choice, in contrast to the more deterministic governance structure and stable static equilibrium applied to alliance theory by transaction cost theorists.

Table 22.1 Differences between different organizational forms

Key features	Hierarchy	Alliance	Network	Market
Normative basis	Employment	Secondment	Complementary strengths	Contract
Communication	Routines	Relational	Relational	Prices
Conflict resolution	Fiat Supervision	Reciprocity and reputation	Reciprocity and reputation	Haggling and the law
Flexibility	Low	Medium	High	High
Commitment	High	High	Medium	Nil
Tone	Formal Bureaucratic	Committed Mutual benefit	Open ended Mutual benefit	Precision Suspicion
Actor preference	Dependent	Interdependent	Interdependent	Independent
Mixing of forms	Informal Organization Profit centres Transfer pricing	Equality Flexible rules Recent systems	Status Hierarchy Multiple partners Formal rules	Repeat Transactions Contracts

Source: Adapted from Powell (1990).

We think the relationships among firms in networks are stable and can basically play the same coordinating and development function as intra-organizational relations. Through relations with customers, distributors, and suppliers a firm can reach out to quite an extensive network. Such indirect relationships may be very important. They are not handled within the transaction cost approach. (Johanson and Mattsson 1991)

Networks of whatever type arise for a number of distinct reasons:

1. To reduce uncertainty. Indeed this motive has been suggested as the prime reason for the development of all institutions. Impersonal relationships in markets are fraught with uncertainty, in that a transaction once made can never be assumed to be repeatable, since it implies no more in relationship terms than is contained in the exchange. Networks imply developing relationships and thus promise more in terms of mutual solidarity against the cruel wind of economic dynamics.

2. To provide flexibility. This quality is offered not in contrast to markets but to hierarchies. Vertically integrated companies establish overheads and production capacity, and in doing so forsake the flexibility of immediate resource reallocation that networks provide.

3. To provide capacity. A firm has certain performance capacities as a result of its configuration. If it is part of a customary network however, such capacity can be considerably extended by involving other network members in the capacity constrained activity.

4. To provide speed to take advantage of opportunities that might not exist for long and may require a fast response. The classical 'window of opportunity' which is open for a short period and then shut forever. An existing network can put together a package of resources and capacities to meet such challenges in a customized response which, in its flexibility and scope, lies beyond the capacity of an unnetworked vertically integrated firm.

5. To provide access to resources and skills not owned by the company itself. Thus, in a network like those found in the clothing industry of Northern Italy (Lorenzoni and Ornati 1988), the strength of one company is a reflection of the strength of its position in its network, and the facility with which it can call on abilities and skills it does not possess itself to carry out tasks necessary to complete a project.

6. To provide information. Network members gain access to industrial intelligence and information of a diverse nature with far greater facility than executives imprisoned in a vertically integrated company. In such firms the 'need to know' principle is far more likely to operate than in networks where all members regard information gathering as one of the principal reasons for establishing themselves in networks. Even in companies that recognize the importance of making their knowledge and experience available to all their members, often by appointing Chief Knowledge Officers as did Coopers and Lybrand, the breadth of knowledge may still be more limited than that embedded in a wide network.

22.5.2 Power and Trust in Strategic Networks

If price is the key regulator and dominant factor in markets, and legitimacy in hierarchies, then power and trust are the factors that dominate network relationships as well as the more formal alliances. They are the dominant factors in any political economy, and networks have many of the qualities of such institutional forms. 'The inter-organizational network may be conceived as a political economy concerned with the distribution of two scarce resources, money and authority' (Benson 1975, cited in Thorelli 1986). To embark on cooperative activity, the domains of companies, i.e. their products, markets, mode of operation, and territories overlap, need to contact each other and perceive the benefit of working together. Until a certain critical mass has been achieved in the level of cooperation and exchange transactions, the alliance or network does not merit the name.

Thorelli (1986) identifies five sources of network power for a member: its economic base, technologies, and range of expertise, coupled with the level of trust and legitimacy that it evokes from its fellow members. It needs to be differentially advantaged in at least one of these areas. All network members, although formally regarded as equals by virtue of their membership, will not have the same degree of power, and it is the linkages between the members, and their respective power over each other in causing outcomes, that determine the culture of the network.

Although networks accord membership to firms, they are not static closed bodies. Entry, exit, and repositioning is constantly going on in networks occasioned by a particular firm member's success or failure and the strength of demand or otherwise for the contribution other member firms believe it can make to their proposed projects. The ultimate justification for the cost to a firm of maintaining its position in a network is the belief that such network activity strengthens its competitive position in comparison to operating on a purely market-based philosophy.

Even networks themselves, however, wax and wane in power. As Thorelli puts it, 'In the absence of conscious coordinative management—ie network management, networks would tend to disintegrate under the impact of entropy.' Networks depend on the establishment, maintenance, and perhaps strengthening of relationships in the hope of profits in the future. In this sense they are different from markets which exist to establish profit today. It is therefore the perceived quality of relationships in networks that matters, since quantitative measures cannot easily be applied to them.

Parts of networks are often appropriable by individuals in a way that technologies and production capacities are not, partly because only the calculative trust stage has been achieved. To that extent, although a firm may join a network to reduce its vulnerability, it may end up replacing one form of vulnerability for another. The successful corporate finance directors of merchant banks in the City of London

depend almost entirely on their networks and are eternally at risk of being bid away to other institutions through a large enough offer. The network, as opposed to other intra-organizational forms, brings with it its own strengths and vulnerabilities. In a turbulent and global economic world however, few players can risk being entirely without networks, or conversely being entirely dependent upon them.

Richardson (1972) sees firms as 'islands of planned coordination in a sea of market relations'. But as Powell (1990) stresses, the sea is by no means clear, and this description of the alternative methods of exchange in economies is of doubtful use. Strong relationships and dense commercial networks have always existed wherever economic exchange occurs, sufficient to make the metaphorical antithesis of solid land and fluid sea an unrealistic one. It would be extreme, however, to blur the distinctions between markets, networks, and hierarchies such that they are rejected as useful categories. At the very least their underlying philosophies differ in essence. In markets the rule is to drive a hard bargain, in networks to create indebtedness for future benefit, and in hierarchies to cooperate for career advancement. As Powell (1990) notes:

Prosperous market traders would be viewed as petty and untrustworthy shysters in networks, while successful participants in networks who carried those practices into competitive markets would be viewed as naive and foolish. Within hierarchies, communication and exchange are shaped by concerns with career mobility—in this sense, exchange is bound up with considerations of personal advancement.

Powell believes that networks score over other governance forms particularly where flexibility and fast response times are needed, 'thick' information is needed, and varied resources are required due to an uncertain environment. He also points out that the social cement of networks is strengthened by obligations which are frequently left unbalanced, thus looking to the future for further exchanges. This differs from other governance forms where the pursuit of exchange equivalence in reciprocity is the norm.

Although trust and its general antecedent 'reputation' are necessary in all exchange relationships, they are at their most vital in network forms. It is true that you need to trust your colleagues in a hierarchy, and you need to trust the trader who sells you a product in a market, at least to the extent of believing that the good is of the declared quality. But in these circumstances tacit behavioural caution and legal remedies can to some degree compensate for doubtful trust in hierarchies and markets, respectively. However, without trust, and a member's reputation on admission to a network, such a mode of cooperation would soon wither, probably into a market form.

Jarillo (1993) looks at a network as more than a rather randomly determined set of business relationships created because its members felt uncertain of the future, and believed that knowing particular differentiated trading partners well, provides a stronger capability than the flexibility that comes with having only market relationships or the costs involved in vertical integration. In Jarillo's view strategic

networks are merely another, and often better way of running the 'business system' necessary for the production and sale of a chosen set of products. By business system he means the stages and activities necessary for designing, sourcing, producing, marketing, distributing, and servicing a product; a form of analysis similar to Porter's (1985) value chain.

From this perspective Jarillo's strategic network requires a hub company to provide scope definition and leadership. It decides if it will carry out a particular activity internally or through network subcontractors. His examples of such a network system are Toyota and Benetton. Conditions that make such a system the preferred solution to vertical integration are, in Jarillo's view:

(1) widely varying optimal scale for different activities in the business system; some activities benefiting from small-scale providers;

(2) varying optimal cultures for the most efficient production of particular activities;

(3) business systems in which innovation most commonly comes from small entrepreneurial companies; and

(4) widely varying expected rates of profitability from different business system activities, as a consequence of their positioning in different industry structures as analysed by a five forces method (Porter 1980).

Jarillo bases his theory of the growth of strategic networks largely on the observation of the current trend towards company downsizing, a major component of which is the replacement of internal non-core functions by subcontracted providers, thereby contracting the size of the core salaried workforce. Frequently, the company contracted to carry out the outsourced activities is a newly formed management buy-out from the previously vertically integrated company. Greater motivation is instilled in the subcontractor at a stroke, better services are provided, greater flexibility is achieved by the hub company, and the size of the company's required capital base is accordingly reduced. There are in theory gains all round, although the motivation of those removed from the parent company may often be damaged, and the feeling of security of those remaining may be compromised.

22.5.3 Types of Strategic Network

Davis, Diekmann, and Tinsley (1994) confirm this movement in their description of the decline and fall of the conglomerate firm in the United States in the 1980s. The authors talk of the firm as an institution being increasingly replaced by a reductionist view of the firm as a network without boundaries. They describe firms of the future as no more than: 'dense patches in networks of relations among economic free agents'. This modern construct is developed further by Snow, Miles, and Coleman (1992) who also claim that the modern firm is becoming: 'a new form of

organization—delayered, downsized, and operating through a network of market sensitive business units—[which] is changing the global business terrain.'

This is clearly Jarillo's strategic network in another guise, although Snow et al. go further. They identify three distinct types of network:

1. *The internal network.* This is a curious identification as a network, since it is described as the introduction of the market into the internal organization of the firm. Thus, activities are carried out within the firm and then 'sold' to the next stage of the value chain at market prices, with the purchaser having the right to buy externally, if he can get a better deal. The activity may also in turn develop third party clients external to the firm.

2. *The stable network.* This is the firm employing partial outsourcing to increase flexibility and improve performance, with a smaller base of permanent employees. It is similar to the Japanese keiretsu in Western form.

3. *Dynamic networks.* These are composed of lead firms who identify new opportunities and then assemble a network of complementary firms with the assets and capabilities to provide the business system to meet the identified market need. Dynamic networks are sometimes otherwise described as Hollow Corporations (*Business Week*, 3 Mar. 1986), since the entrepreneur lacks the capacity to carry out the range of necessary activities from its own resources.

Snow et al. take the network concept further by observing that the change in organizational form leads inevitably to a change in the required qualities of executives. In markets traders need above all to be quick-witted, streetwise, and able to negotiate effectively. In hierarchies executives need a range of personal attributes including leadership qualities, administrative abilities, and diplomatic capacity. An autocratic style although not fashionable is not necessarily an inhibitor to success in many company cultures. In setting up and running networks, however, such a style would almost inevitably lead to the failure of the network or at least to the executive's replacement.

Snow et al. identify the broker as the ideal network executive, and they specify three distinct broker roles:

1. *The architect.* He is the creator of the network or at least of the project in which appropriate firms in an existing network are to be asked to play a part. The architect is the entrepreneur, and dependent upon his creativity and motivational abilities he may be instrumental in providing the inspirational vision that brings a network into being, in introducing new members to it, or merely in resourcing a project from existing network members.

2. *The lead operator.* This broker role is often carried out by a member of a downstream firm in the network, according to Snow et al. He is the manager rather than the entrepreneur, and provides the brain and central nervous system that the network needs if it is to function effectively on a defined mission. As the name suggests, he needs to provide leadership, but in a more democratic style than would

be necessary in a hierarchy, as the members of the team in which he needs to operate are not his employees.

3. *The caretaker.* This role prevents Thorelli's (1986) famous 'entropy' risk being realized. The caretaker will need to monitor a large number of relationships. He will need to nurture, to enhance, and even to discipline network members if they fail to deliver their required contribution. Snow and Thomas (1993) conducted some qualitative research into the validity of these broker roles in networks and found them to be broadly valid. There is no doubt, however, that the network with a strong hub firm at the centre is very different in nature and character to that which is set up amongst firms with greater claims to mutual equality. Even equal partner firms will inevitably be differentiated in terms of their actual power though, and such power relationships will themselves almost inevitably change over the lifetime of the network's operation.

It is difficult to position networks on the cooperative strategy spectrum of ascending interdependence, since some networks exhibit firm-like qualities like the Japanese keiretsu, whilst others are little more than media for the fast transmission of informal industry information. However, the problem becomes easier to solve, if networks are classified into two distinct categories, i.e. the dominated network, where one firm maintains bilateral relations with a number of normally smaller companies, and the equal partner network in which a number of firms develop close relationships with each other, and work together in variable configurations on a variety of projects. These forms approximate to Snow et al.'s (1992) stable and dynamic networks. His third category, the internal network, is regarded as outside the brief of cooperative strategy since it is found in a hierarchy.

22.5.4 The Equal Partner Network

In equal partner networks firms, in Powell's (1987) words, engage in: 'reciprocal, preferential, mutually supportive actions. Reputation, trust, tacit collusion, and a relative absence of calculative quid pro quo behaviour guide this system of exchange. In network forms of organisations, individual units exist not by themselves, but in relation to other units'. Yet they do not submerge their personalities in each other or engage in wide exclusive arrangements with each other. In Pfeffer and Salancik's view (1978) such networks are formed to reduce the level of uncertainty in a firm's perceived environment. Equal partner networks are so named because, unlike in a dominated network, there is no single partner which sets up and controls the network's activities. However, this does not necessarily imply that all partners do in fact have equal power. In all equal partner networks, power relationships are varied and constantly shifting with the fortunes of members. The equal partner network differs from the dominated network also in that it is not a substitute

organizational form to the integrated firm. Rather is it the expression of a set of developed relationships between firms that form a substructure from which competitive organizational entities may emerge.

Figure 22.9 illustrates in a stylized fashion the nature of relationship and contacts between members in equal partner networks in contrast to those in dominated networks. Equal partner networks can be configured and reconfigured to meet changing market opportunities, and often with a different lead partner in the ascendant. This is both their strength and their weakness. Whilst it implies great flexibility, and an ability to respond to changing, often turbulent environments, an equal partner network lacks the permanent brain and central nervous system that will ensure it combative ability against an organization so endowed. Any organization hoping to compete with vertically integrated companies, which possess production and sales capacity and strong identifying brand names, needs to convince the public of its enduring existence. It also requires a leadership capacity to plan and execute strategy, and information systems sensitive enough to convey what needs to be done and to ensure that it is done. This cannot easily be achieved via the loose linkages of an equal partner network, despite its other already identified advantageous qualities. For this reason an equal partner network is more of the nature of a dense set of mutually aware capabilities, than an actual organization form. Such networks may therefore often be in transitory forms which will develop into dominated networks, virtual corporations or even integrated companies in due course. In economies where networks traditionally flourish like Silicon Valley, California, the emergence of new firms out of a deeply embedded network substructure does not disturb the basic network characteristics of the economy.

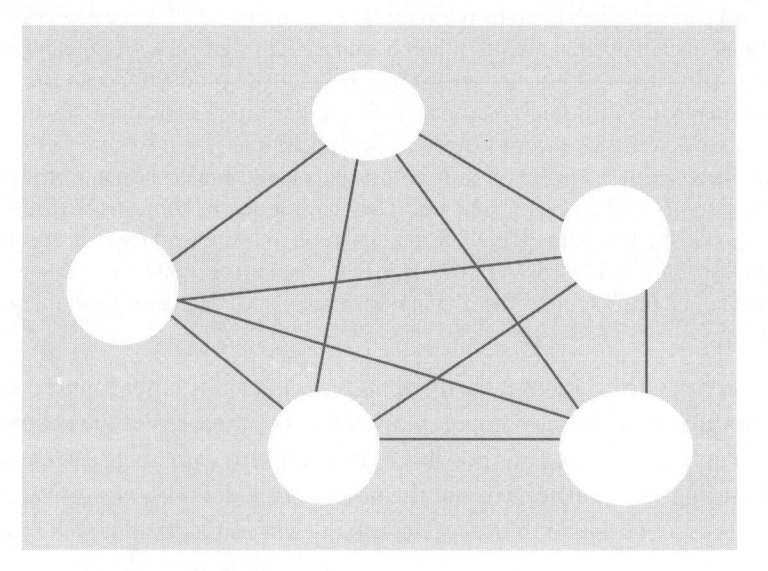

Fig. 22.9 Communications in an equal partner network

22.5.5 The Dominated Network

The dominated network is most frequently exemplified by the Japanese keiretsu (Gerlach 1992) in which a major corporation, e.g. Mitsubishi, exists with a wide and varied network of subcontractors and associated companies, which provide it with services on a regular basis. The network surrounding Rugman and D'Cruz's (1993) flagship firm is similarly a dominated network. The network is regarded by all the institutions concerned as a kind of family with the hub company as the paterfamilias, and the periphery companies as its children. Hub companies often have seats on the boards of the keiretsu companies and may hold a small percentage of their equity. The network structure is used to ensure reliability and quality of supply components, and to make production systems like just-in-time logistics easier to administer.

The dominated network owes its recent growth in the West to two major unconnected factors: the international success in certain high profile markets of industrial Japan, and the fall from grace of the large vertically integrated multidivisional industrial corporation, and its replacement as a favoured paradigm by the downsized, delayered, core competence based 'lean and mean' organization, relying on outsourcing for its production in all functions except those deemed to be strategically vital and close to its core competences.

The Japanese industrial keiretsu represents the archetype of the dominated network. In Gerlach's words (1992):

the vertical keiretsu are tight hierarchical associations centred on a single large parent and containing multiple smaller satellite companies within related industries. While focused in their business activities, they span the status breadth of the business community, with the parent firm part of Japan's large-firm economic core and its satellites, particularly at lower levels, small operations that are often family-run.... The vertical keiretsu can be divided into three main categories. The first are the *sangyo keiretsu* or production keiretsu, which are elaborate hierarchies of primary, secondary, and tertiary-level subcontractors that supply, through a series of stages, parent firms. The second are the *ryutsu keiretsu* or distribution keiretsu. These are linear systems of distributors that operate under the name of a large-scale manufacturer, or sometimes a wholesaler. They have much in common with the vertical marketing systems that some large US manufacturers have introduced to organize their interfirm distribution channels. A third—the *shihon keiretsu* or capital keiretsu—are groupings based not on the flow of production materials and goods but on the flow of capital from a parent firm.

Whilst Gerlach's description of the different types of keiretsu in Japanese industry is clear and categorical, in the complex world of reality the webs of the keiretsu do in fact frequently overlap, and it is possible to have keiretsu with dual centres, the one a manufacturing or trading centre and the other a bank. It is also not unusual for the outer members of keiretsu to deal preferentially with each other as well as with the core company.

Such dominated networks are not unique to Japan, although they are a strong feature of the Japanese industrial system of production and distribution. In the UK Marks & Spencer's relationship with its suppliers has many of the characteristic features of the dominated network including control over quality and supply in exchange for large annual order commitments.

Relationships within dominated networks typically take the form illustrated in Figure 22.10. There is often only limited networking between satellite companies, except in relation to the business of the dominant company. The dominant company may establish formal links with the satellite through a minority shareholding and/or board membership. But this is not always or even generally the case. The advantage of such networks from the viewpoint of the dominant company is that it can rely on regular quality supplies at a pre-agreed price without the need to put up the capital and management resources to create them directly. From the satellite's viewpoint, it can economize on sales and marketing expenditure and have the security of reliable orders and cash flow for its planning purposes, which removes many of the risks from its business. Of course at the same time it also removes some of the autonomy, and if the satellite allows too great a percentage of its business to be with the dominant company it is at risk of ceding all independent bargaining power over such matters as price changes or product development.

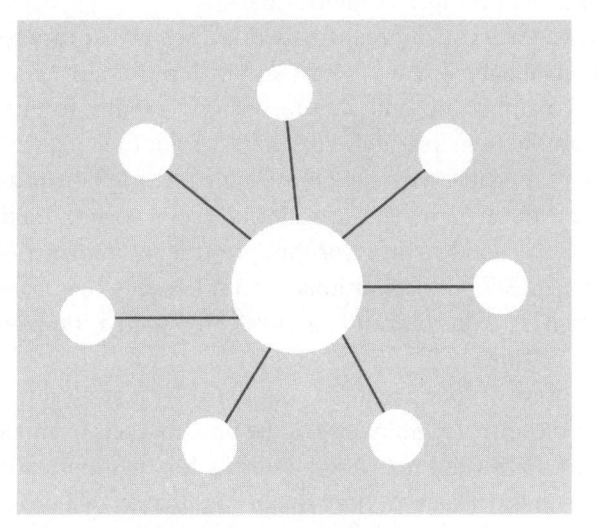

Fig. 22.10 The communication pattern in the
dominated network

22.5.6 An Overview of the Network

Network theory has become prominent in recent years as the basis for new organizational forms, and for the growth of cooperative strategy as a counterbalance to the self-sufficient philosophy underlying competitive strategy theories. At one level however, networks have always been with us. Shortly after any individual starts up a business, or engages in any repeated endeavour, he begins to build up a network out of the associates with whom he interacts. In the business world they will be suppliers, distributors, and perhaps to a lesser extent competitors and customers. He will always consider the degree to which he should outsource some of his potential activities, and the level to which he should deal directly with the customer or develop his sales through a network. In some areas, e.g. Northern Italy, this has traditionally led to strong specialization of activity amongst family firms, and therefore the network as the fundamental underpinning of business activity. In other areas, notably much of the United States, vertical integration has been more the norm until recently, with cooperative networked activity therefore treated with some suspicion.

The degree of prominence networks have received has significantly increased in recent years. This is due largely to the globalization of markets and technologies, leading to the widespread growth of cooperative activity as a necessary strategy, if firms with limited financial strength, focused competences, and limited 'global reach' are to be able to compete in global markets.

An attractive characteristic of many networks then is that they help members to achieve increased global reach at low cost and with minimum time delay. They are flexible in their membership and able to respond rapidly to changing environmental situations. In an increasingly turbulent world, they reduce uncertainty for their members. They enable synergies between members to be captured and provide the conditions for the achievement of scale and scope economies through specialization. They are also good vehicles for the spreading of information and all forms of market intelligence. Under conditions of trust between members, they may also reduce transaction costs, in contrast to vertically integrated companies with internally competitive cultures.

However networks, if they are to be contrasted with vertically integrated companies and with the arm's length nature of the pure markets form, do not score well on all counts. In dominated networks, the risks for the dominant partner are of unlicensed technology leakage, of poor quality assurance, of a possible diffusion of internal feelings of identity and motivation in the outlying companies. There is also the difficulty of communicating tacit knowledge and of achieving a sufficient level of coordination between members in different companies to compete successfully with the systems of integrated companies: the 'singing from several hymn sheets' problem. For the smaller companies in the dominated network, there are the problems of feeling too dominated, and thus of loss of autonomy and motivation,

of lack of promotion opportunities, of insecurity, and of the difficulty in recruiting high quality personnel to small companies with limited prospects.

In equal partner networks the primary problems relate to the lack of a brain and a central nervous system. By their nature they are loosely organized coalitions without a permanent acknowledged leader. Major investment in such networks is difficult to organize, and there is the perpetual tension between trust and the risk of prisoners' dilemma defection by partners, i.e. the potential creation of competitors as a result of too much misplaced trust. There is also the difficulty for a network of driving consistently towards a vision of the future, in the way a successful vertically integrated company can and does.

22.6 THE FUTURE

As Michael E. Naylor, one time boss of General Motors once said, 'There are no facts about the future, only opinions.' It is therefore not possible to tell if the present time is one of transition, in which greater economic turbulence leads to more flexible organizational forms, only to be followed by a period of renewed stability accompanied by the re-emergence of more rigid hierarchies. Or whether the turbulence is here to stay, and the resultant need for strategic flexibility will make flexible cooperative forms of economic organization the dominant ones and ultimately the only naturally selected ones.

The author is inclined towards the second view. The globalizing effects of the Internet alone are likely to create a global strategic market for most industries within the next decade. Yet the variety of peoples, tastes, and needs is likely to persist outside what are called the staple industries leading to the persistence of economic volatility. In a very large market a small swing in demand can involve very large figures for an individual company. The federated enterprise is therefore likely to grow more common in its many varied forms.

Loyalty to integrated companies is likely to continue its decline, and by those companies to their employees. Workers will seek security in their skills rather than in paternalistic corporations, and those skills will need to be broad-based, multi-application skills, and capable of being adapted to meet ever-changing situations and needs. In such a world we are likely to see the decline of hierarchy, of traditional authority, of seniority, and of dogma. In their place will emerge the power that comes from knowledge, from being able to do things, from the ability to 'learn new tricks', and from establishing and maintaining valuable relationships.

This will mean a growing need for the skills that enable people to develop cooperative relationships and produce valued outcomes through them. It is a

world of, often temporary, cooperation to meet changing needs and demands above all through strategic alliances and strategic networks if current trends are to be reliably extrapolated into the future. This will not necessarily mean the death of the multinational, as it has many strong survival qualities. But it is likely to lead to the development of more flexible multinational corporations in specific industries operating side by side with an increasing number of federated enterprises, some of which will preserve their federated form over time, and others of which will be absorbed by the stronger partner or a third party.

The global economy of the future will undoubtedly see a growth of networks in the search for reduced uncertainty in the face of the increasing turbulence of world economic activity resulting from the globalization of technologies and markets. Cooperative strategy will become more prominent. But it can never replace competitive behaviour in the ultimate marketplace, if pressures for efficiencies are to be maintained, and the by now hackneyed slogan to 'cooperate in order to compete' is likely to be heard ever more.

22.7 CONCLUSIONS

Cooperative strategy, whether in the close form of strategic alliances or the more loosely coupled form of networks, requires attitudes and approaches to management quite distinct from those found in hierarchies. It generally emerges when one company finds itself unable to cope with a global or other challenge, because of limitations in its resources and competences, and seeks an ally to reduce its vulnerabilities. Where this new mode of organizing its business is approached flexibly and sensitively by the partners, enduring, successful, and mutually beneficial relationships can be created and maintained. Indeed there are grounds for believing that the future of these more flexible organizational forms as exemplified in alliances and networks is likely to be bright. Such arrangement will not survive, however, if partners play power politics with each other, show lack of commitment, distrust, and lack of integrity and do not make very positive steps to deal with the cultural differences between the partners that will almost inevitably exist. It is these latter mishandled situations that have led to the reported 50 per cent failure rate of recent alliances. The need is to understand the key factors for success in managing alliances as competently as the lessons from management theory in handling integrated hierarchical corporations. They are as different as the contrast between giving orders from a position of authority compared with developing a consensus for action in a community of equals. Only when this difference is appreciated and translated into changed behaviour will the failure rate of cooperative arrangements begin to decline.

REFERENCES

BLEEKE, J., and ERNST, D. (1995). 'Is your Strategic Alliance really a Sale?'. *Harvard Business Review*, Jan.–Feb.: 97–105.

CASTI, J. L. (1991). *Paradigms Lost*. London: Abacus Books.

COYNE, K. P. (1986). 'Sustainable Competitive Advantage: What it is, What it isn't'. *Business Horizons*, 29 1: 54–61.

DAVIS, G. F., DIEKMANN, K. A., and TINSLEY, C. H. (1994). 'The Decline and Fall of the Conglomerate Firm in the 1980s: The Deinstitutionalisation of an Organisational Form'. *American Sociological Review*, 59: 547–70.

GARRETTE, B., and DUSSAUGE, P. (1995). 'Patterns of Strategic Alliances between Rival Firms'. *Group Decision and Negotiation*, 4: 429–52.

GERLACH, M. L. (1992). *Alliance Capitalism*. Los Angeles: University of California Press.

GRANT, R. M. (1991). *Contemporary Strategy Analysis: Concepts, Techniques, Applications*. Oxford: Blackwell Business.

HAMEL, G., DOZ, Y. L., and PRAHALAD, C. K. (1989). 'Collaborate with your Competitors and Win'. *Harvard Business Review*, Jan.–Feb.: 133–9.

HANDY, C. (1992). 'Balancing Corporate Power: A New Federalist Paper'. *Harvard Business Review*, Nov.–Dec.: 59–72.

JARILLO, J. C. (1993). *Strategic Networks: Creating the Borderless Organization*. Oxford: Butterworth-Heinemann.

JOHANSON, J., and MATTSSON, L.-G. (1991). 'Interorganisational Relations in Industrial Systems: A Network Approach Compared with the Transaction-Cost Approach', in G. Thompson, J. Frances, R. Levacic, and J. Mitchell (eds.), *Markets, Hierarchies, and Networks*. London: SAGE Publications, 256–64.

LEVITT, T. (1960). 'Marketing Myopia'. *Harvard Business Review*, July–Aug.: 45–57.

LORENZONI, G., and ORNATI, O. A. (1988). 'Constellations of Firms and New Ventures'. *Journal of Business Venturing*, 3: 41–57.

MATTSSON, L. G. (1988). 'Interaction Strategies: A Network Approach'. Working Paper.

NORTH, D. C. (1996). 'Reflections on Economics and Cognitive Science'. Public lecture, JIMS Cambridge.

OHMAE, K. (1989). 'The Global Logic of Strategic Alliances'. *Harvard Business Review*, Mar.–Apr.: 143–54.

PFEFFER, J., and SALANCIK, G. (1978). *The External Control of Organisations*. New York: Harper.

PORTER, M. E. (1980). *Competitive Strategy*. New York: Free Press.

—— (1985). *Competitive Advantage*. New York: Free Press.

—— (1987). 'From Competitive Advantage to Corporate Strategy'. *Harvard Business Review*, May–June: 43–59.

—— and FULLER, M. B. (1986). 'Coalitions and Global Strategy', in M. E. Porter (ed.), *Competition in Global Industries*. Cambridge, Mass.: Harvard University Press.

POWELL, W. W. (1987). 'Hybrid Organizational Arrangements: New Form or Transitional Development'. *California Management Review*, Fall: 67–87.

—— (1990). 'Neither Market nor Hierarchy: Network Forms of Organisation'. *Research in Organisational Behaviour*, 12: 295–336.

PRAHALAD, C. K., and HAMEL, G. (1990). 'The Core Competence of the Corporation'. *Harvard Business Review*, 90: 79–91.

RICHARDSON, G. B. (1972). 'The Organisation of Industry'. *Economic Journal* 82/Sept.: 883–96.

RUGMAN, A., and D'CRUZ, R. D. (1993). 'The Double Diamond Model of International Competitiveness: The Canadian Experience'. *Management International Review*, 2: 17–39.

SNOW, C. S., and THOMAS, J. B. (1993). 'Building Networks: Broker Roles and Behaviours', in P. Lorange (ed.), *Implementing Strategic Processes: Change Learning and Cooperation*. Oxford: Blackwell.

—— MILES, R. E., and COLEMAN, H. J. (1992). 'Managing 21st Century Network Organizations'. *Organizational Dynamics*, 20: 5–20.

THORELLI, H. B. (1986). 'Networks: Between Markets and Hierarchies'. *Strategic Management Journal*, 7: 37–51.

PART IV

INTERNATIONAL STRATEGY

C H A P T E R   2 3

INTERNATIONAL STRATEGY

DAVID FAULKNER

23.1 INTRODUCTION

THE objectives of this chapter are to explain the rationale for the existence of the multinational corporation, to describe the stages of internationalization, to review the four distinct forms of multinational corporate strategy and structure, and to consider their dynamic nature and relate them to typical contingent circumstances.

The multinational corporation (MNC) has dominated the international business environment at least since World War II. One of the most popular academic rationales for the MNC is that of Dunning's (1974) eclectic paradigm (advantages of Ownership, Location, and Internalization). Rugman, Lecraw, and Booth (1985) provide a different characterization of the same OLI elements used by Dunning by combining the three OLI elements into two factors: firm-specific advantages (FSAs—which include 'O' and 'I') and country-specific advantages (CSAs—which incorporates 'L'). Rugman, Lecraw, and Booth see international strategy formation by MNCs as an outcome of the balance of benefits to the MNC of sets of FSAs and CSAs within each firm. Both Dunning's and Rugman's approaches to explaining the strategic decision-making of international firms assumes that decision-making is based on rationality, and hence on the attempt to minimize transaction costs and factor costs, although in the real world these are not always justifiable assumptions.

23.2 THE RATIONALE FOR THE MNC

Porter (1986) identifies the two key tasks of the would-be international firm as: first, to achieve the optimal form of *configuration* (where to locate value chain activities, which would include CSA issues); and second, type and degree of *coordination* (how to set up the appropriate organization structure and systems to support the actual choice of configuration of the MNC, which would incorporate FSA issues).

In Figure 23.1 *dispersed configuration* means having value chain activities in many countries; while *concentrated configuration* means having value chain activities mostly in the home country. Obviously an array of possibilities exists along that continuum. On the other axis, we use *high coordination* to mean mainly centralized decision-making and *low coordination* to mean mainly decentralized decision-making. Thus, in Figure 23.1 Gillette has a globally dispersed configuration with high centralization of decision-making at MNC headquarters. Nestlé is shown with a dispersed configuration and low coordination; a way of capturing in the matrix Nestlé's multi-domestic MNC structure. We have shown Matsushita of Japan twice: first (top right) as it was structured in the 1970s, with a concentrated configuration and high coordination, which means that it was very centralized in its decision-making and resource-allocation processes at that time; and second (bottom right) as it was by the late 1980s/early 1990s, with a more dispersed configuration and more decentralization of decision-making.

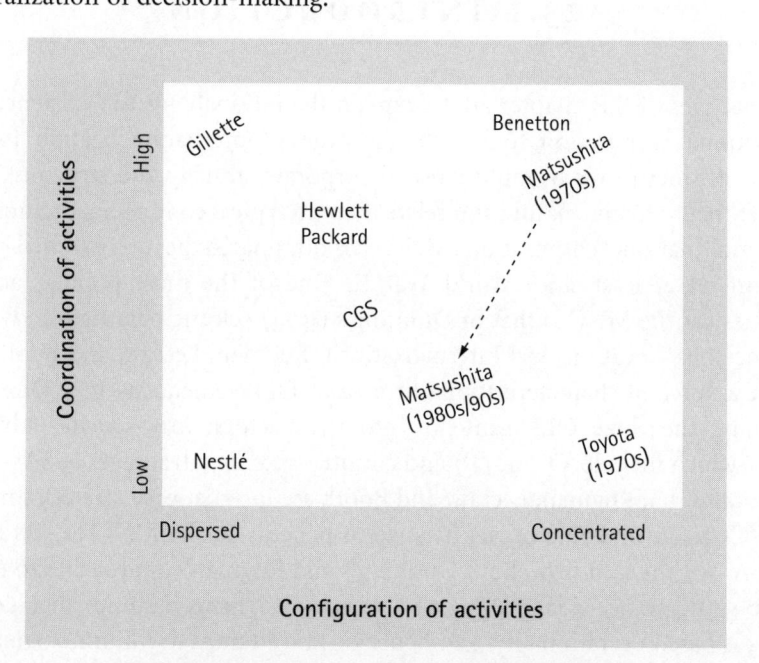

Fig. 23.1 Configuration/coordination matrix

Source: Adapted from Porter (1986).

It would probably be more accurate in discussing the concept of MNC *co-ordination* to move away from simple alternatives such as centralization or decentralization, since such dichotomies do not capture well enough the fluid but clear objective of coordination—to get dispersed activities such as disaggregated R&D departments, production plants, and marketing teams, to truly work together (Porter 1986; Birkinshaw, Morrison, and Hulland 1995). The configuration and coordination of the activities of a multinational corporation on a global scale certainly provide a more daunting and more complex task than is involved in carrying out such activities on a purely national scale. However, as is implicit in the concept of the strategic flexibility of the MNC (Kogut 1985; Buckley and Casson 1998a), MNCs have more choices and options with regard to configuration than are available to a national firm. International strategy choices by an MNC are complex and involve the search for competitive advantage from global configuration/coordination choices throughout the entire value chain of the firm.

This chapter attempts to provide some answers to the question of how MNCs configure and coordinate their international strategies, by examining various approaches to internationalization as a strategy process (Melin 1992; Buckley and Casson 1998b). These will include stages models of internationalization, studies of the link between strategy and structure in MNCs, and more recent organizational models of MNCs. Finally a model will be introduced to summarize and discuss the four basic MNC forms described.

23.3 THE STAGES OF INTERNATIONALIZATION

Vernon's (1966) product life cycle model of the internationalization of a firm suggested that the process of internationalization was likely to take place in stages. First of all, a product is developed and sold domestically. Then it is exported and as demand for the MNC's products grow larger, exporting will be replaced by foreign direct investment (FDI). That will lead to it being produced in the countries in which demand for it has proved large and where factor costs and availability are most advantageous. This stage is thus the growth stage of the life cycle. In the maturity stage production moves to lower wage cost developing economies, and the final stage is decline where the product is imported into the country from which it originally emerged. This is a very stylized model, which assumes that the firm with the new product is starting out from scratch with no existing international

organization. Its basic contribution to theory is to demonstrate how international-ization can cause production to gradually move from the home country.

A somewhat similar stage model was developed in Uppsala by Johanson and Vahlne (1977). They envisaged a firm gradually internationalizing through increased commitment to and knowledge of foreign markets. The firm is therefore most likely to enter markets with successively greater psychic distance (Perlmutter 1969) from that of the home market. Thus, at the outset it sells to countries culturally similar to itself. The model depends on the notion that uncertainty, and hence risk, increases with increasing psychic distance and unfamiliarity.

The problem with this model is that there are many examples of international-izing companies who have merely gone for the large rather than the familiar markets, and many markets at the same time, e.g. Sony, McDonald's, Levis. The contrast is between the so-called 'waterfall' model of global expansion (one country at a time) and the contrasting 'sprinkler' model (many countries at a time). In current markets with ever-shortening product life cycles, and the strategic import-ance of 'time-to-market', there is often insufficient time to adopt the waterfall approach. At all events both of the popular stage models are highly sequential in the stages they describe and are both very deterministic.

23.4 STRATEGY AND STRUCTURE IN MNCs

The first major theory linking strategy and structure in MNCs is identified with Alfred Chandler. This 'structure follows strategy' school first emerged from Chandler's seminal book *Strategy and Structure* (1962) in which he described how a number of major US companies adopted the 'M-form' (multi-divisional) organiza-tion in order to better cope with the need to coordinate activities around the globe. Stopford and Wells (1972), following in Chandler's path, developed a simple des-criptive model to illustrate the typical stages of development for companies pro-gressively moving towards an international organization structure. They saw this as a process driven by two dimensions: the number of products sold internationally, i.e. foreign product diversity; and the importance of international sales to the company, i.e. foreign sales as a percentage of total sales.

Stopford and Wells (1972) suggested that international divisions were set up at an early stage of internationalization, when the figures for both product diversity and percentage of foreign sales were both low. Then, those companies which found that international expansion led to substantial foreign product diversity tended to adopt a worldwide product division structure (pathway (a) on Fig.23.2). Or if companies

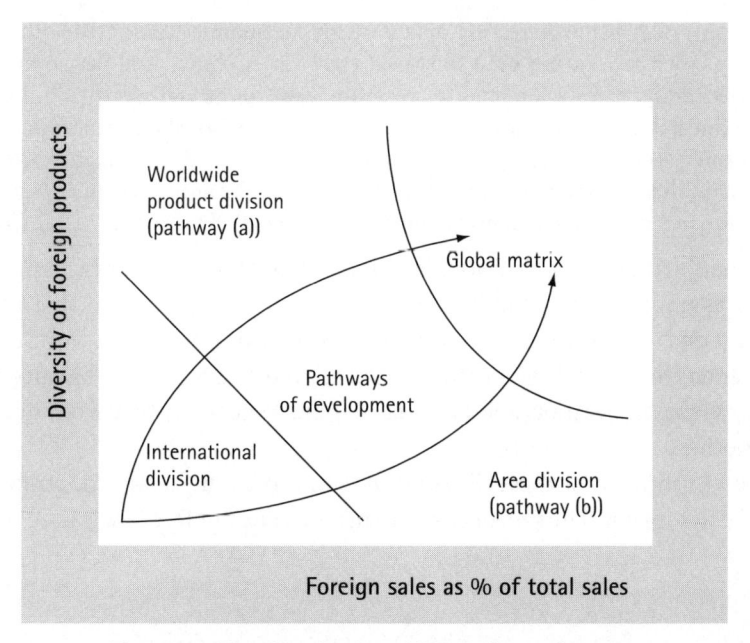

Fig. 23.2 The Stopford and Wells (1972) matrix

expanded overseas without increasing product diversity, they tended to adopt a geographical area structure (pathway (b) on Fig. 23.2). Finally when both foreign sales and the diversity of products were high, a global matrix emerged. Thus, the grid structure of the MNC with a geographic axis and a product group axis emerged. Bjorkman (1989), however, was unable to correlate structures with performance. He therefore concluded that the adoption of new structures was more a matter of fashion than anything else, and resulted from firms copying current organizational trends at any specific time.

23.5 RECENT ORGANIZATIONAL MODELS

Prahalad and Doz (1987) and Bartlett and Ghoshal (1989) are of the newer 'process' school of MNC management. They emphasize control through socialization and the creation of a verbal information network to develop a corporate culture that transcends national boundaries. This school emphasizes *global integration* combined with *local responsiveness.* Both sets of authors have used variations of a *global integration / local responsiveness* framework in their work. Bartlett (1986) described these two major forces and their organizational effect on shaping the international strategies of MNCs as follows:

Some [forces], such as the increasing manufacturing economies associated with global or regional scale demand, or the need to spread escalating technological development costs over shorter product life cycles, tend to create the need for greater global coordination of effort and integration of operations. Other forces, such as national differences in consumer taste or market structure, or host government protectionism or regulation, increase the need for more local differentiation and responsiveness. It is the balance and interrelationship of these two forces that is influential in shaping the organizational task of the MNC. (1986: 369)

All international strategy decisions are made with this trade-off in mind. This approach is not at all deterministic or prescriptive of organization structure; it is contingent on circumstances. The emphasis is on the optimal functioning of MNCs in the markets in which they operate. Figure 23.3 illustrates how the balance of these forces for global integration and national responsiveness can vary from one industry to another.

Figure 23.3 shows how these different industry forces influence the strategic task and hence the appropriate response of the firm. For example, there is little incentive

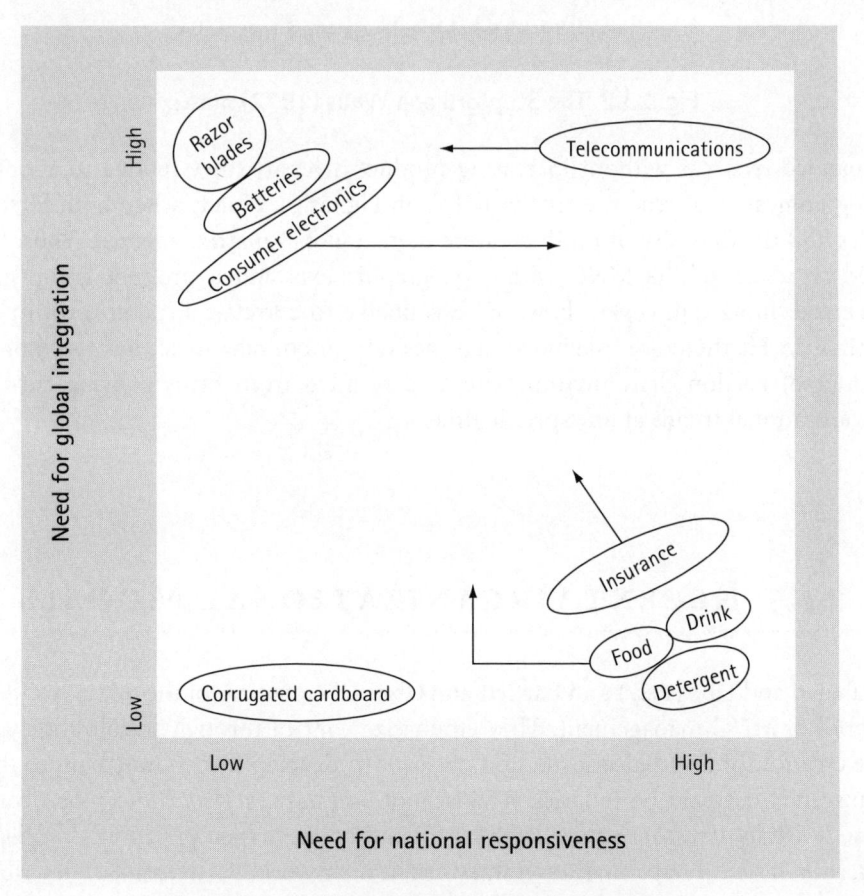

Fig. 23.3 An 'integration–responsiveness' grid

Source: Adapted from Bartlett and Ghoshal (1989).

to build a global scale plant for the manufacture of corrugated cardboard (bottom left in grid) and little basis for differentiating this basic commodity product by national market. By contrast, consumer electronics (top left in grid—together with batteries and razor blades) offers high R&D and manufacturing scale economies, together with standard design opportunities and little need for differentiation by national market. Food products, soaps, detergents, together with some services such as insurance (bottom right in grid), all needed to be adapted to meet local consumer preferences and differences in distribution channels per market, as well as various regulatory requirements. Telecommunications (top right in grid) requires high capital investment and massive R&D costs, but still must meet the variation in technical standards and service levels required by the different national and regional markets. In addition, note the direction of the arrows attached to many of these industry positions. They indicate directions of movement over time for the different industries illustrated, as the forces shaping the industry dynamics shift and change. Each movement around the grid denotes the need for a review of the existing configuration of the MNC, and a corresponding change in its levels of global or regional coordination and integration.

Each of the four extreme corners of Figure 23.3 represents one of the four approaches to being international. Working clockwise around the integration-responsiveness grid from bottom left, these are: international exporter, global, transnational, and multi-domestic.

23.6 INTERNATIONAL STRATEGIES

All international competitors have to be perceived to be at least as good as a local firm providing a product or a service in the local market or they will not be able to sell their products abroad. Poorly organized international competitors may bear higher costs than local competitors, given their more complex structures and systems. Initially also local companies are likely to be equipped with better know-ledge of the local market. Therefore one of the key issues in operating globally is how to organize one's enterprise so that it is possible to compete with local companies in terms of both demand and supply.

In some ways the development of an international competitive strategy is no different from the development of a domestic market competitive strategy. Competitive strategy is about being able to achieve the highest level of customer satisfaction or 'perceived use value' (PUV) at the lowest cost in relation to one's competitors in each product/market, whether the market is national or international. PUV is a

term used to identify the dimensions and attributes that customers value in a product or a service, and which influence their customer buying behaviour (Bowman and Faulkner 1997). Similarly, international corporate strategy is about selecting, resourcing, and controlling the businesses within the corporation. Corporate strategy is about the mix of businesses within the corporation according to market attractiveness and the risk profile of the firm; the overarching organizational structures, systems, and processes to support those businesses; and the investment in necessary firmwide resources and capabilities either by investing internally or acquired by merger and acquisition activity or through participating in alliances with partner organizations. This is so whether the firm is competing nationally or internationally. However, in international strategy there are both additional problems, such as the management of cultural diversity across the organization, and greater opportunities and options, from either leverage or arbitrage as identified by Kogut (1985).

How then is a market defined as national or global? That decision is made by the preferences of customers and the cost structures of the operating firms. If Sony is able to bring its electronic products to the United Kingdom at competitive prices, and UK customers find them acceptable as alternative sources of PUV to those of local suppliers, then the consumer electronic market has become international. This will not of course apply to all products. The market for corrugated cardboard is said to have a radius of about 50 miles. It is a low value commodity in which little differentiation is possible, and once 50 miles have been travelled the local producer is able to realize lower costs than the travelling producer. The same applies to building aggregates. This explains the position of corrugated cardboard on Figure 23.3.

There is then a *strategic market* (Barwise and Robertson 1992) which is defined by the relative homogeneity of consumer tastes, and the possible cost structure of the company that enables it to be a credible competitor over varying distances. Since Levitt's (1983) opening remarks in the debate about global consumers, followed by Ohmae (1985, 1989) and others more recently (Makhija, Kim, and Williamson 1997), it is accepted that with the passing of each year more and more products and services fall into the category of global competition, as similar products and services are sold around the world, as technologies too become global, and as transportation costs become a smaller and smaller percentage of delivered costs.

Strategic issues affecting the four approaches to international strategy fall into three categories:

(1) those that determine which segment to select, and whether or not they involve global competition;
(2) those that affect the company's ability to resource and deliver the product at a competitive price anywhere in the world, i.e. political factors and cost structures (configuration issues);

(3) those that are concerned with how a company should organize itself to control its international activities (coordination issues).

We will deal with each of these in turn.

23.6.1 Selecting Where to Compete

A useful framework to help managers decide how to approach the selection, and eventually, the configuration task in their international strategy is that provided by Ghoshal (1987). He identifies three strategic objectives of any global strategy and three key bases of potential competitive advantage derivable from a global strategy. The resulting framework is given in Table 23.1.

The three basic strategic objectives of a global strategy in Table 23.1 are seen as:

1. *Efficiency,* i.e. carrying out all value chain activities to a required quality at lowest cost. This is the most frequently emphasized objective in the literature. Indeed, it is often the only objective mentioned. Each of the OLI (or FSA/CSA) factors mentioned above need to be considered when reaching decisions about the optimal efficiency of any specific activity.

2. *Risk management,* i.e. managing and balancing the risks inherent in operating in a number of diverse countries, e.g. exchange rate risks, political risks, or raw material sourcing risks. This is very strongly concerned with L (location) or CSA factors.

Table 23.1 Global strategy: an organizing framework

Strategic objectives	Sources of competitive advantage		
	Country differences	Scale economies	Scope economies
Efficiency in current operations	Factor cost differences, e.g. wages and cost of capital	Potential scale economies in each value chain activity	Sharing of resources and capabilities across products, markets, and business
Risk management	Assessment of risk by country	Balancing scale with strategic and operational flexibility	Portfolio diversification
Innovation and learning	Learning from cultural variety in process and practice	Opportunities for technology-based cost reduction	Shared organizational learning

Source: Adapted from Ghoshal (1987).

3. *Innovation learning and adaptation*, i.e. the opportunity to learn from the different societies, cultures, and markets in which one operates.

Ghoshal's organizing framework takes the three types of strategic objective identified above and relates them to what are noted as the three key sources of competitive advantage namely:

1. *National differences*, i.e. competitive advantage can come from exploiting differences in input and output markets in different countries, e.g. low-wage countries are perhaps the most commonly cited examples of such factors, but every other type of national difference should also be considered as part of the strategic flexibility of the MNC. That should include, for example, relative cost of capital, tax regimes, and so on.

2. *Scale economies* provide a source of competitive advantage if one firm is able to adopt a configuration of its activities such that each activity is able to operate at the optimal economic scale for minimum unit costs, especially if competitors fail to do this. Of course, achieving optimal scale economies globally may sometimes lead to dangerous inflexibility. This creates higher rather than lower risk if fluctuating exchange rates alter or destroy these potential economies after plant has been brought on-line to take advantage of them.

3. *Scope economies* are the third source of global competitive advantage. Simple illustrations of economies of scope are found in the use of global brand names like Coca-Cola or McDonald's, but can be found in any area of the firm's activities where resources used to produce or market one product in one country can be reused, virtually without cost, to do the same for other products and in other countries. Technology, IT, any learning or skills are further examples of areas of potential scope economies.

This organizing framework enables the global decision-taker to identify the potential sources of global competitive advantage available to the firm, and to cross reference them to the three basic types of strategic objective, achieving efficiency, managing risk, and enabling learning, with the ultimate objective of deciding where, why, and how to compete internationally.

23.6.2 Resourcing Global Production

Further decisions regarding the configuration of activities on a global scale are concerned with the issue of what parts of the value chain for a product or service should be produced within the company, and what should be outsourced. Configuration also means deciding where such production or other activities should take place—in the home country, the Far East, or elsewhere.

The configuration profile is influenced by a number of barriers that have historically ensured that most markets remained local. However, many of these

are becoming progressively less important. Global products had traditionally been considered by many theorists to have limited potential in many industries, since people in different parts of the world living in very diverse cultures were assumed to have different tastes and values, and therefore to require different products and services to satisfy them. To some extent that is still true; more soft drinks are sold in the United States per head than any other country in the world; more tea per head in the United Kingdom than elsewhere; the Far East consumes more rice than the West; and the West more potatoes than the Far East. Yet such variations are far less common in the manufactured products area. Levitt (1983) comments that 'the same single standardized products—autos, steel, chemicals, petroleum, cement, agricultural commodities and equipment, industrial and commercial construction, banking, insurance, computers, semiconductors, transport, electronic instruments, pharmaceuticals, and telecommunications [are sold] largely in the same single ways everywhere.' While overgeneralized to make his point in a dramatic way, the truth of his comments becomes more accurate with each passing year in an increasingly wide range of industries.

If the limitations on demand for would-be global products are less, we should also consider barriers to the supply of global products and services. The traditional supply-side barriers that make cross-border strategies more difficult still exist in many parts of the world, e.g. tariffs, government regulations, different languages and cultures, and exchange rates. However, some of the drivers behind the perceived regionalization and globalization of markets during the 1980s and 1990s have brought about the marginalization of, or complete elimination of, many of the traditional barriers to trade.

The spread of 'Western' culture through films, videos, travel, and satellite television, and the greater interest in Eastern food, clothing styles, art and music, have done much to homogenize tastes. Many of the effects of the formation of larger trading blocs on the supply side has been significant. International trade agreements such as those in the EU, ASEAN, GATT, Mercosur, and NAFTA areas have led to the reduction of the level of tariffs, and where possible eliminated quotas and domestic subsidies (outside agriculture). Fewer countries now require local majority shareholdings in joint ventures set up with foreign companies, and where they do, the foreign companies have learnt to live with this and operate in a multicultural way. Language barriers remain to some degree, although for good or ill, English is becoming the language of MNCs and of international business, and any company wishing to operate globally has to ensure that its senior executives are proficient in it.

The remaining traditional barriers are transport costs and exchange rates. Transport costs are reducing, but they remain an inhibitor to competitive global trade, the importance of which varies with the value and volume of the article traded. Transport costs are virtually irrelevant to international trade in diamonds, but of considerable importance in limiting such trade as commodity foodstuffs. Exchange

rates, however, will remain of considerable importance, whilst every nation maintains a unique currency and retains the right to devalue or revalue it against other currencies, when the government or the market deems this advisable. To be caught with cash or debtors in a newly devalued or depreciated currency can wipe out any profit at a stroke. Against this background one can appreciate the move to a Europe-wide currency (the 'euro') in the EU, which enabled European trading nations to get rid of internal exchange rate transaction costs across a market size similar to that of the United States or Japan, neither of which have carried these additional costs of trade in their internal market.

Since these barriers to global trade are now so reduced in strength, corporate strategy decisions concerning cross-border trade must be taken as it would be for domestic products, but within the mindset of international strategy. By this we mean fully utilizing the insights of Kogut's (1985) arbitrage and leverage opportunities and competitive and comparative advantage constraints, Dunning's (1998) OLI factors, Rugman, Lecraw, and Booth's (1985) FSA/CSA balance, Porter's (1986) configuration/coordination framework, Bartlett's (1986) integration-responsiveness grid, and so on, to inform the approach to each industry and market.

One approach to general corporate strategy decision-making uses a 'customer matrix' and a 'producer matrix' (Bowman and Faulkner 1997), each of which should be constructed for the strategic market of each product/market. The 'customer matrix' is a tool developed by Bowman and Faulkner (1997) with two axes on the matrix (PUV and price) to assess the market's view of the relative strength of the company's products compared to those of its competitors. Similarly, the 'producer matrix' has axes of effectiveness (arising from competencies) and unit costs. It assesses the 'real' underlying strength of the company in relation to its competitors in terms of its competencies and factor costs. These analyses will show for which markets the company has attractive products. The market size should also be assessed to ensure it is sufficiently interesting for the firm. Since the dimensions of PUV are likely to be different by country, or at least to have different weightings, a separate set of matrices will need to be developed for each country. Perceived price is also likely to be different for each country for reasons of exchange rate, local taxation, and cost of living, and the impact of transport and perhaps other costs will need to be factored into the producer matrix.

23.6.3 Controlling the International Corporation

It is not just the configuration of the value chain that is the key to international competitiveness, it is also the way in which it is coordinated and controlled. In fact since outsourcing, virtual corporations, and networks are in the ascendant as

modern organizational forms, the MNC's international coordination and control capabilities may well be the key to its international effectiveness.

Ghoshal and Nohria (1993) used the integration-responsiveness grid to identify four appropriate organizational forms for coping with the four basic types of MNC strategies: *global, international exporter, multi-domestic,* and *transnational*. Their research placed the following industries in the *global* box: construction and mining, nonferrous metals, industrial chemicals, scientific measuring instruments, and engines. Little national responsiveness was seen as necessary in these industries. Industries appropriate for an *international exporter* strategy low on global scale economies and national responsiveness were: metal industries, machinery, paper, textiles, and printing and publishing. Industries appropriate for a *multi-domestic* strategy high on the need for local adaptation were beverages, food, rubber, household appliances, and tobacco, and those for a *transnational* strategy high on both national adaptation and global scale were seen to include drugs and pharmaceuticals, photographic equipment, computers, and automobiles. Of course as particular industries evolve they may well move boxes. Automobiles, for example, may well be moving into the global box.

Ghoshal and Nohria highlight organizational process as being as important for strategic success as organization structure. They claim that when process environment and organizational form are correctly aligned, MNC performance is higher than when there is a 'misfit' between them. On the process side, they identify structural uniformity as best suited to global environments and organizational forms; differentiated structures to fit multi-domestic environments, integrated variety to fit with the transnational form, and ad hoc variety to fit with international environments.

23.7 THE INTERNATIONAL CORPORATE STRUCTURE MATRIX

The four possible configurations described above are illustrated in the matrix shown in Figure 23.4. This matrix follows a tradition in international business research used and developed by Bartlett, Ghoshal, Doz, Prahalad, and Stopford, amongst others. Although most authors apply varying definitions to some extent, the underlying principles remain the same. In international business there is always a tension between the production efficiency needed to make a standard product and ship it around the world with as little variation as possible at lowest cost, and the marketing need to offer a product to a local market that takes into

account possible local tastes and culture. This tension exists of course in all business beyond the very local at all times, but it is most in evidence in international trade across borders.

The existence of this tension, and the resultant perceived trade-off between global standardization and local adaptation applies in a number of areas. It applies in varying degrees to different industries, e.g. commodities need no local adaptation, wheat is wheat, oil is oil, but a car is not yet an undifferentiated product. It applies also to individual countries. If there is a market for a product in the United States, a similar market may exist in Europe, but more adaptation may be needed for India, Africa, or the Far East. McDonald's do not sell pure beef hamburgers in India for religious and cultural reasons for example.

A similar tension exists between business functions. It is possible for a pharmaceutical company marketing worldwide to carry out all its R&D in one major research site in its home base country. This achieves the greatest economies of scale in terms of running teams of research scientists, and having the hardware resources for them to carry out their research. However, if the company is big enough, it may need more than one R&D establishment in different parts of the world. This is not for reasons of scale economies but for market intelligence-gathering and to give it the necessary flexibility when the market environment changes unexpectedly. The same company may need a small number of production units sited regionally around the world to achieve the minimum economic size for scale economies in production. However, it may well need one sales force per country to develop and use the local market knowledge needed to achieve effective global reach with its portfolio of products, and to gain national and local acceptance. These tensions exist for industries, for markets, and for functions. Relevant balances and trade-offs need to be solved differentially for each contingent set of circumstances. For a company's international strategy to be effective, it must respond to such varying contingencies.

How then should the strategic approach of a multi-product, multi-market global company be organized? There is not one response, but a number of responses to this issue and as environmental circumstances change so will the organizational pressures, and the optimal solutions. Figure 23.4 shows the four most common organizational forms in response to each set of global/local contingencies.

There is some confusion in the international business literature over the appropriate term for firms in the bottom left-hand box. Bartlett and Ghoshal (1989) describe the relevant configurations for the global and the international models in terms which fit this box. The difference is that in their view there may be knowledge transfer from the headquarters unit to local companies in the international model, whereas their global model has a mentality that treats overseas operations as no more than delivery pipelines. What we call multi-domestic, Bartlett and Ghoshal call their multinational: a company that operates with strong overseas companies and a largely portfolio mentality.

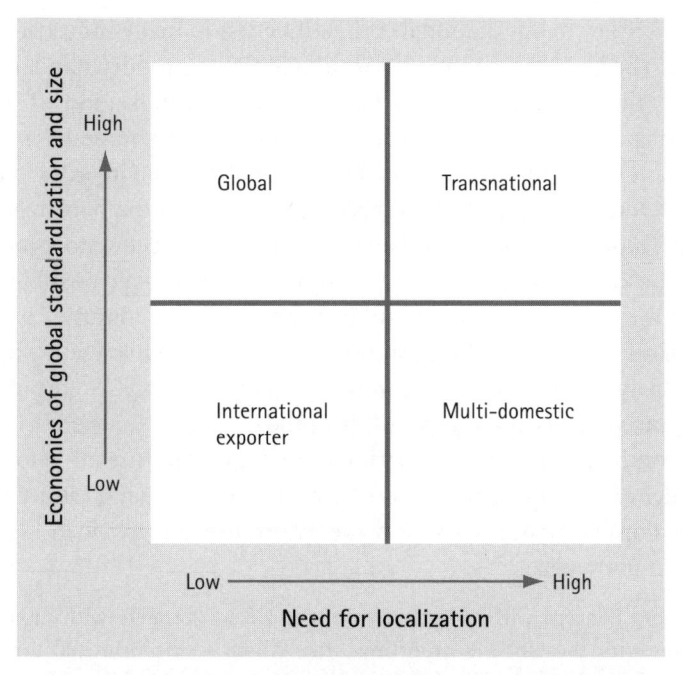

Fig. 23.4 The international corporate structure matrix

We believe that the term 'multinational' should be the umbrella term to describe all company forms that trade internationally, and have a presence in a number of countries. In terms of our matrix this includes the company forms in all boxes of the matrix other than the bottom left-hand box. Let us look at each of the four types in Figure 23.4, starting with the global type.

23.7.1 The Global Company

In the top left-hand box is the *global* company producing standardized products for sale around the world, such as Gillette razors. As a global company, Gillette may not have a major problem. Razor blades need little local adaptation, have an established technological production function, have an easily understandable marketing message, and therefore only sales needs to be handled locally. In this model, the global corporation treats overseas operations as delivery pipelines to a unified global market. Most strategic decisions are centralized at the home country base, and there is tight operational control from the centre. There is likely to be very little adaptation of products to meet local needs. Gillette, Coca-Cola, or Johnson and Johnson's Band-Aid division are all examples of this type of company.

The classical global organization model was one of the earliest international corporate forms that developed, after it became apparent that scale and scope

economies were key to international competitiveness in many industries (Chandler 1962, 1990*b*). The global company built scale facilities to produce standard products, and shipped them worldwide. It is based on the centralization of assets, with overseas demand operations used to achieve global scale in home-base production.

The global corporation may have an international division in order to increase its foreign sales, but the international division is very much the poor relation of the domestic divisions, which are probably further subdivided into product group divisions. The company ships from its home base whenever possible, with very little regard for the differing tastes and preferences of the countries to which it is exporting. This form of organization was typical of the Japanese exporting companies of the 1970s, and is still common in many current US corporations; the Spalding Sport group is an example of this mode.

The predominance in the international strategy literature of a focus on this simple model of the global firm is criticized by Yetton, Davis, and Craig (1995). They target Porter's (1990) work, and the assumptions implicit in his 'diamond' framework in particular:

> Porter's primary concern with the capacity of the US to compete with Japan leads to a preoccupation with the globally exporting firm, which is the principal form by which Japanese manufacturing firms have competed internationally. He focuses not on the complexity of international operations, but on the characteristics of the home base market as a platform for a successful export strategy. Consequently the global MNC is his primary interest.

23.7.2 The International Exporter

By contrast, the firm in the bottom left-hand box, the *international exporter*, may not even think of itself as an international company. It exports opportunistically. Domestic customers are its lifeblood, but it will sell abroad if approached by an international customer, and in times of recession, when overcapacity looms, it may actively solicit international sales to fill its factories. Generally, however, the percentage of its home-based production exported is low, as a percentage of total sales. For many companies this may indeed be a transitional form, as its markets internationalize.

23.7.3 The Multi-domestic Corporation

In the bottom right-hand box is the *multi-domestic* company. Its key characteristics are that of a portfolio of independent subsidiaries, one per country. Such a firm adopts country-centred strategies, and there is relatively little international

coordination. To survive as a multi-domestic, it is important that there be unique product features required per country market and few opportunities for scale economies, since if such economies do exist in large measure the domestic subsidiary will be out-competed by the integrated global firm. In a rapidly globalizing world, traditional multi-domestic firms are becoming rarer, since producing on a global scale and getting local acceptance for a global product are becoming the more powerful competitive stance. An illustration of the old-style multi-domestic is the pre-1970s Philips. The multi-domestic form is sensitive to local needs but may not always achieve possible production scale economies. Although the same company name may be used in all countries in which the firm operates, this may be all that is in common between the various country operations. The products are fashioned to meet local demand and meet local tastes.

A more sophisticated, innovative form of multi-domestic may now be observed in recent years. This *modern multi-domestic* can provide an alternative effective form to the transnational if it concentrates on achieving scale and scope economies that are available to a large corporation. This involves the corporate centre playing a very positive value-adding role to ensure that best practice in one country is successfully transferred to the other countries in which the corporation operates (Anand and Delios 1997). To compete successfully as a multinational organizational form the multi-domestic must of course excel in responding sensitively to local PUV needs. In addition, however, the multi-domestic operates best where the centre is able to establish a degree of 'friendly' competition between country units, where benchmarking is rigorously employed, and where process learning in one country is spread rapidly to the others (Yetton, Davis, and Craig 1995).

Innovation must be similarly spread around the group with vigour, and incentives established for executives to think beyond the confines of their own country business unit for the good of the corporation. Unlike the traditional multi-domestic, the successful modern multi-domestic also has an active centre which carries out its selection task carefully, only entering markets where there is a clear demand for its (standard) products. In Yetton, Davis, and Craig's (1995) words:

Successful multi-domestic corporations de-couple the local, constrained product responsiveness from the global, integrated process and production platforms and manage them separately. In addition they minimize the risk by entering only friendly rather than relatively hostile markets, and outsourcing the local responsibilities to the local management.

This may be through an acquisition by takeover or a joint venture partner.

Traditional multi-domestic forms that sacrifice production economies of scale, yet do not achieve economies of scope, or of learning, innovation, and process do now increasingly appear to be an endangered species. The Philips Group was an example of such a company prior to its repeated reorganizations from the late 1980s on. Management at the centre regarded overseas operations as a portfolio of independent businesses, and the corporate centre did not add value, as in other

MNC organizational forms, including the modern multi-domestic, it is in a unique position to do.

23.7.4 The Transnational Organization Form

Bartlett and Ghoshal (1989) suggested the concept of the '*transnational*' enterprise, a modern form for the MNC with some of the loose network characteristics of a strategic alliance, although ownership is all within the same firm. It is located in the top right-hand box of the Figure 23.4 matrix. Although it does have some home-based exports, it also has a high percentage of foreign production. However, it is not strongly directed from the home-base country. As Bartlett and Ghoshal (1989) explain: 'Managers are being forced to shift their thinking from the traditional task of controlling a hierarchy to managing a network.' The transnational organization seeks to overcome the weaknesses of more traditional models, by moving beyond the global integration/local responsiveness trade-off implicit in the traditional models. To be globally competitive now requires both. Bartlett and Ghoshal (1989, 1990, 1993) have argued that all MNCs must now be locally responsive, with learning as a key requirement for success, whilst also achieving optimal global scale and scope efficiencies. This can only be done by adopting new attitudes to capture knowledge from all parts of the MNC organization and enable it to pass in all directions as appropriate. They also support Ohmae's (1989) view of the desirability of a 'borderless' mindset within the firm. It should be global in mindset rather than, say, a Japanese or US company with foreign subsidiaries. It may indeed have three or more head offices like NEC, as suggested by Nonaka (1989).

To succeed, the transnational form must integrate three flows: first, the company has to coordinate its internal flow of parts, components, and finished goods; second, it must manage the flow of funds, skills, and other scarce resources among units; third, it must link the flow of intelligence, ideas, and knowledge that are central to its innovation and learning capabilities. The transnational may exist more as an aspirational form than a real one as yet, although some organizations such as the Swedish/Swiss ABB or the Japanese NEC are often quoted as examples of the form, and perhaps McKinsey, the management consultancy. It is however the model which attempts to show the real complexity of the optimal coordination processes to achieve global competitive advantage for an MNC. The transnational represents a truly international enterprise, neither owned in one country, nor controlled from one unified corporate headquarters. It is therefore a genuine attempt to find a modern style of MNC capable of embracing the management of complexity, diversity, and change which is the central issue facing all MNCs.

Box 23.1 McKinsey: a mini-case

Few companies meet all the criteria for the pure stereotypes, and there are transitional paths whereby companies restructure themselves from one form to another to meet the changing needs of their global market. The following illustration may help however to clarify the mindsets behind each of the four stylized forms. We use the international strategy consulting firm McKinsey as our illustrative case.

Let us suppose that a financial services company in the City of London approaches the McKinsey London office with a 'request for proposal' mandate for a reorganization study. If this were to have happened in the early 1960s, it may have reached the firm when it was basically an 'international' company (Figure 23.4—bottom left-hand box) The request would have been transmitted to the New York head office. If the proposal were successful, the project would then have been staffed from New York and led by a New York consultant. US analytical models would have been used, largely unadjusted for local conditions, and London people would have been used to provide the necessary local intelligence.

If McKinsey were a 'global' firm (Figure 23.4—top right-hand box), the UK office manager would negotiate the job and global models would be used, i.e. not purely US ones but certainly standardized ones. A New York engagement manager would probably come over with his team to run the study. UK consultants would be invited to New York for training and socialization in the ways and products of the firm. This was largely the situation when the author was a member of the firm in the early 1970s.

If the firm were a largely multi-domestic company (Figure 23.4—bottom right-hand box), the McKinsey name would be used to get the study, but it would then be staffed and run from London, developing a specifically British solution of a bespoke nature without necessarily any contact with the United States. The performance of the London office would be judged by its sales and profits record. Firm-wide training programmes would not be held.

Currently, by the late 1990s however, McKinsey fits fairly closely with the criteria for a transnational firm (Figure 23.4—top right-hand box). In this case there is complex multi-path information flow globally. Projects are staffed from wherever the expertise exists worldwide within the firm. Centres of excellence in particular specialist areas have developed around the world, led by expert individuals and teams. Technological and marketing centres of gravity move, often as a result of forces exogenous to the corporation, in search of any better fit (even if only short term) with particular markets.

In our imaginary illustration the City assignment would be negotiated from London with an international expert on hand. It would then be internationally staffed with the 'best' resources available who would be personally 'bonded' by their identification with the firm culture as developed in particular through international training meetings and work on international project teams. The recommendations would be sensitively tailored to the specific situation but based on firmwide expertise and experience.

Formal organization charts are only one aspect of what binds the transnational organization together. It is held together more strongly by managerial decision-making processes, which depend on information flows. Bartlett and Ghoshal

believe it is not a new organizational form as such that will be needed to meet future global competition, but instead, a new philosophy towards achieving global competitive advantage by transforming existing thinking about local differentiation and global learning in the global enterprise. Clearly, the transnational is a new and more sophisticated concept than earlier organizational forms for the international enterprise. With its emphasis on a network philosophy and the absence of domination by a home-country-based head office, the philosophy can embrace equally well the enterprise based on a network of alliances as it can the integrated corporation. It can be seen, for example, in the approach taken by Fujitsu of Japan to the development of the global Fujitsu 'family' of companies.

Interestingly a similar philosophy is emerging amongst strategic theorists in Japan. Nonaka (1989) talks of the need to manage globalization as a self-renewing process in which information is the key to success. 'Globalization comes about through the interaction of articulated globalized knowledge and tacit localized knowledge, partly through the hybridization of personnel and consequent internalization of learning' (Nonaka 1989).

Nonaka calls this 'compressive management', an interesting echo of Ansoff's (1990) 'accordion' management, similarly devised to deal with the uncertainties of the modern turbulent environment. This process can also lead quite acceptably to a hybridization of the company's headquarters, with perhaps one headquarters in Japan, another in the United States, and maybe a third in Europe. As Contractor and Lorange (1988) have pointed out: 'One model of the MNC sees it as a closed internalized administrative system that straddles national boundaries. An alternative paradigm is to view the international firm as a member of various open and shifting coalitions, each with a specific strategic purpose.'

There is considerable congruity between the philosophical standpoints of Bartlett and Ghoshal, of Contractor and Lorange, and of Nonaka in their rejection for the future of the rigid hierarchy of the traditional MNC, strongly controlled from its home base, even when allowing for local product variation. A world of sometimes shifting but continually renewing informal networks, cross-border partnerships and teams, and strategic alliances, fits well within this philosophy.

23.8 TRANSITIONAL PATHWAYS OF DEVELOPMENT

The development from one international organizational form to another is not merely dependent on the industrial environment, it is also dependent upon

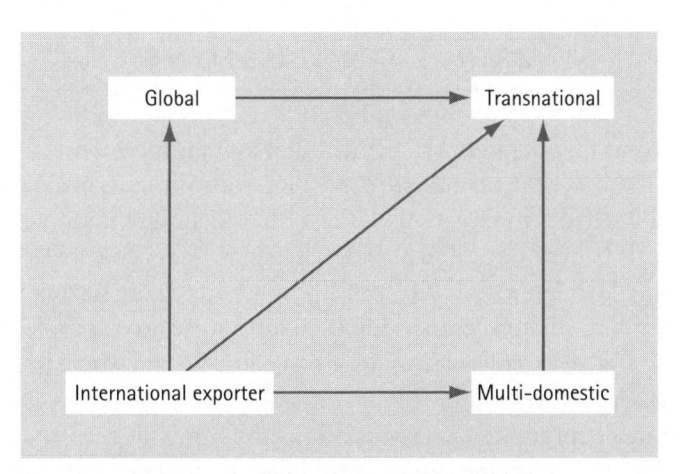

Fig. 23.5 Common organizational forms

how the corporation is currently organized; most forms can be transitional. The arrows on the matrix in Figure 23.5 illustrate the most common directions of transition.

The transition from international exporter to global, and then on to transnational, is perfectly possible as the need for local adjustments becomes apparent as a key requirement for international success. Similarly, a multi-domestic can become a transnational as the country units develop a recognition of, and uses for, each other's skills and abilities, and as shifts in various markets create a need for greater scale economies in certain areas (Malnight 1996).

Transition from a global to a transnational form is also feasible. This shift is about moving from simple global to complex global responses to greater complexity across markets, and less tolerance for simple standardized global products and services. It is also a more efficient use of scarce resources if the organization has the internal capabilities to manage this complex process effectively.

Some transitions would be more improbable. A multi-domestic would find transmutation into a global company or an international one with the required standardization very traumatic, and the corporation might find extreme difficulty in surviving the trauma. Should the transnational form be found to be strategically inappropriate it would also be very difficult to move from a transnational mindset into any of the more centralized hierarchical forms, which are structured to provide lower levels of personal autonomy. However, all four forms need not be transitional. In a more stable environment, they may each represent the optimal organizational form, at least for a period of time.

23.9 Conclusions

It is suggested in this chapter that a firm will adopt an international strategy if it believes that it can achieve a competitive position with any of its businesses in any of the countries it decides to target. Also it will do so if an international strategy will provide it with better ways of achieving efficiency, managing risks, or enabling innovation and learning within the firm. Ghoshal's (1987) organizing framework is helpful in deciding what potential sources of advantage are available for different international strategy configurations, where to compete and where to locate different value chain activities.

Although in all corporate strategy decisions the firm will need to carry out the tasks of selecting, resourcing, and controlling, in carrying out those tasks for international corporate strategy, a greater number of factors would need to be considered, related to both patterns of demand and sources of supply. In relation to basic costs or potential costs, it will need to carefully consider transport (including insurance) costs, and the costs of hedging against the movement of exchange rates. In terms of its overall strength compared with local companies and other international companies operating in the target countries, it will need to evaluate the strength of the various components of its national diamond (Porter 1990) as a source of potential advantage or disadvantage.

The possible relationships between the configuration of the activities of an MNC and how it manages their coordination are critical to its success. In order to consider how to configure and coordinate its activities internationally, Dunning's OLI framework will assist in determining what activities should be carried out at home, and what in other countries. Finally, in coordinating and controlling activities it will need to consider the steps necessary to become an organization structured to succeed in a world with increasingly regionalized or globalized markets, achieving optimal levels of efficiencies, knowledge transfer, and local product sensitivities. In terms of product or service adaptation, it must review the practicalities and costs involved in such organizational adaptation. There is no simple solution offered here. The transnational form, and the modern process-integrated multi-domestic, provide alternative solutions to the fundamental problem of configuring global integration to achieve the optimal levels of scale and scope economies coupled with sensitive local responsiveness. The centralized, standardized global organization still has a powerful role to play meeting clear universal needs.

These frameworks, of course, describe contrasting paradigms. Few actual MNCs fit neatly into one or another. Indeed the decision of where to locate and how to manage each function will be made by the MNC's top management on the basis of contingent circumstances and specific cost-benefit trade-offs. The likelihood of their arriving at a precise organizational form which fits neatly into one of the

particular 'boxes' we have described is low. However, each of these paradigms, describing the different organizational forms, is appropriate for certain specific conditions and offers certain advantages for those conditions.

REFERENCES

ANAND, J., and DELIOS, A. (1997). 'Location Specificity and the Transferability of Down-stream Assets to Foreign Subsidiaries'. *Journal of International Business Studies*, 28/3: 579–604.

ANSOFF, H. T. (1990). *Implementing Strategic Management* (2nd edn.). Hemel Hempstead: Prentice-Hall.

BARTLETT, C. A. (1986). 'Building and Managing the Transnational: The New Organizational Challenge', in M. Porter, *Competition in Global Industries*. Boston: Harvard Business School Press.

——and GHOSHAL, S. (1989). *Managing across Borders*. London: Hutchinson.

————(1990). 'Matrix Management: Not a Structure, a Frame of Mind'. *Harvard Business Review*, July–Aug.: 138–45.

————(1993). 'Beyond the M-Form: Toward a Managerial Theory of the Firm'. *Strategic Management Journal*, 14/Special Issue (Winter): 23–46.

BARWISE, P., and ROBERTSON, T. (1992). 'Brand Portfolios.' *European Management Journal*, 10/3: 277–85.

BIRKINSHAW, J., MORRISON, A., and HULLAND, J. (1995). 'Structural and Competitive Determinants of a Global Integration Strategy'. *Strategic Management Journal*, 16: 637–55.

BJORKMAN, I. (1989). 'Foreign Direct Investments: An Organizational Learning Perspective'. Working paper, Swedish School of Economics and Business Administration, Helsinki.

BOWMAN, C., and FAULKNER, D. (1997). *Competitive and Corporate Strategy*. London: Irwin Books.

BUCKLEY, P. J., and CASSON, M. C. (1998a). 'Models of the Multinational Enterprise'. *Journal of International Business Studies*, 29/1: 21–44.

————(1998b). 'Analysing Foreign Market Entry Strategies: Extending the Internationalization Approach'. *Journal of International Business Studies*, 29/3: 539–62.

CHANDLER, A. D. (1962). *Strategy and Structure*. Cambridge, Mass.: MIT Press.

——(1990a). 'The Enduring Logic of Industrial Success'. *Harvard Business Review*, Mar.–Apr.: 130–40.

——(1990b). *Scale and Scope: The Dynamics of Industrial Capitalism*. Boston: Harvard University Press.

CONTRACTOR, F. J., and LORANGE, P. (eds.) (1988). 'Why Should Firms Cooperate?: The Strategy and Economic Basis for Cooperative Ventures', in *Cooperative Strategies in International Business*. Boston: Lexington Books.

DUNNING, J. H. (1974). *Economic Analysis and the Multinational Enterprise*. London: Allen and Unwin.

——(1998). 'Location and the MNE: A Neglected Factor?'. *Journal of International Business Studies*, 29/1: 45–66.

GHOSHAL, S. (1987). 'Global Strategy: An Organising Framework'. *Strategic Management Journal*, 8/5: 425–40.

—— and NOHRIA, N. (1993). 'Horses for Courses: Organizational Forms for Multinational Corporations'. *Sloan Management Review*, Winter: 23–35.

JOHANSON, J., and VAHLNE, J. (1977). 'The Internationalisation Process of the Firm: A Model of Knowledge Development on Increasing Foreign Commitments'. *Journal of International Business Studies*, Spring–Summer: 23–32.

KOGUT, B. (1985). 'Designing Global Strategies: Comparative and Competitive Value Added Chains'. *Sloan Management Review*, 26/4: 15–28.

LEVITT, T. (1983). 'The Globalisation of Markets'. *Harvard Business Review*, May–June: 92–102.

MAKHIJA, M. V., KIM, K., and WILLIAMSON, S. D. (1997). 'Measuring Globalization of Industries Using a National Industry Approach: Empirical Evidence across Five Countries and over Time'. *Journal of International Business Studies*, 28/4: 679–711.

MALNIGHT, T. W. (1996). 'The Transition from Decentralized to Network-Based MNC Structures: An Evolutionary Perspective'. *Journal of International Business Studies*, 27/1: 43–65.

MELIN, L. (1992). 'Internationalization as a Strategy Process'. *Strategic Management Journal*, 13/Special Issue (Winter): 99–118.

NONAKA, I. (1989). 'Managing Globalisation as a Self-Renewing Process: Experience of Japanese Multinationals'. Paper presented to Oxford colloquium, Templeton College, May.

OHMAE, K. (1985). *Triad Power: The Coming Shape of Global Competition*. New York: Free Press.

—— (1989). 'Managing in a Borderless World'. *Harvard Business Review*, May–June: 152–61.

PERLMUTTER, H. V. (1969). 'The Tortuous Evolution of the MNC'. *Columbia Journal of World Business*, 4: 9–18.

PORTER, M. E. (ed.) (1986). *Competition in Global Industries*. Boston: Harvard Business School Press.

—— (1990). *The Competitive Advantage of Nations*. London: Macmillan Press.

PRAHALAD, C. K., and DOZ, Y. (1987). *The Multinational Mission*. New York: Free Press.

RUGMAN, A. M., LECRAW, D. J., and BOOTH, L. D. (1985). *International Business: Firm and Environment*. New York: McGraw-Hill.

STOPFORD, J. M., and WELLS, L. (1972). *Managing the Multinational Enterprise*. London: Longmans.

VERNON, R. (1966). 'International Investment and International Trade in the Product Cycle'. *Quarterly Journal of Economics*, May: 190–207.

YETTON, P., DAVIS, J., and CRAIG, J. (1995). 'Redefining the Multi-Domestic: A New Ideal Type MNC'. Working paper 95–016 Australian Graduate School of Management, Sydney, NSW.

CHAPTER 24

STRATEGIES FOR MULTINATIONAL ENTERPRISES

ALAN M. RUGMAN

ALAIN VERBEKE

24.1 THE PORTER GLOBAL STRATEGIES

PORTER (1980) has argued that a generic strategy consists of two major choices. First, with regard to the type of competitive advantage being pursued, the choice is between low cost and differentiation. Second, is the choice of the firm's competitive scope, which reflects the breadth of its target market segments; the alternatives are a broad target, covering a whole industry and a narrow target, including only specific segments within an industry.

Based on these two parameters, Porter (1980) has distinguished among three generic strategies: cost leadership, differentiation, and focus. 'Generic strategy' requires a fundamental choice, whether intended or realized, made among alternative patterns of decisions and actions, with a substantial effect on an organization's functioning and performance.

These three types of basic business strategies are known in the business school literature as Porter's three 'generics'. A useful way to visualize these three strategies is in the matrix of Figure 24.1.

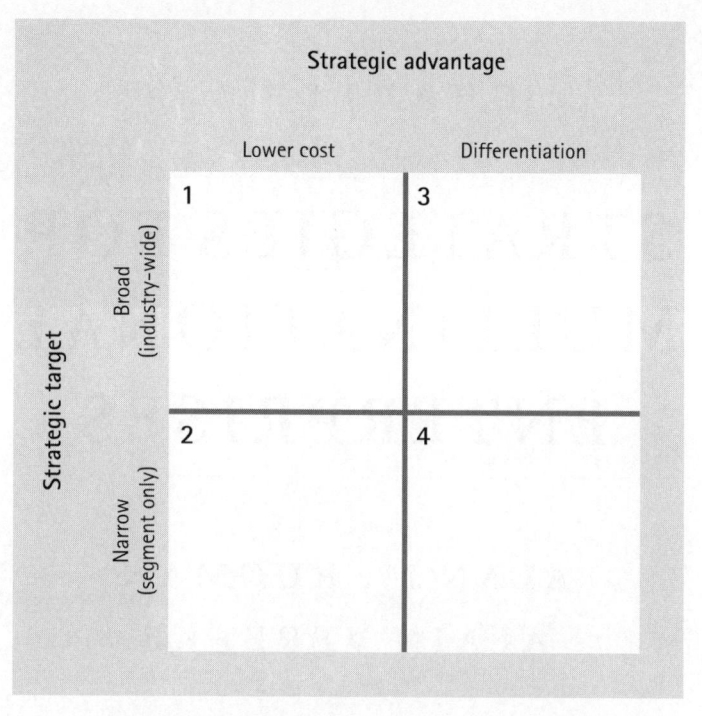

Fig. 24.1 Porter's three generic strategies
Source: Porter (1980, 1985).

With the two axes, for strategic advantage (based on low cost or differentiation) and strategic target (scope of the product line; broad or narrow), it is possible to illustrate the three generic strategies, i.e. quadrant 1 for cost leadership and quadrant 3 for differentiation, with quadrants 2 and 4 for narrow (niched) product lines. There are, in fact, two subcategories of niches; focus-cost in quadrant 2 and focus-differentiation in quadrant 4. To operationalize these generic strategies requires that managers identify the source of their firms' competitive advantage, being aware of how these 'core competencies' are to be created and managed over time.

Porter (1986) has extended this generic strategies framework to take account of the complexities of global competition. Porter states that international strategy is primarily an issue of geographic scope. Porter defines a global industry as one 'in which a firm's competitive position in one country is significantly affected by its position in other countries or vice versa' (Porter 1986: 18). This work suggests that there are in fact four dimensions of competitive scope as shown in Figure 24.2:

(1) segment scope (the range of segments the firm serves);
(2) industry scope (the range of related industries the firm competes in with a coordinated strategy);
(3) vertical scope (the activities performed by the firm instead of by suppliers and channels);

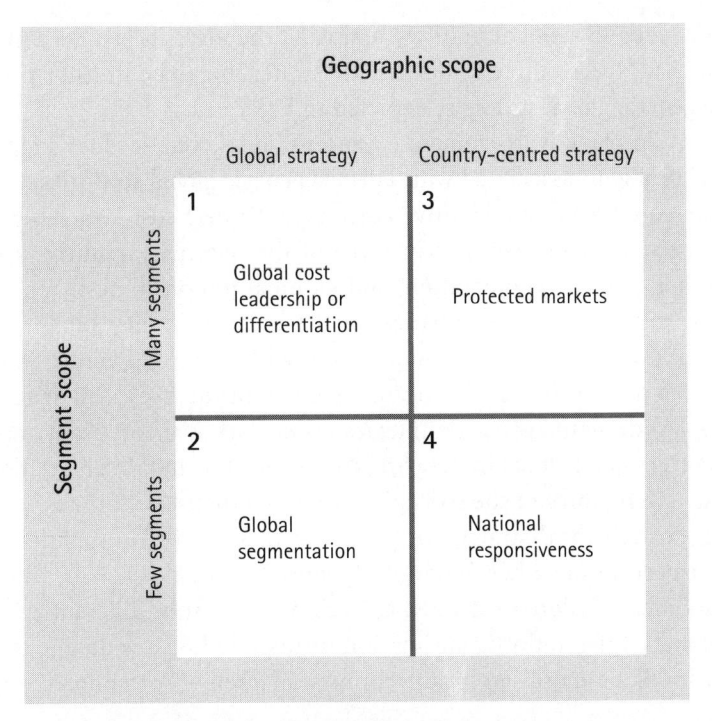

Fig. 24.2 Porter's global strategies

Source: Porter, (1986: 46).

(4) geographic scope (the geographic regions in which the firm operates with a coordinated strategy) (Porter 1986: 22).

Porter's (1986) framework leads to four strategic alternatives for a global industry: global cost leadership or differentiation in quadrant 1; global segmentation in quadrant 2; protected markets in quadrant 3; or what he calls 'national responsiveness' in quadrant 4. Global cost leadership and global differentiation are defined by Porter as 'seeking the cost or differentiation advantages of global configuration/ coordination through selling a wide line of products to buyers in all or most significant country markets' (Porter 1986: 47). Global segmentation is viewed as 'serving a particular industry segment worldwide'.

24.2 THE FIVE GENERIC GLOBAL STRATEGIES

Rugman and Verbeke (1993*a*) and Rugman (1996) have demonstrated how Porter's generic strategies framework can be extended to take into account the issue of

geographic scope in a global industry. Using all the ideas in Figures 24.1 and 24.2, they show that Porter's three initial generic strategies can be transformed into the set of five generic global strategies depicted in Figure 24.3.

This is a simple way to integrate Porter's ideas, but it does highlight two conceptual problems associated with Porter's generic global strategies.

First, the core type of competitive advantage, namely cost leadership or differentiation, becomes indeterminate in three of the five cases, namely: a protected market strategy, global segmentation, and national responsiveness. Yet, in Porter's framework, firms may become 'stuck in the middle' if they pursue both cost leadership and differentiation simultaneously within the chosen geographic and/ or market segment niche. As this occurs in three of the five cases, it implies that Porter's (1980) domestic generic strategies framework is theoretically inconsistent with the Porter (1986) global framework; cost leadership and differentiation cannot distinguish among three of the strategies in the international context.

Second, Porter's third strategy of protected markets is incompatible with the efficiency aspects of the other four global generic strategies. Global cost leadership and global differentiation are defined as 'seeking the cost or differentiation advantages of global configuration/coordination through selling a wide line of products to buyers in all or most significant country markets' (Porter 1986: 47). Global

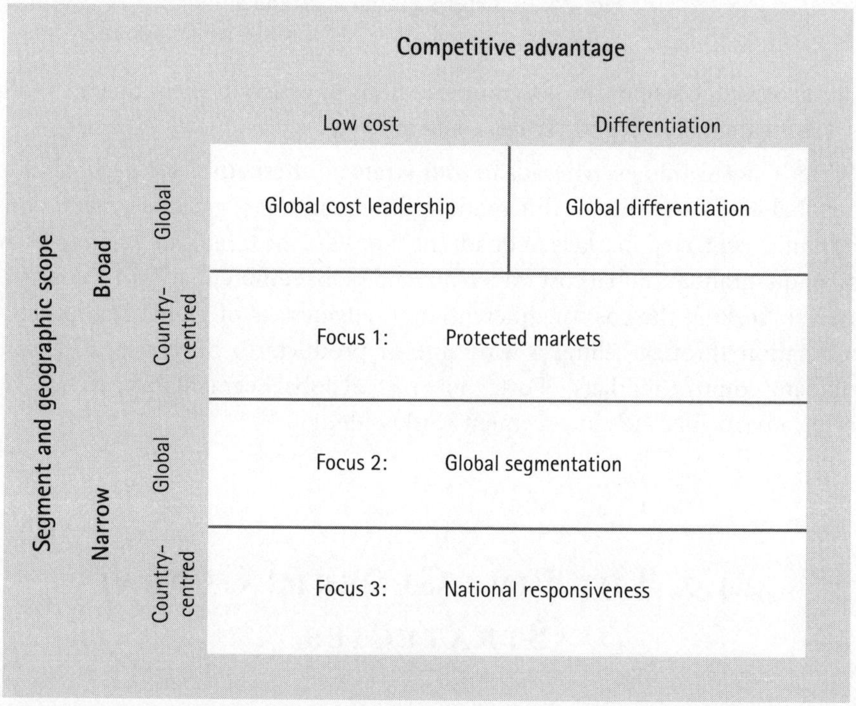

Fig. 24.3 Porter's extended generic strategies framework for global industries

segmentation is viewed as 'serving a particular industry segment worldwide'. National responsiveness for a firm is a 'focus on those industry segments most affected by local country differences though the industry as a whole is global' and it meets 'unusual local needs in products, channels and marketing practices in each country, foregoing the competitive advantages of a global strategy' Porter (1986: 48).

In each of these four cases, efficiency, as measured by relative output/input differentials throughout the value chain, determines a firm's economic performance in terms of survival, profitability, and growth. In contrast, as Porter (1986: 48) recognizes himself, 'protected markets strategies lack a competitive advantage in economic terms, their choice depends on a sophisticated prediction about future government behaviour'. This demonstrates that Porter's extended framework of five generic global strategies based upon two parameters (scope and type of efficiency driven competitive advantage) should not really include the protected market strategy. Thus, a better framework for global strategies is required. We develop this in the next section.

24.3 FIRM-SPECIFIC ADVANTAGES AS GLOBAL STRATEGIES

Rugman and Verbeke (1990, 1992a) and Rugman (1996) have demonstrated that the development and use of firm-specific advantages (FSAs), or the lack of them, reflects the truly generic strategies between which firms need to make a choice in each identifiable pattern of decisions and actions. FSAs include both proprietary know-how (unique assets) and transactional advantages with potential cost reducing and/or differentiation enhancing effects. In a number of cases, it may be difficult to assess the actual impact of an FSA, in terms of cost reduction or differentiation enhancement. Rugman and Verbeke (1991a) have suggested that in such cases, the contribution of an FSA to 'infrastructure development' of the firm should be considered. All strategies that build upon such FSAs or aim to develop new ones are classified as efficiency-based.

24.3.1 Shelter-based Strategies

In contrast, strategies that do not build upon FSAs to achieve a satisfactory economic performance in terms of survival, profitability, growth, or any other

goal considered relevant by decision-makers are classified as non-efficiency-based or 'shelter'-based. If the economic performance of a firm or set of firms does not result from FSAs with cost reducing, differentiation enhancing, or infrastructure building characteristics, this performance must result from 'shelter'-based behaviour.

Shelter-based behaviour reflects instances where firms (a) attempt to impose 'artificial' costs or barriers to differentiation upon (foreign) rivals through government regulation (e.g. tariff and non-tariff barriers) or (b) reduce the market incentives for cost reduction, differentiation enhancement or infrastructure building themselves (e.g. collusive behaviour and cartel formation aimed primarily at exploiting the consumer) or limit the potential effects of these incentives (e.g. government subsidies). In both cases, such strategies may lead to the elimination of workable competition.

Shelter-based strategies are especially significant in the international business context, where firms located in a particular nation may convince public policy-makers that protectionist measures will lead to higher economic welfare in terms of value-added creation or to a special type of public good in terms of the creation of domestic control over strategic sectors, technological spill-over effects, etc. This occurs even where such public goods may be nonexistent or where shelter leads to a substantial reduction in consumer welfare. Rugman and Verbeke (1991b and 1991c) and Rugman (1996) have demonstrated that such strategies may even subvert policies aimed at achieving a level playing field and fair trade, as now frequently occurs in the United States and the European Union.

24.3.2 Efficiency-based Strategies

The distinction between an efficiency-based strategy and a shelter-based strategy is truly fundamental because each strategy builds upon different intellectual premisses as to what constitutes the source of success. In the case of an efficiency-based strategy, consumer sovereignty ultimately determines whether or not the firm will be successful (except in the case of natural monopolies, which do not exist in international business). Strong economic performance reflects the successful creation of value for customers. In contrast, shelter-based strategies reflect behaviour that reduces value of customers, as compared to the situation where efficiency-based strategies would prevail.

The importance of distinguishing between these two types of strategy results from the fact that different 'weapons' are used and different 'rules of the game' are followed in each case. More specifically, firms pursuing a conventional efficiency-based strategy, but faced with shelter-seeking rivals, may suffer in the short run, compared to a situation where all competitors would be engaged in efficiency-based

behaviour. In the short run, shelter-based behaviour will reduce the possibilities for rivals not engaged in such behaviour to exploit their FSAs or develop new ones. Yet, in the long run, shelter obviously works against the firms that build their economic performance on it. Rugman and Verbeke (1993b) and Rugman (1996) explore the ten main reasons why shelter-based strategies may fail in the long run. Further discussion of shelter-based strategies occurs in Box 24.1, while Box 24.2 gives an example of this issue.

Box 24.1 Shelter-based strategies

In practice, it may not always be easy for outside observers to classify a specific pattern of decisions and actions as efficiency-based or shelter-based. There are five main dimensions to consider: need, managerial intent, organizational routines, outcome, and impact on performance.

First, shelter-based strategies are used in international business only as the 'need' arises. This occurs when there is an absence of strong FSAs that would allow firms to beat rivals on the basis of the cost and differentiation characteristics of the products offered. An exception is the case of collusive behaviour when the various firms involved have strong FSAs (e.g. relative to foreign rivals) but attempt to extract rents from consumers through the elimination of competition.

Second, shelter-based behaviour generally results from managerial intentions to engage in such a pattern of decisions and actions but may still contain an emerging component.

Third, specific organizational routines resulting in lobbying efforts may increase the probability of shelter-based behaviour.

Fourth, as in the case of efficiency-based strategies, the goals pursued may not be achieved.

Fifth, government may refuse to provide shelter, thus affecting the firm's performance.

Source: Rugman and Verbeke 1990, 1991b.

Box 24.2 The global shipbuilding industry

The study by Sung Cho Dong and Porter (1986) on the global shipbuilding industry demonstrates Porter's extended generic strategies framework. This analysis demonstrates that firms in the United Kingdom were not able to achieve a satisfactory economic performance after the mid-1950s in spite of strong government intervention in the form of subsidies. In contrast, alleged protected markets strategies in Japan after World War II led to a global cost leadership position. The main reason is that in the United Kingdom and many other European nations, government support was used to provide shelter, i.e. it was not intended and did not lead to a more efficient exploitation of existing firm-specific advantages (FSAs) or the development of new ones. In other words, government support acted as an artificial substitute for strong FSAs, and often resulted from firm lobbying. In contrast, Japanese government support programmes were always intended

Box 24.2 (Continued)

to develop new FSAs and to foster the long run cost competitiveness/differentiation position of Japanese yards. In Japan, government support was used by shipbuilding companies as a complement to their existing FSAs and as a stimulus to generate new ones. These firms pursued efficiency-based strategies.

Source: Rugman and Verbeke 1990, 1992*a*.

24.4 A Framework for Strategies of Multinational Enterprises

Much of the international business literature suggests that, within the efficiency-based patterns of decisions and actions, two parameters can be used to distinguish fundamental subcategories of behaviour, as shown in Figure 24.4. Using the above analysis we can generate the two axes for Figure 24.4; number of home bases and the type of firm-specific advantage (FSA).

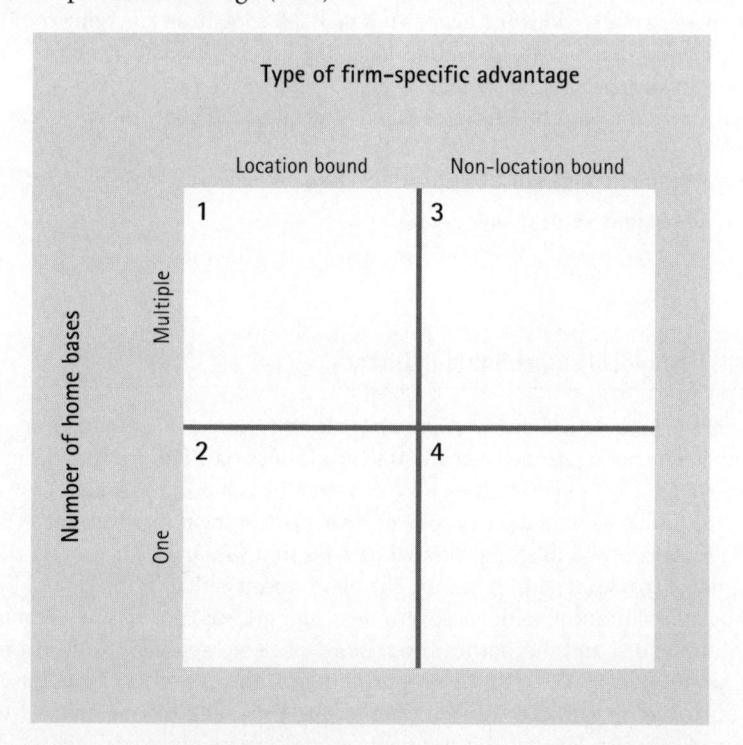

Fig. 24.4 Principal categories of efficiency-based strategies

24.4.1 Firm-specific Advantages

The horizontal axes represents the type of FSAs to be developed or exploited, Rugman and Verbeke (1992*b*) and Rugman (1996). An important distinction exists between location bound FSAs (LB-FSAs) and non-location bound FSAs (NLB-FSAs). The former benefit a company only in a particular location (or set of locations), and lead to benefits of national responsiveness. In the context of international business operations, these LB-FSAs cannot be effectively transferred as an intermediate output (e.g. a tangible or intangible asset) or embodied in the final outputs of the organization, to be sold across borders. In contrast, NLB-FSAs are easily transferred and exploited abroad, whether in the form of intermediate outputs or embodied in final outputs. They lead to benefits of integration in terms of economies of scale and scope and exploitation of national differences. Many authors, including Bartlett (1986), Bartlett and Ghoshal (1989), Doz (1986), Ghoshal (1987), Kogut (1985*a*, 1985*b*), Prahalad and Doz (1987), and Roth and Morrison (1990), have provided the intellectual foundations that led to making this important distinction between two fundamentally different types of FSAs, see Rugman and Verbeke (1991*a*, 1992*a*, 1992*b*).

24.4.2 Home Bases

The second axis is related to the number of 'home bases' used by the firm. A 'home base' is defined by Porter (1990) as the nation where the firm retains effective strategic, creative, and technical control. In addition, it is considered central 'to choosing the industries to compete in as well as the appropriate strategy' (see Porter 1990: 599). Rugman and Verbeke (1993*b*) have demonstrated that a firm may actually have several home bases contributing substantially to the development of new FSAs, so as to improve international competitiveness. It is important to distinguish between the existence of a single home base or multiple home bases in the pursuit of international competitiveness, because it reflects the impact of the country-specific advantages (CSAs) of specific locations on strategic behaviour. A single home base implies the dominating impact of one set of national 'diamond' CSAs on the firm's overall competitiveness, both now and in the future. In contrast, a firm with multiple home bases depends upon decisions and actions taken in various locations and upon the characteristics of these locations.

To the extent that the development and exploitation of NLB-FSAs requires coordination of decisions and actions across borders, a single home base implies direct, centralized control of all foreign operations. In contrast, in the case of a global subsidiary mandate, for example, the 'corporate headquarters' role shifts towards 'managing dispersed strategic processes, ensuring that subsidiary strategies

continue to fit the overall corporation goals and providing the resources and freedom required to support the mandates' (Roth and Morrison 1992: 718). In this case, typical home base activities are concentrated in the various nations where subsidiaries have received global subsidiary mandates.

24.4.3 The Four Cases

In Figure 24.4, four important categories of efficiency-based strategies in global industries are described, which are much more fundamental than the Porter ones. Patterns of decisions and actions in quadrant 1 are typical for so-called *multi-national* firms, as defined by Bartlett and Ghoshal (1989). Here, the different operations in various countries are viewed as largely independent and build their performance on strengths in being national responsive. In quadrant 2, competitive-ness results from having only a single home base and building upon FSAs that lead to benefits of national responsiveness. Here, we find *uni-national firms* that attempt to remain competitive vis-à-vis global rivals in one or a limited set of nations. Quadrant 3 reflects strategies aimed at achieving a superior economic performance through using multiple home bases, each of which builds upon NLB-FSAs. Firms with *global subsidiary mandates*, as described by Rugman and Bennett (1982), Poynter and Rugman (1983), Roth and Morrison (1992), typically fall in this quadrant. The main characteristic of Bartlett and Ghoshal's (1989) *transnational solution* is the simultaneous occurrence of patterns of decisions and actions that fit into quadrants 1 and 3 of Figure 24.4.

Finally, quadrant 4 reflects behaviour typical for both the *global firms* and the *international firms* as defined by Bartlett and Ghoshal (1989). *Global firms* attempt to achieve global scale economies by producing primarily in a single country and exporting products globally as these embody the firm's NLB-FSAs. *International firms* pursue international scope economies and/or benefits of exploiting national differences by transferring know-how across borders and/or by coordinating dis-persed activities placed in different optimal locations. The dispersion of value activities implies global rationalization, whereby each subsidiary specializes in a narrow set of activities in the value chain, see Kobrin (1991).

24.4.4 Examples of the Framework

These four types of efficiency-based strategies appear to reflect the various arche-typal firms engaged in international business as portrayed in the relevant literature. They also represent clearly identifiable patterns of decisions and actions in the pursuit of a satisfactory economic performance. These patterns in fact constitute

alternatives among which choices need to be made, e.g. when reacting to an environmental change such as the 'EC 1992' programme or the North American Free Trade Agreement, even within a single strategic business unit (Rugman 1994).

The framework is more relevant for strategic management purposes than the one of Porter (1986) on the configuration (geographically dispersed or concentrated) and coordination (low or high) of activities. A dispersed as opposed to a concentrated configuration of a firm's activities, in general, does not necessarily carry important strategic implications. What is more relevant is to know where and how the core activities are carried out which will determine the development of new FSAs, and which may be substantially affected by CSAs of the locations where they were developed. Similarly, the framework is more relevant for coordination issues. It is more important to know what the resources are of a firm and its rivals, in terms of LB-FSAs and NLB-FSAs that will lead to either benefits of national responsiveness or benefits of integration, than to observe that some of these benefits, especially scope economies and benefits of exploiting national differences, require coordination across borders in order to be realized.

In related work, Chang Moon (1994) has shown that Porter's configuration/coordination framework is conceptually flawed. Porter (1986: 28) argues that a firm with a geographically concentrated coordination configuration of activities and a high international coordination among these activities pursues a simple global strategy. In fact, in the extreme case, the firm with a concentrated configuration of activities is either a uni-national or exporting firm that does not perform activities in other countries, so that there is nothing to be internationally coordinated. In other words, in Porter's matrix, the concentrated configuration/high coordination quadrant is really an empty cell. Porter argues that 'the simplest global strategy is to concentrate as many activities as possible in one country, serve the world from this home base, and tightly coordinate through standardisation those activities that must inherently be performed near the buyer' (1986: 27). The problem with this statement is that it suggests that some activities must always be performed near the buyer. In reality, a virtually complete concentration of activities in one country makes the international coordination issue redundant in global strategic management.

24.5 INTEGRATING THE LITERATURE INTO THE RUGMAN AND VERBEKE FRAMEWORK

This new framework, developed in greater detail in Rugman and Verbeke (1993b) is a general framework of global strategy. Applications of it to the interaction between

government policy and MNE strategy are summarized in Rugman and Verbeke (1998). Applications to networks and subsidiaries are made in Rugman and Verbeke (2001). Three standard mainstream classifications of multinational strategies in the international business literature are also in accordance with the framework. These are the typologies of international business strategies of Ghoshal and Bartlett (1988*a*) and (1988*b*); of Gupta and Govindarajan (1991), and of Ghoshal and Westney (1993). These typologies are based on the role of the foreign subsidiaries in the R&D process.

24.5.1 Ghoshal and Bartlett

Ghoshal and Bartlett's four types of R&D strategies can be fitted into Figure 24.4 based on the analysis of the preceding sections. First, the local-for-local process (quadrant 1); second, the local-for-global and global-for-global approaches (quadrant 3); third, the centre-for-global process (quadrant 4).

24.5.2 Gupta and Govindarajan

The Gupta and Govindarajan typology also fits in Figure 24.4. The local innovator (quadrant 1), the global innovator and integrated player (quadrant 3), and the implementor roles (quadrant 4) of the subsidiaries in the innovation process are again in accordance with our framework. It is interesting to observe that quadrant 3 of Figure 24.4 includes two types from each of the typologies. In our view, the local-for-global (or global innovator) approach is fundamentally very similar to the global-for-global (or integrated player) process, but the latter approach just reflects a more complex process of creating NLB-FSAs through multiple, highly interdependent, rather than semi-autonomous home bases.

24.5.3 Ghoshal and Westney

Several recent descriptions of strategic decision-making patterns in MNEs suggest that many firms are now moving towards a structure that builds upon multiple home bases and requires the simultaneous development of LB-FSAs and NLB-FSAs. This allows an effective response to the dual requirements of national responsiveness and global integration. One of the main characteristics of this structure is that it can consider all factors contributing to these conflicting demands simultaneously

rather than separately. This new organizational form has been given various names, including the 'transnational' (Bartlett 1986), the 'heterarchy' (Hedlund 1986), the 'multifocal firm' (Prahalad and Doz 1987), and the 'multiple headquarters system' (Nonaka 1990).

Ghoshal and Westney (1993) have identified five characteristics of this new type of firm, namely dispersion, interdependence, tight coupling of sub-units, cross-unit learning, and structural flexibility. The *dispersion* aspect precisely reflects the existence of multiple home bases, e.g. in the area of innovation. The presence of multiple home bases implies that the MNE becomes an integrated network of *interdependent* units that must be *tightly coupled* in order to exploit NLB-FSAs across borders. The development and diffusion of new NLB-FSAs becomes a process whereby the different sub-units of the network need to engage in *cross-unit learning*. However, in order to achieve an optimal balance between the creation and exploitation of both LB-FSAs and NLB-FSAs, *structural flexibility* is required. Structural flexibility means that the management process must be able to change from product to product, from country to country, and even from decision to decision (Bartlett 1986).

The requirement to build upon both LB-FSAs and NLB-FSAs in order to achieve global competitive success is now well established. However, the important question remains whether individual firms require specific linkages with their environment to develop and exploit the required resource base, especially in terms of the NLB-FSAs. In other words, is it sufficient to focus on establishing an intra-organizational network with cross-unit learning or is it necessary to develop strategies regarding the management of an inter-organizational network?

24.6 BUSINESS NETWORKS AND GLOBAL COMPETITIVENESS

In spite of a clear evolution in the direction of multiple home bases, a substantial number of MNEs still operate from a single home base, as is reflected in the work of Porter (1990). Given that NLB-FSAs can be initiated in one or many geographical locations, the important question arises whether their development and diffusion throughout the company requires specific linkages with outside actors.

Figure 24.5 represents this managerial focus on an intra-organizational versus inter-organizational network (horizontal axis), in the situation of both a single and multiple home bases (vertical axis).

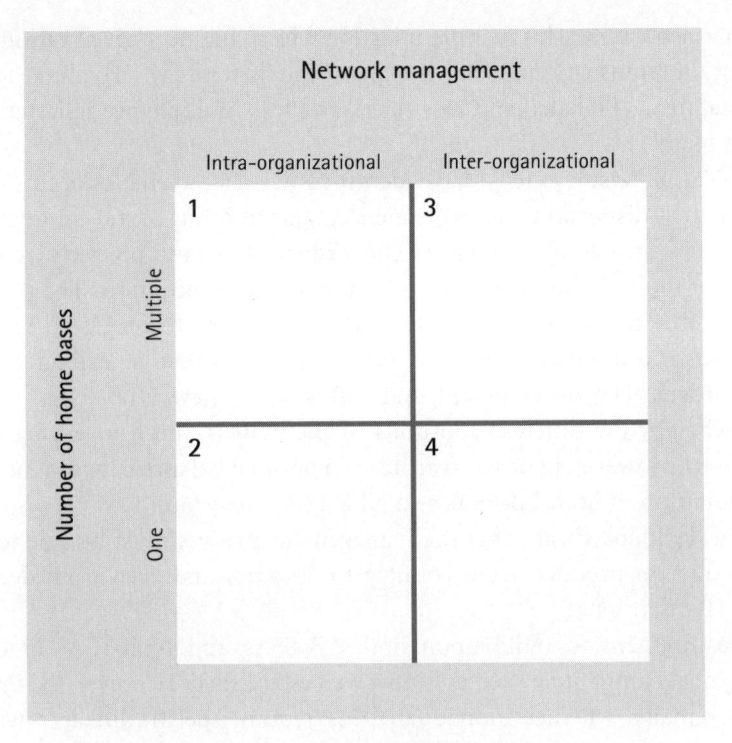

Fig. 24.5 Business networks in international strategic management

24.6.1 MNEs as Hierarchies

The second quadrant (an intra-organizational network and a single home base) reflects a substantial body of primarily economics driven literature on the expansion of hierarchical MNE activity. Vernon's (1966, 1979) product cycle hypothesis; Dunning's (1981) original eclectic paradigm and conventional internalization theory as developed by Buckley and Casson (1976) and Rugman (1981) all attempt to explain the international expansion and success of MNEs building upon the premiss that FSAs are developed in a single location and then diffused internationally through foreign direct investment rather than other entry modes when a number of specific internal conditions (internalization advantages) and external conditions (location advantages) are fulfilled. Williamson's transaction cost approach (1981), building upon the work of Chandler (1962) and Tsurumi (1977), as well as its extensions, see e.g. Teece (1983, 1985), is consistent with this view. The multinational, multidimensional (M) form portrayed in this work describes a very simple intra-organizational network whereby the corporate headquarters organize the firm into semi-autonomous profit units, monitor the (financial) performance of these units, allocate resources to them, and engage in centralized strategic

planning. A clear top down, hierarchical structure is established and no direct interdependences are supposed to exist among sub-units.

24.6.2 MNEs as Networks

Recent extensions of both the eclectic paradigm (Dunning 1988 and 1993*a*) and internalization theory (Rugman and Verbeke 1990 and 1992*b*) have recognized the intra-organizational implications of MNEs functioning with multiple home bases and the limits of the M-form, i.e. quadrant 1 of Figure 24.5. More specifically, in accordance with Hennart (1993), it has been suggested that coordination and control of the internal network should be performed through the use of a mix of hierarchical controls, price controls, and socialization.

Transaction costs associated with operating complex internal networks can be further reduced by introducing procedural justice elements in strategic decision-making processes, see Kim and Mauborgne (1993). Procedural justice appears to be of fundamental importance to achieve attitudes of commitment, trust, and social harmony within the different sub-units of an MNE. This is consistent with the observation of Prahalad and Doz (1987) that 'due process' constitutes a necessary condition for effective strategic decision-making in MNEs.

The complexity of internal network management in the presence of multiple home bases is consistent with the concept of heterarchy as described by Hedlund (1986, 1993) and Hedlund and Rolander (1990). It also explains the rise of several sophisticated coordination and control mechanisms in MNEs (Martinez and Jarillo 1989). This focus on the intra-organizational network of the MNE is sufficient in cases whereby the social context exerts only a limited influence on the sub-units located in different home bases, when they develop new NLB-FSAs.

24.6.3 Inter-organizational Networks

However, the right-hand side of Figure 24.5 takes into account that MNEs may function in complex environments, many elements of which cannot be reduced to the five forces driving industry competition as described in the work of Porter (1980, 1985) on competitive strategy. The influence of the environment on the process of NLB-FSA development in MNEs also requires a richer analysis than the one provided by, e.g. conventional internalization theory where the location advantages characterizing alternative nations or regions are identified, especially within the context of optimal location selection, but where only limited attention is devoted to the dynamic interaction among firm-specific and environmental factors; see Dunning (1993*a*) for an in-depth discussion.

A large body of literature does exist on the creation and management of joint ventures and other types of cooperative agreements in international business, see e.g. Contractor and Lorange (1988), Doz, Prahalad, and Hamel (1990), and Geringer (1991). However, only little has been written on the management of inter-organizational networks with multiple actors in international business, notable exceptions being Dunning (1993*b*) and Westney (1993).

24.6.4 Institutional Theory

Institutionalization theorists have argued that the appropriate level for studying inter-organizational linkages is the so-called 'organizational field', i.e. 'those organizations that, in the aggregate, constitute a recognized area of institutional life: key suppliers, resources and product consumers, regulatory agencies, and other organizations that produce similar services or products' (Westney 1990: 284 and 1993: 56, citing DiMaggio and Powell 1983: 148). The main characteristic of such a network is mutual recognition of the different partners involved. This mutual recognition may lead to isomorphism in cases whereby the different organizations are characterized by resource dependency. Such isomorphism can easily be given a transaction cost interpretation: 'transactions are less costly in time and effort between organizations that are similar' (Westney 1993: 70). If this resource dependency is symmetric, it may lead to the formation of clusters as described by Porter (1990). In the case of asymmetric interdependence, business networks may be formed (see D'Cruz and Rugman 1994; Rugman and D'Cruz 2000).

24.6.5 Porter's Clusters

Porter's (1990) clusters consist of sets of economic actors linked through the elements of the diamond of competitive advantage in a nation (factor conditions, demand conditions, industry characteristics, related and supporting industries). Porter's (1990) work is useful to study the impact of inter-organizational networks on the international competitiveness of firms and industries with a single home base. Although such clusters arise largely unintendedly, as a result of the so-called 'systemic nature of the diamond' (Porter 1990: 148), i.e. the mutual interactions among the various determinants of a single national diamond, it is interesting to observe that Porter focuses primarily on the benefits of these clusters and not on the costs; e.g. as regards the reduction of a firm's autonomy. This is shown in quadrant 4 of Figure 24.5.

Enright (1993) has examined the relationship between localization (geographic concentration) and the coordination of economic activity within industries. He

supports Krugman's (1991) view that there is no single progression or path along which geographically clustered industries evolve. By improving coordination and communication across firms in an industry, localization may influence, but not solely determine, the boundaries of these firms. Enright's case studies of localized industries indicate that surviving industries change organization and coordination mechanisms to reflect changes in the relevant task environment, be they in markets, technology, government involvement, etc. He warns that localized groups of firms will decline if they do not adapt to changing external circumstances. The move towards establishing multiple home bases obviously implies a similar challenge, with MNEs being confronted with fundamentally new environments, as compared to the initial home country environment.

24.6.6 The Flagship Model

Building upon Porter's (1990) cluster framework, Rugman and D'Cruz (2000) have developed the concept of business network as a tool for obtaining a favourable international competitive advantage. This is shown in quadrant 3 of Figure 24.5. This is different from Porter's cluster in two ways: first, the strategic intent of the partners to engage in network formation and second, the asymmetric coordination and control of the network. In their view, a business network consists of a group of firms and non-business institutions competing globally and linked together through resource dependencies. There are five partners in the business network: the flagship firm which is typically a large multinational enterprise, key suppliers, key customers, competitors, and the non-business infrastructure. This last partner includes the service-related sectors, educational and training institutions, the various levels of government, and other organizations such as trade associations, non-governmental organizations, and unions.

The business network is characterized also by the flagship firm's asymmetric strategic control over the network partners in common areas of interest. This asymmetry entails leadership and direction-setting, effectively a 'strategic hand', in setting the priorities of the partners in regard to their participation in the flagship firm's business system. Asymmetric strategic control by the flagship firm is consistent with the idea that international competitiveness demands NLB-FSAs. It is the flagship firm, typically a multinational (MNE), which has the global perspective and resources to lead a business network and to establish the global benchmarks necessary to lead the development of the network. The authors usefully applied this framework to describe international expansion strategies in the telecommunications industry, D'Cruz and Rugman (1994, 2000). However, the important question that is not answered in either of the two frameworks described above is how the form and functioning of inter-organizational networks positioned in

quadrant 4 of Figure 24.5 may be altered, when firms move towards having multiple home bases.

24.6.7 Transnational Networks

In quadrant 3 of Figure 24.5 the main problem facing MNE management thus becomes that each home base may be faced with specific isomorphic pulls that may be conflicting. It is important to realize that the isomorphic pulls faced by a specific sub-unit of an MNE may be entirely unrelated to the development of LB-FSAs in order to become more nationally responsive. The 'local' patterns to be emulated may be those prevailing in subsidiaries of other MNEs or in foreign operations of firms from related and supporting industries. In any case, the process of creating and diffusing NLB-FSAs throughout the intra-organizational network of an MNE may also be influenced by variations in isomorphic pulls arising from inter-organizational linkages. More specifically, in the case of conflicting isomorphic pulls, a local-for-global approach could be established. Here, mimetic isomorphism by each sub-unit in a home base, i.e. its emulation of behavioral patterns considered successful in its specific inter-organizational network, leads to selective coercive isomorphism in the intra-organizational network.

In other words, the activities of sub-units elsewhere in the firm that are dependent on transfers of NLB-FSAs from a particular home base need to conform to what is viewed as legitimate by the sub-unit in that home base. In contrast, in the case of complementarities among isomorphic pulls faced by sub-units in the different home bases, a global-for-global approach when developing new NLB-FSAs may be adopted. Here, it should be emphasized that the relevant isomorphic pulls must not be identical but complementary. Given the existence of complementary versus conflicting isomorphic pulls that characterize the inter-organizational linkages faced by the sub-units in each of the multiple home bases, the question arises what strategies can be pursued by the MNE in order to cope with these external forces.

More specifically, the question is, whether an MNE should simply adopt a reactive strategy, i.e. a strategy of isomorphic flexibility, whereby it attempts to adapt itself as well as possible to existing isomorphic pulls arising from the relevant organizational field in the form of coercive, normative, and or mimetic isomorphism as described by Westney (1993: 55). In this case, isomorphic pulls arising from the external environment largely determine the functioning of the intra-organizational network. An alternative is to change the external network, through a so-called 'institutionalization project' approach. In this case, the intra-organizational network attempts to alter the external network. This problem of optimal 'transnational network' management is explored further in Rugman and Verbeke (1995).

24.7 SUMMARY

Michael Porter's (1980) three generic strategies of cost, differentiation, and focus (in Figure 24.1) were extended by geographic scope and transformed into five generics in the Porter (1986) paper on global strategy, see Figure 24.2. Unfortunately, as shown in Figure 24.3, the resulting strategies are neither global nor generic. One key problem is Porter's peculiar use of the concept of 'national responsiveness'. A new framework for generic strategies was developed in Figure 24.4, in which location bound and non-location bound firm-specific advantages are related to the number of home bases. This generates truly generic strategies for multinational enterprises.

The second half of the chapter developed a new organizing framework to analyse the role of transnational networks in global competition. It demonstrated that the analysis of transnational networks may lead to new insights regarding the sources of sustainable global competitive advantage. Previously, mainstream conceptual models in the international business literature neglected the formation of transnational networks as a condition for global competitiveness. These models, which include the eclectic paradigm (Dunning 1993a), the transnational solution framework (Bartlett and Ghoshal 1989), and the diamond of competitive advantage model (Porter 1990), fail to recognize the major role that transnational networks can fulfil in a context of global competition. The new framework, in Figure 24.4, suggests a classification of transnational network strategies which can incorporate other mainstream literature in international business.

In terms of generic strategies for MNEs, the key problem with the Porter frameworks of domestic competitive strategy (Porter 1980), global strategy (Porter 1986), and the home country diamond of national competitiveness (Porter 1990) is that all of them build upon a single home base. Competitive advantage is achieved by firms using their home base as a staging ground for globalization. Yet, evidence on the activities of MNEs shows that they now operate across multiple home bases rather than the single home base consistent with a Vernon (1966)–Porter (1990) international product cycle approach. In particular, MNEs operate on a triad-regional basis and follow regional rather than global strategies (Rugman 2000). Today, most of the interesting research issues in international business stem from the complexities of organizing an MNE network across multiple home bases (Rugman and Verbeke 2001). The new framework advanced here is a useful starting point for realistic research on MNEs and their network organizational structures.

As shown in Figure 24.5, today, most MNEs function with multiple home bases. The problems faced by these firms to create and diffuse new knowledge go far beyond questions related to solving Porter-type home country–host country conflicts and require finding a balance between developing LB-FSAs and NLB-FSAs. The process of developing NLB-FSAs in an organizational context of multiple home

bases is complicated further by the fact that not only the intra-organizational network must be managed, but also the inter-organizational networks.

Isomorphic pulls arising from inter-organizational linkages in each home base may be conflicting or complementary, as shown in Figure 24.5. The issue is whether an intra-organizational network MNE should adopt a strategy of isomorphic flexibility or make an attempt to alter the external context. Can these two options be pursued simultaneously by a single MNE engaged in transnational network management? Does one option need to be selected, based on the administrative heritage of the intra-organizational network? These organizational issues for MNEs represent some of the unfinished research agenda of international management.

REFERENCES

BARTLETT, C. A. (1986). 'Building and Managing the Transnational: The New Organizational Challenge', in M. Porter (ed.), *Competition in Global Industries*. Boston: Harvard Business School Press, 367–404.

—— and GHOSHAL, S. (1989). *Managing Across Borders: The Transnational Solution*. Boston: Harvard Business School Press.

BUCKLEY, P., and CASSON, M. (1976). *The Future of the Multinational Enterprise*. London: Macmillan.

CHANDLER, A. D. (1962). *Strategy and Structure: Chapters in the History of the Industrial Enterprise*. Cambridge, Mass.: MIT Press.

CONTRACTOR, F. J., and LORANGE, P. (1988). *Cooperative Strategies in International Business*. Lexington, Mass.: Heath and Company.

D'CRUZ, J. R., and RUGMAN, A. M. (1994). 'Business Network Theory and the Canadian Telecommunications Industry'. *International Business Review*, 3/3: 275–88.

DiMAGGIO, P. J., and POWELL, W. W. (1983). 'The Iron Cage Revisited: Institutional Isomorphism and Collective Rationality in Organizational Fields'. *American Sociological Review*, 48: 147–60.

DOZ, Y. (1986). *Strategic Management in Multinational Companies*. Oxford: Pergamon.

—— PRAHALAD, C. K., and HAMEL, G. (1990). 'Control, Change and Flexibility: The Dilemma of Transnational Collaboration', in C. A. Bartlett, Y. Doz, and G. Hedlund (eds.), *Managing the Global Firm*. London: Routledge, 117–43.

DUNNING, J. H. (1981). *International Production and the Multinational Enterprise*. London: George Allen and Unwin.

—— (1988). 'The Eclectic Paradigm of International Production: A Restatement and Some Possible Extensions'. *Journal of International Business Studies*, 19/1: 1–31.

—— (1993a). *Multinational Enterprises and the Global Economy*. New York: Addison-Wesley Publishing Company.

—— (1993b). *The Globalization of Business: The Challenge of the 1990s*. London and New York: Routledge.

ENRIGHT, M. J. (1993). 'The Geographic Scope of Competitive Advantage', Working Paper, Harvard Business School, Mar.

GERINGER, J. M. (1991). 'Strategic Determinants of Partner Selection Criteria in International Joint Ventures'. *Journal of International Business Studies*, 22/1: 41–62.

GHOSHAL, S. (1987). 'Global Strategy: An Organizing Framework'. *Strategic Management Journal*, 8/5: 425–40.

——and BARTLETT, C. A. (1988a). 'Innovation Processes in Multinational Corporations', in M. L. Tushman and W. L. Moore (eds.), *Readings in the Management of Innovation* (2nd edn.). New York: Harper Business, 499–518.

————(1988b). 'Creation, Adoption, and Diffusion of Innovations by Subsidiaries of Multinational Corporations'. *Journal of International Business Studies*, 19/3: 365–88.

——and WESTNEY, D. E. (1993). *Organization Theory and the Multinational Corporation*. New York and London: St Martin's Press.

GUPTA, A. K., and GOVINDARAJAN, V. (1991). 'Knowledge Flows and the Structure of Control within Multinational Corporations'. *Academy of Management Review*, 16/4: 768–92.

HEDLUND, G. (1986). 'The Hypermodern MNC: A Heterarchy?' *Human Resource Management*, 25: 9–35.

——(1993). 'Assumptions of Hierarchy and Heterarchy, with Applications to the Management of the Multinational Corporation', in S. Ghoshal and D. E. Westney (eds.), *Organization Theory and the Multinational Corporation*. London: St Martin's Press, 211–36.

——and ROLANDER, D. (1990). 'Actions in Heterarchies: New Approaches to Managing the MNC', in C. A. Bartlett, Y. Doz, and G. Hedlund (eds.), *Managing the Global Firm*. London: Routledge, 15–46.

HENNART, J. F. (1993). 'Control in Multinational Firms: The Role of Price and Hierarchy', in S. Ghoshal and D. E. Westney (eds.), *Organization Theory and the Multinational Corporation*. New York and London: St Martin's Press, 157–81.

KIM, W. CHAN, and MAUBORGNE, R. (1993). 'Procedural Justice Theory and the Multinational Corporation', in S. Ghoshal and D. E. Westney (eds.), *Organization Theory and the Multinational Corporation*. New York and London: St Martin's Press, 237–55.

KOBRIN, S. (1991). 'An Empirical Analysis of the Determinants of Global Integration'. *Strategic Management Journal*, 12/Special Issue: 17–31.

KOGUT, B. (1985a). 'Designing Global Strategies: Comparative and Competitive Value-Added Chains'. *Sloan Management Review*, Summer: 15–28.

——(1985b). 'Designing Global Strategies: Profiting from Operational Flexibility'. *Sloan Management Review*, Fall: 27–38.

KRUGMAN, P. (1991). *Geography and Trade*. London: MIT Press.

MARTINEZ, J., and JARILLO, J. C. (1989). 'The Evolution of Research on Coordination Mechanisms in Multinational Corporations'. *Journal of International Business Studies*, 20/3 (Fall): 489–514.

MOON, H. C. (1994). 'A Revised Framework of Global Strategy: Extending the Coordination –Configuration Framework'. *International Executive*, 36/5: 557–73.

——RUGMAN, A. M., and VERBEKE, A. (1995). 'The Generalized Double Diamond Approach to International Competitiveness', in A. M. Rugman, J. Van Den Broeck, and A. Verbeke (eds.), *Research in Global Strategic Management*, Vol. 5. *Beyond the Diamond*. Greenwich, Conn.: JAI Press, 97–114.

————(1998). 'A Generalized Double Diamond Approach to Global Competitiveness of Korea and Singapore'. *International Business Review*, 7: 135–50.

NONAKA, I. (1990). 'Managing Globalization as a Self-Renewing Process: Experiences of Japanese MNCs', in C. A. Bartlett, Y. Doz, and G. Hedlund (eds.), *Managing the Global Firm*. London: Routledge, 69–94.

PORTER, M. E. (1980). *Competitive Strategy: Techniques for Analyzing Industries and Companies*. New York: Free Press.

——(1985). *Competitive Advantage: Creating and Sustaining Superior Performance*. New York: Free Press.

——(1986). *Competition in Global Industries*. Boston: Harvard Business School Press.

——(1990). *The Competitive Advantage of Nations*. New York: Free Press.

POYNTER, T. A., and RUGMAN, A. M. (1983). 'World Product Mandates: How Will Multinationals Respond?'. *Business Quarterly*, 47/3: 54–61.

PRAHALAD, C. K., and DOZ, Y. (1987). *The Multinational Mission: Balancing Local Demands and Global Vision*. New York: Free Press.

ROTH, K., and MORRISON, A. K. (1990). 'An Empirical Analysis of the Integration-Responsiveness Framework in Global Industries'. *Journal of International Business Studies*, 21/4: 541–64.

————(1992). 'Implementing Global Strategy: Characteristics of Global Subsidiary Mandates'. *Journal of International Business Studies*, 23/4: 715–36.

RUGMAN, A. M. (1981). *Inside the Multinationals: The Economics of Internal Markets*. New York: Columbia University Press.

——(ed.) (1994). *Foreign Investment and NAFTA*. Columbia, SC: University of South Carolina Press.

——(1996). *The Theory of Multinational Enterprises*. Cheltenham: Elgar.

——(2000). *The End of Globalization*. London: Random House Business Books.

——and BENNETT, J. (1982). 'Technology Transfer and World Product Manufacturing in Canada'. *Columbia Journal of World Business*, 18/4: 58–62.

——and D'CRUZ, J. (2000). *Multinationals as Flagship Firms: Regional Business Networks*. Oxford: Oxford University Press.

——and VERBEKE, A. (1990). *Global Corporate Strategy and Trade Policy*. London: Routledge.

————(1991a). 'Environmental Change and Global Competitive Strategy in Europe', in A. M. Rugman and A. Verbeke (eds.), *Research in Global Strategic Management*, Vol. 2. *Global Competition and the European Community*. Greenwich, Conn.: JAI Press: 3–27.

————(1991b). 'Mintzberg's Intended and Emergent Corporate Strategies and Trade Policies'. *Canadian Journal of Administrative Sciences*, 8/3: 200–8.

————(1991c). 'Trade Barriers and Corporate Strategy in International Companies'. *Long Range Planning*, 24/3: 66–72.

————(1992a). 'Shelter, Trade Policy and Strategies for Multinational Enterprises', in A. M. Rugman and A. Verbeke (eds.), *Research in Global Strategic Management*, Vol. 3. *Corporate Response to Global Change*. Greenwich, Conn.: JAI Press, 3–25.

————(1992b). 'A Note on the Transnational Solution and the Transaction Cost Theory of Multinational Strategic Management'. *Journal of International Business Studies*, 23/4: 761–71.

————(1993a). 'Generic Strategies in Global Competition', in A. M. Rugman and A. Verbeke (eds.), *Research in Global Strategic Management*, Vol. 4. *Global Competition: Beyond the Three Generics*. Greenwich, Conn.: JAI Press, 3–15.

────── (1993*b*). 'Foreign Subsidiaries and Multinational Strategic Management: An Extension and Correction of Porter's Single Diamond Framework'. *Management International Review*, 33/Special Issue 1: 71–84.

────── (1995). 'Transnational Network and Global Competition: An Organizing Framework', in A. M. Rugman and A. Verbeke (eds.), *Research in Global Strategic Management*, Vol. 5. *Beyond the Diamond*. Greenwich, Conn.: JAI Press, 3–24.

────── (1998). 'Multinational Enterprises and Public Policy'. *Journal of International Business Studies*, 29/1: 115–36.

────── (2001). 'Subsidiary Specific Advantages in Multinational Enterprises'. *Strategic Management Journal*, 22/3: 237–50.

TEECE, D. (1983). 'A Transaction Cost Theory of the Multinational Enterprise', in M. Casson (ed.), *The Growth of International Business*. London: Allen & Unwin, 51–62.

── (1985). 'Multinational Enterprise, Internal Governance and Economic Organization'. *American Economic Review*, 75: 233–8.

TSURUMI, Y. (1977). *Multinational Management*. Cambridge, Mass.: Ballinger.

VERNON, R. (1966). 'International Investment and International Trade in the Product Cycle'. *Quarterly Journal of Economics*, 80/2: 190–207.

── (1979). 'The Product Cycle Hypothesis in a New International Environment'. *Oxford Bulletin of Economics and Statistics*, 41: 255–67.

WESTNEY, D. E. (1990). 'Internal and External Linkages in the MNC: The Case of R&D Subsidiaries in Japan', in C. A. Bartlett, Y. Doz, and G. Hedlund, (eds.), *Managing the Global Firm*. New York and London: Routledge, 279–302.

── (1993). 'Institutionalization Theory and the Multinational Corporation', in S. Ghoshal and D. E. Westney (eds.), *Organization Theory and the Multinational Corporation*. New York and London: Macmillan, 237–55.

WILLIAMSON, O. E. (1981). 'The Modern Corporation: Origins, Evolution, Attributes'. *Journal of Economic Literature*, 19/Dec.: 537–68.

CHAPTER 25

GLOBALIZATION AND THE MULTINATIONAL ENTERPRISE

PETER BUCKLEY

25.1 THE MEANING OF GLOBALIZATION

GLOBALIZATION has both affected, and been caused by, the strategies of multi-national enterprises (MNEs).[1] The concept of globalization has become devalued by the ascendancy of use over meaning. Perhaps we should return to markets to give meaning. Broadly, if we envisage three types of markets—financial markets, markets in goods and services, and labour markets—we can envisage each of these moving at a differential speed towards global integration.

Financial markets are already very closely integrated internationally, so much so that no individual 'national market' can have independent existence. Goods and services markets are integrated at the regional level and this coordination is largely policy-driven through institutions such as the European Union, NAFTA, ASEAN, etc. Labour markets however are functionally separate at the national level and here integration is largely resisted by national governments (the UK's opt out of the EU Social Chapter to 1997, examples from NAFTA).

[1] We can simply define a multinational enterprise as a firm which owns and controls assets in more than one country (see Buckley and Casson 1985).

Figure 25.1 shows a highly simplified picture of the world economy. It attempts to show different degrees of integration across various types of market. The suggestion is that financial markets are substantially integrated so that the world financial market can, for many purposes, be regarded as a single market. The market for goods and services is differentiated on a regional basis with 'single markets' either existing or emerging (European Union (EU), North American Free Trade Area (NAFTA), and so on). Such markets are increasingly uniform in regulation, standards, codes of practice (for example, anti-trust), and business behaviour and so they offer the possibility of economies of scale across the market, but are substantially differentiated by these factors (and possibly by a common external tariff) from other regional markets. Labour markets, however, remain primarily national. Governments wish to regulate their own labour market and to differentiate it (protect it) from neighbouring labour markets. Many of the current difficulties in governmental regulatory policy arise from the difficulty of attempting to pursue independent labour market policies in the presence of regional goods and services markets and an international market for capital.

In contrast, multinational enterprises are perfectly placed to exploit the differences in international integration of markets. The presence of an international capital market enables capital costs to be driven to a minimum. The existence of regional goods and services markets enables firms to exploit economies of scale across several economies. Differential labour markets enable costs to be reduced by

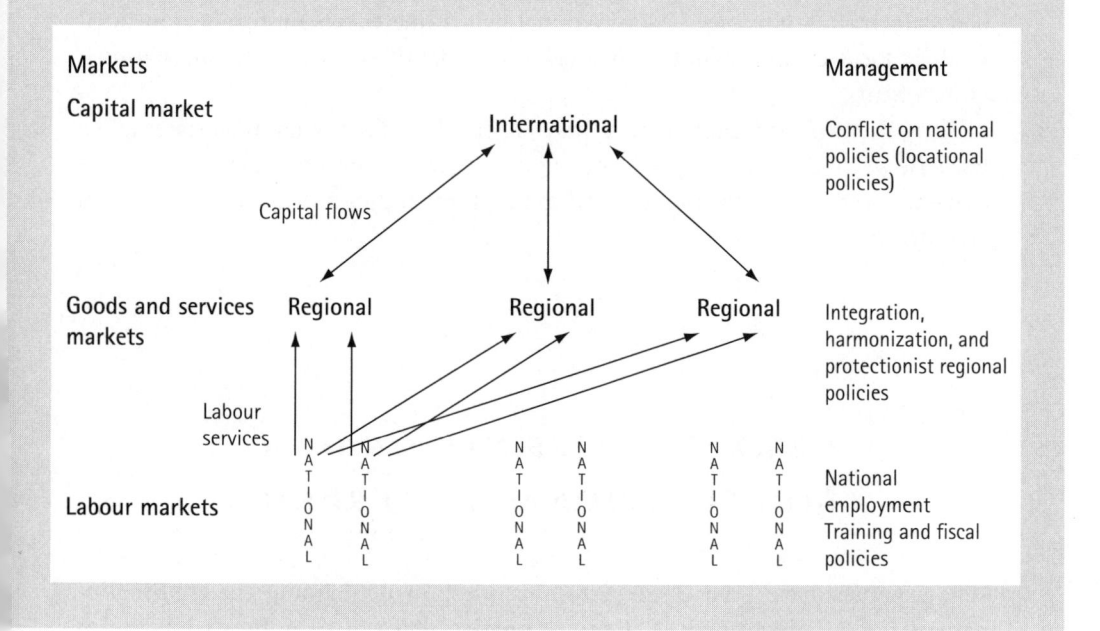

Fig. 25.1 Internationalization of firms: conflict of markets

locating the labour-intensive stages of production in cheap labour economies. Horizontal integration is served by regional goods and services markets, vertical integration by differentiated labour markets and the spatial distribution of supplies of key raw materials. Strategic trade and foreign direct investment can be seen to take place within this overall framework.

The beneficiaries of this differential speed of integration are multinational firms. They can raise capital at the lowest possible cost, reap economies of scale in regional goods and services markets, and segment labour markets by choosing least cost inputs for different spatially separate activities.

National borders do still matter however. A recent study (Rangan and Lawrence 1999) concluded that national borders continue to engender and to coincide with important discontinuities stemming from government policies, geography, and societal differences. Information discontinuities coincide with national boundaries and so create search and deliberation problems for trading and manufacturing firms. These uses also account for the alleged 'home bias' of multinational firms. Foreign direct investment and its variants are the tool by which multinationals bridge cross-border discontinuities. National locations remain distinctive. Policy barriers at the borders, differences in local cultures in the widest sense, and nature and geography contribute to distinctiveness. This, together with the ability of incumbents to keep outsiders at a disadvantage and the first entrant benefits of local firms, reinforce the differentiation of national economies. International competition in product and services markets remains imperfect and international price differences persist because arbitrage is costly. Largely, domestic market conditions determine prices and wages. Multinational firm affiliates remain firmly embedded in their local economy and such local firms identify closely with the national government.

Thus, the two contrasting paradigms of a world of separate national states and a borderless world are incomplete and capture only part of a complex, subtle, and dynamic story. This is the background to the study of the strategy of multinational enterprises.

25.2 THE DEFINITION OF A MULTINATIONAL ENTERPRISE

Whole papers have been devoted to the question of defining the multinational enterprise (Aharoni 1966). Four alternative types of definition would seem to be:

(1) an operating definition, one form of which is the ownership-threshold definition—a firm that owns or controls income-generating assets in more than one country;

(2) a structural definition where multinationality is judged according to the organization of the company;

(3) a performance criterion incorporating some relative or absolute measure of international spread, such as number of foreign subsidiaries or percentage of sales accounted for by foreign sales; and

(4) a behavioural criterion based on the corporation's degree of geocentricity.

Definitions are not right or wrong, just more or less useful. Our definition is the simplest form of a threshold definition—a firm that owns outputs of goods or services originating in more than one country (Buckley and Casson 1985). Consequently, we avoid the issue of defining control and do not necessarily imply that the firm is a foreign direct investor. Thus, we bring new forms of international involvement within the ambit of the theory (Buckley 1985*b*).

25.3 CONCEPTUAL APPROACHES TO THE MNE

25.3.1 The Hymer-Kindleberger Tradition

The initial core of modern theory of the multinational enterprise was a deceptively simple proposition: that in order to compete with indigenous firms, which possess innate strengths such as knowledge of the local environment, market, and business conditions, foreign entrants must have some compensating advantage. This proposition took foreign direct investment away from the theory of capital movements into the theory of industrial organization. For, in a perfect market, foreign direct investment could not exist because local firms would always be able to out-compete foreign entrants.

The initial phase of the Hymer-Kindleberger approach was therefore the search for the compensating advantage that foreign investors possessed. Kindleberger's exposition (1969) examined four main areas of internationally transferable advantages. First, departures from perfect competition in goods markets, including product differentiation, marketing skills, and administered pricing; secondly, departures from perfect competition in factor markets, including access to patented or proprietary knowledge, discrimination in access to capital, and skill differences embodied in the firm (particularly its management); thirdly, internal and external

economies of scale, including those arising from vertical integration; and finally, government intervention, particularly those forms restricting output or entry. Such advantages enable the foreign entrant to overcome its lack of knowledge of local conditions innate in the local firm, which the foreign firm can only acquire at a cost, also serve to compensate for the foreigner's cost of operating at a distance.

We must, however, turn to a second critical element in the Hymer-Kindleberger approach. Given the special advantages that enable the firm to invest abroad successfully (the necessary condition), it remains to be proved that the direct investment is the preferred means of exploiting the advantage (the sufficient condition). The basis for the decision, according to Hymer-Kindleberger, is profitability. In many cases, direct investment will be preferred to either exporting or licensing the advantage to a host-country firm. Exporting will in many cases be excluded by tariff and transport-cost barriers; also, a local producer may be better placed to adapt its product to local conditions and a local presence may have demand-stimulating effects.

The arguments that firms will often prefer foreign direct investment to licensing are more subtle. Hymer (1976) argued that the advantage-possessor cannot appropriate the full return (or rent) from its utilization because of imperfections in the market for knowledge. Such imperfections arise from buyer uncertainty when the buyer is unable to assess the worth of the knowledge until he is in possession of it, lack of an institutionalized market for the knowledge and the dependence of the value of the knowledge on its secrecy. The seller thus cannot induce competitive bids in order to appropriate the full returns. Further factors that favour foreign direct investment over licensing the advantage to host-country firms are the desire for control by the advantage-possessor and the danger that the advantage-seller will create a competitor if the buyer uses the advantage in ways that have not been paid for. Licensing may incur heavy firm-to-firm transfer costs, including costs of policing the transferred property rights (Buckley and Davies 1981)—costs that do not arise in the case of parent-to-subsidiary transfers.

In summary, therefore, this approach suggests that a multinational entrant must possess an internally transferable advantage, the possession of which gives it a quasi-monopolistic opportunity to enter host-country markets. Barriers to trade and barriers that prevent host-country firms from duplicating this advantage mean that foreign direct investment is frequently the preferred form of exploiting the advantage in foreign markets.

It is arguable, however, that the fundamental proposition of the Hymer-Kindleberger approach is not as easily applicable to established multinational firms as opposed to firms becoming multinational. How far do the barriers to entry to foreign market decline as the international spread of the firm widens? Established multinational firms have gained worldwide dominance and developed techniques to learn in advance of local conditions; products, processes, management style, and marketing techniques are continually adapted to local markets. The ability of a

multinational to forecast and adapt is one of the major competitive skills. It is now the only entry into unusually isolated markets (such as China) where the heavy costs of foreignness are still encountered. The advantages of locals in other instances can be discounted in advance by an experienced multinational firm.

The whole concept of firm-specific advantages must therefore be questioned (Buckley 1983a). The concept is artificially attenuated at the point where the firm first crosses national boundaries, or at least has the potential to do so. Firm-specific advantage is a reflection of this cut-off point as a snapshot in time of a dynamic process. The existence of firm-specific advantages depends on a set of assertions on (a) the diffusion of technical and marketing know-how, (b) the comparative advantage of firms in particular locations, and (c) the existence of particular types of economies of scale.

The first set of assertions rests on the size and extent of barriers to the scale of information on the market that are increasingly open to challenge, as are the assumptions on the relatively costless nature of internal information transfer (Teece 1983). The second set of assertions is under threat from the worldwide rise of multinational enterprises. Finally, empirical propositions on economies of scale in research and development, on which firm-specific advantages rest, remain to be proved empirically; there is no guarantee that those who undertake research and development are necessarily the optimum users of its output. Separation through the market of research and its implementation in production may be a better solution. Finally, multinational firms can become locked into outmoded technologies whose institutional rigidities may prevent the creation and absorption of new developments in established firms. This provides opportunities for new-generation products and processes outside existing multinationals that gives flexibility to growth paths and often leads to the emergence of new firms.

The notion of firm-specific advantage is thus short-run when endowments of proprietary knowledge are fixed. In the long run, investment policy is crucial and a dynamic reformulation of industry barriers to entry is necessary to bring about an approach integrating the life cycle of a firm to expansion paths over time (Buckley 1983a).

25.3.2 The Product-Cycle Model and 'The Transnational Corporation'

The product-cycle hypothesis chiefly associated with Raymond Vernon (1966, 1974, 1979) has yielded many insights into the development of the multinational enterprise. The models rest on four basic assumptions:

(1) products undergo predictable changes in production and marketing;
(2) restricted information is available on technology;

(3) production processes change over time and economies of scale are prevalent;

(4) tastes differ according to income and thus products can be standardized at various income levels.

The original model (Vernon 1966) suggested that new products would appear first in the most advanced country (the United States of America) because demand arising from (a) discretionary spending on new products arising from high income and (b) substitution of new capital goods for expensive labour would be most easily transmitted to local entrepreneurs. Consequently, the new product stage, where an unstandardized product with a low-price elasticity of demand is produced on an experimental basis, occurs in the United States of America. The second stage is the maturing product. The product begins to be standardized and the need for flexibility on both supply and demand sides declines. The possibilities of economies of scale lead to expansion in production; this is matched by increasing demand as the product becomes cheaper. The market begins to appear in other advanced countries and is initially satisfied by exports from the United States of America. Eventually cost factors begin to dictate that these foreign markets should be serviced by local production and the emergence of indigenous producers adds a defensive motive to the advantages of investment by US producers. So other advanced countries are the first recipients of US direct investment. In the third stage, a standardized product emerges that sells entirely on the basis of price competitiveness. The imperative now is to produce the product at the lowest possible cost. Consequently, the labour-intensive stages of production are hived off and carried out, via foreign direct investment, in the less developed countries, where labour is cheapest.

Vernon's initial model has the virtues of simplicity and directness. It explains US investment in other advanced countries and the phenomenon of offshore production in cheap labour countries. Despite its advantages in integrating supply-and-demand factors, it has been outdated by events. First, the United States is no longer totally dominant in foreign investment—European and Japanese multinational expansion also needs explanation. Secondly, multinational enterprises are now capable of developing, maturing, and standardizing products almost simultaneously, differentiating the product to suit a variety of needs without significant time-lags.

It was to counter the first objection that Vernon adapted his model to deal with non-US multinational enterprises after virtually admitting the redundancy of the 'simple' model. The modified product cycle (1979) brings the hypothesis much closer to the Hymer-Kindleberger model outlined above, resting as it does on oligopoly and market behaviour. The hypothesis is now concerned to emphasize the oligopolistic structure in which most multinational enterprises operate and their attempts to forestall entry into the industry by new firms. The names of the stages tell the story of the competitive devices used to construct and maintain oligopoly—innovation-based oligopoly, mature oligopoly (price competition and

scale economies), and senescent oligopoly (cartels, product differentiation, and the essential breakdown of entry barriers).

The product-cycle model thus yields many interesting insights into the process of global competition. It has also led to several valuable empirical studies—notably Hufbauer (1966) and Hirsh (1967). However, its over-deterministic and programmatic nature are features that have to be modified in view of the increasing sophistication of global competition (Giddy 1978). In its analysis of the strategy of established multinational firms, the product-cycle approach splits three interdependent decisions: (1) investment in product-development; (2) the method of servicing a foreign market; and (3) the firm's competitive stance in relation to foreign firms. These elements need to be considered simultaneously by multinational enterprises. As the basis for a forward-planning model, the product-cycle hypothesis has been outdated by the existence of experienced firms facing worldwide competition. Modelling of the process by which a beginner becomes an established multinational firm represents a gap in the theoretical framework, despite several empirical studies. Whatever the defects of Vernon's models, their virtues serve to focus attention on a more truly dynamic version of the growth of (multinational) firms.

Vernon's ideas were a major factor in the development of Bartlett and Ghoshal's (1987, 1989) work on 'the transnational corporation'. The threefold imperative of the product cycle: (1) product innovation (product development, technology transfer skills, and competence transmission internationally), (2) closeness to the marketplace ('local' strategies, differentiation and adaptation of products, revenue generation) and (3) cost-based competition (global production, standardization, efficiency-seeking cost-reduction policies) become a key triad for international strategy. Bartlett and Ghoshal took Vernon's threefold strategy imperative, but removed their temporal sequencing. Thus innovation, sensitivity to the local conditions, and global efficiency must be sought simultaneously and continually in order to survive in global competition. The means towards these ends and the trade-off between them remain key issues in the international management literature.

25.3.3 Internalization and the Theory of the Multinational Enterprise

Attempts at integration of the various strands of the theory of the multinational firm have centred on the concept of internalization. The framework of analysis is derived from Coase (1937). It is pointed out in Casson (1985a) that two connotations of this concept exist. One aspect is the internalization of a market where an arm's length contractual relationship is replaced by unified ownership. The other

concerns the internalization of an externality where a market is created where none existed before. Often, internalization of the second kind is a consequence of the first, but logically the two should be dissociated. The excessive generality ascribed to internalization has led to it being described as 'a concept in search of a theory' (Buckley 1983a: 42), but careful distinctions between types of internalization and the incidence of costs and benefits on a firm-by-firm basis lead to concrete propositions on the optimal scope of the firm (Casson 1981; Teece 1983).

The thrust of the concept of internalization is that the actions of firms can replace the market or alternatively augment it. The explanatory power of the concept rests on an analysis of the costs and benefits to the form of internalizing markets, particularly markets in intermediate goods. The predictive power of the concept for the growth and pattern of multinational enterprises is given by a statement of the likelihood of the internalization of the various markets a company faces. The advantages of internalization (and therefore of control by the firm versus the market solution) are given by:

(1) the increased ability to control and plan production and in particular to coordinate flows of crucial inputs;
(2) the exploitation of market power by discriminatory pricing;
(3) the avoidance of bilateral market power;
(4) the avoidance of uncertainties in the transfer of knowledge between parties that may exist in an alternative (market) solution;
(5) the avoidance of potential government intervention by devices such as transfer prices.

Costs arise from communication, coordination, and control difficulties, and the costs of foreignness (Buckley and Casson 1976). Three cases of empirical importance are (a) the advantages of vertical integration; (b) the importance of situations where intermediate product flows in research-intensive industries; and (c) the internalization of human skills, particularly in areas with high returns to team cooperation such as marketing and financing.

Magee (1977) bases his explanation on the ease of appropriability of returns from the creation of information: that is, the ability of the private originators of ideas to obtain for themselves the pecuniary value of the ideas to society. This extension of Johnson's (1970) concept and Arrow's (1962) analysis of the public good nature of proprietary information is linked with an industry cycle to derive expectations on the nature of multinational enterprise development and its ability to transfer technology effectively, particularly to less developed countries (Magee 1977).

Underlying this internalization approach is the view that internal solutions will be sought where international market imperfections would impose costs on firms using those markets. Internalization of markets also imposes severe barriers on new entry. The multinational is thus seen as both responding to market imperfections and creating them. Clearly, strong links with the Hymer-Kindleberger approach

and the product-cycle hypothesis are apparent. Attention to imperfections on intermediate markets should not obscure the role of imperfections in final goods markets, leading to competitive devices such as product differentiation and administered pricing. Multinationals are not passive reactors to imperfections, and internalization decisions interact. The critical role of information as an intermediate product is an important synthesizing element.

The role of multinationals in creating imperfections has not yet been fully incorporated into the theory because more attention has been paid to multinational enterprises' reactions to market imperfections. What is required is a thorough-going theory of barriers to entry for industries and markets. Further, the concept of internalization is a difficult one to measure empirically. The use of internal exports and flows relating to research and development (Buckley and Pearce 1979, 1981, 1984) do not always fully discriminate between this approach and others.

25.3.4 Multinational Enterprises and Location Theory

Any viable explanation of the growth, pattern, and operations (sourcing policies) of inputs and market-servicing policies must include elements of location theory. Under the general rubric above, the multinational enterprise can be seen simply as a major vehicle for the transfer of mobile resources (technology, capital, and management skills) to areas with immobile (or fixed) complementary inputs (markets, raw materials, and labour). Thus, Ricardian endowments enter the theory.

The location-specific endowments of particular importance to multinational enterprises are: (1) raw materials, leading to vertical foreign direct investment; (2) cheap labour, leading to offshore-production facilities; and (3) protected or fragmented markets leading to foreign direct investment as the preferred means of marketing servicing. Location factors therefore enter the theory not only in their own right, as an influence on the relative costs facing a multinational enterprise with a choice of locations, but may also provide the motives for international expansion.

The important connections between location factors and the (internal) organization of multinational enterprises should, however, be given due weight. First, the multinational enterprise will normally be a multistage, multifunction firm and the location of different stages and functions will be subject to different locational influences connected by (international) flows of intermediate products. Secondly, the internalization of markets will affect location in two important ways:

1. The multinational enterprises will have an incentive to minimize government intervention through transfer pricing, for instance, to reduce the overall tax liability by the input of high mark-ups in the lowest tax countries and possibly by altering its location strategy completely to take in a low-intervention tax haven. (For evidence

on the nature and amount of intra-company trade and its determinants, see Buckley and Pearce 1979, 1981, 1984).

2. The increased communication flows in an internal market may bias high communication-cost activities towards the centre—usually towards the source country where critical activities are focused on head office. (A forceful extension of this argument is given by Hymer 1976.)

In his restatement of the product-cycle hypothesis, Vernon (1974) gives a great deal of weight to the interplay between the stage of the industry's development and the relevant locational influences upon it. The location of research activities (in the centre) and the changing locational influences on production provide the dynamic for the theory.

Standard location theory can be shown to be of direct relevance to the strategy of multinational enterprises as illustrated by Dunning's paper on the location of multinational enterprises in an enlarged European Community (1972) (see also Casson (1985b) and Horst's (1972) work on the servicing of the Canadian market by US multinational enterprises). The reduction, removal, or increase of tariffs between nations will alter multinational enterprise market-servicing decisions and cause a restructuring of the location of multinational enterprise activities. This area leads into an interesting discussion centred on the relative comparative advantages of firms and nations and thence to relative bargaining capabilities (Vaitsos 1974; Casson 1979).

25.3.5 Japanese Direct Investment: A Distinct Approach?

Some people believe that Japanese direct investment requires a special approach because of several alleged differences from Western European and US investment (Ozawa 1979a, 1979b). Among these differences are a later takeoff of Japanese investment; a clustering in Latin America and Asia of such investments; the supposed greater labour-intensity of Japanese investment; its openness to joint ventures; and the existence of group-controlled investment (Buckley 1983b, 1985a).

These characteristics have led Japanese analysts to propose alternative explanations specifically related to Japanese conditions. One of the most ingenious is the theoretical framework developed by Kiyoshi Kojima (1978, 1982), Kojima and Ozawa (1984). Kojima's approach has a model of trade-oriented (Japanese-type) foreign direct investment, to distinguish it from anti-trade-oriented (American-type) foreign direct investment. Kojima's aim is to integrate trade theory with direct investment theory and to contrast Japanese-type investment with American-type.

Kojima (1978) begins with the standard two-country, two-factor, two-product Hecksher-Ohlin model of trade. He then introduces Mundell's demonstration that under rigorous Hecksher-Ohlin assumptions, the substitution for commodity-

of-factor movements will be complete. The process for achieving this is that capital—homogeneous (money) capital—flows from the capital-rich to the capital-poor country, perhaps as a response to the imposition of a prohibitive tariff on capital-intensive exportables. As a result, the recipient country becomes more capital-abundant and reallocates its resources so that production of capital-intensive goods expands, and that of labour-intensive goods declines, until equilibrium is reached at a point exactly corresponding to the post-trade situation in the absence of the capital movement. This pattern of output change—that the recipient country's comparatively disadvantaged industry expands and its comparatively advantaged (in terms of its original factor-endowment) industry contracts—is posited in the Rybczynski theorem. Kojima views American foreign direct investment in this light, arguing that the basis for trade is eliminated by outflows of capital from the capital-exporting country's advantaged industry, so foreign direct investment is a substitute for trade.

In the Japanese case, however, Kojima's argument is that the host-country's production frontier expands in such a direction that the (pre-investment) comparatively advantaged industry expands and the comparatively disadvantaged industry contracts, thus enhancing the basis for trade.

This complements case is achieved by the Rybczynski line sloping in an opposite direction (the line linking the original production point and the post-capital inflow production point moves upwards). This effect cannot occur if homogeneous money capital, perfectly re-allocable to any industry, is the norm. Therefore Kojima suggests at this point that direct investment capital is a package involving technical knowledge and human-skill components (including management skills); it is therefore, to some extent, industry-specific. This capital moves to the host country because of comparative advantages in improving productivity in the host country; the resultant increase in profitability adds the motivation. Here Kojima introduces a crucial assumption: that productivity in the host country is increased more through direct investment in the labour-intensive industry than in the capital-intensive industry, because of 'the smaller technological gap and a greater spillover of technology to local firms' (1978: 126). The same amount of output is produced with proportionately smaller inputs of labour and capital. Hicks-neutral technological change is deemed to have taken place.

The critical factor in this model is the disproportionate effect on productivity, when sector-specific capital moves into the host's comparatively advantaged industry. The implicit assumption is that industry-specific public goods have been transferred—the proof of this is Kojima's (1978: 127) statements that the production frontier in the source country remains unchanged 'since the technology and managerial skills do not decrease even when they are applied abroad and since labour and capital are assumed unchanged' in the source country. For Kojima includes the assumption that direct foreign investment involves a negligible transfer of money capital.

The comparative advantage in improving productivity can thus be seen as the result of the combination of internationally mobile inputs transferred by the investing (Japanese) firm that include managerial and organizational skills, with the vital addition of guaranteed access to (Japanese) markets and distributive networks, together with locationally immobile inputs, notably cheap labour. Kojima suggests that because of the sector-specific nature of these productivity-improving resources, it is easier for firms that possess such attributes to relocate abroad (outside Japan) rather than diversify into other domestic industries. Consequently, there is no presumption (unlike product-cycle-type US foreign direct investment) that the outward investors are the leading firms. Indeed, it is suggested that weaker firms, just exposed to exogenous shifts in comparative advantage, will be the most likely to be relocated in less developed countries.

The crucial element in Kojima's explanation of Japanese foreign direct investment is the improvement in productivity in the host country brought about by the infusion of the package of resources involved in Japanese investment. Of key importance is the market access brought by the link with a Japanese distribution network, and the organization skills of Japanese management when working with relatively unskilled or semi-skilled labour. The host-country unit, when taken over or set up by Japanese foreign direct investment, becomes integrated with a marketing network guaranteeing market access. The addition of a Japanese imprint enhances the quality image of the product. Japanese ownership therefore confers immediate benefits.

The specialist skills infused include those developed by Japanese enterprises in response to the particular stimuli they have faced in Japan: notably a cooperative rather than competitive environment, a docile and relatively cheap workforce and skills in organizing high-quality, mass-production systems. The range of industries over which these skills are crucial is very different from those where US and European firms have developed intra-industry specialisms; consequently the industrial structure of Japanese foreign direct investment is different from Western foreign direct investment. It has, however, been differentiated by Kojima more starkly than the version presented here by his concentration on a product-cycle interpretation of American-type foreign direct investment.

Japanese foreign direct investment represents a search for location-specific inputs (stable environment, low transport costs, but chiefly cheap labour) to complement the skills developed by Japanese enterprise. It corresponds to Western, chiefly US, firms' offshore production and exhibits a similar industry structure.

Japanese outward investment must indeed be explained by reference to locational criteria: notably the relative labour costs in nearby less developed countries as compared with Japan. The firm-specific skills of Japanese firms—access to a (worldwide) distribution network, organization ability, and managerial skills—differ significantly from the typical US or European multinational enterprise's strengths.

Consequently, the industrial distribution of Japanese foreign direct investment differs from these other industrialized countries. Differentiation of Japanese foreign direct investment has been exaggerated by its comparison with product-cycle-type US foreign direct investment, which is at most only a subset of that country's outward investment—an explanation that has been outdated by events (Giddy 1978).

25.3.6 Synthesis: A General Theory of the Multinational Enterprise

There are now several candidates for a general theory of the multinational enterprise (see Casson 1987). Among these are Dunning's eclectic theory (1981), (1988), which relies on the ownership/location/internalization paradigm: ownership-specific advantages, location endowments, and internalization advantages. Several unresolved issues remain in this approach. First, the relationship between these three elements and their development over time is unclear and leaves a classification system bereft of a dynamic content. Secondly, the existence of separate (and separable) ownership advantages is doubtful and logically redundant because internalization explains why firms exist in the absence of such advantages.

Rugman (1981) claims that internalization in itself represents a general theory of the multinational enterprise. This is achieved partly by relegating location factors to a footnote by including spatial cost-saving as an internalized firm-specific advantage. Internalization requires restrictions on the relative sizes of internal and external transaction costs to have any empirical content; without a theory of this incidence, it remains tautological.

The markets and hierarchies approach associated with Oliver Williamson (1975, 1981, 1985) has also been advanced as a candidate for a general theory of the multinational enterprise (Calvet 1981). Williamson suggests that his general theory of why firms exist explains the existence of the multinational firm as a special case. Without a theory of the conditions under which one idea-type form (market or hierarchy) will be replaced by the other, only an arid, comparative, static framework remains. The transition from market to hierarchy may be explained by the minimization of transaction costs, once these have been carefully specified (Buckley and Casson 1985). The concept of bounded rationality in management decision-making utilized by Williamson is useful but it sits awkwardly within an essentially neoclassical framework. Further, Rugman's (1981) identification of hierarchy with internal market may be unjustified because internal organization may more closely resemble a perfect market, with transfer prices approximating to shadow prices of a perfect allocation, than the hierarchical mode.

The theory of the multinational firm therefore requires development in several directions before it can be seen to be adequate. First, the fusion between institutional

and neoclassical elements must be made more secure. Secondly, the general area of the economics of business strategy is in need of greater attention. Thirdly, the role of time must be more carefully defined in the relationship between the growth (and decline) of firms, technologies, products, and industries. Finally, the formulation and testing of hypotheses from the theory is an urgent task (Buckley 1988).

Recently, further integration has been achieved between the purportedly incompatible approaches of internalization and market structure theories after Hymer. Buckley (1990) has shown that the two approaches are complementary, not competitive. Hymer himself, in a paper originally (1968) written in French and now republished (Casson 1990), used Coase's framework; the synthesis of the two approaches represents a step forward in theorizing.

25.4 THE CHALLENGE OF GLOBALIZATION[2]

Globalization can also have deleterious effects on MNEs. Most notable is the increase in volatility which globalization brings. The increased volatility in world economy has demanded new strategic choices for MNEs which have the search for flexibility at its core. Key elements of these strategies are:

- uncertainty and market volatility
- flexibility and the value of real options
- cooperation through joint ventures and business networks
- entrepreneurship, managerial competence, and corporate culture and
- organizational change, including the mandating of subsidiaries and the 'empowerment' of employees.

Flexibility may be defined as the ability to reallocate resources quickly and smoothly in response to change. The significance of flexibility is greater, the greater the amplitude and frequency of change in the environment. So far as MNEs are concerned, the impact of change is captured by the volatility induced in the profit stream. The volatility of profit that would occur if the firm made no response to change summarizes the impact on the firm of volatility in its environment.

25.4.1 Increasing Volatility

Competition from Asia was a visible symbol of a less apparent but more fundamental change in the business environment—namely a persistent increase in the

---

[2] This section of the chapter draws on Buckley and Casson (1998).

amount of volatility with which firms have to contend. Volatility has become much greater since the end of the 'golden age'. There are several reasons for this.

The international diffusion of modern production technology has increased the number of industrial powers, and hence increased the number of countries in which political and social disturbances can impact significantly on global supplies of manufactured products. The liberalization of trade and capital markets means that the 'ripple' effects of shocks travel farther and wider than before (Casson 1995: ch. 4). Ripples are transmitted more quickly too: news travels almost instantaneously, thanks to modern telecommunications. Thus, speculative bubbles in stock markets spread quickly around the world. Following the breakdown of the Bretton Woods system, exchange rate fluctuations have created a new dimension of financial volatility too.

As a result, any given national market is now affected by a much wider range of disturbances than ever before. Every national subsidiary of an MNE experiences a multiplicity of shocks from around the world. It is no longer the case that a national subsidiary has to respond to shocks originating in its national market alone. The shocks come from new sources of import competition and new competitive threats in export markets too. While most shocks reveal themselves to firms as competitive threats, new opportunities for cooperation may sometimes be presented as well. The awareness of this sustained increase in volatility has led to a search for more flexible forms of organization.

Increased volatility is not the only reason for greater interest in flexibility. Contemporary culture is very much opposed to building organizations around a single source of monopoly power. The nation state, for example, is under threat from advocates of regional government. The traditional role of the state, to supply defence, can in principle be effected through multilateral defence treaties in which politically independent regions club together for this specific purpose. The demise of the Soviet bloc, and the subsequent political realignment between its member states, may be seen as an example of this kind of cultural change at work. This distrust of monopoly power may be linked to an increase in other forms of distrust, as suggested below.

25.4.2 Opposition to Monopoly

The aversion to internal monopoly is apparent amongst MNEs as well. This movement began in the early 1980s when the powerful central research laboratories of high-technology MNEs were either closed down, shifted to the divisions, or forced to operate as suppliers to 'internal customers' in competition with outside bodies such as universities (Casson, Pearce, and Singh 1991). Headquarters bureaucracies came under attack shortly afterwards, as 'delayering' got underway. The

favoured form of firm has become a federal structure of operating divisions drawing on a common source of internal expertise, but where each division belonging to the federation is free to outsource expertise if it so desires. As with any trend, there has been a tendency for certain advocates to take it to extremes. Just as the 'golden age' was rife with suggestions that oligopolies of hierarchical MNEs would come to dominate world markets, so the 1990s have spawned visions of the 'network firm' and the 'virtual firm'.

25.4.3 Networks and Joint Ventures

The typical US MNE of the 'golden age' was a vertically as well as horizontally integrated firm. In consequence, each division of the firm was locked into linkages with other divisions of the same firm. As Asian competition intensified, there was growing recognition of the costs of integration of this kind.

Commitment to a particular source of supply or demand is relatively low-cost in a high-growth scenario, since it is unlikely that any investment will need to be reversed. It is much more costly in a low-growth scenario, where production may need to be switched to a cheaper source of supply, or sales diverted away from a depressed market. The desire for flexibility therefore discourages vertical integration—whether it is backward integration into production, or forward integration into distribution. It is better to subcontract production and to franchise sales instead. The subcontracting of production is similar in principle to the 'putting out' arrangement described above, but differs in the sense that the subcontractor is now a firm rather than just a single worker.

Dis-integration was also encouraged by a low-trust atmosphere that developed in many firms. Fear of internal monopoly became rife, as explained above. Production managers faced with falling demand wished that they did not have to sell all their output through a single sales manager. Sales managers resented the fact that they had to obtain all their supplies from the same small set of plants. Each manager doubted the competence of the others, and ascribed loss of corporate competitiveness to selfishness and inefficiency elsewhere in the firm. Divisions aspired to be spun off so that they could deal with other business units instead. On the other hand, managers were wary of the risks that would be involved if they severed their links with other divisions altogether. Dis-intermediation is favoured by the growth of electronic commerce.

A natural way to restore confidence is to allow each division to deal with external business units as well as internal ones. In terms of internalization theory, internal markets become 'open' rather than 'closed' (Casson 1990: 37). This provides divisional managers with an opportunity to bypass weak or incompetent sections of the company. It also provides a competitive discipline on internal transfer prices,

preventing their manipulation for internal political ends, and bringing them more into line with external prices. There are other advantages too. Opening up internal markets severs the link between the capacities operated at adjacent stages of production. The resulting opportunity to supply other firms facilitates the exploitation of scale economies because it permits the capacity of any individual plant to exceed internal demand. Conversely, it encourages the firm to buy in supplies from other firms that have installed capacity in excess of their own needs.

The alignment of internal prices with external prices increases the objectivity of profit measurement at the divisional level. This allows divisional managers to be rewarded by profit-related pay based on divisional profit rather than firm-wide profit. Management may even buy out part of the company. Alternatively, the firm may restructure by buying in a part of an independent firm. The net effect is the same in both cases. The firm becomes the hub of a network of interlocking joint ventures (Buckley and Casson 1988, 1996). Each joint venture partner is responsible for the day-to-day management of the venture. The headquarters of the firm coordinates the links between the ventures. Internal trade is diverted away from the weaker ventures towards the stronger ones, thereby providing price and profit signals to which the weaker partners need to respond. Unlike a pure external market situation, the partners are able to draw upon expertise at headquarters, which can in turn tap into expertise in other parts of the group.

A network does not have to be built around a single firm, of course. A network may consist of a group of independent firms instead. Sometimes these firms are neighbours, as in the regional industrial clusters described by Best (1990), Porter (1990), and Rugman, D'Cruz, and Verbeke (1995). Industrial districts, such as 'Toyota city', have been hailed as an Asian innovation in flexible management, although the practice has been common in Europe for centuries (Marshall 1919). As tariffs and transport costs have fallen, networks have become more international. This is demonstrated by the dramatic growth in intermediate product trade under long-term contracts. For example, an international trading company may operate a network of independent suppliers in different countries, substituting different sources of supply in response to both short-term exchange rate movements and long-term shifts in comparative advantage.

Flexibility is also needed in R&D. A firm cannot afford to become over-committed to the refinement of any one technology in case innovation elsewhere should render the entire technology obsolete. As technology has diffused in the post-war period, the range of countries with the competence to innovate has significantly increased. The pace of innovation has consequently risen, and the threat of rapid obsolescence is therefore higher as a result. The natural response for firms is to diversify their research portfolios. But the costs of maintaining a range of R&D projects are prohibitive, given the enormous fixed costs involved. The costs of basic R&D have escalated because of the increased range of specialist skills involved, while the costs of applied R&D have risen because of the need to develop

global products which meet increasingly stringent consumer protection laws. Joint ventures are an appropriate solution once again. By establishing a network of joint ventures covering alternative technological trajectories, the firm can spread its costs whilst retaining a measure of proprietary control over new technologies. The advantage of joint ventures is further reinforced by technological convergence—e.g. the integration of computers, telecommunications, and photography. This favours the creation of networks of joint ventures based on complementary technologies, rather than on the substitute technologies described above (Cantwell 1995).

Joint ventures are important because they afford a number of real options (Trigeorgis 1996) which can be taken up or dropped depending upon how the project turns out. The early phase of a joint venture provides important information which could not be obtained through investigation before the venture began. It affords an opportunity later on to buy more fully into a successful venture—an opportunity which is not available to those who have not taken any stake. It therefore provides greater flexibility than does either outright ownership or an alternative involving no equity stake.

25.4.4 Strategies and Internal Organization of the MNE in a Globalized World Economy

In a very volatile environment the level of uncertainty is likely to be high. Uncertainty can be reduced, however, by collecting information. Flexibility was defined above in terms of the ability to respond to change. The costs of response tend to be smaller when the period of adjustment is long. One way of 'buying time' to adjust is to forecast change. While no one can foresee the future perfectly, information on the present and the recent past may well improve forecasts by diagnosing underlying long-term trends. Collecting, storing, and analysing information therefore enhances flexibility because by improving forecasts it reduces the costs of change.

Another way of buying time is to recognize change as early as possible. In this respect, continuous monitoring of the business environment is better than intermittent monitoring because the potential lag before a change is recognized is eliminated. Continuous monitoring is more expensive than intermittent monitoring, though, because more management time is tied up.

Investments in better forecasts and speedier recognition of change highlight the trade-off between information cost and adjustment cost. This trade-off is particularly crucial when volatility is high. High volatility implies that more information should be collected to improve flexibility, which in turn implies that more managers need to be employed. This is the reverse of the usual recommendation to downsize management in order to reduce overhead costs.

To improve flexibility whilst downsizing management, the trade-off between information cost and adjustment cost must be improved. There are two main ways of doing this. The first is to reduce the cost of information processing through new information technology (IT). The second is to reduce adjustment costs by building flexibility into plant and equipment, both through its design and its location. A combination of IT investment and flexible plant can reconcile greater flexibility with lower management overheads in the manner to which many MNEs aspire.

The information required for strategic decision-making is likely to be distributed throughout the organization. It is no longer reasonable to assume that all the key information can be handled by a single chief executive, or even by the entire headquarters management team. It is difficult to know in advance where the really crucial information is likely to be found. Every manager therefore needs to have the competence to process information effectively. Managers need to be able to recognize the significance of strategic information that they acquire by chance, and to have the power of access to senior executives in order to pass it on. In other words, ordinary managers need to become internal entrepreneurs.

Few entrepreneurs have sufficient information to make a good decision without consulting other people, however. In a traditional hierarchical firm the right to consult is the prerogative of top management. If ordinary managers are to have the power to initiate consultation, and act upon the results, then channels of communication within the firm need to be increased. Horizontal communication as well as vertical communication must be easy, so that lower level managers can readily consult with their peers.

A natural response is to 'flatten' the organization and encourage managers to 'network' with each other. This improves the trade-off between local responsiveness and strategic cohesion (Bartlett and Ghoshal 1987; Hedlund 1993). Unfortunately, though, there has been some confusion over whether flatter organizations remain hierarchies at all. However, as Casson (1994) shows, the efficient managerial processing of information normally requires a hierarchical structure of some kind. The key point is that the more diverse are the sources of volatility, the greater are the advantages of widespread consultation. The less predictable is the principal source of volatility on any given occasion, the greater the incentive to allow consultation to be initiated anywhere in the organization. In practice this means that an increased demand for flexibility is best accommodated by flattening the organization whilst maintaining basic elements of hierarchy.

If flexibility were costless, then all organizations could build in unlimited flexibility at the outset. In practice, the greater flexibility is, the higher transaction costs become. The timing of decisions is absolutely crucial in a volatile environment. The right decision may be of little use if it is taken at the wrong time (Rivoli and Salorio 1996). Committing resources too early to a growing market, for example, means that costs are incurred before adequate revenues can be generated, while deferring until too late means that the market may be permanently lost to

competitors (Buckley and Casson 1981). An important reason for deferring investment is that new information may become available later which would lead to a better decision. This is the central point in the theory of options (Trigeorgis 1996). Investment is often irreversible, in the sense that the resources committed are illiquid, and cannot be fully recovered later through divestment. Deferring a decision on an irreversible investment reduces the risk that the investment may go ahead on a mistaken assessment of the situation (Campa 1994). The more volatile the environment, the more likely it is to change, and hence the greater the advantage of waiting until all imminent changes have occurred.

It would be wrong to infer, however, that investment is always discouraged by volatility. Investment often leads to the discovery of new information. Suppose, for example, that there are two foreign markets, one of which is known to be similar to the other. Investing in the smaller market involves a smaller commitment than investing in the larger one. A by-product of investment in the smaller market is information about the larger market. This information reduces the risk of investing in the larger one. It therefore pays to invest first in the smaller market, even though the prospects are worse than in the larger one, because the experience gained can be used to improve the later, more important, decision. This idea is central to the Scandinavian model of the internationalization of the firm (Johanson and Vahlne 1977).

In general, the growth of an MNE may be understood as a sequence of investments undertaken in a volatile environment, where each investment feeds back information which can be used to improve the quality of subsequent decisions. In this sense, the expansion of the firm is a path-dependent process (Kogut and Zander 1993). Most expositions of path-dependency assume, however, that the choice of path is essentially myopic, in the sense that decision-makers make no attempt to anticipate the kind of information that will get fed back at each stage. This need not be the case, though. An entrepreneurial firm may be able to anticipate how the information that it will obtain in the future depends on the decision that it currently has to make. In this case its managers can exploit the logical structure of this learning process to expand in an optimal manner. The sequence of industries into which the firm diversifies, and the sequence of the countries in which it invests, represents a rational dynamic strategy of growth.

Similarly, strategic divestment in response to competition may also be seen as a consequence of a rational dynamic strategy. In a volatile environment a rational firm will anticipate the possibility of competition by investing in a manner that takes subsequent divestment options into account. It will make only those investments that it is either unlikely to want to divest, or which will be easy to divest because the sunk costs involved are relatively low. The typical investment will involve assets that have several alternative uses, and are easy to sell off to other firms. Since assets of this kind are easy to obtain in the first place, through acquisition, the theory suggests that acquisitions and divestments of highly 'liquid'

or 'non-specific' assets are likely to play a major role in flexible investment strategies. This is one reason why acquisitions and divestments became more common at the same time that international joint ventures (IJVs) became more common too. Both are implications of the strategic pursuit of flexibility in a volatile environment.

The pursuit of sophisticated strategies of this kind requires a great deal of information to be shared within the organization. It is crucial that this information is communicated in an honest manner. Integrity is often assured by repeated interaction, as explained by the theory of non-cooperative games (Kreps 1990). Alternatively, integrity can be assured by cultural engineering (Casson 1991). Cultural engineering within a firm can be effected in two main ways. One is by selecting people who have already been subjected to appropriate cultural influences. This explains why many firms recruit selectively from certain communities, educational institutions, and ethnic groups. Cultural homogeneity not only improves internal communication, but standardizes employees on a uniform set of moral values. The alternative is for the firm to recruit people purely on the basis of competence instead, and standardize the morals through active dissemination of a corporate culture. The first strategy allows the firm to 'free ride' on cultural engineering by other institutions, and reduces the demands on the chief executive's leadership role. The second strategy allows the firm to recruit more widely, and to tailor the moral system to its specific requirements. MNEs will tend to favour the latter strategy because they need to recruit a range of different nationalities, and to combine the expertise of members of very different professional groups.

25.5 THE FUTURE: DYNAMIC MARKET ENTRY

Consider the problem of modelling market entry from a dynamic rather than a static point of view (Chi and McGuire 1996). The most important new point to take into account is that the foreign market can decline as well as grow. Divestment or withdrawal must be considered as serious strategies. Clearly, these strategies do not apply until the market has been entered, but once it has been entered they may need to be used. Static models assume that the market will be constant, while very simple dynamic models, such as Buckley and Casson (1981) only suppose that the market will grow. In a volatile environment a market may grow to begin with, attracting investment, but then go into decline, requiring divestment instead.

Switching between strategies is costly, and the costs depend on both the strategy the firm is switching from and the strategy the firm is switching to. To preserve flexibility, it is important for the firm to choose at the outset strategies whose exit costs are low. This tends to favour exporting over host-country production, and

licensing over internalization. In other words, it reveals foreign direct investment (FDI) as a high-risk strategy.

Switching decisions can be mistaken, however, because the information upon which they are based is poor. Expected switching costs are reduced by avoiding unnecessary switches. Different strategies afford different opportunities for capturing information from the host environment and feeding it back to inform subsequent switching decisions.

FDI offers better opportunities for information capture than either licensing or exporting, since ownership of assets confers ownership of information too. This means, for example, that if volatility caused the market to grow unexpectedly, then the foreign investor would recognize this quickly. Since it is often cheaper to expand existing capacity than to build from scratch, the foreign investor also faces lower costs of capacity expansion than does an exporter who decides to switch to foreign production at this stage. While exporting continues to confer more flexibility in response to market decline, therefore, foreign investment confers more flexibility in respect of market growth.

Is it possible to find a strategy with a better combination of characteristics than either exporting, licensing, or FDI? An IJV may provide the answer (Kogut 1991). Investing in a 50:50 partnership with a host-country producer lays off some of the risks associated with wholly-owned FDI. At the same time information capture remains reasonably good. There is an option to expand capacity if there is unexpected market growth, and a further option to increase commitment by buying the partner out. There is also an easy option to withdraw by selling out to the partner. The partner provides a ready market for divested assets that an ordinary direct investor lacks. There is a down-side, of course—an obvious problem is that the partners may themselves become a source of volatility. This is why trust is such an important element in an IJV. In this way the emphasis on risk management within the new research agenda leads to the emergence of new 'compromise strategies' which would be dominated by more conventional strategies were it not for the 'option value' they possess within a volatile environment.

IJV options can only be exercised once, of course, unless the investor switches back to an IJV arrangement at a later date, when they can be exercised all over again. This explains IJV instability as a rational response to the role that IJVs fulfil. An IJV in which the options are never exercised is probably inferior to a wholly-owned investment, while an IJV where options are exercised at the first available opportunity does not last for very long. When IJVs are chosen because of their option value, it is normally inefficient both to switch out right away or to never switch at all. The optimal timing of a switch is one at which uncertainty about future market growth is dispelled for a reasonable period of time. This implies that the duration of IJVs is, on average, fairly short, and relatively variable.

The globalization of markets has been a major factor in the growth of volatility, as explained above. A feature of many global markets is the use of regional production

and distribution hubs, where several neighbouring countries are serviced from the same location. The regional hub, like the IJV, can be understood as a strategy that offers superior flexibility. Just as an IJV offers a compromise ownership strategy, a regional hub offers a compromise location strategy. Because the hub is nearer to each market than is the home location, it reduces transport costs, and offers better information capture too. Yet because it is close to several markets, it avoids exclusive commitment to any one. If one market declines, production can be switched to other markets instead. Provided the shocks affecting the national markets are independent (or less than perfectly correlated, at any rate) the hub provides gains from diversification. These are real gains that only the firm can achieve, as opposed to the financial gains from unrelated product diversification, which have proved disappointing in the past because they are best exploited through the diversification of individual share portfolios instead.

The two strategies of IJV and hub can be combined. Since one is an ownership strategy and the other a location strategy they can, if desired, be combined directly in an IJV production hub. Closer examination of the issues suggests that this is not normally the best approach, however. The model suggests that a combination of a wholly-owned production hub supplying IJV distribution facilities in each national market is a better solution. A hub facility is too critical to global strategy to allow a partner to become involved, because the damage they could do is far too great. Even with a wholly-owned hub facility, the combination still affords considerable flexibility to divest or withdraw from any single market. The advantage of the combination is that when divesting, the distribution facility can be sold to the partner, while the production capacity can be diverted to markets elsewhere. These options for divestment are combined with useful options for expansion too.

This example illustrates the crucial role that the concepts of flexibility and volatility play in analysing foreign market entry in the modern global economy. Without these concepts, it is impossible to fully understand the rationale for IJVs and production hubs. It is also impossible to understand why these strategies have emerged at this particular historical juncture and not before.

The attacks on New York and Washington on 11 September 2001 have introduced a radical discontinuity into the world system of trade, finance, and investment. This will introduce new elements of political uncertainty to add to the volatility already faced by companies. It is possible that the aftermath of the attacks will represent a setback to the continued integration of markets which globalization represents. This may accelerate regionalization as opposed to globalization (Rugman 2000). It may represent fragmentation of several previously integrated global markets and networks (e.g. international supply chains). It may accelerate the trends towards localization rather than internationalization which were becoming evident in several industrial sectors. The confidence with which international firms face world supply chains and world markets is bound to receive a severe setback. It is indicative of the high levels of uncertainty facing business that a clear future

scenario (or more likely alternative scenarios with different degrees of probabilistic outcomes) is less clear at the end of September 2001 than it was at its beginning.

25.6 SUMMARY

This chapter has connected globalization with an increase in volatility in the world economy. More shocks are being generated, and these shocks are more rapidly distributed around the world system. Multinational enterprises play a role in generating these shocks (by, for instance, relocation decisions), transmitting them (through foreign exchange transactions for instance), and responding to them (reconfiguring activities). These roles can be summed into the requirement for extra flexibility by firms. This imperative has implications for the external environment in which multinational firms operate, for the boundaries of the firm and for the firms' internal organization. These changes feed back to a new round of changes in market and to further global integration. This dynamic system has profound implications outside companies and world markets. Our understanding relies on concepts from the theory of the multinational enterprise, suitably amended for the changed conditions of the globalizing economy.

REFERENCES

AHARONI, YAIR (1966). *The Foreign Investment Decision Process*. Boston: Graduate School of Business Administration, Harvard University.

ARROW, KENNETH J. (1962). 'Economic Welfare and the Allocation of Resources for Invention', in National Bureau of Economic Research, *The Rate and Direction of Inventive Activity*. Princeton: Princeton University Press. Reproduced in D. M. Lamberton (ed.) (1971). *Economics of Information and Knowledge*. Harmondsworth: Penguin.

BARTLETT, CHRISTOPHER A., and GHOSHAL, SUMANTRA (1987). 'Managing Across Borders: New Strategic Requirements'. *Sloan Management Review*, Summer: 6–17.

—— —— (1989). *Managing Across Borders: The Transnational Solution*. Boston: Hutchinson Business Books.

BEST, MICHAEL H. (1990). *The New Competition: Institutions of Industrial Restructuring*. Oxford: Polity Press.

BUCKLEY, PETER J. (1983*a*). 'New Theories of International Business: Some Unresolved Issues', in Mark Casson (ed.), *The Growth of International Business*. London: George Allen & Unwin.

—— (1983b). 'Macroeconomic versus the International Business Approach to a Direct Foreign Investment: A Comment on Professor Kojima's Approach'. *Hitotsubashi Journal of Economics*, 24/1 (June): 95–100.

—— (1985a). 'The Economic Analysis of the Multinational Enterprise: Reading versus Japan?' *Hitotsubashi Journal of Economics*, 26/2 (Dec.): 117–24.

—— (1985b). 'New Forms of International Industrial Cooperation', in Peter J. Buckley and Mark Casson, *The Economic Theory of the Multinational Enterprise*. London: Macmillan.

—— (1988). 'The Limits of Explanation: Testing the Internalization Theory of the Multinational Enterprise'. *Journal of International Business Studies*, 19/2: 1–16.

—— (1990). 'Problems and Developments in the Core Theory of International Business'. *Journal of International Business Studies*, 21/4: 657–65.

—— and CARTER, MARTIN J. (1996). 'The Economics of Business Process Design: Motivation, Information and Co-ordination within the Firm'. *International Journal of the Economics of Business*, 3/1: 5–25.

—— and CASSON, MARK C. (1976). *The Future of the Multinational Enterprise*. London: Macmillan.

———— (1981). 'The Optimal Timing of a Foreign Direct Investment'. *Economic Journal*, 91: 75–87.

———— (1985). *The Economic Theory of the Multinational Enterprise*. London: Macmillan.

———— (1988). 'A Theory of Co-operation in International Business', in Farok J. Contractor and Peter Lorange (eds.), *Co-operative Strategies in International Business*. Lexington, Mass.: Lexington Books, 31–53.

———— (1993). 'Economics as an Imperialist Social Science'. *Human Relations*, 46/9: 1035–52.

———— (1996). 'An Economic Model of International Joint Venture Strategy'. *Journal of International Business Studies*, 27/5: 849–76.

———— (1998). 'Models of Multinational Enterprise'. *Journal of International Business Studies*, 29/1: 29–44.

—— and CHAPMAN, MALCOLM (1996). 'Economics and Social Anthropology—Reconciling Differences'. *Human Relations*, 49/9: 1123–50.

—— and DAVIES, HOWARD (1981). 'Foreign Licensing in Overseas Operations: Theory and Evidence from the UK', in R. G. Hawkins and A. J. Prasad (eds.), *Technology Transfer and Economic Development*. Greenwich, Conn.: JAI Press.

—— and PEARCE, ROBERT D. (1979). 'Overseas Production and Exporting by the World's Largest Enterprises—A Study in Scouring Policy'. *Journal of International Business Studies*, 10/1: 9–20.

———— (1981). 'Market Servicing by Multinational Manufacturing Firms: Exporting Versus Foreign Production'. *Managerial and Decision Economics*, 2/4 (Dec.): 229–46.

———— (1984). 'Exports in the Strategy of Multinational Firms'. *Journal of Business Research*, 12/2 (June): 209–26.

CALVET, A. L. (1981). 'A Synthesis of Foreign Direct Investment Theories and Theories of the Multinational Firm'. *Journal of International Business Studies*, 12: 43–60.

CAMPA, JOSE MANUEL (1994). 'Multinational Investment under Uncertainty in the Chemical Processing Industries'. *Journal of International Business Studies*, 25/3: 557–78.

CANTWELL, JOHN (1995). 'Multinational Enterprises and Innovatory Activities: Towards a New Evolutionary Approach', in J. Molero (ed.), *Technological Innovation, Multinational*

Corporations and the New International Competitiveness. Chur: Harwood Academic Publishers, 21–57.

CASSON, MARK (1979). *Alternatives to the Multinational Enterprise*. London: Macmillan.

—— (1981). 'Foreword', in Alan M. Rugman, *Inside the Multinational*. London: Croom Helm.

—— (1985a). 'Transaction Costs and the Theory of the Multinational Enterprise', in Peter J. Buckley and Mark Casson, *The Economic Theory of the Multinational Enterprise*. London: Macmillan.

—— (1985b). 'Multinational and the Intermediate Product Trade', in Peter J. Buckley and Mark Casson, *The Economic Theory of the Multinational Enterprise*. London: Macmillan.

—— (1987). *The Firm and the Market*. Oxford: Basil Blackwell.

—— (1990). *Enterprise and Competitiveness*. Oxford: Clarendon Press.

—— (1991). *Economics of Business Culture*. Oxford: Clarendon Press.

—— (1994). 'Why are Firms Hierarchical?' *International Journal of the Economics of Business*, 1/1: 3–40.

—— (1995). *Organization of International Business*. Aldershot: Edward Elgar.

—— PEARCE, ROBERT D. and SINGH, SATWINDER (1991). 'A Review of Recent Trends', in M. Casson (ed.), *Global Research Strategy and International Competitiveness*. Oxford: Blackwell, 250–71.

CAVES, RICHARD E. (1996). *Multinational Enterprise and Economic Analysis* (2nd edn). Cambridge: Cambridge University Press.

CHI, TAILAN, and McGUIRE, DONALD J. (1996). 'Collaborative Ventures and Value of Learning: Integrating the Transaction Cost and Strategic Option Perspectives on the Choice of Market Entry Modes'. *Journal of International Business Studies*, 27/2: 285–307.

COASE, RONALD H. (1973). *The Location of International Firms in an Enlarged EEC: An Exploratory Paper*. Manchester: Manchester Statistical Society.

DEMPSTER, MICHAEL A. H., and PLISKA, STANLEY R. (eds.) (1997). *Mathematics of Derivative Securities*. Cambridge: Cambridge University Press.

DIXIT, AVRINASH, and PINDYCK, ROBERT S. (1994). *Investments under Uncertainty*. Princeton: Princeton University Press.

DUNNING, JOHN H. (1972). *The Location of International Firms in an Enlarged EEC: An Exploratory Paper*. Manchester: Manchester Statistical Society.

—— (1977). 'Trade, Location of Economic Activity and the Multinational Enterprise: The Search for an Eclectic Approach', in B. Ohlin, P. O. Hessleborn, and P. M. Wijkman (eds.), *The International Location of Economic Activity*. London: Macmillan.

—— (1981). *International Production and the Multinational Enterprise*. London: George Allen & Unwin.

—— (1988). *Explaining International Production*. London: Unwin Hyman.

—— (1993). *Multinational Enterprises in the Global Economy*. Wokingham, Berks.: Addison-Wesley.

—— (1997). *Alliance Capitalism and Global Business*. London: Routledge.

ERGAS, HENRY (1987). 'Does Technology Policy Matter?' in B. R. Guile and H. Brooks (eds.), *Technology and Global Industry*. Washington, DC: National Academy Press, 191–245.

FRANSMAN, MARTIN (1995). *Japan's Computer and Communications Industry*. Oxford: Oxford University Press.

GERINGER, J. MICHAEL, and HÉBERT, LOUIS (1989). 'Control and Performance of International Joint Ventures'. *Journal of International Business Studies*, 20/2: 235–54.

GIDDY, IAN H. (1978). 'The Demise of the Product Cycle Model in International Business Theory'. *Columbia Journal of World Business*, 13: 90–7.

HEDLUND, GUNNAR (1993). 'Assumptions of Hierarchy and Heterarchy: An Application to the Multinational Corporation', in S. Ghoshal and E. Westney (eds.), *Organization Theory and the Multinational Corporation*. London: Macmillan, 211–36.

HIRSH, SEEV H. (1967). *The Location of Industry and International Competitiveness*. Oxford: Oxford University Press.

HOOD, NEIL, and YOUNG, STEPHEN (1994). 'The Internationalization of Business and the Challenge of East European Business', in P. J. Buckley and P. N. Ghauri (eds.), *The Economics of Change in East and Central Europe*. London: Academic Press, 320–42.

HORST, T. O. (1972). 'The Industrial Composition of US Exports and Subsidiary Sales to the Canadian Market'. *American Economic Review*, 57: 37–45.

HUFBAUER, G. C. (1966). *Synthetic Materials and the Theory of International Trade*. London: Duckworth.

HYMER, STEPHEN H. (1968). 'The Large Multinational "Corporation": An Analysis of Some Motives for the International Integration of Business'. *Revue Economique*, 19/6: 949–73. English version in Mark Casson (ed.), *Multinational Corporations*. Aldershot: Edward Elgar.

—— (1976). *The International Operations of National Firms*. Cambridge, Mass.: MIT Press.

JOHANSON, JAN, and VAHLNE, JAN-ERIK (1977). 'The Internationalization Process of the Firm—A Model of Knowledge Development and Increasing Foreign Market Commitments'. *Journal of International Business Studies*, 8/1: 23–32.

JOHNSON, HARRY G. (1970). 'The Efficiency and Welfare Implications of the International Corporation', in C. P. Kindleberger (ed.), *The International Corporation*. Cambridge, Mass.: MIT Press.

KINDLEBERGER, C. P. (1969). *American Business Abroad*. New Haven: Yale University Press.

KOGUT, BRUCE (1991). 'Joint Ventures and the Option to Expand and Acquire'. *Management Science*, 37/1: 19–33.

—— and ZANDER, UDO (1993). 'Knowledge of the Firm and the Evolutionary Theory of the Multinational Corporation'. *Journal of International Business Studies*, 24/4: 625–45.

KOJIMA, K. (1978). *Direct Foreign Investment: A Japanese Model of Multinational Business*. London: Croom Helm.

—— (1982). 'Macroeconomic versus International Business Approach to Direct Foreign Investment'. *Hitotsubashi Journal of Economics*, 23/1: 1–19.

—— and OZAWA, T. (1984). 'Micro and Macro Models of Direct Foreign Investment: Towards a Synthesis'. *Hitotsubashi Journal of Economics*, 25/1: 1–20.

KREPS, DAVID M. (1990). *Game Theory and Economic Modelling*. Oxford: Oxford University Press.

KRUGMAN, PAUL (1995). *Development, Geography and Economic Theory*. Cambridge, Mass.: MIT Press.

LALL, SANJAYA, and STREETEN, PAUL (1977). *Foreign Investment, Transnationals and Developing Countries*. London: Macmillan.

MAGEE, S. P. (1977). 'Multinational Corporations, Industry Technology Cycle and Development'. *Journal of World Trade Law*, 11: 297–321.

MARRIS, ROBIN L. (1979). *The Theory and Future of the Corporate Economy and Society*. Amsterdam: North-Holland.

MARSHALL, ALFRED (1919). *Industry and Trade*. London: Macmillan.

MELLO, ANTONIO S., PARSONS, JOHN E. and TRIANTIS, ALEXANDER J. (1995). 'An Integrated Model of Multinational Flexibility and Hedging Policies'. *Journal of International Economics*, 39/Aug.: 27–51.

MIRZA, HAFIZ (1986). *Multinationals and the Growth of the Singapore Economy*. London: Croom Helm.

NELSON, RICHARD, and WINTER, SIDNEY G. (1982). *An Evolutionary Theory of Economic Change*. Cambridge, Mass.: Harvard University Press.

OZAWA, T. (1979a). *Multinationalism, Japanese Style: The Political Economy of Outward Dependency*. Princeton: Princeton University Press.

—— (1979b). 'International Investment and Industrial Structure: New Theoretical Implications from the Japanese Experience'. *Oxford Economic Papers*, 31: 72–92.

PORTER, MICHAEL E. (1990). *The Competitive Advantage of Nations*. London: Macmillan.

—— (1991). 'Towards a Dynamic Theory of Strategy'. *Strategic Management Journal*, 12/ Special Issue: 95–117.

RANGAN, SUBRAMANIAN, and LAWRENCE, ROBERT Z. (1999). *A Prism on Globalization*. Washington, DC: Brookings Institution Press.

RIVOLI, PIETRA, and SALORIO, EUGENE (1996). 'Foreign Direct Investment under Uncertainty'. *Journal of International Business Studies*, 27/2: 335–54.

RUGMAN, ALAN M. (1981). *Inside the Multinationals*. London: Croom Helm.

—— (2000). *The End of Globalisation*. London: Random House.

—— D'CRUZ, JOSEPH R., and VERBEKE, ALAIN (1995). 'Internalisation and de-internalisation: Will Business Networks Replace Multinationals?', in G. Boyd (ed.), *Competitive and Cooperative Macromanagement: The Challenge of Structural Interdependence*. Aldershot: Edward Elgar, 107–28.

TEECE, DAVID (1983). 'Technological and Organisational Factors in the Theory of the Multinational Enterprise', in Mark Casson (ed.), *The Growth of International Business*. London: George Allen & Unwin.

TRIGEORGIS, LENOS (1996). *Real Options*. Cambridge, Mass.: MIT Press.

VAITSOS, C. V. (1974). *Intercountry Income Distribution and Transnational Enterprises*. Oxford: Oxford University Press.

VERNON, RAYMOND (1966). 'International Investment and International Trade in the Product Cycle'. *Quarterly Journal of Economics*, 80: 190–207.

—— (1974). 'The Location of Economic Activity', in John H. Dunning (ed.), *Economic Analysis and the Multinational Enterprise*. London: George Allen & Unwin.

—— (1979). 'The Product Cycle Hypothesis in a New International Environment'. *Oxford Bulletin of Economics and Statistics*, 41: 225–67.

WILLIAMSON, OLIVER E. (1975). *Markets and Hierarchies: Analysis and Anti-trust Implications*. New York: Free Press.

—— (1981). 'The Modern Corporation: Origins, Evolution, Attributes'. *Journal of Economic Literature*, 19: 1537–68.

—— (1985). *The Economic Institutions of Capitalism*. New York: Free Press.

WU, SHIH-YEN (1988). *Production, Entrepreneurship and Profits*. Oxford: Blackwell.

PART V

CHANGE

MANAGING STRATEGIC CHANGE

RICHARD WHIPP

26.1 WHY MANAGING STRATEGIC CHANGE?

THE centrality of managing strategic change for contemporary organizations became abundantly clear during the 1990s. The problems it presents for managers are as pervasive as they are challenging. Businesses are confronted by: new bases of competition, the redefinition of whole sectors, and the continual re-establishment of innovative practices by leading companies from across the globe. Whilst micro-electronic and communications technologies offer a platform for new products and services, they also have led to the redrawing of competitive maps and the abandonment of long-established rules of engagement. Change has become the watchword of the era. The ability to handle the implications of such disturbance, at the level of the firm or organization, is highly prized.

A glance at the recruitment pages in the international financial press reinforces the image of change as a critical concern to organizations of all types. The recent advertisement by Jersey Airport is instructive. In seeking to attract a new manager for the airport, the requirements of the position are seen almost exclusively in terms of managing strategic change. As Figure 26.1 shows, this 'change director' will have to address a 'strident technical, financial, and cultural agenda' where all stakeholders embrace this vision. The appointee must convincingly answer the question 'why change' as well as exhibiting commercial flair, understanding of

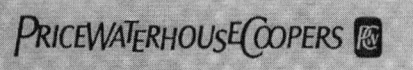

CHANGE DIRECTOR

Who Knows What Tomorrow Brings?

JERSEY   UP TO £70,000

You do. And you'll help take Jersey Airport to a tomorrow that gives full expression to us being the most customer friendly airport in the British Isles. Located in this warm and enticing island off the UK's south coast, we deal with nearly 2 million passengers per year - tourists and business people attracted by Jersey's holiday environment and off-shore financial services industry.

Crystal ball gazing
Our goal, as with other commercial government-run services, is to move from being part of the States of Jersey, to arms length ownership, and to viable financial self-sufficiency. Following an in depth strategic review, we have a strident technical, financial and cultural change agenda to make the airport's commercial potential more than just pie in the sky.

It's that cultural change process that needs someone to take us to where we belong. Reporting to the Airport Director and to the States of Jersey, and as part of the Airport management team, you will send us - employees of all professions, trade unions, and even our managers - on a fundamentally challenging but necessary roller-coaster ride. Your first task will be to get all stakeholders to embrace this vision and convincingly answer the question 'Why change?'

And what of you?
You will have had led change processes where your focus has been on winning spirits, hearts and minds. With a track record of senior management within (or with a high content of) human resources ideally in the service sector, you will also exhibit a commercial flair and a sound understanding of project management.

Developing external public relations and the sharing of views within the airport, you'll liase with a range of the Jersey community's players and work closely with our Head of Human Resources. You'll have a head for the heights of leadership, but not for the clouds - it's the wisdom borne of practical experience we need, not transformation theory.

Your sense of presence and ability to engage people at a time when uncertainty and insecurity are very visible is vital. Likewise, your ability to develop their trust and immerse yourself in the life of the airport, and indeed the island, will do much to determine your success. You will have an eye for systems and processes that deliver, yet still keep your sights on a commercial future.

Your future
If you can lead change for this lifeline service, send your CV to our advising consultants at PricewaterhouseCoopers quoting reference MY2038/ST. For a confidential and informal discussion, call Mohan Yogendran on 0171 939 3895 or Hamish Davidson on 0171 939 3115.

PricewaterhouseCoopers
Executive Search & Selection
Southwark Towers
32 London Bridge Street
London
SE1 9SY
Fax: 0171 378 0647
E-mail: mohan.yogendran@uk.pwcglobal.com

Visit our website at www.pwcglobal.com/executive/uk

Fig. 26.1 Change director

Source: The Sunday Times, 16 May 1999

project management, leadership, and provide 'an eye for systems and processes that deliver' results.

It is striking how the advertisement assumes that the role of manager implies an extensive range of change management skills. A similar picture emerges in other job

announcements from sectors such as finance or health care. The feature which links them all is the breadth of problems faced by organizations in both coping with the implications of their strategic choices and translating such decisions into operational form (see also Box 26.1 below).

Box 26.1 The BBC

The BBC has been described as the UK's most global brand. Its output is known worldwide and its programme makers enjoy the highest of reputations. In the space of just over a decade, however, it has moved from a position of oligopoly to one where viewers now have the choice of hundreds of channels with the advent of digital technology.

During the 1990s the regime of the director-general, John Birt, had emphasized efficiency and productivity in an attempt to bring costs under control. Great weight was placed on the creation of an internal market with elaborate rules and procedures governing relations between departments such as programme makers, journalists, and designers.

The criticism of Birt's reforms were as loud during his period of office as they have been since his departure in 1999. The corporation had become fragmented and individualism was the dominant tone. Market-like exchanges inhibited collaboration and the drive for financial control diminished the energy needed for programme excellence. Serial reorganizations fell into disrepute as they disrupted the efforts of editors and journalists yet seemed to leave senior managers untouched. Identifying the organization's main decision-making processes became impossible.

The BBC now has new executives in post, including Greg Dyke as director-general (after a career in television management) and Gareth Jones, the new director of human resources. Jones has worked as an academic specializing in change management as well as being in charge of human resources at Polygram. Both took up their posts in the past year and agree that the corporation is over-managed and under-led. The BBC, they argue, has to reinvent itself.

The task facing the BBC is a major one. It has to sustain its reputation for excellence as a public-service broadcaster while competing in the new digital environment. There is a clear need to establish a new common purpose which links all staff. The internal market has to be reduced so that rules do not stifle creativity. At the same time, the absence of the stakeholders associated with private businesses must not be allowed to re-create the conditions of the past where BBC staff became notorious for their insularity. The delicate balance between risk-taking and commitment to the organization will have to be created and maintained. All this will have to take place against a labour market which has become particularly volatile with the drawing power of new on-line businesses.

26.1.1 Management Capabilities

While companies have grown more aware of the demands of strategic change, managers appear to be concerned about the readiness of their organizations to

respond. In 1999 the Economist Intelligence Unit and Andersen Consulting questioned 350 senior managers from around the world on the subject of corporate change. Although half had experienced major changes in their business in the past five years, they expected more radical changes by 2010. Only 3 per cent considered their organizations had the techniques to withstand the demands presented by, for example, small, fast-moving knowledge-based companies. Almost 40 per cent cited the skills of people management, communication, and relationship building as lacking in their organization. Only 4 per cent claimed that they were 'very well' prepared for the changes of the next decade.

The results of the survey show how managing strategic change remains a major difficulty in spite of over thirty years of oil price shocks, the advent of new sources of competition from Asian economies, and the appearance of successive waves of so-called 'best practice'. The example of Boeing, the world's most successful aircraft maker, is instructive. Its dominance of its sector notwithstanding, the raft of changes it has to manage over the next five years and beyond is considerable. Seen through the eyes of chairman Philip Condit, this will include: integrating the recently acquired business of McDonnell Douglas; becoming a global rather than a US company; and managing joint ventures with new partners such as those from China. Boeing is candid in admitting that it is impossible to hold on to a 'technological edge'; their advantage will lie in 'human capital' and 'how they run the business'.

As the difficulties facing organizations have multiplied, so academics and reflective practitioners have continued to analyse the pattern of forces involved and to suggest appropriate responses. The broad aim of this chapter is to provide the reader with access to the wealth of approaches to managing strategic change which are now available. Entering the new century, the subject has reached a state of maturity. A succession of schools of thought have emerged, each addressing the problems which confronted their era. Now is an excellent time to synthesize that work and identify the potential problems and solutions for those who have the responsibility of managing strategic change.

The four main sections of the chapter cover these objectives in the following ways. Section 26.2 presents an overview of the field of strategic management and explains how strategic change has become a separate area of specialization. The beneficial merging of techniques and insights from the strategy and organizational fields is a major outcome of recent developments. The pervasiveness of the problem of strategic change has led to the widespread adoption of a change rhetoric by almost every type of organization. The result has been a somewhat restricted vocabulary, reliant on dramatic notions of transformation. In Section 26.3, a more inclusive terminology is offered in the form of a change typology which acknowledges the subtle but vital differences of context and extent of alteration. The specialists who have made use of such distinctions are the subject of Section 26.4. The development of the strategic process perspective has produced arguably the

most penetrating insights into the management of strategic change and its exponents are given separate coverage here. In the light of the difficulties most organizations face in managing strategic change, Section 26.5 examines how leading researchers have grappled with these problems. The section uses the examples of crises, implementation, and resistance. The chapter closes with a consideration of the possible future direction of the subject and the potential sources of analytical and practical innovations. It ends with a summary of the requirements for an organization which is fully able to manage strategic change across different contexts.

26.2 INSIGHTS FROM RESEARCH
AND PRACTICE

The past thirty years of research into the problem of strategic change and how it may be managed look richly textured but uneven. The following pages make reference to such a history and seek to show how different emphases have given rise to contrasting insights. The section will also establish some of the key concepts and terminology which have arisen and are useful for analysing change management. This will lead to the consideration of: the planning orthodoxy of the 1960s; the decision-making frameworks of the 1970s and their links with the cultural, political investigations of change; the reaction by US and European scholars in the 1980s and 1990s to the business policy model's silence on change, which resulted in an alliance between experts on competition, innovation, and organizations. The outcome will be an appreciation of the major ways of explaining the character of strategic change and the options of how to manage it.

Strategic change is in many respects the offspring of the subject of strategy which has grown markedly over the last decades of the twentieth century. Strategy's core meaning had long been encapsulated in Chandler's formula as: the determination of the long-term goals of an enterprise, the allocation of resources, and the courses of action required for meeting those goals (Chandler 1962: 13). Later work has emphasized the need for a strategy to neutralize threats and exploit opportunities (Barney 1997: 27) as well as matching an organization's resources to its environment so as to meet stakeholder expectations. Strategic management is concerned with how strategies are adopted. Managing strategic change refers, therefore, to the management of the changes which specific strategies give rise to and imply.

26.2.1 Planning and Decision-making

In the decades immediately following World War II, the notion of corporate strategy grew strongly, based on microeconomics and the assumptions of rational profit-maximizing behaviour and full information. Heavy emphasis was placed on financial planning (Bourgeois 1996: 5). The corporate strategy tradition has been sustained in various forms down to the present. Since the 1960s and 1970s, however, a stream of enquiry began into how organizations operationalized given strategies. The earliest examples were seen in the work of March and Olsen (1976), who showed how the decisions of managers were seldom wholly rational and that coalition formation led to important trade-offs over outcomes. Their research highlighted how the implementation of strategic decisions could be haphazard and reliant on subjective judgements. Mintzberg's (1978) empirical study of strategy formation and execution concluded that these constituted identifiable change processes which required analysis and management on their own terms.

As interest grew in the full length of the strategic decision-making process, so this attracted the attention of scholars who specialized in the study of the political character of organizations. Their work (see e.g. Pettigrew 1977) shows how interest groups form around strategic issues and compete for resources; the balance of power between them shifts in relation to episodes of change. Negotiation between coalitions occurs as they seek to establish their preferred outcomes. Courses of strategic action are therefore subject to mutual adjustments between those who seek to influence the decision-making process and those who must carry out the strategy. The linking of notions of power and politics to strategic management drew attention to the potential involvement of those from within and outside an organization. Influence is seen as conditional on the organization's dependency on such individuals or units (Hickson et al. 1986).

26.2.2 Cognition and Culture

During the 1970s and 1980s, the recognition of the way strategy development and implementation could be affected by perception and subjectivity led to a wider interest in the role of cognition and culture. The central proposition which emerged was that organizations possess a taken-for-granted and shared framework of attitudes, values, and perceptions. This framework of values enables the organization to interpret the environment in which it operates and helps it to deal with new or complex situations. Choices over strategies are therefore shaped by such value systems and the problems of implementation are addressed within the confines of an organization's culture (Schein 1985). Managers' reactions to the issues which arise in the elaboration and application of a strategy are often conditioned by, for

example, 'organizational routines' which owe their existence to the organization's culture and its historical development.

The application of behavioural and cognitive perspectives to the subject of strategic management led to the concentration by some writers on the role of individuals, usually leaders. The emphasis is upon such an individual's ability to choose a desired future state for the organization which, in turn, suggests a specific strategy and its adoption by others. The vision of some future state may well represent a sharp break with convention and require unfamiliar strategies as far as the organization is concerned. Visionary leaders, it is argued, share the qualities of breaking down traditional thoughts and practices, creating new strategies which draw on the organization's shared values, and communicating new courses of action convincingly to others. The legitimacy of a strategic direction is thereby obtained and the authority for its realization achieved (Trice and Beyer 1986).

An alternative, and by comparison, restrictive view of strategic management grew up alongside but separate to the behavioural approaches. The emphasis is on the limitations which the environment places on an organization's ability to select strategies which match the dominant features of that context. The scope for individual choice is small. When organizations produce variations or new depart-ures in strategy, only those that meet the criteria accepted by the environment survive. Advantages emanating from strategic choices tend to disappear as aware-ness spreads of the innovation and imitation follows (McKelvey and Aldrich 1983).

26.2.3 Strategic Change Processes

The long-term growth of the strategy field has therefore produced a set of influential perspectives on strategic change which have contributed to the literature by concen-trating on decision-making, politics, culture, individuals, and the environment. Many researchers of strategic change are either located within these traditions or draw extensively on their main tenets. This profile is valuable as a guide to how differing emphases have occurred; it is also a reminder of the very different backgrounds of the various authors. The planning approach has relied on academ-ics with economics backgrounds while the political or interpretive schools contain people largely with experience in psychology or behavioural subjects. It is, thereby, an indication of the scope of the problems posed by both the phenomenon of strategic change and the question of what might be relevant to its management.

One way of reinforcing the richness and strength of this field is to dwell on the character of the change processes which the different traditions imply. As Figure 26.2 shows, it is possible to isolate for a moment the organizational level at which change may occur: the micro and the macro. At the same time, one may distinguish whether structural features are paramount in explaining the change process or the

	Structural forms – continuous	Personnel action – discontinuous
Macro level	**Natural selection** An evolutionary process of variation, selection, and retention of structural forms in a population of organizations	**Collective action** A political process of mutual adjustment circumscribed by collective 'working rules' among interest groups
Micro level	**Structural contingency** An evolutionary process of progressive internal structural differentiation and integration	**Strategic choice** Rational process of choice and action by one or a few elite individuals or leaders

Fig. 26.2 Processes of change within orthodox organization theory

Source: Adapted from Van de Ven and Scott-Poole (1987: 39).

actions of people. By combining these aspects in a matrix, four main types of change process are apparent, as indicated in Figure 26.2. The perspectives outlined in the preceding paragraphs can be seen to be emphasizing the different types of change processes found in Figure 26.2. The planning experts and the leadership specialists adopt a more rational strategic choice view of change. By contrast, those who advocate the political or cultural approaches are using a more macro-based, collective action notion of organizational change. It is worthwhile to bear such distinctions in mind when assessing the work of individual authors on the management of strategic change, as will occur in the subsequent sections of this chapter.

26.2.4 Strategic Change and Competition

During the 1980s and early 1990s, dramatic shifts in the nature of competition and the appearance of marked differences in the performance of national sectors made a notable impact on the field of strategic change. The success, in particular, of

Japanese producers of manufacturing and consumer goods internationally, but especially in Western domestic markets, led to a two-stage response. After initial shock, the first actions of US and European commentators were centred on attempts to understand the nature and reasons for the success of the new entrants, such as Honda or Matsushita (Pascale 1990). In spite of the Japanese having no direct equivalent for the English word 'strategy', their apparent ability to manage strategic change became a source of fascination. In due course, admiration for the skills of linking long-range vision, technological innovation, and unprecedented levels of quality, led to a second outcome: a resurgence in interest in the subject of managing strategic change itself.

In truth, the reaction of Western writers appeared to be based partly on anxiety over the continued relevance of their established body of work, and equally on the need for managers and analysts to come up with new techniques of strategic change management to meet the competitive circumstances of the time. The result was a flood of commentary and prescription which often suffered from its shrill tone and meagre evidential base. Peters and Waterman (1982) seemed to be answering the need of US, and later European managers, when they claimed to have discovered the explanation for the 'excellence' of US companies (such as Apple and People's Express) who shone in their sector. In passing, they used their experience at consultants McKinsey to draw on established work on strategic change, especially the cultural and visionary perspectives (see above). Others followed, with the result that transformational change—requiring the complete replacement of the raison d'être of the organization and the bases on which it competed—became a dominant concern. Commentators became obsessed with the exceptional feats of change (as the cover from a contemporary report shows, see Figure 26.3). Subsequent research-led investigations appeared which drew extensively on the ideas of the decision-making, political, cultural, and individual perspectives. Kanter's work (1990), spoke both to the spirit of the times and showed how innovations in strategic management techniques could be achieved through, for example, imaginative approaches to communication, leadership, and influence processes.

The turbulence in competition and the challenge to the previous reputational orders in various sectors in the 1980s and 1990s sparked a fresh interest in strategic analysis, led by students of the microeconomics tradition which had underpinned the earlier strategic planning approach. Porter highlighted the need for organizations to clarify their choice of direction in relation to so-called mutually exclusive 'generic strategies' (such as cost leadership versus differentiation). He later presented a model of extended competition (Porter 1985) which embraced sources of competition from both conventional rivals and sources outside the sector. Others using the micro-economics tradition applied a rejuvenated version of the resource-based theory of the firm to the problem of strategic management. According to the theory, competitive performance is explained by reference to the ability of a firm to maintain a unique collection of capabilities (technological, organizational, and

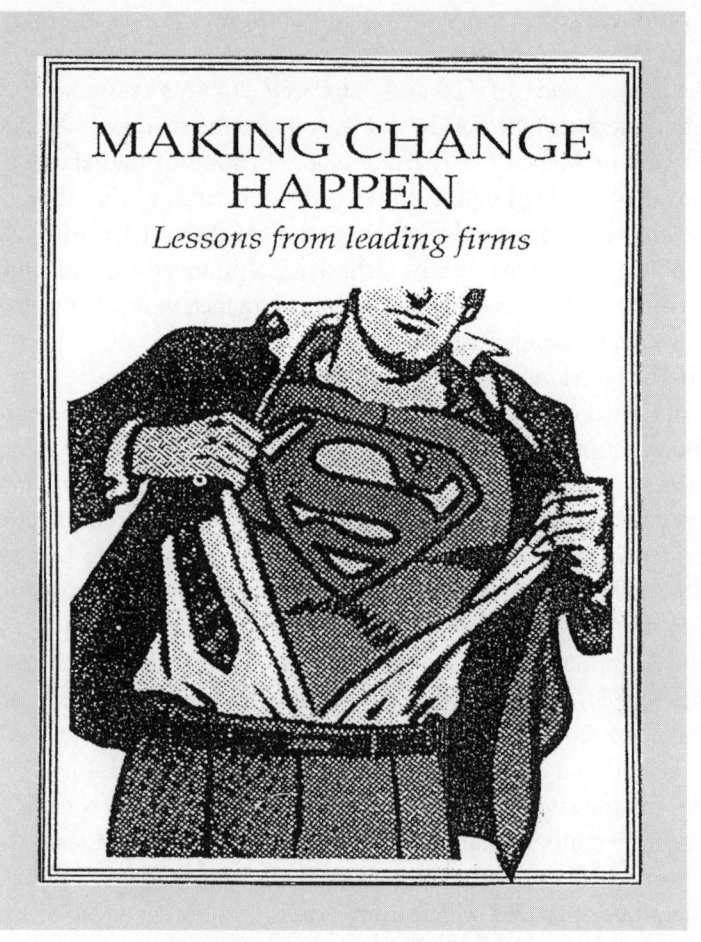

Fig. 26.3 Making change happen

Source: Kinsley Lord (1992: cover page).

financial, for example) by which innovative products or services are delivered and which competitors find difficult to replicate. Others responded by showing how the competence to manage the strategic changes involved is worthy of inclusion in any assessment of competitive performance (Pettigrew and Whipp 1991).

The potential contribution which could be made to the understanding of strategic change by writers from a diversity of backgrounds is formidable. Some see the problem of change as the core issue, others provide insights in a more indirect way while exploring aspects of competition. The inclusive approach adopted in this section points not only to the scale of features with which organizations are confronted when managing strategic change but also to the spread of academic perspectives which may aid explanation. Having surveyed the field, it is necessary to give closer attention to more detailed aspects of strategic change: the first concerns the matter of the language used to describe and comprehend change.

26.3 THE LANGUAGE OF CHANGE

The need to dwell on the nature of change and how it is described is necessary, notwithstanding the wealth of publications on the subject. Partly because of the almost universal recognition of the problem of change management, students and managers alike seldom inspect their assumptions behind the vocabulary they employ. Many of us are guilty of using words such as change and transformation interchangeably without thinking of the loss of clarity. A durable means of describing organizational change is vital if one is to tackle managing strategic change with any precision. This requires an exploration of the contrasts between basic types of change, as well as creating a means of distinguishing the differences in degrees of alteration. The importance of continuity to understanding its opposite—change— also requires attention.

26.3.1 A Change Typology

Change within an organization may vary according to whether the change is localized and small scale as opposed to being organization-wide. In addition, the extent to which the change in question requires new products, knowledge, and ways of operating may be contrasted against change which is based on a recombination of existing elements of the organization. Change may also evoke different orientations by members of the organization, ranging from reactive to anticipatory stances. If these considerations are joined they can be arranged to produce a fourfold categorization of organizational change.

The first is 'tuning'; where the degree of change is slight and adjustments are made to current policies and practices from within the organization. A classic illustration would be Marks & Spencer, until recently the UK's largest and most profitable retailer, which had been able to make such seemingly slight movements a way of life for some thirty years. 'Adaptation' is the second, when a firm is forced to alter in a reactive way to external pressures and stays within the accepted logic of its environment. The reaction of J Sainsbury, the UK supermarket leader (who pioneered own-label products) to the threat of Tesco in the 1980s is an example. The third type, 'reorientation', is when an organization attempts a shift in its core activities, diversifying into a related industry or vertically integrating through the acquisition of a supplier, for example. In the fourth category is 're-creation'. This is the most extreme version of organizational change, where the whole operation is affected and, above all, a fundamental reworking of its reason for existence follows, often resulting in the move into new products or services and their mode of delivery. One of the largest instances is the long overdue move of IBM from its

loyalty to mainframe computers to a concentration on electronic business services after almost disintegrating in the early 1990s.

Figure 26.4 is a useful summary of the main types of change which exist. It has the added advantage of identifying the level at which the change may occur: the strategic or the operational. The figure reminds us that there exists a specific collection of demands around so-called 'expanded reproduction', where the strategy may stay the same but expansion at the operational level is critical. It is important to remember that, in spite of the recent attraction of commentators to transformational change (in the privatization process, for example), organizations can still be faced with the problem of making 'evolutionary transitions'. In other words, a new strategy may be adopted, but it is based on the same commercial precepts and a remixing of existing organizational capabilities. The move of book publishers into electronic formats in the 1990s is a case in point.

It is equally important that the attention to transformational change in the last decade should not eclipse the relevance of continuity or the status quo. Nadler and Tushman (1988) remind us of the subtle distinctions involved between the different types of change which organizations must master. They argue that not all change is 'extraordinary' but that most change consists of fine tuning that enables an

	Degree of change	Organizational/ strategic level	Characteristics
1.	Status quo	Can be both operational and strategic	No change in current practice
2.	Expanded reproduction	Mainly operational	Change involves producing more of the same (goods or services)
3.	Evolutionary transition	Mainly strategic	Change occurs within existing parameters of the organization
4.	Revolutionary transformation	Predominantly strategic	Change involves shifting or redefining existing parameters

Fig. 26.4 Organizational change

Source: Based upon Wilson (1992: 20).

organization to adapt to the movements in its environment. They recognize the extreme nature of transformational change where the organization is dramatically severed from its past: this they call 'framebreaking', a term which applies to the experience of say Chrysler in the 1980s or Apple Computer since 1998. In contrast, the label 'framebending' is given to the way companies make less stark adjustments in structures, systems, or technology and where the organization retains some continuity with the immediate past. Xerox and NCR were leading examples of framebending in Nadler and Tushman's fifteen-year study of 285 companies. It is also worth recording that even where radical shifts are required in strategy, the need often exists for the management to sustain those capabilities which are advantageous for the organization. The oil majors, Shell and Exxon, for example, still have to maintain their skills in oil extraction and distribution while, at the same time, dealing with the pressures of merger and acquisition, supermarket retail competitors or the resurgence of environmental groups. Managing strategic change therefore requires a range of skills in order to meet the demands of the contrasting types of change involved. One way of revealing the extent of these skills is to look more closely at the process view of strategic change.

26.4 A Process View

While the previous section drew out a variety of specialized ways of describing change, here the aim is to highlight a common strength which links most of the established research on change management. The section centres on the appreciation of change as a process and change management in terms of sequences and flows of activity. It is a demanding approach since it is much easier for the manager or researcher to address an event or episode rather than the forces which surround and link them. The insights offered by the process view include the early 'developmental' techniques. They also give rise to Mintzberg's pattern of meaning in a stream of actions, as well as Quinn's revelation of the cumulative impact of fragmented yet incremental small-scale adjustments and Kanter's appreciation of cycles of activity in the production of innovative solutions.

26.4.1 The Behavioural Tradition

The early attempts at developing an overview of strategic change as a process drew heavily on the experts in the field of organizational development. Lewin (1947) and

Lewin	1947	Unfreezing		Changing			Refreezing		
Beckhard and Harris	1987	Present state		Transition state			Future state		
Mintzberg	1978	Recognition	Diagnosis	Search	Design	Screen	Evaluate	Authorize	
Quinn	1980	Sensing	Build awareness	New symbols	Partial solutions	Broaden support	Buffers	Trial concepts	New consensus	Review
Kanter	1990	Question tradition	Raise dissatisfaction	Conviction not vision	Communication		Links to routine issues	Empower	Act on systems that block change

Fig. 26.5 Strategic change processes

later Beckhard and Harris (1987) (see Figure 26.5) are examples of the faith in behavioural techniques of change management. Such work made use of research on group dynamics, for instance. In addition, these writers (and those who later adopted their approach) placed great weight on the ability of managerial action to change organizations towards states of internal equilibrium, if not harmony. Nevertheless, what attracts students of strategic change is the appreciation of the contrasting states which an organization may pass through during such change. In Lewin's case, he argued that action was needed in order to place the organization in a condition where change would be more readily accepted. 'Unfreezing' therefore refers to the questioning and breaking down of accepted practices, structures, and beliefs in order that major change is more likely to occur. 'Refreezing' denotes the actions necessary to ensure the stabilization of the core changes—what is now treated as the institutionalization of new approaches. The popularity of the frameworks of Beckhard and Harris is explained by their similar concentration on not so much the proposed changes but the intervening 'transition state' which an organization should inhabit as a stepping stone to an eventual altered state.

26.4.2 Multi-stage Models

Subsequent process analyses of strategic change have built on the behavioural tradition. They share the conviction that strategic changes give rise to multi-stage processes but have gone on to develop understanding of such sequences by taking account of the plurality of the actors and influences concerned.

Mintzberg (1978) discovered that organizations developed a collection of routines for handling major change (see Figure 26.5), basing his conclusions on
studying both industrial sectors as well as arts institutions and NASA. He shows
the inherent fragility of such processes. Many organizations find their intended
changes are rejected or compromised during the attempts, for example, to establish
recognition of the strategic problem in question, to agree on the diagnosis of the
challenge, or to coalesce around the design of an agreed strategy. Mintzberg was also
clear that in listing the order in which such activities conventionally occurred there
was a risk of oversimplification. It is equally apparent that organizations do not find
these actions taking place sequentially and that some can become locked in almost
continuous loops of 'search' or 'evaluation'. It was these results which, in part, led
Mintzberg to conclude that strategy was in practice the unpredictable pattern in the
stream of these actions.

Kanter and Quinn take seriously the breadth of possible choices and actions
which organizations have generated as they seek to establish new strategies and pilot
them into operational form. Both base their conclusions on conventional research
but share a strong sense of prescription. Quinn leans heavily on his knowledge of US
companies such as Pillsbury, Continental Group, or Texas Instruments. He argues
that strategic changes can be managed but that managers must relate to a fragmented, evolutionary, and intuitive process. In his view, 'the organization probes
the future, experiments, and learns from a series of partial (incremental) commitments' (1980: 58). His full set of potential stages or steps which an organization
might employ is extensive. Almost every conceivable tactical device is laid out for
developing a new strategic idea, ensuring its comprehension and support, and, not
least, the ability to adapt the strategy to events as it is operationalized.

Kanter's approach has many similarities but concentrates more on developing
and implementing strategies which innovate. The popularity of her work is partly
explained by her antipathy to the orthodox methods of linear planning and execution beloved of major corporations. She sees the measurement and reporting
approaches as producing 'rules for stifling change'. In contrast, Kanter offers actions
which not only build on the principles of Lewin, or Beckhard and Harris, but which
are often challenging and counter-intuitive. She observes how businesses do not
necessarily need an external threat to initiate major change. In order to build a
climate for change, the questioning of accepted ways of doing things by managers
who are in touch with external developments may be an excellent way of generating
a productive sense of unease. Raising levels of dissatisfaction is seen as an important
way of challenging complacency and thereby making people more receptive to
change. She was also one of the first commentators to argue that inculcating a
strong sense of conviction for a new course of action within an organization was
more worthwhile than a fully articulated vision. As with Quinn, the point was made
that people are more likely to identify with an initial straightforward sense of
purpose than an elaborate set of very long-term wish lists. She goes on to argue,

for example, on the practical virtues of linking any change effort to everyday issues affecting staff and is realistic concerning the ability of established systems (in accounting or personnel) to block elaborately thought-out strategic change programmes.

It is a measure of the popularity of such process views of change that this way of thinking has been adopted by writers seeking to summarize the nature of contemporary management. Pascale provides a leading instance of the emulation by mainstream management frameworks of strategic change experts. He maintains (1990) that as management techniques have shifted, in order to respond to new forms of competition and organization, so more reliance is placed by managers on process skills rather than mechanical notions of command structures. To him there has been a major 'contextual shift' in management. The past emphasis on consistency, resolving tensions, and identifying fundamental laws in organizations have been overtaken by a recognition of the need for synthesizing process techniques and maintaining constructive tensions.

26.4.3 Implications

A note of caution is, however, required. Clearly the recognition of the centrality of change processes for all types of organization is welcome. What is less evident is how far the full demands of the process view have been recognized and the implications digested.

Concentration by some managers solely on the apparent steps of Quinn's or Kanter's frameworks invariably leads to disappointment. Strategic change projects collapse in spite of the replication of these process models. Such upsets act as a useful warning. In order for the steps identified by Kanter and others to be of use, their application requires an understanding of the inherent difficulties involved and the limitations on managerial action. Whilst the process specialists have assimilated the political and cultural dimensions of the problem, many would-be adopters of their models have not. Contrary to Pascale's assertion of an epoch-making shift in managerial thinking, many managers remain locked in their rational assumptions of the operation of organizations. It is imperative, therefore, that the full implications of the process perspective are accepted if the outputs of this school of thought are to be used productively. This requires acceptance of the way strategic change implies streams of activities through time. The combination of motive forces behind such processes may extend from the personal to the commercial and the accidental. The opportunities for inertia, reversal, or collapse are legion. Apparently logical and highly relevant attempts at strategic change are often the victim of the internal competitive and selection processes of organizations which are anything but objective.

An example illustrates the range of problems contained in strategic change processes, both the objective and the less rational. It concerns Fujitsu and its attempt to redefine itself as a leader in the information industry away from its sprawling collection of high technology businesses. In technical terms the company had been damaged in the mid-1990s by its reliance on selling mainframe computers for the majority of its profits. Under Tadashi Sekizawa the president, the strategic aim of the organization has been to exploit its unique combination of technologies (in telecommunications, computers, and systems) in order to play a leading role in facilitating access to the internet. In achieving this ambition, the company has been confronted by the need to manage multiple streams of activities—some clearly commercial, others more intangible. These include, for example, convincing the company's engineers that in order to attain global standards of excellence, they would have to relinquish their preoccupation with proprietary technology and instead work with so-called 'open platforms'. At the same time, such transformations have seen parallel lines of change in new forms of decision-making, an emphasis on productivity/pay links, a 10 per cent reduction in the workforce to 47,600 and the introduction of a venture business scheme.

The process approach is undoubtedly a demanding one for both academics and practitioners alike. One way of exploring the full relevance of this perspective is to consider some of the main difficulties which confront organizations when managing strategic change.

26.5 CHALLENGES IN MANAGING CHANGE

The emphasis in this section is on the problems which confront people, in all types of organizations, as they seek to manage change and the tools which are useful in solving them. The problems are illustrated by reference to three major issues: the first is crisis management—the most extreme form of change, the second relates to the distinctive requirements of implementation, and the third concentrates on resistance.

26.5.1 Crisis Management

The turbulence in competitive forces worldwide during the 1980s and 1990s produced ample opportunities for organizations in every sector to confront crisis conditions. Some, such as Harley-Davidson in the United States or SAS in Europe,

appeared to relish the challenge and used it to construct new positions in the market based on radical organizational change. The celebration of such cases has also been dangerous, giving rise to the popular wisdom that crises provide excellent opportunities for almost instant corporate rebirth. Yet the way danger and opportunity coexist within a crisis is one of its hallmarks. Whilst the chance to redefine your business may be welcome, managing the requisite changes is usually traumatic.

A crisis is conventionally defined as a life-threatening event for an organization. The immediate trigger may come from a range of sources where the viability of a core product, service, or business unit (and thereby the whole organization) is threatened. The potential for damage to the organization's reputation is extreme. One of the well-known instances comes from Rank Xerox during the 1970s where the one-time leader in 'wet' photocopiers was taken by surprise when Canon introduced dry powder copying machines. Yet as Muller (1985) points out, the attention given to such epoch-making breakthroughs as the dominant cause of a crisis can be misplaced. As Figure 26.6 indicates, there are different types of crisis, each distinguished by the area of the organization in which they occur and the actions required in managing them. Strategic crises relate to fundamental decisions on the direction of the organization. A financial crisis, however, may arise from liquidity issues which prevent the organization meeting immediate financial obligations. Furthermore, organizations in crisis commonly experience more than one of the crisis types seen in Figure 26.6. The resignation of the chairman of General Motors, Robert Stempel, in October 1992 and the crisis which ensued can be traced to heavy losses in three of its divisions, a $12 billion unfunded pension liability, and the inability at the operational level to implement a ten-month recovery programme.

Before looking at the techniques of how to manage the change emanating from a crisis, it is important to note the role which managing change plays in explaining why such life-threatening events for organizations occur in the first place. The inability to manage change is critical. As in the Xerox example, it is relatively easy to identify the external causes of crises: in other words, the movements in technology or industry cycles or the shifts in the fields of extended competition which embrace alternative providers of your organization's product or service. What is less well recognized is the collection of internal defects found in management approaches. The ability to assess the environment in which the firm operates is a vital element of managing change. It involves the skills of not just monitoring events but being able to use the knowledge from all levels of the organization linked to relevant networks. Dramatizing such insights so that the appropriate status is accorded to such new information and ensuring that groups can learn from the experience is vital. Crisis-hit organizations present an opposite profile.

As Starbuck, Greve, and Hedberg (1988) famously showed, crises take root in businesses where such practices are in short supply. Instead, the environment is weakly monitored by staff who share unchanging, subjective views of the outside

Types of crisis management	Actions
Strategic crisis management	Reorientation of the organization strategy: • Retreat/Disinvestments • Consolidation • Diversification
Operating crisis management	Operational solutions (e.g. selling, procurement, production) to: • Improve efficiency • Reduce costs • Boost sales
Financial crisis management	Financial measures: • Bridge liquidity gaps • Change in capital structure
Crisis management during insolvency	Saving the organization through: • Successful composition • Receivership

Fig. 26.6 Types of crisis management

Source: Based on Muller (1985).

world which have remained unchallenged by the inquisitive techniques of Kanter seen in the previous section. This in turn leads to the solidifying of organizational recipes and stock responses. It is noticeable that this pattern is often accompanied by a disproportionate faith in major projects which turn out to be imprudent. Using the example of General Motors, it became apparent that decades of registering 50 per cent of the US car market bred insularity and complacency. The dominance of a finance-based recipe for car making meant the company lost touch with the market and was therefore ill-prepared for the advent of Japanese 'transplant' factories during the 1980s. A late 1980s boom in the US market cushioned its management as they failed to address the underlying weaknesses. The 1990 recession hit the company hard. The experiment of trying to create a '21st century' car company through one project (Saturn) failed to achieve its unrealistic goals.

A sharp contrast exists between organizations which fail to survive and those who take the chance offered by a crisis to take imaginative courses of action. Less successful organizations are guilty of denying that there is a problem or covering it over in the anticipation of a return to normality. They avoid change with the result that internal politics and conflict grows out of control. The fall of Barings in 1995 is a telling instance of this behaviour. Most people know of the activities of Nick Leeson, a futures trader, who accumulated some £50 million in losses which led to the collapse of the bank. What stands out though is that auditors in 1994 had already pointed out the dangers of overexposure in the financial markets by his overriding of internal controls. Yet the split in the organization between the more conventional Baring Brothers Bank division with its blue chip clients, and Baring Securities, the home of its gung-ho brokers, was allowed to continue unaltered. Organizational politics meant that Ron Baker, the head of the financial products group in the securities division, was able to protect the rogue trader.

In general terms, those organizations which cope better with crises rely on change management. This means they are able to combine both immediate decisions to ensure survival, along with longer term action which will inevitably call into question established thinking. Indeed, distinguishing the strategic and other elements of the crisis (see Figure 26.6) is imperative. What is more, some organizations use the crisis period as an almost unique space. Given the severity of the problem, it means staff are more likely to offer new ideas, unconstrained by conventional status hierarchies, and genuinely open up to their environment. It is no accident that the problems in schools in the state or public sector in various countries have given rise to these elements of crisis management seen in the appointment of specialist head teachers and task forces to turn around schools in deprived areas. In 1996, the Ridings School in Halifax was dubbed 'the worst school in Britain'. Peter Clark was brought in as the 'troubleshooter' head, having previous experience of turning around a problem school. Reflecting on his experience, he separates the first few weeks of firefighting (excluding certain pupils, introducing security guards, and establishing communication with the pupils) from the long-term plan based on analysis of, for example, a teaching audit.

26.5.2 Implementation

Research on crisis management provides a strong reminder of the centrality of the issue of implementation, whether it be in connection with extreme circumstances or the conditions associated with more conventional strategic management. In the light of the work of the process experts (see Section 26.4 above), a logical reaction might be that there is little else left to say given the extent of their attention to all phases of the process of strategic change. Although such writers provide a valuable

way of conceiving of the process and its component parts, there are still specific challenges which present themselves as organizations attempt to operationalize strategic plans. Compaq Computer faces the problem of how to move beyond its growth to a $40 billion full-line computer company in the 1990s. The last year has seen profits fall and the emergence of 'deep-seated problems of strategy and execution specific to Compaq' (leader *Financial Times*, 20 Apr. 1999), as it is forced to change its personal computer business model to cope with the direct selling methods of Dell.

Many writers outside management have drawn attention to this problem area. Some point out that, as in biology, transition or mutation is by definition difficult to comprehend and therefore control. In the case of organizations, commentators have moved away from the notion that implementation was merely the logical outcome of the imperatives contained in a given strategy. Hill and Jones (1998: 347) summarize the position well when they observe that implementation refers to the way a company 'creates the organizational arrangements that allow it to pursue its strategy most effectively'. The keynote is on facilitation rather than a command and control approach. Similar conclusions have been reached by those studying processes of technological innovation and their management (Wolfe 1994). Many people follow the emphasis of Bourgeois (1996) on the need to choose between contrasting approaches to implementation; these extend from, on the one hand, 'commander' and 'control' stances to 'collaborative', 'cultural', or 'crescive', on the other. Yet why is implementation so demanding and what are the more effective techniques which can be employed?

The essential problem arises from the non-linear nature of strategic change processes. The everyday labels of planning and execution or the strategic and operational levels are gross oversimplifications. The process, in practice, is resistant to such categorizations, rooted as they are in our natural attempts to reduce their complexity in order to manage them. Certainty is in short supply and predictive powers rare. Most organizations can point to a deliberate strategy or plan seen in its hard copy form. Yet how the ideas and aspirations in that plan emerge and are in due course realized, are governed by the unpredictability of the changing contexts and their interaction with the behaviour of those involved. Implementation processes fail to respect the sequence charts beloved of project managers. The temporal complexity is high. In other words, the process may have irregular, staccato rhythms. Formulation may not be followed by operationalization. Rather, the two may become locked in a circular loop of decision-making and problem-solving because of the assumptions locked into the plan. Clusters of iterative action are common, sometimes resulting in a baffling lack of apparent progress. Where the process derives its energy and momentum from is often hard to uncover let alone manage. As Weick points out, it is a fallacy to believe that the spheres of planning and operationalization are separate and discrete activities. In his words: execution is analysis and implementation is formulation.

Granada, the UK-based television and hotels group, provides a glimpse into the way the inappropriate separation of strategic and operational spheres can be addressed. The group's market value is currently around £7 billion and has enjoyed a tripling of its share price in the last two years. There are four operating divisions: television, TV rental, hotels, and restaurants. Granada's aim is to challenge conventional thinking in each of its businesses. In contract catering they confronted the accepted view that nobody could make more than 4 per cent margins and Granada now achieves 12 per cent. One of the ways this technique has been made to work is through a highly restless management process where the division between the strategic and the operational is hard to discern. Two examples make the point. First, senior executives are deliberately switched between product areas and top managers are allocated clusters of hotels, in order to develop working relations and implementation processes. Second, three-year strategies are turned into annual plans but their operational form emerges from an almost continuous flow of exchanges between Charles Allen, the chief executive and divisional management. This process includes one-to-one sessions where divisional managers are asked, *inter alia*, to identify five high and low points each month. This process involves around 150 people over a year and is not only the main driver of their tenacity in each business but also the source of the insights which will fuel Granada's next strategic direction.

Although it would appear that implementation is largely uncontrollable, since experts emphasize its fragmented and contradictory character, such a negative conclusion would be premature. Those managers who handle implementation well are those who recognize such characteristics and craft their methods accordingly. This requires, in general terms, an acceptance of the iterative and irregular flow of actions and events. A readiness to exploit the accumulation of ideas, partial solutions, and outcomes which arise is invaluable. In addition, those organizations which reflect on Weick's dictum consciously seek out and capture the insights which come from the spontaneous analysis of strategies as they are worked on in the so-called operational forms. Sony's success in consumer electronics, for example, has been shown to rely on the ability to maximize such information and to adapt its strategies and product blueprints as the company seeks to put them to work. As environmental shocks for organizations grow in their frequency and intensity, so previously accepted planning and implementation cycles are unable to cope. Plans are required to be altered throughout the implementation process. In the past this would be considered a deviation. Instead the current climate places a high premium on such 'improvisation' becoming a stock capability.

There also exists a set of techniques which have been proven in use which facilitate the cumulative and improvisational orientation to implementation. First, effort expended in justifying the need for change is time well spent; without it problems of opposition and detachment are simply stored up for later in the process. Second, creating the capacity to mount specific types of change is axiomatic. This may be achieved by a mixture of short-term acquisition of technology or staff, together with

recruitment and development projects which by definition have a longer time scale. The third technique relates to a bundle of devices which include highlighting the role of change manager and the skills required; adjusting status and reward structures to reinforce the objectives implicit in the change process; and creating the means of monitoring the richness of the flows of events and ideas within implementation so that improvisation is timely and well-informed.

26.5.3 Resistance

Acknowledgement of the manifold difficulties which accompany strategic change processes is widespread, as the previous sections demonstrate. In spite of this clear recognition, one aspect remains neglected or at best under-played—the problem of resistance. In part, the absence is explained by the failure of the strategic change field to engage with the phenomenon of power in organizations. Specialists on the subject bemoan the aversion of most managers to tackle the issue directly.

Analysts have long accepted that change of any kind is liable to provoke resistance. Individuals become fearful of either losing their current status, expertise, and possible influence as a result of a new direction in company policy (see Figure 26.7). Inertia is a natural response whereby the intended change can be slowed down and its impact diminished. Organizations as a whole supply different kinds of blockages

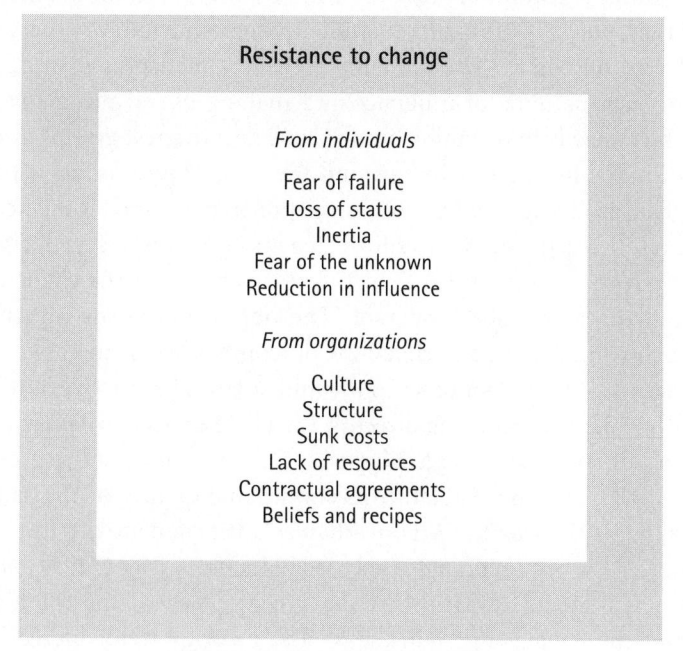

Resistance to change

From individuals

Fear of failure
Loss of status
Inertia
Fear of the unknown
Reduction in influence

From organizations

Culture
Structure
Sunk costs
Lack of resources
Contractual agreements
Beliefs and recipes

Fig. 26.7 Resistance to change

to change, usually of a more indirect kind. Divisional structures may inhibit new collaborative projects, for example, or existing contracts might have established set patterns of behaviour which are contrary to the need to work with new joint venture partners. Chemical industry companies, to take an extreme instance, have become notorious for their obsession with invention rather than commercial logic, where each product division serves a different market, and as a result information flows are poor and management conflict becomes entrenched.

The targeting of corporate culture and its management as the means to resolving these types of resistance has become hugely popular since the late 1980s, partly with the encouragement of some of the main management consultancies. Great faith has been placed in the potential of managers to alter organizational beliefs through the manipulation of language or the inculcation of narratives and representations of appropriate behaviour. After the recent experience of British Airways, and other major businesses who have embarked on high-profile culture change programmes, observers are more sceptical. Temporary movement in everyday behaviour is quite possible but the extent to which the core beliefs of people are capable of manipulation or permanent remodelling is open to question. If the aim is to deal with organization-wide obstacles to strategic change, then an inspection of its political character could be of use. The opportunity is all the more attractive when a leading scholar is convinced that the problems of strategic change are in many instances attributable to failings in developing political will and expertise (Pfeffer 1992: 7).

The reluctance of managers to accept power as a positive feature is understandable when politics is commonly equated with failure or a dysfunctional organization. Put simply, power is the ability to influence the behaviour of others in order to secure preferred outcomes. The difficulty for many managers is in detecting the operation of such patterns of influence and making use of the many associated subtleties which may help or inhibit strategic change. Interest groups or temporary coalitions of individuals crystallize around the main topics found within change processes. The groupings exhibit differing preferences and compete with one another for resources, giving rise to shifting balances of power. It is during strategic change that power relations are at their fullest expression as the chances to secure improved outcomes are more apparent. The opportunities for organizations to engage in such relationships and shape the outcomes are considerable.

The experience of Pearl Assurance in the mid-1990s is instructive, not least in the candour with which its managing director, Richard Surface, explains his approach to the politics of strategic change. Market share was falling as the product range grew too complex and the regulator questioned the quality of the sales process. What is striking is the way the MD overhauled management structures, cut back costs, and halved the product range. He based his action on a political assessment of the company. In short, he identified the power bases of the 'high flyers', the 'anxious', and the 'cynics and refuseniks'. The anxious were offered leadership, while he did not attempt to convert the refuseniks. He argued that it is impossible

to bring all staff with you in a strategic change process. Instead 'coalitions' are needed, starting with those in pivotal jobs, enabling the anxious to follow and the cynics, if they wish, to step aside.

Since open accounts of power and change of this kind are thin on the ground, there are three aspects of the political dimension of strategic change which would repay the attention of change managers: the sources of power, the relevance of external power relations, and the hidden elements of politics.

The conventional wisdom centres on the notions of resource, position, personal, or expert power. These types are based on the ability to control information or access to resources and the advantage of possessing skills or attributes which are in short supply and therefore non-substitutable. The identification of such people, singly or collectively, and the appreciation of their advantages is crucial information which should inform the calculations of any change manager. Conversely, entrusting key parts of a strategic change process to a colleague who did not enjoy robust lines of information, supply, or support should not happen. Furthermore, possession of a source of power by itself is insufficient. What counts is how that potential is used in the change process. In the shifting sands of power relations within that process, those who should be dependent on an expert group (such as computing) can still enhance their position. Channelling information from outside in order to secure your position in the change process is one example.

The external sphere is, in turn, a second aspect of power and deserves separate attention. Dependency is the primary consideration when organizations decide how far they should comply with the demands of outside stakeholders. The relationship is commonly one of a mutual influence process. More importantly, strategic changes will routinely require the cooperation of these stakeholders and even threaten the balance of that process. Those who are adept at resolving the difficulties which result—sometimes called 'boundary spanners'—are able to enjoy some of the strongest versions of power in relation to change projects. Liaison engineers in the engineering and mining industries who have technological knowledge but also deal with suppliers, collaborators, and regulators, often acquire these advantages.

The third area is the more elusive and concerns the way legitimacy is established. In spite of the way politics is equated with overt conflict in organizations, research shows that such disruption is not necessary for the operation of power. It is possible therefore to shape strategic processes by the unobtrusive establishment of procedures, rules, and symbols. In addition, the likelihood of a conducive reception for even extreme changes can be increased by, for instance, the prior construction of key terminology, the establishment of the expertise of key figures, and the development of a language which already embodies some of the core values and aspirations required by the strategic change in question. The skill becomes one of managing meaning as a precursor to the exercise of influence.

Overall, the intention is not to suggest the impossibility of managing strategic change. Rather, the aim has been to highlight some of the more difficult problems which organizations face and to point out some of the more imaginative responses which the field has produced. It also acts as an antidote to the impression given inadvertently by some writers that the accumulated wisdom of the field has in some way diminished the scale of the difficulties of strategic change. Nothing could be further from the truth.

26.6 THE FUTURE

The future of the subject of managing strategic change will be dominated by a set of puzzles. The evolution of organizational and market forms will produce new problems to be solved. Meanwhile, the growth of the specialism will call for a reorientation of how to conceive of the main conceptual frameworks and how to apply them.

26.6.1 New Forms, New Contexts

The shifts in organizational forms which have already begun pose major questions for strategic change analysts. The issue is all the more pointed given that most of the main theories and constructs discussed in the previous sections emerged against a backdrop of the dominant form of large corporations. While such forms will continue to provide abundant change problems to be solved, the growth in alternative types will take centre stage. Microelectronics and communications technology is leading to the disintegration of conventional organization structures. Those previously linked to a single company as, for example, staff, suppliers, or competitors, may now find themselves linked in smaller, possibly project-based ventures or SMEs. Moreover, whilst conventional multi-divisional or matrix organizations may have been in existence for decades, the new forms appear to have much shorter incarnations. It is alleged that the typical Silicon Valley start-up changes form eighteen times in the first year of its existence. Managing such changes will require new approaches.

If the boundaries of organizations have become more porous and the new forms which have resulted look by traditional standards 'disorganized', is the phenomenon a global one? As researchers pursue the answer, a curious paradox has resulted. Although the conventional corporate form is challenged in the West by the changes

just outlined, it still remains the preferred unit of analysis for those who study international business. How large Western and other businesses seek to manage themselves in pursuit of global operations and efficiencies will continue to exercise the minds of strategic change scholars. Yet the experiences and outcomes arising from the transition from managed to free-market economies in Eastern Europe and Asia, for instance, raise the opportunity for studying fresh solutions to the difficulties of implementation. They may also offer sources of innovation relevant to each stage of the change process.

26.6.2 Fresh Perspectives

Academics who are already responding to these phenomena provide some clues as to the future direction of the subject of strategic change. Two instances which are instructive are hyper-competition and complexity theory. Hyper-competition refers to the disruption of existing markets by fast-moving firms who succeed through rapid product innovation and aggressive price and competence-based approaches. Such companies are feeding off the demand by consumers for higher quality but at lower prices, the use of information technology to enter markets, and the collapse of entry barriers to markets following alterations in government policy. The challenge for managing strategic change is profound. Long-term planning becomes even more difficult and sustaining notions of 'vision' is equally questionable. Current wisdom on strategic change has adapted to the need of how to manage a transformation; it has yet to engage with the consequences of fragmented and random competitive shocks which accompany hyper-competition.

In a broadly similar way, adherents of complexity theory have been taking seriously the unpredictability of the internal workings of organizations. The core idea behind the theory is that complex systems, such as organizations, find order within themselves but in unpredictable and haphazard ways. In addition, it is argued that small, localized adjustments trigger sequences of events which have major implications for the entire organization. Managing strategic change may become more reliant on identifying the appropriate 'sense points' for managerial intervention in order to trigger positive change. The example of the 'zero tolerance' policy on petty crime at local level in New York (by William Bratton, police commissioner in the mid-1990s) and its impact on criminality across the city, is a case in point.

Whatever direction the subject of strategic change moves in, and in spite of what new theories are drawn on for assistance, one thing is clear: adopting a singular stance will not be sufficient. Looking at the growth of the subject, those who wrestle with the difficulties of managing strategic change would be forgiven for expecting an assessment of which approach is the most effective or superior. What is more

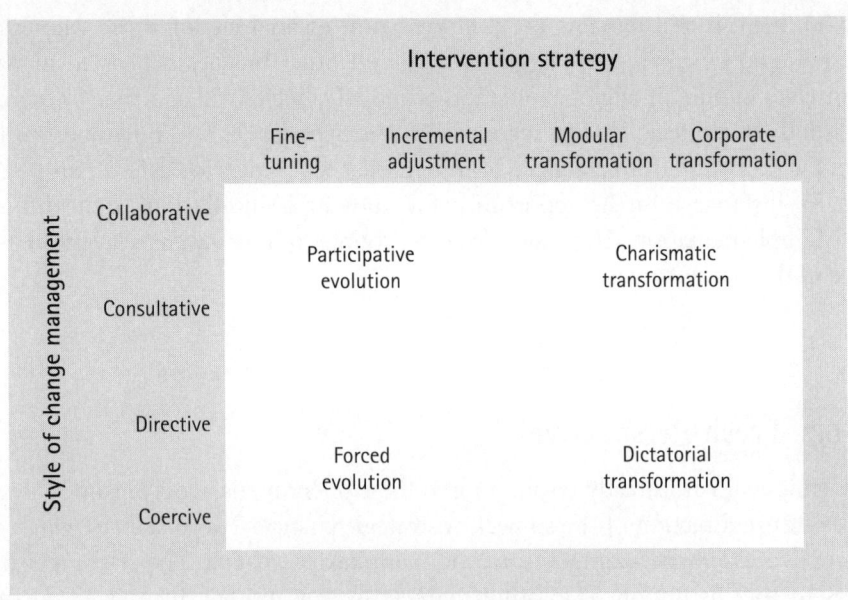

Fig. 26.8 Strategic change matrix

Source: Based on Dunphy and Stace (1994: *passim*).

likely in the future is a continuation of the attempt to link the various perspectives offered by strategic change writers. One example is given in Figure 26.8. The idea behind the matrix is to consider styles of change management against a range of intervention strategies (reflecting the categories discussed in Section 26.3). What becomes clear is the breadth of choices available from even this simple grid. It is this type of approach, where a single business becomes comfortable with mobilizing different techniques to match varying circumstances, which will be more suited to the conditions of hyper-competition. The same must be true for analysts. They should be able to adopt a multi-lens view, deploying combinations of theories and concepts which are able to cope with the existence of more than one type of strategic change process within a single organization over time. Managers and academics alike will have to become at the very least ambidextrous, if not multi-skilled.

26.7 SUMMARY

This chapter has considered the problem of managing strategic change from a variety of standpoints, in order to do justice to its contemporary relevance and its character as a mature field of enquiry. It is apparent that managers continue to

regard strategic change as an area fraught with problems, notwithstanding the rhetoric on some book covers which would seem to indicate otherwise. In order to provide helpful ties between those who research the subject and those who learn by doing, the chapter has attempted to establish four main positions.

The first concerns the longevity of the specialism. What emerges is a subject which has grown over a period of some forty years. In order to engage fully with it one has to appreciate not only its mixed origins but also the different disciplines involved. It is imperative to locate individual authors in their contexts in order to understand their emphases and, above all, to be in a position to make critical use of their insights and to recognize their emphases. The second position established in the chapter relates to the need to reflect on the language of change. Many experts on strategic change are guilty of under-using the full spread of concepts at their disposal. Both practitioners and scholars alike can benefit from employing the distinctions which are required to appreciate the full continuum between transformational change at one extreme and continuity, or the status quo, at the other. The third core feature of the chapter relates to the process view of change. A process perspective has become the bedrock of some of the most notable examinations of strategic change. The aim here was to, in part, celebrate those achievements but also to warn against false impressions of step-like inevitability. Consequently, the fourth objective has been to illustrate some of the enduring problems of managing strategic change and their solutions.

In the light of its continuing relevance and ability to attract attention from commentators of all kinds, the future for the subject is promising. How far that promise is delivered will depend on the extent to which new theories (derived from the social sciences and beyond) are generated to meet the circumstances confronting corporate and less orthodox organizational forms. The ability to ally with those working on related subjects, such as innovation, leading change and project management, will be an additional requirement and of mutual benefit.

References

BARNEY, J. B. (1997). *Gaining and Sustaining Competitive Advantage*. Reading, Mass.: Addison-Wesley.

BECKHARD, R., and HARRIS, R. (1987). *Organizational Transitions: Managing Complex Change*. Reading, Mass.: Addison-Wesley.

BOURGEOIS, L. J. (1996). *Strategic Management from Concept to Implementation*. Fort Worth: Dryden.

CHANDLER, A. (1962). *Strategy and Structure*. Boston: MIT Press.

DUNPHY, S., and STACE, D. (1994). *Beyond the Boundaries*. Roseville, NSW: McGraw-Hill.

HICKSON, D., BUTLER, R., GRAY, D., MALLORY, G., and WILSON, D. (1986). *Top Decisions: Strategic Decision-Making in Organizations*. Oxford: Blackwell.

HILL, C., and JONES, G. (1998). *Strategic Management: An Integrated Approach (4th edn.)*. New York: Houghton Mifflin.

KANTER, R. (1990). *The Change Masters: Corporate Entrepreneurs at Work*. London: Unwin.

KINSLEY LORD (1992). *Making Change Happen: Lessons from Leading Firms*. London.

LEWIN, K. (1947). 'Frontiers in Group Dynamics'. *Human Relations*, 1/1: 5–41.

MCKELVEY, B., and ALDRICH, H. (1983). 'Population, Natural Selection, and Applied Organizational Science'. *Administrative Science Quarterly*, 28: 101–28.

MARCH, J., and OLSEN, J. (1976). *Ambiguity and Choice in Organisations*. Bergen: Universitetsforlaget.

MINTZBERG, H. (1978). 'Patterns in Strategy Formation'. *Management Science*, 24: 934–48.

MULLER, R. (1985). 'Crisis Management'. *Long Range Planning*, 18/5: 38–48.

NADLER, D., and TUSHMAN, M. (1988). 'What Makes for Magic Leadership'. *Fortune*, 6 June: 115–16.

PASCALE, R. T. (1990). *Managing on the Edge*. London: Viking.

PETERS, T., and WATERMAN, R. (1982). *In Search of Excellence: Lessons from America's Best Run Companies*. New York: Harper & Row.

PETTIGREW, A. (1977). 'Strategy Formulation as a Political Process'. *International Studies of Management and Organisation*, 7/2: 78–87.

—— and WHIPP, R. (1991). *Managing Change for Competitive Success*. Oxford: Blackwell.

PFEFFER, J. (1992). *Managing with Power*. Boston: Harvard Business School Press.

PORTER, M. (1985). *Competitive Advantage: Creating and Sustaining Superior Performance*. New York: Free Press.

QUINN, J. (1980). *Strategies for Change: Logical Incrementalism*. Homewood, Ill.: Irwin.

SCHEIN, E. (1985). *Organisational Culture and Leadership*. San Francisco: Jossey-Bass.

STARBUCK, W., GREVE, A., and HEDBERG, B. (1988). 'Responding to Crisis', in J. Quinn, H. Mintzberg, and R. James, *The Strategy Process*. London: Prentice-Hall, 687–97.

TRICE, H., and BEYER, J. (1986). 'The Concept of Charisma', in *Research in Organisational Behaviour*, Vol. 8. Greenwich, Conn.: JAI Press, 118–64.

VAN DE VEN, A., and SCOTT-POOLE, M. (1987). 'Paradoxical Requirements for a Theory of Organizational Change'. Working paper 58/Sept.: 1–83. Strategic Management Research Center, University of Minnesota.

WILSON, D. (1992). *A Strategy for Change: Concepts and Controversies in the Management of Change*. London: International Thompson.

WOLFE, R. (1994). 'Organizational Innovation: Review, Critique and Suggested Research Directions'. *Journal of Management Studies*, 31/3: 405–31.

CHAPTER 27

....

TURNAROUNDS

....

PETER MCKIERNAN

Things do change. The only question is that since things are deteriorating
so quickly, will society and man's habits change quickly enough?

(Isaac Asimov)

27.1 INTRODUCTION

....

THE objectives of this chapter are to explain the process of corporate turnaround, to
develop a six-stage model within the turnaround process, to analyse the behaviour
of senior management during decline and crisis, to analyse the strategic options for
companies in crisis, and to explore the renewal of organizations through the lens of
complexity theory and learning systems.

Corporate[1] cemeteries are littered with collapsed organizations. This biological
and physical debris often reflects an instinctive avoidance of change, despite the
sharpest early warning signals of impending disaster. Organizations, with man at
their cognitive centre, have a limited capacity for change. As Toffler said, when this
is overwhelmed, the capacity is in future shock. Shock stuns the senses and confuses
the corporate mind. Reactions suffer, response is limited and often of inappropriate
design, critical opportunities are missed, and death becomes inevitable.

Thanks are due to Peter Grinyer for his comments. Any errors are my own.

[1] The majority of the academic and practical work on turnaround has been accomplished in the
corporate, profit-centred arena. This chapter follows that focus yet is aware that many of the more
generic issues can be applied to public sector organizational woes.

All organizations endure periods of deteriorating absolute or relative performance. But they don't all die. A judicious strategy, sensible and sensitive leadership, and a capacity for change can often lead to a TURNAROUND in fortunes. But this is a complex and risky world where generic treatments of individual circumstances can lead to ineffective solutions. Each remedy is normally custom-built to take account of particular contextual and cultural conditions. Contextually, the cause may be external, lying in the competitive domain of industry structure or market segment. Culturally, firms are, in Penrose's words, 'unique bundles of resources'. Each one has an individual configuration of human and physical assets bound together by common views, habits, values, and learning systems. Within, the internal causes can be hidden from view and, when viewed, can be ignored. This is a complex and risky world in which to operate. To understand it, the environments coupled with the organization must together be the unit of analysis. The cognition of the senior management team (or dominant coalition) must become the key to analysing behaviour patterns and the treatments must become individual in both content and implementation.

This is an important aspect of our chapter. There is much work elsewhere that focuses on the financial and financing aspects of corporate turnaround (e.g. Slatter and Lovett 1999). This chapter complements these approaches by focusing on the behavioural aspects of the turnaround process. Moreover, it does not attempt to be a guidebook of 'how to' turnaround a company.[2] On the contrary, it aims to give the reader a deeper understanding of the managerial and organizational processes that underpin the turnaround phenomenon.

To reduce the complexity involved in this world, we utilize a linear stage process. This reduction should not be allowed to obscure the drama, emotions, and difficulties involved in reality. Its linearity should not conceal the simultaneous activities enacted in practice and the stages should not lead to robotic diagnostic activity or the proffering of automatic prescriptions to any individual case.

Researchers have identified two main stages in the turnaround process, retrenchment and recovery. First, when the predicament of the organization has been identified and managers are inspired to take action, they tend to retrench or cut back to a manageable core of operations to stem the decline. They catch their breath by buying time and doing what they know best. Second, there usually follows a recovery phase, where organizations take the appropriate and specific actions that return them to previous positions of security. For this chapter, we follow this lead and adopt a six-stage process (see Fig. 27.1) that incorporates these two stages as follows: Causes, Triggers, Diagnostics, *Retrenchment*, *Recovery*, and Renewal.

---

[2] Readers who wish to consult this literature are directed to the narrative style in the John Harvey-Jones coverage of the 'Trouble-shooters', the consultant's guide by Goldston (1992) or the implementation framework in Slatter and Lovett (1999: 99).

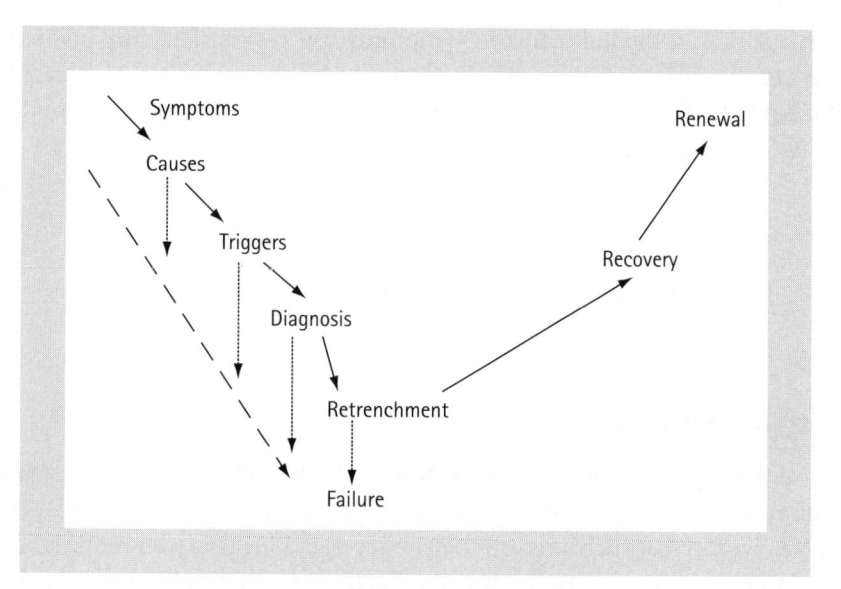

Fig. 27.1 Six stages of turnaround

27.1.1 Causes Stage

Causes of decline are usually described in turnaround literature as common, immediately identifiable internal and external issues such as poor financial control, poor management, and the collapse of key markets. We distinguish between these causes, which we refer to as secondary causes, and a deeper, more fundamental malaise that is related to organizational learning. We refer to these issues as primary causes of decline. The latter have received little attention in theory or practice.

27.1.2 Triggers Stage

Triggering represents the very stimulation of the activity necessary for change to occur. Triggers are needed to activate both a diagnostic process and a call for action. This usually results in a retrenchment phase. However, the complicated political and psychological context of the triggering stage has rendered it a difficult area to research with traditional tools or approaches. Without stimulation however, little diagnosis or action is taken. Hence, we see it as a crucial stage in the process.

27.1.3 Diagnostics Stage

Secondary causes of decline are intuitively and explicitly incorporated into turn-around theory. The theory is shallower in (a) its exposition of symptoms and in (b)

the articulation of the link between symptoms and causes. This link involves the process of diagnosis by senior management and/or their advisers. Hence, we feel that a separate diagnostic stage is necessary due to the significance of good early warning signals and diagnostic processes in informing appropriate action.

27.1.4 Retrenchment: as discussed

27.1.5 Recovery: as discussed

27.1.6 Renewal Stage

Renewal is the completion phase of the process. At the end of the recovery stage, the organization has returned to levels of performance it enjoyed prior to decline. However, we feel that such a return to prior levels is a necessary but not a sufficient condition for a good turnaround process. Such a process should return the organization to a level of performance better than that prior to decline and towards one with greater prosperity and outlook. Such a recovery could be regarded as sustainable. This might be termed a 'genuine turnaround'.[3] In this case, an organization's ability to renew itself through continuous learning would be the sufficient condition and represent an additional stage in the process. With the constant learning in renewal, the lessons of a past deterioration in performance should not be forgotten. The learning loop would then be complete.

This chapter is structured along the lines of the six stages in the turnaround process. First, though, the nature and scope of corporate decline are considered as a background.

27.2 CORPORATE DECLINE

27.2.1 Definition of Decline

Initially, it is useful to distinguish between organizational downsizing and corporate decline. The former is an *intentional* strategic attempt by the firm's executives to adjust organizational size, structure, and scope in the face of diminishing market demand, industry contraction, or supplier overcapacity. The latter is an *uninten-*

---

[3] Slatter (1984) has identified a number of recovery types, including such a sustainable category: (1) no-hopers; (2) short-term survivors; (3) mere survivors; (4) sustainable recoverers.

tional contraction of the strategic discretion[4] of the firm's executives. This will act as our working definition for this chapter.

Discretion pertains to both external and internal factors. Externally, these relate to the structural characteristics of the industry (pace Porter's five forces) and its resource mobility. Other general environmental factors, e.g. political, economic, societal and cultural, technological, legal, and environmental, play a strong role as they influence strategy and operations singly and conjointly. Internally, factors relate to an organization's resource endowment. Discretion depends on the extent to which an organization owns, has access to, uses, and controls the resource base at its disposal.

These resources can be grouped (after Barney 1991) into physical, human, and organizational capital. Managerial discretion varies over each resource and over time. In positive growth phases, executives will have an increasing say in the way things are or should be. In periods of negative growth, discretion contracts as executives lose control over common elements at first and crucial ones later. When all control is lost, then the firm is broken up or allowed to die.

This view of discretion is anchored in the resource-based perspective in strategic management. But the amount of discretion granted to managers by other perspectives in the field differs greatly. Population ecology theory gives executives little control over external or internal factors. Drawing on Darwin's theory of natural selection with its emphasis on births and deaths, it argues that executives have no discretion as organizations are resistant to change and inert. On the other hand, many strategy scholars (e.g. Ansoff, Chandler, and Porter) together with practitioners and consultants argue that, because discretion is abundantly available in all firms, it does not justify separate analysis. They would rather develop tools and techniques to optimize its use in a competitive arena.

The definition of decline adopted here occupies the middle ground between these two extreme views.

27.2.2 Concepts of Decline

Various concepts of decline are highlighted in the literature. These break into four main groups:

(1) decline as a deterioration in resources or stock variables (e.g. personnel, assets, equity, management size, or other variables measured at one point in time);

(2) decline as a deterioration in performance or flow variables (e.g. profits, sales, cash flow, productivity, net income, or other variables that are measured over a period of time).

The sets in (1) and (2) above are easy to operationalize through accessible financial ratios and their analysis leads to logical and comparable results. In many studies, the

---

[4] Discretion in this context refers to the extent of control that managers have over issues and/or resources. The argument in this section owes much to my colleague Urs Neumair.

two sets are combined. Much of the turnaround research uses this data to measure corporate demise. However, its convenience in application is countered by the inherent measurement error due to the window-dressing of accounts, especially in troubled companies. Hence, more detailed studies have paid attention to:

(3) decline as a deteriorating ability to adapt to changing external and internal pressures;

(4) decline as a stage in the organizational life cycle.

The sets in (3) and (4) above place emphasis on behaviour and adaptability in the strategic process of turnaround and so suit the stage-based model well. Clearly comprehensive studies will pay attention to the full set (1–4) in their design.

We now turn our attention to the stages, taking them in a logical and linear order. In reality, some firms in trouble may skip a stage or some stages may occur in parallel. Our arrangement here is mainly for pedagogic purposes.

27.2.3 Symptoms of Decline

Poor performance happens to most organizations. For some, it is a temporary hitch and the strength of their underlying resources and strategy will eventually return them to prosperity. For others, it could represent the early symptoms of a deeper malaise to follow. Some will receive the messages, take action early, and probably recover well. Others will hesitate, perhaps ignore the symptoms and continue into a downward spiral. The deeper and more severe this spiral becomes, then the more incisive and radical the treatment required. If resources are not large or strong enough to endure the treatment, then collapse and failure become inevitable. So the longer symptoms are misread or ignored, the greater the probability of a funeral.

This downward process raises a number of significant issues. First, the role and behaviour of the top management team throughout the decline phase becomes a prime focus of study. In particular, we concentrate on their reaction to signals of ill health, their subsequent decision-making processes, their capacity for groupthink, their deflection of blame, and the resoluteness of their actions. An understanding of this managerial behaviour is necessary to fully grasp both turnaround theory and practice. Hence, we develop this component in Section 27.4.2. Second, the role of the early symptoms of poor performance in the diagnostic process and the distinction between symptoms and actual causes of decline. Third, the separation of actual causes into primary and secondary categories to inform the procedure of any consequent, purposeful action.

27.2.4 Symptom Categories

The symptoms of decline are different from its causes. Because both symptoms and causes are numerous and because their complexity increases as the spiral develops,

this distinction is not always obvious. But it is essential if actions are to be correctly matched to actual causes. Even the experts can be confused: 'Assessing the state of a consumer product, leisure company, service organisation or retailer from a consumer standpoint can fail to uncover the underlying *symptoms that have caused* the problem to develop' (Goldston 1992, emphasis added). Symptoms reflect rather than cause problems initially. They are a sign or indication of the existence of a problem; they may accompany it and serve as evidence of it. Such traces give clues as to what may be wrong in the environment/organization and should guide us to effective treatments. The best analogy is in medicine where high blood pressures and temperatures are symptoms of an illness and accompany it. Doctors who treat the symptoms alone will get poor results.

In organizations, the symptoms may be detected in performance measures like financial ratios. But care must be taken in their interpretation. For instance, a falling profit to sales ratio could be the symptom of a variety of supply and demand side problems and is most likely to be a combination of both. Hence, managers who respond with haste and without systematic analysis to any crisis will end up treating the symptom(s) while the underlying problem(s) continues to erode the resource base or the market position. This makes any consequent recovery action more difficult to implement. Common symptoms are presented in Table 27.1. These are grouped by managerial discretion over the resource category and so signal a potential decrease in discretion over the resources concerned. They are not exhaustive but representative. Many have been witnessed in the not-for-profit as well as the profit sectors. Note, however, that healthy companies who have strong, counterbalancing growth features could display the same symptoms. Again, a comprehensive diagnostic process will help managers to discriminate between the two. We include a separate diagnostics stage at Section 27.5 below.

27.2.4.1 *Public Symptoms*

The symptoms relating to 'financial' resources are relatively easy to measure and so are widely available. They are the ones immediately witnessed and interpreted in the non-specialist, public domain. Academic observers have noted that external stakeholders usually see only such symptoms in the early phases of decline. A cautious management, opaque financial reporting, and clever advisers can deliberately obscure the underlying problems and their severity. Meanwhile, the top management team may or may not be aware of the meaning of these early warning signals. But, cautioned to protect their share price or external credibility, they craft their explanations with care and deliver them with confidence. This behaviour effectively creates a division between those who know the full story and those who do not. The latter could be both external stakeholders and/or other managers within the firm. Even at the most senior level, the dominant coalition may keep key managers out of the information circle for political reasons. Slatter and Lovett (1999) refer to this as

Table 27.1 Symptoms of corporate decline

Physical	Managerial	Behavioural	Financial
Old plant and equipment	Managerial paralysis	Culture of cynicism and fatalism	Decreasing: profit, sales, liquidity and dividends etc.
Problematic access to raw materials	High turnover of good employees	Increase in red tape	Window dressing of accounting information
Repeated failure of product launches	High absenteeism	Retreat internally	Increase debts
Obsolete or hopeless products	Employees withdraw from communal activities	Distorted language and existence of taboo words	Deteriorating gearing, shareholder value
Lack of investment in new technology	High levels of managerial stress	Problems ignored	Public refinancing
Worsening terms of trade	Embarrassing loss of CEO	Reason for problems blamed on others	Raising new funds to fund losses
Major disaster	Emergency board meetings; board conflict	Key executives economical with the truth in public	Financial restructuring plans
	Lack of leadership	No sense of urgency	Breach of banking covenants
	Loss of credibility of senior staff	Lack of strategy	Post-acquisition integration poor
		Declining levels of service	Worsening terms of trade
		Fear	Litigation

Sources: Developed from Grinyer, Mayes, McKiernan (1988), Slatter and Lovett (1999) and Neumair (1998).

the 'reality gap'; the difference between the performance reported and actual performance. We seek to explain this further in Section 27.4.2 below.

Hence the communication of the symptoms is not a simple, one-way 'sender-message-receiver' process. It is one capable of massage and manipulation. A useful analogy emerges from the field of marketing communications and consumer behaviour. This is portrayed in Figure 27.2.

Here, the communications model is a two-way one between the dominant coalition and other parties. Before the symptom message is sent, it has to be encoded (a) in a form of words, figures, images, and pictures to present it in the best light possible. However, two factors can then distort the clarity of the original message.

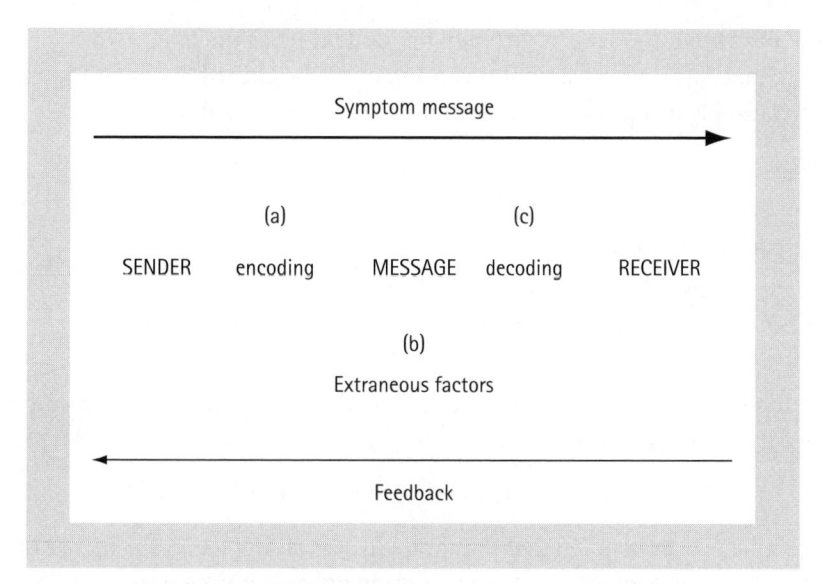

Fig. 27.2 A full marketing communications model

First, there are extraneous factors (b) that can distort the message. For example, the knee-jerk reaction of an influential corporate commentator can reach the receiver before the message and so influence its interpretation. Second, each receiver has a unique psychological profile in use for decoding (c) the message. This, coupled with differential knowledge of the company's affairs, can mean that all recipients do not receive the original message in the same way. Nor is it interpreted in the same way. Hence, the public and private feedback to the company will be varied. In addition, if the encoding has been successful, it will not flood the company with heated and worried responses. The intention is to cap the symptoms and prevent their public exposure from damaging the organization unnecessarily at this stage.

27.2.4.2 *Failure Prediction*

Some researchers have used such publicly available information to try to predict the chances of firms failing altogether. The best known is the work by Altman (1971) who used equations made up of suitably weighted financial ratios to capture the probability of firm solvency. Other researchers have argued that failure can be seen up to five years ahead using such methods, but Altman says two years is a better period. Altman focused on three external and five internal predictors:

External

• change in GNP

Failure rates seem to rise at the same time, or just before, a fall in GNP.

• stock market performance
• money supply

Failure rates seem to move at virtually the same time as the latter two.

We note that Altman's research was conducted in the United States and so may not be generalizable using such macroeconomic variables elsewhere.

Internal

- working capital/total assets (X_1)
- retained earnings/total assets (X_2)
- current profits before interest and tax/total assets (X_3)
- market value of equity and preferred stock/total liabilities (X_4)
- sales/total assets (X_5)

These internal variables all contribute to the dependent variable Z (a company's propensity to fail) as follows:

$$Z = 1.2(X1) + 1.4(X2) + 3.3(X3) + 0.6(X4) + 1.0(X5)$$

A Z score below 1.81 denoted that the company was failing while one higher than 3.0 denoted continued viability. Altman's results were 95 per cent accurate one year prior to bankruptcy and 72 per cent accurate two years prior to the event.

Clearly Altman's early warning system is based on the same public data that can be subjected to massage and manipulation before it is released. Such a process may well disguise the internal problems by yielding a higher than actual Z score. Despite this, Altman's work does provide the pioneering foundations for early warning signals.

27.2.4.3 *Private Symptoms*

Symptoms of decline pertaining to the other two resource categories in Table 27.1, 'human' and 'organizational' capital, are more difficult to measure. They are also more likely to be part of internal reporting systems thus giving top management some discretion on their dissemination. They will not be easy to identify or confirm by external observers. They will differ by industry sector. Moreover, as each organization has a unique culture or unique combination of layers of culture, they will tend to be company-specific. This makes them more difficult for any external observer to generalize from or to compare with indicators from other companies. There is an irony here, as these difficult to measure, externally unobservable symptoms are likely to be more closely related to actual causes of decline than the public symptoms above.

27.3 STAGE ONE: CAUSES

Causes are antecedents that are followed by a certain phenomenon. They are the necessary and sufficient conditions that produce a direct effect. They may be the root of a problem singly or in multiples. They can also exacerbate an existing problem.

Much research on turnaround has been occupied by the identification of the main occurring causes, e.g. poor management, poor financial control, poor product-market positioning, big projects that failed. These 'popular' reasons we will call secondary causes of decline. We distinguish them from their underlying primary causes, which we argue are due to dysfunctions in the corporate learning system. The two sets are illustrated in the model in Figure 27.3. On the one hand, this shows the direction of a good diagnostic process from the trace of observable symptoms to the learning dysfunctions. On the other, it shows the causal direction from primary, through secondary causes to the public and private symptoms.

27.3.1 Secondary Causes of Decline

The majority of turnaround observers have concentrated their efforts on secondary causes of decline. From their work a number of general points emerge:

- Secondary causes of decline are a combination of external and internal factors.
- The majority of secondary causes can be found inside the organization.
- Decline is due to multiple secondary causes.
- There is an automatic tendency to trace all secondary causes back to poor management.

The last point is important for diagnostic reasons. Management is, after all, the ultimate arbiter of a firm's market position and resource base. Poor decisions, inaction, inadequate antennae for the detection of environmental signals are all attributes that could have been done better by existing management. But, to many analysts, this is a convenient reaction to any situation. It rarely provides them with sufficient data to make a proper diagnosis. If they were to believe it, their instinctive solution

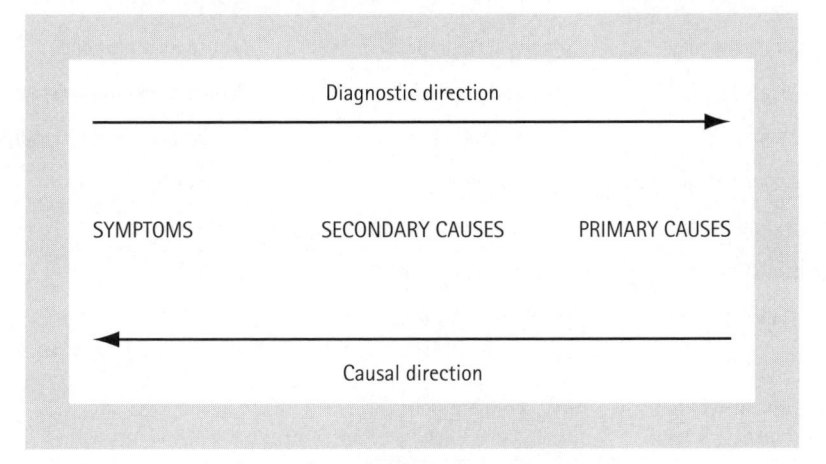

Fig. 27.3 Decline chain factors

Source: Developed by the author from Neumair (1998).

would be to replace the existing management team. This runs the risk of throwing out innocent parties who may be needed in any attempted turnaround. Moreover, it could enable the main problem to go unnoticed elsewhere. The behaviour of management teams during the decline phase will be discussed in Section 27.4.2.

The main secondary causes of decline are outlined in Table 27.2. They are broken down by Financial (largely internal), Demand (largely but not entirely external), and Managerial. Some elements could clearly be incorporated into others, e.g. excess plant capacity and R&D overspend into high cost structure. Here, their individual importance merits a separate mention.

27.3.1.1 *Financial*

A frequently occurring cause is lack of financial control. In particular, this denotes the absence of (especially in small firms) or inadequacy of (especially in larger firms) cash flow forecasts, costing systems, and budgetary control.

27.3.1.2 *Demand*

Two points are worthy of note. First, a distinction needs to be made between a declining trend in demand and a cyclical effect. The former is characterized by

Table 27.2 Main secondary causes of decline

Financial	Demand	Managerial
Poor financial control	Adverse shifts in commodity prices	Poor management
Acquisitions	Changes in market demand	Management unresponsive to change
Poor financial policy	Increased competition	Management problems
Big projects fail	Marketing problems	Poor strategy formulation
Over-trading	Depressed prices	Poor strategy implementation
Poor accounting information	Recessions	Strategic oscillation
Poor gearing	Aggressive market share building	Strike activity
High cost structure	Import penetration	
Excess plant capacity	Technological innovation	
R&D overspend	Bad luck	
Poor working capital management	Government policy	

Sources: Grinyer, Mayes, and McKiernan (1988), Slatter and Lovett (1999), Argenti (1976), Robbins and Pearce (1994a).

changes in product technology, new substitutes, demographic changes, changes in income and its distribution, and political changes. The latter may be part of a general economic and business cycle that will have an impact on all businesses, despite their sector. Second, managerial behaviour in crisis has a natural tendency to blame the cause of decline on external factors so that reputations remain untarnished. To many, import penetration and depressed prices sound like a cover-up for lack of cost competitiveness—an internal malaise over which management has some control.

27.3.1.3 *Managerial*

Perhaps the most frequent cause of decline cited in the numerous studies since the 1960s is poor management. In particular, this emphasizes inability and inaction at the CEO level. But, as the table shows, good strategic management of any organization is critical to its survival, especially in the modern era. It seems that Sun Zi was right when he said, over 4,000 years ago in the 'Art of War', that: 'Weak Leadership can wreck the soundest strategy. While forceful execution of even a poor plan can often lead to victory.'

27.3.2 Primary Causes of Decline

Organizational learning plays a central role in distinguishing failing from surviving companies and lies beneath superior performance. The level of organizational knowledge shapes the way that companies perform. This knowledge has been accumulated through years of learning in the sector and more broadly. This learning directly or indirectly influences the behaviour of the top management team. This learning can fix behaviour in a certain direction, especially if it results from reinforced practice or experience. Luthans (1980) describes learning as 'a relatively permanent change in behaviour that results from reinforced practice or experience'.

27.3.2.1 *Defects in the Learning Process*

Primary causes of decline are the result of defects in the corporate learning process. Learning becomes important when conditions begin to change. Hence, companies with good learning routines will normally be expected to survive, and some to prosper, all other things being equal. Companies with defective routines are more likely to struggle and so to drift down the spiral of decline. The reasons will be different for different firms and are likely to interact in powerful combinations. The main ones are:

• **The Rigidity of Mindsets**

Past experiences can lead management to encode learning into powerful routines that then influence future behaviour patterns. These shared understandings develop

and come to take on a life of their own, constraining subsequent action. They often translate into organizational paradigms.

Kuhn (1970) has argued that belief systems evolve slowly over time. When they become dominant within an organization, they are difficult to change. In many companies, fast change can only occur to such dominant beliefs through strong external pressures (e.g. failure of a main market due to the rapid introduction and acceptance of a new technology) or the autocratic directions of a new CEO. Such change can be described as revolutionary.

These strong paradigms can turn organizations into closed systems. A paradigmatic view of the world embodies procedures for inquiring about that world and stores its observations about that world in a system of 'rules and routines'. These will be referred to consciously or unconsciously for running the business and guiding major strategic decision-making, and will be reinforced as more observations are made. So they possess an internal consistency that makes evolutionary change difficult, if not theoretically impossible. Such a view can represent the construction of the 'only possible world' and, as Golding (1980) says: 'The whole transaction has a tendency to become self-fulfilling. . . . The particular is made general and becomes accepted to the extent that the access to the totality of the larger world, in the shape of possible alternative views, is blocked. Perspectives tend to become ossified.' The paradigm attracts like-minded spirits who, in turn, limit its vision. Their observations are interpreted through the paradigm, forcing them to see only what fits it and so the process of reinforcement perpetuates. Parameters of the real world that do not fit are ignored or rejected, so environmental adaptation is severely limited. The organization is set to ossify. As the mindset becomes more rigid, learning can become an obsolete activity, feared for the potential challenges to the system that it may engender.

• The Inadequacies of Youth

Many young companies fail early. About 25 per cent die before their fourth year and up to 66 per cent of all failures are companies below eight years old. Stinchcombe (1965) offers four reasons for this 'liability of newness':

1. Configuration of role and skills. A new business has to learn much from its environment to configure its learning routines successfully. Its capacity to learn is limited at this stage, especially if the company is in a new industry where the benchmark recipe has not been fully developed.

2. Trust. To survive and develop, new businesses must develop trusting relationships among strangers. This is a tough task when it is young and unknown, and when it may still be trying to develop these internally.

Both elements (1) and (2) above will be strongly influenced by the circumstances at birth. The learning capacity of the firm will be influenced by the template formed by the founding entrepreneur and his/her particular characteristics and ideologies;

and by environmental factors and cultural norms dominant at the time, e.g. location, equity, technology. Neumair (1998) has referred to these as *congenital defects* that are imprinted permanently on the learning routines from the start. The organization can easily 'lock-in' to a faulty recipe unknowingly at an early stage in its life.

3. Interconnection within the routines. The pressure to prime the cash flow with trade at the start of a corporate life occupies the minds of the new dominant coalition. Working out new roles and the relationship between them, new incentive schemes, and a new control and planning framework require a good deal of careful time and attention. This is rarely given in any systematic way. So the establishment of reliable routines lags behind both individual and corporate behaviour in the young firm. Such behaviour will tend to be non-routine, uncontrolled, and emergent.

4. Environmental connections. Ties to the environment are limited in the formative years of a firm's life. The new entity needs to build, from scratch, a whole network of interrelationships with its main stakeholders. This is costly and time consuming.

Elements (3) and (4) above can lead to new firms jumping from one activity to the other in some random way due to their urgent need for revenues. But an over-emphasis on inherent flexibility could lead to a flawed search for effective operating routines through constant iteration, combination, and experimentation. A strong routine may fail to emerge, as rules are continuously re-created. The increased risk associated with decline could also trigger hyperactivity and an enhanced risk-taking mode so reinforcing the young firm's dilemma. Hence, a reliable set of rules fails to emerge.

• **The Overconfidence of Middle Age**

Middle-aged companies can suffer from two distinct but associated problems:

1. Psychology of past success. Success breeds confidence. It instils into organizations a belief that what they are doing and how they are doing it is right. The internal structures and systems that led to success are reinforced as 'the' template for the way of doing things. The organization becomes biased in its selection of rules and procedures towards those that best reflect its successful ones from the past. These 'super rules' and 'super routines' become organizationally legalized. An organization can then 'lock in' to a certain direction of development. Its momentum becomes predictable. If the world remains the same, then success should continue. Even if it changes slightly, then some success within the old systems should be possible.

However, significant environmental changes over time and/or sudden impacts (e.g. changes in technology or government legislation) may demand a different set of routines to those that had been successful in the past. A design gap will emerge

between the newly demanded routines and the 'locked in' routines, based on past success. Miller (1990) has called this the Icarus paradox, where the seeds of destruction lie in the recipe for success. The company is locked in both in terms of the configuration of its 'physical', 'human', and 'organizational' assets and, more importantly, by the inflexibility of the mindsets amid the dominant coalition.

Any search for new rules to cope with the changes will be within an already strong paradigm. The tendency will be for the company to amplify its strengths. It will replace strong rules with even stronger ones, so reinforcing its behaviour. Consequently, weak rules remain untouched and the system only improves at the margin. Experimentation that can lead to the discovery of new rules and routines that are more appropriate to the new conditions are limited by cognition. Managerial discretion will wane as the design gap widens and if the company does not 'unlearn', it will eventually fail.

2. Blind focus and hubris. Corporate development can follow a process of 'punctuated equilibrium' where a period of relative stability is followed by one of dysfunctional change. During stability, rules and routines are developed and if successful, reinforced in an incremental way. During revolutionary times, the existing framework is broken and strategy, structure, power, and control change discontinuously. The phase of stability produces a consistency of rules and routines. Incremental improvements are made in them as some learning takes place. But this learning is based on an incremental improvement (e.g. Kaizen) or adjustment to what exists. With this process, a whole rule and routine set can converge over time to a much-reduced set based upon what works best. The system can become homogeneous as 'rules and routines' are pared back to the minimum. This 'fine-tuning' can have disastrous consequences. For example, in the run up to the Challenger disaster in 1986, NASA had systematically rendered their supplier system 'less redundant, more efficient, cheaper and more versatile' (Starbuck and Milliken 1988). Some parts were continuously reduced in size and weight, and some removed completely. This happened to the O-rings in the solid rocket booster that caused Challenger to disintegrate:

Success breeds confidence and fantasy... managers usually attribute success to themselves and not to luck... [they] grow more confident of their own abilities... and skills, and of their organisation's existing programmes and procedures. The most important lesson to learn from the Challenger disaster is not that some managers made the wrong decisions or that some engineers did not understand adequately how O-rings worked; the most important lesson is that fine tuning makes failures likely. (Starbuck and Milliken 1988)

This convergence process can lead to a focus that is too fine for learning to occur easily. It is usually reinforced when managers think alike within the same paradigm. Disagreement is not heard, ways of improving or broadening the system are not seen, alternative options are not considered, and blind faith is placed in the security

of the system. Janis (1972) termed this phenomenon 'groupthink'. Here, groups of managers reinforce each other's prejudices, emphasize the positives, play down criticism, and, in so doing, reinforce the convergence process.

Managers' past success imbues them with a decision-making arrogance. They can become incautious. Overfamiliarity and overconfidence mix a dangerous managerial cocktail that can lead to a 'hubris effect', forcing them (perhaps against their better judgement) to take on big projects that the system is not capable of coping with. And, as we know from the discussion above, big projects are one of the key secondary causes of failure.

- **The Docility of Old Age**

The youthful and middle-aged corporations above take many actions and may still fail. But companies can also fail due to inactivity or lethargy. This can occur in two ways:

1. Environmental myopia. Poor environmental scanning systems mean that current and future opportunities go unnoticed by some firms. There is a response gap between soft signals of opportunities and threats and the company's ability to detect them and convert them into action. This process can be made worse by a myopic mindset that registers and processes information selectively according to some rigid view of the world. Long-serving executives, who have enjoyed the slowly diminishing returns of previously successful recipes, can be amongst the guiltiest at this practice. Their conservatism could also lead them to a risk averse behaviour in strategic and operating decisions, so investments in new products and processes fail to materialize. This behaviour will be accentuated if the company is spiralling down towards crisis. Here, proactive risk-taking is seen as a strategy of the very last resort.

2. Processing inertia. When signals have been detected and action demanded, the existing set of rules and procedures may be so cumbersome as to delay the effectiveness of the action. This could be due to too many rules and long decision-making routines akin to 'red tape' in the machine bureaucracy. These delay decisions and isolate the market driven urgency through excessive paperwork and committee structures. Final outcomes are likely to be much-diluted offerings, adding to the 'too little too late' excuses.

Hence, primary causes of decline can be seen as problems associated with the organization's learning routines. Faults that might have crept into the system for monitoring and processing environmental signals into new behaviours and actions. This is a much-neglected part of the study of turnarounds. The literature has traditionally focused on symptoms and secondary causes. It has struggled to sort out even this distinction. Yet, what distinguishes surviving from failing companies is the ability to process signals profitably, i.e. the ability to continuously learn. We return to this issue in the final stage of turnaround-renewal.

27.4 STAGE TWO: TRIGGERS

Companies in decline can drift. They may conduct some kind of formal diagnostic process. They may know intuitively what is wrong. However, powerful routines that control behaviour can prevent early action taking place. There could exist some hope that the secondary cause is external, that the decline is cyclical, that it is a temporary blip on the long run performance track. Managers survive in hope that the organization will recover within its existing set of rules and routines. To change them would be a painful process and they are, after all, what the top managers are most comfortable with and know best.

There is thus a stickiness or inertia that can contribute to the crisis. Fombrun (1992) remarks: 'What we loosely term fact consists of powerful forces that obscure management's ability to discern looming threats and so to implement needed changes. These inertial forces derive from crystallized features of firms and the business communities in which they operate.' Close integration of internal capabilities, controls, and culture can dictate conduct and restrict corporate action. Moreover, close ties in business communities with strong recipes can build a momentum, locking the firm into a particular trajectory. The more money, time, and egos that are invested in this trajectory, the greater the resistance to change that develops within the company. When crisis looms, managers naturally hold onto what is familiar. Their existing 'rules and routines' act as a comfort zone, artificially (and temporarily) protecting them from necessary change.

27.4.1 Triggering Change

To achieve change against a strongly held rule and routine system frequently requires a significant jolt. Such a jolt, or trigger for action, can be internal or external to the company. Internally, senior management can recognize the inability of its current system to cope with the situation at hand. Externally, outside stakeholders can exert pressure for immediate change. Yet, there is a more subtle psychological process at work here that is linked to pride and the fear of failure.

We argue that change is triggered in companies because actual or anticipated performance falls below a level that is regarded as acceptable. However, we find in declining companies that managers adjust their expectations of what constitutes acceptable performance downwards, thus postponing the point at which they decide to take action. Hence, inertia and readjustment add to the corporate demise. So, counter to much of the turnaround literature, companies just do not take action in the decline phase. Something must happen that triggers the action. This triggering could be because the continuous decline in actual or relative

performance passes through or falls significantly below an existing level of aspiration. This is illustrated in Figure 27.4.

This aspiration level (after Cyert and March 1963, see Figure 27.4) is an acceptable level of performance that could be influenced by senior management, given their experiences of past performance, or other members of the dominant coalition. Other influences could be by the performances of peer organizations or the perceptions of external stakeholders like banks or the investment analysts of financial institutions. It is rarely quantified in a formal sense. Agents have probably internalized it and instinctively know the level.

The aspiration level can have a strong psychological effect. Companies respond to its presence differently. We illustrate such responses in Figure 27.5. For some (Case A), the very threat of approaching the aspiration level is enough to trigger recovery action. Where inertia is stronger, companies have to pass through it and lie below it before the effect is felt strong enough to trigger action (Case C). Finally, where very strong inertia is present, the company may have to lie significantly below the aspiration level for some time before action is taken (Case D). Clearly, early responders increase their chance of a successful recovery, while late changers stand to risk most of all.

The simple models shown in Figures 27.4 and 27.5 fail to capture adequately the dynamics of change. First, they suggest that the changes undertaken to generate change have immediate benefits and are costless. In practice, neither is true. The actions taken to achieve recovery will tax the deteriorating financial performance even more, causing it to dip below the downward trend before it is reversed

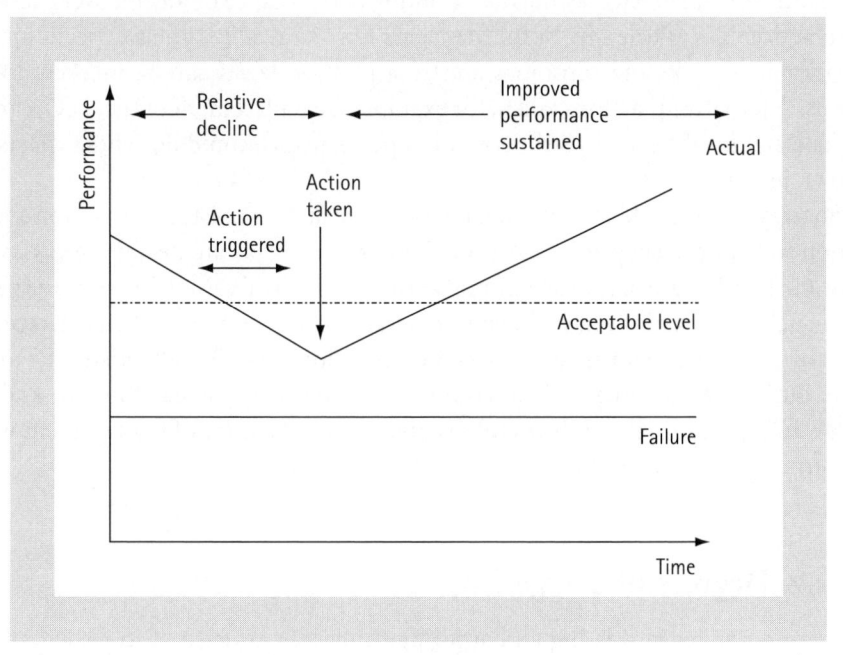

Fig. 27.4 Triggering action

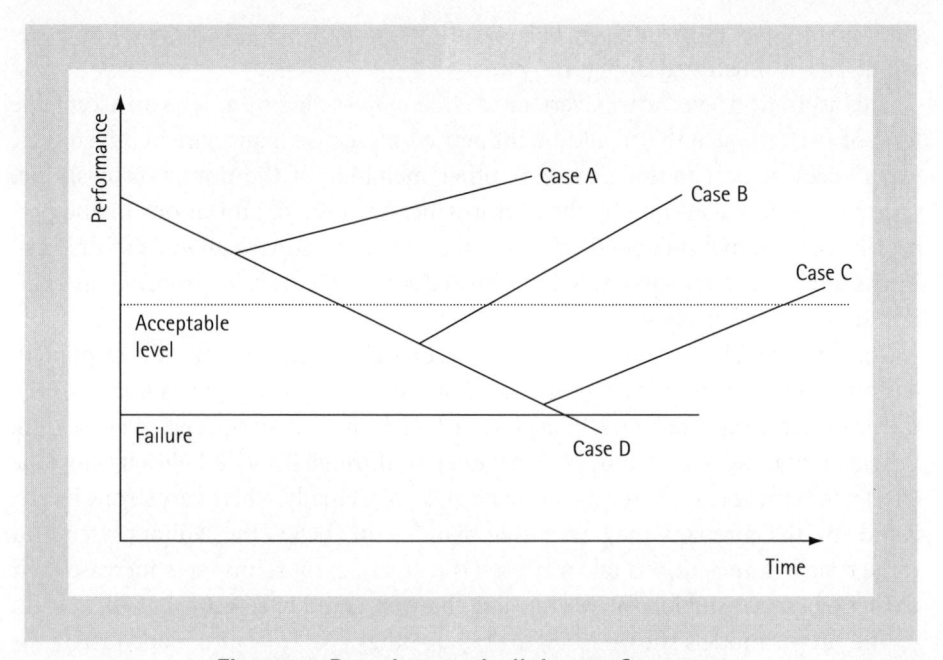

Fig. 27.5 Reactions to declining performance

(Figure 27.6). Again, this emphasizes the dangers of leaving change too late. Second, the graphical representation of the aspiration level suggests that it is a constant phenomenon, unaffected by the deteriorating performance or any recovery actions. In practice, it is affected by both. Managers tend to readjust their expectations of performance as decline continues and so aspiration levels can be marked downwards. Alternatively, actions taken, for example the replacement of the CEO, can lift morale and heighten expectations of what performance could be. These effects are shown in Figure 27.7.

So triggers are needed to provide the initial break from existing systems and force action to happen. They are present in all phases of corporate decline (e.g. Case A, Case C), but the case of the turnaround at the point of real crisis (Case D) is a special one. Such organizations have fallen well below what is deemed to be an acceptable level of performance for them. Unless it takes action soon, it will perish. The forces have built up to a climax as the company approached, passed through, and fell below its aspiration level. It is useful to explore the behaviour of management while the firm cascades down this trajectory.

27.4.2 Degrees of Triggering

There is a danger in treating all corporate recoveries, or even all turnarounds, as homogeneous events from which to generalize. Not all recoveries from decline are

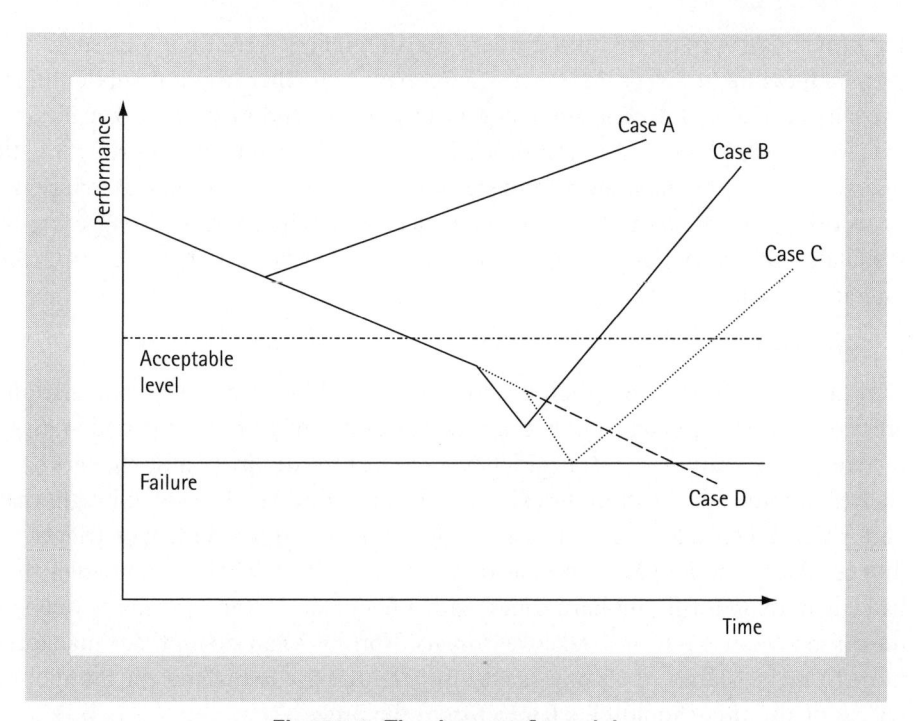

Fig. 27.6 The dangers from delay

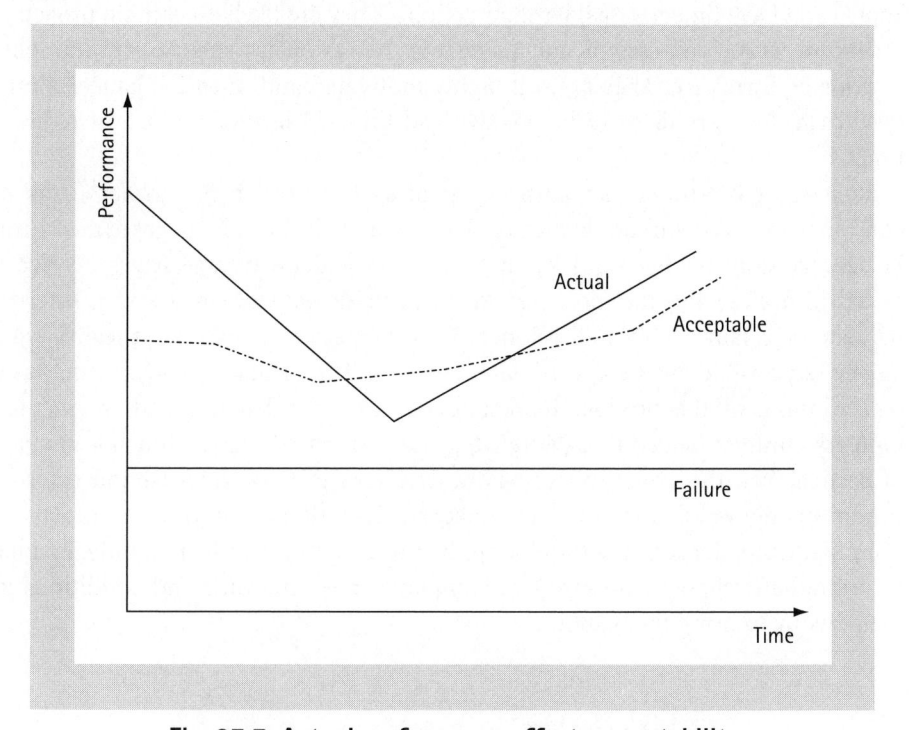

Fig. 27.7 Actual performance affects acceptability

the same. As Figure 27.5 showed, there are differences in timing and so in the preparedness for recovery. Moreover, if we explore further, we find subtle differences in steepness of decline and recovery trajectories and in strategy content and process at each phase. So we can develop the general graphic in Figure 27.6 with research results, and move away from sterile cases to more memorable descriptions. In so doing, we discover that companies need different degrees of triggering to stimulate their activities. Let us describe three recovery trajectories around the aspiration level:

- **Visionaries**

Here, actual performance is slightly above the acceptable level. Such organizations are likely to be anticipatory rather than reactive and may have already tried to make incremental operational or strategic changes to halt the decline. These changes have all been accomplished within the existing rules and routines. The very thought that performance will fall below the aspiration level provides a sufficient trigger to induce effective action. Moreover, as they were reasonably healthy companies that had fallen, temporarily, on hard times, with a fall in share price, the lower value of the company can expose it to takeover threats. Nothing seems to motivate managers more to make changes than pressure from potential predators and the thought of job rationalization should they fall victim to the prey.

Such organizations are some way off the failure zone and impending bank-ruptcy and have time to consider their actions. They are likely to contain proactive managers whose self-esteem and pride will be seriously damaged by thoughts of poor performance. They are still highly motivated and open to change. More-over, cash flows are likely to be positive and this will facilitate efforts at redirec-tion.

Our research[5] shows that such companies are likely to be smaller firms in consumer markets with no divorce of share ownership from management control. Hence, decision-making is quick and direct. They had, on average, fewer secondary causes of decline and the most significant of these was poor marketing. Internal triggers, especially the role of visionary or anticipatory management teams, were largely responsible for the appropriate remedies. The primary change made was a repositioning of the product market focus. Low exit barriers and fragmented industry contexts helped this. Moreover, such visionaries faced a much lower rate of decline than the other groups below. The sum of these internal and external conditions allowed them to make complete reorientations in product market scope. They made broader searches for new opportunities and generally raised their game. Such dramatic changes are rare and companies need the time and conditions in their favour to bring them about.

---

[5] See McKiernan (1992).

• Laggards

These organizations have continued to decline past the point where actual perform-ance breaches the aspiration level. This breach triggers alarm signals in the board-rooms. There is usually a delay in reacting to the situation. Perhaps information systems are not well developed or annual accounting systems, of the type relied on by many small and medium-sized firms, do not provide timely notification of actual performance. Management teams are likely to be mixes of the proactive and reactive, but are generally competent. Theirs is a traditional, sequential reaction to perceived distress.

Secondary causes of decline were more numerous and less operational than for the visionaries. Poor marketing was less of a problem than major market decline. Many industries had matured with concomitant problems of excess capacity and tighter markets. Risky projects that went wrong through poor control exacer-bated the plight of some of these companies. Triggers for action were all internal. Management perceived the gravity of its problems in a reactive way as actual performance breached the aspiration level. Notably, there was an absence of a threatened takeover as an external stimulus. A result consistent with the unattract-ive positions of these firms in mature markets.

Notably, their market declines were sharper than those of the visionary group and they had larger market shares and faced higher exit barriers. But, industry concen-tration was low, suggesting lower competitor reaction to major organizational changes. Their recovery was generally based on cost-cutting and rationalization within their current set of rules and routines. They became more centralized, provid-ing a trimmed down head office with greater decision-making power. These teams planned the succession of their own CEO where this was deemed to be a part of the solution. Only in isolated cases was there any evidence of strategic reorientations. Because the financial impact of rationalization and cost-cutting is fairly immediate, these laggards enjoyed steeper recovery rates than the visionaries.

• Ostriches

These organizations face the real crisis that is stimulated by the threat of extinction. For these ostriches, with their heads in the sand, senior management had not perceived a problem while actual performance declined towards the aspiration level or even after having passed through it. Corporate drift ensued within the comfort of established 'rules and routines'. Even the passing through and exiting below acceptable performance did not provide a big enough shock to shift existing behaviour. The companies continued to drift down to the failure zone. We noted a number of behavioural characteristics during this phase. First, at the beginning of the phase, top management soon entered into denial and refused to accept the existence of a major problem. Second, drift continued to a point where it was obvious to both internal and external observers that a problem had occurred. Senior management then blamed this on other parties or extraneous forces beyond

management's control, e.g. import penetration, high interest rates. This could have been true, but it was highly unlikely. The secondary cause was probably internal, perhaps a lack of investment in competitive production facilities. The reason for the diversion of blame was to protect reputations. Third, as the situation worsened, the firm's leaders began to make public statements that played hard and fast with the truth, perhaps with an intention to shore up the share price and fend off any takeover threat. In addition, accounting information systems were often manipulated to project a better performance through window-dressing. Effectively, senior management was still in denial. Fourth, good managers started to leave. Their moral and ethical principles had been taken to the limit. They saw no future in the firm with present management at the helm and preferred to satisfy their career aspirations elsewhere. This was a crucial juncture for two reasons. First, these were generally youthful managers and just the kind of resourceful and gifted folk required to turn the organization around. Second, in our research, many of these disaffected parties went to work for competitors, so strengthening the opposition just when the host company was at its weakest. Moreover, they went with full knowledge of the customer lists and competence knowledge of the host business.

Meantime, such companies continued to drift close to the point of no return. In the end, external stakeholders had had enough. They had lost faith in the present management team and saw no capacity or willingness to change. Bankers, financial institutions, creditors, and others began to exert pressure for replacement of the top team, especially the CEO. At this point, the very poor performance had triggered the external agents, *not the incumbent management*, into taking action.

In our research, organizations at this late stage faced very sharp declines in performance. Unfortunately, the high exit barriers which confronted them prevented immediate divestment. Any improvements in performance were made manifestly more difficult by the high levels of industry concentration which tended to induce competitor infighting for market share as the industry contracted. These ostriches faced multiple and more major structural problems than the visionaries or laggards. Major declines in their markets were compounded by failures of big projects (though big project failure also occurred in visionary companies, especially when they lacked experience of innovative technology). The major trigger was the threat of extinction made fiercer by predator presence.

In about half these cases though, external agents, including dissatisfied bankers or institutional shareholders, took dramatic action including the replacement of the CEO and other key directors in marketing and finance. Interestingly, in the rest of the sample, the existing senior management was forced by threat of extinction to break out of their traditional 'rules and routines' to enact recovery actions. In general, these involved strong efforts to retrench through rationalization, heavy

cost-cutting, and closures. Firms took multiple actions in parallel. These were aimed at controlling the situation before strategic reorientation could be attempted. However, in some cases where time did not permit such a sequence, strategic measures were enacted simultaneously with operational ones. This was facilitated as decentralized companies took on a more centralized posture in keeping with the widely held belief that autocratic management style is more appropriate in crisis. Decisions could then be taken quickly and lines of command shortened so improving both communication and control.

These three examples serve to illustrate the dangers of treating recovering companies in decline as a homogeneous set. Even those in turnaround situations, faced with the ultimate challenge of extinction, can and do react in different ways. Besides the different 'rules and routines' that are unique to each company, another key reason for treating turnarounds as heterogeneous are the various behavioural characteristics of senior management teams throughout decline and during real crisis. It is important to ask:

1. Why senior management teams, presumably experienced and talented, allow their organizations to spiral down the decline curve to the point of near extinction?

2. How do they react under the pressure and stress of real crisis at this point of near extinction?

27.4.3 Managerial Behaviour in Decline

Much of the literature on organizational decision-making and adaptation stems from the classic work by Cyert and March (1963). It is characterized by a limited, simple search in response to problems; uncertainty avoidance by disregarding unpredictable future impacts; concentration on short-term feedback and negotiated environments; the quasi solution of conflict by sequential attention to goals and local rationality; and the 'use of standard operating procedures and rules' for making decisions. We shall return to the latter notion when we discuss the renewal stage in Section 27.8 below.

These organizations adapt by changes in their aspiration levels—defined as critical values of corporate goals—and through the evolvement of best practice rules. They 'devote little time to long run planning ... and rely heavily on traditional methods, general industrial practice and standard operating procedure for making decisions' (Cyert and March 1963). Such a description is well suited to the 'machine bureaucracies' that operate in mature markets. Problems arise when they face turbulence, say, through the advent of new technology or a major competitive threat. Their historically determined structuration and distributions of power impede the major changes that are necessary in crises. Their systems represent years of investment in distilled knowledge and skills, in trading partners, in physical plant

and equipment, in geographic location and operational systems. Change, then, is likely to be resisted.

This base model has been extended in three ways:

1. The addition of operationally related sets of beliefs or templates (Pondy 1984). These are cultural beliefs about 'how to do business' which are learned through time. In our research on turnaround over the years, we have often heard managers tell us to 'pin your ears back and listen, we have been running this business for 25 years this way, why should we change our style?' Such templates will act as hurdles to change.

2. The addition of a sequential search process. First, responses are delegated to functional areas for incremental operating solutions to be discharged. Second, if solutions do not occur, a wider search ensues leading to cost-cutting in politically vulnerable areas such as general overheads and staff. All this is accomplished within the present set of rules and beliefs. Difficulties must shift to crisis proportions before these are changed or broken. Such events usually lead to the replacement of the top management team, or at least the CEO. This introduces a new dominant coalition with a new set of rules and beliefs more suited to present circumstances.

3. The addition of a process of adaptation to higher learning rules. This is done in two parts. First, through the introduction of a recipe (after Spender 1979) denoting best practice within the industry. This evolves from a small number of firms, is copied more broadly, and becomes the best way of adaptation within the sector. The introduction of new recipes will be resisted to the point of crisis and a new top management with knowledge of it is put in place. Second, through the introduction of systematic, rational models of strategic planning, their indigenous environmental scanning systems, and adaptive structures.

With these developments, the original model can be extended to a sequential search process with higher-level learning rules. The model can then search for solutions at the operating level, move to the administrative level and the strategic level until it locates a solution. This widening search process accords with the natural inclinations of managers to stay within their normal operating patterns, beliefs, and rules (OBRs) as long as possible. This model is presented in Figure 27.8, where this sequential search is illustrated. We develop this model with reference to self-organizing systems and complexity theory in the renewal section at the end of the chapter.

Returning to the three recovery trajectories, we can see how the visionaries have the space and time to enact a full sequence of searches until an adequate solution is found. The laggards jump quickly to cost-cutting and tighter controls initially and then may proceed to strategic switching within the same OBR. Ostriches, however, need to break the mould.

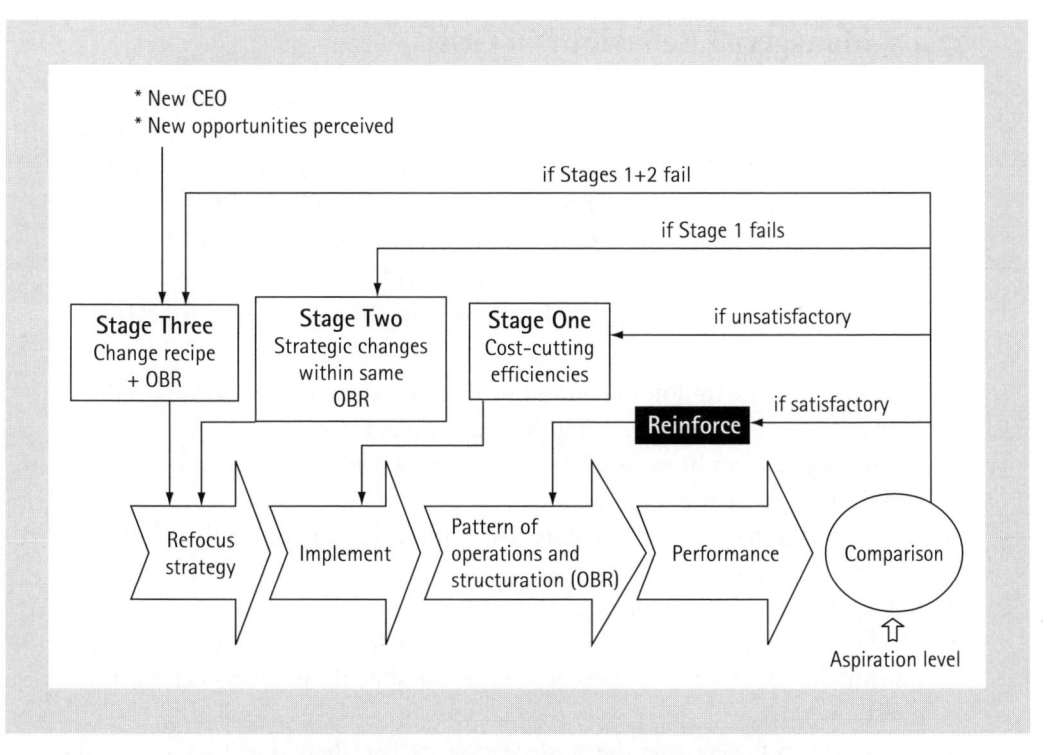

**Fig. 27.8 The extended Cyert and March model
(see Grinyer and McKiernan 1990 for a fuller version)**

27.4.4 Breaking the Mould

The OBRs, as we have seen, can be a significant impediment to change. Great pressure from crisis is required to break the mould. At the heart of the model is the relationship between actual performance and aspiration levels. Performance that fails to meet aspiration levels will trigger a sequential search for solutions. This will begin with tighter control and cost-cutting. Any successes will lead to the adaptation of the OBRs and to their reinforcement. But, if there is no success and performance falls further below the aspiration level, the search widens to more strategic solutions. This may involve changes in the disposition of resources, in the range of products and/or in the markets served. Any changes at this stage are accomplished within the current OBRs. If this stage fails to find an adequate solution, performance will continue to decline so exerting greater pressure for change up to a crisis point. Here, either external or internal agents will dismantle the current way of doing business, smashing the OBRs, and introduce new processes. This action is likely to be both painful and dramatic. The ostrich heads have to be removed from the sand. Major surgery may be required to do this.

27.4.5 Managerial Behaviour in Crisis

Response to crisis varies with the people involved and the type of crisis they face. Turnaround crisis for management can consist of surprise, short decision time, and a high threat to established values. All three can cause stress, increasingly as performance continues to fail. At first, some stress is good; it heightens the senses and can galvanize managers into creative thought and action. However, as the stress mounts beyond a certain point, anxiety can set in with its own deleterious effect on performance. Research[6] has suggested the following characteristics of such situations:

1. An increase in the volume of communications creates an information overload.
2. Management becomes selective in information searches.
3. Danger signals can be ignored as managers see and hear what they want to, conditioned by their own OBRs.
4. Decision-making becomes fragmented with more operational rather than strategic decisions.
5. Managerial tolerance of ambiguity is reduced.
6. The key decision-maker develops a dominant view of the world through which information is interpreted. This view is kept despite information calling it into question.
7. The dominant view may be a stereotype rather than one tuned into the subtleties of the current situation.
8. The personality characteristics of the decision-maker become emphasized, e.g. the anxious become more anxious.
9. There is a trend towards autocratic behaviour.
10. Time perspectives of management are reduced to the 'here and now' and the long term is forgotten.
11. Managers' ability to estimate the consequences of their decisions is impaired.
12. Problems requiring complex solutions are ignored in favour of simple solutions to simple problems.
13. Formal structures can collapse where rules of behaviour no longer seem adequate in the face of an enormous task.

Clearly, managers alter their behaviour, or have their behaviour altered by, crises. It is not always easy to predict how they might do this in any particular situation. The above list is only a guide. What seems to work in these situations is collective sense-making, grounded in communication and trust. But, this has to be built up over a considerable period of time. The actions that will determine the success of later action occur long before decisions need to be made. Starkey (2000), appraising the work of Weick (1995), points out: 'Successful decisions ... depend upon the presence of adequate sense-making processes that can be activated appropriately. It is

---

[6] Based on the work of Slatter (1984), Smock (1955), Milburn (1972), Weick (1995).

essential that this sense-making preparation takes place and that what is learnt is resilient under later pressure.' Unfortunately, the corporate world lags behind the military and the emergency services in taking time out for such preparation.

27.4.5 Triggering Action—Crisis-induced or Managerial Choice?

We have argued that actions for change are not timely. They are held up by the rigidity of internal OBRs. Triggers are necessary to force the action to occur. Our research has identified two stages in the triggering process. First, the gap between aspirations and actual performance grows either due to a fall in performance (as is the case here with declining firms), a rise in aspiration levels (due to a change in CEO, new blood, new markets, a takeover threat, etc.) or a combination of the two. This growing gap causes aspirations to rise within the firm and so creates a climate for change. A second phase kicks in when an event, or series of events, occurs against this climate that triggers change to take place. As we have seen in the Ostrich trajectory, this trigger can be internal when existing managers are galvanized into action by the immediate threat of extinction. Or externally, where creditors may call for extraordinary meetings or predators see a decent set of assets badly managed and take an aggressive posture. The gap creates the climate for change that awaits the trigger or triggers for action.

In theory there could be many triggers for change. The main triggers[7] we discovered were:

- intervention from external bodies
- change of ownership
- new CEO
- recognition by management of problems
- perception by management of new opportunities.

Our research (Grinyer, Mayes, and McKiernan 1988; McKiernan 1992) suggests that the nature of the secondary causes of decline make some triggers more likely to occur than others. From a further analysis of our triggers, we found the following:

- Only a worsening of general market conditions seems to be associated with external intervention.
- Threats of ownership change are associated with internal weaknesses including inflexible autocratic management, poor communication and vision, overly centralized control, poor financial control, high cost structures, poor quality, failed acquisition and big projects.

---

[7] Our research (Grinyer, Mayes, and McKiernan 1988; McKiernan 1992) covered organizations close to the turnaround point but not always at this exact point of crisis.

- New CEOs are also associated with most of the internal weaknesses above, especially where these are attributable directly to weak internal management, e.g. large head offices and bureaucratic systems.
- Recognition of problems by existing management is only correlated with failed acquisitions. This is a serious indictment against existing management and could hardly have gone unnoticed in any internal review.

The results confirm that major pressure has to build before internal management chooses to change. Then, it may only be after a significant dent to pride. In the majority of cases and especially at the point of turnaround, the crisis induced by the widening gap between aspirations and actual performance is detected mainly by external parties that duly exert pressure for change.

27.5 STAGE THREE: DIAGNOSTICS

We have argued that action has to be triggered in declining companies due to different degrees of inertia. The first action to be triggered should be a careful but efficient diagnostic routine. The discussion of such adequate routines is scarce in the management literature. This may be due to its complexity in the turnaround context. Such a routine must concern itself with the complex relationship between symptoms, secondary causes, and primary causes of decline. We noted earlier (see Section 27.2.3) how symptoms present problems for the diagnostic process because of manipulative window-dressing practices, especially when trouble may be brewing. Secondary causes also present our corporate doctors with a quandary. First, they have to sort out the complicated interaction between symptoms and causes. Second, they have to isolate the key problem(s) from the complex interplay between the secondary causal variables themselves. The direction of cause and effect between them is not always obvious:

One might identify intense price competition . . . as a causal factor of decline . . . but is this the real cause or is it the firm's inferior cost position relative to its competitors that is the cause? If *this* is the cause, is it due to lack of market share, or to the firm's conservative financial policy of not investing in modern plant and equipment, or to both? If financial policy is to blame, what causes management to adopt such a policy? . . . In practice, a chain of inter-related causal factors and multiple causes can be identified in most situations. (Slatter 1984)

The identification of the main secondary causal factors requires both a comprehensive array of early warning signals and an excellent diagnostic procedure. The former emerges from a sound scanning system for environmental messages; a well designed management information system and a recognized control framework, e.g.

a balanced scorecard. Guidance on good diagnostic procedures is, however, lacking in the turnaround literature. We suggest that corporate doctors and senior executives could borrow, and learn much, from their medical colleagues.

Research in the medical domain on diagnosis suggests that:

1. Diagnostic techniques differ among health experts. These differences are due to experience, area of specialism, and memory structures.

2. Diagnostic practice tends to follow either a critical or a biased style. The former is characterized by full awareness of detail, careful observations, consideration of ambiguous symptoms, and consciousness that the correct diagnosis is often other than the one initially judged most likely. The latter is characterized by little attention to detail, less careful observations, and over-interpretation of facts supporting the initial hypothesis.

3. The gathering of broader contextual information on the 'enabling conditions' surrounding the acquisition of the illness leads to a higher probability of a correct diagnosis. Such conditions could be age, gender, risk factors from work, behaviour, and hereditary taint.

4. Physicians seeking further information from the relatives of patients make a more accurate diagnosis and a better chance of effective implementation of treatment.

5. A generation of hypotheses based on the broader contextual information to support the sequential gathering of information at patient–physician contact lead to a high degree of accuracy in the diagnostic process.

6. Early information has an overwhelming effect on final diagnosis. The quick generation of hypotheses at the outset of a physician–patient encounter modulates the efficiency and accuracy of the diagnostic process.

7. Diagnostic algorithms exist for the detection of specific afflictions, e.g. urinary incontinence. These tend to follow a root-branch structure in response to yes–no questions.

If we translate the principles inherent in the above findings to the world of corporate decline, they suggest a diagnostic policy of:

- avoiding hasty decisions (2 and 6)
- adopting multiple perspectives (1 and 4)
- making broad initial information searches (2 and 3)
- considering ambiguous symptoms (2)
- generating multiple hypotheses (2, 3, and 5)
- developing diagnostic algorithms for reduction (7)
- testing for Type one[8] and Type two errors (2).

Clearly such principles will be tailored to the particular situation, taking cognizance of prevailing externalities and internal cultures. Further, they are not likely to be a

---

[8] Type one errors are committed when we reject a hypothesis that is true. Type two errors are committed when we accept a hypothesis when it is false.

substitute for the experience generated by professional corporate doctors who have witnessed malaise in company after company and know what works where and when, if not why. But, the principles may guide internal teams towards a better diagnosis early so that the real secondary causes can get the treatment they need before crisis occurs. Moreover, managerial behaviour changes in these conditions where there is added stress and pressure. A simple framework may bring some calm to the storm by providing direction and guidance. Such a framework may even moderate any overconfidence in the professional consultant.

Early warning signals and a good diagnostic routine point the way for further action. Generally, companies retrench back to well-understood or most promising activities and reduce their activities in unrelated areas. However, there are various types of retrenchment policy and companies should adopt those that logically follow on from the discoveries brought about by their diagnostic routines.

27.6 STAGE FOUR: RETRENCHMENT

We note from our discussion on managerial behaviour in decline and crisis, together with our observations of reality in the Ostrich case, the natural tendency of firms to contract to what they know best when crisis hits. Simple, workable solutions to perceived simple problems. Autocratic management, tighter control, cost-cutting, and rationalization all seem to appear as first options. This is the process of retrenchment that has been noted widely in the literature. We must take care not to see this as a homogeneous response.

In our chapter introduction, we emphasized the importance of customizing the response to decline and crisis to individual firm conditions. Common sense tells us that any response to decline should be appropriate to purpose. So we should judiciously diagnose the secondary causes and respond carefully with great sensitivity to individual context. We now explore this issue in detail.

Early turnaround researchers relied on case-based research. A first group (see e.g. Hofer and Schendel 1978) argued that effective turnaround policies should focus on the declining firm's core problems. These could be either operational (not internally efficient) or strategic (poor relative market position). If the cause of decline is inefficient implementation of a sound strategy, then the appropriate solution should focus on increasing efficiency through cost rationalization and revenue generation policies. Equally, if the main problem is poor strategic positioning, then the appropriate solution is strategic reorientation. Managers could get it

wrong by responding to the efficiency problems by changing strategy and the strategy problems by choosing belt-tightening policies internally.

A second group of researchers modelled decline on the sequential search and adaptation route described above (see, for instance, Hedberg, Nystrom, and Starbuck 1976). Here, historically induced inertia needs great pressure to shift managerial cognition from its comfort zone and induce action for change. So the route out of decline is a major realignment of strategy, structure, and belief systems.

From these two groups, we conclude that:

1. Strategic change[9] is central to the turnaround process but likely to be adaptive. Barker and Duhaime (1997) have shown that more strategic change is needed for firms in decline if:

- Their performance decline is steep (very poor performance creates pressure for change).
- External events aid recovery (e.g. economic upswing).
- Their industry is growing.

The roots of a firm's decline can lie in an industry's contraction or be based on firm-specific problems (Cameron, Sutton, and Whetten 1988). In the former, industry decline forces all firms to suffer and solutions are likely to lie in efficiency-seeking policies. In the latter, the industry can be stable or growing but the firm is declining. This suggests poor adaptation with solutions most likely to lie in strategic reorientation.

2. Because of inertia, strategic change will be difficult to implement. Research (see, for instance, the references in note 9) has shown that the extent of strategic change is greater when:

- There is a change of CEO.
- The firm has a diverse portfolio.
- The firm is large.
- The firm has little financial slack.

Taken together, (1) and (2) above suggest that strategic change is central to any turnaround strategy and that its level varies with individual conditions faced and their capacity to implement it. However, a natural reaction to decline is to quickly retrench following some homogeneous recipe. But, the research findings suggest a customized response. Hence, we have to explore retrenchment in more detail, questioning when it is the most efficient and effective response.

---

[9] It is interesting to note that large-scale studies (see e.g. Hambrick and Schecter 1983) that appeared throughout the 1980s and early 1990s, as opposed to the case-based theorists here, failed to find much support for the fact that strategic change was an integral part of a turnaround process. According to Barker and Duhaime (1997), this is due to poor sampling and over reliance on financial ratios and that, according to their research, strategic change is still a key variable in the process.

27.6.1 When Is Retrenchment Appropriate?

Despite the powerful forces constraining strategic change in the rules and routines of the business, logic alone dictates that troubled companies should look to survival and the achievement of a positive cash flow first and foremost. This leads to the classic retrenchment activities of cost rationalization, liquidation, divestment, etc. Once a position of relative safety has been reached, management has to decide how to continue (Bibeault 1982). The choices are clear. Do they attempt recovery in their slimmed down form through some version of their previous strategy (efficiency response) or do they attempt to pursue growth and development with a new strategy (entrepreneurial response)? This logical process suggests the notion of stages in turnaround action with retrenchment preceding any consideration of strategic reorientation.

Retrenchment marks the initial response for firms in crisis situations. The primary objective of the cost and asset reduction exercises is to stabilize the performance decline. The results of this stage should be readily available to internal management and external stakeholders through financial ratios.

Researchers (Pearce and Robbins 1992)[10] have found that:

- Retrenchment is strongly related to turnaround success.
- For firms with very steep decline, both cost and asset retrenchments are necessary for a successful turnaround.
- Cost retrenchment (especially attacks on inventory and interest charges) was indispensable to success.
- Asset retrenchment kicks in when the savings from cost retrenchments fail to stem the decline.
- Firms that saw their main secondary causes of decline as external in origin tended to adopt entrepreneurial responses with success.
- Firms that saw their main secondary causes of decline as internal in origin tended to adopt efficiency responses with success.
- Firms with internal causes retrenched more than others and had more success.
- There is a significant relationship between retrenchment and performance regardless of the secondary cause.

27.6.2 Scale and Retrenchment

The talk of cost and asset reduction in the retrenchment stage is fine when larger firms are the focus of attention. They are likely to have numerous inefficiencies

---

[10] These results have been questioned (Barker and Mone 1994) who argue that retrenchment is a consequence of steep decline and not the cause of an increased performance, and that there is no performance difference between those that retrench and those that do not. However, the original authors (1994b) have pointed to methodological problems in Barker and Mone's study that casts some doubt on their findings.

within internal systems ripe for cost rationalization and diversified product-market portfolios ripe for asset reduction. However, many smaller firms will not possess such opportunities by virtue of their scale. They are likely to have a much-restricted choice of options. However, research (Robbins and Pearce 1994a) has shown that they respond just as dramatically to economic downturns as their larger counterparts. The evidence suggests that:

- Smaller firms made many strategy responses to decline, chiefly in the areas of manufacturing, management, and organization systems and distinctive competencies.
- Firms showed no preference for efficiency responses over entrepreneurial responses.
- Response to decline was through specific functional strategies related to the main secondary causes.
- Retrenchment worked best as a platform for recovery.
- Entrepreneurial responses were less successful than efficiency-based ones, especially those that focused on finance and management activities.

27.6.3 Retrenchment Problems

Clearly, retrenchment is an important and established stage in a turnaround process. But attention has been drawn to the dangers of going too far down this route. A number of problems have been identified:

- Too much cost rationalization may sap employee morale.
- Too much cost rationalization may cause good managers, especially those with much needed marketing skills, to leave.
- Too much cost and asset retrenchment can be resisted by organizational inertia.

An associated phenomenon for firms in decline is a tendency to shift structures from organic to mechanistic. This is known as threat rigidity or mechanistic shift. This increase in organizational rigidity may restrict the organization's ability to be innovative in any recovery solution. Such changes may stifle entrepreneurial responses in particular. Research (Barker and Mone 1998) suggests that:

- Not all firms in turnaround situations react to crisis in this way.
- Mechanistic shifts occur mainly:
  - in smaller firms
  - in firms attempting recovery from low levels of liquidity
  - when a new CEO is introduced following the removal of the previous one by the board.
- Mechanistic shift severely restricts a firm's ability to make strategic changes.

This section has confirmed the position of retrenchment as a separate stage in the process of organizational recovery. Moreover, it has used the research evidence to examine the subtle components of the stage, where it is more successful, how it fares in smaller firms, and what the problems of implementing the stage may be.

27.7 STAGE FIVE: RECOVERY

Recovery represents that phase when the company has successfully negotiated any retrenchment, whether by cost reduction or cost and asset reduction, achieved stability, and is ready to make the decision to progress. Progression is by way of either efficiency or entrepreneurial recovery strategies. The former strategy is important when the main secondary causes of decline are internal. It usually consists of market penetration, segmentation, entry to new markets, acquisitions, and new product development. The latter is important when the main causes of decline are external. It usually consists of liquidation, divestment, efforts to improve operational efficiency, product elimination, and labour rationalization. However, in reality, the choice between the two is not easy. Two sets of factors impinge on the decision:

1. Rigidity of the Current Operating Patterns, Beliefs, and Rules (OBR). We were concerned in the triggers section above with the rigidity of the firm's OBR. Research suggests that dramatic change away from a dominant OBR is a rare occurrence. At the point of stabilization, firms can change their strategies without a change in their OBRs or with an abolition of the old OBR and a fundamental change in ideology. Corporate reactions to decline show a strong tendency for the original OBR to survive in some form whatever the chosen recovery strategy. The process follows a well-trodden pathway. First, changes in strategy are less frequent than minor changes to existing portfolios after retrenchment, e.g. the addition of a better export drive to increase revenues. These are essentially strategic readaptations within the same OBRs rather than radical shifts in the way of doing business. Second, when strategic change occurred, it was more likely to be of the efficiency recovery type. Trading continued within the same OBR but with much trimmed down core business. Entrepreneurial recovery types were rare and their adoption may even have been delayed by the presence of a powerful existing OBR. When they did happen, they were accomplished mainly by acquisitions or by changes in CEO.

In the case of acquisitions, organizations bought into new OBRs in the form of new human organizations, structuration, beliefs, conventions, operating plant, procedures, and networks of relationships of the new business into which they

were entering. This is a more expedient route to adopting new OBRs. For many firms, it has the beauty of allowing the existing OBR to exist, while the new one is kept at 'arm's length' in a new unit or division. Hence, the new need not clash with the old. Over time, the two develop in parallel. The old learns from the new and slowly jettisons its ineffective parts through more divestment of units in which it is still dominant. This is a conservative route to changing the OBR.

The case of a change in CEO tends to be associated with the more radical, but rarer, action of smashing the old OBR completely. This attempt to engineer change from the inside is very painful and the casualties are high. Internal conflict and political games are to the fore. Yet, it is a realization that the old ways of doing business are simply inappropriate for the new era. As they will not or cannot change quickly, then their dissolution is necessary.

Overall, however, we find that old OBRs tend to be rigid, even at the point of stabilization and strategic choice. This can clearly constrain the ability or willingness to become more entrepreneurial and increase the chances of continuation under an efficiency strategy within the same OBR. The situation becomes more complex when we examine Figure 27.9. This shows the combination of recovery strategies and their relationship with the OBRs. Clearly, we expect a close relationship between the adoption of an efficiency strategy under the existing OBR. Equally, the promotion of an entrepreneurial strategy is more likely to come from a new OBR system. The difficulty for the turnaround doctor lies in the other two cells. First, we know that OBRs are rigid but the organization needs an entrepreneurial strategy. It is difficult to imagine that the old OBR could generate and support a new strategy of this type, but it happens. The results are less dramatic than with new OBRs and the trajectory tends to be uncertain and hesitant. Too much hesitation and there is a danger that the old OBR will wander back towards the more conservative efficiency strategy. This is, perhaps, the most dangerous case. Second, the adoption of a new OBR and the pursuance of an efficiency strategy are unusual but also quite thinkable. New manufacturing methods, slimmed down organizational structures, changes in the capital–labour ratio, new product variants would all benefit from new OBRs. Again, performance may not be so dramatic as a new–new relationship.

2. Other Contingent Factors. A number of other factors affect recovery strategy choice. These include:

- Causes of decline. Multiple causes need multiple solutions. In practice, the actual number of generic recovery strategies a firm needs to employ is considerably greater than the actual number of causes of decline.[11] This is a kind of 'reverse synergy' here, peculiar to the turnaround situation. Implementation saps energy and drive and can delay the implementation of entrepreneurial strategies.

---

[11] Readers are referred to Ashby's 'Law of Requisite Variety' that notes that the chances of successfully dealing with change in the external environment are increased if systems have been used to change internally through appropriate coping mechanisms.

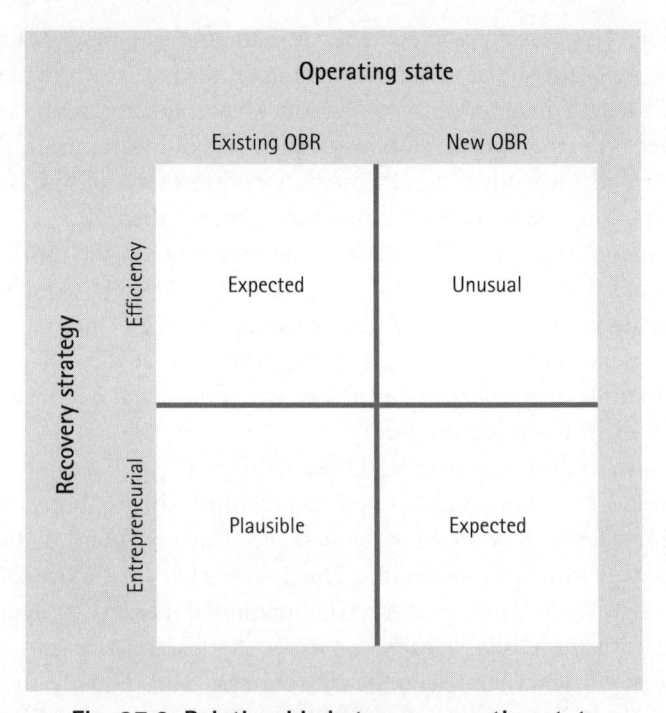

Fig. 27.9 Relationship between operating state and recovery state

- Severity of decline. The steeper the decline, the less the likelihood of spare financial resources sufficient to procure an entrepreneurial recovery.
- Attitudes of key stakeholders. These can act to dictate strategy choice, e.g. governments or banks, or to constrain strategy implementation, e.g. powerful trade unions.
- Industry characteristics. Generally, recovery in industries with high profit potential is higher than in one with low potential. In the former, the chances of opportunities for a successful entrepreneurial strategy are increased. In the latter, few firms will be expanding and there will be no new entrants. So opportunities for getting good prices for divested assets are fewer and such limited cash generation acts to constrain expansion under any recovery strategy. These characteristics can constrain or accelerate recovery strategies and a decent industry appraisal, using Porter's five structural forces analysis (among others, e.g. life cycle), will help sort out the best options.
- Firm's cost-price structure. Sales, volumes, and costs responses will be different in different firms due to their different breakeven points. Coupled with the state of the industry, strategy choices could favour either efficiency or entrepreneurial options.
- External events. Cyclical downturns, global recession, natural disasters, and political or military confrontations over which the company has no control can make the pursuit of any recovery strategy very difficult if not impossible.

As with the diagnostic stage, a good analytical sense needs to be brought to bear on the decision between the two strategy options. In theory, it is straightforward and easy to generate as a set of hypotheses. In practice, the variables interact in a complex manner and make each situation unique. This calls for a customization of the recovery actions to a particular situation.

27.7.1 Generic Turnaround Strategies

Despite our comments above, we find a continual occurrence in the practical literature of 'generic' recovery strategies. In some cases, the authors accompany the lists with an appropriate note of caution. We argue that the adoption of generic recovery strategies, without due diagnosis and diligent analysis of each case, runs a high risk of failure through incompetent design and poor fit.

We have illustrated these generic recovery actions in Table 27.3, where a guide is also provided to indicate the types of conditions under which they might apply. The strategies follow the stages in the text for retrenchment and recovery. However, we have grouped two of them under a general heading due to their broader applicability and importance in any turnaround situation.

27.7.1.1 *Restructure Leadership and Management*

1. Leadership. Leadership has emerged as one of the critical elements of recovery. Not all turnarounds require a new CEO. But, as inadequate top management and the rigidity of OBRs are a major secondary cause of decline, they figure high on any listing. New CEOs bring a new vision, new strategies, new networks, new energy, and most important, new ways of doing things. In time, the latter will become the basis of new OBRs.

They are important symbolically. Internally, because they signal that change is inevitable and a new culture forthcoming as a 'de-freezing' of the old is taking place. Externally, because anxious stakeholders demand change to restore their confidence in the business. This confidence is needed to renegotiate debt, extend credit periods, and raise new capital for the recovery effort.

The type of leader is also important. Leadership traits differ at different stages of the business cycle. During start up and growth phases, an entrepreneurial style fits well. During maturity and early decline, we observe a more traditional approach to management, with plenty of bureaucracy in the system. Finally, under conditions of crisis and turnaround, there is a tendency for more autocracy. The abilities required here are very different from those needed under healthier trading conditions in the business cycle. These include strong leadership and motivational skills; powerful communication ability; flexibility; excellent diagnostic and analytical ability under time constraints; ability to work to a punishing schedule under duress;

Table 27.3 'Generic' turnaround strategies

Strategy	Types of action	Suitable conditions
Retrenchment		
Cost reduction	• Reduce expenses • Stronger financial controls • Intensive efforts to reduce production costs	• Internal causes • Rigid OBRs • Sales 60–80% of break-even • Late stage of decline
Asset redeployment	• Sell assets • Shutdown or relocate units • Debt reduction • Rights issues	• Over-expansion/low capacity use • Sales 30–60% of break-even • Rapid technological change • Entry of new competitors • Decline steep • Late stage of decline • Cost reduction not enough
Recovery		
Selective product-market	**defensive** • Decrease marketing efforts • Divest products	• Over-expansion • High capacity use
	Offensive • Increase marketing efforts • Increase prices • Improve quality/service • Invest in new technology	• External causes • Operating & strategic weaknesses • Early stage of decline
Repositioning	**Defensive** • Niche • Market penetration • Decrease price • Divest products	• Over-expansion • Improved short run profits • External causes • Rigid OBRs
	Offensive • Diversification into new products	• Major decline in market share • External causes face non-diversified firms
General		
Restructure leadership & management	• Replace CEO • Change top managers	• Internal causes • Rigid OBRs • Need to diversify out of industry
Organisation/culture	• Use temporary structures • Change structure • De-centralise • Trim down head office • Alter culture	• Control & communications problems • Facilitate re-positioning • Culture change • Structural change • Universal
Windfall gains	• Management pro-activity	

Sources: Adapted by the author from Slatter (1984), Grinyer, Mayes, and McKiernan (1988), and Hoffman (1989).

and fast implementation skills. Turnaround situations require CEOs to be 'hard and soft' at the same time. Hard, because change will be resisted and unpopular decisions will have to be made, e.g. labour rationalization. Soft because staff that remain need to be motivated and encouraged to play a part in a recovery effort. This is frequently when they are at their lowest ebb, having endured cutbacks under previous leadership regimes for months as the firm declined. Such CEOs are rare. They operate in a power culture and demand direct command and control, typically appropriate to the crisis in hand. They are often described as autocratic. Research (Mueller and Barker 1997) shows how the chances of obtaining a successful turnaround are greater when the CEO also chairs the Board, so increasing power to a virtual monopoly.

Such autocratic styles are necessary while the crisis lasts and until such a point as the organization is safe. Research (Pettigrew and Whipp 1991) shows that such autocratic styles have a sell-by date. They do not work effectively in healthier trading conditions. More democratic leadership styles have to follow once the company is on safe ground. There are a number of reasons for this:

- Staff and management grow tired of the lack of inclusiveness in the autocratic process and by the 'rule of fear' and pressure builds for change.
- Turnaround CEOs are turned on by crisis and lose interest when the company is safe.
- Turnaround CEOs are good at the hatchet part of the process but not so good at repositioning and making progress in growing markets.
- In turnaround situations, internal processes lag behind the numerous actions that have to be taken to stem the crisis so rebuilding is needed.

2. Management. Besides a new CEO, companies need the benefit of broader thinking and vision making among senior management. Moreover, if it is necessary to break the rigidity of the old OBR, other members of the previous dominant coalition will need to be replaced. In many cases, this applies to the functional executive positions of marketing, finance, and R&D. A new team at the top with a committed, positive 'bias for action' and one that stimulates innovative, entrepreneurial behaviour is likely to send out all the right messages to stakeholders and employees. Moreover, having a greater outside interest and control on the Board also increases the effectiveness of a new management team.

Clearly, the severity of the particular situation and its causes will determine whether such a wholesale removal of management is necessary at all. There will be many instances when the experience and knowledge of existing managers will be a boost to the turnaround effort. Any new CEO will have to work alongside and strongly motivate and reward this loyalty through share option or profit-sharing schemes.

Whatever changes are made at this level, it seems clear that a new vision is essential for a successful recovery, accompanied by a drive to achieve it. What is

needed is well-motivated courageous, committed, hard-working, innovative, and positive management and workforce. This can be achieved through many routes—by example of the CEO, personal identification with the goals, by loyalty to and care of staff, by oral and written communication of senior management, through the operating rules of the system, through incentives, or by appointing executives who have those qualities and share the corporate vision.

27.7.1.2 *Windfall Gains*

Windfalls can be defined as changes in circumstances, not engendered by the firm, that help boost the recovery actions. The main windfalls seem to be:

- cyclical upturns in demand
- secular upturns in demand
- government action
- exit of competitor(s)
- favourable exchange rate movements
- luck.

These events can significantly alter the revenue-cost equation for firms and help stimulate recovery. As most of these events tend to have an impact on all firms in the sector, they cannot alone lead to recovery. But they can help by easing the pressure on the financing of the recovery efforts. Some, however, are down to good fortune (luck), e.g. the historic siting of plant in the location of a new industrial development. The trick to understanding luck is the new positive posture that the recovery team adopts. Luck occurs often but is frequently invisible due to tarnished or inaccurate perceptions. This may be especially where an OBR system is very rigid and inflexible in its view of opportunities or when perceptions are altered as in crisis situations. A new team, with a new OBR, can alter perceptions and turn yesterday's ignored opportunities into tomorrow's successful projects.

27.8 STAGE SIX: RENEWAL

The final stage in the turnaround process is renewal. It is one thing to successfully negotiate a recovery from a position of threatened extinction but quite another to be able to sustain it and learn from it. The recovery phase does not contain a one-off set of measures that guarantees improved performance indefinitely. Other measures have to be taken continuously that help maintain and develop the firm's position. This is renewal or continuous learning. It has two parts—continuing characteristics

that have to be maintained for good performance and the development and fostering of an underlying learning culture.

27.8.1 Continuing Characteristics

We have analysed the characteristics of sustained good performance into seven groups; many of these characteristics can be traced directly to the actions taken in the retrenchment and recovery phases. They are:

1. Good management. Features include action orientation, a culture that values people, good internal communications, incentives for the Board and key executives, staying close to customers, strong corporate values, and a Board that is not involved in the day to day running of the business. Perhaps the most striking of these is the continuation of the action-orientation of the recovery phase. The same expenditure of energy and enthusiasm for the task, a confident approach to risk, and a wide search for opportunities.

2. Appropriate organization structure. An important role of organizational structure is to facilitate the effective implementation of management decisions for running the company. The main features include simplicity, lean head office, profit or cost centres with delegated powers, well developed strategic planning systems in larger firms, and regular but informal strategy reviews in smaller firms.

3. Effective financial and other controls. Features here are similar to those in most stable and well run businesses and refer to sound, timely, and comprehensive management information systems, tight liquidity control with good cash flow forecasts, budgetary control, and effective capital budgeting.

4. Sound product-market posture. Much of this activity can be identified as active portfolio management. This requires a broad search for opportunities, a continuous watch on existing markets, and the ability to capitalize on divestment chances. The main features are the investment in growth markets where the firm is competitively strong, maintenance of high market shares in the major business, a focus on the business the firm knows best, maintenance of entry barriers to the main business, and harvesting or divesting competitively weak businesses.

5. Good marketing management. This element is closely related to product market activity above and so its importance is already established. Main features are regular analysis of market research information and its continuous collection, regular analysis segmentation and positioning analysis, systematic search for new markets, regular consultation with key customers, and a strongly motivated and coordinated sales force.

6. High quality maintained. High quality in many global markets is now a given for competitive entry. This means tight quality control systems throughout the value chain, systematic review, and analysis of customer views and competitor

products/services and constantly reiterating the message within the internal culture about zero defects.

7. Tightly controlled costs. Again, these are a prerequisite for survival in most tight markets and represent one of the lasting legacies of the crisis of the turnaround era. Yet, as the firms have learned, tight cost control is not enough. They must continuously invest in new plant, machinery, technologies, training of staff, and R&D. The lesson for many renewal companies was not to confuse costs with investments.

27.8.2 Development and Fostering of a Learning Culture

Research suggests that learning runs through a three-phase model as presented in Figure 27.10.

Learning draws upon experience, memories, and past actions. This knowledge is then processed by individuals or groups and compared with current action through a feedback mechanism. If the feedback is positive and the stimuli strong enough, it may then transfer into a modification of current routines, rules, and patterns that govern behaviour. For many organizations, wedded strongly to past recipes, it is difficult to shift the 'dominant logic' with which they run their operations and develop their strategies. So behaviour changing amid top management teams can be tough.

However, as organizational environments become more dynamic and their constituent variables interact with greater complexity, the need for continuous learning grows. Similarly, there is a need for this learning to accelerate the change in corporate routines to ensure organizational adaptation. In other words, organizations have to learn for change and be adaptive. This means a faster rate of learning and a faster transfer of this learning into the rules and routines that affect behaviour.

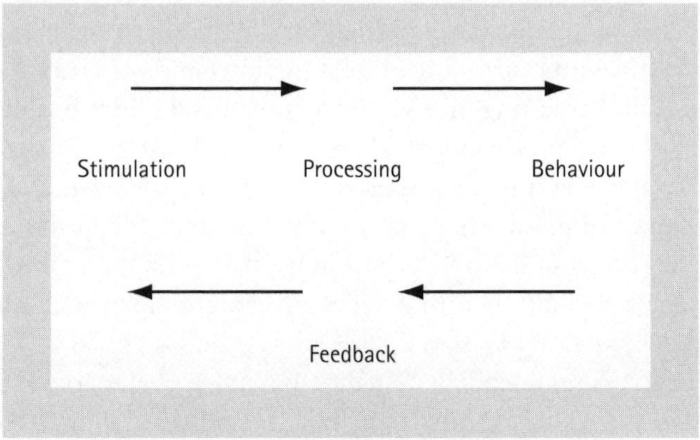

Fig. 27.10 Simple learning loop

Unfortunately, organizational learning theory remains silent on the knowledge processing routine in Figure 27.10. Recent work in open systems theory, cybernetics, and complexity science may help. Here, organizations can be viewed as self-organizing systems (Nonaka 1988). In contrast to a classic machine model, the characteristics of such systems are: 'the ability to continuously renew and recycle their components, while maintaining the integrity of their overall structure and... to reach out creatively beyond physical and mental boundaries in the processes of learning, development and evolution' (Capra 1982). Research in chemistry, mathematics, and biology provides support for the existence of such systems. Recently, research findings in management have provided support for the organizational adaptation position through the discovery of evolutionary drivers existing within self-organizing systems.

The complexity science is a multidisciplinary approach that tries to grapple with the non-linearity, unpredictability, and uncertainty in the behaviour of self-organizing systems. In this branch of the sciences, such systems are known as complex adaptive systems: 'A complex system is a system of a large number of agents that interact with each other in various ways. Such a system is adaptive if these agents change their actions as a result of the events in the process of interaction' (Vriend 1994). This multiplicity of interconnections is responsible for the adaptiveness of such systems, in that any configuration of interconnections constitutes a system state. So any change in environment or internal conditions can be addressed within the system's vast range of possible configurations. Behaviour in these systems tends to move away from extremes of complete order, inertia and stasis, on the one hand, and complete randomness and chaos, on the other. Hence, they would have inherent mechanisms that prevent many of the primary causes of decline (see Section 27.3.2).

Moreover, agents within the system learn to anticipate some of the results of their actions over time through a set of decision rules or 'schemas'. These adaptive agents learn within a classifier system (see Holland 1995 and Neumair 1998). This consists of a system of rules that receives environmental signals and messages and processes them through a system of routines into outgoing signals and messages. The processing element involves a sequential comparison of external messages with the organization's own message memory bank. The classifier system is simply a collection of all the organization's rules and routines and so is unique.

The organization learns through:

- *Exploitation.* The development of its existing rules, strengthening the good ones at the expense of those that do not work well.
- *Exploration.* The search for, and creation of, new rules to improve the existing ones through refinement, continuous improvement, and kaizen. The number of rules in a classifier system is limited and so any new rules have to be better than, and therefore replace, the weaker ones already in the system.

- *Mutation.* A random mutation element operates that can change or modify rules independently of the normal routines. The latter operates to protect the processor from any preoccupation with conservative routines. It is present to 'think the unthinkable'.

Clearly, an organization that solely relied on exploitation for rule development would be closed from new rules and eventually converge on the best of what it had. A process that leads to the kind of myopia discussed in Section 27.3.2. A reliance solely on exploration would yield too many rules for the classifier system to test and implement. The system would become unstable. Any system with low rates of mutation tends to 'in-breeding' and with too much, could tend to chaos. A balance is so required between the learning elements.

This rule-based decision-making is consistent with much of the traditional organizational learning literature. For instance, a general understanding of rules is expressed thus: 'By rules we mean the routines, procedures, conventions, roles, strategies, organisational forms and technologies around which political activity is structured. We also mean the beliefs, paradigms, codes, cultures, and knowledge that surround, support, elaborate, and contradict those roles and routines' (March and Olsen 1989). Because organizational cultures are different, each rule set is unique to that firm as is the learning process associated with it. Hence, any turnaround treatment must also be individual in content and process. Groups of rules have similarities, e.g. the notion of industry 'recipes' (Grinyer and Spender 1979), where discernible patterns of learning can be found among cognate firms in the same sector, e.g. the basis for much modern Northern hemisphere rugby is the New Zealand recipe for playing the game. But the processing of the recipe within firms is usually very different and dependent on the resource base of the entity, e.g. Welsh versus English rugby. In other words, the routines differ: 'it is the routines themselves, and the ability of management to call upon the organisation to perform them, that represents the firms' *business capability*... because routines involve a strong tacit dimension, they may not be easy to imitate. To the extent that this is so, routines contribute to a firm's distinctive competencies and capabilities' (Teece, Pisano, and Shuen 1990).

In addition to rules and routines, the nature of learning is similar between the two approaches. For instance, the exploitation mechanism equates to 'single loop learning' and the exploration mechanism to 'double loop learning' in Argyris and Shon's (1978) widely accepted explanations of how organizations learn. Hence, the basic classifier model proposed by Holland is in agreement with much of the mainstream organizational learning literature. It embodies learning in a set of rules and routines, unique to the organization.

Besides the mainstream, learning under complex adaptive systems equates well with alternative views of the world. In particular, the competing views within organizational epistemology of 'representationist' (the world is given and individuals adapt) and 'autopoietic' (the world is not given but is created by individual

cognition and interaction). In either the adaptive or created worlds, rule-based systems are the mechanisms for living and surviving.

27.8.3 How to Learn to Learn

Classifier learning mechanisms mean that organizations have (a) to maintain a balance among the individual mechanisms (exploitation, exploration, and mutation) and (b) constantly maintain and develop the routines within each. Practically, this translates into careful design of the planning and control systems. In de Geus's (1988) words, 'how to institutionalise learning in the organisational setting'. For instance:

1. Exploitation. The aim here is to make things efficient and do the best learning possible within the existing rules and routines. This could be accomplished through the following:

- development of rules and routines that are based on best practice; and this may not be in the same sector
- routines that consider weak rules as well as strong ones, ensuring that the latter are self-reinforcing
- balance in organizational structure between the mechanistic and organic as appropriate to task and purpose
- an emphasis on loose coupling and decentralization to enhance radical innovation (especially in changing global markets)
- utilization of joint ventures, alliances, internal corporate venturing and federalism for innovation, rule challenge and development
- use of efficiency techniques for good routines, e.g. business process re-engineering, efficient management information systems, cash flow, zero-based budgeting, key performance indicators, activity-based costing, etc.
- use of quality improvement processes in the supply chain, manufacturing and channel management, e.g. key account management
- emphasis on improving 'time to market' throughout the chain.

By this time, staff have endured many necessary changes on the long road to recovery. In the renewal stage, we ask for more change to stay ahead of the game. Clearly, if this process is rushed, staff will begin to feel the effects of fatigue and generally wonder what all the change is for. Moreover, they will begin to ponder when the flow of good results will put an end to further change. If this happens, the turnaround manager needs to slow down and increase the level of communication and training that will emphasize the message that change must become the norm and not the exception in the organization.

2. Exploration. The aim here is to make things effective and lift learning to a second tier above the existing rules and routines. This could be accomplished through the following:

- use of broad scanning of the general and operating environments with deep analysis of the signals and drivers
- constant challenge of the existing rules and routines through:
  - the generation of creative tension
  - the harnessing of the energies of 'fear' and 'aspiration' through artificially generated crises or the stretching of horizons through new visions or 'strategic intents'
  - the making of the status quo more dangerous than unknown futures
  - the institutionalization of doubt and low contentment to sharpen perception
- facilitate experimentation
- share and disseminate new insights and ideas
- analyse failure, accept it, and learn from it
- embrace risk and uncertainty in decision-making
- embrace conflict
- design of control systems that are proactive and pay attention to the acquisition, distribution, interpretation, and storing of new knowledge
- enable managerial sabbaticals for reflection.

3. Mutation. The aim is to avoid ossification in any processing of rules and routines, no matter how well developed the exploratory stage is.

- think the unthinkable on a systematic basis, e.g. through the development of scenarios into deep futures and monitoring of future pathways
- do the opposite of what the figures say now and again
- encourage new blood and youthful ideas
- ensure Board composition and contribution is, and stays, critical and radical
- develop 'skunk-works', fund them, and tolerate their failures.

We thus combine the exploitative, explorative, and mutative elements of learning and fold them into day to day operations. Corporate learning should be a natural process, one given the same time, attention, and investment as any other process in the business. It should become endemic in the culture. It should be the biggest investment.

27.9 THE FUTURE

Research into turnaround tends to go forward in fits and starts. Academic researchers are all pretty well known to each other, as is their work. Practitioners can be flamboyant and charismatic turnaround doctors (e.g. Sir John Harvey-Jones) with

high profiles, or consultants and accountants working diligently but anonymously as part of turnaround teams. For the future, we should endeavour to:

- develop the academic work away from Anglo-American contexts
- develop the academic work away from large, quoted companies towards smaller firms (who arguably need help more)
- reduce the emphasis on 'generic strategies' and focus on research into turn-arounds in specific contexts, e.g. sector, country, size, organizational culture, management styles
- utilize a multidisciplinary approach to inform theory building, e.g. social anthro-pology, social psychology
- marry academic work with that of practitioners
- build large databases with practitioners to encourage a more consistent dissemin-ation of work.

In essence, the study of turnaround is one of multiple perspectives. It incorporates elements from all the subjects of an MBA curriculum. Both academics and practi-tioners need a broad base, the involvement of different specialists and a genuine partnership.

27.10 SUMMARY

This chapter has described the corporate turnaround as a six-stage process consist-ing of Causes, Triggers, Diagnosis, Retrenchment, Recovery, and Renewal. Stage processes are now a generally accepted approach to the subject but here, we add the first three and the last one in an effort to develop the subject area both theoretically and practically. We also pay special attention to the diagnostic events and schema, drawing on medical research and practice for inspiration. Throughout the stages, we have emphasized the importance of understanding the behaviour of the dominant coalition, explaining what actions to expect and when, but, more importantly, why they occur. A central and binding theme has been the emphasis on unique solutions to the unique problems of each enterprise. As learning classification systems and corporate cultures are different for each firm, every turnaround strategy that wishes to optimize its chances of success has to customize its solution. Moreover, it does not end when the company reaches a position of relative safety. To ensure that the same mistakes are not made again, the learning has to happen and be made to happen. That is the ultimate duty of strategic management.

REFERENCES

ALTMAN, E. (1971). *Corporate Bankruptcy in America*. Lexington, Ky: Lexington Books, D. C. Heath.

ARGENTI, J. (1976). *Corporate Collapse: The Causes and Symptoms*. New York: McGraw-Hill.

ARGYRIS, C., and SHON, D. (1978). *Organizational Learning*. Reading, Mass.: Addison-Wesley.

BARKER, V. L., and DUHAIME, I. M. (1997). 'Strategic Change in the Turnaround Process: Theory and Empirical Evidence'. *Strategic Management Journal*, 18: 13–38.

——and MONE, M. A. (1994). 'Retrenchment: Cause of Turnaround or Consequence of Decline?'. *Strategic Management Journal*, 15: 395–405.

————(1998). 'The Mechanistic Structure Shift and Strategic Reorientation in Declining Firms and Attempting Turnarounds'. *Human Relations*, 51/10: 1227–58.

BARNEY, J. (1991). 'Firm Resources and Sustained Competitive Advantage'. *Journal of Management*, 17/1: 99–120.

BIBEAULT, D. B. (1982). *Corporate Turnaround: How Managers Turn Losers into Winners*. New York: McGraw-Hill.

CAMERON, K. S., SUTTON, R. I. and WHETTEN, D. A. (1988). 'Issues in Organizational Decline', in K. S. Cameron, R. I. Sutton, and D. A. Whetten (eds.), *Readings in Organizational Decline: Framework, Research and Prescriptions*. Boston: Ballinger Publishing, 3–19.

CAPRA, F. (1982). *The Turning Point*. New York: Simon & Schuster.

CYERT, R. M., and MARCH, J. G. (1963). *A Behavioural Theory of the Firm*. Englewood Cliffs, NJ: Prentice-Hall.

DE GEUS, A. (1988). 'Planning as Learning'. *Harvard Business Review*, 66/2: 70–4.

FOMBRUN, C. J. (1992). *Turning Points*. New York: McGraw-Hill.

GOLDING, D. (1980). 'Establishing Blissful Clarity in Life: Managers'. *Sociological Review*, 28: 763–82.

GOLDSTON, M. R. (1992). *The Turnaround Prescription*. New York: Free Press.

GRINYER, P. H., and MCKIERNAN, P. (1990). 'Generating Major Change in Stagnating Companies'. *Strategic Management Journal*, 11/Summer Special Issue: 131–46.

—— and SPENDER, J. G. (1979). *Turnaround: The Fall and Rise of the Newton Chambers Group*. London: Associated Business Press.

——MAYES, D., and MCKIERNAN, P. (1988). *The Sharpbenders: The Secrets of Unleashing Corporate Potential*. Oxford: Blackwell.

HAMBRICK, D. G., and SCHECTER, S. M. (1983). 'Turnaround Strategies for Mature Industrial Product Business Units'. *Academy of Management Journal*, 26: 231–48.

HEDBERG, B. K. L., NYSTROM, P. C. and STARBUCK, W. H. (1976). 'Company on Seesaws: Prescriptions for a Self-Designing Organisation'. *Administrative Science Quarterly*, 21: 46–65.

HOFER, C. W., and SCHENDEL, D. (1978). *Strategy Formulation: Analytical Concepts*. St Paul, Minn.: West Publishing.

HOFFMAN, R. C. (1989). 'Strategies for Corporate Turnarounds: What Do We Know about Them?'. *Journal of General Management*, 14/3 (spring): 46–66.

HOLLAND, J. H. (1995). *Hidden Order: How Adaptation Builds Complexity*. Reading, Mass.: Addison-Wesley.

JANIS, I. L. (1972). *Victims of Group Think*. Boston: Houghton Mifflin.

KUHN, T. S. (1970). *The Structure of Scientific Revolutions* (2nd edn.). Chicago: University of Chicago Press.

LUTHANS, F. (1980). 'The Learning Process', in L. L. Cummings and R. B. Dunham (eds.), *Introduction to Organizational Behaviour.* Homewood, Ill.: Richard D. Irwin, 205–27.

MCKIERNAN, P. (1992). *Strategies of Growth: Maturity, Recovery and Internationalisation.* London: Routledge.

MARCH, J. G. and OLSEN, J. P. (1989). *Rediscovering Institutions: The Organizational Basis of Politics.* New York: Free Press.

MILBURN, T. W. (1972). 'The Management of Crisis', in C. F. Hermann (ed.), *International Crises: Insights from Behavioural Research.* New York: Free Press.

MILLER, D. (1990). *The Icarus Paradox: How Exceptional Companies Bring about their own Downfall.* New York: Harper Collins.

MUELLER, G. C., and BARKER, V. L. (1997). 'Upper Echelons and Board Characteristics of Turnaround and Nonturnaround of Declining Firms'. *Journal of Business Research,* 39: 119–34.

NEUMAIR, U. (1998). 'A General Model of Corporate Failure and Survival: A Complexity Theory Approach'. Ph.D. dissertation, University of St Gallen.

NONAKA, I. (1988). 'Creating Organizational Order Out of Chaos: Self-Renewal in Japanese Firms'. *California Management Review,* Spring: 57–73.

—— (1992). 'Turnaround: Retrenchment and Recovery'. *Strategic Management Journal,* 13: 287–309.

ROBBINS, D. K., and PEARCE, J. A. (1994a). 'Entrepreneurial Recovery Strategies of Small Market Share Manufacturers'. *Journal of Business Venturing,* 9: 91–108.

—— —— (1994b). 'Retrenchment Remains the Foundation of Business Turnaround'. *Strategic Management Journal,* 15: 407–17.

PETTIGREW, A. M., and WHIPP, R. (1991). *Managing Change for Competitive Success.* Oxford: Basil Blackwell.

PONDY, L. (1984). 'Union of Rationality and Intuition in Management Action', in P. Shrivastava and Associates (eds.), *The Executive Mind: New Insights in Managerial Thought and Action.* San Francisco: Jossey-Bass.

PEARCE, J. A., and ROBBINS, D. K. (1992). 'Turnaround: Retrenchment and Recovery'. *Strategic Management Journal,* 13: 287–309.

SLATTER, S. (1984). *Corporate Recovery: Successful Turnaround Strategies and their Implementation.* Harmondsworth: Penguin.

—— and LOVETT, D. (1999). *Corporate Turnaround.* Harmondsworth: Penguin.

SMOCK, C. D. (1955). 'The Influence of Psychological Stress or the Intolerance of Ambiguity'. *Journal of Abnormal and Social Psychology,* 50: 177–82.

SPENDER, J. C. (1979). 'Strategy Making in Business'. Ph.D. thesis, Manchester Business School, Manchester.

STARBUCK, W. H., and MILLIKEN, F. J. (1988). 'Challenger: Fine-tuning the Odds until Something Breaks'. *Journal of Management Studies,* 25/4: 319–40.

STARKEY, K. (2000). The Music of Organization or 'Some Like It Hot': A Work in Progress (prepared for the Conference-Workshop 'Conception et dynamique des organisations: Sait-on piloter le changement?', École des Hautes Études Commerciales, Université de Lausanne, 17 Mar. 2000).

STINCHCOMBE, A. L. (1965). 'Social Structure and Organizations', in J. G. March (ed.), *Handbook of Organizations.* Chicago: Rand McNally, 142–93.

TEECE, D., PISANO, G., and SHUEN, A. (1990). 'Firm Capabilities, Resources and the Concept of Strategy: Four Paradigms of Strategic Management'. Working paper, Center for Research in Management, University of California, Berkeley, Dec.

VRIEND, N. J. (1994). *Self-Organized Markets in a Decentralized Economy*. Working Paper No. 94–03–013, Santa Fe Institute.

WEICK, K. (1993). 'Cosmology Episodes in Organizations: Young Men and Fire and the Mann Gulch Disaster'. *Administrative Science Quarterly*, 39: 628–52.

—— (1995). *Sensemaking in Organisations: Small Structures with Large Consequences*. Thousand Oaks, Calif.: Sage.

—— (1998). 'Improvisation as a Mindset for Organizational Analysis'. *Organizational Science*, 9: 543–55.

CHAPTER 28

ORGANIZATIONAL STRUCTURE

RICHARD WHITTINGTON

28.1 INTRODUCTION

ORGANIZATIONAL structures are concerned with the recurrent relationships between the various members of an organization (Donaldson 1996). This includes not just authority and reporting relationships—the simple question of who is in charge. Organizational structures tell us who has the resources; who talks to whom; who is accountable for what; what you can do on your own and what you must do with others; what kinds of career paths are available; and how knowledge flows around the organization. Some of these structures are written down formally, in the organizational chart and other procedures. Many of them are informal, even if often closely linked to formal structures as well. Organizational structures are therefore central to achieving anything in an organization—an essential part of strategy implementation.

Consider any important strategic initiative. Mergers and takeovers immediately raise issues of appropriate structures for integration: should new businesses sit alongside old, or be melded within the whole? Internationalization raises other structural dilemmas: should national structures be stretched to include overseas operations or should overseas units be able to manage themselves autonomously according to local needs? Diversified businesses have their tensions too: how far should head offices intervene to ensure synergy between different businesses, at the

risk of constraining the businesses from pursuing their interests freely and account-ably as they see fit? In short, without fixing the right structure, a strategy is not really done.

The importance and scope of structural issues need to be reasserted. For too long it has been fashionable to dismiss organizational structure as irrelevant and overly formalistic (Waterman, Peters, and Phillips 1980; Pascale 1984). This chapter will assert the continuing importance of structure to thinking about strategy practice. It will also introduce the contingency framework as a starting-point for designing appropriate structures, and apply it to three particularly central strategic issues—growth, diversification, and internationalization. It goes on to address some recent challenges to traditional thinking about large organizations and their structures, namely networks and knowledge management. It then finishes by considering the dynamic nature of structure—the need for continuous, co-evolutionary patching and repatching—and the kinds of skills and capabilities this entails. Structural dynamism is the new agenda for managers and researchers alike.

28.2 THE IMPORTANCE OF STRUCTURE

James Gordon (1978) has written an intriguing book about physical structures—bridges, buildings, dams, and so on—entitled: *Structures, or Why Things Don't Fall Down*. Organizational structures perform an equally important role in human enterprises today. The organizations that dominate our lives are vast and complex entities, employing tens or even hundreds of thousands of people in many different activities all around the globe. We may not always like these organizations, but considered afresh and objectively, they are remarkable constructions. It is structure that holds them together and makes them work.

There are many, though, who argue that the traditional large-scale corporation is now out of date (e.g. Castells 1996; Zenger and Hesterly 1997). According to them, this is the age of entrepreneurs, spin-outs, and networks of small companies. None of these have much need for structure. But as we look out at the business world as it is, there are few signs that the large corporation and its structures are really in decline.

Table 28.1 lists the ten largest corporations by turnover in the world. The measure is turnover—real business—not market capitalization—promised business in the future. For all the talk of a new economy based on e-commerce and networks, these corporations are all pretty old: only four were founded in the twentieth century and the youngest, Wal-Mart, is already about to enter its fifth decade. They are all in rather traditional businesses—four in automobiles. Most important for the structural

Table 28.1 The world's largest firms by revenues, 1999

Rank	Revenues ($bn)	Employees	Foundation date
1. General Motors	176.5	388,000	1908
2. Wal-Mart	166.8	1,140,000	1962
3. Exxon Mobil	163.9	106,000	1882
4. Ford	162.6	364,500	1903
5. Daimler-Chrysler	160.0	466,938	1883
6. Mitsui[a]	118.6	38,484	1673
7. Mitsubishi[a]	117.8	42,050	1870
8. Toyota	115.7	214,613	1926
9. General Electric	111.6	340,000	1892
10. Itochu[a]	109.1	5,306	1858
AVERAGE	140.3	296,049	1876

[a]Trading companies.

Source: The Global 500, *Fortune*, 24 July 2000; Derdack 1988.

issue, these corporations are massive employers. Leaving aside the three Japanese trading companies, their average employment is over 400,000 people. Wal-Mart has more than a million employees. Some of these top corporations are highly diversified: General Electric ranges from turbine generators to media and finance. They all operate in many different national environments, with the four automobile manufacturers each having factories and other operations in North America, Asia, and Europe. On this scale and with this complexity, these corporations still need structure (see Box 28.1 Wal-Mart's structure).

There are plenty more large-scale corporations like these. To give a perspective, new economy companies like Microsoft and Cisco rank only 216 and 409 in the *Fortune* Global 500 list (*Fortune*, 24 July 2000). The message here is this: organizational structures may be changing in the modern world, but they are certainly not going away.

Box 28.1 Wal-Mart's structure

The world's largest private employer, Wal-Mart, operates with a 'divisional' structure (see below). There are four retail divisions: Wal-Mart stores, responsible for the classic American discount retail outlets; the Supercenters division, whose stores combine general merchandise with groceries; SAM's Clubs, the warehouse club operations; and the International Division, responsible for all non-US retailing and representing nearly 14 per cent of total turnover. In addition, there are four specialty divisions: Tire & Lube Express; Pharmacy; Wal-Mart Vacations; and Used Fixture Auctions. Wal-Mart.com, the on-line business, is operated as a separate company.

Source: Wal-Mart Inc. Annual Report, 2000.

28.3 RULES FOR STRUCTURE?

For a long time, the dominant approach to structure has been that of contingency theory (Donaldson 2000). The best form of structure depends upon the particular demands (contingencies) faced by the organization. Structures are designed not according to some universal ideal but according to the particular contingencies that the organization faces. A mismatch between structure and contingencies is likely to lead to poor performance.

Some of the key contingencies that have been proposed are:

- *Organizational size.* The larger the organization, particularly in terms of employees, the more it requires hierarchical levels and specialization according to particular functions (Pugh and Hickson 1976).
- *Operational technology.* Organizations whose key operational technology involves mass production are best organized in a mechanistic and formal manner, whereas small batch producers—typically involving craft skills—can be more organic and informal (Woodward 1965).
- *Organizational environment.* Organizations working in very dynamic and uncertain environments perform best with fluid, organic structures. Organizations in more stable and predictable environments are able to work with mechanistic and formal structures (Burns and Stalker 1961).
- *Diversification strategy.* The more different kinds of business an organization operates in, the more it needs to decentralize its operations into focused and autonomous divisions or business-units (Chandler 1962).
- *Internationalization.* The more international operations are, or the more important adaptation to local market needs, the more the organization will need to decentralize to geographical area units (Stopford and Wells 1972).

According to contingency theory, knowing how contingencies and structures fit together provides the organization with firm rules for structural design.

Contingency theory can be faulted for considering its various contingencies too much in isolation. More recently, advocates of configuration theory (Miller 1986) and the theory of complementarities (Milgrom and Roberts 1995; Whittington et al. 1999; Pettigrew et al. 2002) have proposed more holistic perspectives, where structure needs to match simultaneously with a whole raft of characteristics, from strategy, through systems to technology. In these views, organizational characteristics are complementary, working best when all fitted together. Organizations need to be configured as wholes. As in the Unilever example (Box 28.2 Complementary structural change at Unilever), initiatives in strategy and systems will yield their benefits only when the right structure is put in place. Rather than fitting each individually to different contingencies, strategies, structures, and systems need to be aligned into virtuous circles of complementary reinforcement.

Whether from the point of view of contingencies, configurations, or comple-mentarities, the basic takeaway is clear: structure is a key component in the web of factors determining organizational performance. The following sections will con-sider three key contingencies—growth, diversification, and internationalization—in more detail, before going on to address the implications of an increasingly fast-paced and networked world for traditional contingency thinking.

Box 28.2 Complementary structural change at Unilever

The Anglo-Dutch Unilever is an international food and home and personal care group that radically reorganized in the mid-1990s. Traditionally Unilever had been highly decentralized in character, with a classic 'multi-domestic' structure allowing a great deal of autonomy to the national subsidiary companies. During the late 1980s and early 1990s, the company began to introduce new innovation and strategy systems, at the same time as shifting strategy to focus on core businesses. Strategy and systems were changing, but structural change had to wait until 1996, with the launch of the Shaping for Outstanding Performance programme.

Until 1996 power had been vested in a Special Committee—composed of the Dutch and UK company chairmen, plus the chairman designate—and a fifteen person executive board, comprising functional, product, and regional directors. The structure as a whole was a matrix, with the product 'coordinators' (directors) having prime profit responsibility in Western Europe and the United States and regional directors having profit responsibility in remaining regions. Responsibilities often got blurred. According to an internal document: 'We need clarity of purpose and rôle: the board finds itself too involved in operations at the expense of strategic leadership.'

Shaping for Outstanding Performance abolished both the Special Committee and the regional director level. In its place was put an eight (later seven) person executive committee made up of the chairmen plus functional and category (i.e. food and home and personal care) directors. Reporting to them, with clear profit responsibility, were thirteen (later twelve) Business Group presidents, typically with complete profit responsibility for their category within a particular region. Global strategic leadership was clearly placed at the level of the executive committee; operating performance was the direct responsibility of the business groups.

Beneath this formal structure, international coordination was facilitated by the existence of many formal and semi-formal networks. Research and development was assured by international networks of innovation centres, leadership typically going to centres of expertise rather than automatically to the Netherlands or the United Kingdom. Product and brand networks—International Business Teams—worked globally to coordinate branding and marketing. At the same time, functional networks worked on a succession of projects in order to achieve global coordination on critical issues, such as recruitment and organizational effectiveness. All these networks relied heavily on informal leadership and social processes, as well as increasing investment in electronic mail and databases. Participation was largely determined and funded by the Business Groups rather than corporate headquarters.

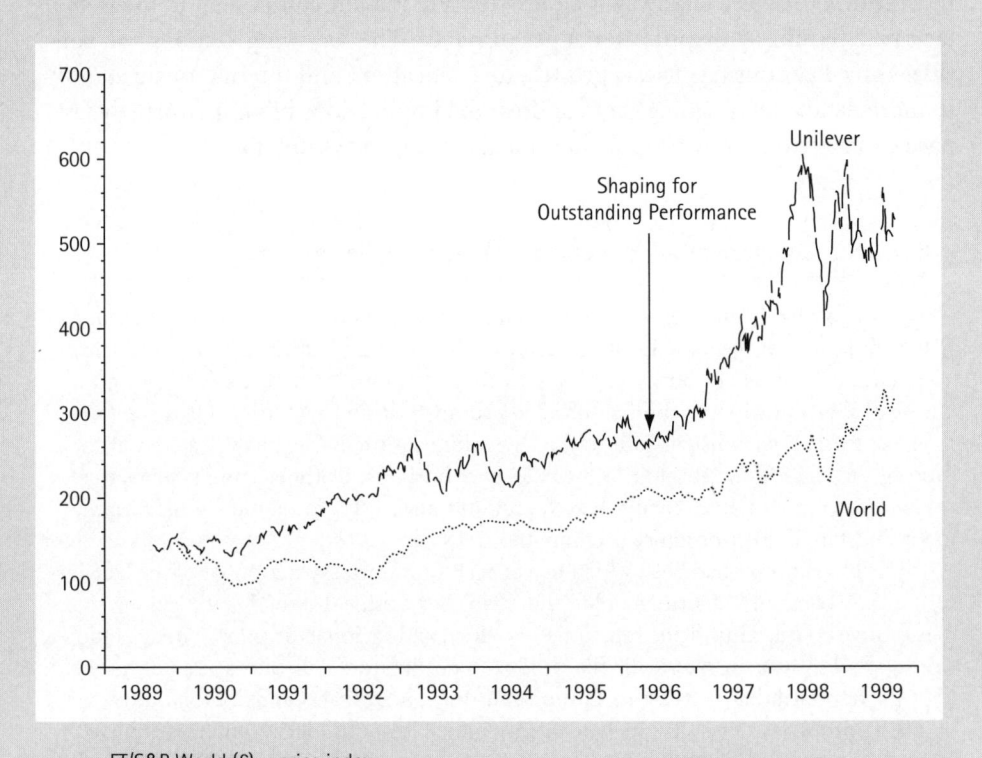

FT/S&P World (£) — price index
Unilever (UK)

Fig. 28.1 Structural change and performance at Unilever

Source: Datastream.

The importance of completing the virtuous circle of complementarities is illustrated here by the timing of performance take-off. In the period preceding the Shaping for Outstanding Performance change, there had been both strategic changes in terms of greater focus on core businesses and systems changes in terms of innovation and strategy formation. But only when the circle was completed by structural change did the share price start to significantly outperform the world index. Unilever's value more than doubled in the two subsequent years. Structure pays.

Source: Adapted from Whittington and Mayer (2001).

28.4 GROWTH AND STRUCTURE

A classic finding from contingency theory is that organizational size—whether measured by employees or sales—is strongly correlated with elements of structure (Pugh and Hickson 1976). The larger the organization, the more hierarchical levels it

typically has. The larger the organization too, the more it can afford functional specialists—in other words, instead of everybody mucking in, setting up specialized functions and departments. This finding on size has crucial implications for successful growth strategies.

Larry Greiner (1998) has identified regular patterns of crisis and reordering in the ways in which organizations grow (see Figure 28.2). Crises are frequently because of structure—sometimes too little, other times of the wrong sort. Thus, the first stage of a new organization is typically one of growth through the exercise of creativity, the realization of the original entrepreneurial idea. As the organization grows larger and older, it risks the first crisis, that of leadership. The founders have to abandon their original informality and introduce some managerial structures. Growth is restored on the basis of a stronger sense of direction, until the next crisis hits. Now the problem is of autonomy: too much structure is smothering initiative and creativity. The solution is to delegate, introducing more decentralized structures. These succeed for a while, until problems of control and integration arise. The solution this

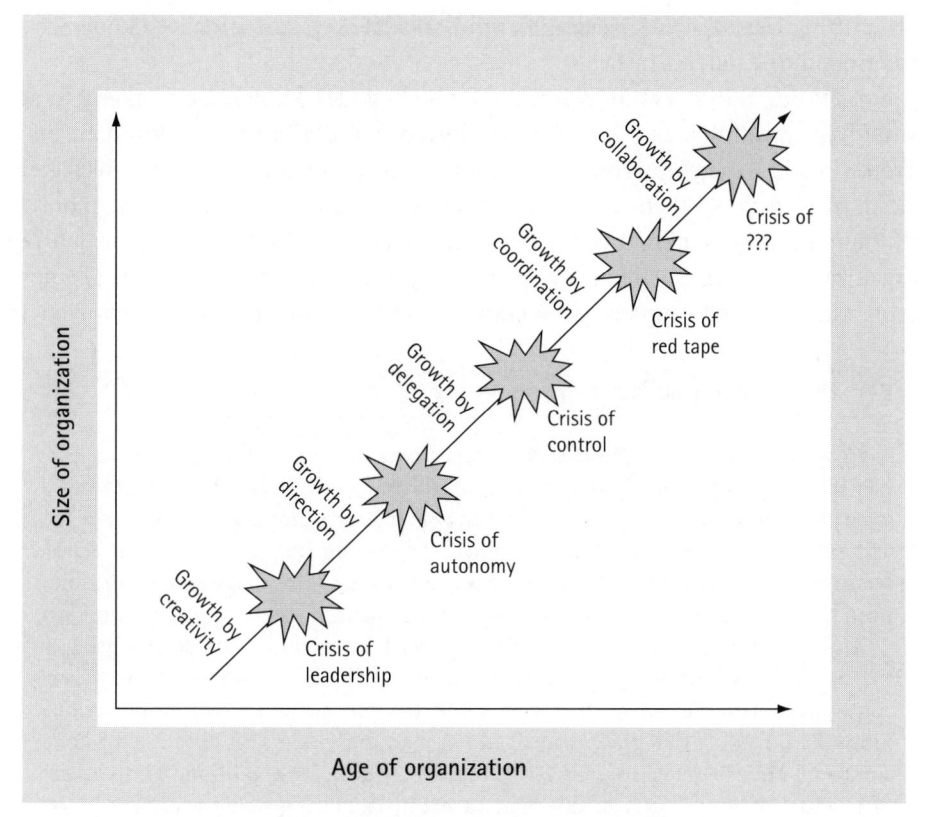

Fig. 28.2 The five stages of growth

time is to put in coordinating structures, with cross-departmental liaison and company-wide controls. Soon the organization runs into a crisis of red tape. Here the way forward lies in developing a spontaneous and collaborative spirit that is capable of oiling the wheels of formal structure. Rather as in theories of configurations or complementarities, culture is necessary to making structures work smoothly.

Sometimes structure can be seen as a barrier to growth and enterprise: it sounds too much like bureaucracy for its own sake. Management guru Tom Peters (1992), for instance, celebrates 'disorganization', 'chaos', and 'mess'. Management theorists such as Barrett (1998) and Hatch (1999) invoke jazz as a metaphor for organizing, urging improvisation within minimal structures. Close reading, in fact, reveals that these advocates of chaos and improvisation are always careful not to throw out structure altogether: they just want the right structure and not too much of it. This is the message of Greiner's (1998) model too. Getting the structure right is critical to strategic growth, and the right structure changes as the organization gets larger. Anticipating the structural demands of rapid growth was essential to the success of the world's first large-scale Internet browser company, Netscape (see Box 28.3 Structuring Netscape). As Netscape's Jim Barksdale says, the trick is to know when to bring on the bureaucrats.

Sometimes, too, structure is resisted by high-skilled knowledge workers. In accounting, consulting, and law firms, for instance, the norm has traditionally been professional partnerships. Here accountants, consultants, and lawyers are given great freedom to develop their practices as they see fit, with control exercised loosely through the democracy of the partners. Growth has brought these loosely structured organizations under pressures for change: Big Five accounting firms typically have more than 100,000 employees, operate all over the world and are involved in

---

Box 28.3 Structuring Netscape

Netscape was founded (as Mosaic Communications) in 1994. Within five years, it was a half-billion dollar company and the fastest growing software company of all time. A large part of its success was down to two things: first, the readiness of founders Jim Clark and Marc Andreeson to hire as their chief executive Jim Barksdale, an experienced senior manager with IBM, AT&T, and Federal Express; second, Barksdale's readiness from the first to impose structure and systems on the explosively successful company.

Barksdale summed up his philosophy: 'The trick is to know when do you bring on the bureaucrats. There's a stage in a company's life where it's fine to be loosely-controlled. There's another stage where you have to get more and more serious.' From the first, he put in place control and accounting systems 'fit for a billion-dollar company'. He also quickly decentralized the rapidly growing organization into a series of product divisions, broken down in turn into smaller groupings called 'divlets'. Divisions and divlets could get on with their complex and fast-moving tasks, while providing the clarity of reporting and accountability essential for control.

Source: Cusumano and Yoffie 1998.

consulting, information technology, and even legal services. According to Hinings, Greenwood, and Cooper (1999), the appropriate model in these large, multinational professional service organizations is increasingly that of the 'Managed Professional Business'. Here professional partnerships become subject to the kinds of specialization and hierarchy normal in any other large enterprise. 'Partners-in-charge' are introduced, taking responsibility for practice areas (such as audit, tax, etc.) little different from conventional departments or divisions. Specialists are also hired, typically from outside the profession, to take responsibility for key functions such as marketing or human resources. Rational planning systems are imposed to give the firms strategic coherence. The structural transformation of engineering consultancy Ove Arup is quite typical of this kind of move to the style of Managed Professional Business (see Box 28.4 Ove Arup's structural reformation).

Growth strategies, then, inescapably increase the need for structure as they enlarge the scale of operations. Hierarchical layers increase and functional specialization emerges. Some activities tend to become more centralized; others are decentralized within formal frameworks. Growth, however, does not necessarily lead to bureaucratization in a simple negative sense. Peter Blau (1972) has shown that the proportion of administrative staff as a whole tends in fact to fall with increased size. There are economies of scale in bureaucracy, so that growth actually reduces bureaucratic intensity. Structure and bureaucracy are not pernicious parasites on growth. As Greiner (1998) insists, structures are essential to successful development for all kinds of business, whether traditional manufacturing, Internet start-up, or knowledge-intensive service industry.

Box 28.4 Ove Arup's structural reformation

Ove Arup was founded in London as a one-man engineering consultancy in 1946. By the 1990s it had 6,000 employees in more than 50 offices in over 40 countries around the world.

The company had started as a traditional partnership. In 1992, however, it became a private company, owned by two trusts: an employee trust and a company trust. Profits are shared. The company also addressed its structure. In the early 1990s, the company still had 50 different units all reporting directly to the main 'Partnership Board'. However, there was a feeling that the multinational and multidisciplinary whole was now drifting apart. The solution was the 'Reformation' initiative, launched in 1995. The Partnership Board was replaced with a Policy Board, responsible for strategy and a new 'statement of intent'. Five operational boards were established to manage different parts of the business: Operations, Civil Engineering, Industrial Engineering, Building Engineering, and East Asia. Skill networks, market networks, and project teams worked across these divisions in order to ensure collaboration and cohesion. Centralized initiatives on computer systems and human resources provided the necessary common infrastructure.

Source: Fenton and Pettigrew 2000.

28.5 DIVERSIFICATION AND STRUCTURE

One of the key means of growth over the last one hundred years has been strategies of diversification. Although during the last decades of the century there may have been some reversal of diversification in the United States—(Markides 1995)—in Europe it looks as if diversification has continued to be an increasing phenomenon through the whole post-war period. Whereas in 1950 around about one-third of the largest corporations in France, Germany, and the United Kingdom were diversified, by the 1990s the proportion was around two-thirds or more (Whittington and Mayer 2001). Diversification is a key structural contingency. As corporations grow more diversified, they become both bigger and more complex: not just more business, but new businesses of sometimes many different kinds. This puts a lot of strain on the two traditional forms of organization: the functional structure and the holding company (Chandler 1962; Williamson 1975).

The functional structure is centralized by the principal functions of the business—sales, production, finance, and so on. A typical example is the DuPont corporation immediately after World War I (see Box 28.5 DuPont discovers the M-form). The problem for the functional structure is coping with the complexity of diversification. Departments and their chiefs have to be equally able to deal with functional issues arising from potentially a very wide range of businesses. In the DuPont example, making and selling explosives was a very different matter to making and selling paints.

Box 28.5 DuPont discovers the M-form

The history of the DuPont chemical company illustrates the importance of getting the structure right for diversification (see Chandler 1962). At the beginning of the twentieth century, it was relatively undiversified, an explosives company producing dynamite. DuPont enjoyed boom times during World War I, of course, but the company's management was shrewd enough to realize that the explosives business would not for ever enjoy such high demand. Accordingly, they diversified into dyestuffs, paints, and more obscure products of the time such as pyralin and fabrikoid, all with good peacetime prospects. However, it retained its old centralized 'functional' structure to manage this new range of products. The heads of the sales and production functions were responsible for everything from explosives to paint (see Figure 28.3(a)). The

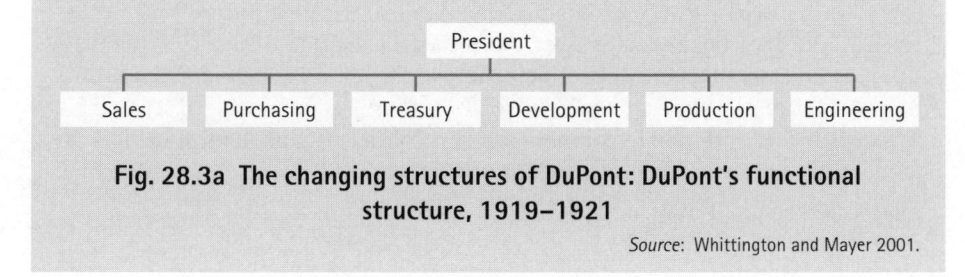

Fig. 28.3a The changing structures of DuPont: DuPont's functional structure, 1919–1921

Source: Whittington and Mayer 2001.

result was chaos. DuPont plunged into losses after the war: the only profitable business turned out to be explosives. The problem was not the strategy—diversification made good sense—but the structure with which to manage it. As Chandler (1962: 314) famously put it: 'unless structure follows strategy, inefficiency results'. The solution DuPont adopted in 1921 was to decentralize into separate divisions for each product (see Figure 28.3(b)). Effectively, DuPont was the first company in the world to hit upon this structural solution to the problem of diversity. DuPont has kept essentially the same product divisional structure ever since (see Figure 28.3(c)).

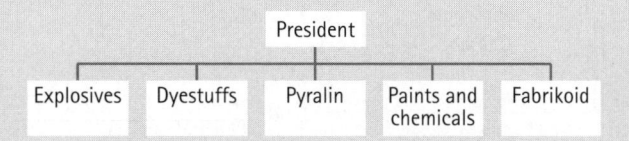

Fig. 28.3b The changing structures of DuPont: DuPont's new divisional structure, August 1921

Source: Whittington and Mayer 2001.

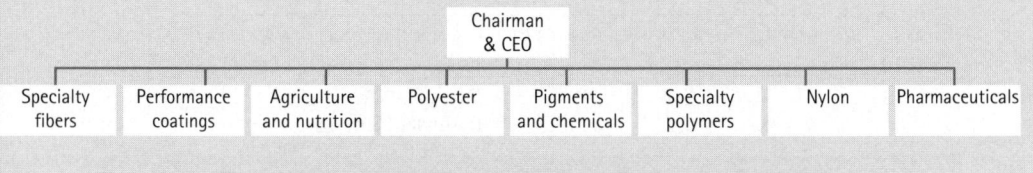

Fig. 28.3c The changing structures of DuPont: DuPont's divisional structure, 1999

Source: Whittington and Mayer 2001.

The holding company structure, on the other hand, is highly decentralized. Subsidiary businesses have a great deal of autonomy, not being integrated within common accounting and other systems and often being only partially owned. The result is that it is hard first to compare the performance of the different businesses and then to exert the kind of control necessary for policing performance and shifting resources to the most promising opportunities. A typical example of a traditional holding company is the French luxury goods Financière Agache group in the mid-1990s (see Figure 28.4). Here, the largest part of the business, LVMH, is a quoted company under minority ownership (45%), operating with separate systems from its ultimate parent (Whittington and Mayer 1997). Partial ownership and quoted subsidiary statuses inhibit optimal structure, so that the Guerlain perfume operation stands apart from LVMH's perfume division and Christian Dior and Celine are separate from the couture division.

According to contingency theory, diversified corporations can solve the dilemma between over-centralization and under-centralization by adopting the

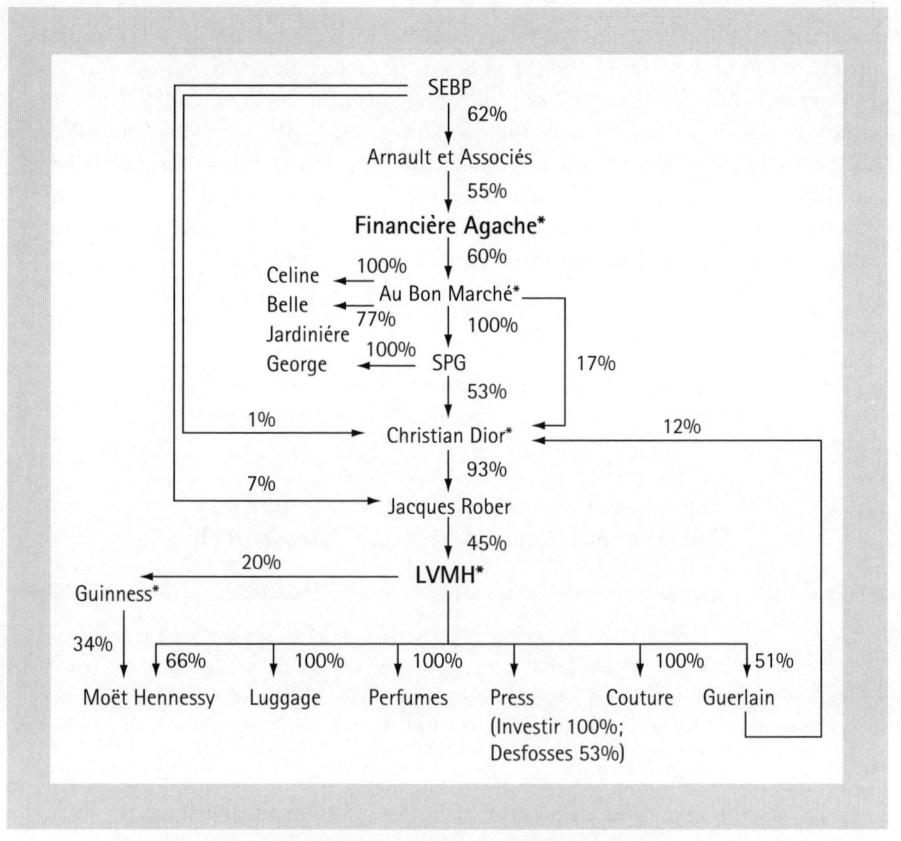

Fig. 28.4 The Financière Agache holding company structure
*Quoted companies

Source: Adapted from Whittington and Mayer (1997).

multi-divisional structure (often called 'the M-form'). Instead of trying to control everything from the centre, the multi-divisional structure separates operational responsibility for the individual diversified businesses from strategic responsibility for the make-up and performance of the overall corporate portfolio. Operational responsibility is decentralized to the heads of divisions—distinct business units, organized around products or regions—while strategic responsibility is kept firmly at the centre. The centre does not meddle in operations, but simply holds divisional heads accountable for performance. The centre installs the necessary common systems to monitor divisional performance and to ensure that resources are directed according to opportunity and strategy. The contrasting patterns of centralization and decentralization in the multi-divisional structure and the alternative functional and holding structures are illustrated in Figure 28.5.

The advantages of the multi-divisional (M-form) structure over the functional and holding structures are as follows (Williamson 1975):

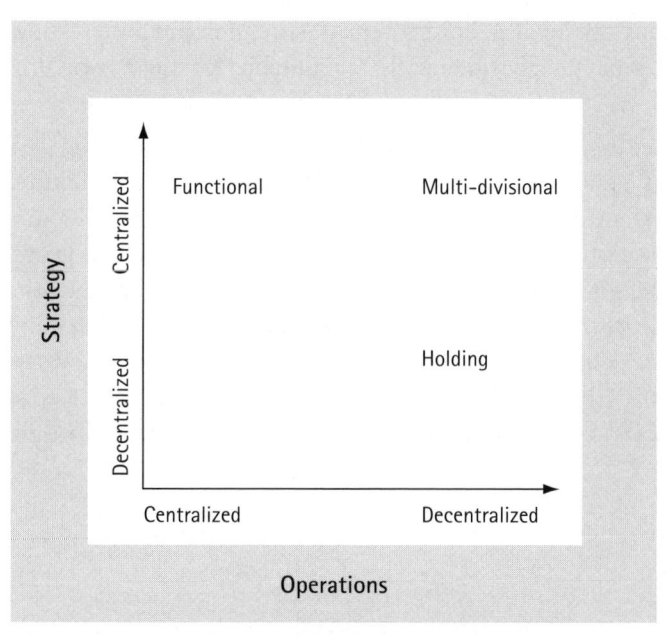

Fig. 28.5 Types of organizational structure

Source: Whittington and Mayer 2001.

1. Responsibility for overall corporate strategy is clearly placed with corporate executives undistracted by operational concerns.

2. Operational complexity is reduced, because the business is divided into discrete, specialized, and smaller business units (divisions).

3. Responsibility for operational businesses is clearly with divisional managers, who can be held accountable for performance outcomes, reducing the need for central intervention.

4. Experience of running divisional business units is good training in the general management skills needed for running the corporation as a whole.

The way in which the centre actually operates its overall strategic control may vary. Goold and Campbell (1987) demonstrate degrees of central intervention and responsibility with their notion of 'strategy styles'. These range from a 'Strategic Planning' style, in which the centre takes a very directive role in strategy formation for divisions, to the 'Financial Control' style, which is hands-off regarding divisional strategies so long as they meet corporate financial objectives. In any case, the decentralization of operations and retention of ultimate strategic control at the corporate level remain the defining principles of the multi-divisional.

Recently, however, the sharp distinctions of the multi-divisional have come under some criticism (Ghoshal and Bartlett 1998*a*):

1. Managements can become too detached from the operational realities of the businesses, simply running things 'by the numbers'.

2. Divisions divide: it is hard to create synergies and foster knowledge transfer between separate divisions each accountable for their own profit performance.

As we shall see when we discuss networks, these limitations can be partly addressed by new developments within the traditional multi-divisonal structure.

In fact, it seems that nowadays, most large businesses have divisionalized structures of some sort, whether organized according to products or geography. Figure 28.6 shows the spread of the divisional organization in Europe over the second half of the twentieth century. Although the French and Germans still retain more loosely knit holding company structures, it is clear that in the major Western European economies the trend has been overwhelmingly towards the clear separation of strategic and operational responsibilities embodied by the multi-divisional structure.

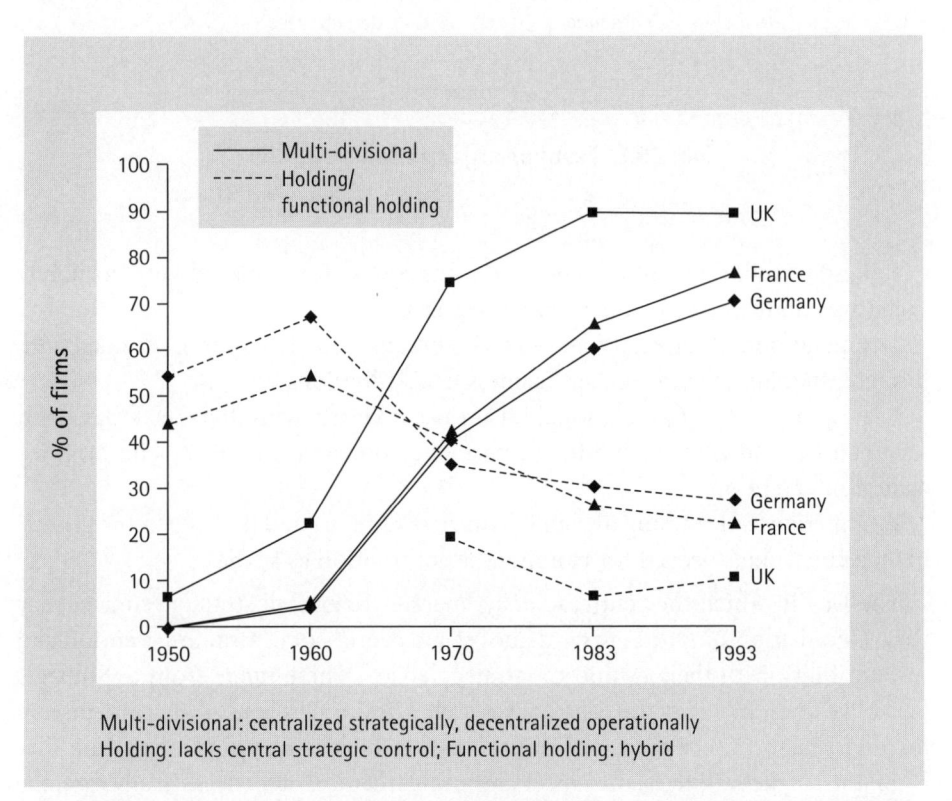

Multi-divisional: centralized strategically, decentralized operationally
Holding: lacks central strategic control; Functional holding: hybrid

Fig. 28.6 Organizational structures in large Western European industrial firms, 1950–1993

Source: Whittington and Mayer 2001.

28.6 Internationalization and Structure

Internationalization is another key strategy of growth and again a critical contingency for structure. International operations add a whole extra dimension to the complexity of running a large, diversified business. Thinking here has been moving fast in recent years, particularly in response to some critiques of the traditional multi-divisional structure.

The classic model is provided by Stopford and Wells (1972). Here the four main structural alternatives are as follows:

(1) simple international division, where all international activities are grouped together and operate alongside traditional product divisions (see Wal-Mart example above);

(2) area divisions, where different products are grouped within a particular area (see Unilever example above);

(3) worldwide product divisions, where divisions are based upon products with worldwide scope, regardless of particular areas (see Ove Arup example above, excepting its East Asia operational board); and

(4) a matrix ('grid') structure, in which area and product divisions are given equivalent status and managers on the ground report to both area and product divisional managers (see ABB example below).

In the Stopford and Wells model, the key contingencies for choosing between these structural alternatives are:

(1) foreign product diversity; and

(2) the percentage of foreign sales.

Thus, companies with high foreign sales but low diversity are best able to handle internationalization within area divisions. However, area divisions are unable to cope with high diversity: in this case, worldwide product divisions may be more appropriate. The matrix structure might be introduced to help where there is both high internationalization and high diversification (see Figure 28.7).

Ghoshal and Bartlett (1998b) add a further two key contingencies, more concerned with the sources of competitive advantage than the simple split of business by foreign sales or product diversity:

• *The need for global coordination and integration.* This is often important where there are major scale economies, so that the efforts of all countries need to be integrated, or where there is a need for coordinated responses to aggressive international competitors.

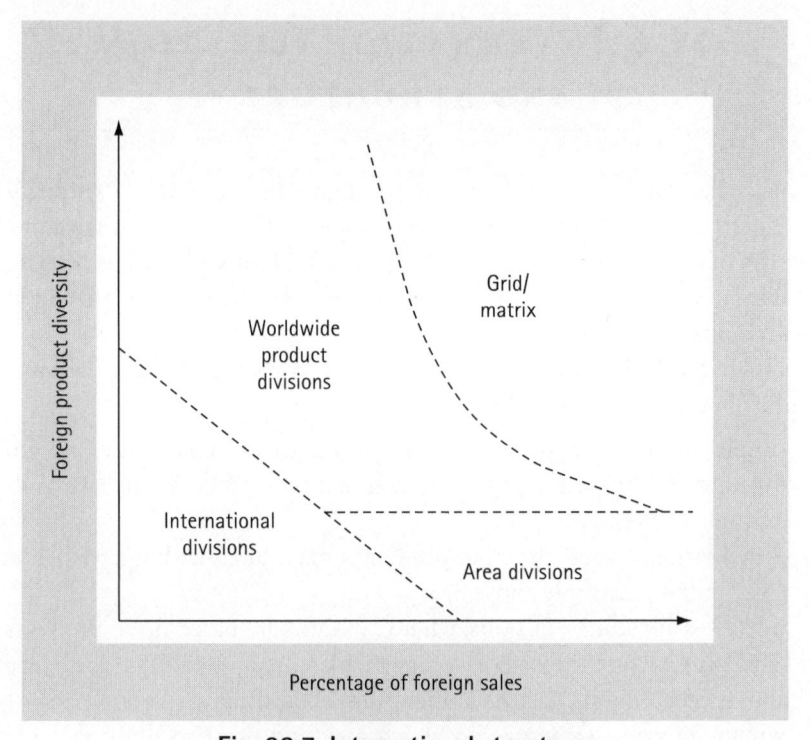

Fig. 28.7 International structures

Sources: Adapted from Stopford and Wells (1972) and Egelhoff (1988).

- *The need for national differentiation and responsiveness.* This is often important where competitive advantage is to be had from adapting to local tastes and needs or building local relationships.

More recently, Ghoshal and Bartlett (1998*b*) have offered an alternative to the traditional kinds of divisional structure, one that builds on the notion of the matrix. This 'transnational' form is proposed as an 'integrated network'. The transnational's aim is to transcend the stark dichotomy between worldwide product divisions pursuing scale economies and area divisions based on local responsiveness. Areas and products are linked together in networks of mutuality and interdependence, rather than simple hierarchies of control and reporting. Network relationships facilitate the flow of knowledge, a key resource in contemporary competition. Global best practice can be informed by experience from around the world and in turn adapted to the particular requirements of local operations (see unileves, Box 28.2).

Figures 28.8 and 28.9 compare the three basic international structures: the headquarters is at the centre, national subsidiaries on the periphery, with the shading indicating where leadership lies. In the traditional area divisional organization (termed 'multi-domestic' by Ghoshal and Bartlett 1998*b*), responsibility for product, marketing, and similar decisions rests with the geographical

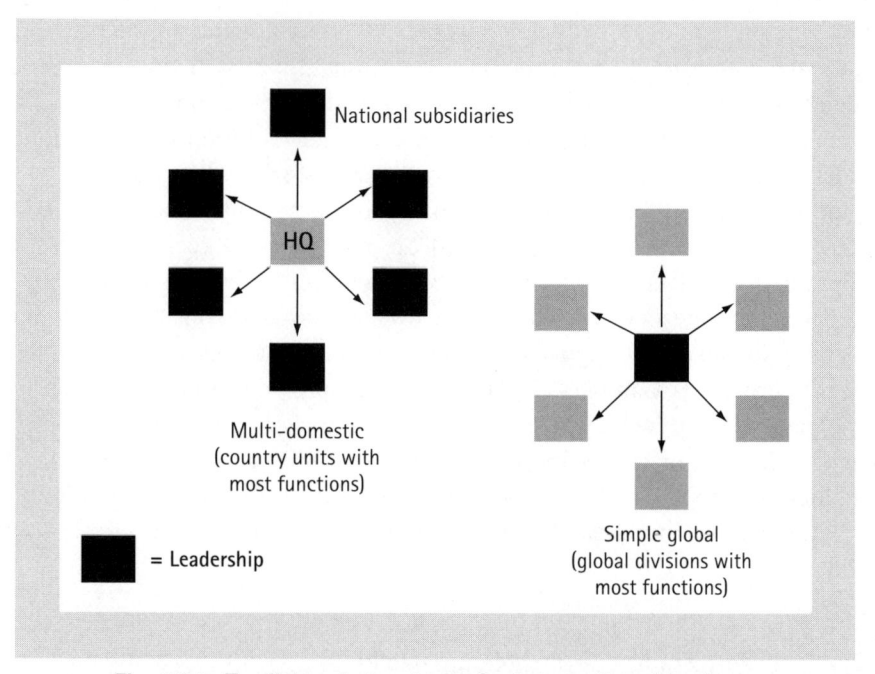

Fig. 28.8 Traditional structures for international business

Sources: Adapted from Ghoshal and Bartlett (1998*b*).

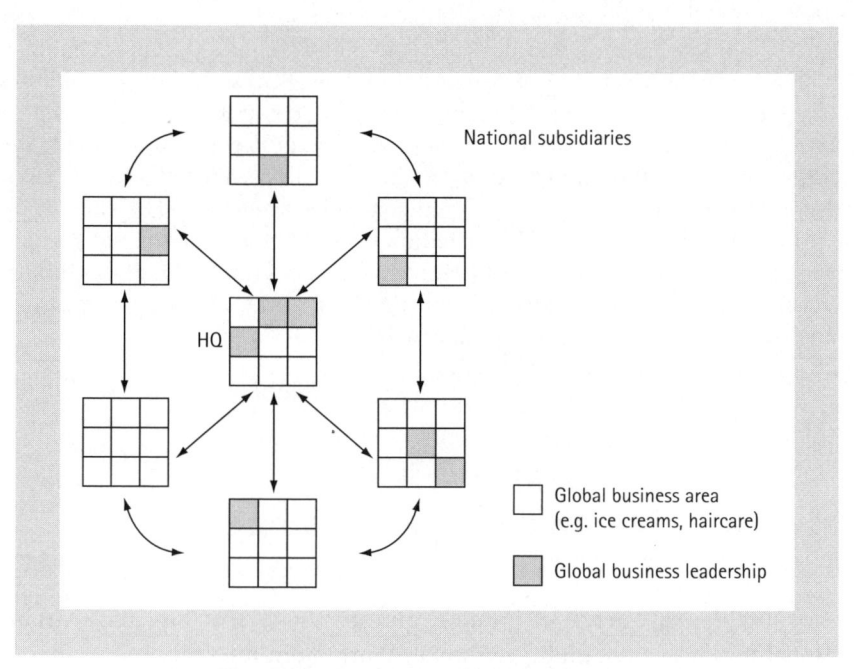

Fig. 28.9 The transnational structure

Sources: Adapted from Ghoshal and Bartlett (1998*b*).

areas, whether countries or regions. In the classic worldwide product divisional organization (simple global structure, in Ghoshal and Bartlett's terminology), leadership is at the central headquarters, with little discretion for geographical areas. As can be seen from Figure 28.9, however, leadership in the transnational is neither necessarily at headquarters (as in a classic worldwide product divisional organization) nor in the local areas (as in the classic area divisional organization). Instead, leadership is 'polycentric', based on many centres, typically determined according to the location of greatest expertise. Global business leadership for one particular category (e.g. ice cream) will be based in one territory; global leadership for another category (e.g. hair care) will be based in a quite different territory. Procter & Gamble's Organization 2005 provides a good illustration of such transnational 'polycentricity' (see Box 28.6 Polycentricity at Procter & Gamble). Instead of everything being either centralized to Procter & Gamble's headquarters in Cincinnati, or decentralized to countries, global responsibility for particular product areas has been delegated to different centres across the world.

Box 28.6 Polycentricity at Procter & Gamble

By 1998, Procter & Gamble was finding itself repeatedly outpaced by its competitors—most gallingly by Unilever, whose Persil products were taking share and innovating faster than P&G's Ariel and Daz. The company announced its major reorganization, 'Organization 2005', under the auspices of its old chief executive John Pepper but to be taken forward in 1999 by new chief executive Durk Jager. P&G shifted responsibility for its seven core product areas from four regional units into seven global business units (GBUs). Baby care, health care and new ventures, beauty care and tissues and towels were to be centred at P&G's headquarters in Cincinnati; leadership for fabric and home care would go to Brussels; feminine protection in Kobe; and food and beverage would be based in Caracas. GBUs would have full responsibility for profits, product design, brand equity, and product sourcing. Market development organizations (MDOs) were to collaborate with the GBUs to tailor products to local markets, but would typically be centralized on a regional rather than national basis.

Sources: Press, especially *Information Week*, 25 October 1999.

28.7 Networks and Structure

It is not just the experience of Western multinationals that has put a strain on traditional notions of the multi-divisional. Working in international markets and the success of Asian competitors in particular have exposed Western business thinking to alternative forms of organization—particularly the loose networks of

overseas Chinese business and the keiretsu of Japan (Hamilton and Biggart 1988; Li 1998).

Neither the Japanese keiretsu nor Chinese networks rely upon the same clear hierarchies and hard-and-fast distinctions of traditional Western divisional organizations. Keiretsu members are typically linked through webs of mutual minority shareholdings. Keiretsu vary, but typically these interlocking shareholdings are not large enough to give any company control but do provide a sufficient sense of interdependence and joint-destiny to ensure long-term cooperative relationships (Lai 1999). The Mitsubishi keiretsu, with roots back to the nineteenth century, does not integrate its various members into a coherent structure. Instead, it is organized as a web of cross-shareholdings uniting thirty main companies—including Mitsubishi Motors, Mitsubishi Electric, Kirin Breweries, and Tokio Marine & Fire Insurance—with no clear strategic apex. The traditional keiretsu are now under pressure to change, but new ones may be emerging. Since 1981, Masayoshi Son has constructed a new Japanese-based keiretsu in the form of the Softbank Corporation. With substantial stakes in 300 Internet companies such as Yahoo!, E*Trade, and Buy-com, Softbank has become a 'cyber keiretsu' worth $200 billion in February 2000 (see Figure 28.10).

Networks of various kinds are also important within the Chinese world. The particular modernization path of mainland China has produced what Boisot and Child (1996) describe as a form of 'network capitalism'. Both late imperial and Communist China were dominated by powerful states in which useful connections were essential to economic effectiveness. As China moved towards a more market-oriented economy during the 1990s, economic resources were decentralized but still heavily dependent on their linkages to state institutions. Although central direction

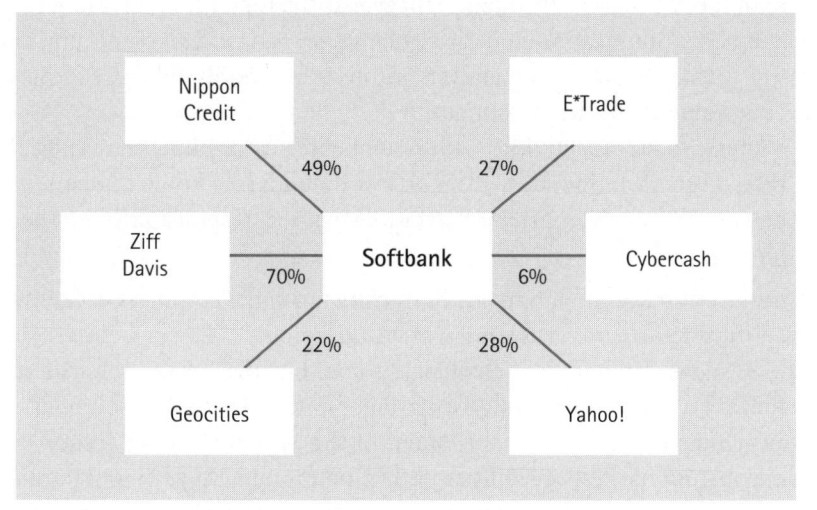

Fig. 28.10 Softbank: a cyber–keiretsu?

Source: www.softbank.com.

reduced, it was valuable still for managers to retain old relationships between enterprises in order to assure quality and reliability. The dependability of these old relationships enables Chinese managers to rely upon loose networks of independent but relationship-based contracting instead of formal ownership and control as under Western notions of appropriate organization. Something similar happens even amongst the overseas Chinese, where networks may be based upon family membership, shared origins in the same village, or old friendships (Whitley 1999). Again, there is no unambiguous control, nor even necessarily clear boundaries between different enterprises, but there is a sense of trust and mutuality that allows for highly flexible and dynamic subcontracting and partnership.

Many Western firms are increasingly adopting similar kinds of network models in preference to the rigid integration of all activities within the formal structures of the organization itself. Lorenzoni and Baden-Fuller (1995) cite the prominent examples of Benetton, Nike, and Sun, all working strategically with networks of partnerships and subcontractors. The apparent success of these alternative Asian models, and experiments with the integrated networks of the transnational, now move some influential theorists to argue that business must go 'beyond the M-form' (Bartlett and Ghoshal 1993).

Hedlund (1994) has proposed an N-form model for organizing activities retained within the boundaries of the large-scale corporation. The term 'N-form' implies a strong reliance on networks and networking. He identifies seven key characteristics of the N-form:

(1) putting things together, i.e. combining rather than dividing;
(2) temporary constellations of people, rather than permanent structures;
(3) the importance of direct interaction between people at the middle rather than indirect liaison through managers at the top;
(4) lateral communication and dialogue rather than vertical communications;
(5) top managers acting as catalysts, protectors, and architects of knowledge communication and investment;
(6) strategic focus on activities with potential for combining knowledge, rather than diversification into fields with low potential for knowledge integration;
(7) heterarchy (many centres of decision-making responsibility) rather than hierarchy.

A consistent feature of these N-form characteristics is the emphasis on knowledge, both as critical resource and as source of authority.

Hedlund's (1994) model is a challenging one, but may exaggerate the scale of contemporary organizational transformation. None of Hedlund's seven characteristics undermine the fundamental element of the M-form, the separation of strategic and operational responsibilities. Whittington and Mayer (2001) argue that N-form does not so much go 'beyond' the multi-divisional as develop its essential properties still further. As in Table 28.1, 'the network multi-divisional' is simply

Table 28.2 Evolving types of multi-divisional

	Investor	Managerial	Network
Origins	1920s	1960s	1980s
Key resource	Capital	Scale and Scope	Knowledge
Key technique	Accounting Ratios	Planning	Exchange
Key function	Finance and Accounting	Corporate Planning	Human Resources
Structure shape	Pyramid	Pear	Pancake
Examples	DuPont	General Electric	ABB

Source: Adapted from Whittington and Mayer (1997).

another step in the evolution of the basic multi-divisional form. Whereas once financial capital and the physical resources of scale and scope were critical to the corporation, now it is the successful management of knowledge. In the 'network multi-divisional', exchange of knowledge is the key technique, rather than accounting ratios or traditional top-down planning. Human resource management is critical, for it is within people that knowledge lies, through people that it is created, and between people that it is exchanged. While the traditional 'investor-multi-divisional' took on the hierarchical shape of the pyramid, and the 'managerial multi-divisional' grew pear-shaped as new layers of middle managers proliferated for planning and coordination, the shape of the new 'network multi-divisional' is more like that of a pancake: flat, flexible, and with the emphasis on the horizontal and the circular rather than the vertical and the hierarchical.

The Swiss-Swedish engineering company ABB under the leadership of charismatic Percy Barnevik has often been advanced as an example of new forms of organization, beyond the M-form (Handy 1992; Ghoshal and Bartlett 1998a). In fact, its recent history appears to reaffirm the enduring merits of the traditional divisional organization (see Box 28.7 ABB—Beyond the M-form?). After a few years of experimentation with radical decentralization within a matrix or transnational framework, in 1998 ABB moved very much closer to a traditional product divisional structure, in which product divisions such as power generation or power transmission dominate over the traditional national holding companies.

Whether beyond the M-form or not, an emphasis on flexibility rather than rigidity is a common theme throughout all these accounts of contemporary organizations (Volberda 1998). Barnevik's successor at ABB, Goran Lindahl, has declared that the company's new divisional structure is not likely to stay in place for more than five years (Whittington, Pettigrew, and Ruigrok 2000). Contingency theory's static language of fit needs to be extended to a more dynamic language of 'co-evolution',

Box 28.7 ABB—Beyond the M-form?

During the 1990s, European engineering group ABB was frequently cited as a new model of organization, an exemplar of Bartlett and Ghoshal's (1993) slogan 'beyond the M-form'. In August 1998, however, ABB announced a major reorganization, apparently taking the company back to a product divisional structure.

ABB was formed in 1988 from the merger of the Swedish ASEA group and the Brown Boveri company of Switzerland. At the time, this was the largest cross-border merger the world had ever seen, bringing together companies operating around the world and with combined employment of 170,000 people. Chief executive Percy Barnevik quickly imposed a matrix structure on the company. The two key dimensions were business segments (such as Power Generation, Power Transmission, and so on) and geography—initially based on countries, but rationalized over the 1990s into three main regions. A simplified version of ABB's matrix structure as it stood in 1997 is provided in the Figure 28.11(a).

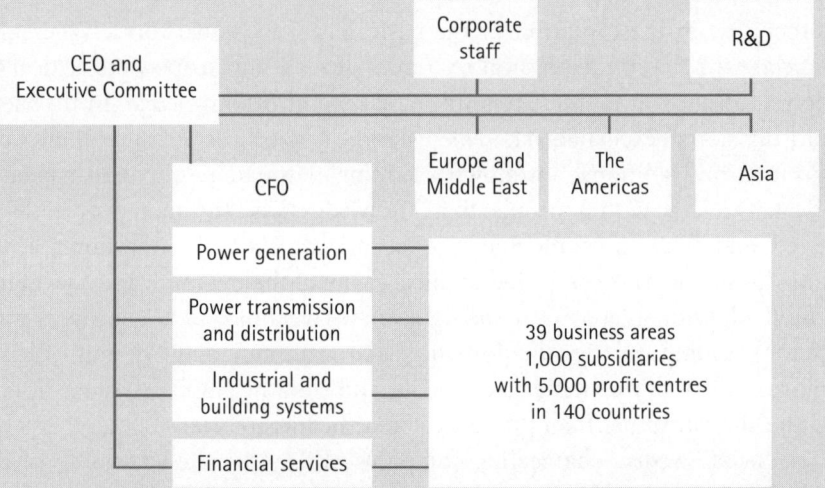

Fig. 28.11(a) ABB group organizational chart, 1997

Source: Adpated from Ruigrok et al (2000).

However, this matrix was just the framework for Barnevik's structural innovation. He imposed a radical decentralization, so that the company was divided into 1,100 separate companies with an average employment of 200 people. These companies were in turn split into 3,500 profit centres, with about 50 people each. The small size of these companies and profit centres was designed to improve responsiveness and make everyone aware of financial performance. These small units were also necessarily interdependent, typically forced to share resources and knowledge in order to operate effectively. There would be little help from above. The new head office, in Zurich, had only 100 people. Corporate functions, such as Research & Development, were decentralized to the major companies and obliged to sell their services on an internal market. Essential roles

for top management in this decentralized matrix were to foster an understanding of common purpose, to provide the infrastructure for cooperation and to facilitate cross-unit knowledge-sharing and learning. Cross-Company Teams and multi-level, multi-business Open Spaces meetings were two of the mechanisms designed to ensure networking across structural boundaries.

While lauded as a model in the business schools, ABB was experiencing considerable frustration with its structure by the late 1990s. Ruigrok et al. (2000) identify three principal problems. It was hard to push coherent segment growth strategies on a global basis; the internal market was creating transfer pricing disputes and delays; the regions were growing too powerful, creating 'regional principalities'. When a new chief executive took over from Barnevik, one of his first actions was to abolish the regions and restructure the business segments into seven, more focused product divisions. The ethos of cross-business cooperation was to continue, but, according to Ruigrok et al. (2000), within the structural framework of a 'network multi-divisional'.

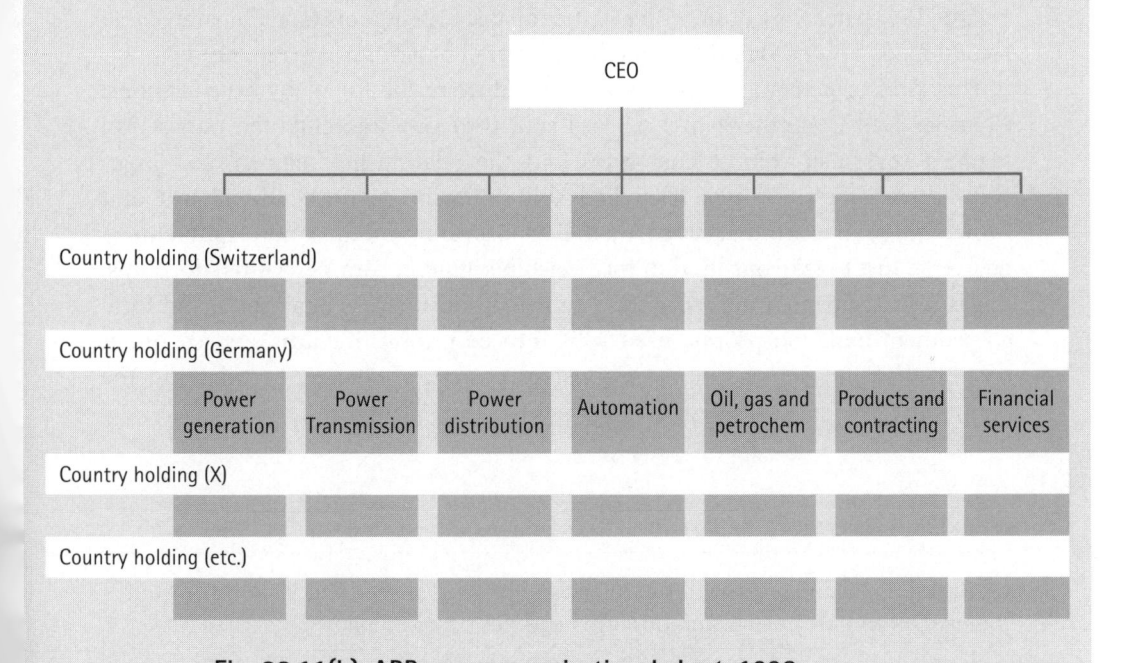

Fig. 28.11(b) ABB group organizational chart, 1998

Source: Adapted from Ruigrok et al. (2000).

Principal sources: Bartlett and Ghoshal 1993; Barham and Heimer 1998; Ruigrok et al. 2000.

representing organizations as continuously responding to shifting demands put upon it by complex environments (Lewin, Long, and Carroll 1999). Co-evolution-ary structural change and its implications are themes developed further in Eisen-hardt and Brown's (1999) notion of organizational 'patching'.

28.8 DYNAMIC STRUCTURES

Markets, technologies, and competition now are moving faster than ever before. As Galunic and Rodan (1998) note, for Joseph Schumpeter the production of new things depended essentially on the capability to combine and recombine existing materials in novel ways. At the heart of business innovation, therefore, lies the ability to reconfigure the existing organization to bring different parts together in new combinations.

According to Eisenhardt and Brown (1999), the importance of innovation and the contemporary pace of change requires a different view of organizational structure—not one of static solutions, but of constantly revised structural combinations. They call the process of continuous structural change 'patching'. Here the organization is regarded as a patchwork quilt, with patches capable of being constantly separated and recombined in order to find new and better overall patterns of organizing.

This kind of patching is an inescapable feature of life for many organizations. Consider Dell Computers. In 1994 Dell split into two segments: the transaction segment for small volume customers and the relationship segment for larger volume customers. By 1996 Dell had split into six segments. Eisenhardt and Brown (1999) report that since then Dell has announced a new split almost quarterly. Just to take one kind of relationship segment, commercial relationships, this is now segmented into corporate and small business, federal, state, and local government and non-profits, itself split into education, medical, and so on. A possibly less innocent account of constant structural change, highlighting the politics involved, is illustrated in Box 28.8 Microsoft 'Reorgs'.

Box 28.8 Microsoft 'Reorgs'

Michael Drummond (1999: 95–6), a close observer of software giant Microsoft, remarked on the company's notoriously frequent 'reorgs' as follows:

Microsoft constantly boils with internal reorganisations, often causing monumental disruptions and sweeping realignment of duties. [Bill] Gates is said to tolerate reorgs because they allow burned-out employees a chance to get recharged in new areas, which stokes competitive fires and keeps the giant company nimble.

Some joke that reorgs are used to force programmers to clear off their desks periodically.

The official reason for reorgs, however, is that by reallocating company resources, Microsoft can make better products. 'They're in response to market conditions and how we can best meet needs of customers', says Microsoft spokesman Tom Pilla. 'This is a very fast-paced industry. Any company that isn't constantly re-evaluating itself isn't going to be around very long.'

A reasonable explanation, but one that might not penetrate far enough. Others inside the company say many Microsoft reorgs were the result of massive political tectonics and power grabbing between Brad Silverberg's Windows group and Jim Allchin's Windows NT army.

There is a crucial shift in thinking involved in 'patching': structural change is normal. The mentality should shift from striving for once-and-for-all structural design solution towards building the internal skills and capabilities required for coping with continuous structural change. Eisenhardt and Brown (1999) suggest several key characteristics required by organizations likely to be involved in constant processes of 'patching':

- Organizational modularity. It is easier to combine and recombine businesses that are discrete and stand-alone, rather than enmeshed in many relationships across the corporate portfolio or with the centre.
- Detailed and standardized metrics. It is easier to grasp opportunities for patching and to implement them if all businesses across the portfolio use standardized metrics that give real insight into the business and which facilitate quick integration.
- Compensation parity. Parity in compensation packages across the portfolio will ease the process of reassigning managers to new patching solutions and make them less insecure at the prospect of further changes in the future.

These are the more formal conditions for successful patching, but there are human ones as well. Schoonhoven and Jelinek's (1990) study of how managers cope with the constant changes of high-tech organizations like Hewlett-Packard, Intel, and Motorola provides pointers towards the kind of human capacities required of managers working with patching and repatching. Constant structural change requires:

- an attitude that change is normal, stability dangerous
- an embedded readiness to be self-critical and to search for improvement
- a culture of trust and cooperation, so that structural change is not reduced to turf protection and aggrandizement
- an ability to work with transitional and quasi-formal structures, such as teams, task forces, and dotted-line relationships.

We are reminded here that structures are about people, and work only so well as their constituents are capable.

28.9 THE FUTURE FOR ORGANIZATION STRUCTURES

The need for organization structures does not look like going away in the coming years. So long as there remain large and complex organizations like

Daimler-Chrysler or General Electric, good structures will be essential to competitive success.

However, if present trends provide at least a hint about the future, we can suggest some features of structure that will become more important. Structure will increasingly be designed around the creation and communication of knowledge within the corporation, rather than simple control. Inasmuch as they impede these critical knowledge processes, traditional structures based on control are likely to be self-defeating. Accordingly, structures will become flatter, more horizontal, and polycentric rather than rigid and hierarchical. The tension between segmentation into discrete units for purposes of accountability and interdependence for the sake of knowledge combination will be resolved more often in favour of the latter than the former. Networks of all kinds—internal and external, formal and not-so-formal—will become an endemic feature of organizational life. Centrality in networks rather than formal hierarchical position will become crucial to personal power and the capacity to get things done. Formal structures anyway will be constantly changing, as organizations go through continuous processes of 'patching' and 'repatching'.

In these conditions, what will make the difference between a structure working well and a structure working badly will be not so much the structure itself as the skills and attitudes of the managers working within them (Whittington 2001). Structures will rarely have the time to bed-down, so that key relationships become clear and start to operate smoothly as experience grows. Managers will have to learn to manage plural and ambiguous relationships; they will have to cope with the uncertainties and disruptions of continuous structural change. Managers striving constantly to impose permanence, clarity, and order will make the new kinds of organizations fail. Managerial capacity to cope with structural change and ambiguity becomes a critical contingency in the design of organization structures.

This implies a different focus for both practice and research. Academics and consultants have searched before to define the most appropriate structures. But if structural solutions are temporary responses to shifting challenges, so they must constantly be moving towards imperfection. The future for thinking about organization structure is to worry less about the structures themselves, more about the people who must manage them. Structures will work better as we improve managers' capacities to cope with chronic structural inadequacies and repeated structural change. Managers need to become skilled performers of structure and structural change. Understanding and developing effective structural design *processes* (Goold and Campbell 2002) will be at least as important as advocating and formalizing particular design *solutions*.

The overall message is that structure will continue to be a central feature of organizational life. So long as that remains the case, the point is not to attack structure as 'bureaucracy', but to make structures work better (Adler 1999).

28.10 SUMMARY

Organization structure is a key element in the strategists' tool-kit. Without the right structure, strategies will fail. Contingency theory provides some initial guidelines for how structures should be designed. According to contingency theory, strategy, size, technology, and geographical scope are all likely to be critical in the design of appropriate structures. But contingency theory does not provide categorical or final answers. It will always take managerial judgement, both to assess the relative importance of one contingency over another where they conflict, and to appreciate changing contingencies over time.

Some contingencies seem to be becoming more important, for example knowledge-intensity. New ways are emerging to manage sometimes conflicting contingencies, for example the transnational in managing the tension between the global and the local. Contingencies are seen now to be embedded by much more complex and multilateral organizational relationships than before, as illuminated by new theories of configurations or complementarities. National cultures and institutions may modify contingent arrangements, and ideas such as the network may be extended from one regional context to international business more widely. Finally, the somewhat static designs of traditional contingency theory have to give way to the more dynamic processes of patching required by the fast-changing business world of today. Managerial capabilities in managing continuous structural change become increasingly important.

Nevertheless, the central message of contingency theory provides a fundamentally useful reminder. There is no ultimate, universal and ideal structural model—M-form, N-form, or whatever. Structures need to be tailored to the specific demands of an organization's situation. In a fast-paced world, enduring success will rely upon continuous co-evolution between structure and situation. Addressing the dynamics of structure should be high on the agenda of managers and academics alike.

REFERENCES

ADLER, P. S. (1999). 'Building Better Bureaucracies'. *Academy of Management Executive*, 13/4: 36–50.

BARHAM, K., and HEIMER, C. (1998). *ABB: The Dancing Giant*. London: Pitman.

BARRETT, F. J. (1998). 'Creativity and Improvisation in Jazz and Organizations: Implications for Organizational Learning'. *Organization Science*, 9/5: 605–22.

BARTLETT, C., and GHOSHAL, S. (1993). 'Beyond the M-Form: Toward a Managerial Theory of the Firm'. *Strategic Management Journal*, 14/Winter Special Issue: 23–46.

BLAU, P. (1972). 'Interdependence and Hierarchy in Organizations'. *Social Science Research*, 1: 1–24.

BOISOT, M., and CHILD, J. (1996). 'From Fiefs to Clans and Network Capitalism: Explaining China's Emerging Economic Order'. *Administrative Science Quarterly*, 41/4: 600–29.

BURNS, T., and STALKER, G. M. (1961). *The Management of Innovation*. London: Tavistock.

CASTELLS, M. (1996). *The Rise of the Network Society*. Oxford: Blackwell.

CHANDLER, A. D. (1962). *Strategy and Structure: Chapters in the History of American Industrial Enterprise*. Cambridge, Mass.: MIT Press.

CUSUMANO, M. A., and YOFFIE D. (1998). *Competing on Internet Time: Lessons from Netscape and its Battle with Microsoft*. New York: Free Press.

DERDACK, T. (1988). *International Directory of Company Histories*. Chicago: St James Press.

DONALDSON, L. (1996). 'The Normal Science of Structural Contingency Theory', in S. Clegg, C. Hardy, and W. Nord (eds.), *The Handbook of Organizational Studies*. London: Sage.

——(2000). *The Contingency Theory of Organizations*. Thousand Oaks, Calif.: Sage.

DRUMMOND, M. (1999). *Renegades of the Empire: How Three Software Warriors Started a Revolution behind the Walls of Microsoft*. London: Vision.

EGELHOFF, W. G. (1988). 'Strategy and Structure in Multinational Corporations: A Revision of the Stopford and Wells Model'. *Strategic Management Journal*, 9: 1–14.

EISENHARDT, K., and BROWN, S. (1999). 'Patching: Restitching Business Portfolios in Dynamic Markets'. *Harvard Business Review*, May–June: 72–81.

FENTON, E., and PETTIGREW, A. (2000). 'Integrating a Global Professional Services Organization: The Case of the Ove Arup Partnership', in A. Pettigrew and E. Fenton (eds.), *The Innovating Organization*. London: Sage.

GALUNIC, D. C., and RODAN, S. (1998). 'Resource Recombinations in the Firm: Knowledge Structures and the Potential for Schumpeterian Innovation'. *Strategic Management Journal*, 19: 1193–1201.

GHOSHAL, S., and BARTLETT, C. (1998a). *The Individualised Corporation*. London: Heinemann.

————(1998b). *Managing Across Borders: The Transnational Solution*. (2nd edn) New York: Random House.

GOOLD, M., and CAMPBELL, A. (1987). *Strategies and Styles*. Oxford: Blackwell.

————(2002). *Designing Effective Organizations: How to Create Structured Networks*. London: Wiley.

GORDON, J. E. (1978). *Structures, or Why Things don't Fall Down*. London: Penguin.

GREINER, L. (1998). 'Evolution and Revolution as Organizations Grow'. *Harvard Business Review*, 76/3: 55–68.

HAMILTON, G., and BIGGART, N. (1988). 'Market, Culture and Authority: A Configurative Analysis of Management and Organization in the Far East'. *American Journal of Sociology*, 94/Suppl.: 52–94.

HANDY, C. (1992). 'Balancing Corporate Power: A New Federalist Organization'. *Harvard Business Review*, Nov.–Dec.: 59–72.

HATCH, M. J. (1999). 'Exploring the Empty Spaces of Organizing: How Improvisational Jazz Helps Redescribe Organizational Structure'. *Organization Studies*, 20/1: 75–100.

HEDLUND, G. (1994). 'A Model of Knowledge Management and the N-form Corporation'. *Strategic Management Journal*, 15/Summer Special Issue: 73–90.

HININGS, C. R., GREENWOOD, R., and COOPER, D. (1999). 'The Dynamics of Change in Large Accounting Firms', in D. Brock, M. Powell, and C. R. Hinings (eds.), *Restructuring the Professional Organization*. London: Routledge.

LAI, G. M.-H. (1999). 'Knowing Who You are doing Business with in Japan: A Managerial View of Keiretsu and Keiretsu Business Groups'. *Journal of World Business*, 34/4: 423–48.

LEWIN, A., LONG, C., and CARROLL, T. (1999). 'The Coevolution of Organizational Forms'. *Organization Science*, 10/5: 335–550.

LI, P. P. (1998). 'Towards a Geocentric Framework of Organizational Form: A Holistic, Dynamic and Paradoxical Approach'. *Organization Studies*, 19/5: 829–62.

LORENZONI, G., and BADEN-FULLER, C. (1995). 'Creating a Strategic Center to Manage a Web of Partners'. *California Management Review*, 37/3: 146–64.

MARKIDES, C. C. (1995). *Diversification, Refocusing and Economic Performance*. Cambridge, Mass.: MIT Press.

MILGROM, P., and ROBERTS, J. (1995). 'Complementarities and Fit: Strategy, Structure and Organizational Change in Manufacturing'. *Journal of Accounting and Economics*, 19: 179–208.

MILLER, D. (1986). 'Configurations of Strategy and Structure: Towards a Synthesis'. *Strategic Management Journal*, 7: 233–49.

PASCALE, R. (1984). 'Perspectives on Strategy: The Real Story Behind Honda's Success'. *California Management Review*, 24: 47–72.

PETERS, T. (1992). *Liberation Management: Necessary Disorganization for the Nanosecond Nineties*. London: Macmillan.

PETTIGREW, A., WHITTINGTON, R., VAN DEN BOSCH, F., MELIN, L., RUIGROK, W., SANCHEZ-RUNDES, C. (2002). *Innovative Forms of Organizing: Complementarities and Dualities*. London: Sage.

PUGH, D., and HICKSON, D. J. (1976). *Organization Structure in its Context: The Aston Programme 1*. Farnborough, Hants: Saxon House.

RUIGROK, W., ACHETENHAGEN, L., WAGNER, M., and RÜEGG-STÜRM, J. (2000). 'ABB: Beyond the Global Matrix towards the Network Multi-divisional Organization', in A. Pettigrew and E. Fenton (eds.), *The Innovating Organization*. London: Sage.

SCHOONHOVEN, C. B., and JELINEK, M. (1990). 'Dynamic Tension in Innovative High Technology Firms: Managing Rapid Technological Change through Organizational Structure', in M. von Glinow and S. Mohrman (eds.), *Managing Complexity in High Technology Firms*. Oxford: Oxford University Press, 90–115.

STOPFORD, J. M., and WELLS, L. T. (1972). *Managing the Multinational Enterprise: Organization of the Firm and Ownership of Subsidiaries*. London: Longman.

VOLBERDA, H. W. (1998). *Building the Flexible Firm: How to Remain Competitive*. Oxford: Oxford University Press.

WATERMAN, R. H., PETERS, T. J., and PHILLIPS, J. R. (1980). 'Structure is not Organization'. *Business Horizons*, 23/3: 14–26.

WHITLEY, R. (1999). *Divergent Capitalisms*. Oxford: Oxford University Press.

WHITTINGTON, R. (2001). 'Corporate Structure: From Policy to Practice', in A. Pettigrew, H. Thomas, and R. Whittington (eds.), *The Handbook of Strategy and Management*. London: Sage.

——and MAYER, M. (1997). 'Beyond or Behind the M-Form? The Structures of European Business', in D. O'Neal, H. Thomas, and M. Ghertman (eds.), *Strategy, Structure and Style*. Chichester: Wiley.

————(2001). *The European Corporation: Strategy, Structure and Social Science*. London: Oxford University Press.

WHITTINGTON, R., PETTIGREW, A., and RUIGROK, W. (2000). 'New Notions of Organizational "Fit" ', T. Dickson (ed.), *Mastering Strategy*. London: Financial Times/Prentice Hall.

—— —— PECK, S., FENTON, E., and CONYON, M. (1999). 'Change and Complementarities in the New Competitive Landscape'. *Organization Science*, 10/5: 583–600.

WILLIAMSON, O. E. (1975). *Markets and Hierarchies: Analysis and Antitrust Implications*. New York: Free Press.

WOODWARD, J. (1965). *Industrial Organization, Theory and Practice*. London: Oxford University Press.

ZENGER, T., and HESTERLY, W. (1997). 'The Disaggregation of Corporations: Selective Intervention, High-Powered Incentives and Molecular Units'. *Organization Science*, 8/3: 209–22.

CHAPTER 29

STRATEGY INNOVATION

PETER J. WILLIAMSON

29.1 WHY STRATEGY INNOVATION?

ASK yourself the question how many corporations have been able to maintain shareholder returns in the top quartile of the peers in America's S&P 500 or Britain's FT 100 each year for an unbroken run of five years or more? Since the early 1990s, the answer is less than 5 per cent of the corporations in each index. Over the past few decades the number of firms able to sustain consistently above-average shareholder returns over an extended period has been declining.

These are humbling statistics. They suggest that there are powerful processes at work that undermine the capacity of almost any single business model (a systemic combination of value and cost drivers) to go on creating value indefinitely. We call this process 'strategy decay'. As we will see below, strategy decay may occur because competitors undermine the early differentiation in a business model by imitating it. It may occur because changes in technology or customer taste or behaviour render an existing business model obsolete as a way of making money. Competitors emerge with the proverbial 'better mouse trap'. Changes in customers' lifestyles eliminate demand for the product or service. Innovative competitors completely transform the economics of the business, as we have seen in the case of Direct Line insurance, dealing a body blow to transitional higher cost and/or less convenient ways of providing the product or service.

In the face of strategy decay, a corporation can only go on generating new wealth for its shareholders (or ultimately survive) if it can go on renewing its business models in such a way as to create new and distinctive sources of competitive advantage.

The process of business model renewal is what we term 'strategy innovation'. It is not simply about improvements to a product line or service offering or incremental reductions in costs. Strategy innovation constitutes a fundamental innovation in the company's business model; a significant change in the way it makes money that opens up new sources of competitive advantage.

In practice it is sometimes difficult to draw a precise line between product, service, or technological innovation, on one hand, and strategy innovation, on the other. However, a useful rule of thumb in identifying whether something is a strategy innovation is to ask whether or not it constitutes a change to some combination of three dimensions of a business model:

- who the company serves (a change to its customer base)
- what the company offers to its customers (a change to the offering)
- how the company provides value to its customer (a change to the activity chain and the value and/or costs associated with each activity).[1]

Examples of strategy innovation would include Dell Computer's strategy of combining on-line ordering and specification with the capability to offer the buyer a computer customized to their particular needs; Monsanto's introduction of genetically modified seeds that were selectively resistant to its proprietary herbicide (which allowed a change in the proposition to farmers as well as requiring a fundamental shift in the activity chain that necessitated the integration of the seed supply chain with that for herbicides); and Enron's morphing of its gas pipeline business into an integrated energy trading operation that replaced a simple supply chain with a sophisticated market for energy that flexibly matched customers and suppliers (but also led to an increase in risk that was ultimately fatal).

This kind of strategy innovation is the antidote to the decay of existing business models. It provides new sources of competitive advantage. But just because a strategy is innovative, does it mean that it will create value and wealth? Success comes only from matching the right strategy innovation to a particular set of market conditions at the right time. So even if a corporation becomes successful at churning out a series of strategy innovations before its existing business model reaches the point of deep decay, it may not generate shareholder value. To beat the curse of strategy decay, it needs to launch a strategy innovation that catches the wave of a dynamic market at the right time. Since market evolution, and the changing technological, consumer behaviour, and competitive forces that drive that evolution are often highly uncertain, launching the right strategy innovation at the right time is obviously a challenging task.

---

[1] This definition was proposed by Markides 2000.

In this chapter we explore how a company can go about improving its chances of successfully meeting this challenge of continually renewing its business model by creating a flow of profitable strategy innovations launched into the market at opportune times. The first step towards meeting this challenge is to understand how far and how fast a company's established strategy is decaying and therefore how urgently the launch of a strategy innovation is required.

29.2 MEASURING STRATEGY DECAY

Most of us put off going to the dentist as long as possible: it is one of those things we never quite get around to. Those well-polished pearls look fine from the outside because the decay is within. When the pain comes, it comes with a 'bang' because that unseen decay is already so well advanced it has hit a sensitive nerve. Strategy decay works much the same way because traditional measures of performance frequently tell us everything is fine, until we hit the nerve and our world starts falling apart. Worse still, even when the decay is already severe, workhorse metrics like ROCE and ROI may be signalling that our strategy is working better than ever!

An important reason why traditional metrics are not good at warning of strategy decay is that when we measure profitability we do not ask whether the profit is the result of creating new value or whether we are just milking out the positions we, or our management forebears, have previously put in place. In other words, how much of today's profits are coming from creating new value and how much of our reported profits are really the rents we are collecting on the assets we inherited?

Remember all those companies who were riding on a profit wave of pagers in the early 1990s? As new customers signed up, sales soared while the high fixed costs of building the pager network were spread ever more thinly. Profits leapt. Once the sign-on discounts started to expire and customers paid full price, profits continued to a steady upward trend. Having established their customer base, some operators decided to raise the tariffs. Both absolute earnings and profitability rose still further. Management was congratulating itself on the performance of their brilliant strategy.

But underneath, the danger signs were already plainly evident for those who knew where to look. Profits were rising fastest at the very time that the rate of new subscriptions had begun to go slow. A slowdown in new subscriptions was great for profitability because there were fewer people on introductory discounts, so total

profits rose rapidly. Then the installed base started to erode as the number of defectors to the new, mobile telephone technology exceeded the rate at which new customers signed up. Yet profits continued their upward trend as the price increases to 'leverage our installed base' kicked in. Management and shareholders were sanguine, drawing confidence from traditional profit metrics like ROS and ROCE that said everything was going swimmingly.

In fact, as the champagne corks popped, strategy decay was already well advanced. Without realizing it, those pager companies had moved from creating new wealth to milking out their existing base. As subscriber defections began, the same fixed costs had to be spread over fewer users. But the resulting rise in unit costs had been masked by the expiry of sign-on discounts and tariff hikes—sources of the milk they were siphoning off. Profits steadily grew even though the underlying economic engine had already gone quietly into reverse; a negative spiral of rising unit costs had taken root.

One fateful day management woke up and found that the reliable growth in profits as sign-up discounts lapsed was no longer there. With a falling subscriber base, price increases were out of the question. With no way of increasing revenues and a heavy base of fixed costs, profit growth stalled. The milk had run out. As the impact of defections accumulated, profits then went into reverse. The unseen strategy decay had eventually reached the nerve.

Now you may believe that strategies in many industries do not decay; one basic strategy has served the same company for many years or even decades. But, consider the following simple statistic: how many of the companies in the S&P 500 managed to consistently deliver total shareholder returns (TSR) in the top quartile for more than five years to 1999? The answer is 9 out of 500.

Clearly, strategies do decay. If we cannot rely on traditional profit measures to tell us when a strategy is decaying how do we know? What are the early warning signs of strategy decay?

29.2.1 Four Measures of Strategy Decay

Four basic measures can be used to help diagnose strategy decay:

(1) divergence between revenue growth and earnings growth;
(2) rising ROCE but falling P/E multiple;
(3) a high ratio of rents to new value creation; and
(4) convergence of strategies in the industry.

If a company scores in the danger zone on these measures, especially where several point in the same direction, it should be concerned that its strategy is showing signs of decay.

29.2.1.1 *Divergence between Revenue Growth and Earnings Growth*

For a year or two, maybe even a few more, profits can grow very much faster than revenues. We often see this phenomenon in the turnaround of companies in trouble. The same thing happens when margins rise either through higher prices or squeezing costs. But few companies are in the enviable position that they can go on getting price increases over and above the rate of inflation in their costs year after year for decades.

The plain fact is that there is a limit to how much profit even the best managed, most efficient company can squeeze out of any fixed amount of revenue. (A fact economists call the law of diminishing returns.) As a member of the US Federal Reserve once put it so beautifully: 'things that cannot go on forever do eventually stop.'

Therefore if a company's revenue growth has been consistently falling behind its profit growth year after year, it needs to worry that it will soon hit the limit. The capacity of its strategy to generate future profit growth will be in deep decay.

The same holds true if revenue is growing faster than profits year after year. That means the company is working a bigger and bigger operation successively harder for a smaller and smaller increment to the bottom line. Its wheels are spinning. Again the capacity of its strategy to generate future profit is in decay.

Put the things together and it becomes clear that if the *ratio* of a company's earnings growth to revenue growth diverges a long way from '1' for an extended period (say five or ten years), then its strategy is probably decaying. Profits growing at a slightly faster clip than revenue is good, but when you see earnings growth or revenue growth outstripping the other year after year that should be a warning sign.

Now, of course, the test 'a long way from 1' is inherently subjective. So to understand how to use the measure in practice, we need to look at some data.

Consider these data on the ratio of profit growth to revenue growth over the five years to 1998. For companies like Danone (1.08), Glaxo Wellcome (1.00), Loreal (0.94) or Nokia (1.14), and Tesco (0.89), earnings and revenue were pretty much in balance over the medium term (the ratio was close to 1).

But over the same five-year period some companies saw earnings growing at tens or even hundreds of times faster than revenues: like Bass (25 ×), Cadbury Schweppes (17 ×), GKN (25 ×), or KLM (38 ×). Ask yourself how long that can go on? Squeezing dramatically more out of the same revenue base. It looks as if they are milking out the businesses with a fire hose. This is a warning sign for strategy decay. The capacity of the strategy to generate earnings growth in the future looks extremely doubtful.

On the other end of the spectrum, we have companies seeing rapid growth in revenues, while profit growth has stalled so that their ratio of earnings growth to revenue growth in the five years to 1998 is well below 1. Examples include British Telecommunications (0.26), Fiat (0.53), and Lafarge (0.39). Just as for those

companies for which the ratio was very high, these low statistics are also a sign of strategy decay. The value creation potential of these companies' strategies is just about spent; they can grow revenue, but only by practically 'giving incremental products and services away' at close to zero profit.

The bottom line: if a company's ratio of earnings growth to revenue growth consistently diverges from '1' by a large margin, either way above or way below (say, over 2 or less than 0.5), then there are probably problems round the corner because its strategy is decaying from within.

29.2.1.2 Rising ROCE but Falling P/E Multiple

When a company breaks yet another record in the return it delivers on its capital employed (ROCE reaches new heights), the managers may be congratulating themselves. But if, at the same time, its price/earnings ratio (P/E) is falling, the market is telling them something: 'You may be earning record profits now, but we are going to mark down your share price because we don't think you can continue to deliver this rate of return long term.' That is another way of saying, 'We believe your strategy is in decay.'

The reason is simple: if a company is delivering strong earnings on its assets today, but the multiple of those earnings investors are willing to pay for its shares (which are a claim on your future earnings) is going down (a falling P/E), it can only be for one of two reasons. Either investors think the risk associated with those future earnings has increased; or they are expecting your future earnings to tail off. In either case, their assessment is that your strategy is in a process of decay.

Again, consider the data depicted in Figure 29.1. Cadbury Schweppes, Cable and Wireless, and Pirelli increased their ROCE consistently between 1993 and 1998, but their P/E ratio fell during this period. What are investors telling these companies? You may be squeezing more and more profits out of your strategy, but you are draining blood from the veins, year on year your strategy is decaying further.

Worse still, of course, if both ROCE and P/E ratio are falling. This was the case for companies like Fiat, TI Group, and De La Rue. In this case, investors were not only seeing a decline in earnings today, they were telling the company they expect its returns to decline in the future as well.

The message is clear: if a company is earning more on its capital but its P/E has stalled or is declining, that company's strategy is probably decaying. If both ROCE and P/E are falling, its strategy is, well, 'decayed'.

29.2.1.3 A High Ratio of Rents to New Value Creation

The third measure of strategy decay is to take a hard look at whether you are a creator of new value or a rent collector. Again, looking at traditional profit measures does not give us any answers to this question: to a historic cost accountant, value creation and rents are all the same, they both represent 'profits'. But from a strategic

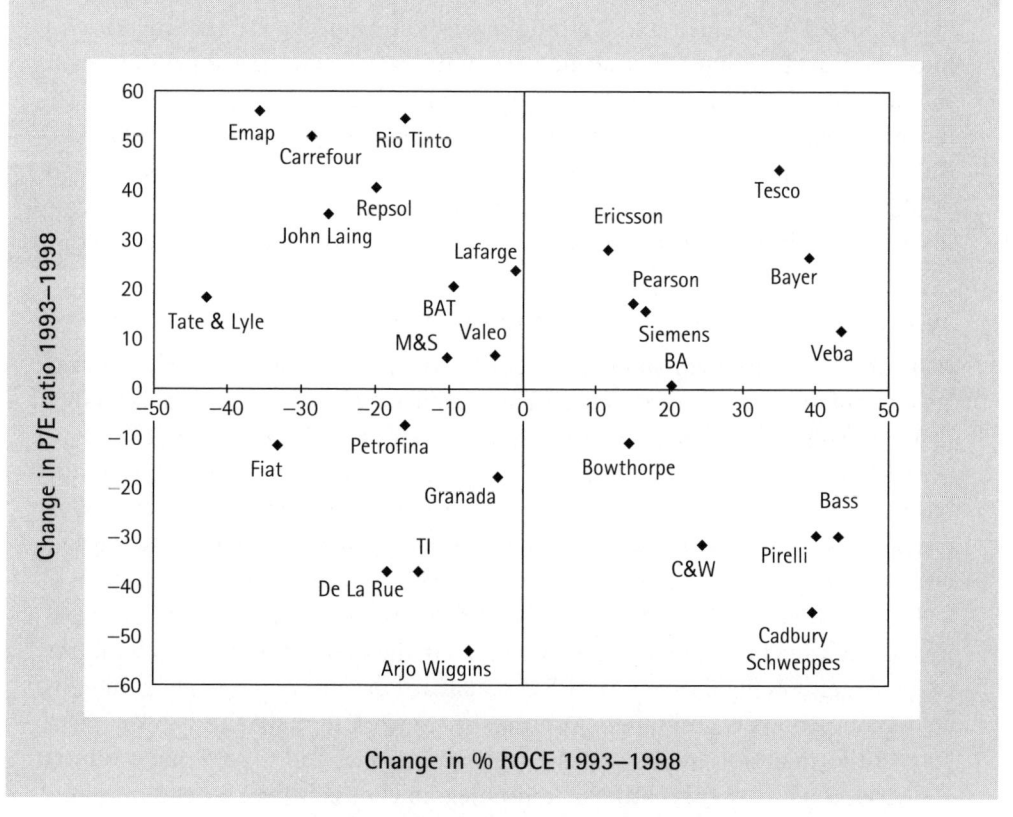

Fig. 29.1 ROCE, P/E, and strategy decay

standpoint, rent collection is very different from value creation. This is because most strategic assets on which a company collects rents sooner or later begin to depreciate. When this happens, the profit-generating capacity of a strategy that is based on those strategic assets begins to decay. Once the property begins to collapse, so do the rents.

It is not an easy task to judge how much of any year's profit comes from rents versus new value creation. But, even if this cannot be done with pinpoint accuracy, it is a worthwhile discipline. Filling in the following table is a first step:

Source of Rent (Strategic Asset)	% of Current Profit
Patents	
Installed base	
Long-term contracts	
Competencies more than 5 years old	
TOTAL	

If the total number you come up with is more than 50 per cent, then the majority of your reported profits are rents. Nothing wrong with being a good rent collector, as long as you are building new strategic assets and creating new value for customers at the same time. If you are not replenishing and extending the asset stock, then you are living off a legacy that, one day, will run out. The higher that percentage of rents gets, the more you need to worry about how long those old strategic assets will go on yielding those rents in the face of depreciation and expiry. A high proportion of rents in current profitability, therefore, is another danger sign of potential strategy decay.

29.2.1.4 *Convergence of Strategies in the Industry*

In a survey of more than 500 CEOs, sponsored by MCI, a majority of corporate leaders said that the strategies of the industry leaders had become more alike, rather than more dissimilar over the past several years. This should be a red flag. Remember back to Economics 101 and that idea of 'perfect competition'—everyone in the business following an identical strategy. You may also remember the textbook result: every company in the industry only made just enough profit to survive and no more. It is the business equivalent of a subsistence economy.

The final indicator of strategy decay, therefore, is convergence between a company's strategy and those of its main competitors in the industry. One ready indicator of convergence is the degree to which the standard deviation in operating margins across competitors is declining. Two forces are at work to make this happen. First, competitive imitation means that the major companies end up offering products and services where there is little for consumers to choose between; hence they buy and price, the industry becomes 'commoditized' and margins decline towards a common minimum. Second, higher cost, less competitive firms are either forced out of the business or are acquired so that scale and operating efficiency become prerequisites simply to remain in the business. As costs find a lower floor, there is pressure to lower prices in the quest for marginal volume. Margins are squeezed.

Figure 29.2 presents the data for the computer software and insurance broking industries. In insurance broking the strategies of the main players seem to be converging; operating margins are becoming more similar and the average margin is falling. By contrast, in industry computer software, the players seem to be coming up with innovative strategies which push their operating margins out above those of competitors.

29.2.1.5 *A Composite Measure*

If we put these four indicators of strategy decay together, you can make an assessment of a company's Strategy Decay Rate (SDR)—a measure of how fast your strategy is running out of steam. If you average a score of 'somewhat' or 'yes', you are in the danger zone.

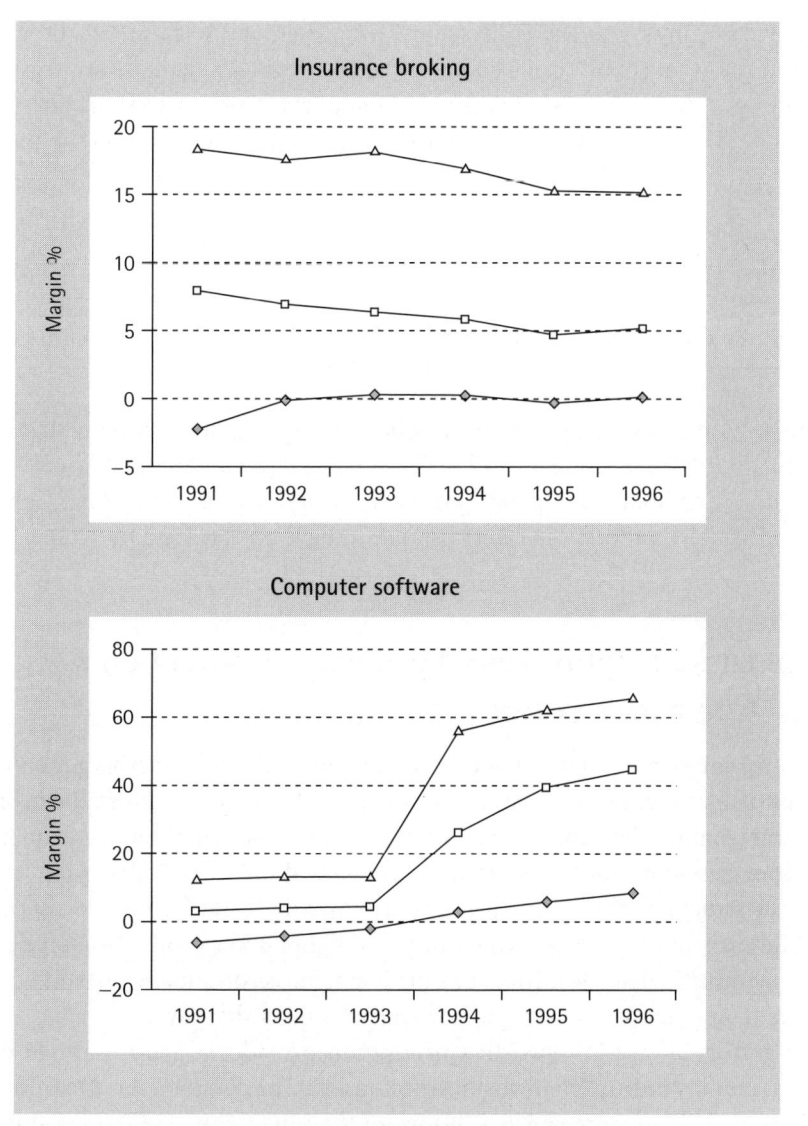

Fig. 29.2 Strategy convergence and divergence

Indicator	No	Somewhat	Yes
Ratio of earnings to revenue growth over five years diverges from 1 by a wide margin (> 2 or < 0.5)			
Rising ROCE and falling P/E (or both falling) over last five years			
High percentage of my profits are 'rents' on old strategic assets			
Standard deviation in margins across competitors in my industry is below average			

Assessing whether your strategy is decaying

So if a company's strategy is decaying, what can it do about it? Even more importantly, what actions can a company take to begin renewing its strategy before strategy decay becomes too advanced? One important answer to these questions is to build and actively manage a rich portfolio of strategic 'options on the future'.

29.3 STRATEGY AS OPTIONS ON THE FUTURE[2]

In this section we begin by illustrating what happens when a company that lacks a sufficient portfolio of strategic options faces strategy decay. We then discuss what a strategy that embodies a coherent portfolio of options for the future might look like, and sketch a process managers can use to develop this kind of strategy.

29.3.1 Lack of Options as a Powerful Constraint on a Company's Future

Successful companies often get ahead of their competitors by focusing their efforts on a particular segment of customers or geographic market so that they come to know more about the behaviour and needs of these potential buyers than anyone else. They design a profit-generating engine, based on a particular price, margin, and cost structure, that is in turn underpinned by a set of investments in the capability to source, produce, distribute, and support a product or service that these customers value. Over time, this profit engine is continually fine-tuned, often reaping economies of scale, scope, and learning along the way.

The history of the Woolworth Corporation provides a good example of this process. Frank Winfield Woolworth, who founded the company in 1879, pioneered the idea of selling merchandise at no more than five cents. He refined this 'five-and-dime' profit engine to become a finely-tuned general merchandising machine. Initial concepts of 'no-frills' service, focus on cheap products, and items that were non-perishable, provided the core. The Woolworth Corporation subsequently developed its competencies in managing a very wide product range, while keeping stock-turn high by carrying only the most popular, 'standard' varieties of each product; competencies in site selection and development; and the logistics to reap economies of scale from a chain of stores.

When he died in 1919, Woolworth boasted a chain of 1,081 stores with sales of $119 million (an incredible figure for its day). The power of the formula was reflected in

[2] For a more detailed discussion of this topic, see Williamson 1999.

the company's headquarters building at 233 Broadway in New York which was, at 792 feet, the world's tallest building until the Chrysler building was completed in 1930. After World War II the company continued to improve this winning formula, adding new competencies in the management of advertising, consumer credit, and self-serve, and site selection and management in the new retailing environment of the suburbs of American cities.

Woolworth's strategy had the advantages of focus: it was able to deepen its existing competencies and incrementally expand both its competency base and its knowledge of different market environments (such as suburban retailing). However, competitors were developing retail formats that required both competencies and market knowledge that were outside the 'box' in which Woolworth was operating. Competitors like Wal-Mart were introducing general merchandise, discount superstores, on one flank, and speciality 'category killers' (like Toys-R-Us) were attacking, on the other.

Despite seeing its overall sales figures declining in real terms, year after year (recall our measures of 'strategy decay' above), Woolworth failed to invest in creating the new capabilities or understanding of different market behaviours that would give it options to expand its business into either superstores or speciality retailing. When, in the late 1980s, Woolworth eventually did try to respond with its own discount and speciality stores, it ran into a hidden constraint: while the strategy made sense, it had not built the depth of capabilities and market knowledge necessary to gain competitive advantage in these new areas against determined rivals. Woolworth, in fact, did not really have the option to change its strategy quickly, since it had not invested in creating new capabilities and knowledge outside its existing formula. Thus, for example by 1995, Woolworth was forced to sell its new speciality stores 'Kids Mart' and 'Little Folks', established in the early 1990s, because of poor profitability. The company had become a prisoner of its past.

In 1993 Woolworth closed 400 stores in the United States and sold its 122 Canadian Woolco stores to Wal-Mart. In 1997 Woolworth closed its last general merchandise store in the United States. It had refined and polished its economic engine and deepened its narrow range of competencies into almost perfect extinction. By and large, the company had invested in new strategic options too late given the time necessary to build the stock of competencies and knowledge of new formats necessary to give it a launching pad to pursue a new strategy, combined with the fact that, by then, competitors were already well established.

In fact, Woolworth had invested in one new strategic option that arguably saved the company when, in 1974, senior managers had decided to back an experiment into speciality retailing branded 'Foot Locker'. The pilot in speciality retailing lay more or less dormant as a small venture for almost a decade. But when growth in the market took off, in the wake of growing health consciousness among the American population in the 1980s, Woolworth was able to exercise this option to rapidly build a chain of athletic-shoe stores, using the new capabilities in retailing of

athletic footwear and its knowledge of this market segment it had already accumulated in the Foot Locker venture. It subsequently introduced new formats, including Lady Foot Locker in 1982 and Kids Foot Locker in 1987. Over time, Woolworth opened over 7,100 of these speciality stores and in June 1998 it changed its corporate name to 'Venator Group', reputedly to convey an image of virile sportsmen. In some ways this is an example of successfully repositioning a company whose core business had become obsolete. But, in fact, Woolworth paid a high price for failing to recognize the hidden constraint on its strategy choices and under-investing in the creation of new strategic options soon enough. It is now a much smaller company, a contraction perhaps best epitomized by the fact that it now occupies only half the floors in that famous New York skyscraper, which it sold in April 1998.

From the late 1980s, the company had set itself challenging new missions. But in the quest to achieve them, its managers kept bumping up against two important constraints: they did not really understand the different set of customers they would need to attract to achieve a new, broader strategy, nor did they have the capabilities to deliver the advantages necessary to compete with rivals who were already established. When they decided to respond to loss of sales caused by changes in the market that were, by then, well established, managers at F. W. Woolworth kept hitting the dual constraints of narrow capabilities and lack of a deep understanding of new potential markets. They had expanded their ambitions, but they had not invested in enough real options soon enough to replace their dying profit engine. They were caught in the box depicted in Figure 29.3.

To avoid becoming a prisoner of these hidden constraints, it is necessary for a company to maintain a portfolio of new options for its future by building new capabilities and simultaneously expanding its knowledge of new market segments and customer behaviour.

These options on the future may take various forms. The option may take the form of:

(1) an idea for a new opportunity that has been thought through, but not tested;
(2) an experiment or pilot that has been conducted to test a new business model or market proposition; or
(3) a venture where the pilot has been launched as a stand-alone business, but not yet scaled up, or rolled out into a fully fledged division.

The choice of whether to maintain an option on the future as an idea, as an experiment, or as a business involves a trade-off between cost, on one hand, and speed, on the other. If the option is maintained as an idea, we minimize the cost of the option—maintaining an idea does involve much investment. But the speed with which we can exercise that option and its power as a launching pad for a new business is limited by the fact that we have not tested the idea or developed it into a business venture. By contrast, if we decide to develop every option we want to maintain in our portfolio right through to the point where it has been launched as

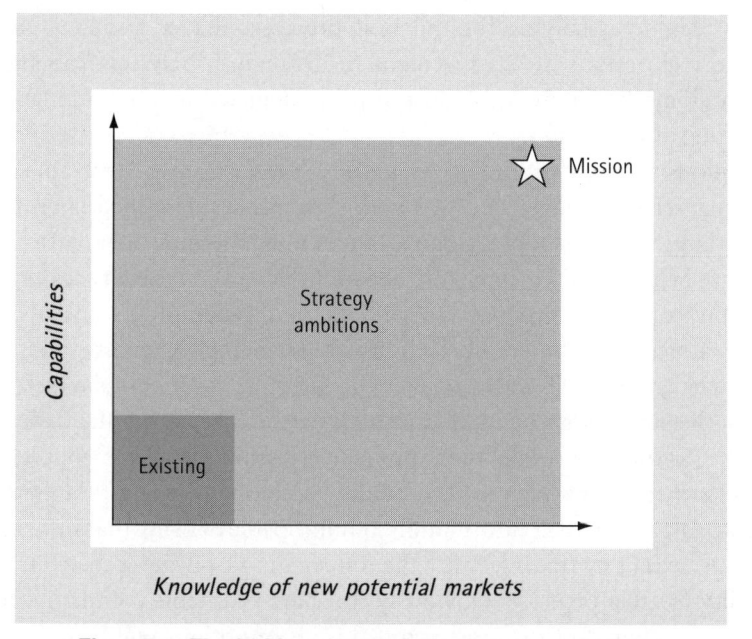

**Fig. 29.3 The hidden constraints: narrow capabilities
and market knowledge**

a venture, the total investment required could be huge. Developing the option
through to the venture stage, however, has the advantage that it will be much
quicker to scale up when we detect the environment makes it opportune to exercise
the option by scaling it up into a fully fledged business (as Woolworth did when it
decided to scale up the Foot Locker venture into a business of over 7,000 stores
almost a decade after its initial pilot of a single store). As we will see later, it makes
sense for a company to maintain a portfolio of options on the future at different
stages of development depending on their assessment of the trade-off between
investment cost and the likely benefits of positioning themselves to react faster
than the competition.

Provided the outcome of uncertain developments in the market falls within the
range of its portfolio of options, the company will be in a position to exercise one or
more of the options that turn out to be relevant. Exercising such an option will
allow it to reposition its strategy rapidly when changes in the market environment
make this necessary in a way not otherwise open to it. Thus, by creating strategic
options, some of which turn out to be relevant to the future, the company will be in
a position to outperform its competitors who have not made these investments.
Alternatively, it will be in a better position to close the competitive gap with rivals
who, for historical reasons, already possess the necessary capabilities and market
knowledge (because, for example, they happen to be serving a particular segment of
the market that subsequently 'takes off').

With a view to specifying the different processes that a company can use to expand its real options, it is convenient to distinguish between 'capability constraints' and 'market knowledge constraints' as depicted by the boundaries of the 'existing' box in Figure 29.3.

The options available to some companies are not seriously constrained by their stock of market knowledge. Through various processes described later, they have created a large internal pool of knowledge about potential new customers and competitive behaviours. This may include knowledge about new types of potential users of the company's products or services, new geographic segments, existing users whose needs and buying behaviour are changing, or competitors who are trying to 'change the rules of the game'. The dilemma these companies face is that having market knowledge, by itself, can still leave the company with too few ways to exploit that knowledge (other than, perhaps, by selling it to someone else). This might be termed the problem of the 'trader': a company aware of a great deal of potentially valuable market information, but incapable of using that information to create value, except by trading either the information or using it to arbitrage some commodity (see Figure 29.4). Obviously there are profitable companies based on trading information, but for most firms, this set of options will be too narrow to allow them to leverage much of their existing competence base and therefore to support an adequate return on their existing asset and skill bases.

To avoid the problem of a set of capabilities that is too narrow to exploit the knowledge of different markets and customer behaviours that such a company continues to amass, it needs to find a way to systematically expand its pool of value-

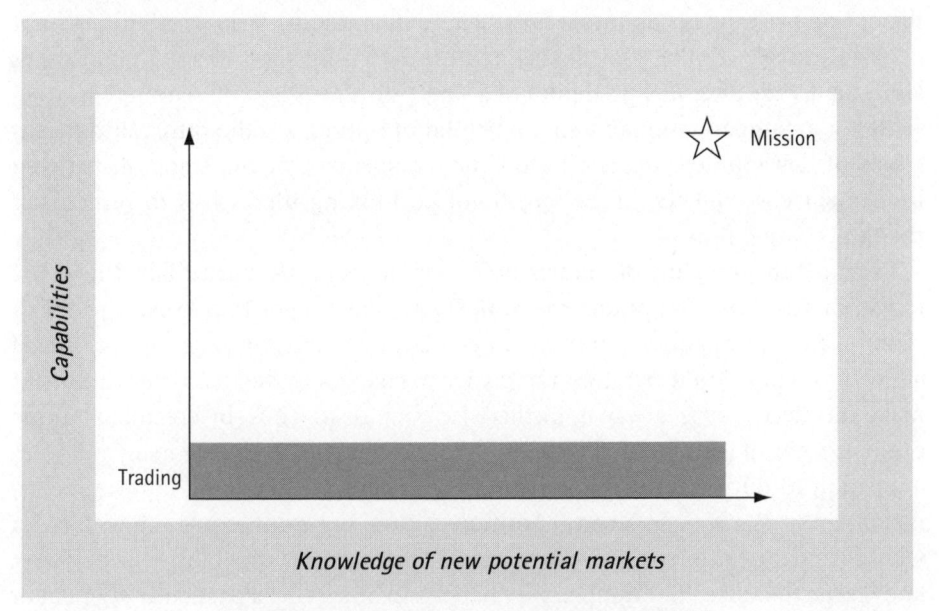

Fig. 29.4 The trader—'aware but incapable'

creating capabilities (adding, for example, the capability to manufacture products, or deliver services that utilize that market knowledge). A company that arguably found itself in this situation is the veritable British trading house, Inchcape. Its geographic reach extended from South-East Asia through to the Americas, the Caribbean, India, Europe, and Africa with interests in over 500 companies in 44 countries. It became a professional distributor, marketer, and seller of products and technologies of its 'principals' (the owners of the branded products and services it traded) and as a provider of specialist services. As a 'trader' it successfully expanded its options into new markets along the horizontal dimension in Figure 29.4. But as the principals for whom Inchcape acted as agent became more familiar with the behaviour of local markets, wanted more control over their market positioning, and built up the scale necessary to cover the fixed costs of their own local operations, they began to integrate forwards into Inchcape's business. As a traditional 'trader', it had few places to turn. With finely honed trading skills, but lacking the breadth of capabilities to add value in other ways, its strategic options were tightly circumscribed. Some of Inchcape's competitors, like Swire Pacific, for example, had invested more in creating new options by developing new capability sets in areas such as property development and airline management. By the time pure 'trading' as a mechanism for extracting profit from local knowledge came under serious threat, Swire was able to exercise the option to use these expanded capabilities to extract an increasing proportion of total profit from their local knowledge in new ways (INSEAD 1993; Kennedy 1996).

Some companies have the opposite problem of Inchcape: they have created a formidable set of capabilities that are prisoners of their lack of market knowledge. This problem is depicted in Figure 29.5. AT&T during the period immediately after the demerger of the Bell operating companies is a good example. The company had a formidable set of capabilities in technology, communications infrastructure, and experience in sales and customer service. As a result of a long period of domestic regulation and the presence of government monopolies overseas that constrained the markets open to them, however, much of the potential of AT&T's capabilities was imprisoned by a lack of market experience outside the long-distance, voice, and data sector in the United States. These constraints meant that AT&T capabilities had under-utilized capacity. More specifically, given the set of options AT&T had available given the regulatory constraints and its existing pool of market knowledge, the marginal costs of deploying its capabilities across a broader range of market segments and value-creating services remained below the expected marginal revenues to be obtained.

Gradually, in parallel with deregulation at home and abroad, AT&T has opened up new strategic options by building its knowledge base about the markets for new domestic services and users in national markets overseas. It was thus able to increase the effective capacity utilization of its existing capabilities.

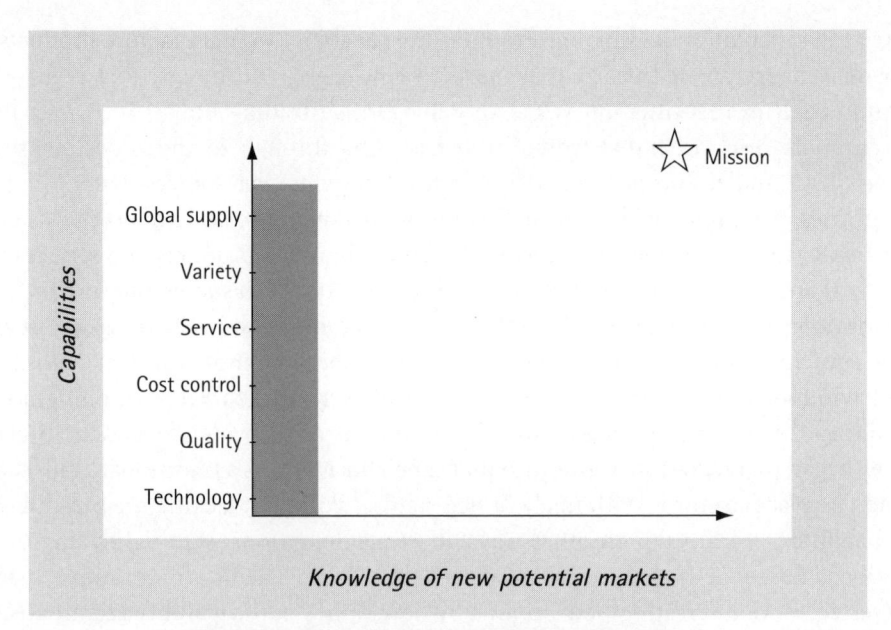

Fig. 29.5 The prisoner—'capable but unaware'

To develop new strategic options, therefore, two sets of processes may be required. First, a set of processes that fundamentally expand a company's capability set. Second, a set of processes that expand a company's knowledge of new markets and market behaviours.

It is important to recognize, however, that opening up new options does not necessarily imply 'unrelated', or even 'related' diversification in the traditional senses (see e.g. Lubatkin and Chatterjee 1994). In the case of Woolworth, the relevant options turned out to be new retailing formats which could be seen as a type of related diversification, likewise, for the comparison between Inchcape and Swire Pacific. But, alternatively, new options can often involve finding new ways to deliver either enhanced value to, or reduce the costs of serving, an existing customer segment such as Monsanto's use of biotechnology to replace traditional chemicals in its weed control business or Schwab's introduction of 'E-Schwab' as an alternative to execution through its telephone call centres. In almost every case, however, the creation of new options involves some combination of fundamentally extending the company's existing capabilities base and, at the same time, its knowledge of customer and market behaviour. In the case of E-Schwab, for example, a series of new capabilities around the design and management of an Internet interface between the customer and Schwab's internal systems was required. Many of the customers for E-Schwab will be users of the existing telephone trading system. But those customers are likely to behave differently in an environment of electronic trading. Schwab needed to understand, for example, what customers will pay a price premium for in a world of electronic commerce

and how this will change Schwab's ability to build customer loyalty (INSEAD 1998).

Equally, this is not an argument for companies to develop an infinite number of capabilities, or that exploiting them across every market they can learn about is the ideal strategy. Such approaches would eventually drown in diseconomies of complexity as the variety of activities the organization was called upon to handle increased (Schoemaker 1990). As we will see below, there is an optimal portfolio of options that a company needs to create in order to strike the right balance between the cost of creating and maintaining an option and the pay-offs in terms of the ability to reposition itself more rapidly and at lower costs than if it had not invested in those options.

These observations raise two further questions: 'What would these processes actually look like inside a company' and 'how broad a range of options does it make sense to create?' It could be argued in the case of F. W. Woolworth, for example, that the company was continually expanding its capabilities and knowledge of customer behaviour within its existing retailing format and that its error was to limit the range of new options it created to a set that was untenably narrow, given the rate and nature of changes occurring in its industry. We turn to both of these questions below.

29.3.2 Putting in Place Processes to Build New Strategic Options

As we have seen, the process of creating new strategic options involves some combination of expanding the company's knowledge about new, potential markets or customer behaviours while simultaneously building new capabilities. These processes need to be designed in such a way as to keep the costs of building and maintaining the portfolio of strategic options to a minimum—a particularly important factor given that many of the options are likely to remain unexercised.

Cost-effective methods of expanding knowledge about new potential markets and customer behaviours include mechanisms to leverage the knowledge inside customers and suppliers, learning from 'maverick' competitors and from related industries.

Market research is perhaps the most obvious way to leverage knowledge inside customers. But as a source of raw material from which to fashion new options, traditional market research suffers from the limitation that it is often bounded by the current perception and orthodoxies of the bulk of existing consumers. To create new options it is often better to focus on customer complaints, as a means to understand where customers feel the existing offering is falling short and in what ways—shortfalls that will suggest options for new sources of value-added or

additional services. Likewise, in creating new options in the spheres of industrial products or business users, it can be valuable to find a customer who has articulated an unserved need and partner with that customer to solve it. The geographic periphery of the company's existing markets or concentrations of highly sophisticated customers, where products and services designed to serve a home market are likely to require most adaptation, can also be fruitful sources of knowledge about potential new customer segments or emerging customer behaviour. To create options from this information requires a company to ensure it has the right environment for the broader potential of these adaptations to be recognized. Finally, options thinking suggests that a company may enter a new market simply to learn knowledge that is potentially relevant for its global operations, rather than earn profits from that market directly. Options thinking would view the costs of being in such a market as an investment the company was making in expanding its portfolio of strategic options.

Partnerships with leading-edge suppliers, exchange of technical information, or purchase of minority equity stakes in suppliers with potentially innovative technologies are processes that can help to provide the raw material to generate new options. Likewise, there is mileage in scanning related industries for potentially applicable technologies, service systems or patterns of changing customer behaviour as a means of providing the raw material to generate new options.

Finally, take particular notice of 'maverick competitors', by continually asking 'who is breaking the rules in the industry?'. Taking the narrow view that your company has a single strategy, from which sales and efficiency must be optimized, means that these competitors are often dismissed as irrelevant 'because they aren't in our market' or they are 'following a different strategy'. As a source of ideas for investment in the creation of a portfolio of strategic options on the future, however, the behaviour of maverick competitors can be a gold mine.

An analogous set of processes need to be put in place to build the new capabilities that will allow a company to expand its strategic options. In her seminal book *Wellsprings of Knowledge*, Leonard-Barton (1995) analysed the processes involved including building a company's capabilities base through problem-solving, experimentation, importing knowledge, and implementing and integrating new capabilities. The combination of capability-building initiatives involved in a Total Quality Management System is a good example. These include physical and technical systems, managerial system, and values and norms, all aligned to the process of building a new capability, in this case 'quality'.

Figure 29.6 illustrates how Acer has used these types of processes to grow from inauspicious beginnings as a small electronics company in Taiwan to become the third largest supplier of personal computers in the world.

Just like their competitors, Acer lacked a reliable crystal ball to forecast the future. But they did have a broad sense of which markets they would have to learn about to expand their strategic options. They knew that they would never have the option to

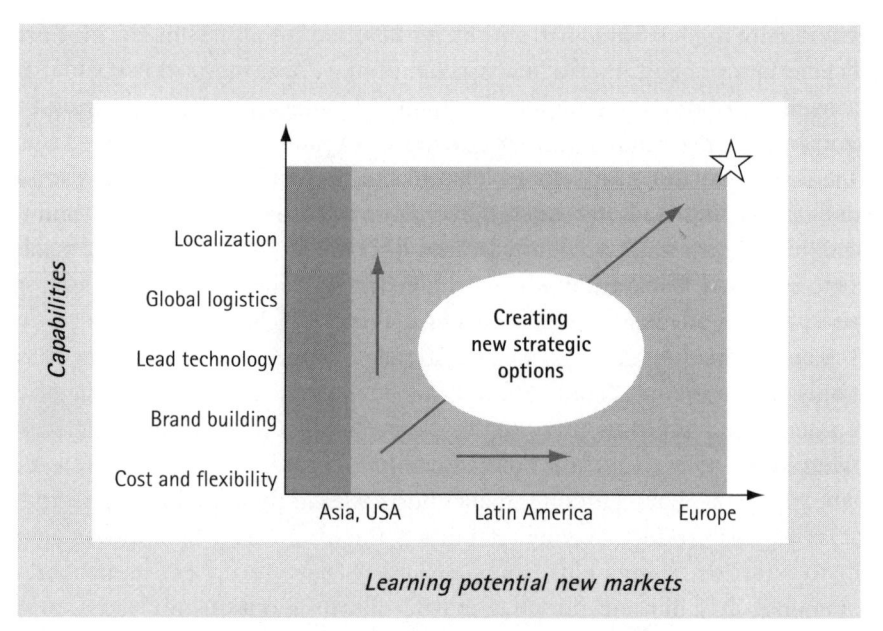

Fig. 29.6 Creating strategic options at Acer

become a global player if they failed to enter the US marketplace. Obviously the United States is a large marketplace in real terms. But more importantly, Acer recognized that because the United States was home to the world's most sophisticated buyers of personal computers, understanding these customers would give Acer a head start against competitors in other markets around the world. In other words, understanding the US market would open up many options for Acer both to respond more rapidly and to lead change as other markets followed the American lead. According to Stan Shih, Acer's Chairman, this is an important reason why Acer has maintained its presence in the US market despite sometimes extended periods of local financial losses (INSEAD 1997).

Acer also knew it would be suicidal to attack the established PC giants across a broad front, so they next concentrated on getting an understanding of the Asian consumers in their own back yard. Most of the major suppliers of PCs had traditionally sold only to the 'high-end', high-price segment of Asian markets. Acer set out to develop the capabilities, products, and consumer understanding to allow them to access the much lower price mainstream markets in Asia. After rounds of redesign of their products to cut costs, interspersed with test marketing, Acer learned how to sell computers to the mass market segment in emerging Asian economies ahead of their competitors. This opened up new options to enter other low-price, emerging markets like Mexico, South Africa, and Russia.

Acer did not follow a strategy of straight-line forecasting based on its existing products and procedures. In fact, when it entered a new market it did not always know exactly what product it would sell to whom. Its initial investment in entering

a market amounted to buying an option. Rather than simply selling the products it had to the kinds of customers it had served at home, Acer invested in partnerships with local distributors and suppliers designed to maximize its opportunities to learn about the market and further develop its capabilities. In the United States, partnerships with discount retailers taught Acer how to use a previously under-served channel. Its alliance with California-based Frog design helped build its capability to develop non-traditional computer designs and 'ergonomics'. It subse-quently exercised this option when it launched the unconventional, sleek, grey 'Aspire': a multi-media home PC which became a best seller.

In Mexico where the conventional wisdom of competitors like IBM and HP was that only large corporates could afford branded personal computers, while private consumers bought low-quality clones, Acer invested with its local partner in working with small- and medium-sized companies to discover, and then to fill, a specific gap in the market among smaller businesses. It then used its capabilities to create a suitable product. Having established a new option, it then moved aggres-sively to exercise it, building its market share in Mexico to 32 per cent by 1996.

Of course, Acer did not end up exercising all of the options it created. In 1996 Acer effectively acquired an option on the Russian market by building an assembly plant across the border in Lappeenranta, Finland from which it could efficiently supply computers to Russian distributors. In fact developments in Russia during 1996 and 1997, including the rapid emergence of strong, domestic competitors, meant that the Russian market became markedly less attractive than at the time Acer made the investment and much of the Russian aspect of the option remained unexercised. However, given Finland's membership of the European Union, the resulting excess capacity could be easily transferred into other European markets (*Economist* 1997). This example illustrates another important factor to keep in mind: as far as possible the option should be designed to minimize the costs incurred should you decide not to exercise it.

Fundamental to Acer's approach was a view that strategy is about creating options on new markets. Likewise, Acer kept on expanding its capabilities in successive waves. It began by exploiting its basic capabilities in low-cost manufacturing and flexibility to rapidly introduce new technology as a supplier of components and sub-assemblies to other suppliers of personal computers. Recognizing that this positioning con-strained its strategic options, the company changed its name to Acer in 1987 and began to invest in its brand. It also realized that to break out of a 'me-too' cycle and compete with the global leaders, it would need access to leading-edge technology. It gained this access through joint ventures in core components with leading companies like Texas Instruments and MBB, a subsidiary of Daimler-Benz.

When Acer began to localize final assembly of its computers, siting assembly lines inside its major markets, it did not precisely forecast how this move would impact its business. It was buying an option that would allow it to rapidly respond to changes in exchange rates and relative labour costs, as well as the opportunity to

reduce the stock of finished goods in its pipeline. But local assembly, along with its growing understanding of customers and improved IT capabilities that allowed it to access customer information directly from its retailers, combined to create a new option. It was now possible for Acer to receive the specifications of a customized PC from a retailer and rapidly assemble it to order. It decided to exercise this option when it introduced its 'fast-food' model of computer supply, in which computers were prepared to order by assembling different combinations of standard components in an analogous way to a 'fast-food' restaurant.

Figure 29.6 illustrates this process whereby each wave of Acer's initiatives opened up a new and broader set of options for positioning the company in the future. No amount of planning could enable it to pinpoint exactly which of those options it would exercise in an uncertain future. Unlike Woolworth or Inchcape, however, it had created an expanded strategic space in which it could manoeuvre as future conditions unfolded.

29.3.3 Optimizing the Portfolio of Strategic Options

Clearly it usually costs money to open up new strategic options. A company must therefore choose a bounded portfolio of options to create. So how does a manager know if he or she has created the right portfolio of strategic options for the future?

The good news is that you can answer this question without pretending to be able to forecast the exact volume of sales, prices, or input costs five years hence. But traditional spreadsheets with spurious accuracy to two-decimal places five years into the future have to be set aside. Instead, to begin creating the right set of options we need to take a view on two sets of factors:

1. Broadly what alternative capabilities might we need to profitably meet our probable customers' needs in the future (e.g. digital or analogue technology, localization or individual customization, high levels of variety, reduced lead times, bundled products and services, and so on)?

2. Which potential future markets (geographic, customer, or non-user segments) or new customer behaviours (such as how customer behaviour will change with the growth of e-commerce) will it be important to start learning about so that we have the option to respond to them in the future?

At this 30,000-ft level, far above the detail of unit sales and prices, we can probably forecast with reasonable accuracy. It is interesting to note that in 1984, for example, John Naisbitt analysed 6,000 local newspapers in the United States to isolate ten 'mega-trends'. They were developments like the fact that 'customers would demand a combination of high-tech combined with high-touch', that 'globalisation would mean a combination of more shared production with more cultural assertiveness in individual markets', and that there would be an 'option explosion' in which

customers across more and more industries would demand not just 'chocolate or vanilla', but a huge variety of alternative product or services specifications (Naisbitt 1984). Most of these broad 'predictions' came to pass, largely because they were not predictions at all, but trends already underway that simply gathered pace with the passage of time. They are exactly the kinds of views on the future that companies would need to know to assess the set of capabilities market knowledge necessary to generate a sound portfolio of strategic options. Asking, for example, what kind of capabilities we need to build to increase our options to provide future customers with massively more variety; what does this mean for our operations, for our inventory systems, for our salesforce training? The answers will obviously differ industry by industry and company by company, but we can make a fair guesstimate of what they are.

Various techniques exist to develop this list of the alternative capabilities that a company might need to develop and the market environments or customer behaviours it might need to understand in order to cope with most of the major directions in which its industry might develop. One popular approach is 'scenario planning', pioneered by the Hudson Institute, in which a series of alternative, internally consistent scenarios of how the market and industry structure might develop, and what the implications for sources of competitive advantage might be, are built (see e.g. McNulty 1977; de Gues 1988). In their book *Competing for the Future*, Hamel and Prahalad suggest isolating potential 'discontinuities' by looking for the likely collision of different trends that will create a step-change in the environment (Hamel and Prahalad 1994: 145). An example of such a discontinuity is the combination of changing lifestyles creating a demand for news broadcasts at any time 24 hours a day, the emergence of a new cable media distribution channel, and the development of low-cost satellite communications to allow reporters to despatch their stories without the need for a network of large local bureaux, that opened the way for CNN to become a feasible proposition.

Once a list of alternative new capabilities and market environments and behaviours that might figure in the future has been accumulated, a table of the main alternatives a company is likely to face can be created. An example of such a table of contingencies for a competitor in the mobile telephone industry is illustrated in Table 29.1.

Table 29.1 illustrates the fact that not all combinations of future potential discontinuities and possible capabilities required to underpin competitive advantage will be technically feasible (Internet-mobile telephony convergence and analogue technology, for example). Once the feasible options have been identified, planners must then decide whether or not to make the investment necessary to include a particular option in the company's portfolio. Looking at Table 29.1, for example, each competitor will have to decide whether or not to include Option 3 and Option 8 in its portfolio by investing in the continued development of analogue technology. These decisions should be result of three considerations:

Table 29.1 Designing a portfolio of options for the mobile telephone business

Capability requirement/ market discontinuity	Analogue engineering	Digital GSM engineering	Other digital engineering
Mobile telephones competing to replace fixed-line services inside large corporations		Option 1	Option 2
Emergence of lifestyle uses and the mobile telephone as a 'fashion accessory'	Option 3	Option 4	Option 5
Internet, voice, and data applications converge		Option 6	Option 7
Entertainment media/ mobile telephony convergence	Option 8		Option 9

(1) the costs of creating and maintaining the option;
(2) the estimated probability that the options will be exercised;
(3) the probability that creating the option will itself spawn future options, even
     if it remains unexercised (e.g. a company may value Option 3 or Option 8 not
     for its direct profit-making potential, but because of its capacity to open up
     future options that rely on analogue technology).

When strategy is viewed as the creation of options on the future, minimizing the costs of creating and maintaining options becomes a critical managerial concern. The costs of creating and maintaining options can be reduced by careful design of efficient experiments, test marketing, and prototyping, sharing the costs in partnership with interested customers or suppliers, and by leveraging the new information sources, like maverick competitors or adaptation taking place on the geographic periphery of the organization, that were discussed above.

In attempting to optimize the company's portfolio of options it is also important for management to make a clear distinction between the cost of investing in the option and the cost of exercising that option (the latter being the costs of scaling up the option into a profit-generating business). In the case of Woolworth, for example, the costs of its initial experiment to establish its first 'Foot Locker' store were the costs of creating an option to move into this type of speciality retailing. If this option had been left unexercised, the cost would have amounted to writing off the cost of this experiment. The cost of exercising the option that experiment

created included all of the investments required to establish and operate a competitive chain of stores that achieved the minimum efficient scale for this business. The cost of Acer's option on the Russian market amounted to the investment in its Finnish plant less the expected present value of cash it could obtain from selling the production elsewhere in Europe if it decided to leave the option to enter Russia unexercised. The costs of exercising its Russian option, meanwhile, would have included the costs of investing in brand building and distribution capacity in Russia, and so on. This distinction is critical because the decision whether or not to include a particular option in the company's portfolio should be made by comparing the estimated value of that option with the *cost of creating the option*, not with the costs of exercising it.[3]

It is also worth noting that, by viewing the first role of good strategy as the creation of a portfolio of options for a company's future, the success of that strategy does not rest on the ability to predict the continuance of any single trend. As we have already noted, depending on the future environment, not all of our options will be exercised. However, those that we discard are not wasted, but will have served the useful purpose of insuring against an uncertain future.

29.3.4 Corporate Renewal and the Strategy Innovation Pipeline

As we noted above, the cost of creating and maintaining an option also depends on the form in which the option is maintained: as an idea, as an experiment, or as a venture. To position itself for continuous renewal in the face of a changing environment, it makes sense for a company to maintain its portfolio of options in different states of development and to manage the flow of investment into each option depending on the way the environment seems to be moving and how fast. As an option looks more likely to be exercised it will pay to invest more in it, thus moving the option from the idea stage, through experimentation towards a stand-alone venture. Managing a portfolio of options, therefore, involves actively creating and managing a 'pipeline' of options as different stages of development. Such a 'pipeline of strategic options' is depicted in Figure 29.7.

Some options will need to be pushed through the pipeline rapidly, if the likelihood of exercising them increases. Others may lie 'dormant' for an extended period, or possibly indefinitely, if the environment never evolves in a way that justifies their exercise. Each individual option will also need to be managed differently, depending on its stage of development: ideas will need to be managed differently from experiments or ventures.

---

[3] The subject of valuing real options is a large topic in its own right that there is insufficient space to cover here. For relevant techniques and methods, see e.g. Amram and Kulatilaka 1999.

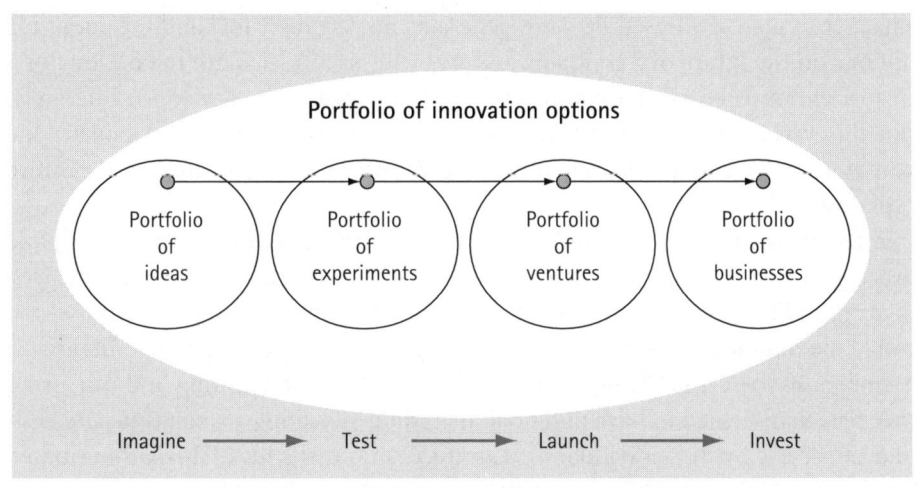

Fig. 29.7 The strategy innovation pipeline

29.4 MANAGING THE STRATEGY INNOVATION PIPELINE

Managing a pipeline of options for strategic innovation and renewal involves four main activities:

(1) finding mechanisms to fill the pipeline with different ideas that are possible options on the future;

(2) managing four sub-portfolios of options at different stages of development: ideas, experiments, ventures, and business;

(3) managing the toll gates and transitions by which an option receives further investment to move through the pipeline;

(4) exercising the option by scaling it up into a substantive business within the corporation's portfolio of business activities.

We examine each of these activities below.

29.4.1 Filling the Strategy Innovation Pipeline

A survey of strategy innovation in twenty-five companies undertaken in 1999 by the author found that in most companies there was no lack of ideas that potentially represent innovative options on the future. But most of these ideas were left in 'limbo'; they remained little more than flashes of inspiration in the heads of individuals or small groups because there was no process to develop these ideas. Many companies had 'suggestion schemes'. While these were effective for

small, incremental ideas they were generally not attuned to handling ideas for options on the future of a company and its business model. With the backing of a strong, entrepreneurial champion, some of these ideas were developed internally. But this was very much a 'hit or miss' process. Others were taken outside the corporation by entrepreneurial former staff and became seedlings for venture capitalists.

A few companies, such as Royal Dutch Shell, have developed a more systemic process to collect ideas for options on the future. In Shell's case this involved inviting individuals to sketch out their idea on a simple one-page form which would be submitted to a 'GameChanger' panel of six peer-group individuals. Members of the GameChanger Panel were tasked with expanding and nurturing the ideas that seemed to have potential, including allocating a small time and cash budget for use by the individual or team to flesh out the idea. Shell also initiated 'just do it' meetings in which individuals or teams with ideas for options as to how to develop Shell's business in a particular area were invited to bring their ideas to a common forum for further development and initial funding.

All ideas submitted were logged by Shell in the portfolio of ideas for options on the future. Some lay dormant. Others were pushed forward. In this way the portfolio was actively managed.

29.4.2 Managing a Portfolio of Ideas

Having amassed a portfolio of ideas and put in place mechanisms to encourage a continuous flow of new options into this portfolio, the ideas must be managed, evaluated, and developed. But when an option is in the form of an idea, it is at an early stage in its gestation. It is therefore inappropriate to apply the same criteria as used to assess an established business. That would be the equivalent of asking a 6-month-old baby to run a marathon. The criteria for assessing the quality of an idea as an option on the future should not be based, for example, on the quality of a proverbial five-year spreadsheet laying out future forecasts of its profitability in existing market conditions. Given the role of an option as a way of dealing with future uncertainty, it will be more important that the idea is capable of acting as a launching pad into a new technology or market segment that might take off, than its prospects of making a return on the assumption that current trends continue.

Viewed as options on the future, ideas will be valuable if they:

(1) are capable of dealing with possible discontinuities in technology or con-
    sumer behaviour;
(2) provide new types of customer benefits; or
(3) are scalable should the option be exercised.

Given the low cost of maintaining an option as an idea, an optimal portfolio of ideas must be judged by the extent to which it allows a company to 'cover the bases' of alternative scenarios or 'states of the world' it may face. This judgement can be based on:

(1) the number of ideas;
(2) whether they cover the major discontinuities (technological, consumer, competence); and
(3) the likely scalability of the ideas in the portfolio relative to the size of the existing business.

Before an option in the idea portfolio can make the transition to the stage of an experiment (justifying the higher investment required) three conditions must be met:

(1) the ability to articulate a viable business model around the idea (a value proposition, revenue source, and major cost drivers);
(2) an experiment to begin to identify the major assumptions that would make the option viable and attractive; and
(3) a team with the right mix of skills to conduct this experiment (either physical or virtual) to test the potential of the idea as an option on the future.

29.4.3 Managing a Portfolio of Experiments

Once it has been decided to develop an option to the stage of experimentation, a new set of criteria become relevant to managing it. These include:

(1) the ratio of learning over the cost of the experiment;
(2) how conclusive the results of the experiment are in determining the viability of the option;
(3) whether the experiment is successful in identifying the critical preconditions under which it would make sense to exercise the option.

Again the quality of the portfolio of options a company has at the experimental stage will be determined by whether the portfolio covers the major technological or market discontinuities the company could face and whether, taken as a total portfolio, the options are of sufficient potential scale to match the need to grow or replace the corporation's existing business models in the face of strategy decay.

The decision to invest further to push a particular option past the experimental stage and to launch it as a venture, meanwhile, depends on:

(1) how soon demand is likely to emerge (this might be proxied, for example, by whether a lead customer can be identified for the option);
(2) demonstrated proof of concept, including a potential revenue stream; and
(3) support of a suitably qualified team.

29.4.4 Managing a Portfolio of Ventures

Once the decision has been taken to push an option to the stage of becoming a venture, the task is to refine and prove the feasibility of exercising the option by scaling it up into a profitable business and to identify under what conditions exercising the option would make sense.

In many cases these assessments of whether the venture represents a viable option for scaling into a significant business cannot be made on the basis of the existing profitability of the venture. It may be, for example, that the venture will never be able to achieve profitability at small scale. Instead the critical criteria for assessing a venture are:

(1) its potential to create significant value as a new business if the environment moves in a particular direction;

(2) its potential to act as a profitable alternative to an existing business model should changing conditions accelerate decay of the current profit stream;

(3) the risks involved in successfully scaling up the venture even if the right constellation of market conditions were to fall into place.

An optimal portfolio of ventures for a company, meanwhile, will be such as to cover the main technological and market discontinuities it may face (or potentially benefit from in the future). Overall the strategy innovation pipeline should cover these environmental contingencies with a set of options such that the maturity of the options in the overall portfolio would allow the company to be in a position to exercise each option when required. Thus, technological or customer changes that are likely to evolve only in the longer term should be matched with options in the pipeline at the idea stage. Short-term technological or market contingencies meanwhile need to be matched with options at the venture stage of maturity so that they can be exercised at short notice as a solid platform to rapidly build or reposition a significant business.

29.4.5 Exercising an Option by Scaling It Up to Become a Substantive Business

When a previously uncertain change in the market environment actually comes to pass, it will make sense to exercise one or more of the options in the portfolio. This means investing the resources and competencies necessary to scale the option up into a full-fledged business unit. Typically this involves the infusion of:

• cash

• relevant competencies from the existing businesses (brand building capabilities, for example)

- operational skills required to drive up efficiency and manage a large-scale, possibly complex business
- an 'organizational home' within the corporation and associated reporting structure.

Once scaled up, the criteria for evaluation are no longer those used for an option: the business needs to judged by more traditional measures of an established, ongoing business such as revenue growth, profitability, return on capital employed, Economic Value Analysis (EVA), and so on. What was an option throughout its life to date has now entered the portfolio of businesses that makes up the corporation revenue and profit-producing engine. It has cleared the various hurdles described above and reached the end of the pipeline shown in Figure 29.8. This completes the strategy innovation cycle.

In a world that often seems to assume that maximum speed is always the right strategy, it is important to recognize that it may be wrong to push an option through to a full-scale business too early, especially if this means closing off other options in the process.

Monsanto, for example, single-mindedly drove through to full-scale launch its strategy for rewriting the role of the herbicide business using genetically modified (GM) seeds. Rather than retaining a portfolio of options distributed between portfolios of ideas, experiments, and ventures, it chose a single strategic innovation and simply 'went for it'. When the environment unexpectedly turned increasingly hostile to GM-based products, starting in Europe and spreading back to the United States, it was left boxed into a corner. Monsanto closed off other options too early and drove its idea of GM seeds linked to its herbicide range rapidly through the strategy innovation pipeline before the market was ready. This left the company seriously damaged and looking for a 'rescue partner' with which to merge.

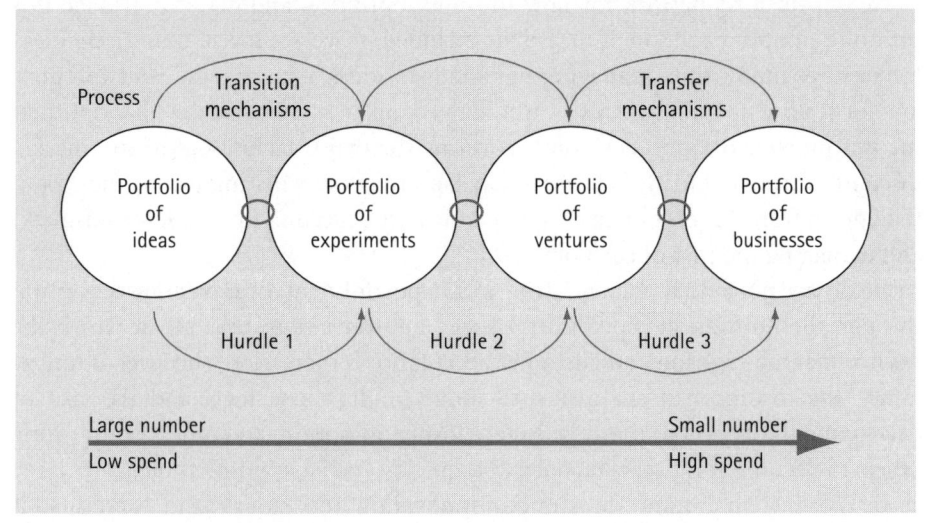

Fig. 29.8 The life cycle of an option on the future

Its competitor, BASF, by contrast, created a new biotechnology division comprising seed companies, biotechnology expertise, and speciality chemicals capabilities. This new division was charged with coming up with a portfolio of options that BASF might exercise in the future to take advantage of emerging biotechnologies. Rather than choosing a single strategic innovation and rapidly scaling it up, it set about building a pipeline of options at different stages of maturity to maximize readiness to launch successful strategy innovations as the fog of market uncertainty began to clear.

29.5 SUMMARY

In this chapter we began by sketching out what strategy innovation is and why it is a necessary capability for companies to develop in the fight against strategy decay. We developed a set of indicators a company can use to assess the extent and speed of strategy decay in its existing business model. This establishes the size of the 'gap' that strategy innovation must fill and the speed with which the new business model must be scaled up into a fully fledged profit generator.

But faced with uncertainty about the future directions of technology, consumer behaviour, and market evolution, it is extremely dangerous for a company to bank its future on a single strategy innovation. Instead, it needs to develop a portfolio of options on the future made up of a pipeline of alternative strategy innovations at different stages of maturity from ideas, through experiments, to ventures.

We set out a framework for how to build, optimize, and actively manage this portfolio of options on the future. This included processes for sourcing new ideas for strategy innovation, managing portfolios of ideas, experiments, and ventures, and for scaling up a venture into a full-fledged business unit. We saw that optimizing this pipeline of options involves covering the major technological and market discontinuities a company believes it may face. It involves distinguishing the cost of the option from the cost of exercising it (the cost of scaling up to a large business) and managing the cost of each option.

Finally, we noted that managing the option portfolio involves pushing the option through the innovation pipeline at a speed appropriate to the rate at which the environment is evolving and customer acceptance is increasing, the level of uncertainty, the readiness of an option to move to the next stage, and the cost of developing the option to the next stage. Closing off options too quickly or pushing others to become a full-scale business too quickly can have a downside just as large as developing an option for strategy innovation too slowly and exercising it too late.

REFERENCES

AMRAM, M., and KULATILAKA, N. (1999). *Real Options: Managing Strategic Investment in an Uncertain World*. Boston: Harvard Business School Press.

DE GUES, ARIE (1988). 'Planning as Learning'. *Harvard Business Review*, Mar.–Apr.: 70–4.

Economist, The (1997). 'Laptops from Lapland'. *The Economist*, 6 Sept.: 89–90.

HAMEL, G., and PRAHALAD, C. K. (1994). *Competing for the Future*. Boston: Harvard Business School Press.

INSEAD (1993). 'The Inchcape Group (A): The End of an Era'. Case study No. 04/93–317.

—— (1997). 'The Acer Group: Building an Asian Multinational'. Case study No. 01/98–4712.

—— (1998). 'E*Trade, Charles Schwab and Yahoo!: The Transformation of On-line Brokerage'. Case study No. 05/98–4757.

KENNEDY, C. (1996). 'Can Two Hongs Get It Right?' *Director*, Feb.: 34–40.

LEONARD-BARTON, D. (1995). *Wellsprings of Knowledge*. Cambridge, Mass.: Harvard University Press.

LUBATKIN, M., and CHATTERJEE, S. (1994). 'Extending Modern Portfolio Theory to the Domain of Corporate Strategy: Does it Apply?' *Academy of Management Journal*, 37: 109–36.

McNULTY, C. A. R. (1977). 'Scenario Development for Corporate Planning'. *Futures*, Apr.: 14–22.

MARKIDES, CONSTANTINOS C. (2000). *All the Right Moves*. Boston: Harvard Business School Press.

NAISBITT, JOHN (1984). *Megatrends*. New York: Simon & Schuster.

SCHOEMAKER, P. J. (1990). 'Strategy, Complexity and Economic Rent'. *Management Science*, 36/10 (Oct.): 31–43.

WILLIAMSON, P. J. (1999). 'Strategy as Options on the Future'. *Sloan Management Review*, 40/3 (Spring): 117–26.

PART VI

FLEXIBILITY

CHAPTER 30

GAME THEORY IN STRATEGY

J. H. POWELL

30.1 INTRODUCTION

THE contribution of game theory to our understanding of economic and other social processes during the latter half of the twentieth century has been immense and even a superficial survey of the associated literature is a task beyond the limits of this chapter. Instead, we shall concentrate on an understanding of the relevance of certain key types of game to strategy. For example, we will examine the relevance of *iterated games* to the reputation-building process in an industry. Stylized games like *Chicken* and *Rendezvous*, where participants are, respectively, in irremediable opposition and in complete (but defective) cooperation, mirror many strategic processes and inform our thinking about pre-commitment and norms of expectation, respectively. Examination of situations where equilibrium among the participants is achieved by adopting an evolutionary stable strategy (*Hawks and Doves*) shapes our thinking about the level of analysis of our strategic intent. Lastly, the latest methods of representing specific conflict/cooperation relationships between companies are discussed in order to show that game theory is capable of doing more than discussing strategic situations in general, and can, in fact, be used for specific action planning.

30.2 The Development of Game Theory

30.2.1 The Games We Play

Man has played games for many thousands of years. Bronze Age graves, for example, have been found containing a simple pebble-moving game related to the modern-day African game of *mancala*. Generally speaking, these pastimes involve direct (if stylized) confrontation between the participants: what one player wins the other loses. The games we consider here, however, are neither so trivial in their effect nor so unidimensionally confrontational. Like the relations between companies, where a competitor in one situation can be a partner in another, real-life games are an intimate mixture of cooperation and conflict.

The essential concept of a game in the sense we understand it here is that two or more players are struggling over a limited (but not necessarily fixed) resource. The struggle is to win resources by achieving a cooperative agreement and/or by application of some sort of force. An example might be two companies seeking to agree over the work-share of an important project. Coercion is undoubtedly present, but there is nevertheless a sincerity of intent, since, if they do not agree a work-share, they are unlikely to be able to implement the project. A second example of this hybrid cooperative/competitive behaviour is the struggle for a number of companies to control market share. To the extent that the market is fixed in size, they are undoubtedly in direct opposition one with the other. To the extent, however, that they can cooperate (even tacitly and implicitly) to increase the total size of the market, say by introducing a new technology or de facto standard desired by the customer, they are in cooperation.

The early work on game theory was carried out by von Neumann and Morgenstern (1944). The scope of its attention is interesting. It deals with both parlour games, such as poker, and with more 'businesslike' games such as bargaining and the formation of coalitions in negotiation. Many of the contemporary themes of game theory as a part of economics can be traced back to this important work, but as we look back today on the scope of game theory, it has a breathtaking reach which it would have been difficult to predict at its birth.

Game theory probably reached its apotheosis, at least in public perception, in the 1960s, when, led by the work of Thomas Schelling (1960) and the RAND corporation, it was seen as enormously influential in the formation of the grand nuclear strategy of the Cold War. The essential idea of 'strategic' thinking, in the strict sense of seeking a 'self-consciously interactive' solution (Ghemawat 1997: 8) stems from this era. The concept of zero-sum games, where the resources fought for by the participants are fixed, achieved common usage as a proxy for the mutually assured destructive intent of the nuclear stand-off. Game theory's role as a means of understanding military and global political conflict still con-

tinues, but we shall concentrate on the more general economic and social applications.

The strongest line of development from von Neumann and Morgenstern's seminal work has been in the application of game theory to strictly economic problems, to the extent that in 1994 the Nobel Prize in Economic Science went to three game theoreticians, Nash, Harsanyi, and Selten. The work of these three, together with that of Shapley reflects the enormous progress made by economics in addressing general technical questions of game theory, but thousands of other papers reflect the search by economists for specificity and accuracy in their models. The spread of these models is very wide indeed, extensive work being carried out into, for example, negotiation and bargaining, voting power, sequential games (where moves are carried out in turn), infinite games, multi-person duels, the role of information, collective action in bargaining, and many other topics of a similar nature. To most strategic managers, however, these topics are largely inaccessible, since they are voiced in a mathematical language that only specialists can appreciate. Nevertheless, it would be an error to dismiss them as irrelevant to strategy, since the work underpins all of the more directed material accessible to the strategist.

A second line of development has been the application of game theory to more general social studies, exemplified by the work of Brams (1994) and Binmore (1994). Here we see a treatment less mathematical and dealing with such diverse topics as reputation, threat, deterrence, and altruism. Axelrod's (1984) study of cooperation among trading entities in a computer environment also falls within this category. An associated area of study is the application of game theory to biological evolutionary studies, one aspect of which is discussed below (in the game *Hawks and Doves*) when we examine the tactics and behaviour of birds in winning food in order to throw light on the extent to which we should see strategy as a reactive response to a series of specific situations or as a structure for the adaptation of policy. To use more familiar terminology, should we see our core competences as a bundle of skills allowing us to react successfully to a series of market situations or as a capacity at a higher level of analysis allowing us to adapt our strategies, or, indeed, our concept of what constitutes a strategy in response to the policy environment in the industry?

A third line of development has been in the generation of situation-specific models. Most of the economic and social models are, because of their purpose, archetypal in nature—they provide stereotypes of behaviour, which allows us to understand the essential structure of negotiations, for example—but, because of their need for generality, they do not often possess the specific detail needed for a particular management problem. This does not, of course, render them impotent. It is merely that their intent is descriptive rather than normative. Into this former category of specific models falls the work of Fraser and Hipel (1984), Howard (1971, 1998), and others (Bennett 1980, 1986; Powell 1999).

30.2.2 Classification of Games

It is useful to have some sort of method for classifying strategic games. One instinctively feels that there are inherent structural differences between:

(1) a number of competitors each simultaneously trying to decide on their investment strategies for product/market development; and

(2) two companies seeking to agree over work-share for one of a series of large projects.

In the first case information is very definitely not shared among the participants. Play is simultaneous, in that there is no natural ordering sequence of investment decisions for the group of competitors and the participants cannot (either by legislation or self-interest) have mutually binding agreements.

In the second case the players are part of a sequence of binding agreements, since they hope to cooperate in the future as well as on this particular project. They also have a much greater degree of sincere communication between them than in the first case. These considerations and others below form a sound basis for classifying games.

- *Are moves in the game sequential or simultaneous?* There is a distinct difference in thinking style between that required when you move and then the opponent moves, knowing what you have done, and when both players make their tactical choices simultaneously (or, more precisely, without prior knowledge of the other's choice). In the first case, the situation requires you to think '*What will my opponent do in reaction to my move?*' In the second, simultaneous, case you each have to decide what the opponent is going to do right now, but recognizing that each of you, in calculating your current move, will be taking into account that the other is predicting his opponent's (i.e. your) move.

    An example of the importance of sequential games is that of deciding whether first mover advantage can be realized when a number of firms attempt to enter a new market. On one argument, if a firm can defend aggressively the initial position (or indeed has a reputation for having defended a position aggressively in the past), there will be first mover advantage. Scale economies grow as initial market share is lifted by the initial rapid growth of an immature market and the first mover takes the rent on his or her entrepreneurial foresight. On other occasions, where the technical basis for the initial entry cannot be defended, the second mover has the advantage, since it may well be less costly to retro-engineer a product than to have invented and innovated it.

    A particularly rich case study of a sequential game covering the battle between BSB and Sky Television over the UK satellite TV market in the early 1990s can be found in Ghemawat (1997).

- *To what extent are the players competing or cooperating?* In some games the participants are struggling over a fixed asset and one player's gain is the other's

loss. Such a situation (known as zero-sum) necessarily leads to a degree of aggression not present where the contested resource is expandable through co-operation. This cooperation is not necessarily overt or even, on occasions, obvious to the participants. Take the case of companies selling competing project support software, say, a risk management tool. The market for these expensive software packages is limited by the major projects which are available for bidding, and so in some respects these companies compete in a zero-sum fashion and will be optimizing their moves so as to bring down the other as much as to enhance their own position, since these objectives amount to the same thing.

On further examination, however, the single project confrontation is seen to be part of a larger more cooperative game, since there is a component of one company's action which helps the other, since any market development activity helps all software manufacturers by raising the generalized perceived need among clients.

To see that such behaviour is truly strategic in nature, one should observe the advantage gained by large telecommunications companies such as BT who embraced enthusiastically the European PTT standard setting of the late 1980s, thereby gaining a considerable entry barrier in the subsequent battle for European telecommunications business. If you set the standard, you may well 'leak' some technical information to competitors, but collectively the early standard setters are better fitted to defend the technical position that they have collectively created. The latecomer has to invest to compensate.

- *Is the game a one-off or will the players meet again?* Whether or not the game is repeated bears enormously on the strategy for its solution. In situations where a one-off agreement has to be made, the temperature can become very high indeed. Any takeover, for example, where the negotiators do not expect to gain any position in the new company, say because they will be retiring on their share options, is likely to be more aggressive than one where the direct initial confrontation is attenuated by knowledge that 'we all have to rub along' in the new company. Behaviour of participants is, therefore, altered if they expect to have to use concepts like trust or reputation in their future business dealings. On the other hand, if, as in the stock markets of the 1980s, the concept of dog eat dog applies, there is no future value in dealing other than aggressively with another participant.

  There is another reason why repeated trading with the same participants alters behaviour, and it bears strongly on our strategic behaviour. If we have traded with a company before, we have a better chance not only of predicting their behaviour but of gaining insight into their competences. It could be argued that avoiding trading with the same companies is a way of protecting the tacit skills of the firm. Certainly the reverse is true. It is a well-known tactic on the part of certain very large companies to carry out due diligence[1] on a

---

[1] The process of determining the value of a target company to protect shareholders' interests before a deal is struck.

target company a number of times. In a sense they are in bad faith on the first occasions. Even though they intend to make an offer eventually, they are using two separate mechanisms of influence—first, they are gaining a better view of the target's competences and hence a more accurate valuation. Secondly, they know that the behaviour of the target is altered because they, too, dare not assume that this is a single, one-off engagement between the management teams.

- *Do the players have the same information?* There are some parlour games, such as chess, where players possess the same information, but in business this is a rare situation indeed. Generally speaking, business people see information as one of the assets with which they manipulate situations towards their advantage. Hirschleifer and Riley's (1992) comprehensive book on the subject deals with many aspects of asymmetry of information in economic and business situations, mostly from a game theoretic viewpoint. We might, for example, seek to withhold from a potential strategic partner the true value which we place on the relationship in order to obtain favourable terms for alliance. We wish to release information to our advantage but to withhold information which acts against our interest, and so do others with whom we deal.

  Our deceit, however, is so natural and understandable that partners will be very sceptical of our utterances and will tend to rely only on those actions or commitments that are real. In particular, two phenomena known as *screening* and *signalling* model this need for us to judge others on deeds rather than words.

  Signalling is the act of a player who has more information than another and who wishes to convince the other players that he is not bluffing in claiming this valuable knowledge. In order to be convincing, the first player must carry out an act which can only be interpreted as being in his interest if the claim to knowledge is, in fact, correct. Let us imagine that we are trying to convince predators that we are determined to protect our position. One component of an entry barrier is well understood to be the willingness of an incumbent to react aggressively to intrusion, say by prompt and aggressive court action to protect a patent. We could make loud noises in the press, but this could be interpretable as bluff. Instead, we recruit expensive patent lawyers, saying in effect, 'Look, we are going to react aggressively to any attack on our patent. If we were bluffing, it would not be worth our while having this high paid help, but because we are going to defend our position it makes sense for us to make the commitment.' *Screening*, used in the sense of testing or filtering, is the demand by a less-informed participant that the other make an objective commitment that cannot be interpreted as bluff.

- *Can the rules of the game be changed?* Most business games involve an establishment of the rules prior to some actual play, and if those rules are not in our favour, self-evidently we will be put at a disadvantage. Strategically, therefore, it is

important to take part in the pre-game that sets those rules. Many takeover battles in restricted markets have a pre-game component where the Mergers and Monopolies Commission is asked by one contender or another to rule on whether a bid would be allowed. Usually the issue is whether an acquisition by the potential buyer would create an inappropriate domination of the market. There are many examples of this, including the break-up of the Ferranti companies in the mid-1990s and the hostile bid by Royal Bank of Scotland for NatWest bank in December 1999. In some cases (and Ferranti is a good example), winning or losing the pre-game is tantamount to winning or losing the game itself because if a takeover were allowed in principle, the subsequent bidding war would be a foregone conclusion because of the superior financial strength and commitment of one of the parties.

The European PTT standard setting discussed briefly above can also be seen as a pre-game.

- *Are cooperative agreements binding?* There is a convention in game theory that situations where the parties are able to enter into enforceable agreements to take joint action are called *cooperative* games whereas those where the parties cannot enter into an enforceable agreement are called *non-cooperative* games. This is rather misleading, since it seems to imply that no cooperation can result without binding agreements. This is not the case. It is perfectly possible for parties to agree on joint action in the non-cooperative case, so long as it remains in their individual and separate interests to act in the agreed (but non-enforceable) fashion. One might think that the majority of business situations are, in this sense, cooperative ones, but very often agreements with very powerful bodies such as governments are so unbalanced that they become in effect non-cooperative games. A small company carrying out consultancy work for a foreign government might think that the government will be bound by normal rules of commercial contracting. This is not the case necessarily, and the government may be forced by the actions of its own legislature to renege on a contract signed. Any assumption that a game is cooperative should be carefully audited; we are far better seeking stable solutions which maintain agreements through beneficial self-interest rather than relying on externally stabilizing influences. An example of this is two firms setting out on a strategic relationship, say to share markets or bundle deliverables. Of course, they will establish a legal agreement between them, but the real stability in the relationship is produced by early establishment of jointly beneficial business, so that they each see a benefit in making the relationship work.

30.3 Strategic Action: Cooperation and Conflict

30.3.1 General versus Specific

Game theory's relevance to strategy does, of course, depend on what one means by strategy. The approach taken here is that the remit of strategy is not merely the long-term, wide span of control of the affairs of companies, but also includes the management of short-term events, often involving relatively limited resources, on which the future of the firm can, nevertheless, turn. Certainly game theory has a role to play at this level of analysis, providing generalized descriptive advice which allows us to make sense of the actions of others in an aggregated sense. Rather than model the behaviour or hypothesize about the motivations of specific competitors, we discuss them as archetypes. Thus, in the examples already given, the concept of pre-games can inform our general thinking about how we approach any attempted takeover, namely as a multi-stage engagement.

Not all strategy is of that aggregated type, however. Just as in warfare, where strategy is generally seen to involve the wide sweep of whole armies over continents, there are occasions when a small band of determined men[2] can turn a war. Similarly, in business strategy there will be occasions where an isolated relatively small-scale event (the failure to take over a company, the establishment of a PTT standard) can turn the future for a company. It is unwise to concentrate exclusively upon the generally applicable strategic theory at the expense of the specific interaction which may prove to be of critical importance. It is wise to distinguish between the small and the unimportant.

The difficult thing, naturally, is to determine which specific events are the most important. In the main part, such insight marks out the strategic mind from the more mundane and is a matter of subjective capacity, but the interaction between scenario planning, a ubiquitous approach to future sensemaking, and discrete space games, discussed below, presents some prospect of assisting us in this task. Here we see a game theoretical modelling approach to specifics being placed within a more subjective, global view of the future, so that the former provides the necessary detail to produce management action plans while the latter forms the context for that specific modelling.

30.3.2 Nature of Strategic Cooperation/Conflict

The relations between companies at the strategic level are not to be understood as either wholly conflictual or wholly cooperative. If we consider the nature of the

---

[2]   ...or indeed, a band of small determined men.

relationship between an important buyer and a critical supplier, we see that it is an intricate dance, where both are bound into cooperation because of the costs of disengaging. The buyer would bear the extra costs of setting up anew the quality standards already in place with the incumbent supplier and that supplier would bear the costs of having to change to meet the demands of a new buyer, to say nothing of the costs of finding that new buyer in the first place. They are, however, to some extent also in conflict since, simplistically, the one wants to supply at a high price and the other to buy at a low price.

Where there is a degree of mutuality, communication between the participants will be freer than where conflict is present, and this freedom and sincerity of communicative regard lead to accessibility of one party's rationality by the other.[3] Since game theory generally relies on an assumption of economic rationality on the part of the participants, this is an important issue. The structuring capacity of game theory provides us with a means of judging the validity of our assumptions about the other's rationality. Signalling and screening are examples of this process. Where communication is defective, game theoretic models provide us with the basis for predicting another's behaviour and consequently of hypothesizing about their otherwise inaccessible value system.

30.4 KEY CONCEPTS OF GAME THEORY

30.4.1 Normal and Extensive Form

Table 30.1 shows a duopoly game in what is known as normal or matrix form. It represents the investment choices for two companies in an existing market, namely *invest in process* to reduce price, *invest in quality* to improve differentiation, or make *no investment*. Along the left-hand side are the tactical choices for Row Inc. (who chooses which row of the matrix is played) and along the top are the choices for Column PLC (who chooses which column is played). Each cell of the matrix contains the return to Row and Column, respectively, as a percentage of the existing market. Because of the different inherent capabilities of the firm the pay-offs are not symmetrical. If both choose *no investment*, the entry barriers to a new entrant will fall and so the bottom right-hand cell shows a reduced total return to the existing sellers of 30 + 30 = 60%. The game is thus not zero-sum.

---

[3] The reverse is easy to see. If we are not in sincere communicative regard with another, there is a real possibility that, since we will have defective information on the value system of the other, we will judge actions which are, in fact, consistent with the other's value system, as irrational because they do not comply with our erroneous assumption of the other's value system.

Table 30.1 Normal form game of product/market investment, pay-offs to
(Row, Column), respectively

		Column PLC		
		Invest in process	Invest in quality	No investment
Row Inc	Invest in process	(50, 50)	(30, 70)	(85, 15)
	Invest in quality	(60, 40)	(45, 55)	(80, 20)
	No investment	(25, 75)	(20, 80)	(30, 30)

What should they do? Column figures this way. 'If I look at each column in turn I can determine the worst thing that could happen if I make each choice. If I pick *invest in process*, my worst case is if Row chooses *invest in quality*, which gives me a return of 40%. If I choose *invest in quality* Row could choose *invest in quality*, too, in which case I would get a market share of 55%. If, finally, I choose *no investment*, Row might choose *invest in process*, when I would get only 15%. My safest choice, then, is to choose *invest in quality*, so that I will get at least 55%.'

Row, by similar reasoning, also reaches the conclusion that the safest bet is to *invest in quality*. This type of interactive arguing is characteristic of simultaneous games and is often called mini-max reasoning, since it seeks the least worst solution under uncertainty about the competitor's tactics. Note that the reasoning does not depend on Column assuming that Row moves later or earlier. It is as if the moves are made simultaneously, although in practice it may be that they are sequential, but no one notices the effect in the market until after the investment is made.

If the investment decisions were made sequentially, one could draw the matrix out in what is called an extensive form. Figure 30.1 shows the same game, but this time assuming that Row moves first and Column has the advantage of responding when Row's move is known.

Row now thinks in this fashion. 'If I choose *invest in process* Column would be stupid not to choose *invest in quality* for a return of 70%. If I choose *invest in quality* Column will have to choose *invest in quality* too, since this gives them the greatest return of 55%. If I choose *no investment*, Column will gain a 80% market share by choosing to *invest in quality*. The best of these for me is if I *invest in quality*, and Column does the same, giving me a return of 45% and Column 55%.' Note that the style of thinking here is subtly different, since in each conditional case, Row can know what Column would have done in response to Row's initial move. In a sense Row is 'rolling back' from the twigs of the tree to determine the best first move, and this process can be done whatever size of tree is being considered.

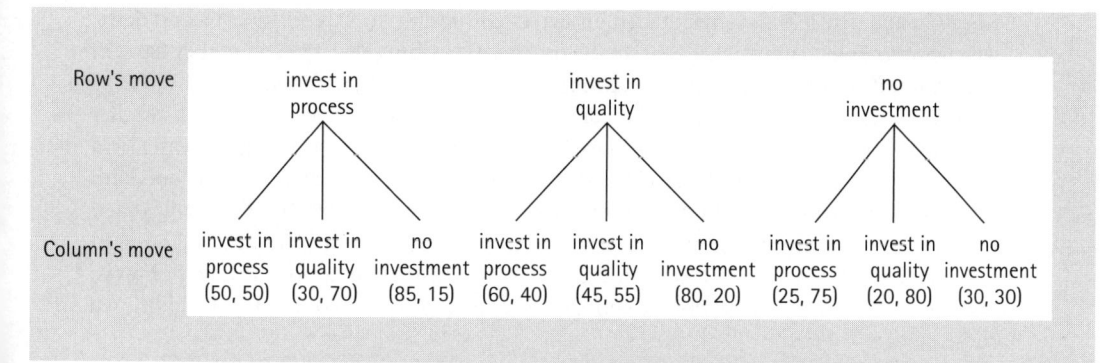

Fig. 30.1 Extended game tree for product/market investment game, payoffs to (Row, Column) respectively

30.4.2 Equilibrium

The concept of equilibrium in game theory is a central one, and presents very knotty problems mathematically. We can see its essence, however, in the simple, stylized game of Table 30.1. An equilibrium solution is a set of tactical choices by the participants such that no party is motivated to move away through their own action alone. Consider the game of Table 30.1, and look at the options for each player with respect to the central cell (*invest in quality, invest in quality*). Column has the option of moving left or right, but in each case the market share is reduced from 55%. Similarly, Row could move up or down, but in each case the return will be either 30% or 20%, both of which are less than the return to Row Inc. of 45% in the central cell.

In many cases an equilibrium solution is not found in this simple form and what is called a mixed strategy has to be adopted. This occurs when making any single choice makes one predictable, and the best tactic is to choose a judicious random mixture of tactical choices in order to mislead the competition.[4]

30.4.3 Iterated games

Some games only exhibit stability when played over and over again. Consider Table 30.2, an example of the ubiquitous *Prisoners' Dilemma*, originally described in terms of two criminals in separate cells deciding whether to betray one another and turn Queen's evidence. It portrays the choices to CheatCo Ltd and TrustCo Inc. with respect to their adherence to an agreement prior to its being formalized. The situation is this:

---

[4] Penalty takers in soccer do not always choose the same side, and neither do the goalkeepers in response. They are both adopting mixed strategies.

CheatCo and TrustCo have negotiated an agreement jointly to exploit their technologies, which are complementary. Naturally, in the process of reaching that agreement they have, in good faith, exposed certain of their capabilities to the other. One of them, say CheatCo, is then approached by a third party who alleges that TrustCo is in conversation with another company with a view to reneging on CheatCo. If TrustCo were to sign an agreement with a third party, they would already have the advantage of the information released in good faith during the negotiation. The third party offers a similar arrangement to CheatCo, saying that it may not be quite as advantageous to CheatCo to renege than to stay with TrustCo, but how can CheatCo be sure TrustCo will remain loyal? Asking TrustCo, of course, will be pointless, because if they were untrustworthy enough to renege, lying would be of little additional consequence.

Should CheatCo themselves renege on the agreement with TrustCo, and betray TrustCo's good faith for the greater gain of the new agreement?

Table 30.2 shows the dilemma. The cells contain the pay-offs to TrustCo and CheatCo, respectively. If they both remain in cooperation (call this C,C) they will gain $100 m each, whereas if either defects (C,D or D,C), the defector will gain more ($130 m), while the betrayed partner will get only $50 m. CheatCo therefore thinks, 'If I remain in good faith and TrustCo betrays us, we will lose heavily. I have no choice therefore but to cheat.' TrustCo, in the meantime, is going through the same thought process. They do not know whether CheatCo are really in good faith, and so have little choice but to renege as well. As a result, neither party sticks with the agreement (D,D), even though the total profit would have been greatest and each now does worse than if the interim agreement had stuck.

Why then do we not behave in this fashion? There are a number of reasons. First, the game structure is somewhat artificial, in that we have the cover of non-disclosure agreements precisely to prevent this situation. Secondly, rightly or wrongly, companies do build up personal trust between negotiators, so that they feel that they have insight into the integrity of their opposite numbers. Most significantly, however, is the effect of iteration. Imagine what would happen if TrustCo and CheatCo were to look ahead and realize that they were inevitably going to be put into such situations of mutual exposure to betrayal over and over

Table 30.2 *Prisoner's dilemma* game, pay–offs to (TrustCo, CheatCo), respectively

		CheatCo	
		Cooperate	Defect
TrustCo	Cooperate	(100, 100)	(50, 150)
	Defect	(150, 50)	(80, 80)

again, perhaps because the industry contained only a few mutually dependent firms. They would then come to the conclusion that, because in the long run it is better to take the return of $100 m each from cooperating rather than the $80 m from defecting, it is better to stick with the agreement rather than take the short-term advantage of cutting and running.

It is worth noting, however, that if a participant believes that this is the last time the agreement will be offered, it is advantageous at that point to renege. It is only if they expect to trade repetitively for the indefinite future that the iterated Prisoners' Dilemma (or IPD, as it is called) has a solution stable in (C,C), where both parties keep their words.

30.4.4 Information and Common Knowledge

Information can be argued to be at the very heart of game theory and of strategy itself. Whole topics in strategy concern themselves with the approaches needed to gain long-term advantage through technology strategy and core competence approaches in general. These are deliberate attempts to gain an asymmetry in information in the strategic game which can then be turned into competitive advantage. Many excellent texts deal with the game theoretic aspects of this endeavour, including those of Hirschleifer and Riley (1992) and of Rasmusen (1989).

An important issue in strategy is the extent to which the players see the rules of the game as well defined, or whether they are able to invent a new set of options which the other players do not see. The important work of Bennett (1980) and others (Rosenhead 1989) in hypergames, in which different players may see and use different tactical options, provide an important link between the generalizable archetypal games of economics and the strategists' need for specific answers to specific problems. Even hypergame structures, however, cannot insulate us against the consequences of failing to see tactical options on the part of an opponent which redefine the very structure of the game.

30.4.5 Rationality

Game theory generally makes fairly sweeping assumptions about the rationality of participants. It is almost always assumed that players have common knowledge of the rules, and that each is attempting to maximize a return, usually expressed financially, by the end of the game. Players are assumed to be faultless calculators of what is best for them, too. While this may appear somewhat optimistic, it does at least produce an analysis where the opponent is using the best armoury at his disposal. There are other assumptions about players' abilities to see a number of

moves ahead and it is not necessary to assume that this decision horizon is limitless. In practice the problem is to know on what basis a limited decision horizon may be assumed.

It is important, also, to understand what this rationality concept does not assume. It is not necessary, for example, to exclude acting in someone else's interest, or to assume that they have to act solely on a financial basis. The weighting of options for OXFAM, for example, would have to include some measure of the emancipatory benefit to be gained by others through a particular business posture, but in all other respects game theoretic concepts just as easily apply to the cooperation between charities and to their battles for the compassionate pound in our pockets as between more conventional profit-making organizations.

30.5 SOME IMPORTANT TYPES AND EXAMPLES OF GAMES

30.5.1 Chicken—Pre-Commitment

Two companies, AspirantCo and ImproverCo are addressing a new foreign market where there is no opportunity for collaboration. Entering the new market will require investment, but if they have a free run at the market the investment will be less than if they both attempt to enter. We can model this situation by a simultaneous move, normal form game like Table 30.3.

The pay-offs reflect the fact that if the market entry is unopposed, the entrant will make a profit of $1 m and the declining company will lose credibility if it is seen not to have taken advantage of what in retrospect will be seen by shareholders to have been a

Table 30.3 Market entry *Chicken* game, pay-offs to (ImproverCo, AspirantCo), respectively

		AspirantCo	
		Fight	Decline
ImproverCo	Fight	(−2, −2)	(1, −1)
	Decline	(−1, 1)	(0, 0)

perfectly viable opportunity. If, on the other hand, both companies decline, the shareholders will be more likely to take the view that the opportunity was never a viable one and the damage will be less. We also assume that it is worse for the two companies to compete in the market because the cost of fighting is less than the likely return.

A game of this structure has no equilibrium, since it is in each party's interest to move away from any emergent agreement. For example, if we start with a position (*Decline, Decline*) where neither exploits the market, each party, separately, has a motivation to move either to *Fight, Decline* or to *Decline, Fight*. AspirantCo has the power to move to *Decline, Fight* for a gain of $1 m (remember that neither will care about the other's gain or loss). Similarly, ImproverCo could move unilaterally to *Fight, Decline* at a gain of $1 m. *Decline, Decline* is therefore not a stable position in that at least one of the parties will have both the motivation and the unilateral power to move away from it. Similar arguments show that none of the other states is stable.

This game is well known in the game theory literature. It is called *Chicken* and derives from a potentially fatal teenage pastime of driving cars down a narrow road towards one another. A player wins if he does not swerve. Swerving is seen as a loss of face. Similarly in our market entry game of *Chicken*, declining to enter when the other company makes a success of the prospect is bad for our shares. We swerved and lost face.

It would be a mistake to think that there is no solution to the game, however. There is a kind of solution, and it informs our strategic thinking about pre-commitment to action. Morris (1992) discusses the 'super-tactic' of pre-commitment, which, in the context of the teenage tearaways, involves being seen to be totally committed to not swerving. The player chains the wheel in the forward position and arranges to be seen to be drinking heavily from a bottle of spirits, in order to give the strong impression that no rationality will be brought to bear. Hence, the other player must assume that he will employ *Fight* and that as a result the only rational response will be to *Decline*. While amusing in a macabre sort of way, Morris's super-tactic does work. In market terms, we would replace the fixing of the steering wheel by a set of prior commitments to exploit the market, say by being seen shaking hands with the President of the country and signing a committing technology transfer deal to which we are committed *even if we choose not to enter the market*. Thus, we are committed to fighting and our competitor will see that he has no option rationally but to accept our commitment and decline to fight.

In strategic terms, showing prior commitment in situations where our actions could be disarmed through the fear of consequences can be seen as raising entry barriers, showing determination in the face of any subsequent action by the competitor. It also has an effect on companies' choice of differentiation basis when high profile research and development programmes signal commitment to a particular line of differentiation, sending signals to warn off others who might

otherwise seek to share an undifferentiated market. An example of this is the distinct separation between US military aircraft programmes (concentrating on conventional high agility fighters) and UK military aircraft R&D (specializing in VTOL[5] aircraft such as the Harrier). The United States could have chosen to fight, and develop VTOL technology, but in the face of a determined and very public espousal of VTOL development by both the UK industry and government, it decided instead to take a licence (in effect) to build the McDonnell Douglas AV8B.

30.5.2 Evolutionary Games

So far we have considered only those situations where individual players make rational decisions on the basis of their economic self-interest. We have noted that the assumption is always that the players will behave as if they had perfect calculating ability; that they both see and act upon whatsoever tactical choices are best for them. To reflect our imperfections in the real world, however, we need a model which reflects what happens when a population displays different game-theoretic behaviours, some successful, some less so and then have the opportunity to learn from their experiences.

The approach developed for this purpose is known as evolutionary game theory, and it represents an important means by which strategists can understand the growth of strategic concepts in industries.

General evolutionary theory relies on three elements:

- variation of behaviour or response to the environment (mutation)
- testing for success (fitness)
- retention of the effect of success and failure (heredity).

In our vocabulary, members of an industry will try out variations of strategic approaches, will succeed or fail thereby, and on that basis of perceived fitness others in the industry will adopt the successful approaches and the successful approaches will propagate.

The essential difference between this approach and that of conventional game theory is that in evolutionary game theory the behaviour (known as the phenotype) is a result of something inherent in the member of the population whereas in the latter, the behaviour is the result of calculation. The focus of evolutionary game theory is how populations behave rather than tracking the rational decision-making of an individual. One starts with a population containing certain proportions of members following one behaviour or another and observes how those proportions alter as the effects of the success of the various behaviour come to bear. A behaviour is referred to as being an *evolutionary stable strategy* if a population

---

[5] Vertical take-off and landing.

adopting that behaviour cannot be invaded by a mutant behaviour. It should be noted that the mechanism by which successful strategies come to represent relatively greater fractions of the whole is fundamentally different from the mechanism in biology. In the latter the mechanism is breeding success; here it is the observation and adoption of successful behaviours by participants. In a sense this book is part of that process. To the extent that you, as a business person, are convinced by the case studies and theories presented here, you will adopt them and they will form thereby a slightly increased fraction of the whole body of accepted knowledge about business strategy. The emergent topic of memetics (Blackmore 1999) discusses the ways in which identifiable components of our assumptions and knowledge propagate around a population and offers some promise of a coherent theory of knowledge propagation around a knowledge community.

30.5.2.1 *Prisoners' Dilemma—Cooperation and Reputation*

The Prisoners' Dilemma discussed above had an undesirable, but perfectly rational solution; although the defection of both parties did not lead to an attractive result, the players were forced by their inability to communicate and hence achieve a binding agreement into acting in their local self-interests. In other words, if we are never to meet our prospective business partner again, acting in our narrow and ephemeral self-interest pays more than adhering to any higher and longer term moral imperative. Principles cost money, at least in the short term and without the prospect of retaliation.

An examination into the effect of playing the game over and over again, however, gives a very different result. The work of Robert Axelrod (1984) in studying the performance of computer opponents trading in an evolutionary computer environment is accessible and very relevant to relationship strategies in business. Axelrod set up a population of algorithms trading one with another according to a Prisoners' Dilemma pay-off matrix. Participants remembered the past history of trading, so that if you had previously reneged on me I would be able to recall it. That then leaves open the prospect of expanding the tactical options available to participants beyond the simple decision to cooperate or defect. Now we can adopt policies which react to previous trading experience. For example, one policy might be *Never Forgive*, where once another player defected on you, you would always defect in subsequent trading with that player. Another might be *Tit for Tat*, where whenever a fellow trader defected, you would defect only on the next trading opportunity. Axelrod encouraged the readers of a popular science magazine to offer policies and trialled them over a large number of trading events in his computer environment.

The most successful policy was *Tit for Tat*, in that over many trades a player who followed that policy gained the greatest return over any other policy. Axelrod then set up another computer environment and invited participants to propose policies aimed specifically at beating *Tit for Tat*. Again, *Tit for Tat* won, primarily because

the programmes that beat it only did so by small amounts, and they did not do at all well against other policies. *Tit for Tat* also did well in an evolutionary computer environment, where populations of policies were played against one another to see which were the most successful. In this environment, too, although *Tit for Tat* did not do well at first, as other 'nastier' policies met up with other vindictive policies, they effectively neutralized one another and *Tit for Tat* came through as the dominant phenotype in the population.

This has something to say about our attitudes to industrial (network) strategy. We rely to a great, often hidden extent on trust and reputation in our strategic intercourse. Clearly, if we are to establish good trading relations with strategic partners we need to have mutual trust, but we are often tempted to renege on agreements for short-term gains. We should not do so if we are likely to be meeting those partners again and again in our industry. Similarly, if we are cheated upon, we should not leave the sin unchallenged as such behaviour will indicate no penalty for subsequent potentially unreliable partners.

30.5.2.2 *Hawk–Dove game*

The *Hawk–Dove* game is one of the earliest in evolutionary game theory. It deals with a population of birds who inhabit forest clearings where they compete for food. Whenever two birds alight on a piece of food in the clearing, they fight or share the food depending on their type. If a bird predisposed to fighting (a Hawk) meets a non-fighting bird (a Dove), the Hawk wins most of the food. If, however, two Hawks arrive at the food they will use more energy fighting for the food than it contains and they will both lose. Similarly, if two Doves arrive at a piece of food, they will have to share the food, but they will not use any energy fighting. Given that better-fed birds will breed more, how will the populations of Hawks and Doves evolve over time?

The analogy here is with firms who have to decide how to behave when a market opportunity presents itself. To what extent should they fight for the market opportunity and to what extent should they only prosecute opportunities where the opposition is not aggressive? One can see that a single Hawk in a population of

Table 30.4 *Hawk–Dove* game, pay-offs to (A, B), respectively

		B	
		hawk	dove
A	hawk	(−1, −1)	(9, 1)
	dove	(1, 9)	(5, 5)

Doves will always win relative to the Doves, because it will always win all the food whereas each Dove–Dove meeting implies a sharing of the food. If, however, a Dove finds itself in a population of Hawks at first glance it will always lose, in that it will be left only with the scraps after each engagement, which the Hawk wins. The issue here, though, is not the absolute increase in energy gained by the Dove, but the amount gained relative to the Hawks, who will be starving because they are using more energy fighting than the food is worth. The Dove is making a small net relative gain and as a result it breeds slightly better than a Hawk, and the population of Doves increases.

The population settles out into a balance between Hawks and Doves. If the population swings towards one type of behaviour, the other phenotype will be slightly advantaged and the fraction of that behaviour will increase to bring the balance back. In corporate terms, if we are in a very aggressive environment where projects appear in a sequence and other firms always fight to the death over work-share, we may well be better off taking a somewhat supine position, accepting a smaller 'piece of the action' but at smaller cost to ourselves. For example, some buyers demand 'fly-offs'[6] when contracting larger projects. One response is to put investment into this highly uncertain bidding process and take the competitors head-on and the other is to look for small workshares from the resulting winners, taking a smaller return, but using much less resource in the process. Contractors in these environments can be clearly seen to fall into two groups—those who fight aggressively for leadership (i.e. majority work-share) and those who act as substantial subcontractors for, say, production or specialized contributions. Often these 'Doves' are as large and successful as the 'Hawks' but their core competences are very different, the latter having highly developed bidding teams skilled in fighting the 'Hawk–Hawk' game.

30.5.3 Bargaining

Bargaining in game theory means the agreement to share a fixed resource among parties—it is a partitioning exercise rather than necessarily the haggling which is its common language meaning. Western approaches to bargaining between parties assume that each party is out to get the most at the expense of another. Oriental concepts, however, stress that each party should leave the bargaining table happy with the result. Game theory has components of both.

Bargaining is, indeed, a strategic concept. The decision of how long to wait for strategic agreement to bundle technologies in the face of a rising risk that a third company will beat you to the market meets all the recognized criteria for a strategic

---

[6] A contracting scheme where bidders have to make huge risk investments to develop prototypes which are then trialled one against the other, the winner taking full control of the project.

issue. It is of long-term importance, it involves large resources, it has high uncertainty, etc. Similarly, obtaining a fair division of resources within the divisionalized firm is not just a matter for a synoptic CEO to determine. The CEO may propose, but the divisional MDs dispose. If they are not content with the allocation of resources, they are unlikely to be following a business plan with which they can have confidence. Consequently, the allocation is a negotiation, albeit one which is strongly shaped by the corporate centre.

A key concept is the BATNA (Thompson 1998: 24). Standing for *Best Alternative To a Negotiated Agreement*, it is the best you can get if you do not agree. Imagine you are the representative of a firmware company which has developed an operating system for a massively-parallel quantum computer. You are in negotiation with the brand new company formed by the inventors of the quantum computer. Together you can access a $10 billion market based on public key encryption, secure funds transfer, advanced aerodynamics, and electromagnetic calculations. If you try to sell your OS to another computer manufacturer the platform will be less capable, allowing you a share in a smaller market worth only $500 k. On the other hand, your potential computer partner cannot exploit his computer at all without an OS but will be able to apply for academic development funds for some $100 k. Your BATNA is $500 k and his is $100 k. Note that this is very different from the investment that each has made to get to the negotiation. You might each have invested equal amounts, say, $1 m each, but as far as the BATNA is concerned that, so to speak, is history.

Figure 30.2 shows a negotiation between two parties, A and B, who want to share an asset, V (say, the profits from a joint market exploitation). The axes represent the amounts each takes away from the negotiation. Clearly neither can take more than V, and so no agreement is possible above the line VV, but within the triangle OVV any agreement is feasible. Player A, however, will not agree if the agreement allocates her less than her BATNA, V_A and player B will not agree if she receives less than V_B. We can foresee that if the parties start at the worst situation for both, where they both achieve only their BATNAs, it is in their cooperative interest to move up and to the right towards the line VV, upon which all the best joint solutions will lie, since all of the profit V is then allocated. The best negotiated solution, F, will then lie along the intersection of a straight line through the BATNA point with the line VV. Note that this does not define the negotiated solution uniquely, since the slope of the line PF is not defined. This slope is set by the relative powers which the parties have over one another. It is easy to assume that in a 'fair' negotiation, this should be equal, so that they each take an equal part of that resource V over and above the BATNAs. Life, however, is not necessarily fair, and the different parties will have powers over one another which cannot be included in such a simple theory. For example, the negotiation may be between two companies who have existing contracts which are asymmetrical—one may be a supplier to a larger company, for example. Nevertheless, this simple negotiating model can tell us a number of relevant things about our strategic approach.

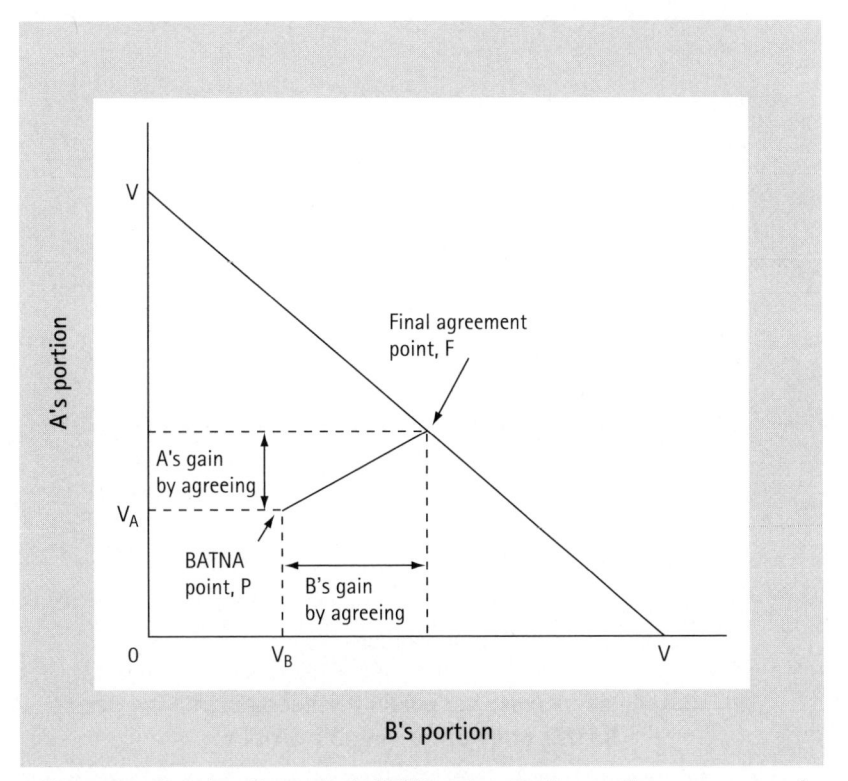

Fig. 30.2 Starting from the BATNA point, P, the parties move up and right towards a final negotiated position which is better for both of them than their BATNAs

First (as player A), we can base our strategy on increasing the slope of the line PF. This represents a straightforward increase in our negotiating power in the discussions. Apart from specific techniques used in the negotiation itself, which do not fall within strategy as generally understood, we can act strategically so as to place ourselves in a more persuasive position. For example, we might have access to competences either through our own organic development or through exterior relationships with partners, to which the other party to the negotiation does not have access. In this respect, then, core competence theory is seen not just as a process of winning and husbanding bundles of skills to improve competitive advantage per se, but also as a power play in obtaining advantageous relationships with partners.

Secondly, we can act strategically so as to increase our BATNA. This will move the BATNA point from P to P* (see Figure 30.3) and the resulting agreement can be seen to be more favourable to us, player A. What, strategically, would constitute a raising of our BATNA? Imagine that we are negotiating a joint entry to a foreign market with a prospective partner, who is bringing channels to market where we bring an existing product or technology. Perhaps we are thinking of jointly offering our product to the Japanese market, where knowledge of local distribution networks

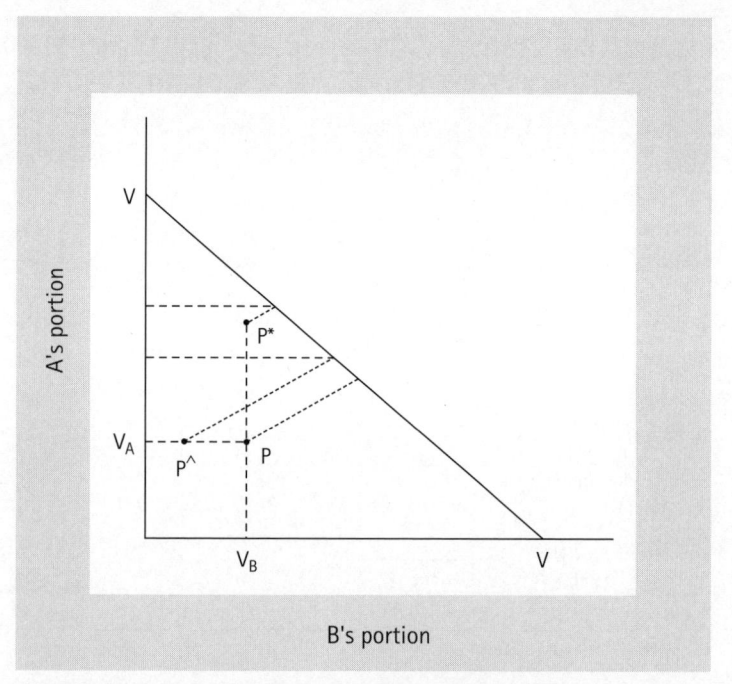

**Fig. 30.3 A can increase her portion either by increasing her
BATNA or by decreasing B's BATNA**

and practices is particularly difficult for a new entrant to access. If we have no other development path for our product, our BATNA is low—we have no alternative but to do a deal with somebody or we will not be able to realize fully the investment we have made in our product. To raise our BATNA we could carry out similar negotiations aimed at another market, say South America. By having a real alternative to doing the deal with our Japanese partner, we raise our BATNA and increase the likely value of the deal to ourselves. Such an argument would lead us, in terms of strategic product/market development, to adopt multiple opportunities and we would have to balance in our development strategy the advantages of being put into a good negotiating position against the inevitable costs of multiple options investigation.

Third, the result is likely to be more in our favour if we can find a way to reduce the other party's BATNA. Figure 30.3 shows that if we can move point P to the position $P^\wedge$ by reducing the value of the other party's fall-back position, we will gain in the final outcome. We might do this in our market exploitation example by tying an existing relationship into this negotiation, say, by pointing out to the other party that failure to agree a joint position here will endanger continuing work for them on existing products.

Negotiation and bargaining, then, can be seen to be of material importance to strategy, particularly in respect of network strategy and the externalities of the firm.

We have only been able to touch the surface of this complex topic and the interested reader is recommended to consult Leigh Thompson's comprehensive book on the topic (Thompson 1998), which deals not only with the game theoretic structure of negotiating, but also with the socio-dynamics and practicalities.

30.5.4 Rendezvous Games—Focal Points

A certain class of games, called assurance or rendezvous games, deals with situations where the participants wish to cooperate but are unable to communicate directly. An example often quoted (Jervis 1978) is the strategic relationship between the USSR and the US in the arms races of the last century. Each had the opportunity either to invest in strategic nuclear assets or to invest that fraction of their GDP in social improvement. There are two stable solutions: either both should invest in nuclear assets or both should not. Clearly the latter is the preferred solution, but because of the atmosphere of distrust and ideological conflict between the two super-nations, communication between them was necessarily defective. It could be argued that the ideological basis of their relationship provided a focal point of expectation of conflict, so that each could not believe that the joint social invest-ment solution was a safe one.

A game which examines this focal point issue in more detail is *Rendezvous*. Two parties, Emma and Dai, have arranged to meet in a particular city, say Cardiff, at noon on a specific date. On the way to the meeting each realizes that they have failed to specify where they are to meet. What should each do?

This is clearly a cooperative game where communication is defective. If we imagine that there only two places to meet in Cardiff (the steps of the National Museum and the main railway station, for example) we can see the essential structure of the game. See Table 30.5.

Each party now has a dilemma, since they each want to choose the same rendezvous as the other. The nature of the solution lies in understanding what

Table 30.5 *Rendezvous* game, pay–offs to (Emma, Dai), respectively

		Dai	
		Museum	Station
Emma	Museum	(10, 10)	(0, 0)
	Station	(0, 0)	(10, 10)

knowledge or preconceptions the other has. Dai (as one might imagine) knows Cardiff rather well, but Emma does not and Dai knows this. He therefore has to assume that Emma will not know of the National Museum as an obvious rendez-vous, and therefore will assume that she will go to the main railway station. Emma has no such choice to make. She does not know the city and therefore will choose some focal point obvious to anyone who does not know Cardiff. In this case, then, the game solves itself because of a peculiarity of the two parties, but in general the solution is more difficult and depends on the extent to which one player's focal points are accessible to the other. One can work to improve this visibility. A farsighted parent may well say to a child in a busy Christmas department store, 'If you get lost, go to the toy department and stay there. I'll find you', thus predeter-mining a focal point.

A number of strategic situations are structurally similar to the *Rendezvous* game, and the approach of establishing or discovering common focal points amongst groups of participants is helpful. Consider, for example, the behaviour of an industry consisting of prime contractors and subcontractors tendering together to a community of buyers. The civil engineering industry follows this form. In tendering for civil engineering contracts, buyers and contractors are concerned with (among other things) the management of project risk, and there have emerged a small number of risk management packages (ProMap, Risk Man, etc.) to help with this. Investment in each of these packages is demanding both in terms of initial investment in the software and in the extensive training required for engineering and project staff. It is not feasible, even for very large companies, to run more than one package. As a result the contractors can be viewed as being in a rendezvous game. The subcontractors and primes want the same risk management package in order to minimize nugatory investment, but each package has its advocates and each its detractors. In time, of course, de facto standards emerge whereby successful prime contractor/subcontractor teams succeed using particular approaches and propagate them thereby. One can view these dominant frames as the focal points of the *Rendezvous* game of software investment, and the wise subcontractor in such an environment spends time detecting the fashion in these affairs in order to provide a natural solution to a series of *Rendezvous* games with prime contractors.

Achieving agreement between SBUs on technology strategy in a divisionalized company is a further example of focal points. To the extent that the SBUs share natural foci of understanding, either in terms of desirable overall corporate object-ives or simply at the level of common technological frames of reference, agreement will be more easily reached between them, and it may well be more efficient for the corporate centre to concentrate upon engendering and uncovering focal points rather than attempting to prescribe the specific nature of the agreement to be reached.

30.5.5 Discrete Space Games—From the General to the Specific

It will not have escaped attention that, in the main part, the games described so far have presented generalized, almost archetypal, conclusions. They are very good at presenting generalizable results and patterns of thought but are rather less good at offering actions specific to a strategic problem. There is another group of games deriving from the operational research (OR) community (as opposed to economics) which are aimed at modelling specific situations, strategic in nature, but requiring detailed management agenda setting and action planning.

These OR game structures see the world as consisting of a network of states which may or may not be realized according to the various powers and motivations of the participants to bring them about. In many respects they present an extension of the scenario planning view of the world, where planning can be viewed as navigation around a set of futures. Our management agenda then consists of such things as deciding which of the futures we prefer, what we have to do to pursue trajectories which lead to those desired end-points, and what we have to do to unravel the plans of other parties who may wish to divert our progress.

In the games examined so far, the states of play have been defined by the tactical choices made by the players. An alternative view is that the tactics stem from the likely outcomes and our reaction to these likely states of affairs. In drama theory (Howard, Bennett, et al. 1992; Bennett and Howard 1996; Bennett and van Heeswijk 1997; Howard 1998), for example, players adopt positions identifying their initial and subsequent negotiation points, and analysis consists of examining the abilities of players to move between these positions in order eventually to come to some sort of resolution. A key element of the analysis is the identification and treatment of characteristic dilemmas for players. For example, a player may experience a *cooperation dilemma* when joint action is needed to move together with another player to a mutually advantageous new position. As in the Prisoners' Dilemma, there will be a natural suspicion of the other's intent and ability to renege to his short-term advantage. Drama Theory provides a structuring process by which these dilemmas can be resolved to provide a mutually beneficial (or at least stable) solution. The method has been applied to company situations and to political problems such as the recent Bosnian conflict and is frequently used in the military context. The episodic nature of negotiation, through initial exposure of positions, realization of dilemmas and resolution to outcomes is reflected naturally in the Drama Theory structure and, significantly, the game positions are not defined by the players' tactics, but rather the other way around. What the players have to do to resolve their dilemmas results from consideration of the game structure.

The same generative approach can be seen in Powergraph (Powell 1999). Here, the first step is to establish a set of possible outcomes for the situation which form a network of states. See Figure 30.4. This is done by consideration of the motives and

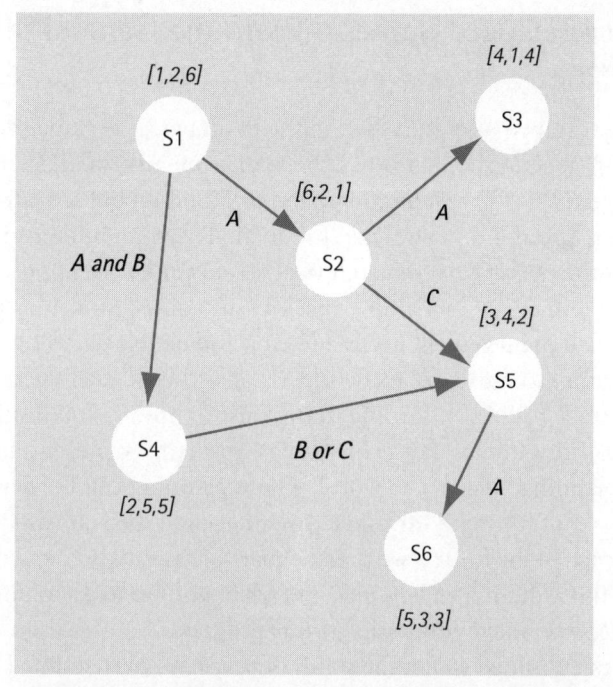

Fig. 30.4 Powergraph network structure. Players'
utilities for each state are shown thus: [A, B, C]. Here
A will choose to move from S1 to S2. C will choose
to move from S2 to S5. A will then choose
to move from S5 to S6

interests of the participants. Next we consider the ability of the participants to move the game from one state to another. Sometimes these transitions can be brought about by a player on her own, sometimes only in combination with others. A map of the conflict can then be drawn which shows the possible states of affairs and who has control over the transitions between those states. Consideration is then given to the preferences of the players between the various states. Clearly, if a player is to utilize his power to move from one particular state to another, this must be seen by him to be desirable as well as being within his power. Both power and motivation are necessary for a transition to take place.

The result is a kind of map of the game where the likely paths around the map can be examined. Even quite complex conflict/cooperative situations can be easily modelled. Using the map we can ask very directed questions leading to management action plans, such as:

- Bearing in mind the state(s) we prefer, what do we have to do in order to force the transitions we want? Whom (if anyone) do we have to carry with us?
- What can the competition do to prevent these transitions we desire? Whom can we influence to block those moves?

- What transitions will the competition be trying to engender? Who do they need to carry with them? What can we do to prevent these transitions?
- Can we create new states which resolve conflicts of interest and objective?
- These kinds of questions lead naturally to the very directed kind of action plans needed to manage high energy inter-company conflicts such as hostile takeovers, major project struggles, and the like.

Box 30.1 The Battle for Trafalgar

Situation

In early 1993 BAe Systems and Services were strengthening their position in the defence naval market and were tracking two major projects, a frigate, called at the time CNGF (Common New Generation Frigate) and a submarine, a replacement for the Trafalgar Class nuclear submarine called B2TC (Batch 2 Trafalgar Class). BAe had been expecting the CNGF programme to appear after the submarine tender, and so it came as a surprise when the CNGF programme took a leap forward. The company had to review its commitment to potential partners in the two parallel programmes.

The clear front runner on the submarine programme was Vickers Ship Engineering Limited (VSEL), a company with a good track record in submarine design and manufacture. Relationships between BAe and VSEL had been good, with a history of joint project work and a growing mutual respect stemming from common work on the feasibility phase of B2TC. VSEL were clear that they wanted BAe in their CNGF team because of BAe's surface weapons and system engineering capability. While VSEL were prepared to include BAe in 'their' submarine programme, and could see some advantages in a joint approach, they were confident about their ability to prosecute the submarine programme without major additional help. VSEL were determined to bid for both programmes.

On the frigate programme the situation was somewhat different. GEC Naval Systems, with their access to experienced shipyards, were the front runner, but perhaps not so clearly as were VSEL on the submarine programme. GEC saw advantages in having BAe on the frigate team. They were keen to deny VSEL any advantage on the submarine programme and could see their probabilities of a win on the submarine programme increasing if the innovative approaches of GEC and BAe were to be joined.

At a meeting to decide BAe's teaming, the Commercial Director offered the following argument. 'It doesn't make sense for us to bid with anyone but the most likely winner. As a result we should offer to team with GEC on the frigate and with VSEL on the submarine.' The Managing Director agreed. 'We have things to offer each of them and I don't intend to increase the risk of losing by going on either project to a likely loser.'

Reluctantly, the Project Director prepared work-share agreements which offered BAe's services to GEC on the frigate alone and to VSEL on the submarine alone.

Was the Commercial Director right?

The Explosion

The Managing Director spoke to GEC the following afternoon. They took the news fairly well that BAe were available for the frigate but not for the submarine.

At a big institutional dinner in London that evening, the BAe MD took the chance to break the good news to VSEL that BAe would be happy to join them in their submarine bid. Of course, they must understand that, as GEC were the front runners on the frigate, BAe would have to go with them. The VSEL Chairman was most unhappy. 'You expect us to include you in our submarine bid while you compete with us for the frigate business we desperately need to keep our yard open. I don't think so.'

The BAe MD retired to consider the position. If he now approached GEC for a position on the submarine as well, his negotiating position would be very weak.

What went wrong?

The Model

Figure 30.5 shows the Powergraph model of the dilemma.

There are seven states.

- *Start*   before any offer is made
- *Submarine only*   where BAe has approached VSEL alone
- *Frigate only*   where BAe has approached GEC alone
- *Split*   the commercial director's position, where GEC is the frigate part-
                     ner and VSEL is the submarine partner
- *Freeze-out*   where BAe has no position
- *GEC alliance*   joined with GEC on both projects
- *VSEL alliance*   joined with VSEL on both projects

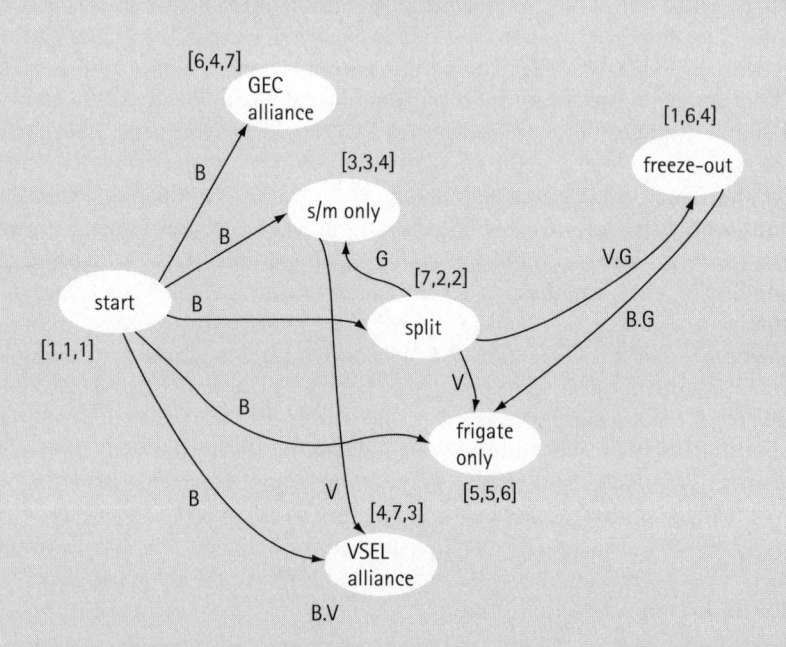

Fig. 30.5 Powergraph model of battle for Trafalgar. B = BAe, G = GEC, V = VSEL. Utilities of each state shown thus: [B, V, G]

The controlling players' symbols, *B*, *V*, and *G* are attached to the relevant transitions. The only transitions which are shown in this simplified diagram are those where a player has both the power to move and has the motivation so to do. Thus, we see that once BAe makes the *split* offer the other two players have control over the situation. VSEL, in particular, has the power to reject the *split* position and (because the chain of command was shorter) did so immediately, putting the game into the state *frigate only*, less desired by BAe than either of the alliance states. BAe could have achieved a state more highly valued (6 against 5) if they had offered an alliance to GEC straight away, but the game structure shows that

- *Split* is unstable
- once having given the initiative away by offering split, if VSEL reject the offer there is no recovery from the moderately acceptable *frigate only* position
- if GEC had acted to reject *split* uncharacteristically quickly, there was a recovery path to an alliance with VSEL.

What happened

BAe negotiated with GEC and achieved an adequate work share on the frigate programme. Their submarine market position was shaky and the continuing desire to play in this important market led to an abortive attempt to purchase VSEL.

Shortly after that attempted purchase the results of the submarine competition were announced.

GEC won on merit and price.

30.6 APPLICABILITY AND LIMITATIONS: A PATCHWORK OF THEORIES

Game theory is a way of thinking. It requires that we should take into account that we live and manage within a system structure, in which others have interests, some of them legitimate. Our actions are no longer to be seen as being optimizing in the limited sense that we decide what we want and then plan unilaterally to achieve it because other strategists are taking their own views, and we have no alternative but to take their actions into account. This system approach is what game theorists refer to as 'strategic thinking' and in many respects it aligns itself well with the relativist concepts of core competence, for example, in strategy. Our competences are not seen as being bundles of skills measured in any absolute sense, but must be judged relative to others' competences and in a context of opportunity. There are problems, however, inherent in the economic game theory approach.

Ghemawat sums up the essential difficulties of migrating game theory from its home in economics into the adjacent field of strategic management. 'Game theory

has taken over industrial economics but has barely had an effect on the applied field of business strategy. The gap that has opened between game theory's formidable analytical advances and its lackluster empirical applications appears to be a large part of the reason.' (Ghemawat 1997: 27). Rumelt, Schendel, and Teece (Rumelt 1991) summarize this problem of the 'semi-detachedness' of game theory in terms of the different perspectives of economists and strategists. They claim that

- The strategic phenomena themselves lie outside the domain of economic game theorists.
- The game theorists seek to explain events and mechanisms rather than to establish their normative effect.
- Game theory has a natural focus on a few economic variables to the exclusion of those variables well known to strategists as having practical importance, such as technology, politics, and organization, limits its testability and even its utility in business.
- The degree of rationality required to achieve game theoretic equilibrium may well be too demanding.
- Game theory tends to focus on external transactions while the source of competitive advantage tends to be internal.

Other writers, too, are concerned about the ease with which game theory gravitates to the most mathematically convenient assumptions for players' rationality. Almost always the assumptions of complete rationality and ability to calculate are made, whereas there is clear evidence (Camerer, Johnson, et al. 1993) that in a social context rationalizing behaviour is limited by concepts of fair play and equity and extremes of return to any player tend not to be realized. Shubik comments that 'even if we have a full description of "the game" we have to make an inductive leap based upon our social perceptions as to what we wish to consider to be a solution.' (Shubik 1983: 12). In our application of the theory to strategy, then, we should be aware that what we consider to be an appropriate solution is highly conditioned by our collective socialized understanding of strategic behaviour, i.e. by ethics, norms of behaviour, and business expectations.

Game theory is also very distinctly end-directed in a way that most of strategy is not. 'Rationality is cast as a means–end framework with the task of selecting the most appropriate means for achieving certain ends' (Heap and Varoufakis 1995), whereas much of contemporary strategic writing stresses the need for adaptation and responsiveness to developing situations.

In general terms, Shubik sums up the situation concisely. '[I]n the current state of game theory there does not appear to be a uniquely agreed upon set of assumptions concerning intent or behaviour but there are many different solution concepts and a patchwork of partial theories which have been more or less justified in certain usages' (Shubik 1983: 12). This observation remains valid today; we should view game theory's contribution to strategy in two different forms.

1. It provides a set of schemata for the understanding of the interaction between archetypal elements of the interactive business system in which strategy is developed and implemented. In this respect we should not expect direct and specific guidance on, say, negotiating behaviour or oligopoly effects in our industry at this time. Rather, we should see game theory as a structure of economic archetypes of behaviour upon which we can generalize and build, incorporating our own knowledge of the specifics of our situation. In spite of its abstraction, this contribution is at least as useful as that of any essentially descriptive theory.

2. We note that strategy is a grounded subject and demands grounded answers. Strategic managers seek to manage and consequently to act in the world, and quite reasonably expect specific solutions to real-world problems. Game theory has the ability to achieve this specificity through (among others) the discrete space modelling approaches discussed above. Additionally, these specific models do allow us to combat the difficulties inherent in assuming global rationality since, because of our detailed knowledge of the situation, we may be in a better position to identify likely failures of rationality or calculation in the competitor. No such assumption is safe in a generalized model.

30.7 FUTURE DEVELOPMENTS

The dramatic sweep of game theory through economics has produced an intricate richness of models which are generally accepted to fall short of the needs of strategists. 'Game theorists, dissatisfied with the sensitive dependence of their predictions on the detailed protocols of games, are trying to develop predictions that hold more generally. Unfortunately it has proved impossible so far, to satisfy this craving for generality without sacrificing specificity' (Ghemawat 1997: 18). There is little doubt that this search for specificity will continue and form a strong component of the applied game theory agenda. There are arguments against this 'natural' agenda, however.

1. There is an assumption that the generalized game theoretic models fall short of requirements, in some sense, because they do not deal with specifics. This is to mistake their purpose which is not to provide some universally applicable model of behaviour which can be migrated without adaptation into the domain of management so much as to provide modalities of thought which we can combine, using the nuts of our experiences and the bolts of our knowledge of the particularities of the situation.

2. There appears to be an inherent difficulty in moving from a general game theoretic model to a specific one. The characteristics of the models which give their generalizability lead to an arbitrariness in the specific modelling. Fudenberg and

Maskin (1986), for example, illustrate that one can persuade one particular type of game theoretic model, the non-cooperative one, to provide any behaviour one desires by assuming different kinds of incomplete information in it.

In spite of these difficulties, strategy will seek for specifics, but it is likely to find them not in an extrapolation of generalized economic models but in two topics addressed in this chapter, namely economic game theory and discrete models.

There is a widely held assumption that we live in a world of historically unsurpassed uncertainty, change, and chaos. While one might offer the observation that times were pretty uncertain and trading conditions fast moving in middle Europe for most of half a millennium, we undoubtedly have to cope with a highly dynamic environment and, moreover, one where the contacts between trading entities, because of improved communications and globalization, are more frequent. These are the very conditions in which the assumptions of evolutionary game theory thrive. We can confidently expect strategic thinking to be informed as general evolutionary economic theory and knowledge management come together. Specifically, the impact of memetic thinking (Blackmore 1999) on the horizontal strategy of a company, and particularly in terms of the strategy for innovation and adaptation to competitive environments, is bound to be extensive. This interaction between the competitive advantage of the firm and the information flow in the environment around it sees the firm being defined as much by the information which flows in and out of it as by its traditional definitions as a social construct, a bundle of skills or a nexus of contracts. The crucial difference is that in the memetic concept it is the information which is engaged in game theoretic behaviour as much as the competing firms.

Lastly, the OR-derived modelling methods provide real hope of specificity in strategic management. The joint mobilization of scenario planning methods more flexible in approach and more ambitious in their intent alongside modelling methods like drama theory and Powergraph approaches have a real possibility of providing practising strategic managers with specific answers to strategic problems.

References

AXELROD, R. (1984). *The Evolution of Cooperation*. Harmondsworth: Penguin.

BENNETT, P. (1980). 'Hypergames: Developing a Model of Conflict'. *Futures*, 12: 489–507.

—— (1986). 'Beyond Game Theory—Where?' in P. Bennett (ed.), *Analysing Conflict and its Resolution*. Oxford: Oxford University Press, 43–70.

—— and HOWARD, N. (1996). 'Rationality, Emotion and Preference Change: Drama-Theoretic Models of Choice'. *European Journal of Operational Research*, 92/3: 603–14.

—— and VAN HEESWIJK, S. (1997). *Using Software for Confrontation Analysis: A Case Study in Food Safety Policy*. IMA Conference Working Paper at IMA Conference, Wadham College, Apr. 1997–09–29.

BINMORE, K. (1994). *Game Theory and the Social Contract*, Vol. 1. *Playing Fair*. Cambridge, Mass.: MIT Press.

BLACKMORE, S. (1999). *The Meme Machine*. Oxford: Oxford University Press.

BRAMS, S. (1994). *Theory of Moves*. Cambridge: Cambridge University Press.

CAMERER, C. (1991). 'Does Strategy Research Need Game Theory?' *Strategic Management Journal*, 12: 137–52.

—— JOHNSON, E., RYMON, T., AND SEN, S. (1993). 'Cognition and Framing in Sequential Bargaining for Gains and Losses', in K. Binmore (ed.), *Frontiers of Game Theory*. Cambridge, Mass.: MIT Press, 27–48.

CAVES, R. (1994). 'Game Theory, Industrial Organisation and the Quest for Competitive Advantage'. *Journal of Business Economics*, 1: 11–14.

FRASER, N. M., and HIPEL, K. (1984). *Conflict Analysis: Models and Resolutions*. Amsterdam: North Holland.

FUDENBERG, D., and MASKIN, E. (1986). 'The Folk Theorem in Repeated Games with Discounting and with Incomplete Information'. *Econometrica*, 54: 533–54.

GHEMAWAT, P. (1997). *Games Businesses Play*. Cambridge, Mass.: MIT Press.

HEAP, S. H., and VAROUFAKIS, Y. (1995). *Game Theory: A Critical Introduction*. London: Routledge.

HIRSCHLEIFER, J., and RILEY, J. (1992). *The Analytics of Uncertainty and Information*. Cambridge: Cambridge University Press.

HOWARD, N. (1971). *Paradoxes of Rationality*. Cambridge, Mass.: MIT Press.

—— (1998). 'N-person "Soft" Games'. *Journal of Operational Research Society*, 49/2: 144–50.

—— BENNETT, P. G., BRYANT, J., and BRADLEY, M. (1992). 'Manifesto for a Theory of Drama and Irrational Choice'. *Journal of Operational Research Society*, 44: 99–103.

JERVIS, R. (1978). 'Co-operation under the Security Dilemma'. *World Politics*, 30: 167–214.

MORRIS, P. (1992). *Introduction to Game Theory*. New York: Springer Verlag.

POWELL, J. (1999). 'Powergraph—a Network-Based Approach to Modelling and Managing Corporate Strategic Conflict and Co-operation'. *Journal of Operational Research Society*, 50/7: 669–83.

RASMUSEN, E. (1989). *Games and Information*. Oxford: Blackwell.

ROSENHEAD, J. (ed.) (1989). *Rational Analysis for a Problematical World*. Chichester: J. Wiley.

RUMELT, R. P., SCHENDEL, D., and TEECE, D. (1991). 'Strategic Managemnt and Economics'. *Strategic Management Journal*, 12/Special Issue: 5–29.

SALONER, G. (1991). 'Modeling, Game Theory and Strategic Management'. *Strategic Management Journal*, 12: 119–36.

SCHELLING, T. (1960). *The Strategy of Conflict*. Oxford: Oxford University Press.

SHUBIK, M. (1983). *Mathematics of Conflict*. Amsterdam: Elsevier.

THOMPSON, L. (1998). *The Mind and Heart of the Negotiator*. London: Prentice-Hall.

VON NEUMANN, J., and MORGENSTERN, O. (1944). *The Theory of Games in Economic Behaviour*. Princeton: Princeton University Press.

CHAPTER 31

STRATEGY, HEURISTICS, AND REAL OPTIONS

BRUCE KOGUT
NALIN KULATILAKA

31.1 LOOKING INWARD AND OUTWARD

STRATEGIZING is the application of heuristic frames to analyze the world and to generate normative evaluations of potential avenues of implementation.[1] Yet, like many professional schools caught between academics and application, strategy research is often ambivalent about the implications of valuing the development of heuristics. Because a test of a good heuristic is its application, the relevant community by which to evaluate such contributions appears often to be the commercial world.

This tension is probably more functional than commonly realized. Professional schools of business share, as Simon noted, commonalties with schools of design, e.g. engineering or architecture. Strategy research reflects competing ideas about

We would like to thank Carliss Baldwin for many helpful comments, and managers of Lucent for a reality check on some ideas.

[1] This chapter is based on Kogut and Kulatilaka (1992; revision 1994); the published version Kogut and Kulatilaka (2002) considers in more depth organizational theories.

how the world looks, or what the world needs.[2] However, like their counterparts in engineering or architecture, strategy researchers distinguish themselves from practitioners by their attention to an articulation of theory and
evidence.

One of the most important bodies of strategic ideas at large today are associated
with the notions of capabilities or core competence. The book by Gary Hamel and
C. K. Prahalad *Competing for the Future* has sold more copies than any other
Harvard Business School book. The resource-based theory of the firm, which has
seized the intellectual agenda from industry analysis, views the unique capabilities
of the firm as the cornerstone of sustainable rents. Ned Bowman (1995) has made
the distinction between strategies that look in the mirror and those that look
through the looking glass. It is not surprising that during a time of restructuring
and re-engineering, strategy researchers should shift the emphasis from industry
analysis to the internal sources of competitive advantage. The international competition and the introduction of information technologies have, as the extensive
literature on American competitiveness has documented, generated considerable
competitive pressures on corporations.

This emphasis on looking in the mirror begs the question of how to choose
among alternatives. Hamel and Prahalad (1994) essentially invert this framing by
proposing the concept of white spaces in the topography of existing businesses to
identify valuable avenues of exploration. This language is strongly reminiscent of
the commonly made distinction between exploitation and exploration (see Hedlund
and Rolander 1990 and March 1991).

We propose that the real options literature provides an appropriate theoretical
foundation for the heuristic frames suggested as ways to identify and value capabilities. Since capabilities are platforms that create a generic set of resources, they
represent investments in future opportunities. The distinction between exploitation
and exploration has an exact correspondence in the difference between net present
value and option valuation. The attractiveness of real option thinking is only
superficially in the obvious characteristic of forcing managers to think about the
value of flexibility in response to uncertain events. The more fundamental contribution is to require that the valuation placed upon a strategy is derived from
dynamic equilibrium prices in the market. In effect, real option valuation marries
the resource-based view with industry positioning by disciplining the analysis of the
value of capabilities by a market test.

We proceed by first characterizing what are heuristics and how real option theory
and core competencies are related through the concept of capabilities. Capabilities
reflect irreversible investments, because of the costliness of transforming the organizational knowledge in a firm. We illustrate these ideas through a stylized mathematical description of the problem of adopting radical change. This formalization

---

[2] Mintzberg (1990) suggests there are no less than ten schools of strategic planning.

clarifies that the benefit of a real options heuristic is the imposition of a market test to derive the valuation of capabilities.

31.2 HEURISTICS

A good heuristic has four qualities: it is easy to use, easy to communicate, provides a better direction than ones currently employed, and motivates people who have to implement the strategy. The Boston Consulting Group growth matrix is the canonical heuristic. It requires only two data inputs of market growth and relative position. The famed ideograph of stars, dogs, question mark, and the cash cow have an Orwellian Rosebud value, i.e. they are comprehensible and memorable.[3] The implementation leads to a clear motivation. As the CEO of General Electric stated, the objective of GE's business units is to be number 1 or 2 in world markets. However, the not-so-minor drawback is that the heuristic often gives the wrong direction.

Because heuristics are intended to be used, they have many qualities that upset the norms of academic research. The objections come from all quarters. Sociologists point out that such heuristics reflect prevailing norms of style or conceptions of control. Cognitive psychologists note that heuristics are prone to type 1 and 2 errors, that is, managers ignore evidence of misfit and overstate the possibility of success. Social scientists are quick to criticize the absence of formal theory and empirical evidence.[4] Ad hoc field research indicates that well-educated Ph.D. business faculty members frequently moan over the humiliation of teaching heuristic frames that are not clearly derived from their formal education.

Heuristics are useful because formal theory often does not suggest operational rules, or is not credible, for the problems decision-makers confront in actual conditions. Since they are intended to guide action, heuristics are designed to motivate. From a normative perspective, overestimation is an evolutionary attractive property for assembling human effort; an emphasis on sober assessment screens out people who are most likely inclined to act.[5] Because they are meant to influence action, they are biased toward current conceptions of the world; they are also liable to be dispensed as these conceptions change.

---

[3] This aspect of communicability has been underestimated. However, in an increasingly more integrated 'community of practitioners', the importance of ideographic and metaphoric communication is critical to the success of information technology implementation and performance.

[4] For overestimation bias, see Kahneman and Lovallo (1993); for a discussion of a lack of theory, see Simon's (1992) discussion of the professional school. These biases are critical to understanding why managers are loathe to 'kill an option'.

[5] An interesting set of statistics are MBA entrance data. Whereas Wharton MBAs score at the top of the GMAT percentiles, their GPAs are usually around B+. These are smart people who do not like to study too much.

Heuristics have the advantage of countering some cognitive biases, but at a cost. In a study on plant scheduling, Bowman (1963) found that managers would do better if they used linear estimates from their experience rather than tried to optimize in response to each situation. In real time, the search for optimal strategies can be too costly or liable to be influenced by recency effects (e.g. the arrival of new information). Kunreuther (1969) modified these findings that rules cued to selective environmental information improve actual decision-making.

One of the merits of a heuristic is its real-time utility. Studies on innovation show remarkable trade-offs between costs and time for innovations (Scherer 1967; Mansfield 1988). Field research and experimental evidence show ample evidence that people rely upon rules of thumb and known routines in situations constrained by time, even for simple problems for which there exist optimal rules. Because decisions must be made, managers and firms often transfer these sub-optimal rules to settings that are poorly suited to these proven heuristics.[6] The limits to the robustness of a heuristic are usually experiential, because the theory is rarely explicit or is ignored.

31.3 HEURISTICS AND STRATEGIZING

The history of strategic planning tools documents the applicability and limitations of heuristics. Following distinctions made in cognitive science, we separate a heuristic into its cognitive frame and the rules of search. A cognitive (or heuristic) frame refers to the 'representation' of the problem and solution space. The heuristic rules of search are the algorithms by which solutions are found in the represented solution space.[7]

Table 31.1 compares three cognitive frames for developing business strategies. The BCG cash flow matrix 'works' to the extent that the theory of scale and experience driving down cost is the proper characterization of value creation. From the initial data, it bootstraps from observations on market growth and relative positions to evaluate whether a firm can dominate a market. Though a fairly simple heuristic, it shared the common bias of its times that size drives success, as opposed to the more modest inference that size is the outcome of success.[8]

---

[6] See Allison (1971) on frames; psychology experiments of Bartlett (1958) and Cohen and Bacdayan (1994) for evidence on schemata and sub-optimal transfer.

[7] See Minsky (1985: 74, 243–53) for an example. The definition of heuristic search is discussed in Bowman and Moskowitz (2002).

[8] For examples of this bias, see Chandler (1962) and Servan-Schreiber (1969). Only in light of this backdrop is it possible to understand the contribution of Piore's and Sabel's (1984) counter-revolution in thinking about size and performance.

Table 31.1 Strategizing as cognitive frames

Cognitive frame	Theory	Initial data	Analysis	Implementation
Experience curve (BCG)	Scale and experience drivers	Attractive (growing) markets	Relative market position	Dominance by scale
Industry analysis	Industrial economics	Industry forces	Cost or differentiation strategies	Value-chain exploitation
Capability	(Real options)	Intended strategy	Core competence	Exploratory business strategies

Porter (1980) developed his industry analysis in the immediate aftermath of the oil shock and during a period of depressed corporate profitability. Its theory is derived from an industrial economics that appears as antiquated by contemporary advancements, but reflects the preoccupations of a time when the historical peaking of oligopolistic measures of concentration suggested that industry structure deeply influenced corporate performance. It is, in many ways, an inevitable implication of the BCG analysis that a world in which a few firms grow to dominance should lead to a focus on how to attain the conditions of structural stability. The initial data on industry forces serves to inform (though the mapping is not clear) the choice between low-cost and differentiation strategies. The implementation proceeds through an evaluation of the value-chain, with the criterion being contribution to profit. Compared to the requirements of the BCG growth matrix, the methodology is intensive in the use of data.

The core competence concept arose in the late 1980s during the height of re-engineering propelled by acquisitions and new information technologies. It is a direct response to the reputed financial pressures from financial markets dominated for the first time by institutional investors (see Useem 1996). The formulation by Hamel and Prahalad (1994) suggests that the initial data are in the spirit of understanding the intended strategy of the firm that should be grounded in a distinctive competence.[9] This competence is defined by three attributes: it should be 'extendable' to multiple markets, it should be hard to imitate, and it should satisfy a derived customer demand (Hamel and Prahalad 1994: 202-7).

The theoretical foundations to this view are several, from the reasoning on why knowledge is hard to imitate to the evolutionary theories of firm growth. From a decision theoretic perspective, the core competence framing lends itself readily to a

---

[9] Selznick (1957) was one of the first to develop the idea of distinctive competence, which was absorbed into the language of the early business policy literature, as well as of writings on the value-added chain.

real option interpretation. A real option is defined by an investment decision that is characterized by uncertainty, the provision of future managerial discretion to exercise timing, and irreversibility.

These three elements are jointly required for the application of a strategic options heuristic. An option has value only if there is uncertainty, though defining the relevant source of the uncertainty is not trivial. An operationally important element of design is the provision of discretion, such as the staging of an R&D project to correspond to discrete points of go–no go decisions.

Irreversibility is an easily overlooked feature and signifies the inability to cost-lessly revisit an investment or decision. A classic example is the BCG categorization of the 'dog' product division which a firm should divest, assuming there is a market. However, the ability to divest a poorly performing division is, as Winter (1987) observes, rarely exercised without incurring a loss on the original investment. In this context, irreversibility is the inability to recover the investment costs already expended for the product division.

31.4 Capabilities as Strategic Options

This definition of a core competence as a strategic option is close to the argument put forth by Barney (1986) regarding the resource-based view of the firm. To Barney, the creation of entrepreneurial rents is fortuitous. If managers understood the value creation process, the knowledge through imitation would lead to the immediate erosion of these rents.[10] The presence of a strategic factor market serves to arbitrage the value of these assets to guarantee a competitive return. (We return to this observation later to motivate the explicit use of a traded security for valuation of a real option.)

The important difference between this early statement of the resource-based view of the firm and core competence is the latter's insistence on the value of a resource as derived from its future but uncertain use. In the sense that Barney relies on market valuations to back into his identification of unique assets, he is consistent with the view that the market values the use of these assets in reference to their potential use by firms bidding for their ownership. But he makes an incomplete inference, namely, that these firms must have differential information. An equally plausible insight is that firms differ in their opportunity set, inclusive of the organizational features that are costly and time-consuming to acquire. Consequently, some firms will discover

---

[10] The inimitable observations in Barney are more fully explicated in a related literature on knowledge of the firm. See Zander and Kogut (1995) and Szulanski (1995) for empirical studies that measure inimitability, or tacitness.

profitable projects, where the 'excess rents' are earned on their organizational, not physical capital, assets.

Real option theory bridges the positioning and core competence by dynamically deriving the value of capabilities simultaneously from two discrete operating states: their value as 'is' and as 'could be'.[11] The 'as is' evaluation is a net present valuation based upon an evaluation of the range of possible pay-offs to operations currently in place. The option value is derived from the discretion to alter these operations to take advantage of future opportunities. In this simultaneous valuation of both operating states (they are clearly dependent), the analysis derives the valuation by creating a shadow security based on the market value of the strategic factor.

It is the identification of the opportunity set, as established through market valuations, that should drive the identification and valuation of core competence. Some writers fail to make this observation altogether. For example, Teece, Pisano, and Shuen write:

We define those competences that define a firm's fundamental business as core. Core competences must accordingly be derived by looking across the range of a firm's (and its competitors') products and services . . . The degree to which a core competence is distinctive depends on how well endowed the firm is relative to its competitors, and how difficult it is for competitors to replicate its competences. (1997: 516)

This statement is, however, rather problematic. It derives a core competence from the description of a firm's businesses, and in comparison to competitors. Finally, it notes that distinctiveness depends on a firm's endowment and the difficulty for the assets to be copied.

The missing element in this analysis is, of course, value. A firm may be well endowed with patents making it difficult for competitors to imitate. However, the important question is whether these endowments, which we might also call more generically the knowledge of the firm, is useful not only to current, but also to future applications. This question is not answered by a notion of dynamic capabilities, or of combinative capabilities, unless the normative criterion is the identification and investment in core competences in reference to their potential uses. This objection is not petty, for it is easy to imagine that without market discipline on the analysis, the potential candidates for core competence quickly multiply.[12]

There is another way to think about this problem, suggested by Winter (1987), as a broader formulation along the lines of optimal control. Winter (1987: 180–1) states, 'From evolutionary theory comes the idea that a state description may include organizational behavioral patterns or routines that are not amenable to

---

[11] See Dixit and Pindyck (1994) and Amram and Kulatilaka (1999) for extensive discussions on the application of real options.

[12] One of the authors visited an optical fiber business unit of a large company. In response to a question about core competence, the factory and business managers identified the capability to quickly code the fiber in color packaging.

rapid change, as well as . . . more conventionally defined assets. It is by this route that a variety of considerations that fall under the rubrics knowledge and competence may enter the strategic state description.' This suggestion seems odd, for optimal control requires an excessive belief in the rationality and knowledge of decision-makers, a belief that Nelson and Winter (1982) have strongly criticized. However, it is not a bad heuristic frame (Winter uses this term) if some of the insights of a capabilities approach are properly specified. A conventional formulation is to describe the characteristics of the state description and allow the decision-maker discretion over a few control variables, e.g. technologies or output. A transformed formulation deprives the decision-maker of control over some variables and, in effect, captures the constraints and opportunities of capabilities through a richer description of the given state in a decision context.

Consider the example of flexibility through the installation of new automated equipment. A conventional approach assumes that this technology enters into the description of the state and provides the decision-maker with the choice of whether to exercise flexibility. However, a new capability is not determined by the capital purchase but by the presence of an organizational system that identifies and supports such flexibility. Because technology can be bought, or peopled hired into a firm, it is the organizational constraints that are often the most binding. Robert Stempel, the former head of General Motors, noted: 'We've tried automation without knowledgeable workers, and it doesn't work. We put a tremendous amount of automation and electronics into our Cadillac plant in Hamtranck. And we couldn't run it because our people didn't understand what we were asking them to do.'[13] The study by Ittner (1996) found that a major problem in the exercise of flexibility at General Motors was that the accounting system focused on unit labor cost variances; there was no measure for whether flexibility was under- or over-utilized.

This accounting problem is reflected also in the capital budgeting problem. Just like accounting variances do not measure flexibility properly, net present value techniques wrongly estimate the value of building capabilities.[14] The important insight into the failure at General Motors is that new technology and organization are complements. Even though technology can be purchased, the organizational complement requires a longer period of experimentation and gestation. In other words, the organizational value of capabilities depends upon the potential uses of flexibility in future but uncertain states.

---

[13] *Fortune*, 1992; cited by Bernard Wolf and Steven Globerman, 'Strategic Alliances in the Automotive Industry', mimeo, York University, 1992. See also the discussion in Ittner and Kogut (1995).

[14] Winter (1987) suggests net present value as a measure, which is appropriate for the case without uncertainty. Most surveys on the use of capital budgeting techniques show that almost all large corporate firms use net present value calculations for investment decisions. See Kogut and Kulatilaka (1992) and Baldwin and Clark (1992, 1994) for a discussion why investment in capabilities is not a net present value of cash flows but a real option valuation.

It is, consequently, reasonable to think of a firm's technology and organization as forming a coherent and dynamic set of capabilities whose value is derived from their value in future and stochastic states of the world. Such capabilities as speed of production or the ability to produce a particular quality are created through the possession of a set of technologies and of organizing principles. Given these capabilities, the firm is endowed with the resources that may be exploited strategically in the market.

31.5 NEW CAPABILITIES AS ORGANIZATIONAL DISCONTINUITIES

It is useful, before starting, to explain why investments in capabilities are irreversible because of the tight coupling of technology and organization. The close relationship between organizing principles and technology is apparent in standard definitions in the literature on innovations and organizational sociology. Scott (1995: 227) defines technology as including 'not only the hardware used in performing work but also the skills and knowledge of workers, and even the characteristics of the objects on which work is performed'. Scott's definition encompasses the standard economic distinction between new products and processes and the embodiment of human capital formation in better techniques and products.

By technology, then, we mean the physical and human capital stock; by organization, we mean the way physical capital and people are jointly coupled through organizational routines, processes, incentive schemes, and governance structure. For example, a system of mass production consists of the serial placement of capital equipment coupled with an assembly line of workers performing standardized tasks and under staff supervision. The technology is embedded in the equipment; the organizational knowledge is the principle by which work is arranged and supervised in conjunction with the use of this technology.

An area of debate has been whether to treat major technological innovations as radical or incremental. The organizational literature, especially Tushman and Anderson (1986), has offered the resolution that these innovations can be characterized as radical or incremental depending upon whether they destroy or enhance a firm's competence (see also Henderson 1993). This resolution raises the more fundamental problem that a firm, by its ability to recruit new engineers and managers, should have the capacity to alter its technological competence. The costs of switching to a technology should, by this reasoning, consist of the costs of hiring new individuals trained in the new science or engineering technology. Yet,

clearly, the difficulty of adopting new capabilities cannot be explained by the relatively open recourse to the labor market in most advanced capitalist countries.

This reasoning ultimately leads to the consideration that the radicalness of an innovation has less to do with the novelty of the technology than its conformity with existing knowledge of the firm, i.e. the ways by which work is organized and power is distributed. Since the way work is organized will vary by firms, then the radicalness of a technological innovation cannot be determined independent of a particular organizational context. Switching, or adoption, costs are strongly contingent on the current organization of work.

If radicalness of a technological innovation is a question of the organization, it follows that the potentially most radical kinds of innovation are those which alter directly the method by which work is organized. New ways of doing things are often difficult to understand and implement. They also pose, by their very nature, threats to the existing agreement on the allocation of power.[15]

To draw out why, consider the very important literature in organizational behavior concerning the suitability of particular organizational and technological combinations. One of the most perplexing questions in organizational behavior is the failure to identify clear matches between technologies and organizational structures. Yet, the findings are rather ambiguous in this regard. The line of work begun by Woodward and later the Aston school that linked performance to particular technological and organizational combinations has not resulted in clear relationships. Indeed, the most robust finding appears to be between organizational size and output volume rather than between particular structural and technological configurations. Indeed, even the findings between size and authority relations have been found to be sensitive to contextual variables, such as culture.[16]

Dosi and Kogut (1993) proposed that the failure to find robust relationships has been due to the tendency to theorize element-to-element correspondence, such as high volume production with vertical hierarchy[17] (see Figure 31.1a). The empirical results do not show that these are complements when other factors are controlled. Alternatively, the correspondence might be set-to-set, where a set of organizational practices maps onto a set of technologies. The data might not reveal that A and B exist as complements; all we observe is A and C and D and B. Complementarities need not be unique between any given technology or organization, but they still should be relationally bounded. The recent findings by MacDuffie (1996) on 'bundles' of human resource practices in auto plants indicate that there is a logic that relates organizing practices to each other, and to technologies (see Figure 31.1b).

---

[15] Nelson and Winter (1982), consequently, refer to organizational routines as 'truces'.

[16] See the review given in Dosi and Kogut (1993) and the summary of the work comparing US and Japanese organizations (Lincoln 1993).

[17] This point is implicit in the lattice formulation of Milgrom and Roberts (1990), where a firm's choice is constrained by technical complementarities. It is, however, difficult to see the implications from their formulation for the many studies on organizational performance.

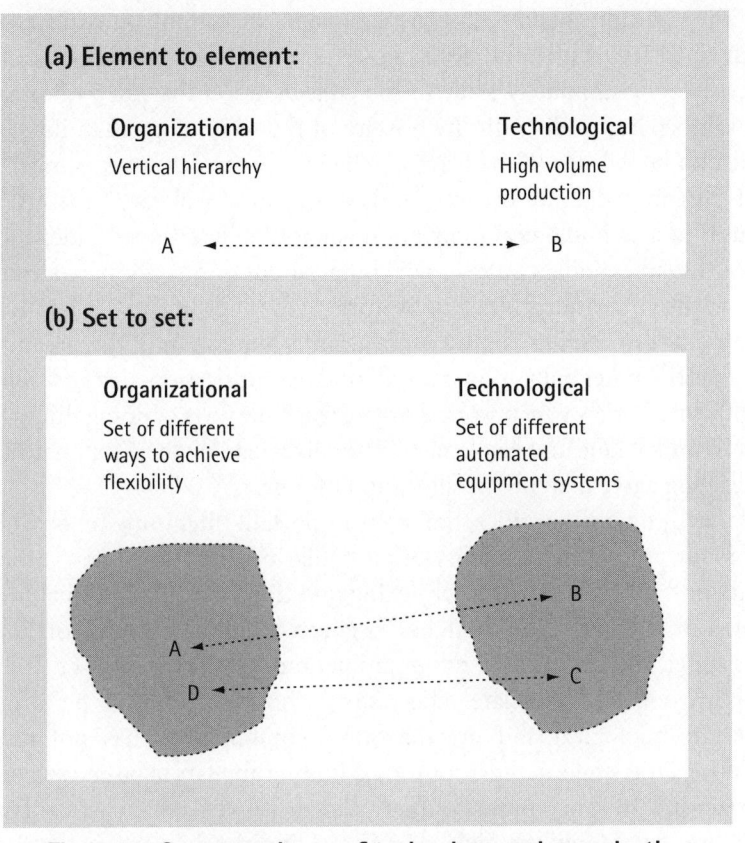

Fig. 31.1 Correspondence of technology and organization

As suggested in the opening citation of Robert Stempel, the experience of General Motors and other car manufacturers, as confirmed in MacDuffie's study, is that adopting the new capabilities of flexibility and speed requires changes in automation and organization. Between these two sets, there are many functionally equivalent complements, but there are no unique element-to-element correspondences.[18]

This description captures also the idea of co-evolution of technology and organization through two key features. First, technology and organization do not represent random assignments, nor is their coupling simply at the discretion of managers. Rather, the matches of a technology and organizing principle are constrained to reasonable set-to-set correspondence. However, within these 'developmental' constraints (to borrow from biology), improvements in technology and organization are correlated through experiential learning. For example, the intro-

[18] A good example of the linking of capability and technology is modular design, in which modularity provides an option to improve a product by component; however, the product design has to be backed by an organizational structure to allow specialization. See Baldwin and Clark (1993).

duction of mechanical equipment to move the incomplete chassis from one line to the next required the organizational innovation to increase the 'tightness' of the coupling of serial work processes in the factory. In other words, technology and organization are dynamically coupled in their evolution.

The tight coupling of technology and organization means that the costs of organizational change means that firms will persist in their old ways beyond the recommendation of the net present value. This persistence defines a range of inertia, or what we call a hysteresis band. Because organizational change is disruptive and hence discontinuous, managers hesitate to change radically their organizations, hoping perhaps that future states of the world would provide more appealing environments.

Figure 31.2 provides a simple illustration of this point. A firm can choose between two complementary systems, called low and high variety. The important issue is whether the relative value of gaining the capability of variety is enough to offset the costs of discontinuous change. The choice of capabilities is, as we depict it, derived from the market price placed on variety. Because of uncertainty over the evolution of the value of variety and the costs of adoption, managers rationally might choose to persist with inferior techniques before they are confident of future developments.

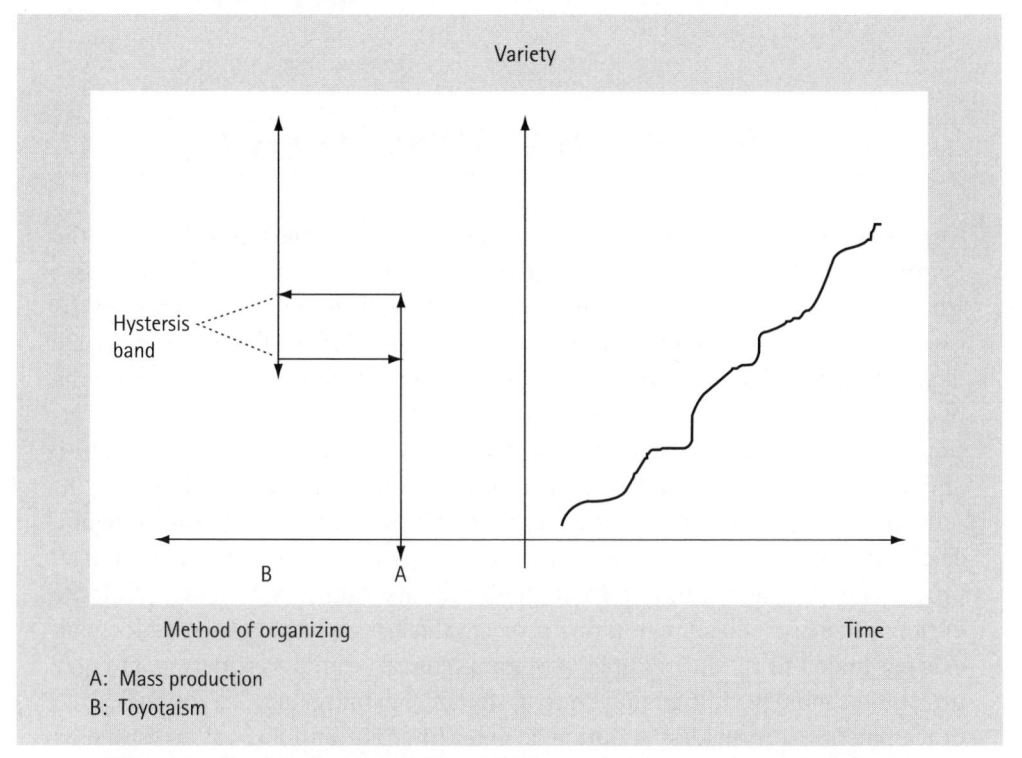

Fig. 31.2 The implications of hysteresis on the choice of new techniques

In the analysis below, we develop a modeling framework by which to examine this hysteresis band and the complementarity of organization and technology contingent upon a stochastic parameterization of the environment. The formal description explains how investments in organizational and technological capabilities are derived from their evaluation in the market. We suggest that knowledge accumulates in terms of two activities: competence in the use of particular technologies and in the organizational capability by which this technology is applied.

The problem facing the firm is to choose this set such that it tries to maximize its value in reference to its expectations on the evolution of prices and innovations in capabilities. In this formulation, the nature of the environment and strategy play an important role in shaping the capabilities of the firm. This problem is dynamically complex, as the firm must consider not only how its choice influences current profits, but also the learning of future capabilities.

This descriptive formulation clarifies two central claims. The current capability set and prevailing environment and market structure influence the choice and performance of a set of capabilities. The second claim is that there is a set-to-set correspondence between families of technology and organization that bound the feasible bundles of practices; but there is no unique element-to-element correspondence between a particular organizational practice and technology.

31.6 A FORMAL DESCRIPTION

The market price of a similar firm provides the most direct link between the performance of a capability set and prevailing market conditions. This market price is not the value of the core competence. Rather, it permits a valuation of the organizational capability by identifying a correlated asset in the relevant 'scarce factor' market. Value of a capability is then inferred (at times calculated) from the observed price dynamics that replicate the pay-off to the real option. This replication is the device through which market discipline is imposed on the identification and selection of core capabilities, thus imposing financial market discipline.

To elucidate the intuition, consider again the framing of a real options problem. The organizational assets of a firm provide an option to spend a fixed amount to procure a new capability by purchasing a physical asset at the end of one year. If the option is exercised, then the resulting project value has the risk characteristics of an existing traded firm. For example, a pharmaceutical firm is considering an entry into biotechnology. It currently has a strong capability in conventional drug development that provides an option to enter into biotechnology at an estimated cost. This cost is idiosyncratic to this firm. However, once it enters into the market,

its new business carries a market risk similar to other biotechnology firms. This example illustrates why the price of other firms does not give the value of the core capability, since the cost of entry is idiosyncratic to each firm. However, the price dynamics of other firms provide information on the factors (e.g. risk) that drive the value of the option to enter in this market.

The value of a financial option depends on the current share. Black, Merton, and Scholes derived this value through an option pricing formula. The simple, but critical innovation was their eventual recognition that by composing a replicated portfolio, the value of the option could be perfectly tracked by a levered position in the traded stock. Therefore, a risk-free portfolio can be constructed by holding a combination of the stock and options.[19] Hence, once the range of possible future stock prices is known (from its volatility), the market price of the option can be inferred by risklessly discounting the possible option pay-offs.

In many instances, there may not be a traded security whose price perfectly tracks the value of the resulting capability. In such cases, we can use one of two possible tracks to retain the market discipline. First, there may be a bundle of pure assets (an index) that captures risk characteristics of the capability. For example, 'crack spread' on crude oil as a proxy for the gross operating margin of an oil refinery; the SOX/SXE equity index of semiconductor manufacturers serves as a proxy for the value of the production from a chip fabricating plant. Second, the value of the capability depends on the price of product or factor prices whose risk is spanned by traded assets in the economy. The value of the capability then is obtained by explicitly specifying the profit function using these prices as an argument.

A simple example is a microprocessor, whereby a quality-adjusted price can be expressed as the ratio of price to the processing speed (or 'mips' for millions of instructions per second). An increase in processing speed implies that the price for one 'mips' has declined. This quality-adjusted price of the output enters the profit function. Thus, the price dynamics of chips directly drives the expected cash flow from operating the 'as is' assets and from possibly exercising the option to exploit the 'could be' investment.

31.6.1 The Economic Environment and Quality-Adjusted Prices

Let us use this last example to specify, descriptively, the method by which the price dynamics of the scarce factor is inferred through observations on a traded output. We then will take this description of the price dynamics to derive the profit function. Once we have this profit function, we then can describe the qualitative properties of how an investment in new organizational capabilities influences the

---

[19] As the stock price fluctuates, the portfolio weights to reflect the changing sensitivity of the value of the option to the stock price.

definition of a core competence. The fundamental conclusion of this exercise is to motivate the definition of a core competence as the capabilities that provide the best response to prevailing market opportunities.

In order to identify and value a core competence, we must specify the evolution of the quality-adjusted price which we call θ. However, since θ is not a pure security but is the observed price of a scarce factor, its price characteristics need not necessarily evolve according to its equilibrium risk characteristics. Local supply and demand conditions and technological innovation determine the evolution of θ. In particular, the expected rate of appreciation of θ may be different from its risk-adjusted equilibrium rate of return. Hence, the risk-neutral dynamics of θ will depend not only on the risk-free rate of interest but also on the difference between the equilibrium and actual growth rates of θ.[20]

We assume θ to be exogenously determined and characterize its evolution by stochastic process

$$\Delta\theta_t = \underbrace{\mu(\theta_t, t)\Delta t}_{\text{Deterministic growth}} + \underbrace{\sigma(\theta_t, t)\Delta Z_t}_{\text{Smoothly evolving uncertainty}} + \underbrace{\kappa\ dq}_{\text{Discrete innovations}}$$

where μ is the expected growth rate of θ, σ is its instantaneous volatility, ΔZ_t is standard Normal distributed, dq is a Poisson process with intensity parameter λ and κ is the random percentage jump amplitude conditional on the Poisson event occurring.[21]

This discrete-time process captures the main features of the notion of a scarce factor market with technological innovation.[22] The drift term reflects the expectations regarding technological progress. For example, the performance of memory semiconductors follows a fairly predictable path, with performance improvements occurring every few years and prices declining subsequently.

Changes in the quality-adjusted price may also reflect unpredictable shifts in consumer preferences. For example, an increase in oil prices would lead consumers to prefer cars which save on fuel consumption. As long as these changes are fairly smooth, it seems reasonable to capture this uncertainty in volatility.

Other changes may be more radical, such as the arrival of new organizational innovations. These changes would appear as a sudden jump in price to a firm. Recall that these are quality-adjusted prices. The introduction of assembly-line methods at Ford appeared to competitors as a sudden decrease in price. However, as Raff and Bresnahan (forthcoming) show for the history of the automobile, part of the competitive effect of new techniques was accomplished through changes in quality,

---

[20] This is analogous to a dividend on a stock or convenience value derived from a commodity. See chapter 13, Hull (1997) for a general model on valuing derivative securities. More extensive treatments can be found in Dixit and Pindyck (1994) and Amram and Kulatilaka (1999).

[21] More generally, we could define this process in vector form over a set of Wiener processes. See Merton (1976).

[22] For reasons of exposition, we work in discrete time.

holding the nominal price the same. They estimate that quality-adjusted prices fell by 5 per cent a year from 1906 to 1940; about 60 per cent of this decline was due to falling production costs and 40 per cent to improved quality. We capture these impacts of innovative change by allowing price to evolve in response to quality and process innovations.

A market-traded proxy for the quality-adjusted price of computer chips can be constructed as the price index of chip-making firms. Such an index will span the relevant risk characteristics. The rate of return on the index will proxy the equilibrium return. However, to the extent that the growth rate of the quality-adjusted price deviates from the traded index, we correct the actual price process. This deviation will enter into the risk neutral representation of the option pricing model as a shortfall from equilibrium akin to a convenience yield.[23]

Since the total risk characteristics of the quality-adjusted price, θ, is similar to that of the proxy variable, the volatility can be estimated from the market for the chip company stock index. In fact, options contracts on such an index (SOX/SXE) are traded at the Philadelphia Stock Exchange. The implied volatility of these options provides a market source for information on the standard deviation (σ) given in the above equation.

31.6.2 Profit Functions

Having described the evolution of quality-adjusted prices, we can now turn to describing the relationship between capability sets of the firm and its profit function. Consider a firm that has the set of capabilities c, where $c \in C$ is the set of all feasible capabilities.[24] The firm faces exogenously determined 'quality-adjusted prices', θ. The single-period profit obtained when operating under the set of capabilities c and facing prices θ_t is denoted $\Pi(\theta_t, c)$. This simple description captures the idea that firms are heterogeneous and their profits are determined both by the price of output and their organizational capabilities.

Given this set of capabilities and the realization of θ, we examine how the firm chooses its investment and production strategy. As an example, consider the case where C contains 'mass' and 'lean' production families with their associated organizational structures. Each family of production techniques can contain many distinct technologies. They are, however, coupled with the same organizational structure. Hence, a technology family refers to all technologies that can be operated within a single organization.[25]

---

[23] See McDonald and Siegel (1984); an application of adjusting for the shortfall can be found in Kogut and Kulatilaka (1994b).

[24] C will include technological and organizational characteristics as well as learning opportunities.

[25] For now we assume that families do not overlap, in that each technology can only belong to a single family. This assumption can be easily relaxed.

Suppose the firm is currently employing technology in the 'mass' production family, i.e. $c_m^i \in c_m \in C$. The firm's problem is to decide what capabilities it should use in the current period. Specifically, its choices are (a) continue using c_m^i; (b) continue in the same family but make incremental technological improvements by employing a better mass production technique, c_m^i; or (c) make discontinuous organizational switch and employ lean production technique, c_l^k. Choices (a) and (b) reflect 'as is' evaluations; only (c) involves a 'could be' alternative.

Furthermore, a capability provides a dynamic representation of the firm. A firm's capabilities not only serve to meet the current demands but also place it in a position to make further investments to launch new products to meet changing demand conditions. A capability endows the firm with an ability to change. A static profit function, therefore, cannot be a complete description of a capability. The description of capability must capture the dynamics that determine the type, level, and timing of investment needed to transform capabilities over time.

In other words, we must consider explicitly the costs of switching from one capability to another, be it from mass into lean, or conventional pharmaceutics to biotechnology, from a current capability such as mass production to a technique in the lean production family. Switching from one capability to another incurs large costs due to reorganization.[26] We denote these large organizational costs of switching as Δ_{ij}. For example, the cost of switching from c_n (mass production) to c_l (lean production) can be denoted as Δ_{ml}.

Within an organizational capability, however, switching costs are small, but not insignificant. At the same time, continuing within the same family enables the firm to capitalize on local learning effects. If the firm continues in c_m^i or moves to a better mass technique c_m^j, then it will subsequently learn by doing. However, switching from the ith to the jth technology may still incur technological costs. We define the local learning benefits in mass production as $-o_{mm}$ and technological switching costs δ_{ii}.

To summarize the magnitude of switching costs between all combinations of capabilities and technologies, we denote the cost of switching from c_m^i capability to c_l^j will be

$$\delta_{ml}^{ij} = \underbrace{T_{ij}}_{\text{Technological change}} + \underbrace{\Omega_{ml}}_{\text{Organizational learning}}$$

where

$$T_{ij} = \begin{cases} \overbrace{\delta_{ij}}^{\text{technological cost}} & \text{if } i \neq j \\ \underbrace{-\delta_{ij}}_{\text{technological learning}} & \text{if } i = j \end{cases} \qquad \Omega_{ij} = \begin{cases} \overbrace{O_{ml}}^{\text{organizational cost}} & \text{if } m \neq l \\ \underbrace{-O_{mm}}_{\text{organizational learning}} & \text{if } m = l \end{cases}$$

[26] For simplicity we are assuming that switching across organizations only incurs organizational costs. In effect, we assume that switching from any mass technology to any lean technology incurs the same cost. This can easily be generalized to include both technological and organizational costs.

Table 31.2 T_{ij} and Ω_{lm} switching cost pairs

| | | c_m | | c_l |
		c_m^1	c_m^2	c_l^3
c_m	c_m^1	[− −]	[− +]	[+ +]
	c_m^2	[+ −]	[− −]	[+ +]
c_l	c_l^3	[+ +]	[+ +]	[− −]

Consider a special example where mass production family c_m contains two technology modes c_m^1 and c_m^2 and lean production family c_l contains a single technology mode c_l^3. Table 31.2 presents the switching matrix containing the technological and organizational cost pairs. A negative entry indicates learning value from continuing to use the same technology or organization. A larger sign reflects a larger value.

More generally, the diagonal elements in the switching cost matrix will contain negative entries indicating the learning value.

We can now write down the firm's maximization problem. Each set of capabilities c_m^i has an accompanying profit function that is obtained by solving the usual profit maximization problem:

$$\Pi\left(\theta, c_m^i\right) = \max_{y \in c_m^i} \theta.y$$

where θ is a vector of quality-adjusted input and output prices and y is the vector of input and output levels that are determined by the capability set.

This simple expression indicates that the firm's ability to choose the best strategy is contingent on its organizational resources.

31.6.3 Critical Capability Set

31.6.3.1 *Static Profit Maximization when there are no Switching Costs*

To fix ideas, let us first consider the static case where the firm maximizes its single-period profits. Suppose the firm can costlessly obtain any feasible capability in C. Then we can define a static capability c^* as

$$c^*(\theta) = \underset{c \subseteq C}{\mathrm{argmax}} [\Pi(\theta, c)]$$

(Argmax simply picks the capability that achieves the optimal response for a given θ.) In our simple example, c^* picks an element from either mass or lean families depending on the respective profit functions and the particular realization of θ.

31.6.3.2 Static Profit Maximization with Switching Costs

Consider now the case where switching between capabilities involves costs, e.g. corporate or business reorganization. The critical capability set depends not only on θ and the characteristics of the various profit functions, but also on the currently employed capability set. For instance if the firm is currently using c_m^i, the optimal single-period profit-maximizing capability set is given by the solution to the following problem:

$$\Pi\left(\theta_t, \ c_m^i\right) = \max_{c_l^j \in C} \left[\Pi\left(\theta_t, \ c_l^j\right) - \delta_{ml}^{ij}\right]$$

Figure 31.3 illustrates this choice in the special case where mass and lean families each contain only a single technique. In a costless world, the lean technique dominates globally the mass technique. However, with switching costs, the relevant comparison is between the profit function of the currently employed mass technique and the profits of the lean technique net of switching costs. When θ falls below the intersection point θ^*, the static decision rule calls for switching families.

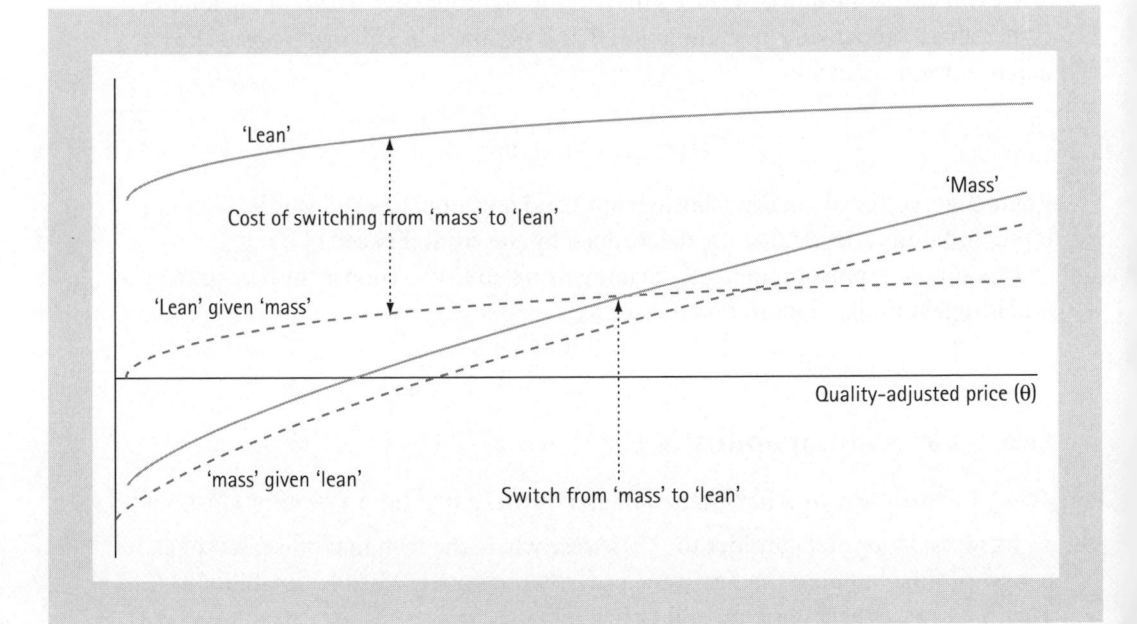

Fig. 31.3 Choice of capability set 'static case'

31.6.4 Dynamic Value Maximization

The static analysis ignores the impact of the current capability choice on future choices. When future values of θ evolve stochastically, the current decision influences all future decisions as well. The decision by a mass producer of cars to invest in flexible manufacturing using lean production runs the risk that the American market suddenly decides to buy large recreational vehicles made best by standard mass production techniques. But now they face the problem that they are invested in lean manufacturing, and cannot easily switch back. The tight coupling of organization and technology is essential to understanding why capabilities radically change the understanding of strategy as not only market competition, but as the selection of competence.

The way to incorporate the implications of future switching is to write out explicitly the problem over time. To do this, we no longer work directly with profit functions, but instead with a value function. While technically this problem is often hard to solve, its formulation is both intuitive and insightful. At a point in time (t), this formulation treats the present value of all future benefits given optimal future behavior, as represented by the value function $V(\theta_t, c_m^i)$. The value function is the solution of the well-known Bellman equation:

$$V\left(\theta_t, c_m^i\right) = \max_{c_l^j}\left[\left(\Pi\left(\theta_t, c_l^j\right) - \delta_{ml}^{ij}\right) + \rho E_t\left[V\left(\theta_{t+1}, c_l^j\right)\right]\right]$$

where c_m^i is the current capability pair (consisting of technology i and organization m) and j and l are chosen from the set of feasible technologies and organizations at time $t+1$.

The Bellman equation indicates that in each period the producer contemplates switching into a new capability. If it chooses capability c_l^j, it realizes benefits of $\Pi\left(\theta_t, c_l^j\right)$, but pays switching costs of δ_{ml}^{ij}, and then arrives at the following period with value function $V(\theta_{t+1}, c_m^j)$. This value depends on the capability chosen, c_l^j, as well as on the value of the state variable next period, θ_{t+1}. Because θ_{t+1} is still unknown at time t, we take expectations; we also discount at rate ρ.

In each period, the producer chooses the capability c_l^j that maximizes the value of the project. This can be interpreted as the *dynamic capability*. More formally, we define the dynamic capability as

$$c^{**} = \text{argmax}_{c_l^j}\left[\left(\Pi\left(\theta_t, c_l^j\right) - \delta_{ml}^{ij}\right) + \rho E_t\left[V\left(\theta_{t+1}, c_l^j\right)\right]\right]^{27}$$

In the absence of switching costs, the solution to this optimization problem is simple: choose in each period the capability c_l^j that maximizes $\Pi(\theta_t, c_l^j)$ in that

---

[27] For present purposes we ignore issues of risk. See Pindyck (1991) and Kulatilaka and Marcus (1992) for a treatment of the systematic risk in θ.

period. This is the static critical capability discussed earlier. However, the presence of switching costs makes a forward-looking analysis necessary. The probability distribution of future prices affects the current choice of technology and organization.

This definition of a dynamic capability defines our reinterpretation of a 'core competence'. Core competence is the capability set (i.e. combination of organization and technology elements) that permits the firm to choose the optimal response for a given price realization of the strategic factor.

31.7 HYSTERESIS AND COSTLY SWITCHING

With the above concepts, we can now analyze more fully the hysteresis band first given in Figure 31.2. If a firm is unable to choose the optimal response, these conditions lead to a competency trap that is expressed by a hysteresis band. In Figure 31.4, the profit functions for two capability sets and the resulting hysteresis band are graphed. Since the dynamic analysis takes into account the impact of a current switching decision on all future switching decisions the hysteresis band is wider than in a static analysis.

For the costless switching case, the switch occurs exactly at where the two functions cross. The presence of switching costs has two effects: static and hysteretic. The static costs results in the switch occurring at the value of θ where profits associated with the new mode justify the costs of adopting new organizational capabilities of lean production. θ would have to decline past this point of switching in order to justify the switching costs back to mass production.

The band between the switching costs is underestimated by looking only at static costs. Because of the possibility that θ may revert back to previous values (e.g. due to a sudden drop in oil prices favoring gas-guzzling cars), the firm persists in its current mode and waits to see how prices evolve in the future. At some point, however, θ takes on values that justify not only the one-time switching costs but also the probability-weighted costs attached to switching back. The range of inaction associated between switching in and out of a capability set is what is defined as the 'dynamic hysteresis band' depicted in Figure 31.4.[28]

---

[28] For an analysis of hysteresis effects of foreign direct investment under fluctuating exchange rates, see Kogut and Kulatilaka (1994a).

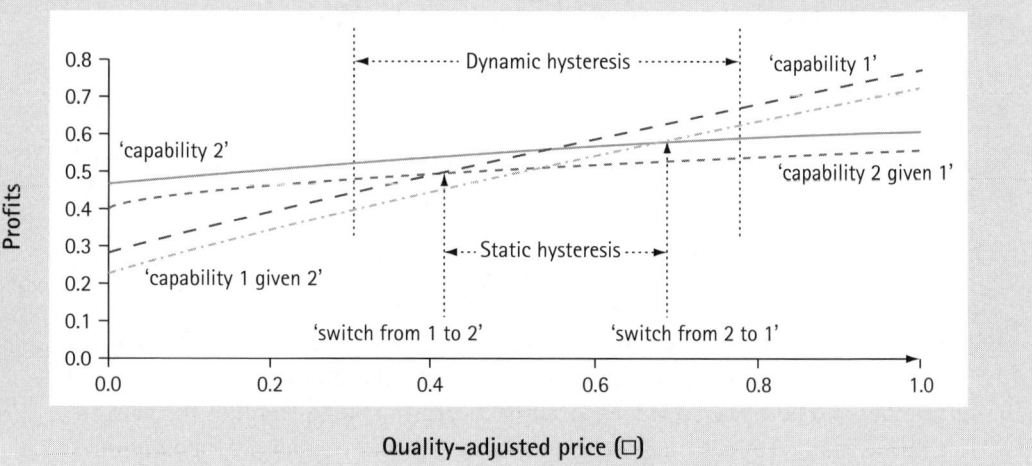

Fig. 31.4 Static and dynamic hysteresis

31.8 COMPETENCY TRAPS AND
LEARNING TO LEARN

Owing to the benefits of learning by doing, the firm's capabilities improve dynamically. In effect, the profit function can be described as shifting outward over time. By staying in its current activities, the firm becomes increasingly more competent. Techniques of mass production are expressed in well-understood routines that couple technology and people through known organizing principles of work.

The danger remains, of course, that θ will suddenly jump to a range or cross a critical threshold in which the firm's competence is no longer profitable. In a sense, its accumulated learning in the old techniques is a 'competency trap'. By improving in mass production, it is less attractive to change organizational capabilities. Hence a firm might rationally preserve its way of doing things, because it has become so good at doing the (now) wrong thing. Dougherty (1995) has labeled this 'core incompetence'. Exploitation of current knowledge drives learning by doing; the pitfall is that this learning increases the rigidity of the firm.

To speed its transition to new techniques, the firm may decide proactively to allocate funding to exploration by experimenting with new techniques. This diversion of resources slows down its accumulation of learning with the current technology. At the same time, it increases the value of the option to switch to new

capabilities by lowering the costs of switching. To characterize this wider menu of choices, Figure 31.5 depicts the decision of a firm that has accumulated a particular breadth of knowledge in the current production techniques, as well as in learning derived from experiments with new methods. (We can think of these experiments as 'joint ventures', such as the Nummi venture between General Motors and Toyota.)

The net effects of learning are ambiguous and depend upon the rate by which new knowledge is gained through learning by doing relative to experimentation. In Figure 31.6, this comparison is graphed by showing the upward change in profit-functions over time due to these two learning effects. By construction, we show the gains to experimentation dominating learning by doing.

We can expect that the attractiveness of experimentation increases with time for two reasons. First, the drift of prices leads to the expectation that over time, the old techniques should be scrapped. Secondly, it is reasonable to think of the gains to learning as marked by eventual declining returns. As the 'technological opportunities' of the current capabilities are exhausted, the attractiveness of exploring in the new set of techniques should increase.

We expect, therefore, that investments in learning should follow a cyclical pattern. Indeed, the historical record suggests that the early experiments in mass

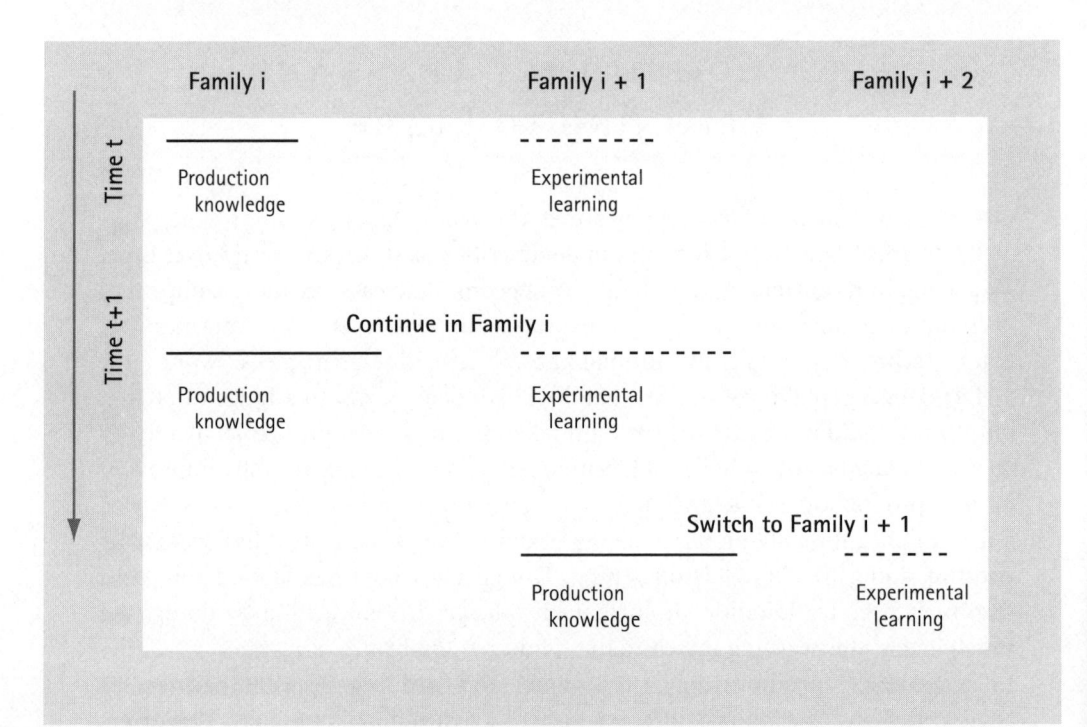

Fig. 31.5 Expanded capability sets

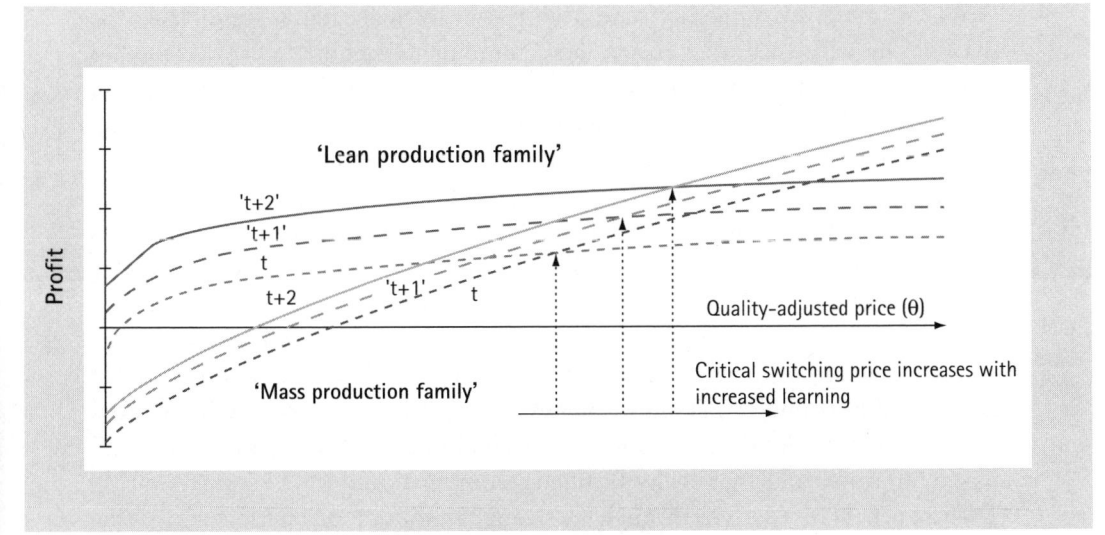

Fig. 31.6 Effects of learning

production gradually dwindled. It would be consistent with this view to expect that the investments in incremental learning so often attributed to Japanese firms should also decline over time, as these opportunities are exhausted. It is not necessary to stipulate that for cultural reasons, Japanese firms are better learners than American firms are. Rather, in a particular cross-section of time, Toyota had *more* to learn about how to expand its capabilities than Ford, which had after 60 years explored most of the terrain of how to organize mass production of standardized products. When there are few gains to exploration, allocation to exploitation of current capabilities dominate investments in incremental learning.

31.9 COMBINATIVE CAPABILITIES

Our portrayal of exploitative learning by doing as a process of discovering better matches between organizational and technological elements suggests a dynamic by which knowledge accumulates through recombination. This characterization of learning implies that the capabilities of firms can improve by a modular design. In this case, there is a higher order strategy rested upon the combinative capabilities of a firm to dynamically readjust its knowledge (Kogut and Zander 1992).

We can make this similarity more transparent by analyzing in more detail the dynamic by which learning accumulates through recombination. This point is implicit in the argument of Baldwin and Clark (1993, 2000) that the benefits of modularity are realized through exercising the embedded options to ratchet up improvement. They note that modularity allows for a better process of 'mix and match' through an improved understanding of subsystems.

An intuitive way to understand their model is to compare two kinds of strategies of throwing dice.[29] Let the score on each die indicate performance. The first strategy is to toss both dice, and then to accept or reject the total. The second is to toss each separately, and apply the same decision rule to each die separately. The first strategy reflects an *integrated* design; the second, a *modular* design. The modular design allows for the possibility that one die scores a 5, while the other only a 2. In this case, the designer may decide only to toss the second die. By this process of mix and match, improves in design evolve through recombination.

These benefits are derived through the strong assumption that performance is the sum of independent draws, i.e. the outcome of tossing a die. There are two important implications from dropping independence of the draws. The first is that the benefits fall, because the experiments are correlated. Behaviorally, correlation in experiments captures realistically the limitations of any firm in designing independent projects; statistical correlation reflects the bias of managers in the projects they are willing to support.

The second implication is that interdependence makes the design problem more difficult. For by fixing one of the dice, the performance contribution of the second module is dependent not simply on its own efficiency, but also on its interaction with the first module. As a consequence, the optimization of a given set of modules does not guarantee that this evolutionary process can ever arrive at a 'best' system. However, the notion of correlation also expresses tightly the idea that irreversibility is derived from the rigidity of competence in managing a particular set of interdependent organizational and technological elements.

This insight of correlated performance underscores why exploratory search is required. Implicit in any modular design is a system constraint. If the overall system performance is inferior to competing systems (e.g. lean production), then evolutionary learning through recombination within a given capability set leads to a competency trap. It is this evolutionary characterization of the learning process that provides the behavioral basis to the concept set-to-set correspondence as defining a capability set.

---

[29] This exposition is due to Per-Goeran Persson's remarkable student paper written for a course on organizational design at the Stockholm School of Economics. His Monte Carlo simulation of the following description is available on request.

31.10 How Good a Heuristic?

Strategic option theory is obviously a complex heuristic to apply. However, much like the BCG growth matrix does not need to measure costs, a core competence heuristic does not (always) need to value the option. Instead, through identifying the value of the competence as derived from market price of correlated assets, strategic option theory disciplines the core competence analysis to understand valuation as sensitive to competitive forces. These forces tend to limit the potential exploitation of a competence through a consideration of the effects on price and competition.

There are, however, several important complications to a strategic option heuristic. These complications provide important insight into the use of strategic options, and they also suggest the sub-optimal transfer of the heuristic to inappropriate settings. For illustration, we consider three problem areas.

31.10.1 Competitive Interactions

The valuation of a strategic option requires an identification of a market price by which to derive the replicate of the underlying asset. In financial markets, this price is easily given by stock or future prices. An important and reasonable assumption is that exercising the option does not influence the value of the replicating portfolio.

This assumption does not hold always for strategic options for two reasons. First, by exercising an option to enter a market, a firm often influences prices through increasing supply. Second, by entering (or exiting) a market, competitors will alter their behavior. As a result, the market price is endogenous to the decision whether to exercise the option.

This problem is partly resolved by recognizing that the value of θ reflects the assessment on entry.[30] But this assumption hardly provides insight into the identity of possible entrants and their strategic behavior. A structural approach is explicit regarding the nature of future competition. Kulatilaka and Perotti (1998) follow this approach by evaluating the decision to launch a new technology in the context of different conjectures about market structure. This solution marries the industry structure analysis to core competence, but through the stipulation that the analysis is forward-looking rather than focused on current market structure.

---

[30] This endogeneity is similar to the work done on currency rate dynamics when traders form expectations on central bank policy. See the essays in Krugman and Miller (1992).

31.10.2 Why Not Switch Now?

The hysteresis band, we have suggested above, is influenced by the extent to which a firm has locked into a tightly-coupled system. Another explanation seeks to explore a question—often under-theorized in strategy research—concerning who gains from a decision to switch. Baldwin (1982) showed, for example, that owners would maintain inefficient plants in a bargaining setting to threaten workers from seeking higher wages. Kulatilaka and Marks (1988) analyzed why owners might choose to persist in an older, non-flexible technology as a way to signal a credible commitment to workers over wages. Both of the above papers suggest that bargaining strategies increase the value of maintaining older technologies and hence widen the hysteresis band.

A related issue is the difference between innovators and imitators. In the case of innovation, the profit windfall means that the bargaining problem is dividing a larger pie; Ford could win acceptance by increasing wages to $5 a day (see Raff 1988). For imitators, adoption is in the midst of declining revenues; there is less to redistribute and hence bargaining is more of a zero-sum game for some parties. The situation facing imitators is more of an end game, where bankruptcy is a credible outcome. In this context, switching to new practices is more an issue of survival than improving fitness relative to rivals. These concerns form the central debate in the strategic thinking in Europe and elsewhere on whether firms should insist on flexible labor markets as a policy to respond to international competition.

31.10.3 Stock Options as Compensation

This notion of flexibility in employment is often also extended to flexibility in compensation. There is a frequent belief that a large firm could be more flexible to seize opportunities if employees' compensation was contingent on outcomes. There are, however, two major problems to such an argument. Putting in option-like compensation clauses results in high variance of compensation for managers in comparable positions. As almost all studies on compensation show, pay and performance are not closely linked because it is demoralizing; employees do not believe that differentials reflect ability and they find the social comparison to be unfair. The implications for promoting what should be the source of gain to a firm—namely, sustained coordinated and cooperative behavior—are invidious.

Second, compensation by options does not encourage flexibility. As Lambert, Larcker, and Verrecchia (1991) found, managers treat options that are in the money as wealth, and they consequently do not want to take decisions that eradicate their value. Unless a compensation scheme can be designed so that every decision is linked to a contingent payment, compensation by options is a disincentive for flexibility.

Excessive incorporation of options in compensation is a heuristic, while appealing in its financial language in an age of institutional investors, whose application is detrimental.

31.11 Conclusions

Real option analysis provides the theoretical foundations to heuristics derived core competence. It offers the improvement by conditioning an understanding of competence in relation to a market test (e.g. Barney's notion of a strategic factor market) and by putting the organizational dilemma in central stage as the leading explanation for the irreversibility of investments in capabilities. In a narrow sense, it denigrates discounted cash flow analysis as the principal tool of understanding the value of a firm. But more profoundly, the recognition that the coupling of people and technology is a source of considerable option value challenges simplistic notions of firms as 'pure asset plays'.

It is reasonable to also ask whether the formal theory itself is liable to be implemented through a more usable heuristic framing. Reducing the mathematical formulation to linear approximations, e.g. the proposal by Bowman and Moskowitz (2002), makes this framing more plausible to the manager. However, the larger challenge remains whether the rigor of using an assessment of market valuation of options leads to heuristic frames that improve the quality of strategizing.

Through the link to the value of the embedded knowledge in organizational assets, the treatment of capabilities as strategic options deflects, ironically, a purely financial evaluation of the firm. Because organizations consist of coupled systems, the value of the firm is not reflected in the present value of its constituent parts, but in the combinative potential (i.e. the option value) of deploying these capabilities for innovation in existing markets or for addressing new markets.

The implications of modularity as maintaining the option to recombine capabilities has an intuitive appeal to current trends in flat and flexible organizations.[31] It suggests that firms are dynamic systems consisting of the complex coupling of technology and people through organizational design. The ironic conclusion to the sustained application of financial modeling to firms is that in the end, the fundamental basis of the value of the firm is its organizational capability to exploit current and explore future opportunities.

[31] Baldwin and Clark (1993) provide an interesting discussion and model of the value of modularity as options under the assumption of independence among the modules or development projects. An issue that cannot be pursued here is the observation that the value of the firm rests in managing the dependence among these modules; otherwise, a policy of outsourcing, e.g. a Toyota production system, can equally manage independent modules for eventual downstream assembly.

References

ALLISON, GRAHAM T. (1971). *Essence of Decision: Explaining the Cuban Missile Crisis.* Boston: Little, Brown.

AMRAM, MARTHA, and KULATILAKA, NALIN (1999). *Real Options: Managing Strategic Investments in an Uncertain World.* Boston: Harvard Business School Press.

BALDWIN, C. Y. (1982). 'Optimal Sequential Investment when Capital is Not Readily Reversible'. *Journal of Finance*, 37: 763–82.

—— and CLARK, K. (1992). 'Capabilities and Capital Investment: New Perspectives on Capital Budgeting'. *Journal of Applied Corporate Finance*, 5: 67–82.

—— —— (1993). 'Modularity and Real Options'. Boston: Harvard Business School, Working Paper, #93–026.

—— —— (1994). 'Capital Budgeting Systems and Capabilities Investments in U.S. Companies after World War II'. *Business History Review*, 68/1: 73–109.

—— —— (2000). *Design Rules: The Power of Modularity.* Cambridge, Mass.: MIT Press.

BARLEY, STEPHEN (1990). 'The Alignment of Technology and Structure through Roles and Networks'. *Administrative Science Quarterly*, 35: 61–103.

BARNEY, JAY (1986). 'Strategic Factor Markets: Expectations, Luck, and Business Strategy'. *Management Science*, 32/10: 1231–41.

BARTLETT, FREDERIC (1958). *Thinking.* New York: Basic Books.

BOWMAN, EDWARD (1963). 'Consistency and Optimality in Managerial Decision-Making'. *Management Science*, 9: 310–21.

—— (1995). 'Strategy History: Through Different Mirrors'. *Advances in Strategic Management*, 11: 25–45.

—— and MOSKOWITZ, GARY (2002). 'The Use of Options Analysis in Strategic Decision-Making'. *Organization Science*, forthcoming.

CHANDLER, ALFRED (1962). *Strategy and Structure.* Cambridge, Mass.: MIT Press.

COHEN, MICHAEL, and BACDAYAN, PAUL (1994). 'Organizational Routines are Stored as Procedural Memory: Evidence from Laboratory Study'. *Organization Science*, 5: 554–68.

DIXIT, AVINASH, and PINDYCK, ROBERT (1994). *Investment Under Uncertainty.* Princeton: Princeton University Press.

DOSI, GIOVANNI, and KOGUT, BRUCE (1993). 'National Specificities and the Context of Change: The Co-evolution of Organization and Technology', in B. Kogut (ed.), *Country Competitiveness: Technology and the Organizing of Work.* New York: Oxford University Press, 249–62.

DOUGHERTY, DEBORAH (1995). 'Managing Your Core Incompetencies for Innovation'. *Entrepreneurship, Theory, and Practice*, 19: 113–35.

HAMEL, GARY, and PRAHALAD, C. K. (1994). *Competing for the Future: Breakthrough Strategies.* Boston: Harvard Business School Press.

HEDLUND, GUNNAR, and ROLANDER, DAG (1990). 'Action in Heterarchies: New Approaches to Managing the MNC', in C. A. Bartlett, Y. Doz, and G. Hedlund (eds.), *Managing the Global Firm.* New York: Routledge.

HENDERSON, REBECCA (1993). 'Underinvestment and Incompetence as Responses to Radical Innovation: Evidence from the Photolithographic Alignment Equipment Industry'. *Rand Journal*, 24: 248–70.

Hull, John, C. (1997). *Options, Futures, and Other Derivatives* (3rd edn). Upper Saddle River, NJ: Prentice-Hall.

Ittner, Chris (1996). 'Exploratory Evidence on the Behavior of Quality Costs'. *Operations Research*, 44/1: 114–30.

——and Kogut, Bruce (1995). 'How Control Systems Can Support Organizational Flexibility', in Edward Bowman and Bruce Kogut (eds.), *Redesigning the Firm*. New York: Oxford University Press, pp 155–82.

Kahneman, Daniel, and Lovallo, Dan (1993). 'Timid Choices and Bold Forecasts: A Cognitive Perspective on Risk Taking'. *Management Science*, 39: 17–31.

Kim, Dong-Jae, and Kogut, Bruce (1996). 'Technological Platforms and Diversification'. *Organization Science*, 7: 283–301.

Kogut, Bruce, and Kulatilaka, Nalin (1992). 'What is a Critical Capability?', Reginald H. Jones Working Paper, Wharton School.

————(1994a). 'Options Thinking and Platform Investments: Investing in Opportunity'. *California Management Review*, 36/2: 52–71.

————(1994b). 'Operating Flexibility, Global Manufacturing, and the Option Value of Multinationality'. *Management Science*, 40: 123–39.

————(2002). 'Capabilities as Real Options'. *Organization Science*, forthcoming.

——and Zander, Udo (1992). 'Knowledge of the Firm, Combinative Capabilities, and the Replication of Technology'. *Organization Science*, 3: 383–97.

Krugman, Paul, and Miller, M. (eds.), (1992). *Exchange Rate Targets and Currency Bands*. Cambridge: Cambridge University Press.

Kulatilaka, Nalin, and Marcus, Alan (1992). 'Project Valuation under Uncertainty: When does DCF Fail?', *Journal of Applied Corporate Finance*, 5/1: 92–100.

——and Marks, Stephen (1988). 'The Strategic Value of Flexibility: Reducing the Ability to Compromise'. *American Economic Review*, 78: 574–80.

——and Perotti, Enrico (1998). 'Strategic Growth Options'. *Management Science*, 44/8: 1021–31.

Kunreuther, Howard (1969). 'Extensions of Bowman's Theory on Managerial Decision-Making'. *Management Science*, 16: 415–39.

Lambert, Richard, Larcker, David, and Verrecchia, Robert (1991). 'Portfolio Considerations in Valuing Executive Compensation'. *Journal of Accounting Research*, 29: 129–49.

Leach, J. Chris (1994). 'Good and Bad Variance in Valuing Production and Technological Expenditure Programs or Are Real Options Really Options?' Mimeo, Wharton School.

Lincoln, James (1993). 'Comparison of Japanese and US Organizational Structures', in B. Kogut (ed.), *Country Competitiveness: Technology and the Organizing of Work*. New York: Oxford University Press, 54–74.

McDonald, Robert, and Siegel, Daniel (1984). 'Option Pricing When the Under-lying Asset Earns a Below-Equilibrium Rate of Return: A Note'. *Journal of Finance*, Mar.: 261–5.

MacDuffie, John Paul (1996). 'Human Resource Bundles and Manufacturing Perform-ance: Flexible Production Systems in the World Auto Industry'. *Industrial and Labor Relations Review*, 48/2: 197–221.

Mansfield, Edward (1988). 'Speed and Cost of Industrial Innovation in Japan and United States'. *Management Science*, 34: 1157–68.

MARCH, JAMES (1991). 'Exploration and Exploitation in Organizational Learning'. *Organization Science*, 2: 71–87.

MERTON, ROBERT C. (1976). 'Option Pricing When Underlying Stock Returns are Discontinuous'. *Journal of Financial Economics*, 3./Jan./Mar.: 125–44.

MILGROM, PAUL, and ROBERTS, JOHN (1990). 'The Economics of Modern Manufacturing: Technology, Strategy, and Organization'. *American Economic Review*, 80: 511–28.

MINSKY, MARVIN (1985). *The Society of Mind*. New York: Simon and Schuster.

MINTZBERG, HENRY (1990). 'Strategy Formulation: Schools of Thought', in J. Frederickson (ed.), *Perspectives on Strategic Management*. New York: Harper Business, 105–236.

NELSON, RICHARD R., and WINTER, SIDNEY G. (1982). *An Evolutionary Theory of Economic Change*. Cambridge, Mass.: Harvard University Press.

PINDYCK, ROBERT S. (1991). 'Irreversibility, Uncertainty, and Investment'. *Journal of Economic Literature*, 29/3: 1110–52.

PIORE, MICHAEL, and SABEL, CHARLES (1984). *The Second Industrial Divide*. New York: Basic Books.

PORTER, MICHAEL (1980). *Competitive Strategy: Techniques for Analyzing Industries and Competitors*. New York: Free Press.

RAFF, DANIEL (1988). 'Wage Determination Theory and the Five-dollar Day at Ford'. *Journal of Economic History*, 48: 387–99.

—— and BRESNAHAN, T. F. (forthcoming). 'Plant Shutdown Behavior during the Great Depression and the Structure of the American Motor Vehicle Industry'. *Journal of Economic History*, forthcoming.

SCHERER, F. M. (1967). 'Research and Development Resource Allocation under Rivalry'. *Quarterly Journal of Economics*, 81: 359–94.

SCOTT, W. RICHARD (1995). *Institutions and Organizations*. Thousand Oaks, Calif.: Sage.

SELZNICK, PHILIP (1957). *Leadership in Administration: A Sociological Interpretation*. Evanston, Ill.: Row, Peterson.

SERVAN-SCHREIBER, JEAN-JACQUES (1969). *The American Challenge*. New York: Athenaeum.

SIMON, HERBERT (1992). *The Sciences of the Artificial*. Cambridge, Mass.: MIT Press, seventh printing.

SZULANSKI, GABRIEL (1995). 'Unpacking Stickiness: An Empirical Investigation of the Barriers to Transfer Best Practice Inside the Firm'. *Academy of Management Best Paper Proceedings*, 437–41.

TEECE, DAVID, PISANO, GARY, and SHUEN, AMY (1997). 'Dynamic Capabilities and Strategic Management'. *Strategic Management Journal*, 18: 509–34.

TUSHMAN, MICHAEL, and ANDERSON, PHILIP (1986). 'Technological Discontinuities and Organizational Environments'. *Administrative Science Quarterly*, 31: 439–65.

USEEM, MICHAEL (1996). *Investor Capitalism: How Money Managers are Changing the Face of Corporate America*. New York: Basic Books.

WINTER, SIDNEY (1987). 'Knowledge and Competence as Strategic Assets', in D. Teece (ed.), *The Competitive Challenge—Strategies for Industrial Innovation and Renewal*. Cambridge, Mass.: Ballinger, 159–84.

ZANDER, UDO, and KOGUT, BRUCE (1995). 'Knowledge and the Speed of the Transfer and Imitation of Organizational Capabilities: An Empirical Test'. *Organization Science*, 6/1: 76–92.

STRATEGIC FLEXIBILITY

CREATING DYNAMIC COMPETITIVE ADVANTAGES

HENK W. VOLBERDA

32.1 CRISIS IN STRATEGY: ESCAPING THE RED QUEEN RACE

As we entered the twenty-first century, strategy as a field of study has fallen on hard times. Changing competitive environments are forcing companies in almost every sector to re-examine their strategy and organizational form. There seems to be a growing consensus among managers that the path to success leads away from traditional strategy prescriptions advocating top-down control, formal planning, and rational industry-analysis. Managers and practitioners are heralding flexibility as the new hallmark of organizational excellence. Moreover, the business literature on strategic change is replete with prescriptions and directives with regard to successful strategic transformations, often summarized in terms of catchy statements, such as *downsizing* the corporation; *re-engineering* the business process; *outsourcing* of non-core activities; *benchmarking* the core activities; creating *multi-functional project teams*; *empowering* employees; increasing the *workforce flexibility*

(multi-skilled workers); expanding the externalized workforce (temporary workers); replacing highly specialized machinery for *flexible manufacturing systems*; and developing *multi-purpose* information systems.

Despite all the business literature offering these signposts for new flexible modes of managing and organizing, the discipline of strategic management seems to play a minor role in this debate. To what degrees are these trends commented on so widely yet empirically little studied, woven together into a coherent strategic approach? Is there just one type of flexible firm? Does every firm face the same competitive challenges? How should we design a flexible corporation?

Up till now, managers in today's competitive environment were engaged in strategic experiments without the guidance of an appropriate theory or framework. Many one-time industry leaders that failed to keep up with the accelerating pace of industry change have started large-scale strategic transformations and increasingly experimented with new flexible forms. Yet, these 'best managed' firms of the 1970s and 1980s, such as IBM (ongoing reorganizations resulting in a 13 per cent reduced headcount by 1993), Xerox (numerous reorganizations in the 1980s), and Philips (launching of the Centurion project in 1990 resulting in the elimination of 67,000 jobs over a three-year period) have been partly successful in transforming their traditional organizations. They all restructured themselves by using a slash-and-burn approach, cutting staff to the bone without thinking about how the work gets done and rationalizing their portfolios without supporting promising new lines of business. The enforced corporate anorexia made these companies thinner and more efficient, but did not really make them more flexible (Hamel and Prahalad 1994: 11). One sometimes has the feeling that in these large-scale transformations it is forbidden to mention the word 'strategy' at all. In this respect, former Philips' CEO Jan Timmer claimed that not strategy but the client was the most important for initiating the Centurion change project. Similarly, the German CEO of Daimler-Benz, Jürgen Schrempp, aggrieved after many difficult questions about the direction of the company commented 'Strategie kann man nicht essen'. Also John Kay (see Chapter 2) rightly reasoned in the *Financial Times* (1998) that 'Strategy' is the most misused word and in daily practice often associated with expensive, inefficient, and prestigious. Considering the killing competition nowadays, companies do not like the S-word anymore. In this connection, Kay poses in a bantering way that the sentence 'I am a strategist' should be translated as 'I have a large office, a high salary, and the ear of the CEO', 'I am a strategy consultant' means 'our fees are very high', and 'this is a strategic investment' implies 'we are going to lose a lot of money on this project'.

In a reply to this devaluation of the strategy concept, management futurologists have tried to show us a rough sketch of successful companies in the new competitive landscape, including the virtual corporation (Davidow and Malone 1992); the hollow corporation; the dynamic network form (Miles and Snow 1986); the hypertext organization (Nonaka and Takeuchi 1995); the platform organization (Ciborra 1996); and the shamrock organization (Handy 1995). Most of these studies, however,

have tried only to justify and rationalize successful adaptive organizational forms (e.g. Sun Microsystems' virtual organization, Dell Computer's dynamic network, Sharp's hypertext form, Olivetti's platform organization, or F international's electronic shamrock). However, the transience of successes of manufacturing companies such as DAF, Fokker, and more recently, IT companies such as Baan and World On-Line have proven that there is no permanent successful strategy.

Do we have to conclude then that strategy is passé? Or even worse, that the key question in strategic management, namely: 'Why does one company outperform the other?' (Porter 1991) cannot be answered? In other words, firms are caught in a competitive race of more of the same in which in the end only losers remain. Instead of long, stable periods in which firms can achieve sustainable competitive advantages, competition is increasingly characterized by short periods of advantage punctuated by frequent disruptions (D'Aveni 1994). Competitive advantages are continuously eroded by actions of other players which lead again to higher levels of competition and the need to react faster. In the end, these dynamic interactions between firm learning and adaptation, on the one hand, and higher levels of competition and selection, on the other hand, cancel each other out. This is often dubbed an 'arms race' or 'the Red Queen effect' (Kauffman 1995) after the comment to Alice, 'It takes all the running you can do to keep in the same place' (Carroll 1946). Companies adapt faster and faster, but as a consequence of the resulting increase in competition they do not make any progress (see Box 32.1). Similar dynamic strategy concepts are *hypercompetition* (D'Aveni 1994) and *coevolution* (Lewin and Volberda 1999).

How can firms escape the Red Queen effect in which there is no place for sources of competitive advantage? What has strategy to offer in these highly competitive

Box 32.1 The Red Queen effect

'Now! Now!' cried the Queen. 'Faster! Faster!' And they went so fast that at last they seemed to skim through the air, hardly touching the ground with their feet till, suddenly, just as Alice was getting quite exhausted, they stopped, and she found herself sitting on the ground, breathless and giddy.

The Queen propped her up against a tree, and said kindly, 'You may rest a little now.'

Alice looked round her in great surprise. 'Why, I do believe we've been under this tree the whole time! Everything's just as it was!'

'Of course it is,' said the Queen. 'What would you have it?'

'Well, in *our* country,' said Alice, still panting a little, 'you'd generally get to somewhere else—if you ran very fast for a long time, as we've been doing.'

'A slow sort of country!' said the Queen. 'Now, *here*, you see, it takes all the running *you* can do to keep in the same place. If you want to get somewhere else, you must run at least twice as fast as that!'

Source: Carroll 1946: 178–9.

environments? Although we have to re-evaluate the assumptions of traditional static strategy models, there is great unanimity among strategy scholars that the need for strategic thinking in these hypercompetitive environments is even greater than ever. According to Porter (1996), in his article 'What is strategy', those beliefs that competitive advantages are at best temporary are 'dangerous half-truths, and they are leading more and more companies down the path of mutually destructive competition'. In his argument, downsizing, restructuring, re-engineering, and benchmarking often only improve operational effectiveness, but do not provide strategic advantage. Likewise, Hamel and Prahalad (1994) contended that instead of 'more of the same' or 'try harder' approaches ('How to be better'), firms should fundamentally reconsider their core activities ('How to be different'). Not a static strategy, but strategic renewal and industry transformation are much more important. Elsewhere, Hamel (1996) preaches strategy as revolution; creating new industries and breaking the existing rules of the industry. This implies that not a fixed strategy but strategic flexibility is the source of success. Strategic flexibility may help firms to escape the Red Queen effect in which all competitive advantages are cancelled out by increasing competition.

In this chapter, we first explore the concept of flexibility in theories of strategic management (Section 32.2). Subsequently, we provide a more dynamic approach in strategic management in which strategic flexibility is considered as a constructive friction between change and preservation, in particular between routines and dynamic capabilities, learning and unlearning, administration and entrepreneurship (Section 32.3). On the basis of this paradox of flexibility, we develop a strategic framework that distinguishes the building blocks needed to analyse and discover viable strategic positions in various competitive environments (Section 32.4). In this framework, flexibility is a managerial as well as an organization design task. The managerial task involves the creation of capabilities for situations of unexpected disturbance (Section 32.4.1). On the basis of the variety of these capabilities and speed of response, four types of flexibility are distinguished: steady-state, operational, structural, and strategic flexibility. The organization design task concerns improving the responsiveness of the organization, which depends on the creation of the right conditions to foster flexibility (Section 32.4.2). We consider various technological, structural, and cultural barriers to flexibility. The challenge for management is thus to develop dynamic capabilities that enhance flexibility and to have an adequate organizational design to utilize those capabilities. In other words, a flexible organization must possess some capabilities which enhance its flexibility to avoid becoming rigid, but it must also be anchored in some way in order to avoid chaos.

On the basis of this strategic framework of flexibility, we distinguish alternative flexible forms that connect different types of competitive environments with effective types of flexibility and organization designs: the rigid, planned, flexible, and chaotic form (Section 32.4.3). Moreover, various trajectories of organizational failure and success in meeting various levels of competition are derived from this

typology (Section 32.5). Application of this framework within large companies shows us dual trajectories of transformation for coping with hypercompetition: revitalization of core activities together with radical transformation for developing new activities (Section 32.6). On the basis of these ongoing tensions between exploitation and exploration in multi-unit firms we distinguish four more permanent corporate forms for creating strategic flexibility: the network, the dual, the oscillating, and the balanced corporation (Section 32.7). They illustrate that companies in highly competitive environments have various choices for winning the Red Queen race (Section 32.8).

32.2 FROM STRATEGIC MANAGEMENT TO STRATEGIC FLEXIBILITY

Over the past thirty years, strategic management has become established as a legitimate field of research and managerial practice. In the evolution of strategy research, a diversity of partly competitive and partly supplementary paradigms or models have emerged (cf. Volberda and Elfring 2001). For a long time, however, these models ignored the concept of flexibility. They focused instead on how firms should develop sound strategies by means of systematic forecasting, planning, and control. While it is true that organizations must pursue strategies for purposes of consistency, they must also discard their established competencies in response to a changed environment. When environmental changes become increasingly undefined, fast-moving, and numerous, it is risky to rely upon conventional strategic management approaches. Therefore, more recent descriptive strategy perspectives consider flexibility as a strategic asset in situations in which anticipation is impossible and strategic surprise likely (cf. Aaker and Mascarenhas 1984; Quinn 1980; Sanchez 1995). In this section, we will consider major developments within the strategy field and their contribution to flexibility.

32.2.1 The Linear Model: Rigidities of Strategic Planning

Historically, an organization's strategy has been thought of as an integrated plan. The most frequently cited definitions of organization strategy are provided by Andrews (1971) and Chandler (1962), and emphasize concepts such as goals, resource allocation, and especially plans. These concepts form the essential

elements of the *linear model* of strategic management (Chaffee 1985), corresponding to what others have called the 'planning' (Mintzberg 1973), 'rational' (Peters and Waterman 1982), 'rational comprehensive' or 'synoptic' (Fredrickson 1983) approach.

This model still pervades the literature on the process of strategic management. In this sequential process, 'strategy formulation' precedes 'strategy implementation'. Emphasis is on planning 'What to do', rather than on planning 'What the organization might be capable of doing in the future'. As a consequence, the content of strategy (i.e. 'in which direction do we change the firm's position in the environment?') dominates the process in the linear model, while the process itself is often underestimated or oversimplified. The linear model assumes there are no problems with implementing strategy after it has been formulated.

Regarding strategy formulation, the role of the management is that of a 'rational actor' issuing directives from the seat of power. The model assumes that an exhaustive analysis can be undertaken before action is taken, and requires that management holds a considerable amount of power and has access to complete information. Regarding implementation, the role of the management is that of an architect, designing administrative systems to orchestrate implementation and to push the organization towards goal achievement. By manipulating the systems and structures of the organization in support of a particular strategy, however, the management may be trading off important strategic flexibility. 'Should an unforeseen change in the environment require a redirection of the strategy, it may be very difficult to change the firm's course, since all the "levers" controlling the firm have been set firmly in support of a now-obsolete game plan' (Bourgeois and Brodwin 1984).

Thus, where environmental uncertainty is high, it may prove effective in the long run to refrain from the linear model described above. Whereas in a stable environment we can permit deliberate formulation and execution of strategy, many situations now involve strategic surprises that do not give sufficient warning to permit deliberate planning (Burton 1984). A stable environment increases the likelihood that the critical variables can be identified, and it allows plans to be developed regarding the relationship between those variables and the organization. On the other hand, a highly unstable environment makes it difficult to achieve the level of certainty needed by rational models to be effective.

According to the linear model, however, increased environmental uncertainty can be addressed by a more comprehensive decision process. Instead of relatively fixed strategic programmes, which are in essence extrapolations of former trends, management has to develop action strategies and to concentrate on certain essential strategic issues, both of which have to be regularly revised (Ansoff 1980: 132–48). In addition, in situations of more extreme uncertainty, management has to develop contingency plans in which decisions are assessed and prepared that deviate from decisions which are part of the long-term plan (Linneman and Chandran

1981). Contingency plans are complementary plans; that is, they are based on developments that are relatively unlikely, but are very important should they occur (see for a more detailed treatment Chapter 11 on scenario planning). These 'What if' approaches are widely understood and growing in technical sophistication as a result of computer modelling (Burton and Naylor 1980). Indeed, these various planning tools are able to cope with more uncertainty. Yet, they are not sufficient to assure the viability of the organization. There is a limit to an organization's planning repertoire, due to organizational inertia. A firm can change its plan yearly, monthly, or daily, but the one-sided focus on planning is insufficient and leads in many cases to organizations becoming ever more rigid. For instance, an increase in the number of planning forecasts of the Central Planning Department of Philips Semiconductors in Eindhoven resulted only in larger inventories and higher prices for the plants. It has been suggested that even if an organization has significant resources, attempting to be comprehensive may result in achieving tomorrow's solution to yesterday's problem (Braybrooke and Lindblom 1970: 121).

Attitudes towards planning and analysis should therefore be biased towards new ways of thinking in order to compensate for the one-sided tendency of corporate planners to produce highly formalized and ritual-like planning procedures. In this context, Pennings (1985: 20) and Starbuck (1983) warned against the institutionalization and routinization of formal planning systems, which might lead a life of their own, uncoupled from relevant strategic events. In such circumstances, strategy becomes the job of an increasingly specialized planning department that is divorced from the everyday business. Numerous examples can be found in the public sector where planning systems are imposed upon the organization by legislative moves or in large private corporations where planning systems are imposed by executive order. For instance, in the 1970s and early 1980s, strategic planning was the gospel at GE. The company's elaborate controls ranged from detailed monthly budget approvals to an annual strategic planning review that required six to eight months of preparatory research and analysis (Tichy and Sherman 1994). Jack Welch's success started when he dismantled this rigid strategic planning system and slimmed down the corporate planning group. Instead of directing a business according to a detailed GE-style strategic plan, Welch believes in setting only a few, clear overarching goals.

Considering these arguments, we might conclude that in the linear approach, there is no room for flexibility. At most, flexibility represents a management capacity for quickly developing plans to anticipate new developments. However, we argued that in situations of radical change, attempts to adopt planning would only paralyse the organization. The annual planning rituals within corporations restrict their creative potential; options are fixed and new options are not noticed. That is, planning is the least flexible of the strategy-making modes. Its obsession with rationality leads to a further refinement of the planning mechanism that is the cause of the problems.

32.2.2 The Adaptive Model: Opportunistic Behaviour and Flexible Resources and Capabilities

Surprisingly enough, it was Ansoff (1978), one of the founders of the linear model, who suggested that the level of environmental change was increasing and giving rise to strategic surprises, making strategic anticipation and strategic planning of the sort that proceeds in an outside-in, market-to-product development manner no longer useful. According to Ansoff, the planning concept of strategy had to be re-examined because uncertainty limits the ability of the organization to pre-plan or make decisions about activities in advance of their execution. Because of this effect, organizations must develop flexibility. The more uncertain the situation, the more an organization will need flexibility as a complement to planning (cf. Thompson 1967: 148). Therefore, Ansoff (1978) asserted that in these situations the use of traditional action strategies ('In which direction do we change the firm's position in the environment?') would be increasingly supplemented and sometimes replaced by preparedness or flexible configuration strategies ('How do we configure the resources of the firm for effective responses to strategic surprises?'). Rather than adhering single-mindedly to a predetermined set of goals and course of action, it is better to be capable of adapting to a variety of possible events, exigencies, or unpredictable states of nature (Burton 1984).

In line with this emphasis, Mintzberg and Waters (1985) argued that the focus should not be placed on deliberate planning and control, but on developing an organizational capacity for strategic thinking and learning, which means being open and responsive. From this capacity, strategies emerge which are not guided by explicit a priori intentions. Patterns or consistencies are realized despite, or in the absence of, intentions. Nevertheless, the emergence of these ex post strategies does not mean that management is out of control, only that it is open, flexible, and responsive. 'Such behaviour is especially important when an environment is too unstable or complex to comprehend, or too imposing to defy. Openness to such emergent strategy enables management to act before everything is fully under-stood—to respond to an evolving reality rather than having to focus on a stable fantasy' (Mintzberg and Waters 1985: 271). As an example, Mintzberg and Waters proposed that a distinctive competence cannot always be assessed on paper a priori; often, it has to be discovered empirically by taking actions that test where strengths and weaknesses really lie.

The different modes of strategy discussed above are depicted in Figure 32.1. The relationship between environmental turbulence and comprehensiveness of planning activities is presented as a reversed U-form. In a relatively stable environment, strategic management can be limited to the development of strategic programmes, which are based on the extrapolation of trends. There is no need to change the organization. When the environment becomes more unstable, strategic programmes are insufficient and have to be supplemented with strategic issue management or even

contingency planning. Besides strategic programmes, management has to focus on certain relevant issues and initiate organizational activities regarding these issues. If these programmes and issues have to be revised too often, contingency planning is more suitable. For every possible change, a plan has to be developed and the organization must be well organized in order to anticipate these various plans. However, in a highly unstable environment, planning activities create more problems than they solve. The associated uncertainty is not amenable to formal objective assessment. Therefore, organizational activities are substituted for planning activities in order to create a flexible configuration of resources. These preparedness strategies result in a more spontaneous organization. Figure 32.1 shows that in situations of high environmental uncertainty, deliberate planning becomes less important while organizing for flexibility becomes more important.

Preparedness strategies are part of the *adaptive model* of strategic management, a term also used by Mintzberg (1973) and Chaffee (1985). In this model, strategic management is depicted as a messy, disorderly, and disjointed process around which competing factors contend. Lindblom (1959), Mintzberg (1978), and Quinn (1980) contributed substantially to this approach by doing more descriptive strategy research instead of prescriptive research. Their contributions are founded largely on the notion of cognitive limits of rationality as described in the early work of Herbert Simon and James March (March and Simon 1958).

On the basis of these insights, it was Lindblom (1959) who first claimed that policy-making in government is an incremental process of 'muddling through' that is distinct from the linear rational perspective, since different sub-units display a disorderly proliferation of preference orderings and divergent views of cause–effects relations. Lindblom's arguments have generally been supported by other management scientists. For example, in his ground-breaking *Harvard Business Review* article 'Good Managers Don't Make Policy Decisions' Wrapp (1967) argued that disjointed incrementalism is also found in business firms. Years later, Quinn (1980) concluded that this 'non-rational' incrementalism is logical because of the inherently iterative nature of strategic decisions and the resultant need to make and remake them. In his in-depth study of nine large corporations facing major changes, Quinn concluded that the successful firms were those in which the strategist was able to adjust incrementally to changes in customer needs or in which the internal structures and processes were appropriate.

The adaptive model differs from this linear model in several ways.

- *Facilitating bottom-up initiatives.* The linear model still works on the assumption that the CEO, management, or planning group can design an explicit 'grand' strategy for the entire enterprise based on a highly top-down, deliberate, analytical process. Honda's successful entry in the American motorcycle market demonstrates that sound strategies are not always explicitly formulated. The opportunities to experiment within Honda, the trial and error behaviour in design, and the

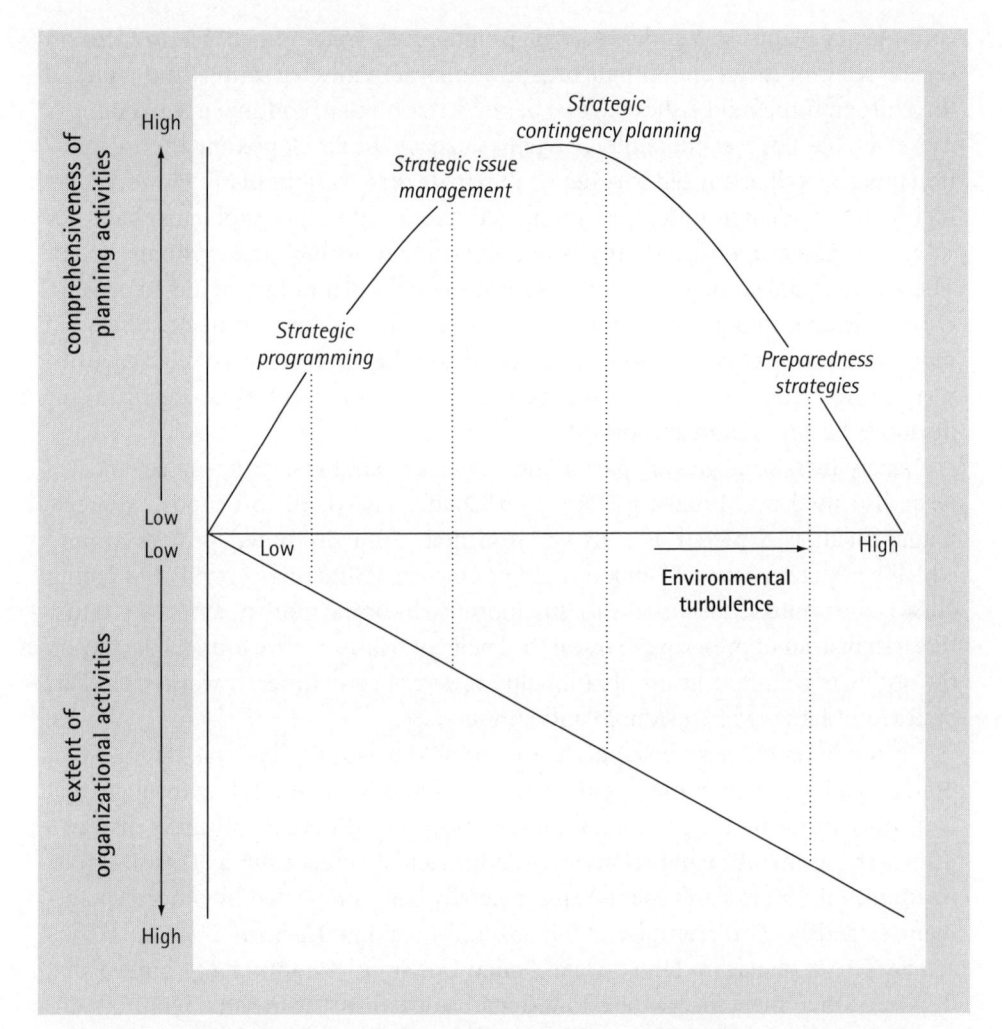

Fig. 32.1 Different modes of strategy depicted as a constellation of the degree of environmental turbulence, the comprehensiveness of planning activities, and the extent of organizational activities

Note:

Strategic programming	extrapolation of trends without changing the organization
Strategic issue management	besides programmes, also focusing on relevant issues and initiating activities in line with these issues
Strategic contingency planning	developing plans for every possible change and transforming the organization in order to anticipate possible developments
Preparedness strategies	decreasing planning activities, and increasing organizational activities in order to get more strategic mileage out of the organization in case of strategic surprises

firm's lack of a hierarchical structure suggest that perhaps the most effective process of strategic management is through originating, developing, and promoting strategic initiatives from the bottom up (Pascale 1984). Other researchers (Bower 1970; Burgelman 1983; Quinn 1985) further developed this bottom-up

perspective. They demonstrated that in large diversified firms strategy emerges from the bottom-up initiatives of individuals or small groups, while the role of top management is often restricted to retroactive legitimizer. More recently, on the basis of ABB's recent success Bartlett and Ghoshal (1993) have argued for a more proactive perspective; the role of top management in this predominant bottom-up process is to challenge the status quo, while the middle line is concerned with horizontal linking and leveraging of capabilities across units. These divergent findings illustrate that strategy is less centralized in top manage-ment, more multifaceted, and generally less integrated than in the linear model. The adaptive model therefore asserts that strategic management is an organiza-tion-wide activity in which each management level has to contribute in its own way (Van Cauwenberg and Cool 1982).

- *Keeping options open.* A second difference follows from the relative unimport-ance of advance planning in the adaptive model (Chapter 31 by Kogut and Kulatilaka deals more thoroughly with strategic options). Top management initially formulates guidelines in more general terms. These are designed to steer the organization in the increasingly turbulent and therefore uncertain environment and to maintain a flexible position vis-à-vis the large number of unknown future events. Specific proposals formulated in technical and economic terms typically emanate from front-line management, while middle management faces the difficult task of integrating both activities. Since the formulation and the implementation of specific strategic initiatives do not originate at the same hierarchical level, and since different hierarchical levels are found to be relatively independent, it is inevitable that strategy can develop only in an incremental way. Strategic management is necessarily a fragmented process, whereby initiatives arise from different subsystems and top management defines strategies as broadly as possible and leaves options open as long as possible.

- *Maintaining flexibility of resources and managerial capabilities.* The adaptive model does not deal with decisions about goals as emphatically as the linear model. Instead, it tends to focus the manager's attention on resources and capabilities, and the goals are represented by alignment of the organization with the environment. If markets are in a state of flux, then the internal resources and capabilities of a firm appear to be a more suitable basis for strategy formula-tion than the external environment (Grant 1996). For instance, Honda had no superior strategy for entering the US motorcycle market, but it had unique dealer-network capabilities and superior engine expertise. In this conception, organizational flexibility depends on the inherent flexibility of resources available to the firm and on the firm's managerial capabilities in applying these resources to alternative courses of action (Sanchez 1995). Honda was able to apply its engine expertise in different end-products like motorcycles, cars, snowblowers, and lawnmowers. Similarly, Citibank is able to move rapidly to acquire other banks' portfolios and credit cards, adjust rates and prices, and target specific customer

niches in promotional campaigns largely because of its continuing investment in general-purpose information-processing capabilities (Boynton and Victor 1991). In the linear model, such investments in flexible and general-purpose processing capabilities without known specific product returns would be considered signs of inefficiency. In the adaptive model, however, such investments create an asset for strategic surprise (see also Chapter 31).

The emphasis on the flexibility of resources deployed and managerial capabilities are further developed in the resource-based theory of the firm (Penrose 1959; Learned et al. 1969). This approach does not consider the firm as a black-box guided by the strategist, but as a bundle of firm-specific 'resources' which can lead to superior 'performance' (see also Sanchez's treatment of resources in Chapter 12). Although most of the proponents of the resource-based approach originally considered only pure physical resources, a shift can be seen towards more interest in 'intangible resources', 'tacit knowledge', and 'capabilities' (cf. Quinn 1992; Itami 1987; Teece, Pisano, and Shuen 1997). The more a firm can exploit its resources in various end-markets, create access to a broad knowledge base, and build up a variety of capabilities, the more flexible it becomes.

In summary, the adaptive model of strategic management requires an a priori flexible configuration of resources in order to facilitate ex post emergent strategies. In situations of fundamental uncertainty, the management has to keep options open and to build in flexibility in order to adapt to and successfully handle unforeseen contingencies and exogenous shocks. In this regard, flexibility is a strategic asset for facilitating effective responses to 'unanticipated' changes.

32.2.3 The Interpretative Model: Varying Strategic Schemas

Some discussion remains about the nature of incrementalism within the adaptive model. What exactly drives adaptation? How can small, resource-limited firms successfully adapt to competitive change while some corporate giants with plentiful resources and many strategic options cannot? For instance, how could a smaller company like Canon manage to make such a huge dent in Xerox's market share? Why was Sharp more successful in the electronic calculator business than Texas Instruments? Apparently, strategic options and flexible resources are not a sufficient basis for adaptation. The explanations for what drives adaptation vary from those who see adaptation as a result of cognitive schemas (Weick 1979), paradigms (Johnson 1987), or cultural idea systems (Smircich and Stubbart 1985).

Adaptation requires that participants are able to make sense of their environment and know what to adapt to. In other words, the question of what drives adaptation depends on the socially constructed reality of organizational participants. That is, reality is defined through a process of social interchange in which perceptions are affirmed, modified, or replaced according to their apparent congruence with the

perceptions of others. Weick (1979) described this process as enactment. Members of organizations actively form or enact their environment through their social interaction. A pattern of enactment establishes the foundation of organized reality, which in turn has effects in shaping future enactments. Strategy in this *interpretative model* might be defined as strategic schemas or frames of reference that allow the organization and its environment to be understood by organizational stakeholders (cf. Bettis and Prahalad 1995; Chaffee 1985: 93). These strategic schemas lead to calculated behaviour of participants in non-programmed situations (Van Cauwenberg and Cool 1982). As such, stakeholders are motivated to believe and act in ways that are expected to produce favourable outcomes for the organization.

The most essential question for management becomes one of how to develop adequate strategic schemas that enable the firm to create or adapt to competitive change. The choice of schemas and interpretations becomes a creative and political art. Novel and interesting schemas may stimulate novel and interesting environments that can in turn preface novel and interesting strategic initiatives. For instance, when Sharp entered the electronic calculator business, it did not have an established strategic schema in the home appliance business, its main business. The calculator division of Sharp thus enjoyed a high degree of freedom in the strategy formulation process and was able to refine its strategic schema independently. While Sharp was able to refine its strategic schema, Texas Instruments could not change its schema. In TI, there already existed a sophisticated strategic schema in the semiconductor business, and its electronic calculator business was heavily dependent on the semiconductor division. When applied to the new business, the strategic schema which worked so well for TI in the semiconductor business led to failure.

Smircich and Stubbart (1985) argued that companies might be able to enlarge their capacities for novel interpretations by varying schemas systematically. Strategic management in this approach involves creating and maintaining systems of shared meaning that facilitate organized action. Similarly, Hamel and Prahalad (1994) discussed the concept of strategic intent: ambitious goals that stretch far beyond the temporal bounds of strategic plans. According to them, successful firms simply have more foresight, and are capable of imagining products, services, and entire new businesses that do not yet exist.

Nonetheless, too much control or too narrow an organizational set of beliefs and assumptions can prevent valuable strategic initiatives from rising from the front line, while too little guidance can result in destructive chaos. Organizations with very strong cultures usually suffer from xenophobia (Ouchi 1981). That is, they resist deviance, retard attempts at change and tend to foster homogeneity and inbreeding. IBM is an excellent example of a strong culture. Its strategic schema revolved around a set of unseen assumptions about the centrality of the mainframe business. This mainframe logic was strongly preserved in IBM's culture. The resulting cultural blocks hampered IBM's efforts to refashion its basic beliefs and assumptions in line with changes in the computer business.

As the above arguments imply, flexibility means that strategic schemas must be broad enough to encourage strategic initiatives and narrow enough to suppress counterproductive actions. In this sense, a flexible organization is an organization with a core set of beliefs of a relatively high order and yet rather heterogeneous sets of beliefs at other levels (Peters and Waterman 1982). That is, there must be a 'constructive tension' between that which is necessary to preserve and that which must be changed (Kanter 1983), such as that between the need for managers to question and challenge and the preservation of core values and the organizational 'mission'.

32.2.4 Flexibility from a Strategic Perspective

On the basis of these developments in strategic management, flexibility has become a strategic asset in strategic management theories. In Table 32.1 these developments within strategic management are illustrated.

Table 32.1 Developments within strategic management and their contributions to organizational flexibility

Strategic management		
Linear model	*Adaptive model*	*Interpretative model*
Planning strategies	Flexible configuration strategies	Strategic schemas
In which direction do we have to change the firm's position in the environment?	How do we have to configure the resources of the firm for effective responses to unanticipated changes?	How do we give meaning to our activities for participants and stakeholders?
Problem area: establishing long-term goals	Problem area: developing flexible resources and capabilities	Problem area: creating and maintaining broad strategic schemas
Methods: long-term planning, SWOT analysis, determination of sustainable competitive advantages	Methods: analysing firms' resources and managerial capabilities	Methods: managing culture by concentrating on values, symbols, language, and dramas
Flexibility is a management capacity for quickly developing plans	Flexibility is an organizational capability for facilitating emergent, spontaneous strategies	Flexibility is an imaginative capacity for creating strategic schemas broad enough to encourage strategic initiatives

Traditionally, a strategic manager is portrayed as a planner, an implementer of structure, and a controller of events who derives ideas from information. However, in a highly turbulent environment, the prescriptive assertions of the linear model are no longer tenable. As a consequence of more descriptive strategy research, the strategist's task is defined as organizational in the adaptive model and imaginative in the interpretative model. These developments have contributed substantially to the concept of flexibility, which from a strategic perspective means creating a flexible configuration of resources for facilitating emergent strategies and creating strategic schemas which enhance the creation of multiple interpretations. It results in a process of the management of 'unintended order' (Mintzberg and Waters 1985) or 'controlled chaos' (Quinn 1985), in which change as well as stability is possible. That is, the organization can respond to surprises and initiate novel actions, but is also able to resist certain changes or to squash destructive initiatives.

32.3 THE PARADOX OF FLEXIBILITY: TENSIONS BETWEEN EXPLOITATION AND EXPLORATION

Theories of strategic management showed us that flexibility requires change and preservation. But how do firms reconcile the conflicting forces for change and stability? How do they promote order and control, while having to respond, renew, and learn? Expanding worldwide competition, fragmenting markets, and emerging technologies force established firms to renew themselves continuously by transforming stagnant businesses and creating new sources of wealth through new combinations of resources (Guth and Ginsburg 1990). On the other hand, short-term competitive forces require them to maximally exploit their existing capabilities and competencies.

Those tensions have been variously described in the strategy literature as change versus preservation (cf. Poole and Van de Ven 1989; Volberda 1996), adaptation versus selection (cf. Lewin and Volberda 1999), and exploration versus exploitation (cf. March 1991; Levinthal and March 1993). Examined less frequently is how firms deal with these tensions over time. There has been relatively little focus on the specifics of how firms develop firm-specific competencies and how they renew them to shifts in the industry. We will investigate dynamic theories that may provide answers for how to deal with these tensions.

From an evolutionary perspective, organizations accumulate know-how in the course of their existence. They become repositories of skills that are unique and often difficult to transfer. These skills are the source of both inertia and distinctive competence. The inertia results from sunk costs in past investments and entrenched social structures, and also to organization members becoming attached to cognitive styles, behavioural dispositions, and decision heuristics. The accumulated skills that render firms inert also provide opportunities for strengthening their unique advantages and further improving their know-how. The potential benefits include greater reliability in delivering a sound and comprehensible product and many economies of efficiency and routine (Miller and Chen 1994: 1).

Among the best-known proponents of such an incremental view are evolutionary theorists (see Chapter 4) as well as researchers within the resource-based theory of the firm (see Chapter 12). In their *Evolutionary Theory of Economic Change*, Nelson and Winter (1982) present firms as repositories of routines which endow them with a capacity to search. Yet the same routines suppress attention span and the capacity to absorb new information by spelling out behaviour that permits search only for new ideas that are consistent with prior learning. In a similar way, the firm in the *resource-based theory* is seen as a bundle of tangible and intangible resources and tacit know-how that must be identified, selected, developed, and deployed to generate superior performance (Penrose 1959; Learned et al. 1969; Wernerfelt 1984). These scarce, firm-specific assets may lead to a core competence with a limited capacity to change. Just as with the evolutionary theory of economic change, the resource-based theory assumes that *firms are stuck with what they have and have to live with what they lack*.

While the suppression of choice is probably a condition for the efficient exploitation of a core competence, many studies show that in highly competitive environments a core competence can become a core rigidity (Leonard-Barton 1992; Burgelman 1994) or *competence trap* (Levitt and March 1988; Levinthal and March 1993). Firms develop core rigidities together with highly specialized resources to enhance profits at the price of reduced flexibility (Volberda 1996). GM, IBM, and DEC have encountered these traps (see Box 32.2). They have become prisoners of their deeply ingrained routines and irreversible, fixed assets, turning their formerly distinctive competencies (big cars, mainframe computers, minicomputers) into new problems to be resolved.

Box 32.2 GM's competence trap: extreme exploitation

General Motors' core competence throughout the 1980s and early 1990s is illustrative. It reinforced the mistaken belief that cars are status symbols and that styling is more important than quality. Further, finance exerted a tremendous dominance over the entire organization. The emergence of one dominant elite narrows the frame in which learning occurs. This kind of limited learning hampers search and filters away significant

amounts of relevant uncertainty, diversity, and change signals. Consequently, the organization is motivated to transform ill-defined problems into a form that can be handled with existing routines. GM rewarded only volume and simply ignored quality. The inability of the organization to solve new, significantly different problems derived from this retardation of organizational learning. Mistaken perceptions of the customer and the tight financial instruments led to complacency, myopia, and, ultimately, decline. Money became a substitute for innovation, past success turned into dogma, and maintenance of the status quo became the measure of success.

Sources: *Fortune* 1994, 1995.

In a sense, the incremental view of developing competitive advantage based on maximal exploitation has the unintended consequence of building inertia that threatens survival in a Red Queen race. Teece, Pisano, and Shuen (1997), therefore, have suggested that the relative superiority of firm-specific resources and routines cannot be taken for granted and that, from a normative perspective, the firm must always remain in a dynamic capability building mode, in which the firm retains its capacity to renew, augment, and adapt its core competence over time. Similarly, Utterback and Abernathy's (1975) model posits that a firm which does pursue the evolution of its processes and products to the extreme may find that it has achieved the benefits of high productivity only at the cost of decreased flexibility and innovative capacity. It must face competition from innovative products that are produced by other flexible firms. NCR's focus on its established line of business, electromechanical cash registers, and ignorance of electronic machines is illustrative. From 1972 to 1976, it lost 80 per cent of the market for cash registers to more flexible manufacturers of electronic products. Likewise, GM was reluctant to design and build compact cars for fear this niche would cannibalize its big-car business. The strong focus on exploitation of existing opportunities leads to the proliferation of routines that become institutionalized in planning and control systems and shared norms and values. The organization maximally adapts (static fit) and becomes very vulnerable when unexpected changes do occur. Learning and search processes take place only within narrow norms and values (single-loop learning) and result only in small, incremental changes (see Figure 32.2). Managers in these kind of organizations are mainly caretakers that are highly risk-averse and have a strong preference for stability.

Successfully competing in dynamic product markets requires resources, capabilities, and strategies that are intrinsically different from those likely to lead to competitive success in more stable markets (cf. Sanchez 1993). In the strategy field we see an increased attention to the dynamic capability approach (Volberda and Elfring 2001; Chapter 13 by Tallman) in which the emphasis is on exploring new opportunities (March 1991). However, the returns associated with exploration are distant in time and highly variable, while the returns associated with exploitation are proximate in time and more certain. It implies that management should not

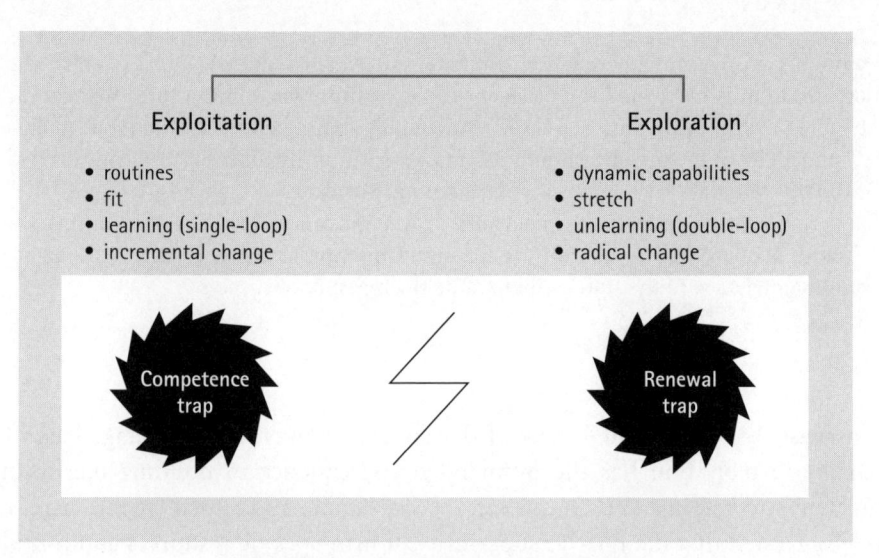

Fig. 32.2 The paradox of flexibility

completely adapt to the existing environment (fit), but create some slack in the organization (in terms of redundancies in resources and overlapping work roles) and the ambition to go for hardly reachable goals (stretch). Instead of tight fits, management has to look for loose fits in which there is some stretch for change (see Figure 32.2). With this leeway the organization can experiment and unlearn old, inadequate routines. It may result in radical changes initiated by managers with a more entrepreneurial profile (Stevenson and Gumpert 1985).

Still, it is debatable if companies that maximally explore will win the Red Queen race. Exploration can have dysfunctional effects too. 3M, a company with a superior track record in exploration of new opportunities, has found important drawbacks to overinvestment in renewal: patient financial and intellectual resources, an environment that encourages people to work around and even defy their superiors, and a determination to let the company follow where its scientists and customers lead (*Fortune* 1996). The company does not have a clear strategy; the development and introduction of a product merely evolves. Patience, for example, has cost 3M dearly in the magnetic-storage business (diskettes, videotape, and audiotape). Still, 3M held on because the business supported technologies it needed elsewhere. A well-articulated strategy could have helped 3M work its way to a quicker and less drastic resolution of the long-simmering problems in its imaging and electronic storage businesses. Too much exploration creates instability as a consequence of overreactions and excessive information searches. The organization exaggerates the importance of local errors and becomes overresponsive to fads and fashions. Continuous adjustments may waste resources on 'noise' in environmental signals. They result in chaotic organizations that cannot retain a sense of identity and continuity over time (Weick 1979: 215). Chronic exploration destroys the identity or shared idea system

of the organization. It creates a vicious circle that results in a *renewal trap* characterized by potentially serious problems with conflict of authority, unclear responsibilities, inadequate controls, lack of direction and shared ideology, and, consequently, greater scope for chaos and inefficiency (Volberda 1996, 1998). The decline of Apple Computer, once the hip flagbearer of high tech, is illustrative (see Box 32.3).

Box 32.3 Apple's renewal trap: extreme exploration

Apple created the legend of two kids in a garage inventing a computer and then building a company where the old corporate rules were scrapped: no dress or hair codes, no formal meetings. This anarchic culture facilitated renewal, but also fostered chaos and conflict. It led to many clashes between the creators, or the 'technical wizards', and the experienced managers hired to run marketing and finance. Year after year, key decisions such as licensing the Mac operating system were postponed, reversed, or avoided completely as various executives and factions tried to push their own agendas.

Source: Business Week 1996.

How can firms excel in a Red Queen race of dynamic competition? Figure 32.2 already showed us overexploitation of existing opportunities as well as overexploration of new opportunities are dysfunctional for the firm and lead to a competence trap or a renewal trap. Overexploitation ends in organizational rigidity. By focusing on planning, the organization eliminates all strategic choice. Once an optimal fit is achieved, search for new strategies tends to decline. The organization accumulates repertoires of programmes, and grows insensitive to change signals. The limited search of single-loop learning facilitates the development of a set of 'distinctive competencies' that allow the organization to develop incremental innovations. Its routines and standard operating rules, however, eliminate organizational potential: the organization is doing what it had been doing more efficiently, but is unable to question the appropriateness of its actions. Consequently, planning strategies are reinforced and errors in beliefs and norms remain. The organization is dominated by a tendency towards conservatism, delay in decision-making, and ossification. The accumulated inertia may well be so significant that it threatens the firm's survival when environments change irreversibly.

On the other hand, overexploration ends in chaos. It increases the firm's potential to deal with emergent problems in the form of expanded search and a higher level of curiosity. The associated double-loop learning, which goes together with totally new values and norms, encourages radical innovations. Nonetheless, the focus upon destroying the value of existing approaches may result in instability as a consequence of overreactions and excessive information searches. Continuous adjustment of strategic schemas and reallocations of resources may waste energy

on 'noise' in environmental signals. Consequently, the firm is transformed into a chaotic organization that cannot retain a sense of identity and continuity over time.

To sum up, extremity in either direction of the paradox between exploration and exploitation creates dysfunction in the form of rigidity or chaos. Only flexible firms that somehow solve the paradox of exploitation versus exploration may win the Red Queen race of dynamic competition. The difficulties of the flexibility paradox are illustrated by the tensions between the two main divisions of KLM Royal Dutch Airlines, the KLM Passenger and KLM Cargo divisions (see Box 32.4). To be flexible, an organization must possess attributes that are simultaneously contradictory, even mutually exclusive (see Figure 32.2).

Both contradictions of the paradox of flexibility are accepted and present. Both operate simultaneously. In her study of high-tech firms in the Silicon Valley, Bahrami (1992) showed that emerging flexible enterprises were able to manage opposing tensions. They facilitated creativity, innovation, and speed while maintaining coordination, focus, and control. They could accommodate opposing tendencies and yet function as coherent and cohesive firms. Similar tensions also seem to confront many established corporations (cf. Bartlett and Ghoshal 1988). Percy Barnevik, former CEO of ABB, describes the firm's challenge as dealing with tensions such as global versus local, big versus small, and centralized versus decentralized. British Petroleum's challenge is how to reinforce corporate control while allowing its constituent businesses much greater speed and response. In this connection, Andrew Grove of Intel introduced the metaphor 'agile giant'; big enough to win global wars of products, technology, and trade, while moving like a small company.

Box 32.4 The tensions between exploitation and exploration within KLM

KLM is a one-system company, that is, its divisions share the same resources, namely airplanes. Within the passenger division, the focus is on exploitation: achieving tight cost reductions by essentially doing more of the same activities. By contrast, within the Cargo division the emphasis is on exploration. This means doing new things in new businesses such as offering an increasing number of added value services to customers (transporting dangerous goods, live animals, or expensive paintings), attracting new customers, and providing non-transport related logistic services (subassembly of components, stock maintenance). According to Jacques Ancher, former Executive Vice President of KLM Cargo, 'Our greatest challenge is to let go; there is no place for a command and control culture. We have to be prepared for mistakes, and be prepared to learn from them. This requires an entirely different mindset to the one we had last year: it demands nothing short of fundamental change.' The KLM board, however, faces the question of how to reconcile exploitation (tight cost reductions) and exploration (new businesses) in one single company. The new cost-cutting programmes initiated by Chairman Leo van Wijk seem inescapable in the airline industry but have the negative effect of eliminating exploration.

32.4 A Strategic Framework of Flexibility

Although rivalry-reducing strategies and traditional organizational forms have worked well in the relatively stable environments of the past, the globalization of markets, rapid technological change, shortening of product life cycles, and increasing aggressiveness of competitors have radically altered the ground rules for competing in 2002 and beyond. Instead of long, stable periods in which firms can achieve sustainable competitive advantage (static competition), competition is increasingly characterized by short periods of advantage punctuated by frequent disruptions (dynamic or Red Queen competition). The strategic behaviour and underlying organizational forms of successful firms in these hypercompetitive environments (D'Aveni 1994) have received much attention recently.

On the basis of the dynamic theories in strategic management discussed in Section 32.3, we develop an integrated framework that relates competitive environments, type of managerial capabilities, and organizational conditions. In this framework, changing competitive environments require fundamentally new management and organizing principles, resulting in alternative flexible forms (see Figure 32.3). Competitive changes force firms to move more quickly and boldly and to experiment in ways that do not conform to traditional administrative theory. In order not to be competed away by the Red Queen effect, firms have to continuously develop and adapt new sources of advantage, thus being the fastest runner in the Red Queen race. This dynamic process requires new modes of managing and organizing to enable firms to explore new opportunities effectively as well as exploit those opportunities efficiently, to change their strategic focus easily as well as develop some strategic direction, and to change their dominating norms and values as well as correct deviations from essential norms and values. How can firms reconcile these conflicting forces?

The framework proposed here suggests two important tasks required to resolve the paradox of flexibility. First, it is argued that flexibility is a *managerial task*. Can managers respond at the right time in the right way? In this connection, the concern is with the variety and speed of managerial capabilities that endow the firm with flexibility; for example, manufacturing flexibility to expand the number of products the firm can profitably offer in the market or innovation flexibility to reduce the response time for bringing new products to market. Secondly, the framework suggests that flexibility is an *organization design task*. Can the organization react at the right time in the directed way? The concern here is with the controllability or changeability of the organization, which depends on the creation of the right conditions to foster flexibility. For instance, manufacturing flexibility requires a technology with multi-purpose machinery, universal equipment, and an extensive

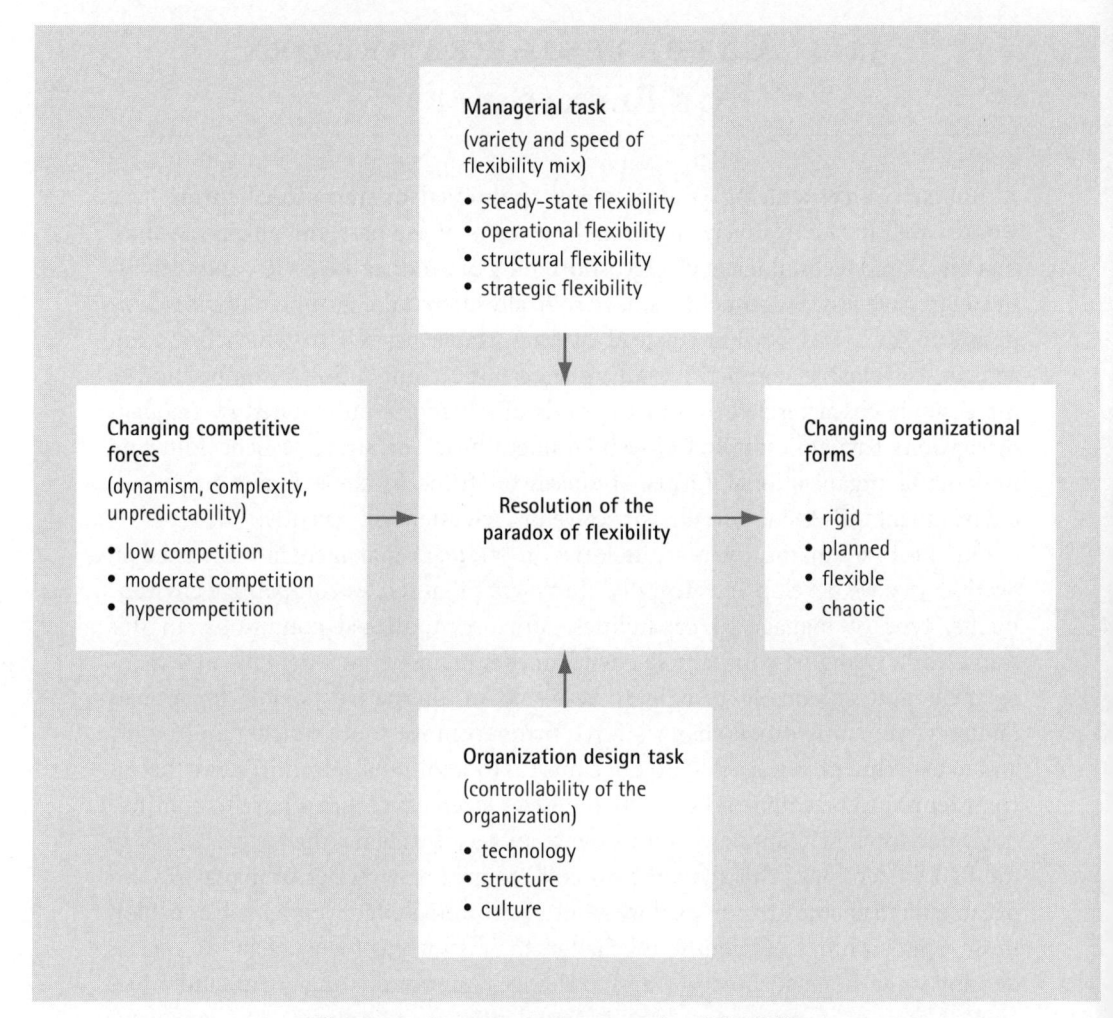

Fig. 32.3 A strategic framework of flexibility

operational production repertoire (cf. Adler 1988). Similarly, innovation flexibility requires a structure of multifunctional teams, few hierarchical levels, and few process regulations (cf. Quinn 1985).

Combining the managerial and organization design tasks involves a process of matching and resolving paradoxes. Management must develop dynamic capabilities that enhance flexibility, and the firm must have an adequate organizational design to utilize those capabilities. Consequently, management must cope with a constructive tension (Kanter 1983) between developing capabilities and preserving organizational conditions, which can be considered the building blocks of flexibility. Different companies put these building blocks together in very different ways. From this framework we can therefore obtain several alternative flexible forms, each of which reflects a particular way of coping with the paradox of change

and preservation. We will now first elaborate on the management and organization design task of flexibility. Subsequently, we will distinguish various flexible forms.

32.4.1 The Managerial Task: Developing Dynamic Capabilities

As a managerial task, flexibility involves the creation or promotion of capabilities for situations that generate unexpected disturbance. Figure 32.4 shows two core components of this managerial task, variety and speed.

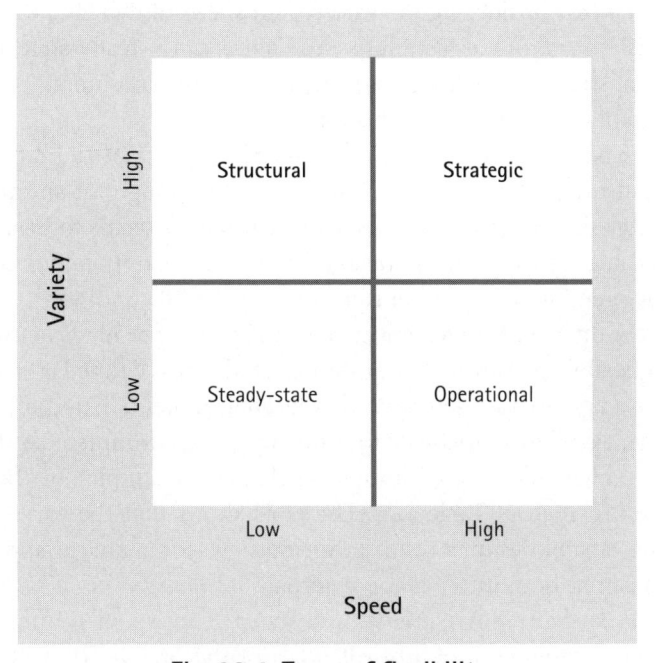

Fig. 32.4 Types of flexibility

Variety of managerial capabilities. Both the currently used arsenal of capabilities and the collection of potential flexibility-increasing capabilities that are not yet activated are important. Currently used capabilities have already been deployed for the purpose of flexibility. The possible emergence of opportunities or threats requires management to have some potential capabilities as insurance against risk (see Scott 1965). Ashby (1964) demonstrated that to be able to respond to all circumstances, a firm must have a variety of capabilities at least as great as the variety of disturbances in the environment. In a turbulent environment, management needs an extensive, multidimensional collection of capabilities. Variety can be in terms of either the quantity (the number) of capabilities or the quality of capabilities (such as temporary versus durable flexibility-increasing capabilities).

For instance, the training of multi-skilled personnel results in a durable improvement in flexibility, whereas the contracting out of certain peripheral activities or 'hire-and-fire' employment practices results in a temporary improvement in flexibility. Temporary flexibility-increasing capabilities lead to a reduction of the potential for use once allocated, but durable flexible capabilities are not restricted in use.

Speed. Management may have the necessary capabilities, but may not be able to activate them in time. Flexibility is not a static condition, but a dynamic process. Speed is therefore an essential factor of organizational flexibility.

The dynamic capabilities that endow the firm with flexibility are manifested in the '*flexibility mix*'. Considering the variety and speed of dynamic capabilities, we can distinguish four types of flexibility (see Figure 32.4): steady-state, operational, structural, and strategic. Each type represents a simple combination of more/less variety of capabilities and fast/slow response.

Steady-state flexibility (low variety, low speed) consists of static procedures to optimize the firm's performance when the levels of throughput and the nature of throughput remain relatively stable over time. It hardly seems to be a real type of flexibility because under steady-state conditions there is only minor change and a relatively low premium on speed of response to external conditions.

For the other three types of flexibility, a distinction can be made between internal and external flexibility (Ansoff 1965). Internal flexibility is defined as management's capability to adapt to the demands of the environment. External flexibility is defined as management's capability to influence the environment so that the firm becomes less vulnerable to environmental changes. Examples of these types of flexibility are provided in Table 32.2. The table shows that the variety and speed of managerial capabilities may result in various levels of managerial manoeuvring capacity and can be both internal and external.

Operational flexibility (low variety, high speed) consists of routine capabilities that are based on present structures or goals of the organization. It is the most common type of flexibility and relates to the volume and mix of activities rather than the kinds of activities undertaken within the firm. The routines used are directed primarily at the operational activities and are reactive. Operational flexibility provides rapid response to changes that are familiar. Such changes typically lead to temporary, short-term fluctuations in the firm's level of activity. Although the variety in the environment may be high, the combinations of conditions are sufficiently predictable for management to develop routine capabilities to reduce uncertainty.

Operational flexibility can be internal or external. Examples of internal operational flexibility are the variation of production volume, the building up of inventories, and the maintenance of excess capacity. For instance, vertically integrated fashion apparel firms like Benetton or The Limited have developed 'quick-response' capabilities aimed at shortening the manufacturing cycle, reducing

Table 32.2 Examples of internal and external types of flexibility

	Internal	External
Routine manoeuvring capacity	Internal operational flexibility • variation of production volume • building up of inventories • use of crash teams	External operational flexibility • use of temporary labour • multi-sourcing • reserving of capacity with suppliers
Adaptive manoeuvring capacity	Internal structural flexibility • creating multifunctional teams • changing managerial roles • alternations in control systems	External structural flexibility • purchasing of components from suppliers with a short delivery time (JIT) • purchasing of subassemblies from suppliers (co-makership) • developing of subcomponents together with suppliers (co-design)
Strategic manoeuvring capacity	Internal strategic flexibility • dismantling of current strategy • applying new technologies • fundamentally renewing products	External strategic flexibility • creating new product-market combinations • using market power to deter entry and control competitors • engaging in political activities to counteract trade regulations

inventory levels, and enabling manufacture in response to sales during the season (Richardson 1996). These routine capabilities in rapid learning, communication, and coordination supplant traditional core competencies in design and fashion sense. Rather than bet on a few designs from the most savvy designers, these firms try out many designs, quickly imitate others, and continue to produce what sells. Though product innovations and demand changes are rapid and somewhat unpredictable, introducing new products and responding to changing demands are routine manoeuvring in fashion apparel. New styles and designs do not usually require new types of inputs or process technologies. The object of this kind of internal operational flexibility is a more efficient, less risky operation in a volatile end market. In addition to these internal types, external operational flexibility can be achieved by contracting out certain peripheral activities, using temporary labour to adjust the size of the workforce to shifts in product demand, or obtaining resources from more than one supplier.

Structural flexibility (high variety, low speed) consists of managerial capabilities for adapting the organization structure, and its decision and communication processes, to suit changing conditions in an evolutionary way. When faced with

revolutionary changes, management needs great internal structural flexibility or intra-organizational leeway to facilitate the renewal or transformation of current structures and processes. Examples of internal structural flexibility are horizontal or vertical job enlargement; the creation of small production units or work cells within a production line; changes in organizational responsibilities; alterations in control systems; the use of project teams; and the transformation from a functional grouping to a market-oriented grouping with interchangeable personnel and equipment.

Structural flexibility can also be external in terms of inter-organizational leeway in supporting and sheltering new technologies or developing new products or markets. Examples include various forms of JIT purchasing, comakership, co-design, or even joint ventures and other coalignments. By increasing structural relations with outsiders, the organization can engage more easily in new developments. This type of flexibility is perfectly illustrated by Nordvest Forum, a group of 46 small- and medium-sized firms in and around the city of Alesund on the north-west coast of Norway (Hanssen-Bauer and Snow 1996). In order to cope with hypercompetitive environments, these regional firms developed network relationships that expedite the learning process and help the member firms to upgrade their adaptive capacity so that they can compete more effectively in both the national and international marketplaces. More extreme examples of superior external structural flexibility include large dominating firms or strategic centres such as Nike, Nintendo, Sun Microsystems, and Toyota (Lorenzoni and Baden-Fuller 1995). These firms responded to increasing competition by forming tight network organizations in which they perform only a few unique functions along the value chain and outsource the remaining functions to specialist partners. Such relationships can be temporary, as in the case of a past alliance among IBM, Intel, and Microsoft in the computer industry, or it can endure, as in the long-standing relationships between Nike and its production partners in the athletic footwear and apparel industry (see Chapter 22 for a more elaborate treatment of alliances and networks by Faulkner). From the focal firm's standpoint, external structural flexibility raises interesting questions about the relative efficacy of internal versus external avenues towards new products, technologies, and knowledge. When management retains the opportunity to modify the structural relationship and leave a relationship that no longer meets its needs (external structural flexibility), external avenues can be very attractive. If not, internal avenues by means of internal structural flexibility are more appropriate.

Strategic flexibility (high variety, high speed) consists of managerial capabilities related to the goals of the organization or the environment (Aaker and Mascarenhas 1984). This most radical type of flexibility is much more qualitative and involves changes in the nature of organizational activities. It is necessary when the organization faces unfamiliar changes that have far-reaching consequences and needs to respond quickly. The issues and difficulties relating to strategic flexibility are by definition unstructured and non-routine. The signals and feedback received from the environment tend to be indirect and open to multiple interpretations, 'soft' and

'fuzzy'. Because the organization usually has no specific experience and no routine answer for coping with the changes, management may have to change its game plans, dismantle its current strategies (Harrigan 1985), apply new technologies, or fundamentally renew its products. Its response may also be external, for example influencing consumers through advertising and promotions (Mascarenhas 1982), creating new product market combinations (Krijnen 1979), using market power to deter entry and control competitors (Porter 1980), or engaging in political activities to counteract trade regulations. New values and norms are necessary and past experience may not provide any advantage. The creation of new activities in new situations may be very important. For instance, Regional Bell Operating Companies (RBOCs) that were spun off from AT&T developed strategic flexibility from international expansion activities because the international managers in the unregulated side of the business questioned past practices, raised new assumptions about the organization, and promoted significant changes in strategy. The transfer of strategic capabilities from international operations to domestic network operations was helpful in awakening wireline operations to the realities of coming competition and the need for employees to be flexible, strategic thinkers (Smith and Zeithaml 1996).

32.4.2 The Organization Design Task: Creating Adequate Organizational Conditions

The ability to initiate the repertoire of managerial capabilities depends on the design adequacy of organizational conditions, such as the organization's technology, structure, and culture. Those conditions determine the organization's controllability or responsiveness. If management tries to increase the flexibility repertoire beyond the limits of organizational conditions, the controllability of the organization will diminish.

Designing the appropriate organizational conditions requires identifying the type of technological, structural, or cultural changes necessary to ensure effective utilization of managerial capabilities. For many service and manufacturing organizations, recent developments in *technology* have created a range of programmable automation systems and general information systems that seem to afford much greater flexibility potential (Adler 1988; Ittner and Kogut 1995). In this connection, 'technology' refers to the hardware (such as machinery and equipment) and the software (knowledge) used in the transformation of inputs into outputs, as well as the configuration of the hardware and software. The design of technology can range from routine to non-routine, corresponding to the opportunities for routine capabilities. Richardson's study (1996) of fashion apparel firms shows those firms that redesigned their technology by implementing new information technologies

such as CAD/CAM equipment and EDI developed a much greater potential for operational flexibility.

Increases in controllability might also involve changes in *organizational structure*. Organizational structure comprises not only the actual distribution of responsibilities and authority among the organization's personnel (basic form), but also the planning and control systems and the process regulations of decision-making, coordination, and execution. The structural design of the organization can range from mechanistic to organic (Burns and Stalker 1961), corresponding to the opportunities for adaptive capabilities.

Many large corporations are undertaking organizational restructuring to increase their responsiveness (a more detailed discussion can be found in Chapter 28 by Whittington). For instance, Xerox was able to exploit its superior technological and market capabilities after fundamentally changing its organizational architecture by creating business divisions with self-organizing teams and developing new reward and recognition systems (Howard 1992). Similarly, Smith and Zeithaml (1996) illustrated that the newly developed capabilities of two Regional Bell Operating Companies (RBOCs) could be successfully deployed after drastic restructuring and organizational redesign.

Not only structural changes, but also cultural changes may be necessary to increase the controllability of the firm. *Organizational culture* can be defined as the set of beliefs and assumptions held relatively commonly throughout the organization and taken for granted by its members (Bate 1984). Essential features of such beliefs are that they are implicit in the minds of organization members and to some extent shared (Hofstede 1980). These beliefs may constrain managerial capabilities by specifying broad, tacitly understood rules for appropriate action in unspecified contingencies (Camerer and Vepsalainen 1988). The organizational culture can range from conservative to innovative, depending on the slack within the current norms and value systems for strategic capabilities.

The beliefs and assumptions of the organizational culture also play a central role in the interpretation of environmental stimuli and the configuration of organizationally relevant strategic responses (Johnson 1987). Does the organization see new strategic options? Can it deviate from present patterns? The more innovative the culture, the greater the leeway for strategic flexibility within the organization. Hence, many large Western corporations such as GE, Philips, and ABB have not only restructured themselves, but also tried to change their corporate cultures. After downsizing and delayering, GE started its famous workout programme, best-practice sessions, and change acceleration programme (Tichy and Sherman 1994). In the same way, Philips' Centurion programme started with an efficiency drive but was followed by a cultural revitalizing module initiated by the concern committee, Values and Behaviour (the Philips Way). An even more radical cultural change was attempted by ABB, which developed a 21-page 'Mission, Values, and Policy' booklet referred to inside the company as the policy bible when it formed its global matrix

structure. Moreover, Craig's (1996) study of two players in the Japanese beer indus-try reveals that cultural change is also an important issue in Japanese companies. Asahi initiated and Kirin responded to hypercompetition by not only working on their functional structure, but also reconsidering their intolerant culture. Both firms fundamentally changed their corporate culture by corporate identity and empowerment programmes.

32.4.3 A Typology of Alternative Forms for Coping with Hypercompetition

Our strategic framework shows that the managerial task and the organization design task have to be matched with various levels of competition to achieve effective flexibility (see Figure 32.3). From our framework we can obtain four ideal types: the *rigid, planned, flexible,* and the *chaotic* form. Each type represents a particular way of addressing the flexibility paradox of exploration versus exploit-ation, and some are more effective than others.

32.4.3.1 *The Rigid Form: Strategic Programming*

In a rigid organization management has a very restricted flexibility mix dominated by simple procedures (steady-state flexibility). Its choice and variation possibilities are limited; improvisation is forbidden in the organization. The mature technology (routine), the functionalized and centralized structure with many hierarchical layers (mechanistic), and the monotonous and narrow-minded culture (conserva-tive) do not allow potential for flexibility and result in a fragile and vulnerable organization (see Figure 32.5).

In a static, simple, and predictable environment, we often find rigid forms. In such non-competitive environments, firms have established positions that enable them to develop absolute sustainable competitive advantages and generate excessive profit potential. In such environments, there is little need for managers to expend effort on a flexibility mix or for the organizational conditions to generate potential for flexibility. Too much flexibility is a nuisance. Strategy is in the rigid form limited to the development of strategic programmes, which are mainly based on extrapo-lation of existing trends.

32.4.3.2 *The Planned Form: Strategic Planning*

The *planned form* also has a narrow flexibility mix, but its variety of routines and organizational responsiveness are less limited than in the rigid organization. The flexibility mix consists mainly of specific rules and detailed procedures, which are sophisticated and complex and require an extensive information-processing

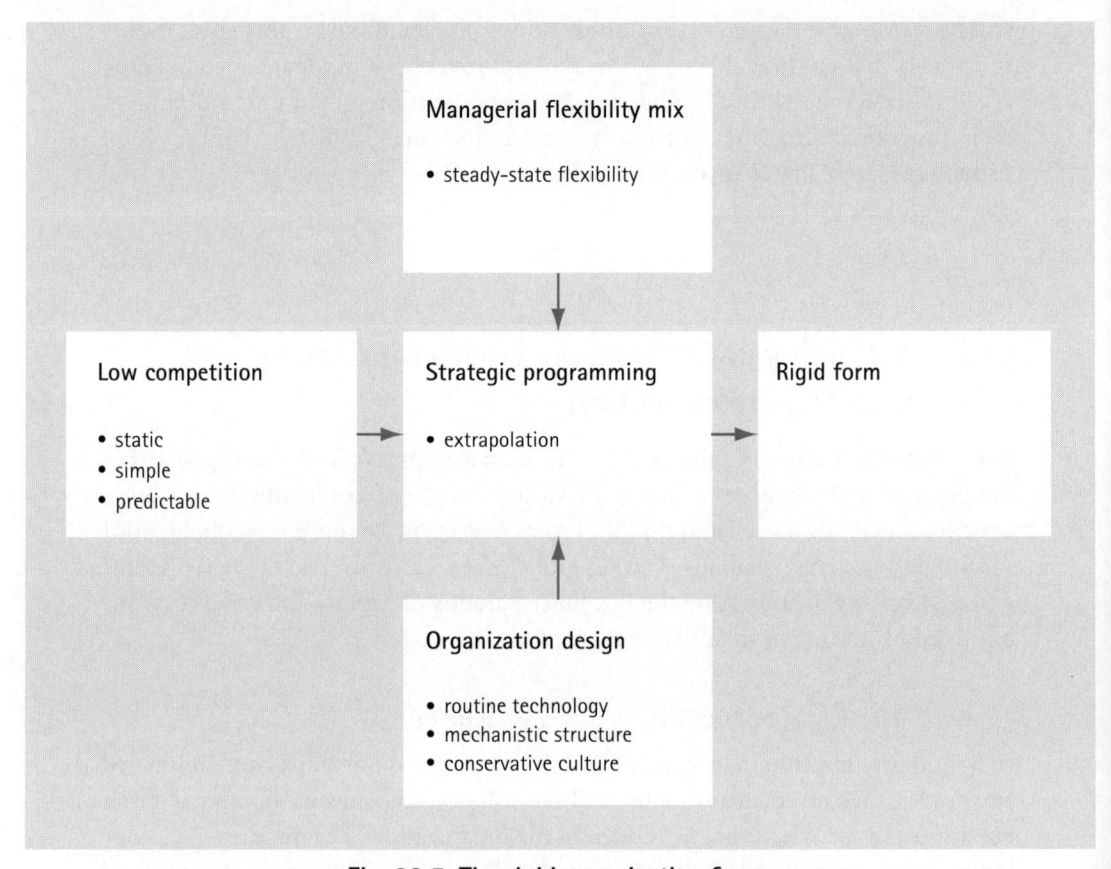

Fig. 32.5 The rigid organization form

capacity. Moreover, for every possible change, management has developed a certain routine (superior operational flexibility). The rigidity of this organizational form is not a result of the technology or the basic organizational structure, but of strong process regulations such as standardization, formalization, and specialization, and very detailed planning and control systems. Also, the shared cultural beliefs and assumptions of its members give very little leeway for deviant interpretations of the environment, and dissonance is potentially threatening to the organization's integrity. This form resembles the 'ideal-type' bureaucracy of Weber (Perrow 1986). As long as the organization encounters no unexpected changes, its controllability is high. However, if changes occur that are not anticipated in the planning repertoire and are threatening to the idea system shared by its members, the result is a situation known as '*strategic drift*' in which consciously managed incremental changes do not necessarily keep pace with environmental changes (Johnson 1988: 88). The incremental changes result only in further attempts by the firm to perfect its process regulations and basic beliefs and assumptions. These attempts increase organizational inertia, and rigidity sets in.

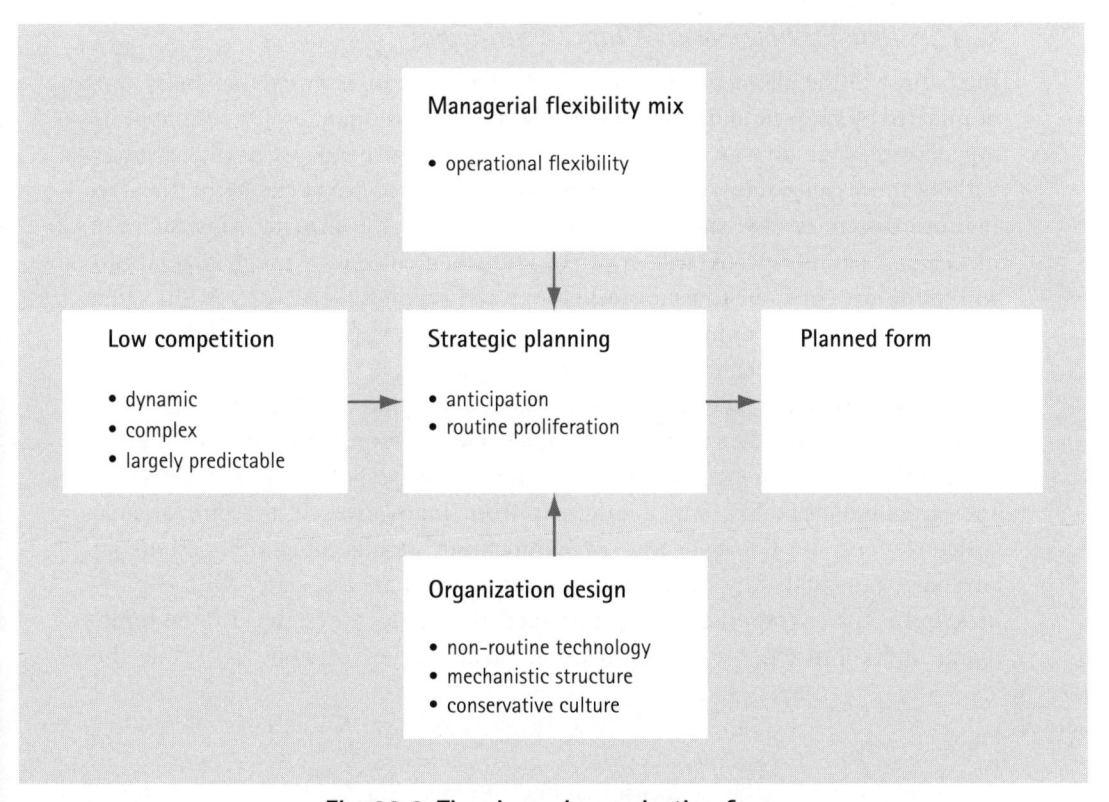

Fig. 32.6 The planned organization form

The planned form is very adequate for firms coping with moderate competition. For survival in such dynamic and complex but largely predictable environments, managers must activate many sophisticated routines to cope with complex changes. They need a potential for operational flexibility originating from a non-routine technology. In such moderately competitive environments, firms seek to establish stable 'oligopolies' by implicit collusion or developing sustainable competitive advantages (D'Aveni 1994: 224). The creation of strong entry and mobility barriers can reduce intra-industry rivalry. Competition may be characterized by relatively long periods of incremental, competence-enhancing changes (Tushman and Anderson 1986). Although competitive changes can be very dynamic and complex, they may be predictable to a large extent and various routines (ranging from simple to sophisticated) can be developed. Management therefore needs an extensive information-processing capacity to anticipate complex changes and to facilitate the development of routines (see Figure 32.6). Strategic management in the planned firm involves scanning the environment (think on *early warning systems*), reducing rivalry and systematically developing strategic plans.

32.4.3.3 *The Flexible Form: Adaptive Strategies*

In contrast to the planned form, the *flexible form* has an extensive flexibility mix dominated by strategic and structural flexibility. In addition, its ability to change its organizational conditions is reasonably high. It effectively adapts to disturbances without the organization losing its distinctiveness. Resistance to signals of threat to the idea system is low; the innovative culture helps the firm to constructively incorporate new perspectives. They can be implemented easily through adaptations within the current (non-routine) technology and (organic) structure. At the same time, it develops some dominance over its environment to preserve its identity, and effects a balance between exploration and exploitation.

Flexible forms are effective in fundamentally unpredictable environments, which may also be dynamic and complex (see Figure 32.7). In such hyper-competitive environments, management must activate both strategic flexibility and structural flexibility, which originate from innovative culture and organic structure. The escalating degree of competition results in short periods of advantage punctuated by frequent disruptions, which are associated with departures from current approaches that reduce the value of established commitments and competence and require fundamentally new capabilities. While the

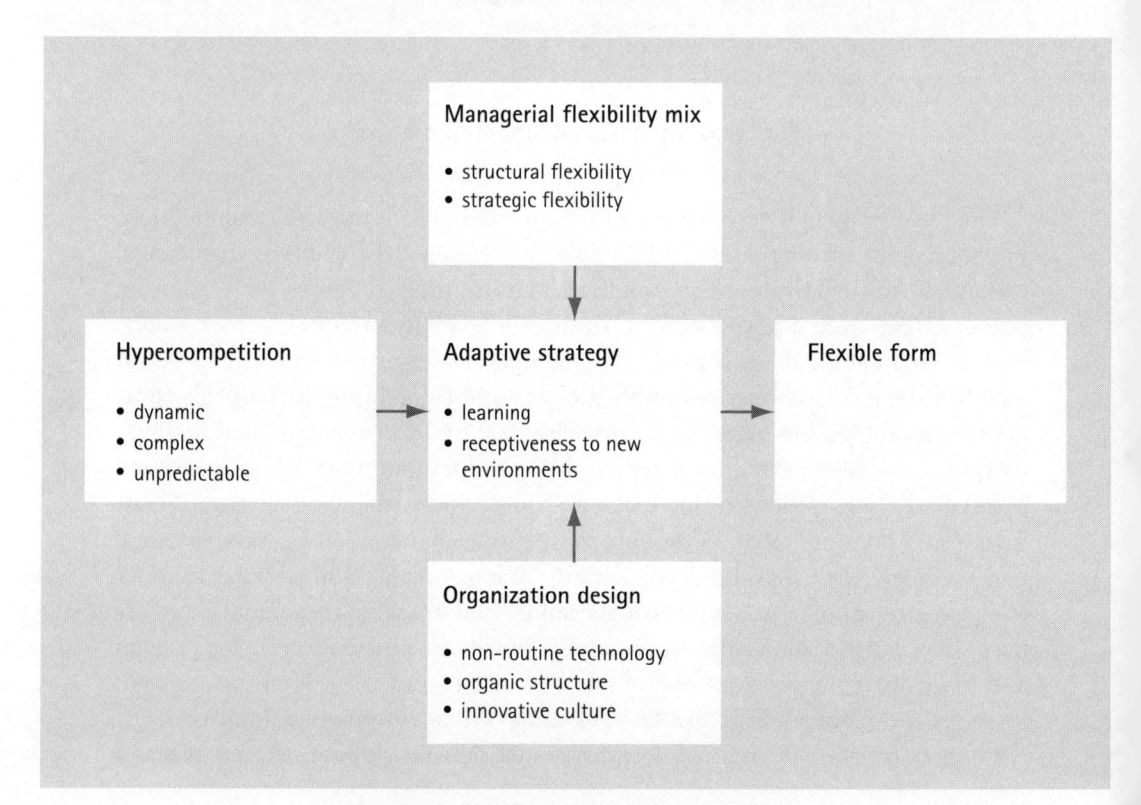

Fig. 32.7 The flexible organization form

liability-of-newness problem plagues new firms confronting moderate competition within well-established markets, the liability of age and tradition seriously constrains established successful firms confronting hypercompetition (Stinchcombe 1965; Tushman and Anderson 1986). Hypercompetition is facilitated by the disequilibrium-creating activities of firms that are capable of breaking new ground, pioneering new fields, promoting radical innovation, and partially or completely transforming the organization in the process. Instead of building on current routines as a part their operational flexibility, such firms develop high levels of structural and strategic flexibility.

Strategic management in such flexible firms requires intelligence-gathering and information-processing directed towards enhancing the receptiveness to new environments and increasing the learning capacity of management. The signals and feedback received in such unpredictable environments are very indirect and open to multiple interpretations. Extrapolation or other conventional management tools are not useful in this context. The problems are by definition unstructured and non-routine and the scarce information is very soft and fuzzy. New values and norms are necessary and past experience may not provide any advantage. It involves a change in the criteria of evaluation; past practices need to be questioned, new assumptions about the organization have to be raised, and significant changes in strategy have to be considered.

32.4.3.4 *The Chaotic Form: Spontaneous Strategies*

Finally, the *chaotic form* has a very extensive flexibility mix dominated by strategic flexibility, but is totally uncontrollable (see Figure 32.8). In organizations with this form, the possibilities for variation are unlimited because there is no anchorage within a set of basic organizational conditions. The innumerable initiatives for change are impossible to implement. Chaotic organizations have no distinct technology, stable administrative structure, or basic shared values stemming from their organizational culture. Consequently, the environment can push a chaotic organization in any direction. A chaotic organization's lack of administrative stability is caused by *strategic neglect*, which denotes the deliberate tendency of managers not to pay attention to the administrative structure of the organization (Burgelman 1983: 234–7). As a consequence of the lack of strong strategic orientation and a stable structure managers' decision-making capacity is greatly reduced. Decisions are delayed although the situation requires an immediate decision.

On the basis of our framework, we can argue that flexible modes are most likely to prosper in dynamic rugged landscapes with many peaks as sketched out by the Red Queen, planned modes in sloping hilly landscapes with moderate competition, while rigid modes seem only to survive in quiet valleys with stable competition. The chaotic mode seems to be locked in a Red Queen race, without being able to sustain competitive advantages. The chaotic mode tries to move faster than the company

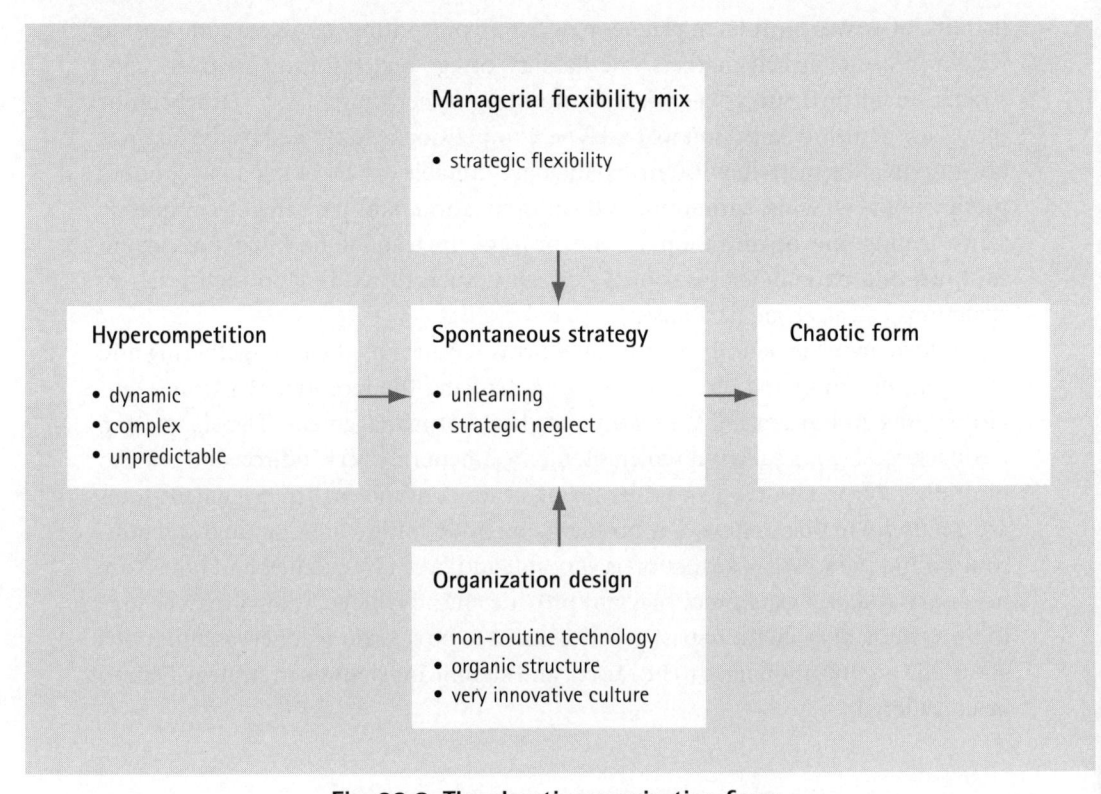

Fig. 32.8 The chaotic organization form

can actually do. Management overreacts to competitive change and the organization is unable to respond. Although the chaotic form has a negative connotation, this mode can however be helpful for regulated firms that are confronted with increasing competition. To unlearn old routines and existing monopolistic mindsets, the chaotic mode can be an effective temporary alternative. In particular, resource-rich firms can use chaotic forms to quickly develop new capabilities in their unregulated business.

32.5 SINGLE TRAJECTORIES OF REVITALIZATION

In the previous chapter, we developed a strategic framework that distinguishes the building blocks needed to analyse and discover new flexible forms. Various alterna-

tive forms enable firms to initiate or respond successfully to different kinds of competition. None of these forms, however, creates a permanent solution. Shift may occur in the level of competition, and the organization has to prevent itself from overshooting and becoming extremely rigid or chaotic. On the basis of the extensiveness of the flexibility mix (simple routines versus dynamic capabilities) and the controllability or responsiveness of the organization (low versus highly controllable), we can distinguish various trajectories for coping with changing levels of competition (see Figure 32.9).

32.5.1 The Natural Trajectory of Routinization: Decreasing Levels of Competition

The most likely trajectory firms go through is a transition from a chaotic state to flexible, planned, and rigid forms (see Figure 32.9). During this process of decreasing levels of competition, management's increased capacity to process information facilitates the proliferation of routines, thus creating natural trajectories. These trajectories correspond with those in Nelson and Winter's evolutionary theory

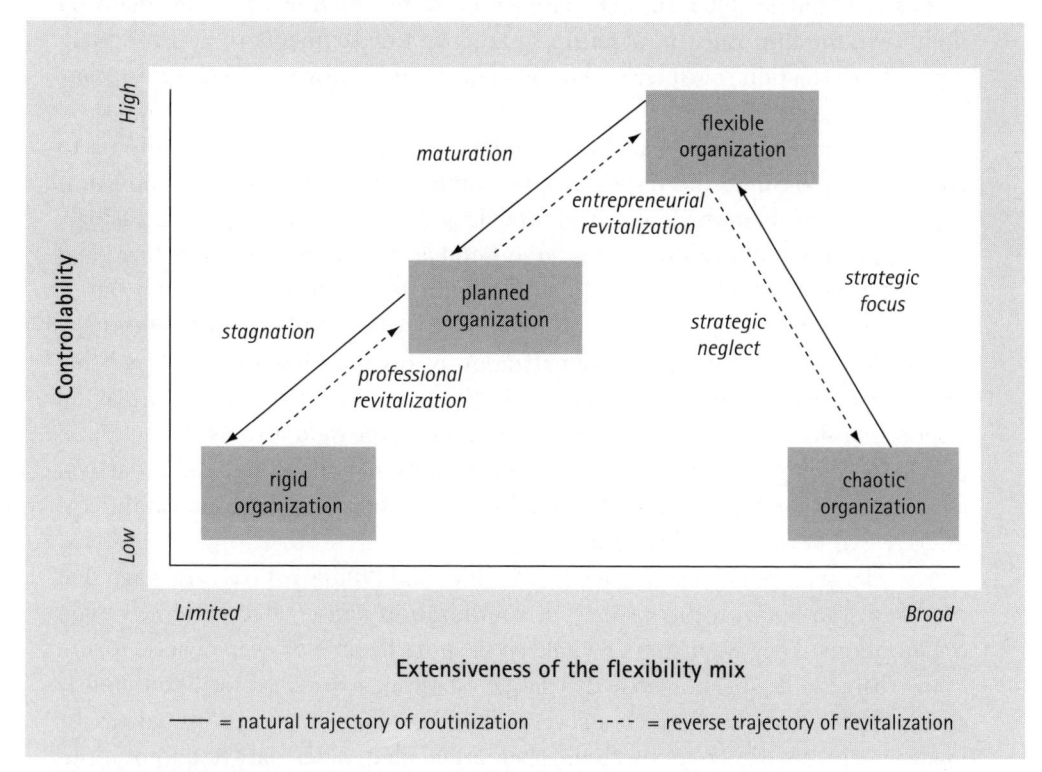

Fig. 32.9 A typology of alternative flexible forms for coping with hypercompetition

(1982), which holds that radical change becomes less possible as the organization ages. The natural trajectory of routinization suggests that starting entrepreneurial firms and new ventures operate chaotically in order to develop new capabilities. This state of loose and unsettled relationships is organic and responds easily to environmental change, but necessarily has slack and is inefficient (Utterback and Abernathy 1975: 641). To 'get off the ground', this form must be sufficiently well organized to change from a chaotic state of random, disconnected, and uncoordinated impulses. This transition requires a capacity for achieving some degree of *strategic focus*.

As the level of competition decreases, the flexible organization faces a crisis. It must become more efficient in its operations to extract greater benefit from the changes that it introduced previously, and to exploit its existing knowledge and opportunities. These change efforts are particularly important if the organization is to stay ahead of its imitators and other competitors, which are busy enhancing their competencies. The transition from a flexible form towards a planned form can be portrayed as a process of *maturation* (Miller and Friesen 1980: 285). Maturation requires a greater need for the firm to professionalize and institutionalize its intelligence-gathering and information-processing functions, and to integrate efforts of its decision-makers by formal means (process regulations). Whereas managers in the flexible form may have gathered information quite informally on their own, the firm must now set up systems and departments to gather certain types of information routinely and to disseminate this information to appropriate decision-makers.

However, in the process of adapting and refining the organizational conditions to efficiently exploit time and response opportunities, the planned organization runs the risk of losing its strategic and structural flexibility as it concentrates increasingly on accumulating and optimizing a large number of operational procedures and routines (operational flexibility). In such circumstances, it may become progressively more rigid. In this progression toward *stagnation* (Miller and Friesen 1980: 283–4), the routinization and systematization of organizational conditions bring bureaucratic momentum, traditions, and resistance to change. These all play an important role in boosting conservatism. As a result, the rigid form is characterized by a reduced emphasis on product-market innovation, risk-taking, and proactiveness. The rigid form has pursued the development of specialized routines at the cost of decreased flexibility and innovative capacity.

Many large corporate giants such as GE, IBM, and Philips realized years ago that they went too far with this process of routinization and created extremely rigid organizations. They want to be revitalized in more flexible or even chaotic forms. Many theorists doubt, however, that large, established firms can self-consciously change themselves very much or very often, or that conscious initiatives by management are likely to succeed. They argue that older, larger corporations must die off, like dinosaurs, to be succeeded by a new breed better adapted to its

environment, in much the same way that has characterized biological evolution. Others, like Kanter (1994) and Baden-Fuller and Stopford (1994), have demonstrated that mature firms can become flexible enough to balance corporate discipline with entrepreneurial creativity. In fact, there are many routes mature corporations might take to effect this goal. On the basis of our typology, we will provide a more systematic analysis of alternative trajectories directed towards 'revitalization' of mature or declining organizations. Such trajectories are most likely to be effective in extremely turbulent environments.

32.5.2 The Reversed Trajectory of Revitalization: Escalating Levels of Competition

For many organizations, the transition from a chaotic state towards a rigid organization can be regarded as a natural trajectory. A transition in the reverse direction can also be perceived as a trajectory, though it may not be as easy to achieve or seem as 'natural' as the former process (see also Chapter 29 by Williamson on strategy innovation). Such trajectories of revitalization, initiated for creating temporary disequilibria, are most likely to be effective under situations of hypercompetition. Some likely trajectories are considered based on flexibility studies within the Dutch Postbank, Philips Semiconductors, and the Dutch National Gas Corporation (see Figure 32.10)

The dangers for rigid organizations in non-competitive environments stem from their increasing vulnerability to the occurrence of major change in their environments, and from the exhaustion of profitable opportunities obtainable in these niches. As these organizations are confronted by low and diminishing returns from established product lines and rapidly escalating competition from numerous rivals in the same field, they must seek to exploit opportunities flowing from more unstable environments, or attempt to generate major innovations. Confronted with escalating levels of competition, they face the task of shifting back towards the flexibility mix and the organizational conditions of the planned organization. This transition, or *professional revitalization*, involves the comprehensive and often dramatic movement away from traditions, conservatism, and rigidity and towards adaptiveness, vigilance, and diversification (Miller and Friesen 1980: 281). Such a trajectory was evident within the Administrative Department of the Dutch National Postbank, which was recently privatized. In the past, its main line of business had been retail banking because of restrictions imposed by the Dutch government. It provided mostly standardized services to more than six million account holders. After it was deregulated, it intended to provide more customized services as a part of corporate banking. It was confronted, however, with increasing national and international competition, new information technologies in banking, increased pressure on interest margins, and the introduction of new banking-related services.

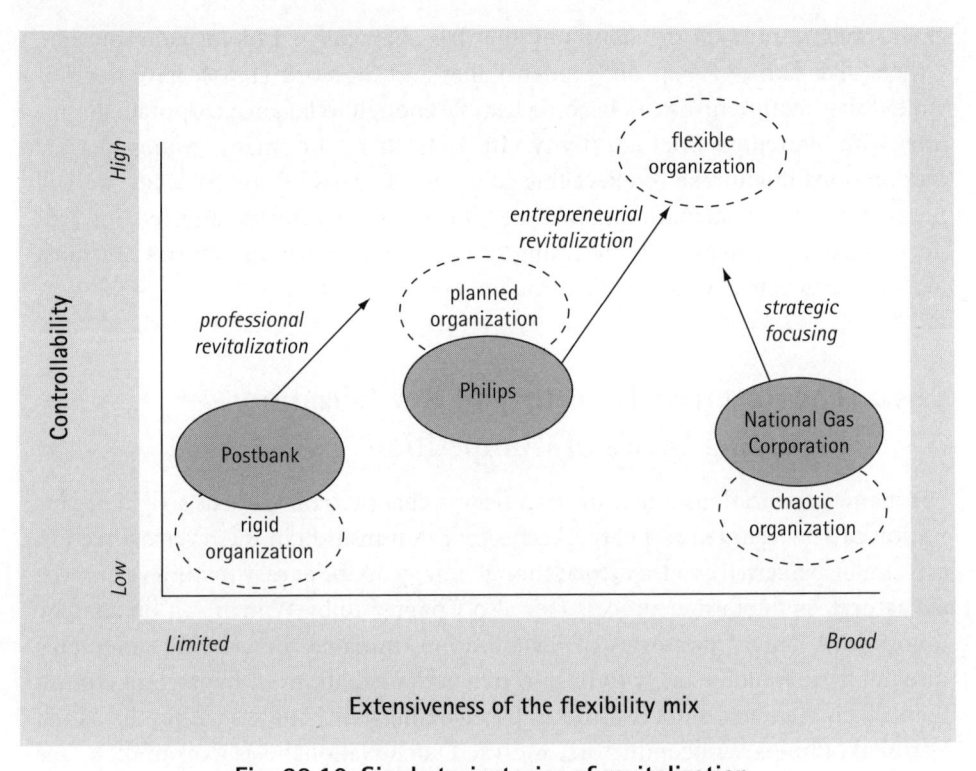

Fig. 32.10 Single trajectories of revitalization

The Administrative Department of Corporate Accounts, which was bureaucratically organized for a non-competitive environment, had to adopt a more comprehensive flexibility mix dominated by operational flexibility, which in turn originated from a more adaptive technology (broadly applicable information systems) and a larger operational production repertoire by employees.

When professional revitalization proves inadequate, the planned organization must transform itself further into a more flexible form. Although planned forms have developed a great number of complex routine capabilities, they are seriously handicapped when confronted with hypercompetition. This change in the composition of the flexibility mix can be realized only if the organization moves towards even more flexible or multi-purpose technologies, develops a more organic structure, and adopts a more heterogeneous, open, and externally oriented culture. Such efforts help to promote asymmetry within the previous organizational form while propelling the organization towards the creation of new temporary advantages better suited to hypercompetitive environments. This process of *entrepreneurial revitalization* is promoted by such changes as new leadership composed of visionary entrepreneurs, reduction of process regulations (specialization, formalization), loose organizational forms (grouping by target market, flat structure, and broad management tasks), a more open external orientation, and a high tolerance for ambiguity.

A transition of entrepreneurial revitalization occurred within Philips Semiconductors. The rapidly escalating competition in cost and quality (price erosion and unforeseen volume developments) and in timing and know-how (introduction of plastic diodes, release of higher voltages version, new crystal types, and the advance of integrated circuits in the application markets) forced the firm to increase its structural and strategic flexibility to more easily exploit unknown opportunities in those hypercompetitive areas. It effected this entrepreneurial revitalization by radically transforming itself from a bureaucratic, conservative company into an innovative and responsive one (see Figure 32.10). Managers initiated autonomous task groups, created interdisciplinary marketing-production-development teams, used less formal planning and control systems, developed a unique logo for the plant, and organized social events, special training, and a news bulletin for employees. The combination of these efforts made the transformation possible.

If the organization successfully transforms itself, it faces the opposite danger of overshooting its target and becoming chaotic. For example, the R&D Department of the Dutch National Gas Corporation had unlimited potential for flexibility, but managers could not capitalize on it. In other words, the department was too flexible. The department had many initiatives for new research, but it could not implement them because it had no clear administrative structures or shared values stemming from its culture. Nor did it have adequate information about man-hours, costs, or technical progress per project. The schizophrenia of the department resulted in distorted information that managers could not use to make appropriate decisions. Consequently, various environmental forces (board, internal clients) could force the department in any direction. This *strategic neglect* resulted in a lack of decisiveness about research priorities, a fragmented structure, and a loose constellation of subcultures. As Kanter (1988: 195) pointed out, creating change requires some stability. Organizational structures and cultures must allow continuity and preserve the organization in the midst of change. In particular, Kanter proposed that strong social ties and strong beliefs in fundamental values create stability for the organization. If successful revitalization is not anchored in stability, it runs the danger of provoking chaos.

32.6 Dual Trajectories of Revitalization in Multi-Unit Organizations

So far, our typology was applied to a division or business unit with only one line of business. However, evidence of corporate transformations in regulated companies

suggests that if multiple levels or multiple parts are considered, dual trajectories of transformation for coping with hypercompetition can be found in a single company. We will consider these dual trajectories because they illustrate how large, established firms can create flexibility to cope successfully with increasing competition.

32.6.1 Dual Trajectories within American Baby Bells

Building on our typology, Smith and Zeithaml (1996) found two different trajectories within the same Regional Baby Bells Operating Company (RBOC). Before 1984, local telephone service activities were protected within the rigid organizational form and natural monopoly status of AT&T. After divestiture, the RBOCs shifted their core activities into more planned modes, but in their unregulated business they created more chaotic modes. In other words, the two distinct areas followed two different trajectories: professional revitalization of core telephone activities, and strategic neglect and subsequent focusing of early chaotic international activities (see Figure 32.11).

The traditional wireline activities could be initially characterized as rigid because they still operated in highly regulated environments, had received a windfall local

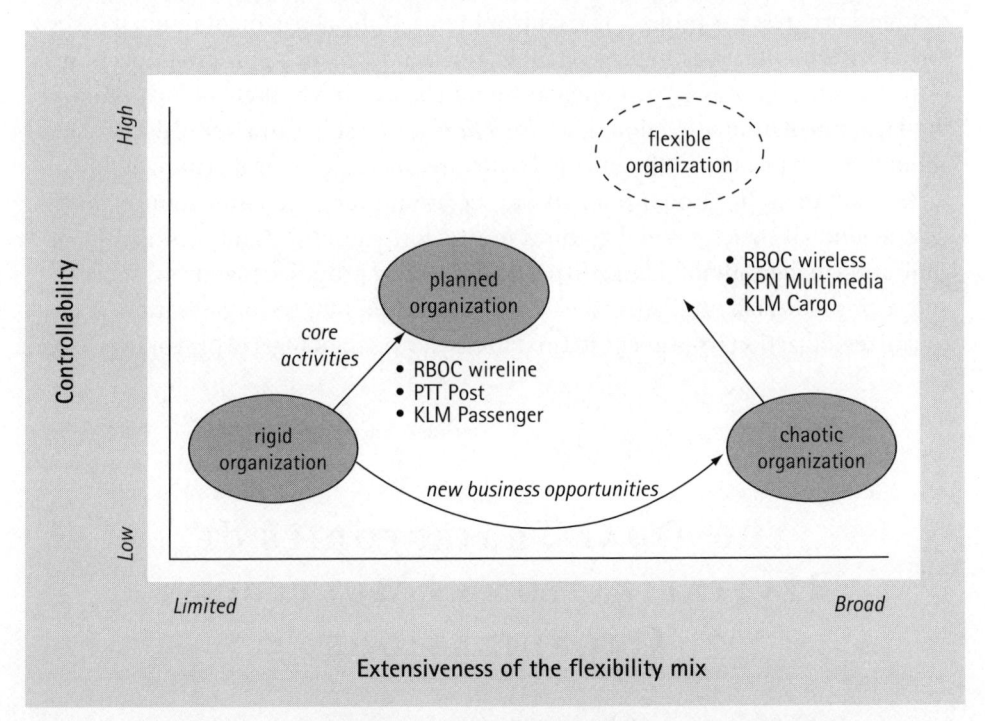

Fig. 32.11 A dual-trajectory revitalization for multi-unit firms facing extreme competition

rate in 1984, and held a monopoly in local service. In the early 1990s the management efforts of two RBOCs resulted in a transition from extreme rigidity towards a more planned organizational form (reduction of domestic regulations, establishing incentive-based rate making) in the regulated side of the RBOCs' business. While managers in these two firms were trying to understand their new regulatory environment, they had neglected many of their more speculative unregulated activities, such as international expansion. Lack of supervision allowed chaotic forms, but top management intervention and focusing enabled international managers in these firms to develop some flexible modes with a high level of strategic flexibility: fast start-ups of new, international entrepreneurial ventures, flexibility in bidding on deals and partner selection, and learning about technologies such as a digital cellular and bypass operations. These 'marketing mavericks' and 'corporate renegades' led the development of new learning and new capability development from international activities. They determined that they could not continue to manage with their existing monopolistic mindset, in which they controlled all aspects of the business, and that they had to learn to react quickly to changes in international opportunities.

The fact that these two RBOCs now complain about their 'split brain' personality is not surprising given their two trajectories: one through chaos and another through a more planned mode. Within both RBOCs, the flexibility in international activities contrasted with the more planned nature of the rest of their activities. One RBOC solved this paradox by knitting the regulated and unregulated sides into an integrated whole (synthesis), whereas the other accepted the paradox by splitting the company in two (spatial separation) to increase both parts' chances for survival. In the integrated RBOC, the cross-fertilization was helpful in awakening the wireline operations to the realities of coming competition (Smith and Zeithaml 1996: 395). The CEO of this organization tried to change the conservative culture under which the regular side of the business had operated for many years by integrating the learning, experiences, and capabilities of managers of unregulated activities into the regulated activities. The CEO of the other RBOC believed that its regulated and unregulated units would have better chances of developing appropriate types of flexibility by refocusing their activities rather than meshing them together.

Recently, many large corporations (e.g. AT&T, Nedloyd, ITT, Unisys, Vendex) have split up into separate parts in order to separate well-developed planned core activities from new flexible growth activities. Other large established corporations have split off flexible parts of their rigid or planned core, such as EDS from GM, Eastman Chemical from Eastman Kodak, and Sprint Cellular from Sprint. Many other large established corporations will probably also divest because it seems that shareholders value extreme spatial separation of planned and flexible forms more than some kind of balanced corporation.

32.6.2 Dual Trajectories for Coping with Increasing Competition: TNT Post and KLM

The dual-trajectory model of organizational transformation may be of value to other regulated companies, such as electronic utilities, railway, and post companies that must address dramatically changing competitive forces. In increasingly competitive environments (e.g. the introduction of competition in a nearly monopolistic industry), areas of chaos should perhaps be created or tolerated by top management, while core activities should move along a revitalization path. Similar trajectories were found in the Dutch PTT Post (see Box 32.5).

Box 32.5 Dual migration paths within the Dutch PTT Post

The Dutch PTT Post, in the meantime TNT Post, was one of the largest divisions of KPN and made up of several business units (letters, parcel service, mediaservice, international, EMS, logistics, philately) and joint ventures (Post Offices, GD Express Worldwide, Interpost Group of Companies). It was preparing itself for the transition from a highly regulated environment to a more competitive one. To revitalize its core activities and exploit new growth opportunities, it initiated several change projects such as Mail 2000, Tele-present, and New Formulas for the Post Office network. In the Mail 2000 project it worked together with A. T. Kearny on improving its competencies in physical transport and distribution of mail, still its core business. By automating the sorting process and reducing the number of sorting hubs, it increased the steady-state and operational flexibility of its primary process. In the Post Office project, it adopted a McDonald's formula to focus on the client. Despite this professional revitalization of its core activities, it realized, however, that the amount of mail it will deliver will further decrease due to other communication means, that its margins will diminish, and that wages and inflation increase. To compensate for decreasing revenues and increasing costs of the traditional planned post organization, it needed new growth areas. To develop these areas, it started various chaotic projects such as the tele-present project with outside partners, VNU (a Dutch publishing firm) and RTL (a European mediaservice company). In this project it helped develop a new service: clients could give orders to send gifts, a kind of tele-shopping. The service was located in a new developed business unit, namely mediaservice. It required the development of a call centre, a tele-present information system, warehousing (PTT Logistics), and distribution (Parcel Service). For PTT Post, this project formed an entry avenue into the electronic superhighway and the development of data distribution capabilities. In addition, this venture was the forerunner of a multi-mall project, in which clients could order products in a virtual store. Nonetheless, in the consolidation of this project, the corporate management of KPN decided to position Tele-present in the KPN Multimedia Division, which is a 50–50 per cent joint venture of PTT Post and PTT Telecom. In order to develop data warehousing and distribution capabilities, PTT Post could learn much from the PTT Telecom Division, which had already coped with tough competition for several years.

This dual trajectory can also be found in less regulated companies such as KLM, which faces extreme competition (see Box 32.6). While KLM's Passenger Division is working on a trajectory of professional revitalization (continuously improving service levels, reducing overall costs, and increasing operational flexibility in terms of flight capacity and personnel), its Cargo Division went through a radical transform-ation from a rigid to an extremely chaotic organizational mode (offering an increased number of value-added services to customers, attracting new customers, and

---

Box 32.6 Radical transformation of KLM Cargo

KLM Cargo, a division of KLM Royal Dutch Airlines, is one of the world's leading air cargo carriers. It intends to rank among the top three customer-driven suppliers of high-quality transport, distribution, and information services worldwide. It has embarked on a radical change programme, turning itself inside out in the process, to fulfil this mission.

A major step in this endeavour occurred in 1989 with the development of the KLM corporate programme Vision '93, which led to the reconfirmation of the airline's core activities and the creation of two divisions: passenger and cargo. In 1994 KLM Cargo launched the 'Division in Transition' programme, which incorporated not only issues of strategy and structure but the determination to effect behavioural change throughout the organization. Until then, KLM's main cargo activities were made up of predomin-antly generic transport services, which are packaged and supplied to the end-user. The margin on these generic services has been slowly eroded: carriers can provide these services only if the highest priority is given to efficiency. Moreover, KLM Cargo did not know who its clients were, and their customers—the freight forwarding agents—fre-quently turned out to be their competitors. KLM Cargo's new strategy was therefore based on end-customers that are prepared to pay extra for value-added products, the exact nature of which differs from client to client. This move towards an organization that will be able to offer yet more added value to clients required a shift from Air Network, which offers a distributed network with a central hub, to Air Logistics or even Full Logistics. Essentially, all providers of base commodities (airlines, truckers, shipping lines) find that the further they move downstream towards the customer, the more their perspectives need to shift from mono-modal to multi-modal, and from basic transportation services to more complete logistics service options.

In realizing this fundamental change, the creation of an entirely different mindset was most important. It now had to perceive itself as provider of integrated logistics instead of an airline operator with only transport and distribution services. This unlearning of its old strategic schema and relearning of a new one required it to invest heavily in flexible capabilities to provide a variety of customized added-value services. Furthermore, it decided to fundamentally redesign the organization. Thus, it flattened the organization and arranged its functions into three disciplines (Operations, Sales, and Customer Service), five business units (Cargo Service Centres, which perform handling activities; Mail; IT; Logistics; and a Special Cargo Unit, which is responsible for such cargoes as perishables, valuables, and live animals); and seven staff departments. The obvious reason for this structural change was to get closer to customers, cutting down the bureaucracy, and empowering people to act innovatively and swiftly.

Box 32.6 (Continued)

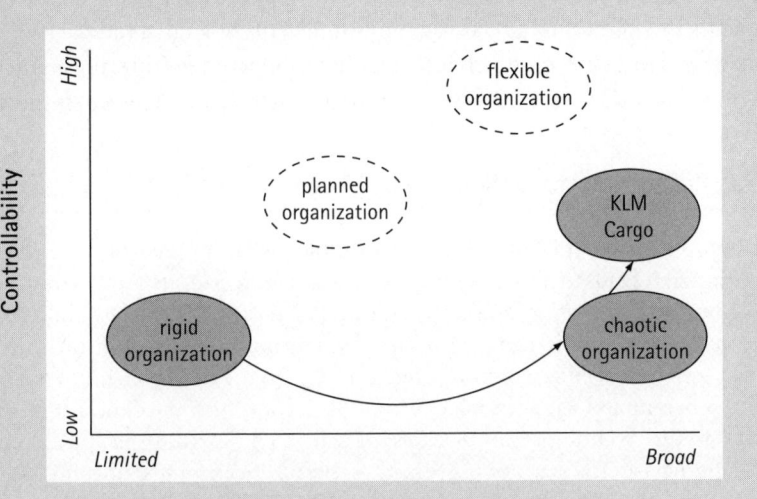

Extensiveness of the flexibility mix

Fig. 32.12 KLM Cargo: a trajectory of radical transformation

In less than one year, it had managed to change its geographic hierarchical structure into a flat dual structure with central functional departments and autonomous business units. Everybody had to reapply for new management positions and managers often had to move from one continent to another. Furthermore, it created self-organizing teams in the factory. In order to facilitate these fundamental changes, management organized awareness courses, training seminars, and interactive workshops.

While this radical change from a rigid towards a chaotic state created momentum for change, however, it also caused some major problems. First, the applicability of both information systems and the skill repertoire of employees (rigidity of technology) to new services was very limited. Moreover, the splitting of the Division into functional departments (Sales, Operations, and Customer Service) and five business units (Cargo Service Centre, Mail, IT, Logistics, and Special Cargo) resulted in large sequential interdependencies and fights about who owns the customer. Furthermore, there was much resistance from lower-level managers who were not involved in the change process (cultural values). In order to exploit its newly developed capabilities, management standardized the service portfolio (commodities, specialties, and customized) and developed a more transparent structure in which a new department of business systems was responsible for more efficient coordination. In addition, management tightened its strategic vision and developed a code of conduct for communicating the common cultural values in KLM Cargo. After the transformation, KLM Cargo could be positioned somewhere between the flexible and the chaotic mode (see Figure 32.12).

providing non-transport related logistic services) and is now slowly shifting towards a more flexible mode (categorizing the service portfolio, a more transparent structure, tightening the strategic vision, and developing Cargo values and a code of conduct).

For these dual trajectories to succeed, top managers must be able to tolerate the presence of initially chaotic modes so that learning takes place. On the other hand, they should have some business intuition of when to intervene, focus on certain activities, give additional resources, or terminate activities.

Moreover, one may ask when it is appropriate for management to choose a sequential revitalization from a rigid to a planned to a flexible mode, and when it should choose to radically transform the organization from a rigid to a chaotic to a flexible mode. Our data suggest that a radical transformation is less time-consuming, but more risky because the scope of change is large and the content of change is most difficult (Baden-Fuller and Volberda 1997). It requires the organization to transform quickly and in a holistic manner, which carries severe dangers. There is a risk that the organization will disintegrate into chaos. Sequential revitalization will therefore be most effective when the firm is not concerned with speedy reaction. By contrast, radical transformation will be more effective when there is a pressing need for the organization to respond collectively.

32.7 RECONFIGURATING THE MULTI-UNIT FIRM: NEW PERMANENTLY FLEXIBLE CORPORATIONS

How can firms win the Red Queen race of permanent change and increasing competition? From our typology, trajectories of organizational 'success and failure' in meeting various levels of competition were obtained. In the old mode of competition in which firms' attention is directed towards reducing the level of competition, a natural trajectory of routinization is most likely. In the new mode of rapid, escalating hypercompetition, a trajectory of revitalization is more likely to be successful. To be front runner in the hypercompetitive environments of the Red Queen, firms must continuously increase the variety and speed of their flexible capabilities as well as their organizational responsiveness. Of course, we have to realize that both trajectories have their pitfalls.

The risk of a trajectory of routinization is that it will transform the firm into a rigid form as a result of strategic drift. The surplus of operational flexibility, consisting of sophisticated routines, creates inertia in the form of a very mechanistic structure

and a very narrowly focused culture. Growing resistance in an organization to 'deviant' interpretations of the environment reflects a tendency towards 'overbalance' of the rigid form. On the other hand, a trajectory of revitalization risks turning a firm into a 'chaotic form' as a result of 'strategic neglect'. The surplus of structural and strategic flexibility in this situation can lead to unfocused actions with dysfunctional results. The chaotic form's lack of administrative structures, sense of direction, shared beliefs, and institutional leadership is characteristic of a tendency towards 'underbalance' of the chaotic form.

How should multi-unit firms reconcile the conflicting forces of exploitation and exploration? They have to cope with different levels of competition at the same time and need efficient exploitation as well as superior exploration (see Chapter 19 by Prahalad and Doz). In terms of our typology, these organizations need properties of the flexible, planned, or even chaotic forms at the same time or in different portions of the corporation. Is there a more permanent solution? We distinguish in this section four corporate responses for combining in some way the elements of exploration and exploitation (see Figure 32.13): opposition (network corporations), spatial separation (dual corporations), temporal separation (oscillating corporations), and synthesis (balanced corporations).

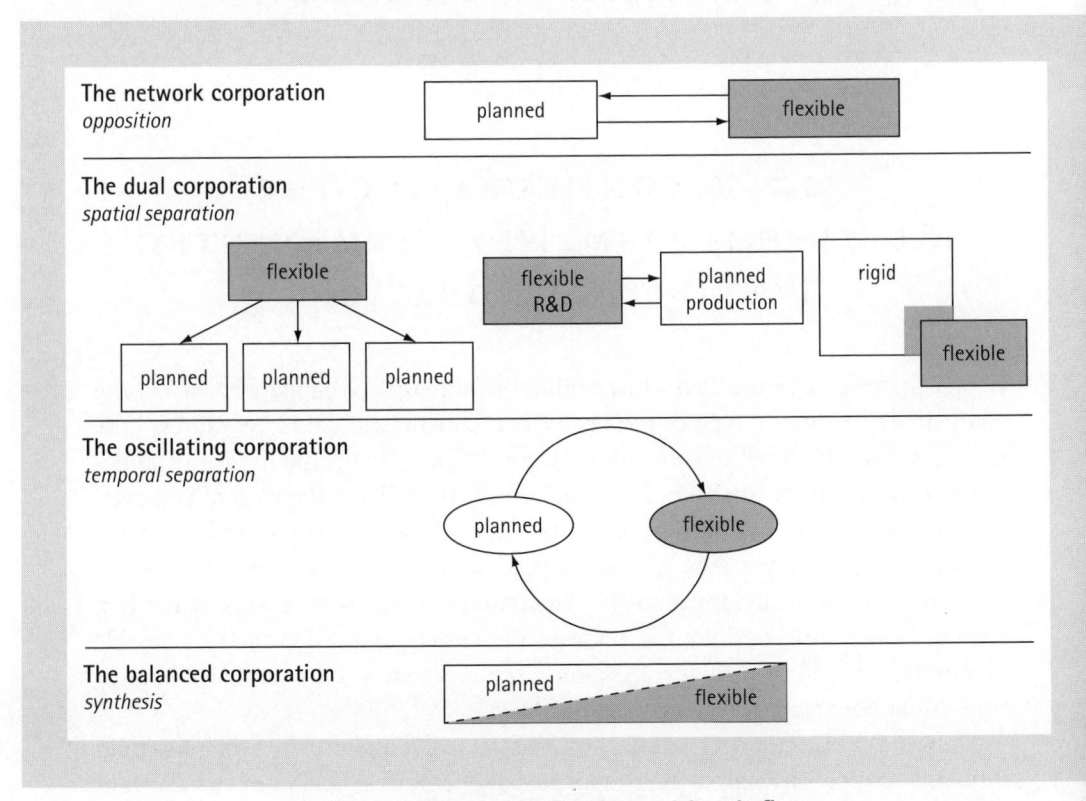

Fig. 32.13 Permanent flexible multi–unit firms

32.7.1 Opposition: The Network Corporation

Most corporations find it difficult to combine the discipline of a planned form with the openness of a flexible form. The network corporation accepts the tension between change and preservation, but believes that the opposition between exploitation of routines (planned mode) and exploration of new flexible capabilities (flexible mode) cannot be solved within the firm. Thus, it outsources the problem of change or preservation to others (Baden-Fuller and Volberda 1997). It is essentially a broker of planned, flexible, or even chaotic organizational modes linked in a variety of complex ways (Miles and Snow 1986). Resolving the paradox of change and preservation can take place in the network because there is no longer a clear distinction between competition outside the organization and cooperation inside (see Figure 32.13 (a)). Rather, the partners in the network experience both competition and cooperation. Competition is a driving force for change, but cooperation helps ensure resources and stability. This view was also espoused by Ouchi (1981) in his discussions of clans of organizations. The social pressures to aspire to higher achievement and the resources of the network provide industrial clans with powerful mechanisms for resolving the flexibility paradox of change and preservation. However, the same features which give these networks strength, especially the strong social bonds, can also slow radical change. That is, corporate networks run the risk of becoming tight networks in which there is no real opposition or constructive tension between change and preservation.

Many will recognize this corporate network form as an approach that has been embraced by a small, but growing number of highly successful companies over the past decade. The UK-based Amstrad, which has battled successfully against much larger firms in the consumer electronics and computer industries, is illustrative. It has built market share for an expanding range of high-tech durables that are developed and manufactured with heavy dependence on outsourced components, subassemblies, and other inputs (Bartlett 1993). Another example is Nike, which has strategic flexibility in capabilities focused tightly on product design and marketing, and externalizes almost all 'planned' manufacturing and distribution functions. To achieve flexibility in what they do without incurring high costs or losing efficiency, these central firms create alliances among smaller naturally flexible firms (Lorenzoni and Baden-Fuller 1995).

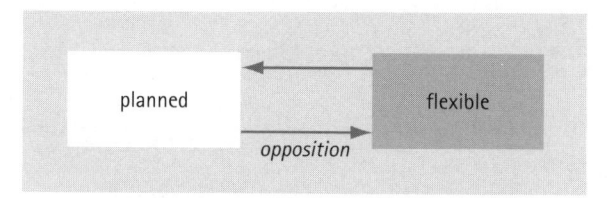

Fig. 32.13(a) The network corporation

32.7.2 Spatial Separation: The Dual Corporation

In the network, participating firms do not solve the exploration/exploitation paradox but focus on one of its two components. Another way to deal with the flexibility paradox is to solve it within the corporation by simultaneously developing flexible and planned modes in different portions of the corporation. In these 'dual' corporations, one horn of the paradox operates at one level of analysis, while the other horn operates at a different level. Spatial separation can occur by level, function, and/or location. Level differences are related to hierarchy (e.g. top versus middle versus front-line managers), functional differences are caused by the distinctive functions performed, processes applied, or knowledge used (e.g. marketing, production, engineering) and location differences are influenced by geography or business unit (see Figure 32.13(b)).

An example of a *level* distinction can be found in the traditional M-form, in which top management operates in a flexible mode and has a high absorptive capacity for exploring new business opportunities (Chandler 1962). In this setting, the divisions operate best in the planned mode for maximally exploiting these business opportunities; they change only as a result of the strategic intent of top management. The new corporate form of GE emerging from Jack Welch's redesign efforts is a more sophisticated version of such a hierarchically divisionalized structure (Miles, Coleman, and Creed 1995). Yet, we can also think of corporations in which the strategic exploration of new opportunities takes place at the lowest level; interactions with the market and demanding clients cause front-line managers to call into question their norms, objectives, and basic policies. Corporate management operates in the planned mode, which permits it to persist in its set policies and achieve formulated objectives, which change as a result of autonomous behaviour of front-line managers. This reversed hierarchy can be found in 3M.

Separation by *function* can be found in nearly all corporations. Usually, production departments operate in a rigid or planned mode for reasons of efficiency and scale, marketing departments operate in a more flexible mode since they are exposed to various customer demands, while R&D departments that are engaged in highly unpredictable research projects operate in a chaotic mode. More extreme

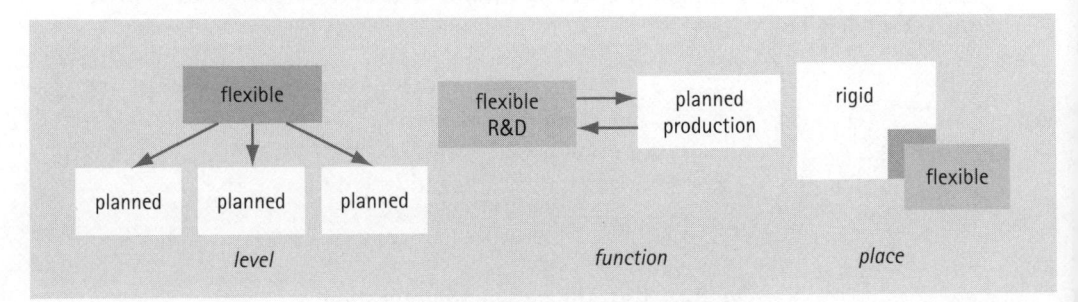

Fig. 32.13(b) The dual corporation

examples of functional separation for solving the flexibility paradox can be found in Honda and KLM Cargo. In order to make functional tensions visible, Honda broke itself apart in a far more radical fashion than had ever occurred in its industry (Pascale 1990). R&D and Engineering were split into two separate companies. While Honda Motor Company (with sales and manufacturing) is the parent, and primary customer, each of the three companies now has its distinct identity and specific organizational mode. The tensions between these companies, each highly independent, yet interdependent, are not suppressed, but serve as the engine of change and renewal.

Similarly, KLM Cargo decided to split its Cargo Factory (handling, warehouse management, and flight network control), in which volume and efficiency are most important, from the business units, in which service, market penetration, and the development of new logistic services dominate. The functional separation allows each business unit to respond to various well-defined markets, but still share in processes and technologies.

Yet, dividing a corporation into its functional parts can result in dysfunctional tensions and a fragmented organization that has lost its synergies. In Honda, the shared culture is strong enough to handle stress without tearing. In KLM Cargo, the lack of this increased the need for setting rules and guidelines on how to use shared assets. Management thus decided to create a new unit, Cargo Business Systems, which is responsible for coordination, systemization, and organization of the core processes.

A third way of spatial separation is by *location*. In almost every diversified firm, one sees asymmetry between high-growth businesses and older, mature operations. That is, mature divisions confronted with moderate competition operate in a planned mode, whereas some new divisions developed to create or counter hyper-competitive disruption may operate in a flexible or even chaotic mode (cf. Galunic and Eisenhardt 1996). We can distinguish separation by location in different degrees, varying from the creation of skunk works (Peters and Waterman 1982), corporate ventures (Fast 1979; Burgelman 1983) to even completely new venture departments. At the simplest level, we can think of isolating a flexible unit from a rigid operating core. This principle was applied at IBM when the IBM PC was developed, as the mainframe logic was strongly preserved in IBM's culture and prevented entry into the new PC market. While at first IBM was very successful with this isolation strategy, it found that transferring these new capabilities from the flexible mode to the rigid operating core was very difficult. IBM could not exploit these capabilities in its operating core because it lacked communication channels and common mental frames. Similarly, Eastman Kodak, Philips, and Xerox have had only modest success from their internal venturing and new business development programmes.

A more complicated form of separation involves the continuous splitting off of groups into separate organizations. Hewlett Packard, Johnson & Johnson, and

Origin are examples of corporations that have developed a system of small, semi-autonomous units, and encourage entrepreneurs to pursue their ideas in new separate divisions, while the older, more established divisions provide continuity and stability (Mintzberg and Westley 1992). Overall, the organization appears to be in a perpetual stage of adaptation, never really rigid or planned as long as new units are being regularly spun off from the older ones. This process is best described as a regular cell fission, characterized by ongoing entrepreneurial revitalization. However, the downside to this cell structure is that such corporations may become overly divisionalized, and have problems with exploiting synergies across certain businesses. Because of continuous fission, these organizations lose their identity and become uncontrollable.

Approaches of spatial separation by location seem to assume that the parent organization can continue to operate in a planned fashion, while a flexible sub-unit of the organization is permitted to undertake pioneering (e.g. R&D) endeavours. Nonetheless, to the extent that the relevant environment for the organization as a whole has been transformed from moderate competition towards hypercompetition, the crisis confronts the entire organization and requires a comprehensive response, not a partial one. Although the creation of a separate flexible unit accelerates progress in new areas of opportunity, it often leads to problems of morale, disruption, and reassimilation (MacMillan 1985). Consequently, exploiting the new opportunities can be slow and frustrating (cf. Burgelman 1983). Sometimes, a dramatic corporate-wide transformation may be necessary to temporarily explore new flexible capabilities. The limitations of spatial separation brings us to temporal separation as a way to survive in a Red Queen race of increasing competition.

32.7.3 Temporal Separation: The Oscillating Corporation

Whereas opposition and spatial separation consider exploration and exploitation occurring contemporaneously, temporal separation resolves the flexibility paradox over time. Periods of operational flexibility and tight organizational conditions (planned mode) are alternated with periods of strategic and structural flexibility and loose organizational conditions (flexible mode). In this perspective, the oscillating corporation is being sequentially manipulated into the flexible mode that stimulates the proposal of radical innovations and then back into the planned mode, which enhances adoption of incremental innovations (see Figure 32.13(c)). In periods of change, there are radical transformations across the whole organization.

In making the distinction between the two different phases, almost all recognize that during periods of preservation, a firm can develop some new operational capabilities alongside the exploitation of the specialized routines. This process

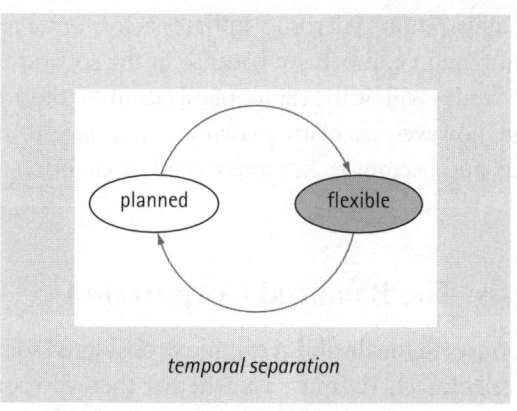

Fig. 32.13(c) The oscillating corporation

will be one of incremental development. However, there will be moments where change and preservation cannot co-exist; these will occur when the trajectory becomes competence-destroying (Tushman and Anderson 1986). At such moments, the organization cannot simultaneously exploit the old and develop the new, but has to 'choose' (perhaps unconsciously) between radical change and slow decline.

For small entrepreneurial firms, this dynamic alternation between flexible and planned organizational modes is part of their existence and competitive advantage. Their lack of tight commitments and relatively low sunk costs enable them to easily undertake radical change. For large corporations, complete transformations are much more complicated and nearly impossible. Nonetheless, Kanter (1994) used case histories from companies such as Kodak and Apple Computer to argue that US corporate giants can learn to change. In addition, using examples of mature UK firms (Richardson, Edwards, and Hotpoint), Baden-Fuller and Stopford (1994) observed that although triggers for change may have to come from many quarters and may take time to gather speed, the state of the whole organization can change from rigidity to flexibility. Case histories of large capital-intensive corporations such as DSM Chemicals, Shell, and Unilever that operate in cyclical industries also give us examples of firms that have been successful in managing alternate cycles of convergence and divergence. However, the periods of change for these companies were infrequent and relatively short as compared to periods of preservation. In Unilever, for instance, over the last twelve years there have been three periods of sharp upheaval followed by periods of comparative stability (cf. Maljers et al. 1996). By contrast, for corporations facing more hypercompetitive environments, the exploitation of capabilities becomes extremely difficult, while the periods of change are more frequent (cf. D'Aveni 1994). Instead of long, stable periods in which corporations can achieve sustainable competitive advantage, hypercompetition is increasingly characterized by short periods of advantage punctuated by frequent

disruptions. As an illustration, Microsoft initiates a corporate redesign every eight months in order to remain competitive because in the software industry, the fully flexible company of today will be the rigid organization of tomorrow. In the process of frequent change, however, oscillating corporations have to prevent themselves from 'overshooting' and becoming extremely rigid or chaotic.

32.7.4 Synthesis: The Balanced Corporation

The corporate responses to the flexibility paradox considered so far leave each of the two extremes basically intact. We must ask whether there are corporate forms that make a synthesis of flexible and planned organizational modes at the same time and at the same level possible (see Figure 32.13(d)).

Applying the insights of our strategic framework of flexibility, a balanced corporation can choose to compensate for its mechanistic structure by encouraging and promoting cultural heterogeneity. Consequently, the firm will experience a constructive tension between strategic change and structural preservation. If, on the other hand, an organization wants to compensate for the proven structural flexibility of its organic structure, it can seize upon the various devices used to solidify and extend a more homogeneous cultural pattern. Doing so will result in a tension between structural change and strategic preservation. Some large corporations such as 3M, HP, and Motorola have developed structures and cultures to achieve this balancing act (see Box 32.7). Against their minimal structures, they developed a strong culture dominated by corporate values like trust, respect for individuals, uncompromising integrity, and teamwork.

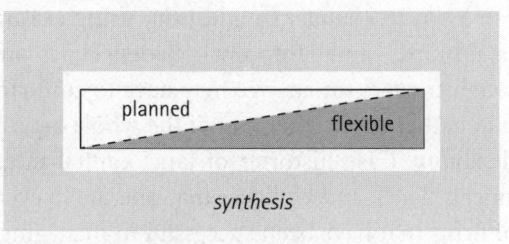

Fig. 32.13(d) The balanced corporation

Box 32.7 Balancing acts in 3M, HP, and Motorola

3M, for example, continually reassesses the barriers to flexibility that tend to develop over time. In order to overcome core rigidities, 3M has a formal goal of having 30 per cent of its sales derived from products that are new or have been substantially modified in the past four years. HP and Motorola are also pursuing structures and cultures that are more focused on building new competencies. Like 3M, these companies decentralize

decision-making at the team and divisional level, and encourage spin-off projects. In addition, they constantly seek ways of making their current technology obsolete in order to push the innovation envelope of their assets. For example, 70 per cent of HP's sales is represented by products introduced or substantially modified in the past two years. Similarly, the development of the Motorola Integrated Radio Services is projected to effectively supplant Motorola's lucrative cellular handset business.

Other corporate forms that come close to the balanced corporation are the hybrid forms. An example of such hybrid forms is the hypertext organization (Nonaka and Takeuchi 1995). Based on successful Japanese companies, the hypertext organization is a parallel structure that combines the steady-state flexibility of a hierarchical bureaucracy with the strategic flexibility of the flat, cross-functional task force. For instance, Sharp has a hierarchical business layer, but the company exploits its project-team layer, which is a completely independent, parallel structure when it comes to new-product development. Even more complicated and diffuse is Olivetti's platform corporation in which there is the coexistence of a multiplicity of organizational forms (Ciborra 1996): managers may operate within two or more organizational modes at the same time. The firm has much latitude for surprise and change, but retains the underlying bedrock of the collective cognitive schemas of participating managers.

Weick (1982), however, noted that compromise responses might be detrimental to the total flexibility of the corporation because they usually dominate other alternatives, since they are often acceptable to those with competing interests. Should these corporations have to cope with a changed environment, they might not be able to develop the right responses, since they have retained only composite alternatives. Superior flexible firms have to continually reflect on their exploration/exploitation ratio in order not to fail as a result of chronic forms of exploitation or exploration in the Red Queen race. We have showed various options to remain permanently flexible.

32.8 STRATEGIC FLEXIBILITY IN THE NEW LANDSCAPE OF THE TWENTY-FIRST CENTURY

In this chapter, we described successful and unsuccessful ways to win the Red Queen race of dynamic competition. As is clear from the empirical studies in this chapter, however, there will never be one best way to achieve flexibility in hypercompetitive environments. The trajectories discussed indicate that firms can arrive at the

flexible form through strategic focusing of the chaotic mode or through entrepreneurial revitalization of the planned mode. In addition, the flexible form itself can be achieved in different ways, thus suggesting equifinality. There are several equally good ways to match high variety and speed of managerial capabilities with an adequate organization design to resolve the constructive tension between developing capabilities and preserving stability within the organizational conditions.

The intention of this chapter is to develop theory on strategic flexibility and stimulate debate that goes beyond theory about traditional strategy in stable competition. Since a dramatic and far-reaching shift has occurred in the nature of competition in most industries, bureaucracy is no longer the appropriate form of organization and the emergence of new organizational forms can be expected (Lewin and Stephens 1993). We should consider what forms might characterize flexible organizations in the twenty-first century. In these new forms strategy means not reducing rivalry and proliferating routines, but rather learning from competitors and developing new capabilities. What will these future flexible firms that combine still higher levels of exploration and exploitation look like?

Many (cf. Clegg 1990; Kanter, Stein, and Jick 1992) have predicted that the future will be dominated by small flexible firms that will be predominantly service- or information-oriented and apply automated production and computer-based technology, informal and decentralized structures, and loose and tolerant cultures. Our framework and typology, however, suggest a much larger variety of effective flexible forms over which managers exercise some choice. Moreover, we think that planned or even rigid modes will still exist. They will, however, be viable only as long as they are part of network or dual corporations in which the forces of stability are counterbalanced by change. These units will be most effective when the organization needs to contain the risk of change and is not concerned with speedy reactions. Nonetheless, our typology seems to suggest that successful firms will generally move along a diagonal of increasing variety and speed of managerial capabilities together with higher levels of organizational responsiveness (see Figure 32.14). In this connection, the oscillating and balanced corporation, which allow the whole organization to adjust to competitive change more holistically and quickly, seem to be more promising. Without constant adaptation, however, the fully flexible firm of today will become the rigid firm of tomorrow. Firms must continuously increase the variety and speed of their flexible capabilities as well as their organizational responsiveness. Doing so requires innovation in managerial capabilities (flexible manufacturing, JIT, multi-sourcing, quick-response, product development capabilities) together with innovations in organization design (CAD/CAM, FMS, delayering, teaming, empowerment, corporate identity).

But how can firms reinvent themselves as they move along the flexibility trajectory? Unfortunately, most managers try only to copy existing successful forms rather than create new flexible forms. Consequently, their firms can at best be as good as their competitors, but never outperform them. The conceptual underpinnings of

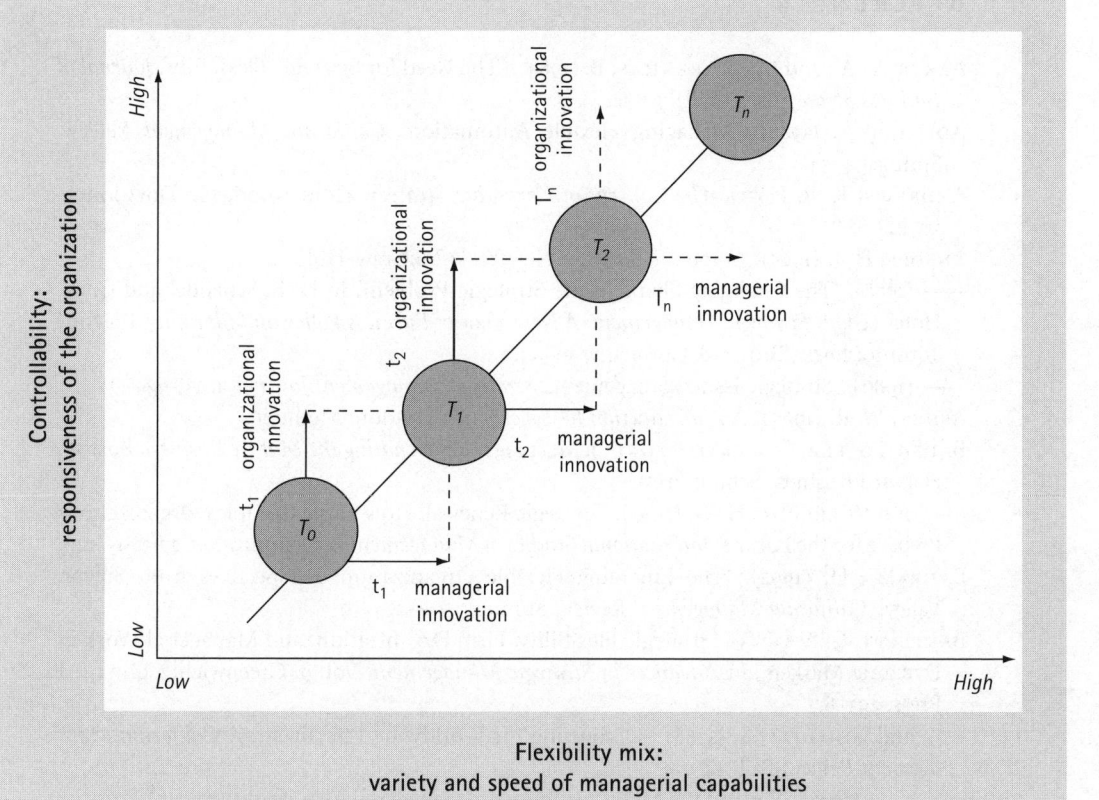

Fig. 32.14 The flexibility trajectory of successful firms of the twenty–first century

the viability of new flexible forms in situations of hypercompetition has not been discussed properly. Nevertheless, the strategic framework and typology of alternative flexible forms developed in this chapter may provide researchers a useful guide for the discovery of effective strategies and organizational forms in the new world of hypercompetition. Moreover, managers and practitioners can use our framework and typology proactively in order to build flexible firms of the future. The superior strategic flexibility of these new forms may open up new sources of competitive advantage. Competitive advantages of firms tend to be competed away quite quickly because many are players in a Red Queen race. Long-term superior performance is achieved not through static strategies aimed at providing sustainable competitive advantage, but by strategic flexibility in order to continuously develop and adapt new dynamic sources of advantage, and thus being the fastest runner in the Red Queen race.

References

AAKER, D. A., and MASCARENHAS, B. (1984). 'The Need for Strategic Flexibility'. *Journal of Business Strategy*, 5/2 (Fall): 74–82.

ADLER, P. S. (1988). 'Managing Flexible Automation'. *California Management Review*, Spring: 34–56.

ANDREWS, K. R. (1971). *The Concept of Corporate Strategy*. Homewood, Ill.: Dow Jones-Irwin.

ANSOFF, H. I. (1965). *Corporate Strategy*. New York: McGraw-Hill.

—— (1978). 'The Changing Shape of the Strategic Problem', in D. E. Schendel and C. W. Hofer (eds.), *Strategic Management: A New View of Business Policy and Planning*. Boston/Toronto: Little, Brown & Company, 30–44.

—— (1980). 'Strategic Issue Management'. *Strategic Management Journal*, 1: 131–48.

ASHBY, W. R. (1964). *An Introduction to Cybernetics*. London: Methuen.

BADEN-FULLER, C., and STOPFORD, J. M. (1994). *Rejuvenating the Mature Business*. Boston: Harvard Business School Press.

—— and VOLBERDA, H. W. (1997). 'Strategic Renewal: How Large Complex Organizations Prepare for the Future'. *International Studies of Management & Organization*, 27/2: 95–120.

BAHRAMI, H. (1992). 'The Emerging Flexible Organization: Perspectives from Silicon Valley'. *California Management Review*, Summer: 33–52.

BARTLETT, C. A. (1993). 'Strategic Flexibility, Firm Organization, and Managerial Work in Dynamic Markets', in *Advances in Strategic Management*, Vol. 9. Greenwich, Conn.: JAI Press, 293–8.

—— and GHOSHAL, S. (1988). 'Organizing for Worldwide Effectiveness'. *California Management Review*, Fall: 54–74.

—— —— (1993). 'Beyond the M-Form: Toward a Managerial Theory of the Firm'. *Strategic Management Journal*, 14/Special Issue: 23–46.

BATE, P. (1984). 'The Impact of Organizational Culture on Approaches to Organizational Problem-Solving'. *Organization Studies*, 5/1: 43–66.

BETTIS, R. A., and PRAHALAD, C. K. (1995). 'The Dominant Logic: Retrospective and Extension'. *Strategic Management Journal*, 16/1: 5–14.

BOURGEOIS, L. J., III, and BRODWIN, DAVID, R. (1984). 'Strategic Implementation: Five Approaches to an Elusive Phenomenon'. *Strategic Management Journal*, 5: 241–64.

BOWER, J. L. (1970). *Managing the Resource Allocation Process*. Boston: Harvard Business School Press.

BOYNTON, A. C., and VICTOR, B. (1991). 'Beyond Flexibility: Building and Managing the Dynamically Stable Organization'. *California Management Review*, Fall: 53–66.

BRAYBROOKE, D., and LINDBLOM, C. E. (1970). *A Strategy of Decision: Policy Evaluation as a Social Process*. New York: Free Press.

BURGELMAN, R. A. (1983). 'A Process Model of Internal Corporate Venturing in the Diversified Major Firm'. *Administrative Science Quarterly*, 28/June: 223–44.

—— (1994). 'Fading Memories: A Process Theory of Strategic Business Exit in Dynamic Environments'. *Administrative Science Quarterly*, 39: 24–56.

BURNS, T., and STALKER, G. M. (1961). *The Management of Innovation*. London: Tavistock.

BURTON, R. M. (1984). 'Variety in Strategic Planning: An Alternative to the Problem-Solving Approach'. *Columbia Journal of Business*, Winter: 92–8.

——and NAYLOR, T. H. (1980). 'Economic Theory in Corporate Planning'. *Strategic Management Journal*, 1/3: 249–63.

Business Week (1996). 'The Fall of an American Icon'. 5 Feb.: 32–9.

CARROLL, L. (1946). *Through the Looking Glass* and *What Alice Found There*. New York: Grosset & Dunlap.

CAMERER, C., and VEPSALAINEN, A. (1988). 'The Economic Efficiency of Corporate Culture'. *Strategic Management Journal*, 9: 115–26.

CHAFFEE, E. E. (1985). 'Three Modes of Strategy'. *Academy of Management Review*, 10/1: 89–98.

CHANDLER, A. D., Jr. (1962). *Strategy and Structure*. Cambridge, Mass.: MIT Press.

CIBORRA, C. U. (1996). 'The Platform Organization: Recombining Strategies, Structures, and Surprises'. *Organization Science*, 7/2: 103–18.

CLEGG, S. R. (1990). *Modern Organizations—Organization Studies in the Postmodern World*. London: Sage Publications.

CRAIG, T. (1996). 'The Japanese Beer Wars: Initiating and Responding to Hypercompetition in New Product Development'. *Organization Science*, 7/3: 302–21.

D'AVENI, R. (1994). *Hypercompetition: Managing the Dynamics of Strategic Maneuvering*. New York: Free Press.

DAVIDOW, W. H., and MALONE, M. S. (1992). *The Virtual Corporation*. New York: Harper Collins.

FAST, N. D. (1979). 'The Future of Industrial New Venture Departments'. *Industrial Marketing Management*, 8: 264–73.

Fortune (1994). 'GM's $11,000,000,000 Turnaround', 17 Oct.: 30–42.

——(1995). 'GM: Some Gain, Much Pain'. 20 May: 46–50.

——(1996). '3M Fights Back', 5 Feb.: 42–7.

Financial Times (1998). 'Strategic Advantage', John Kay, 5 Aug.

FREDRICKSON, J. W. (1983). 'Strategic Process Research: Questions and Recommendations'. *Academy of Management Review*, 8/4: 565–75.

GALUNIC, D. C. and EISENHARDT, K. M. (1996). 'The Evolution of Intracorporate Domains: Divisional Charter Losses in High-Technology, Multi-divisional Corporations'. *Organization Science*, 7/3: 255–82.

GRANT, R. (1996). 'Prospering in Dynamically-Competitive Environments: Organizational Capability as Knowledge Integration'. *Organization Science*, 7/4: 375–87.

GUTH, W. D. and GINSBURG, A. (1990). 'Corporate Entrepreneurship'. *Strategic Management Journal*, 11: 5–15.

HAMEL, G. (1996). 'Strategy as Revolution'. *Harvard Business Review*, July–Aug.: 69–82.

——and PRAHALAD, C. K. (1994). *Competing for the Future*. Boston: Harvard Business School Press.

HANDY, C. (1995). *The Age of Unreason*. London: Arrow Business Books.

HANSSEN-BAUER, J., and SNOW, C. (1996). 'Responding to Hypercompetition: The Structure and Processes of a Regional Learning Network Organization', *Organization Science*, 7 (4): 413–27.

HARRIGAN, K. R. (1985). *Strategic Flexibility*. Lexington, Mass.: Lexington Books.

HOFSTEDE, G. (1980). 'Motivation, Leadership and Organization: Do American Theories Apply Abroad?' *Organizational Dynamics*, Summer: 42–63.

HOWARD, R. (1992). 'The CEO as Organizational Architect: An Interview with Xerox's Paul Allaire'. *Harvard Business Review*, 70/5: 106–21.

ITAMI, H. (1987). *Mobilizing Invisible Assets*. Cambridge, Mass.: Harvard University Press.

ITTNER, C. D., and KOGUT, B. (1995). 'How Control Systems Can Support Organizational Flexibility', in E. Bowman and B. Kogut (eds.), *Redesigning The Firm*. New York: Oxford University Press, 155–80.

JOHNSON, G. (1987). *Strategic Change and the Management Process*. Oxford: Basil Blackwell.

—— (1988). 'Rethinking Incrementalism'. *Strategic Management Journal*, 9/Sept: 75–91.

KANTER, R. M. (1983). *The Change Masters*. New York: Simon & Schuster.

—— (1988). 'When a Thousand Flowers Bloom: Structural, Collective, and Social Conditions for Innovation in Organization'. in B. M. Staw and L. L. Cummings (eds.), *Research in Organizational Behavior*, Vol. 10. Greenwich, Conn.: JAI Press, 169–211.

—— (1994). *When Giants Learn to Dance: Mastering the Challenge of Strategy, Management and Careers in the 1990s*. London: Routledge (Reprint).

—— STEIN, B. A., and JICK, T. D. (1992). *The Challenge of Organizational Change: How Companies Experience It and Leaders Guide It*. New York: Free Press.

KAUFFMAN, S. A. (1995). 'Technology and Evolution: Escaping the Red Queen Effect'. *McKinsey Quarterly*, No. 1: 118–29.

KRIJNEN, H. G. (1979). 'The Flexible Firm'. *Long Range Planning*, 12/Apr.: 63–75.

LEARNED, E. P., CHRISTENSEN, C. R., ANDREWS, K. R., and GUTH, W. (1969). *Business Policy: Text and Cases*. Homewood, Ill.: R. Irwin.

LEONARD-BARTON, D. (1992). 'Core Capabilities and Core Rigidities: A Paradox in Managing New Product Development'. *Strategic Management Journal*, 13/Special Issue: 111–25.

LEVINTHAL, D. A., and MARCH, J. G. (1993). 'The Myopia of Learning'. *Strategic Management Journal*, 14/ Special Issue: 95–112.

LEVITT, B., and MARCH, J. G. (1988). 'Organizational Learning'. in W. R. Scott (ed.). *Annual Review of Sociology*, Vol. 14. Palo Alto, Calif.: Annual Reviews, 319–40.

LEWIN, A. Y., and STEPHENS, C. U. (1993). 'Designing Postindustrial Organizations: Combining Theory and Practice', in G. P. Huber and W. H. Glick (eds.), *Organizational Change and Redesign*. New York: Oxford University Press, 393–409.

—— and VOLBERDA, H. W. (1999). 'Prolegomena on Coevolution: A Framework for Research on Strategy and New Organizational Forms'. *Organization Science*, 10/5: 569–82.

LINDBLOM, C. E. (1959). 'The Science of "Muddling Through"'. *Public Administration Review*, 19/ Spring: 79–88.

LINNEMAN, R. E., and CHANDRAN, R. (1981). 'Contingency Planning'. *Managerial Planning*, Jan./Feb.

LORENZONI, G., and BADEN-FULLER, C. (1995). 'Creating a Strategic Center to Manage a Web of Partners'. *California Management Review*, 37/3: 146–63.

MACMILLAN, I. G. (1985). 'Progress in Research on Corporate Venturing: 1985'. Working Paper, NY University, Center for Entrepreneurial Studies.

MALJERS, F., BADEN-FULLER, C., and VAN DEN BOSCH, F. (1996). 'Maintaining Strategic Momentum: The CEO's Agenda'. *European Management Journal*, 14/6: 555–61.

MARCH, J. G. (1991). 'Exploration and Exploitation in Organizational Learning'. *Organization Science*, 2: 71–87.

—— and SIMON, H. (1958). *Organizations*. New York: Wiley.

MASCARENHAS, B. (1982). 'Coping with Uncertainty in International Business'. *Journal of International Business Studies*, 13/2: 87–98.

MILES, R. E., and SNOW, C. C. (1986). 'Organizations: New Concepts for New Forms'. *California Management Review*, 28/3 (Spring): 62–73.

—— Coleman, H. J., Jr., and Creed, W. E. D. (1995). 'Keys to Success in Corporate Redesign'. *California Management Review*, 37/3: 128–45.

Miller, D., and Chen, M. (1994). 'Sources and Consequences of Competitive Inertia: A Study of the U.S. Airline Industry'. *Administrative Science Quarterly*, 39: 1–23.

—— and Friesen, P. (1980). 'Archetypes of Organizational Transition'. *Administrative Science Quarterly*, 25/2: 268–300.

Mintzberg, H. (1973). 'Strategy-Making in Three Modes'. *California Management Review*, 16/2 (Winter): 44–53.

—— (1978). 'Patterns in Strategy Formation'. *Management Science*, 24: 934–48.

—— (1994). *The Rise and Fall of Strategic Planning*. New York: Free Press.

—— and Waters, J. A. (1985). 'Of Strategies, Deliberate and Emergent'. *Strategic Management Journal*, 6: 257–72.

—— and Westley, F. (1992). 'Cycles of Organizational Change'. *Strategic Management Journal*, 13: 39–59.

Nelson, R. R., and Winter, S. G. (1982). *An Evolutionary Theory of Economic Change*. Cambridge, Mass.: Harvard University Press.

Nonaka, I., and Takeuchi, H. (1995). *The Knowledge-Creating Company*. New York: Oxford University Press.

Ouchi, W. G. (1981). *Theory Z: How American Business Can Meet the Japanese Challenge*. Reading, Mass.: Addison-Wesley.

Pascale, R. T. (1984). 'Perspectives on Strategy: The Real Story behind Honda's Success'. *California Management Review*, 26/3: 47–86.

—— (1990). *Managing on the Edge*. London: Penguin Books.

Pennings, J. M. (1985). 'Introduction: On the Nature and Theory of Strategic Decisions', in J. Pennings (ed.), *Organizational Strategy and Change*. San Francisco: Jossey Bass, 1–34.

Penrose, E. T. (1959). *The Theory of Growth of the Firm*. New York: Wiley.

Perrow, C. (1986). *Complex Organizations: A Critical Essay*. (3rd edn) New York: Random House.

Peters, T. J., and Waterman, R. H., Jr. (1982). *In Search of Excellence*. New York: Warner Books.

Poole, M. S., and Van de Ven, A. H. (1989). 'Using Paradox to Build Management and Organization Theories'. *Academy of Management Review*, 14/4: 562–78.

Porter, M. E. (1980). *Competitive Strategy: Techniques for Analyzing Industries and Competitors*. New York: Free Press.

—— (1991). 'Towards a Dynamic Theory of Strategy'. *Strategic Management Journal*, 12: 95–117.

—— (1996). 'What is Strategy?'. *Harvard Business Review*, Nov.–Dec.: 61–78.

Quinn, J. B. (1980). *Strategies for Change: Logical Incrementalism*. Homewood, Ill.: Richard D. Irwin.

—— (1985). 'Managing Innovation: Controlled Chaos'. *Harvard Business Review*, 63/3: 73–84.

—— (1992). *Intelligent Enterprise: A Knowledge and Service Based Paradigm for Industry*. New York: Free Press.

Richardson, J. (1996). 'Vertical Integration and Rapid Response in Fashion Apparel'. *Organization Science*, 7/4: 400–12.

Sanchez, R. (1993). 'Strategic Flexibility, Firm Organization, and Managerial Work in Dynamic Markets', in *Advances in Strategic Management*, Vol. 9. Greenwich, Conn.: JAI Press, 251–91.

——(1995). 'Strategic Flexibility in Product Competition'. *Strategic Management Journal*, 16/Special Issue: 135–60.

SCOTT, B. W. (1965). *Long-Range Planning in American Industry*. New York: American Management Association.

SMIRCICH, L., and STUBBART, C. (1985). 'Strategic Management in an Enacted World'. *Academy of Management Review*, 10/4: 724–36.

SMITH, A. D., and ZEITHAML, C. (1996). 'Garbage Cans and Advancing Hypercompetition: The Creation and Exploitation of New Capabilities and Strategic Flexibility in Two Regional Bell Operating Companies'. *Organization Science*, 7/4: 388–99.

STARBUCK, W. H. (1983). 'Organizations as Action Generators'. *American Sociological Review*, 48: 91–102.

STEVENSON, H. H., and GUMPERT, D. E. (1985). 'The Heart of Entrepreneurship'. *Harvard Business Review*, 64/Mar.–Apr.: 85–94.

STINCHCOMBE, A. L. (1965). 'Social Structure and Organizations'. in J. G. March (ed.), *Handbook of Organizations*. Chicago: Rand McNally, 142–93.

TEECE, D. J., PISANO, G., and SHUEN, A. (1997). 'Dynamic Capabilities and Strategic Management'. *Strategic Management Journal*, 18: 509–33.

THOMPSON, J. D. (1967). *Organizations in Action*. New York: McGraw-Hill Book Company.

TICHY, N. (1983). *Managing Strategic Change*. New York: Wiley & Sons.

——and SHERMAN, S. (1994). *Control Your Destiny or Someone Else Will*. New York: Harper Business.

TUSHMAN, M. L., and ANDERSON, P. (1986). 'Technological Discontinuities and Organizational Environments'. *Administrative Science Quarterly*, 31: 439–65.

UTTERBACK, J. M., and ABERNATHY, W. J. (1975). 'A Dynamic Model of Process and Product Innovation'. *Omega*, 3/6: 639–56.

VAN CAUWENBERG, A., and COOL, K. (1982). 'Strategic Management in a New Framework'. *Strategic Management Journal*, 3: 245–64.

VOLBERDA, H. W. (1996). 'Toward the Flexible Form: How to Remain Vital in Hypercompetitive Environments'. *Organization Science*, 7/4: 359–74.

——(1997). 'Building Flexible Organizations for Fast-moving Markets'. *Long Range Planning*, 30/2 (Apr.): 169–83.

——(1998). *Building the Flexible Firm: How to Remain Competitive*. Oxford: Oxford University Press.

——and BADEN-FULLER, C. (1998). 'Strategic Renewal and Competence Building: Four Dynamic Mechanisms', in G. Hamel, C. K. Prahalad, H. Thomas, and D. O'Neal (eds.), *Strategic Flexibility: Managing in a Turbulent Environment*. Chichester: Wiley, 371–89.

——and ELFRING, T. (2001). *Rethinking Strategy*. London: Sage.

WEICK, K. E. (1979). *The Social Psychology of Organizations* (2nd edn). Reading, Mass.: Addison-Wesley.

——(1982). 'Management of Organizational Change among Loosely Coupled Elements'. in P. S. Goodman and Associates (eds.). *Change in Organizations: New Perspectives in Theory, Research, and Practice*. San Francisco: Jossey-Bass, 375–408.

WERNERFELT, B. (1984). 'A Resource-Based View of the Firm'. *Strategic Management Journal*, 5: 171–80.

WRAPP, H. E. (1967). 'Good Managers Don't Make Policy Decisions'. *Harvard Business Review*, 45/5 (Sept.–Oct.): 91–9.

Subject Index

a priori intentions 454, 458

3M 38, 57, 59, 84, 464, 494, 498–9

ABB 47, 48, 49–50, 57, 76, 87, 333, 339–41, 457, 466, 474–5
   lean matrix 81–4, 85–6
   parenting advantage statement 90

absorption integration 110, 113

access to resources, and strategic networks 143

Acer 366–9, 372

acquisitions *see* mergers and acquisitions

adaptation 247, 458–9, 496

adaptive model 454, 455–8, 460–1, 478–9

administration
   heritage 35
   processes 58–9

advantages
   country-specific (CSAs) 170, 191
   firm-specific (FSAs) 187–91, 194–5, 196, 200, 201–2

ageing of companies 280–3
   and crises 325–6

Airbus Industrie 134

Alcatel 66, 68

American Express 66

Amstrad 493

Andersen Consulting 240

anergy 75–6

AOL Time Warner 38, 99

Apple Computer 249, 497

archetypes 390

Arthur D. Little (consultancy) 3

ASEAN 206

aspiration level 283–91, 285–6

asset-stripping 100, 107

assets 462
   invisible 32
   organizational 428–9

asymmetry 484, 495
   and game theory 388

AT&T 363, 473, 474, 486–7

Atlantic Richfield 75

automation 423

autonomy
   crisis of 325
   organizational 110, 112

AXA (insurance) 132

BAe Systems and Services 408–11

balanced corporation 11, 451, 492, 498–9, 500

balanced portfolio 24, 25, 37

Banco Santander 133, 134

banks, Dutch 483–4

Barings Bank 256

barriers
   exit 290
   to global trade 168–70

BASF (biotechnology company) 378

BATNA (Best Alternative to a Negotiated Agreement) 402–4

BBC (British Broadcasting Corporation) 239

beating the specialists paradox 79–80

behavioural perspective 242–3, 249–50

Bellman equation 435–6

benchmarking 447

Benetton 52, 146, 338, 470–1

Berkshire Hathaway 31, 33

bid premium 103–4, 108

biotechnology 24, 364, 377–8

blind focus 282–83

Boeing 240

Boston box 3

Boston Consulting Group (BCG), matrix 3, 23, 24, 418, 419–20, 421, 441

bottom-up initiatives 455–7

boundaries of firm, fuzzy 262–3

boundary spanners 140, 261

"boundaryless" behaviour 59

bounded rationality 219

BP (British Petroleum) 75, 466
branding, joint 76
break-ups 28–9, 36
brewing industry 475
British Airways 52, 55
BTR (manufacturing company) 92
building blocks 477–80
bureaucracy 476, 500
    in Managed Professional Business 326–7
    structure seen as 326
business schools 18
business selection 56–7
business-level strategy 2
buy-outs 28

Canon 59, 62, 81–4, 85, 86, 87, 254, 458
capabilities 32–3, 417–18, 420–1, 450, 457, 458,
        500
    combinative 439–40
    critical capability set 433–4
    managerial 239–41, 469–70
    narrow 359–60
    as organizational discontinuities 424–8
    and parenting opportunities 80
    switching costs 431–5
    technology 423–4
    value-creating 362–3, 369–72, 422, 429
capability constraints 362
capability-building initiatives 366–9
capacity, and strategic networks 143
Cargill 47–8
cell structure 472
centralization 328, 331
    of functions and services 76–7
Challenger disaster (1986) 282
change 8–10
    and competition 244–6
    degrees of 286–91
    language of 247–9, 265
    management and 344
    multi-stage change models 250–2
    operational 248
    patching (continuous structural change) 341,
        342–3, 344, 345
    and preservation 461
    process view 9
    resistance to 259–62, 291–2
    transformational 9
    triggering 269, 284–6, 284–96
chaotic form 450, 464–6, 479–80
Charles Schwa 52
chemical industries 91

China 48, 137, 211
    business networks 337–8
Chrysler 249
Cisco 321
Citibank 457–8
clans, industrial 493
clarity, structural 57–8, 65
cluster framework (Porter) 198–9
CNN 52, 370
co-design 472
co-evolution 339–41, 345, 426–7, 449
co-makership 472
co-operation 493
coalition formation 384
cognitive frames 419–21
cognitive limits of rationality 455
cognitive perspective 242–3
cognitive science 419
cognitive styles 458, 462
Cold War 384, 405
collaborations, strategic
    alliances 134, 135
combination benefits, and value creation 106
commitment, in strategic alliances 139
communication
    and corporate decline 273–5
    in multinational enterprises (MNEs) 225, 227
    in strategic alliances 140
company failures 280–3
Compaq Computers 257
compensation, flexibility in 442–3
compensation parity 343
competence-destroying change 497
competence-enhancing change 496–7
Competency trap 436–9, 462–3, 465
competition 244–6, 461–6, 467, 493
    and change 244–6
    imperfect 209
    perfect 356
competitive advantage 5, 122–4, 126, 449, 463,
        477, 501
    and business network 199–200
    diamond 198–9, 201
    and invisible assets 32
    and strategic fit 137
    and strategy innovation 350
competitive interactions 441
competitive strategy 5, 165–6
    international 165–71, 178–81
complementarities theory 322–4
complex strategic integration 49
complexity, diseconomies of 365

complexity science 311
complexity theory 9, 263
comprehensiveness of planning 454
configuration
    and international firms 160–1
    of portfolio 49
configuration/coordination matrix 67–71,
        160–1, 193
conglomerates 2, 19–21, 35
    performance problems 21
conservatism 483
constraints
    developmental 426–7
    market knowledge 361, 362
    organizational 423
constructive tension 460, 468
contingencies 322–4, 345
contingency plans 452–3, 455
contingency theory 9, 322–325, 329–30,
        339–40, 345
continuity 64, 264
continuous fission 496
control, crisis of 325–6
controllability 474
controlled chaos 461
convergence
    process 282–3
    of strategies 356, 357
Cooper Industries 29
cooperation
    motivation for 118, 128–32
    rationale for 118, 119–28
    and value chain 128, 146
coordination, and international firms 160–1
core businesses 27–9
core competencies 29, 31–3, 47–8, 385, 417,
        420–22, 462
    definition 430, 436
    and game theory 411
    and parenting advantage 91–2
core incompetence 437–8
core rigidity 462
Corning 47
corporate decline 270–6
    definition 271
corporate development 280–3
    and value destruction 77
corporate drift 289–90
corporate giants 482–3, 497
corporate learning process 279
corporate raiders 18, 26, 27, 37, 73
corporate redesign 498

corporate restructuring 28–9
corporate strategy 2–6
    framework 88, 91
    and parenting advantage 87–91
corporate ventures 495
corporate-level strategy 3–4
corporations
    diversified 17–18
    network 11
country-specific advantages (CSAs) 191
    and firm-specific advantages (FSAs) 170
Courtaulds 31
crises 253–5
    and ageing of companies 325–6
    autonomy 325
    control and integration 325–6
    leadership 325
    red tape 326
crisis management 253–6, 294–6
cultural barriers 490
cultural fit 137, 139–40
culture 458, 474–5
culture clashes, in mergers and
        acquisitions 113–14
customer matrix 170
customers, complaints 365–6
cyclical industries 495

Daimler-Chrysler 55, 321, 448
decentralization 26, 32, 79–80, 86, 322, 329,
        498–9
    China 337–8
decision theory 420–1
decision-making 242
    and adaption 291–3
    and communication 462
decline
    causes of 269–70, 276–83
    concepts of 271–2
    and managerial behaviour 291–3
    symptoms of 272–6
Dell Computer 257, 342, 350, 449
demand, and corporate decline 278–9
demergers 36
design, and bias 440
design processes 344
developmental constraints 426–7
differentiation 397–8
    generic strategies 183–4, 186
    national 334
Direct Line insurance 349
discounted cash flows (DCF) analysis 443

dispute resolution, in strategic alliances 140
distinctive competence 420, 462, 465
distribution 48–9
diversification 3, 6, 54
    challenge of 36–8
    coherent 46
    and opening up new options 364–5
    and portfolio planning 25
    related 3
    strategy 322
    and value destruction 74–5
diversification strategies 18–21
diversified corporations 17–18
diversified form 488
divestment 101, 107, 421, 487
divisions see multidivisional structure
        (M-form)
dominant coalition 9, 268
dominant logic 11, 30, 33–6, 38–9
double-loop learning 465–6
downsizing 26, 64, 146, 147, 270, 447
drama theory 407, 414
DSM Chemicals 497
dual corporation 11, 451, 492, 494–6
dual trajectories 485–91
DuPont corporation 328–9
Dutch National Gas Corporation 483, 485
Dutch Postbank 483–4
Dutch PTT Post 488
dynamic approach 501
dynamic capabilities 463, 468
dynamic capability 435–6
dynamic network 448
dynamic value maximization 435–6

e-commerce 320, 364–5
    and parent companies 92–3
early warning systems 477
Eastern Europe 263
Eastman Kodak 495, 497
eclectic paradigm 159, 180, 196, 197, 219
economic value analysis (EVA) 62, 377
efficiency, and global generic
        strategies 167, 187
electronics industry 91–2
Emerson 81–4, 85, 86, 87, 92
enactment 458–9
enlightened self-interest paradox 79
Enron 350
entrepreneurial creativity 482, 483
entrepreneurial form 497
entrepreneurial revitalization 484–5, 496

entry costs 428–9
environment, organizational 322
environmental myopia 283
environmental turbulence 452, 454, 456, 461,
        483
equifinality 500
equilibrium 393, 397
EU (European Union) 129, 193, 206, 207, 216,
        368
evolutionary learning 440
evolutionary stable strategies 398–9
evolutionary theory 420–1, 422–3, 462,
        481–3
evolutionary transitions 248
exchange rates 169–70
    European currency 170
    volatility 221
expanded reproduction 248
expansion paths 211
expectations, organizational 59–60
exploitation 311, 313, 417, 451, 461–6
exploration 311, 313–4, 417, 451, 461–6
exploration/exploitation ratio 499
Exxon-Mobil 75, 249, 321

F International 449
factor costs 159, 180
failure prediction 275–6
family ownership 152
fast-food model 369
"feel for the business" 80
Ferranti 77, 389
financial control 34, 278, 331
financial markets, and mergers and
        acquisitions 96–8
financial motives, mergers and acquisitions
        99–100
Financiere Agache group 329, 330
firm-specific advantages (FSAs) 187–91,
        194–5, 211
    and customer-specific advantages
        (CSAs) 170
    and generic strategies 187–90
    location and non-location bound 191, 195,
        196, 200, 201–2
five forces model (Porter) 11, 146, 148
flagship firms 199–200
flexibility 8, 10–12, 47, 450
    in compensation 442–3
    costs of 225–6, 423
    and foreign market entry strategies 229–30
    internal and external 470

isomorphic 200, 202
operational 470–1, 482, 491–2
in research and development 223–4
strategic 472–3, 478
and strategic networks 143
strategic perspective 460–1
structural 472, 478
and technology 423
flexibility capabilities 500
flexibility mix 470
flexibility trajectory 500–1
flexible configuration strategies 454
flexible corporation 448
flexible form 450–1, 478–9
focal points 405–6
Ford Motor Co. 60, 321, 442
forecasting 224, 366, 367–8
    failure 275–6
    'mega trends' 369–70
foreign direct investment (FDI) 161–3
    Japan 216–19
formal planning systems 447
framebending 249
France, mergers and acquisitions 112
Fujitsu 178, 253
functional structure 328–9

game theory 6, 11
    asymmetry 388
    and core competencies 411
    critique 411–13
    equilibrium 393, 397
    evolutionary 398–401
    future development 413–14
    history 384–5
    key concepts 391–6
    mixed strategy 393
    Prisoners' Dilemma 119–22
games, specific
    Chicken 383, 396–8
    Hawks and Doves 383, 385, 400–1
    Prisoners' Dilemma 393–5, 399–400
    Rendezvous 383, 405–6
games, types of
    classification 386–9
    competition/cooperation 384, 385, 386–7,
        389
    discrete 407–11
    evolutionary 385, 398–401
    extensive form 391–2
    iterated 387–8, 393–5
    network 407–11

non-cooperatives 389, 414
    normal form 391–2
    one-off 387–8
    sequential 385, 386
    simultaneous 386, 392
    zero-sum 384, 387, 391
gatekeepers and gateways 76
GBUs (global business units) 336
General Electric (GE) 21, 29, 46–7, 48, 59, 132,
        321, 418, 453, 474, 494
    value creation logic 51–2, 54, 67–8
General Mills 28
General Motors 93, 253, 255, 321, 423, 426, 438,
        462–3
General Signal 28
generic strategies 7, 183–4, 201, 245
    cost leadership 183–4, 186
    differentiation 183–4, 186
    and efficiency 187, 188–90
    and firm-specific advantages (FSAs) 187–90
    focus 183–4
    and geographic scope 185–7, 201
    Porter's framework 183–5, 201
    for recovery 305–7, 308
    shelter-based strategies 187–8, 189–90
geographic scope, and generic strategies
        185–7, 201
Gillette 160, 173
GlaxoSmithKline 96, 105, 106
global companies 171–4
    see also multinational corporations
        (MNCs)
global firms 192
global integration/local responsiveness
        matrix 163–5
global production, resourcing 168–70
global segmentation 185–7
global structure 333, 334–6, 345
global subsidiary mandates 192
global village 129
globalization 6, 7, 119, 129, 152, 153–4
    challenges of 220–7
    and homogenization of tastes 169
    and mergers and acquisitions 116
    volatility 220–1, 229–30
goal compatibility, and strategic alliances 140
Gould 55, 56
governance processes 4, 44–5, 53–4
    and fairness 63
    mixed signals 64
    non-negotiable 63
    tailor-made 63

Granada (leisure group) 258
grid structure *see* matrix structure
growth
    earnings 353–4
    and organizational structure 324–7
    revenue 353–4
growth conferences 85
growth share matrix 3
Gulf & Western 20, 21

Hanson plc 29, 31, 33, 34, 35, 47, 48–9
    value creation logic 49, 50, 53, 54, 59, 62
hardware 473
Harley-Davidson 253–4
harmony 61–6
    and substantive issues 64–6
heartland businesses 86, 90
heuristics
    and cognitive biases 419
    cognitive frames 419–21
    qualities of 418
    strategic option theory 416–43
    testing 416–17
Hewlett-Packard 49, 53, 59, 62, 343, 495–6,
        498–9
hierarchy
    and levels of integration 127, 145
    and multinational enterprises (MNEs)
        196–7, 219
    and organizational size 322, 324–7
    and spatial separation 494
hilly landscapes 479
holding company structure 328, 329
holding integration 111, 113
hollow corporation 448
home bases 191–2, 195, 200, 201–2
Honda 245, 455–6, 457, 495
horizontal organizations 30–1
hub companies 146, 150, 228–9
hubris, managerial 108–9, 115, 282–3
hybrid organizations 126
hypercompetition 263, 449–50, 451, 467,
        475–80, 500–1
hypergames 395
hypertext organization 448, 499
hysteresis band 427–8, 436–7, 442

IBM 32–3, 66, 247–8, 448, 459, 472, 495
Icarus paradox 282
imitation
    and innovation 442
    and strategy decay 349

implementation 256–9
improvisation 258
Inchcape 363, 364, 369
incrementalism 455, 457, 458, 496–8
India 48
industrial districts 223
industrial (network) strategy 400
industry analysis 420
industry consolidation 47
industry foresight 52–3
inertia 252, 259, 284–6, 453, 462, 465, 476, 491
    processing 283, 284, 299
information
    in games 386, 395
    as intermediate product 214–15
    sharing across boundaries 59
    and strategic networks 143
    transfer of 211
innovation 10
    and global strategy 167
    and imitation 442
    incremental 424–5
    radical 424–5
    and strategy decay 349
    see also strategy innovation
innovation pipeline 10
innovative culture 463
insights, value creation 81–4, 90
institutional theory 198
institutionalization project approach 200
intangible resources 458
integrated design 440
integration 5–6
    absorption 110, 113
    after mergers and acquisitions 109–12
    complex strategic 49
    crisis of 325–6
    global 333
    holding 111, 113
    horizontal 208
    levels of 127–8
    opposition to 222
    preservation 111, 112
    symbiosis 111, 112
    vertical 208, 222
integration-responsiveness grid 171
Intel 343, 466, 472
internalization
    and internal markets 222–3
    and market structure theory 220
internalization theory 196, 197
international exporters 171–4

see also multinational
  corporations (MNCs)
international firms 192
international strategy 6–8
  competitive scope 184–5
international trade theory 124
internationalization 54, 322
  and organizational structure 333–6
  stages of 161–2
interpretative model 459–61
intuition 18, 251
investment
  irreversible 417, 421, 424–5
  law of diminishing returns 353
  in learning 437–9
  returns on 349
  in strategic options 360–1
  see also foreign direct investment
    (FDI)
investment choices 391–2
invisible assets 32
irreversibility 417, 421, 424–5
ISC Group 77
isomorphism 200, 202
Itochu 321
ITT 19–20, 21, 62

Japan
  brewing industry 475
  foreign direct investment 216–19
  global companies 174, 178
  incremental learning 439
  keiretsu 124, 127, 147, 148, 150–1, 337
  mergers and acquisitions 112
  strategic alliances 137
  and strategic change 244–5
JIT (Just In Time) purchasing 472, 500
job enlargement 472
Johnson & Johnson 57, 495–6
joint ventures 133–4, 135, 140, 198, 222–4, 227,
    228–9, 438, 472

K Mart 66
keiretsu 124, 127, 147, 148, 150–1, 337
KKR (buy-out specialist) 31, 84
KLM Airlines 466, 488, 489–91, 494
know-how 187, 462, 485
knowledge
  embedded 443
  management 107–8
  tacit 108, 458
  transfer 106, 107–8, 211

knowledge workers 326–7
Kodak 53, 54–5, 66

labour markets, national regulation
    207–8
language of change 247–9, 265
leadership *see* management
learning
  incremental 439
  net effects 437–9
learning culture 310–14
learning systems 9
legitimacy 261
Levis 52
licensing agreements 127, 210, 227–8
life-cycle model
  and internationalization 161–2
  product 211–13, 216
limitations, management 66–7
linear model 451–3, 460–1
linear stage process 268
linkages
  cross-company 85
  influence 75–6
  interbusiness 48–9
Litton Industries 19–20, 21
localization 199

M-form (multidivisional structure) 328–33,
    338–41, 494
McDonalds 162, 168, 172
McKinsey (business consultancy) 3, 101,
    176–7, 245
Managed Professional Business 327
management
  behaviour 273–6, 279, 291–3, 291–5
  bounded thinking 83
  capabilities 239–41, 457, 469–70
  compressive 178
  crisis 253–6
  and crisis 325
  dealing with crisis 294–6
  entrepreneurial 43, 225
  general management skills 18–19
  hubris 108–9, 115
  knowledge 107–8
  leadership styles 305–8
  limitations of CEO 66–7
  motivation 100–1
  and organizational structure 344
  portfolio 25, 28
  public image 67–9

management (*cont.*)
    role of CEO 4, 35, 43, 61–6, 69–70, 100–1,
        307–8
    'stick to the knitting' 27–9, 38
    strategic management styles 33–6
    strategic networks 147–8
    strategy innovation pipeline 373–8
    and structural change 344
    turnover 113
    visionary 243
management process school 18–19
managerial cognition 300
managerial discretion 270–1
managerial task 467–8, 469–73
market, conflicts 207
market development organizations
        (MDOs) 336
market efficiency 102, 104
market evolution 350
market knowledge constraints 361, 362
market research 365
marketing mavericks 487
markets
    access to 130–1, 145
    development of 359–60
    regionalization 207
    reliance on 12
    strategic 166
Marks & Spencer 151, 247
mass production 431–3
matrix structure 333, 334, 340–1, 474–5
Matsushita 57, 160, 245
maturation 482
maverick competitors 366, 371
mechanistic shift 301
mechanistic structure 491–2
mega-trends 369–70
memetics 399, 414
mergers and acquisitions 5, 95–116, 227
    activity and drivers 96–8
    differences between 96, 103–4
    and divestiture 26
    employee resistance 112–15
    failure rate 115
    geographical differences 112
    and globalization 116
    merger waves 96–8
    motives for 98–101
    performance 101–3
    post-acquisition integration 109–12
    regulation 98
    and value creation 103–9

and value destruction 77
    volume of 95, 96–8
    wealth generation 101–2
Mergers and Monopolies Commission 389
Merrill Lynch 29
Mexico, computer industry 368
Microsoft 67–8, 321, 472, 498
    'reorgs' 342
mindsets
    'borderless' 176
    rigidity 279–80
Minebea 91–2
minerals business 74–5
mini-max reasoning 392
mission 460
Mitsubishi 150, 321
    keiretsu 337
Mitsui 321
modular design 440
modularity
    as options 443
    and patching 343
monopolistic mindsets 487
Monsanto 24, 350, 364, 377
motivation
    for cooperation 118, 128–32
    heuristics and 418
    for mergers and acquisitions 98–101
Motorola 51–2, 53, 54, 60, 343, 498–9
muddling through 455
multi-domestic structure 171–6, 323, 333,
        334–6
    see also multinational corporations
        (MNCs)
multi-stage change models 250–2
multi-unit firm 491–9
multidivisional structure
        (M-form) 328–32, 338–41, 494
    advantages 331
    alternative forms 333, 339
multinational corporations (MNCs)
        154, 159
    'borderless' mindset 176
    rationale for 160–1
    stages of development 162–3, 178–9
multinational enterprises (MNEs) 201
    communication 225, 227
    different models 193–5
    general theory 219–20
    as hierarchies 196–7, 219
    opposition to internal monopoly
        221–2

as strategic networks 197–200
strategy framework 190–200, 201
and variation in integration 207–8
multinational firms 192
mutation 312, 314

NAFTA (North American Free Trade
    Association) 193, 206, 207
national advantage 208
natural trajectory of routinization 481–3
NatWest 389
NCR 249, 463
negotiation, of mergers and acquisitions
    114–15
Nestle 131, 160
net present value 423
Netscape 326
network capitalism 337–8
network corporation 11, 457, 492, 493
network form (N-form) 338–9
network multidivisional 339
network theory 142
networking 85
networks
    centrality in 344
    multidivisional 323–4
    and organizational structure 336–41
    relationships 334
    see also strategic networks
niches, and generic strategies 184
Nike 52, 338, 472, 493
Nintendo 472
Nordvest Forum 472

obsolescence
    and strategy decay 349
    value creation logic 55–6
oil industry 3
    value-destroying interventions 74–5
oligopolies 477
Olivetti 499
operating patterns, beliefs and rules
    (OBRs) 292–3, 302–3
operational flexibility 470–1, 482, 491–2
opportunity set 422
opposition 492, 493
option explosion 370
option pricing formula 429
option theory 226, 365–6
options 457
    and heuristics 417
    strategic see strategic options

organic growth, and mergers and
    acquisitions 96
organization design task 5, 467–8, 473–5,
    500
organizational assets 428–9
organizational conditions 468, 473–5
organizational costs 126–7
organizational culture 474–5
organizational downsizing see downsizing
organizational environment 249–53,
    322
organizational forms 249–53
    differences between 142–3
organizational learning 269, 279–83
organizational recipes 255, 259
organizational renewal 5
organizational structure 9, 474
    definition 319–20
    and diversification 328–32
    future development 343–44
    and growth 324–7
    importance 320–1
    and internationalization 333–6
    and knowledge workers 326–7
    and management 344
    and networks 336–41
    rules 322–4
    and technology 421–8
Origin (corporation) 496
oscillating corporation 11, 451, 492, 496–8,
    500
outsourcing 168, 170–1, 447, 493
    of central services 79–80
Ove Arup (engineering consultancy)
    327, 333
over-exploitation 464–6
overheads, and value creation 83
ownership
    advantages 219
    family 152

pagers 351–2
paradigms 458
    organizational 280
paradox 468–9
    flexibility 461–6
parent companies 4, 6, 72–93
    10% versus 100% paradox 78–9
    and e-commerce 92–3
    successful 81–6
    value creation 73
    value-destroying interventions 72–8

parenting advantage 5, 36, 47, 87–8, 90
    and core competencies 91–2
    statement 90–1
parenting characteristics 85–6, 90
parenting opportunities 80, 89–90
    reasons for 89
parenting similarities 47
parenting theory 4–5
patching (continuous structural change) 341,
        342–3, 344, 345
patents 85
path-dependency 226
Pearl Assurance 260–1
perceived use value (PUV) 165–6, 170, 175
perfect competition 356
performance, acquisition 101–3
pharmaceutical industry 172
Philips Group 47, 60, 175–6, 453, 474, 483, 484,
        485, 495, 498–9
planned form 450, 475–7
planning 242, 243–4
    formal systems 22
    and parenting characteristics 85
    portfolio 23–5, 27
    strategic 21–2
    value-based 26–7
planning and control systems 453
platform organization 448–9
politics 243–4, 260–2
polycentricity 336
portfolio
    'balanced' 24, 25, 37, 91
    core 29
    management of experiments 375, 378
    management of ideas 374–5, 378
    management of ventures 376, 378
    optimization 359–72, 378
    risk-free 429
portfolio configuration 44, 45–6
    and value creation logic 54–6
portfolio logic 49–50
portfolio management 25, 28
portfolio planning 23–5, 27, 36–7
portfolio school 3–4
post-entrepreneurial corporation 31
power 260–2
    in strategic networks 144–6
Powergraph 407–11, 414
pre-commitment 389, 396–8
preparedness strategies 454, 455, 456
preservation integration 111, 112, 461, 497,
        498

price dynamics 429–31
price/earnings ratio 354
principal/agent theory 79
process regulations 482
process view 9, 243–4, 249–53, 256–7, 265
Proctor and Gamble 33, 48
    polycentricity 336
producer matrix 170
product cycle hypothesis
    modified 212–13, 216
    oligopoly 212–13
product development 83
professional revitalization 480–5, 489
profit functions 429–33
profit metrics 351, 352
profits, static profit maximization 433–4
project teams 472, 499
Prudential 29
public goods 214
public image 67–9
punctuated equilibrium 282

quality-adjusted prices 429–31
quiet valleys 479

radical innovation 424–5
radical transformation 491
rationality 395–6
re-creation 247–8
re-engineering 447
re-orientation 247
real option theory 11, 417, 421, 422
reality gap 273–4
recipes 312
    faulty 281
    introduction of 292
recovery 268, 302–8
recovery trajectories
    laggards 289
    ostriches 289–90
    visionaries 288
Red Queen effect 449–50, 467
Red Queen race 451, 463, 464, 465, 466, 467, 479,
        491, 496, 499, 501
red tape, crisis of 326
redundancies, after mergers and
        acquisitions 114
regionalization 201, 221, 229
    of markets 207
regulation
    labour markets 207–8
    of mergers and acquisitions 98

relatedness 45–9, 92 n., 104
  types of 46–9
renewal 270, 307–14
renewal trap 465
rents, and value creation 354–6, 421–2
reputation 400
research and development 494
  flexibility in 223–4
  as parenting characteristic 85
resistance
  to change 259–62
  to mergers and acquisitions 112–15
  to structure 326
resource allocation 22–3, 32
resource dependency theory 124–5
resource sharing, and value creation 105
resource-based theory of the firm 3, 123–4,
    245–6, 417, 421–2, 458, 462
restructuring 28–9, 38, 106
retrenchment 268, 269, 298–302
return
  on capital employed (ROCE) 352, 353,
    354
  law of diminishing returns 353
reversed trajectory of revitalization
    483–5
revitalization 480–5, 489, 491, 496
rigid form 450, 475, 476, 492, 500
Rio Tinto 36
risk
  and global strategy 167
  spread of 91
  and strategic alliances 131
rivalry 500
routines 251, 462, 477
  interconnection within 281
  and resistance to change 281, 284, 292
routinization 481–3, 491
Royal Bank of Scotland 133, 134, 389
rugged landscapes 479
rules of search 419
Russia, computer industry 368, 372

Sainsburys 247
SBUs 32, 58, 59, 193, 322, 406
scale, economies of 47, 48–9, 75–6, 168,
    173–4, 208, 209–10, 211, 333, 386
scarce factor market 428–31
scenario planning 370, 390, 414
schemes 311
schizophrenia 485
Schwab 364–5

scope
  economies of 168, 173–4
  international strategy 184–5
screening 388, 391
Sears 66
self-interest
  enlightened 79
  and external advisers 108–9
  managerial 100–1
self-organising systems 311
sense making 294–5
separation by function 494–5
separation by location 495–6
September 11 attacks 229–30
sequential revitalization 491
sequential search processes 292, 293, 299
sequential transformation 491
services, value-added 365
shamrock organization 448–9
share price, bid premium 103–4, 108
shared beliefs 459
shareholder returns 349, 352
shareholder value 26–7, 37
Sharp 458, 459, 499
Shell 75, 249, 497
  strategic options 374
shelter-based strategies 187–8, 189–90
shipbuilding industry 189–90
signalling 388, 391
single-loop learning 463, 465
situation-specific models 385
size, organizational 322
skills transfer 106, 107–8
skunk works 495
Slater Walker 20
SmithKline Beecham
    (now GlaxoSmithKline) 96, 105, 106
Softbank Corporation 337
software 473
Sony 162, 166, 258
Southwest Airlines 52
Spalding Sport Group 174
spatial separation 394–6, 493
  and hierarchy 494
speciality retailing 359–60, 361, 371–2
speed 377, 470
  and strategic alliances 131–2, 143
spinoffs 36
split brain personality 487
spontaneous strategies 479–80
stable environment 463
stagnation 482

stand-alone influence 75, 78–9
Standard Oil 75
standardized metrics 342
start-ups, entrepreneurial 116
steady-state flexibility 470
"stick to the knitting" 27–9, 38
stock options 442–3
strategic alliances 5–6, 118, 125–6, 127–8,
        132–41
    collaborations 134, 135
    commitment 139
    complex 133, 135
    consortium 134–5
    cultural fit 137, 139–40
    dimension 132, 135
    dispute resolution 140
    evolution 135, 141
    and external forces 128–30
    focused 132–3, 135
    future development 153–4
    and goal compatibility 140
    and internal conditions 130–2
    and limited competition 138
    management 135–6, 139–41
    and mergers and acquisitions 96
    and risk 131
    selecting partner 135–8
    and speed 131–2
    strategic fit 34, 35, 136–7
    trust 139
    and uncertainty 125
    see also joint ventures
strategic assets 462
strategic change
    Japan 244–5
    processes 243–4, 249–50
    significance 237–9
strategic control 34
strategic cooperation, and
    conflict 390–1
strategic divestment 226–7
strategic drift 476, 491
strategic fit 34, 35, 136–7
    and value creation 104–5
strategic flexibility 451–61, 472–3, 478
strategic focus 482
strategic framework 450
strategic initiatives 457
strategic interdependence 109–10, 112
strategic issue management 454, 456
strategic management 33–6, 451–61
strategic markets 166

strategic motives, mergers and acquisitions
        98–9
strategic neglect 479, 485
strategic networks 6, 7–8, 125–6, 141–53,
        222–4
    business networks 199–200
    dominated networks 150–1
    dynamic 147–8
    equal partner networks 148–9
    future development 153–4
    and global competitiveness 195–200
    inter-organizational 197–8
    internal 147–8
    leadership 147–8
    MNEs as 197–200
    power and trust 144–6
    rationale for 143
    stable 147–8
    strengths and weaknesses 152–3
    transnational 192, 200, 201
    types of 146–8
strategic options
    creation of 365–9, 372
    and diversification 364–5
    exercising 371–2
    and future development 358–65
    heuristics 416–43
    investment in 360–1, 371
    portfolio optimization 359–72, 378
    scaling up 376–8
    valuation 441
strategic planning 21–2, 34, 451–3,
        475–7
    as management style 331
strategic programming 454–5, 456, 475
strategic re-orientation 298–9
strategic relationships 389
strategic renewal 10
strategic schemas 459
strategic thinking 384–6, 411
strategy 241
    convergence 356, 357
    corporate-level 22
    simplifying management 22
    see also strategic change
strategy decay 349–50
    constraint on future development 358–65
    measurement 351–8, 378
    Strategy Decay Rate (SDR) 356–8
strategy formulation 452
strategy implementation 452
strategy innovation

and competitive advantage 350
  definition 350
  pipeline 372–4, 378
  see also innovation
strategy styles 331
stretch 65, 464
structural clarity 57–8, 65
structural flexibility 471–2, 478
structure, organizational *see* organizational
    structure
suggestion schemes 373–4
Sun Microsystems 338, 449, 472
sustainable competitive advantage 463, 477,
    499, 501
Swatch 52, 55
Swire Pacific 363, 364
Swissair 55, 56
switching costs 431–5, 436–7, 442
symbiosis integration 111, 112
synergy 3, 29, 30–1
  and cooperation 128
  and value destruction 75–6
synergy school 3–4
synthesis 487, 492, 498–9

tacit knowledge 108, 458
takeovers 96
  threat of 288, 289
  see also mergers and acquisitions
technology 473–4
  and flexibility 423
  global 129
  and organizational structure 322,
    421–8
temporal separation 492, 496–8
Tesco 247
Texas Instruments 33, 91, 368, 458, 459
Textron 19–20, 21
TNT Post 488
Total Quality Management (TQM) 366
Toyota 146, 321, 438–9, 472
Toys-R-Us 359
traders 362–3
trajectories 481, 483
transaction costs 126–7, 131, 159, 180
transfer costs 210
transformational change 9, 240, 249
transition states 250
transnational corporations 7–8, 31, 171–4,
    176–8
  see also multinational corporations (MNCs)
transnational networks 192, 200, 201

transnational structure 334, 335, 336, 345
triggering, degrees of 286–91
triggering change 269, 284–6, 284–96
trust 280
  in strategic networks 139, 144–6
tuning 247, 248–9
turnarounds 9, 111

unbundling 100, 106
uncertainty
  and strategic alliances 125
  and strategic networks 143
uni-national firms 192
Unilever 36, 84, 134, 333, 336, 497
  complementary structural change 322,
    323–4
unintended order 461
United Kingdom, mergers and acquisitions
    112
United States
  business management 19–20
  computer industry 367
  foreign direct investment (FDI) 211–12,
    216–17, 218
unpredictability 468

value chain 420
  and cooperation 128, 146
value creation 35–6, 44–5, 49
  by parent companies 73, 74
  conditions for 80–1
  generic mechanisms 105–8
  insights 81–4, 90
  and rents 354–6
  and strategic fit 104–5
  undermining factors 349
value creation logic 50–2
  dynamic evolution 52–4
  and internal governance 56–61
  obsolescence 55–6
  and portfolio configuration 54–6
value destruction
  by parent companies 72–8
  factors in 78–81
value of flexibility 423
value function 435–6
value gaps 26
value-based planning 26–7
values and behaviours 60–1
ventures
  portfolio of 376, 378
  see also joint ventures

virtual organizations 170–1, 222, 448–9
visibility 69
volatility
    exchange rate 221
    globalization 220–1, 229–30
    of options 431

Wal-Mart 48, 52, 320–1, 333, 359
    structure 321
wealth generation, mergers and
        acquisitions 101–2

Welch, Jack 46–7, 51, 59, 67, 418, 453, 494
windfall gains 307
Woolworth Corporation 358–60, 361, 364, 365,
        369, 371–2
work cells 472
World Trade Organization 129

xenophobia 459
Xerox 249, 254, 448, 458, 474, 495

Name Index

Aaker, D. 451, 472
Abernathy, W. 27, 463, 482
Abhriq, N. 171
Achetenhagen, L. 340, 341
Adler, P. 344, 468, 473
Aharoni, Y. 208
Alberts, W. 27
Aldrich, H. 243
Alexander, M. 35–6, 72 n., 73 n.
Allison, G. 419 n.
Altman, E. 275–6
Amram, M. 372 n., 422 n., 430 n.
Anand, J. 175
Anderson, P. 424, 477, 479, 497
Andrews, K. 17, 18, 19, 20, 22, 451, 458, 462
Angwin, D. 110, 111
Ansoff, H. 22, 30, 178, 271, 452, 454, 470
Aquilar, F. 34
Argenti, J. 278
Argyris, C. 312
Arrow, K. 214
Arup, O. 327
Arzac, E. 27
Ashby, W. 469
Ashforth, B. 114
Attiyeh, R. 21
Axelrod, R. 385, 399

Bacdayan, P. 419 n.
Baden-Fuller, C. 338, 472, 483, 491, 493, 497
Bahrami, H. 466
Baiman, S. 79
Baldwin, C. 423, 426 n., 440, 442, 443 n.
Barham, K. 341
Barker, V. 299, 300 n., 301, 307
Barnevik, P. 76
Barney, J. 241, 271, 421, 443
Barrett, F. 326
Bartlett, C. 31, 35, 57, 61, 163–4, 170, 171, 172, 176, 177–8, 191, 192, 194, 195, 201, 213, 225, 331,

332–6, 338, 339, 340, 341, 419 n., 457, 466, 493
Barwise, P. 166
Bate, P. 474
Beckhard, R. 250, 251
Bennett, P. 192, 385, 395, 407
Benson 144
Berg, N. 20, 22, 23
Berkovitch, E. 100
Berry, D. 73
Best, M. 223
Bettis, R. 25, 29 n., 33–4, 49, 63, 459
Beyer, J. 243
Bhagat, S. 28
Bibeault, D. 300
Biggart, N. 337
Binmore, K. 385
Birkinshaw, J. 161
Bjorkman, I. 163
Black 429
Blackmore, S. 399, 414
Blau, P. 327
Bleeke, J. 101, 105, 141
Boisot, M. 337
Booth, L. 159, 170
Boston Consulting Group 3, 418
Bourgeois, L. 242, 257, 452
Bower, J. 23, 456
Bowman, C. 166, 170
Bowman, E. 417, 419, 443
Boynton, A. 458
Bradley, M. 407
Brams, S. 385
Braybrooke, D. 453
Bresnahan, T. 430–1
Brodwin, D. 452
Brown, S. 341, 342, 343
Bryant, J. 407
Buckley, P. 8, 161, 226, 227
Burgelman, R. 49, 53, 55, 456, 462, 479, 495, 496

Burns, T. 322, 474
Burton, R. 452, 453, 454

Calori 114
Calvet, A. 219
Camerer, C. 412, 474
Cameron, K. 299
Campa, J. 226
Campbell, A. 3, 4, 30, 31, 32, 34, 35–6, 47, 72 n., 73 n., 331, 344
Cannella, A. 113, 114
Cantwell, J. 224
Capra, F. 311
Capron, L. 107
Carroll, L. 449
Carroll, T. 341
Cartwright, S. 114
Casson, M. 161, 196, 206 n., 209, 213–14, 216, 219, 220, 221, 222, 223, 225, 226, 227
Castells, M. 320
Casti, J. 119–20
Chaffee, E. 452, 455, 459
Chandler, A. 22, 162, 174, 196, 241, 271, 322, 328, 419 n., 451, 494
Chandran, R. 452–3
Chang Moon 193
Chatterjee, S. 28, 30, 364
Chen, M. 462
Chi, T. 227
Child, J. 112, 337
Christensen, C. 22, 458, 462
Christensen, K. 29 n.
Ciborra, C. 448, 499
Clark, K. 443 n.
Clegg, S. 500
Coase, R. 213, 220
Cohen, M. 419 n.
Coleman, H. 142, 146–7, 494
Collis 4
Contractor, F. 178, 198
Cool, K. 457, 459
Cooper, C. 114
Cooper, D. 327
Coyne, K. 122
Craig, J. 174, 175
Craig, T. 475
Creed, W. 494
Curran, J. 27
Cyert, R. 285, 291, 293

D'Aveni, R. 449, 467, 477, 497
Davidow, W. 448

Davies, H. 210
Davis, G. 146
Davis, J. 174, 175
Davis, S. 57
Day, G. 23
D'Cruz, R. 150, 198, 199, 223
De Gens, A. 313, 370
de Vries, M. K. 66
Delios, A. 175
Derdack, T. 321
Devine, M. 34
Diekmann, K. 146
DiMaggio, P. 198
Dixit, A. 422 n., 430 n.
Donaldson, L. 319, 322
Dosi, G. 46, 425
Dougherty, D. 437
Doz, Y. 3, 4, 35, 49, 53, 57, 163, 171, 191, 197, 198, 492
Drucker, P. 18–19, 22
Drummond, M. 342
Duhaime, I. 49, 299
Dunning, J. 159, 170, 180, 196, 205 n., 209, 210, 211, 214, 215–16, 219, 220, 223
Dunphy, S. 259
Dussauge, P. 137

Egelhoff, W. 334
Eisenhardt, K. 54, 341, 342, 343, 495
Elfring, T. 451, 463
Enright, M. 198–9
Ernst, D. 101, 105, 141
Evans, P. 32

Fast, N. 495
Faulkner, D. 5, 7, 112, 166, 170, 472
Fenton, E. 327
Finkelstein 102
Flanagan, D. 104
Fombrun, C. 284
Franks, J. 77 n.
Fraser, N. 385
Fredrickson, J. 452
Fried, Y. 114
Friesen, P. 482, 483
Fudenberg, D. 413–14
Fuller, M. 128

Galunic, D. C. 53–4, 67, 342, 495
Garrette, B. 137
Geneen, H. 20, 21
Geringer, J. 198

Gerlach, M. 150
Gerstner, L. 22
Ghemawat, P. 384, 386, 411–12, 413
Ghoshal, S. 31, 35, 57, 61, 163, 164, 167–8,
        170–2, 176, 177–8, 180, 191, 192,
        194–5, 201, 213, 225, 331, 332–6, 338, 339,
        340, 341, 457, 466
Giddy, I. 213, 219
Ginsburg, A. 461
Globerman, S. 423 n.
Golbe, D. 97
Golding, D. 280
Goldston, M. 273
Goold, M. 2, 3, 17 n., 21, 31, 34, 35–6, 47, 72 n.,
        73 n., 331, 344
Gordon, J. 320
Govindarajan, V. 194
Grant, R. 29, 32, 123, 457
Green, S. 73
Greenwood, R. 327
Greiner, L. 325, 326, 327
Greve, A. 254
Grinyer, P. 274, 278, 293, 295, 308, 312
Grove, A. 55
Gumpert, D. 464
Gupta, A. 194
Guth, W. 22, 458, 461, 462

Hall, W. 21, 23, 25
Hambrick, D. 101, 108, 113, 114, 299 n.
Hamel, G. 3, 32, 47, 52, 53, 65, 91, 125, 198, 370,
        417, 422, 448, 450, 459
Hamermesh, R. 21, 23, 24, 25
Hami, H. 32
Hamilton, G. 337
Handy, C. 122, 339, 448
Hanssen-Bauer, J. 472
Harrigan, K. 473
Harris, R. 77 n., 250, 251
Haspeslagh, P. 24, 25, 32, 47–8, 59, 105, 109, 115
Hatch, M. 326
Haunschild, P. 109
Hayes, R. 27
Hayward, M. 101, 108
Healy 103
Heap, S. 412
Hedberg, B. 254, 299
Hedley, B. 24
Hedlund, G. 197, 225, 338, 417
Heimer, C. 341
Heller, R. 20
Henderson, R. 424

Hennart, J. F. 197
Hesterly, W. 320
Hickson, D. 242, 322, 324
Hill, C. 257
Hinings, C. 327
Hipel, K. 385
Hirsch, S. 213
Hirschleifer, J. 388, 395
Hof, R. 33
Hofer, C. 24, 298
Hoffman, R. 308
Hofstede, G. 474
Holl 102
Holland, J. 311, 312
Horst, T. 216
Howard, N. 385, 407
Howard, R. 474
Hufbauer, G. 213
Hull, J. 430 n.
Hulland, J. 161
Hymer, S. 209–11, 212, 216

INSEAD 363, 365, 367
Itami, H. 458
Ittner, C. 423, 473

Janis, I. 283
Jarillo, J. 145–6, 197
Jelinek, M. 343
Jemison, D. 32, 105, 109, 115
Jensen, M. 28, 73, 79
Jervis, R. 405
Jick, T. 500
Jilling, G. 75
Johanson, J. 142–3, 162, 226
Johnson, E. 412
Johnson, G. 29 n., 458, 474, 476
Johnson, H. 214
Jones, G. 257
Jones, T. 19
Judelson, D. 20

Kahneman, D. 418 n.
Kanter, R. M. 26, 30–1, 75 n., 245, 249, 250,
        251–2, 460, 468, 483, 485, 497, 500
Kaplan 101
Kauffman, S. 449
Kay, J. 448
Keller, J. 33
Kennedy, C. 86, 363
Kiechel, W. 32
Kim, K. 166

Kim, W. Chan 63, 197
Kindleberger, C. 209–11, 212
Kinsley, L. 246
Kobrin, S. 192
Koch, R. 36
Kogut, B. 11, 161, 166, 170, 191, 226, 228, 416 n.,
    421 n., 423 n., 425, 431 n., 436 n., 439, 473
Kojima, K. 216–18
Koontz, H. 19
Kreps, D. 227
Krijnen, H. 473
Krugman, P. 199
Kuhn, T. 280
Kulatilaka, N. 11, 372 n., 416 n., 422 n., 423 n.,
    430 n., 431 n., 435 n., 436 n., 441, 442
Kunreuther, H. 419

Lai, G. 337
Lambert, R. 442
Langlie, A. 19
Larcker, D. 442
Larsson 102
Lawrence, P. 57
Lawrence, R. 208
Learned, E. 22, 458, 462
Lecraw, D. 159, 170
Lehrer, M. 55
Leonard-Barton, D. 366, 462
Levinthal, D. 461, 462
Levitt, B. 462
Levitt, T. 129, 166, 169
Lewin, A. 341, 449, 461, 500
Lewin, K. 250, 251
Li, P. 337
Lincoln, J. 425 n.
Lindblom, C. 453, 455
Linneman, R. 452–453
Long, C. 341
Lorange, P. 22, 178, 198
Lorenzoni, G. 143, 338, 472, 493
Lovallo, D. 418 n.
Lovett, D. 268, 273–4, 278
Lubatkin, M. 114, 364
Lubove, S. 28
Luchs, K. 2, 17 n., 30
Luffman, G. 30
Luthans, F. 279

McDonald, R. 431 n.
MacDuffie, J. 425, 426
Mace, M. 22
McGuire, D. 227

McKelvey, B. 243
McKiernan, P. 9, 274, 278, 288 n., 293, 295,
    306
MacMillan, I. 496
MacMillan, W. 48
McNulty, C. 370
McTaggart, J. 27
Magee, S. 214
Makhija, M. 166
Maljers, F. 497
Malnight, T. 179
Malone, M. 448
Mansfield, E. 419
Marceau, J. 19
March, J. 242, 285, 291, 293, 312, 417, 455, 461,
    462, 463
Marcus, A. 435 n.
Markides, C. 45, 328, 350 n.
Marks, S. 442
Marshall, A. 223
Martinez, J. 197
Mascarenhas, B. 451, 472, 473
Mattsson, L. -G. 132, 142–3
Mauborgne, R. 63, 197
Mayer, M. 324, 328–32, 338–9
Mayes, D. 274, 278, 295, 308
Meakin, E. 414
Meckling, W. 79
Melin, L. 161, 322
Merton, R. 429, 430 n.
Milburn, T. 294 n.
Miles, R. 142, 146–7, 448, 493, 494
Milgrom, P. 322, 425 n.
Miller, D. 66, 282, 322, 462, 482, 483
Milliken, F. 282
Mintzberg, H. 27, 242, 250, 251, 417 n., 452, 454,
    455, 461, 496
Mone, M. 300 n., 301
Montgomery, C. 4, 29 n.
More, T. 26
Morgenstern, O. 384
Morris, P. 397
Morrison, A. 161, 191, 192
Moskowitz, G. 419 n., 443
Mueller, G. 307
Muller, R. 254, 255
Musky, M. 419 n.

Nadler, D. 248–9
Naisbitt, J. 369–70
Narayanan, M. 100
Naughton, T. 114

Naylor, T. 453
Nelson, R. 423, 425 n., 462, 481–2
Neumair, U. 270 n., 274, 277, 281, 311
Nonaka, I. 176, 178, 311, 448, 499
Norburn, D. 99
Nystrom, P. 299

Ohmae, K. 129, 166, 176
Olsen, J. 242, 312
Ornati, O. 143
Ouchi, W. 459, 493
Ozawa, T. 216

Palepu 103
Pascale, R. 245, 252, 320, 456, 495
Pearce, J. 278, 300, 301
Pearce, R. 215–16, 221
Pennings, J. 453
Penrose, E. 268, 458, 462
Perlmutter, H. 162
Perotti 441
Perrow, C. 476
Perry, N. 19
Persson, P. -G. 440 n.
Peters, T. 27, 245, 320, 326, 452, 460, 495
Pettigrew, A. 242, 246, 306, 322, 327, 339
Pfeffer, J. 124, 148, 260
Phillips, J. 320
Pindyck, R. 422 n., 430 n., 435 n.
Piore, M. 419 n.
Pisano, G. 312, 422, 458, 463
Pitkethly, R. 112
Pondy, L. 292
Poole, M. 461
Porter, M. 18, 26, 28, 30, 75 n., 77 n., 105, 128, 135, 146, 160, 161, 170, 174, 180, 183–7, 189, 191, 192, 193, 195, 197, 198, 199, 201, 223, 245, 271, 420, 449, 450, 473
Powell, J. 6, 385, 407
Powell, W. 142 n., 145, 148, 198
Poynter, T. 192
Prahalad, C. K. 3, 4, 32, 33–4, 35, 47, 49, 52, 53, 57, 63, 65, 91, 125, 163, 171, 191, 197, 198, 370, 417, 420, 448, 450, 459, 492
Pugh, D. 322, 325

Quinn, J. 21, 249, 250, 251, 252, 451, 455, 456, 458, 461, 468

Raft, D. 430–1, 442
Ramanujam, V. 30
Rangan, S. 208

Rappaport, A. 27
Rasmusen, E. 395
Reed, R. 30
Reimann, B. 27
Richardson, G. 145
Richardson, J. 471, 473–4
Riley, J. 388, 395
Ringbakk, K. 22
Ringman 7
Rivoli, P. 225
Robbins, D. 278, 300, 301
Roberts, J. 322, 425 n.
Robertson, T. 166
Rodan, S. 53, 342
Rolander, D. 197, 417
Rosenhead, J. 395
Roth, K. 191, 192
Ruback 103
Ruegg-Sturm, J. 340
Rugman, A. 159, 170, 185–7, 188, 189–94, 196, 197, 200, 201, 219, 223, 229
Rugner, A. 150, 198, 199
Ruigrok, W. 322, 339, 340, 341
Rumelt, R. 3, 29 n., 46, 92 n., 412
Rymon, T. 412

Sabel, C. 419 n.
Sadtler, D. 36
Salami 102
Salancik, G. 124, 148
Salorio, E. 225
Sanchez, R. 451, 457, 458
Sanchez-Rundes, C. 322
Schechter, S. 299 n.
Schein, E. 242
Schelling, T. 384
Schendel, D. 24, 298, 412
Scherer, F. 419
Schoemaker, P. 365
Schoenberg 5, 98, 108, 113, 114
Scholes 429
Schoonhoven, C. 343
Schumpeter, J. 7, 342
Scott, B. 469
Scott, W. R. 424
Scott-Poole, M. 244
Selznick 420 n.
Sen, S. 412
Servan-Schreiber, J. -J. 19, 419 n.
Seth, A. 29 n., 104
Shanley 113
Sherman, S. 67, 453, 474

Shetty, Y. 19
Shleifer, A. 28
Shon, D. 312
Shubik, M. 412
Shuen, A. 312, 422, 458, 463
Shulman, L. 32
Siegel, D. 431 n.
Simon, H. 416, 418 n., 455
Singh, S. 221
Slater, J. 20
Slatter, S. 268, 270 n., 273–4, 278, 294 n., 296, 308
Sloan, A. 22
Slopford, J. 483, 497
Smircich, L. 458, 459
Smith, A. 473, 474, 486, 487
Smock, C. 294 n.
Snow, C. 142, 146–7, 448, 472, 493
Spender, J. 292, 312
Stace, D. 259
Stalk, G. 32
Stalker, G. 322, 474
Starbuck, W. 254, 282, 299, 453
Starkey, K. 294–295
Stein, B. 500
Stephens, C. 500
Stevenson, H. 464
Stimpert, J. 49
Stinchcombe, A. 280, 479
Stopford, J. 162, 171, 322, 333, 334
Stubbart, C. 458, 459
Sudarsanam 102
Sung Cho Dong 189
Sutcliffe, B. 26, 73
Sutton, R. 67, 299
Szulanski, G. 53, 421 n.

Takeuchi, H. 448, 499
Tallman 463
Taubmann, C. 47–8, 59
Taylor, W. 86
Teece, D. 46, 196, 211, 214, 312, 412, 422, 458, 463
Thomas, A. 19
Thomas, H. 29 n.
Thomas, J. 148
Thompson, L. 402, 405, 454
Thorelli, H. 144, 148
Tichy, N. 67, 453, 474
Tiegs, R. 114
Tinsley, C. 146
Trautwein, F. 30

Trice, H. 243
Trigeorgis, L. 224, 226
Tsurumi, Y. 196
Tushman, M. 248–9, 424, 477, 479, 497

Useem, M. 420
Utterback, J. 463, 482

Vahlne, J. -E. 162, 226
Vaitsos, C. 216
Van Cauwenberg, A. 457, 459
Van de Ven, A. 244, 461
van den Bosch, F. 322, 497
van Heeswijk, S. 407
Vancil, R. 22
Varadarajan, P. 30
Varoufakis, Y. 412
Veiga 114
Vepsalainen, A. 474
Verbeke, A. 7, 185–7, 188, 189–90, 191, 193–4, 197, 200, 201, 223
Vernon, R. 161, 196, 201, 211–12, 213, 216
Verrecchia, R. 442
Very 114
Victor, B. 458
Vishny, R. 28
Volberda, H. 11, 339, 449, 451, 461, 462, 463, 465, 491, 493
Von Neumann, J. 384
Vriend, N. 311

Wagner, M. 340, 341
Waterman, R. 27, 245, 320, 452, 460, 495
Waters, J. 454, 461
Weick, K. 257, 294, 458, 459, 464, 499
Weisbach 101
Wells, J. 75 n.
Wells, L. 162, 322, 333, 334
Wernerfelt, B. 3, 462
Westley, F. 496
Westney, D. 194–5, 198, 200
Whetten, D. 299
Whipp, R. 8–9, 246, 307
White, L. 97
White, R. 25
Whitley, R. 19, 338
Whittington, R. 9–10, 322, 324, 328–32, 338–9, 344
Williamson, O. 10, 196, 219
Williamson, P. 328, 358 n.
Williamson, S. 166
Wilson, D. 248

Winter, S. 46, 421, 422–3, 425 n., 462,
        481–2
Winters, P. 33
Wolf, B. 423 n.
Wolfe, R. 257
Woodward, J. 322, 425
Wrapp, H. 455
Wrigley, L. 46

Yagil 97
Yamanouchi, T. 85
Yetton, P. 174, 175
Young, D. 26, 34, 73

Zander, U. 226, 421 n., 439
Zeithami, C. 473, 474, 486, 487
Zenger, T. 320